ANOTHER KNOWLEDGE IS POSSIBLE

Reinventing Social Emancipation: Toward New Manifestos

VOLUME 3

ANOTHER KNOWLEDGE IS POSSIBLE

Beyond Northern Epistemologies

Edited by

Boaventura de Sousa Santos

VERSO

London • New York

First published by Verso 2007
This edition published by Verso 2008
Copyright in the collection © Verso 2007, 2008
Copyright in the contributions © the individual contributors 2007, 2008

The moral rights of the authors and editor have been asserted

1 3 5 7 9 10 8 6 4 2

Verso
UK: 6 Meard Street, London W1F 0EG
USA: 180 Varick Street, New York, NY 10014-4606
www.versobooks.com

Verso is the imprint of New Left Books

ISBN-13: 978-1-84467-256-1

British Library Cataloguing in Publication Data
A catalogue record for this book is available from the British Library

Library of Congress Cataloging-in-Publication Data
A catalog record for this book is available from the Library of Congress

Printed in the USA by Quebecor World, Fairfield

Contents

Preface

This book is the third in a series of five volumes that present the main results of an international research project that I have conducted under the title *Reinventing Social Emancipation: Towards New Manifestos*. The project's core idea is that the action and thought that sustained and gave credibility to the modern ideals of social emancipation are being profoundly questioned by a phenomenon that, although not new, has reached in the past decades such an intensity that it has effected a redefinition of the contexts, objectives, means, and subjectivities of social and political struggles. This phenomenon is commonly designated as globalization. As a matter of fact, what we usually call globalization is just one of the forms of globalization, namely neoliberal globalization, undoubtedly the dominant and hegemonic form of globalization. Neoliberal globalization corresponds to a new system of capital accumulation, a more intensely globalized system than previous systems. It aims, on the one hand, to desocialize capital, freeing it from the social and political bonds that in the past guaranteed some social distribution; on the other hand, it works to subject society as a whole to the market law of value, under the presupposition that all social activity is better organized when organized under the aegis of the market. The main consequence of this double change is the extremely unequal distribution of the costs and opportunities brought about by neoliberal globalization inside the world system. Herein resides the reason for the exponential increase of the social inequalities between rich and poor countries, as well as between the rich and the poor inside the same country.

The project's assumption is that this form of globalization, though hegemonic, is not the only form and that, in fact, it has been increasingly confronted with another form of globalization. This other form, an alternative, counter-hegemonic form of globalization, is constituted by a series of initiatives, movements, and organizations that combat neoliberal globalization through local/global linkages, networks, and alliances. Their motivation is the aspiration to a better, fairer, and more peaceful world, which they deem possible, and to which they believe they are entitled. This form of globalization is as yet still emerging. Its most dramatic manifestation occurs annually with the World Social Forum of Porto Alegre, six of which have already taken place (Porto Alegre, 2001, 2002, 2003; Mumbai, 2004; Porto Alegre, 2005; and the polycentric World Social Forum of 2006, which took place simultaneously on three continents, in Caracas, Bamako, and Karachi.

To my mind, this alternative globalization, in its confrontation with neoliberal globalization, is paving a new path towards social emancipation. Such a confrontation, which may be metaphorically characterized as a confrontation between the Global North and the Global South, tends to be particularly intense in countries of intermediate development, or, in other words, semi-peripheral countries. It is, therefore, in these countries that the potentialities and limits of the reinvention of social emancipation manifest themselves more clearly. This is the reason why four of the five countries in which the project was conducted are countries of intermediate development in different continents. The five countries in question are: Brazil, Colombia, India, Mozambique, and South Africa.

The new conflicts between the Global North and the Global South occur in the most diverse domains of social, economic, political, and cultural activity. In some of these domains, however, the alternatives created by counter-hegemonic globalization are more visible and consistent, not only because the conflicts in them are more intense, but also because the initiatives, movements, and progressive organizations there have reached higher levels of consolidation and organizational density. I selected the following five domains or themes to be analyzed in each of the five countries included in the project: participatory democratic practices; alternative production systems; emancipatory interculturality and cultural and cognitive justice and citizenship; the protection of biodiversity and the recognition of rival knowledges against neoliberal intellectual property rights; and new labor internationalism. To learn about the choice of countries and themes, as well as the assumptions underlying the project and the challenges it aims to face, the reader should see the general introduction in the first volume of this collection.[1]

The series is constituted of five volumes.[2] The first three volumes deal with the above-mentioned five themes. To be sure, the themes are not watertight; there is intertextuality, now implicit, now explicit, among the different books.

This volume, the third in the collection, tackles the struggles and politics of recognition of difference that in the past three decades have been confronting imperial identities, false universalisms, the coloniality of power, and imperial epistemology, all of which are as germane to historical capitalism as the exploitation of wage labor. The struggles and movements pursuing alternative conceptions of human rights, collective rights, cultural rights, as well as the rights to local self-determination are analyzed. New forms of racism and of reactionary multiculturalism are confronted with an emancipatory politics of cultural difference.

In light of both the global mercantilization of modern technical and scientific knowledge under way and the more and more unequal access to information and knowledge it causes, the confrontation among rival knowledges acquires special relevance. Such a confrontation derives also from the latest advances in biology, biotechnology and microelectronics, which have transformed the wealth of biodiversity into one of the most precious and sought after "natural resources." Since most of this biodiversity is located in countries of the South and is sustained by popular, peasant, or indigenous knowledges, the issue (and the conflict) consist in deciding how to protect such biodiversity and such knowledges from the voracity with which scientific, technological, and industrial knowledge transforms them into patentable knowledge objects. The struggles and movements for the recognition of popular knowledges concerning biodiversity, medicine, environmental impact, and natural calamities are analyzed through a variety of case studies.

The introduction to this volume, penned by myself, João Arriscado Nunes, and Maria Paula Meneses, provides the theoretical and analytical framework for the topics dealt with in the book. The main debates on multiculturalism, cultural citizenship, and on the relations between science and alternative knowledges, are reviewed, and an argument in favor of the emancipatory recognition of both cultural differences and the epistemological diversity of the world is put forward.

The book is divided into five parts. In the first part, entitled *Multicultural Citizenship and Human Rights*, five case studies highlight, from different perspectives, the tension between individualistic liberal conceptions of law, rights, and grassroots, collective and intercultural conceptions of human dignity that are susceptible of being translated into the language and practice of emancipatory human rights. They investigate such questions as human rights and their reconstruction beyond the Eurocentric matrix, the new forms of legal pluralism associated with globalization, the relationship of globalization to redefinitions of sovereignty, the right to self-determination as fought for by indigenous peoples, and the creation of spaces for new transnational solidarity around them.

In Chapter 1, I examine the increasing importance of the discourse on human rights as the new emancipatory vocabulary of progressive politics. I explore the conditions under which human rights, one of the creations of

Western modernity, could be appropriated by a politics of emancipation that takes both the recognition of cultural diversity and the common affirmation of human dignity into account. This process is illustrated through an investigation of a possible dialogue between three conceptions of human dignity, the first based on human rights in Western culture, the second on *dharma* in Hindu culture, and the third on *umma* in Islamic culture. I then present the concept of *ur-rights* as a possible foundation for a radical intercultural politics of rights.

In Chapter 2, Shalini Randeria deals with the role played by international institutions, NGOs, and social movements in their complex interactions with the state and the emergence of new forms of legal pluralism associated with the "fractured sovereignty" of peripheral and semiperipheral states within the context of globalization. Base the argument on the case of India, the author examines the ways in which the state participates, in a contradictory manner, both in the constitution of the neoliberal order and in (covert or overt) resistance to it. Social movements, in their turn, either oppose the state as an agent of neoliberal globalization and seek the support of international organizations against state policies, or mobilize sectors of the state—such as judicial power—to oppose neoliberal policies.

In Chapter 3, Carlos Frederico Marés de Souza Filho draws upon the author's professional experience during the time when he was responsible for the affairs of indigenous populations for the Brazilian state and reflects upon this practice. Through an analysis of several struggles for the recognition of the collective rights of indigenous peoples and for their institutional visibility, Souza Filho shows how the emancipatory cause of recognizing the right of indigenous populations to a collective existence has involved different forms of confrontation with the state, all of which had varying degrees of success and which were, to a large extent, rooted in the past history of the processes of colonization and the occupation of territory. Territoriality is, without a doubt, a fundamental element in the affirmation of these collective rights, and one that conflicts with liberal conceptions of ownership.

In Chapter 4, by Lino João de Oliveira Neves, this topic of territoriality is further developed in light of indigenous peoples' struggles for land demarcation in Brazil, specifically in the Amazon region, where the largest indigenous population is concentrated. Neves analyzes the differences between the emancipatory practices of "self-demarcation" and the practices of integrating indigenous peoples into processes of "participatory demarcation," which are subordinated to the logic of the state and its agents. There is an emphasis on the confrontation between the symbolic universes, epistemological systems, and rival knowledges that these initiatives express and through which both indigenous practices and the practices of the actors and institutions of the larger society are articulated.

In Chapter 5, Luís Carlos Arenas also presents a situation in which the affirmation of collective rights is inseparable from that of territorial roots. Arenas traces the struggle that, since 1993, has set the U'wa, a small indigenous community in northeast Colombia, against the designs of an American petroleum company, the Occidental Petroleum Corporation (OPC). The struggle of the U'wa gained national prominence and gradually generated movements and initiatives of international solidarity. Throughout the struggle, legal challenges relating to the rights of indigenous peoples had a decisive influence on the process. This study aims to respond to a set of questions that have a much wider scope than the specific case under investigation: how can a forgotten, isolated and barely visible community become the object of worldwide attention? Why were activists and the media so attracted to the case? What lessons can be learned from a local process that became global?

Part II, entitled *The World's Local Knowledges*, focuses on two of the central epistemological debates of our time: the internal plurality of modern scientific knowledge (different ways of conceiving and practicing science); and the interconnections and conflicts between scientific knowledge and other knowledges. These topics are further detailed in Parts III and IV.

In Chapter 6, Laymert Garcia dos Santos analyzes the "cybernetic turn" that, in his opinion, has sealed the alliance between capital and science and technology and transformed technoscience into a powerful motor of accumulation converting the entire world into raw material at the disposal of technoscientific work. The centrality of the concept of information has blurred the distinction between nature and culture, as illustrated by the informational transformation of the access to genetic patrimony. With a specific reference to the Brazilian case, this transformation is critically analyzed by Santos in so far as it dominates the conflict that, throughout the 1990s, unfolded between the different conceptions regarding the access to and the use of biodiversity and the traditional knowledges associated with it.

Chapter 7 is authored by Shiv Visvanathan. It deals with the debate between tradition and modernity in India, focusing on the field of science and technology in both colonial and post-colonial times. For a long time, the state-promoted ideology of modern science and technology as the sole source of progress has been confronted by grassroots movements that seek to defend the epistemological wealth of the country, a conflict that has become most intense in recent times with regards to the issue of genetic diversity. Visvanathan illustrates the different possibilities of dealing with this conflict in the work of the Indian chemist C. V. Seshadri. He discusses the innovative ways in which Seshadri drew on both modern science and traditional knowledge while refusing to give an exclusive privilege to either of them.

For Seshadri, India needed neither a rigid theory of the modern nor an ossification, an orientalizing, or a "museumification" of tradition.

In Chapter 8, João Paulo Borges Coelho discusses the tensions between scientific knowledge and traditional peasant knowledges in the case of "natural calamities"—extreme climatic events such as droughts, torrential rains and floods, and tropical cyclones—to which Mozambique has been severely subjected in the last thirty years. According to Coelho, the Mozambican case shows clearly how state policies (based on scientific and technological hypotheses) adopted in response to emergency situations (as well as to prevent such situations) are far from being merely technical operations. For the author, an efficacious response actually capable of minimizing the destructive effects of natural calamities must be based on a plural network of knowledges in which scientific knowledge and peasant popular knowledges cooperate.

The third part, entitled *From Biodiversity to Rival Knowledges*, is devoted to the question of biodiversity and the new conflicts between scientific knowledge and other (popular, indigenous, peasant) knowledges that it has sparked in recent years in the wake of the biotechnological revolution. The intensity of these conflicts derives from the new fusion between knowledge and capital accumulation brought about by both the life-sciences industry and the concentration in gigantic transnational corporations of the production of bio-industrial products related to agriculture, foodstuffs, and health.

Chapter 9, written by Margarita Flórez Alonso, deals with the complex question of how to protect the traditional knowledges that relate to biological diversity in the context of an aggressive globalization of North-centric conceptions of intellectual property rights that have been geared to defend the interests of biotechnological companies. She asserts that traditional peoples and communities have protected their knowledge to a greater or lesser extent, depending on their internal norms and mores. These should prevail over any legal construct of the Western world. According to Alonso, we should reject this type of protection because it does not arise from any of the real needs of traditional peoples and communities, but rather from Western society's desire to frame these social and cultural systems in different formats of property rights and thus to define "owners" with whom they may sign contracts or make deals.

In Chapter 10, Vandana Shiva claims that, while biodiversity and indigenous systems of knowledge meet the needs of millions of people, new systems of patents and intellectual property rights (IPRs) are threatening to appropriate these vital resources and knowledge systems from the Third World, as well as to convert them into the monopoly of Northern corporate interests. As an example, she describes how multinational corporations that have promoted the use of chemicals in agriculture are now looking for biological options. In the search for new markets and for control over the biodiversity base for the production of biopesticides and chemicals, these corporations are claiming IPRs on *neem*-based biopesticides. According to Shiva, the past decade's movements and struggles against biopiracy have now begun to have an impact. These movements are about both the rights of communities to be the producers of knowledge, food, and medicine and the rights of citizens to have access to basic needs. They are, by their very nature, pluralistic in content and form.

In Chapter 11, Arturo Escobar and Mauricio Pardo analyze the struggles by indigenous and Afro-descendent peoples in the Pacific region of Colombia to secure control over their historical territories by organizing resistance against the rapid advancement of powerful global economic agents that have the support of the state. Black and indigenous organizations have challenged the government in order to obtain legal recognition of their lands and authority and to counter the actions of the timber, mining, and palm oil industries as well as government projects that aim to build roads, hydro-electric plants and ports in the region. The positions of these organizations regarding nature and biodiversity are to be understood in the broader scheme of their political objectives. Indigenous peoples' control of their lands constitutes the focus of their struggle, which also includes respect for their cultural specificities, the autonomy to decide their future, and the protection of their traditional knowledge.

Part IV, entitled *The Resistance of the Subaltern: The Case of Medicine*, is devoted to another social field of conflicts, tensions, and interconnections among rival knowledges that has gained international prominence in the last two decades: the relations between modern and traditional medical knowledges and practices.

Chapter 12, by Thokozani Xaba, deals with the socio-cultural impact of the marginalization of traditional medical practices in South Africa both in terms of the cultural loss of the holistic approach and of the egalitarian nature of indigenous medicines and in terms of the incapacity of modern medicine to satisfy the health care needs of African populations. Political institutions represented by the state, religious institutions represented by missionaries, and medical and pharmaceutical institutions representing "scientific" medicine have all converged to eliminate any competition emanating from traditional practices. Xaba analyzes the ups and downs of the limited recognition granted to traditional medicine in the post-apartheid period and argues that traditional medicine must be recognized on its own terms as complementary to modern biomedicine.

In Chapter 13, Maria Paula Meneses analyzes the complex relations between modern biomedicine and traditional African medicine on the basis of empirical research conducted in Maputo (Mozambique). According to her, the two paradigms of medical knowledge have different conceptions of health and illness, of the relationship between cure and prevention, and of the interconnection between an individual's health problem and his/her community, both past and present. For Meneses, traditional medicine is not a remnant of the past; rather, it is being reinvented as an alternative modernity. This explains why traditional medicine continues to attract not only patients from rural areas but also patients from urban areas who, with their modern problems and expectations, seek treatment, protection, and success. Whenever possible, people resort to both traditional and modern medicine. To account for this, Meneses proposes the concept of "intermedicine."

As with all of the other volumes of the collection *Reinventing Social Emancipation*, this volume ends with commentaries (Part V), one by Yash Ghai and another by Tewolde Berhan Gebre Egziabher.

In Chapter 14, Ghai's engaging commentary focuses on the first five chapters, which deal with the complex and tense relationship between universal human rights and the recognition of cultural and ethnic differences. Drawing on his vast international experience in constitution-making, and without ruling out the emancipatory possibilities of interculturality in the field of human rights, Ghai cautions against the possible dangers of relativism and of abuses by authoritarian political leaders eager to invoke cultural specificity in order to legitimate gross violations of basic human rights.

In Chapter 15, Egziabher's equally eloquent commentary focuses on the last eight chapters. It traces the historical roots of the epistemological conflicts between the North and the South, concentrating on the most recent concerning biodiversity and intellectual property rights. Drawing on his vast experience as an expert representing the African positions on these issues and cautioning against the introduction of genetically modified plants, Egziabher defends the creation of a global regime of community rights as a form of resistance against the global imposition of a North-centric legal monoculture of intellectual property rights.

As I have already mentioned, this volume is the third in a series of five volumes. A brief reference to the remaining volumes is therefore in order.

The first volume, entitled *Democratizing Democracy: Beyond the Liberal Democratic Canon* (Verso, 2005), is concerned with high-intensity forms of participatory democracy emerging in the global South. The main thesis of this book is that the hegemonic model of democracy (liberal, representative democracy), while prevailing on a global scale, guarantees no more than low-intensity democracy, based on the privatization of public welfare by more or less restricted elites, on the increasing distance between representatives and the represented, and on an abstract political inclusion made of concrete social exclusion. Parallel to this hegemonic model of democracy, other models have always existed, however marginalized or discredited, such as participatory democracy or popular democracy. Recently, participatory democracy has attained a new dynamics. It has engaged primarily subaltern communities and social groups that, propelled by the aspiration to more inclusive social contracts and high-intensity democracy, struggle against social exclusion and the suppression or trivialization of citizenship. By this I mean local initiatives in urban or rural contexts that gradually develop bonds of inter-recognition and interaction with parallel initiatives, thus giving rise to the formation, as yet embryonic, of transnational networks of participatory democracy. To my mind, one of the major conflicts between the North and the South will increasingly result from the confrontation between representative and participatory democracy. Such a confrontation, often shown in representative democracy's systematically denying the legitimacy of participatory democracy, will be resolved only to the extent that such a denial is replaced by the development of forms of complementarity between the two forms of democracy that may contribute to deepen both one and the other. Such complementarity serves to pave one of the ways to the reinvention of social emancipation.

Volume II, entitled *Another Production is Possible: Beyond the Capitalist Canon* (Verso, 2006), deals, on the one hand, with the non-capitalist production alternatives that for the past two decades have been gaining new life in their resistance to the social exclusion and wild exploitation brought about by neoliberal globalization, and, on the other hand, with the new struggles of workers against such exploitation, which signal the emergence of a new labor internationalism. Alternative models to capitalist development, generally known as solidary economy or social economy, are analyzed, and case studies of popular economic organizations, cooperatives, communitarian or collective land management and associations of local development are presented. Also analyzed are the new forms of the conflict between capital and labor, derived, on the one hand, from the end of the Cold War and, on the other, from the fact that in the last three decades labor has become a global resource, though without the emergence of any globally organized labor market. From this disjunction has resulted the weakening of the union movement as we know it. Meanwhile, it is clear today that labor solidarity is reconstituting itself under new forms, on both local and national levels, and on a global level as well. The book deals in detail with some of these new forms.

Volume IV, entitled *Voices of the World*, is different from the previous volumes. Rather than focusing on the scientific and social analysis of alternatives, it focuses on the discourse and practical knowledge of the protagonists of such alternatives. One of the core concerns of the project *Reinventing Social Emancipation* is to contribute to renovating the social sciences (see the general introduction to the first volume). One of the paths of renovation resides in confronting the knowledge the social sciences produce with other knowledges—practical, plebeian, popular, common, tacit knowledges—which, although being an integral part of the social practices analyzed by the social sciences, are always ignored by the latter. In this book, voice is given to the leaders and activists of social movements, initiatives and organizations, many of which are studied in the previous volumes. To this effect, long interviews were conducted and transcribed.

Finally, Volume 5, provisionally entitled *Reinventing Social Emancipation: Toward New Manifestos*, presents my theoretical, analytical, and epistemological reflection upon the major themes of this project and its main results. In addition, it reflects as well on the project itself as the construction of a scientific community under conditions and according to rules largely outside the conventional models.

Sixty-one researchers participated in this project; more than fifty-three initiatives were analyzed. A project of such proportions was possible only thanks to a demanding series of conditions. In the first place, adequate funding was available; I am grateful to the MacArthur Foundation for financial support. Second, the project was made possible by a number of coordinators, one in each country, who helped me to select the themes and researchers, and finally to bring the various strands of the research to conclusion. I was fortunate enough to have the collaboration of Sakhela Buhlungu in South Africa, Maria Célia Paoli in Brazil, Mauricio García-Villegas in Colombia, Shalini Randeria and Achyut Yagnik in India and Teresa Cruz e Silva in Mozambique. My most heartfelt gratitude to all of them.

This project would not have been possible without the support of a dedicated and highly competent Secretariat. Sílvia Ferreira, Paula Meneses and Ana Cristina Santos shared administrative, scientific, and editorial tasks, but they all did a little bit of everything. In the course of three years, they accomplished a remarkable amount of work, creating the best conditions to make my meetings with the country coordinators and the researchers productive, to meet all of the researchers' needs and requests, and to facilitate the production of all the texts. Theirs was a Herculean task, and I am only too happy to mention this here in order to keep it from lying buried in the many pages of this series of books.

This project was based at the Center for Social Studies of the School of Economics of the University of Coimbra and greatly benefited from the support of the Executive Committee and its administrative staff. As usual, a very special word of thanks must go to Lassalete Simões, my closest collaborator and dear friend of more than ten years. She is the recipient of my most deeply felt gratitude.

The solidarity shown throughout by the governing bodies of the School of

Economics of the University of Coimbra was always encouraging, as were the sympathy and support of my colleagues in the Department of Sociology, a gift all the more appreciated for being increasingly so rare in academic institutions. My sincere thanks to all of them.

Several translators collaborated with me in this volume, and I would like to thank all of them: Amanda Hammatt, David Hedges, Karen Bennett, John Avelda, Jonelle Weinrich, and Peggy Sue. Very special thanks to Mark Streeter, on whose generous time and competence I counted during the last phases of the preparation of the manuscript, and whose outstanding job as a copy-editor was invaluable.

Maria Irene Ramalho was ever an unobtrusive presence during the execution of this project. Thanking her, no matter how emphatically, would always be less than adequate. She alone knows why.

Boaventura de Sousa Santos

Notes

1 Boaventura de Sousa Santos, ed. (2005). *Democratizing Democracy: Beyond the Liberal Democratic Canon*. London: Verso.
2 Besides this English edition, this series is also being published in Brazil (Civilização Brasileira), Mexico (Fondo de Cultura Económica), Italy (Città Aperta Edizioni), and Portugal (Afrontamento).

INTRODUCTION

Opening Up the Canon of Knowledge and Recognition of Difference

Boaventura de Sousa Santos, João Arriscado Nunes,
and Maria Paula Meneses

The main argument of this book is that there is no global social justice without global cognitive justice. Probably more than ever, global capitalism appears as a civilizational paradigm encompassing all domains of social life. The exclusion, oppression, and discrimination it produces have not only economic, social, and political dimensions but also cultural and epistemological ones. Accordingly, to confront this paradigm in all its dimensions is the challenge facing a new critical theory and new emancipatory practices. Contrary to their predecessors, this theory and these practices must start from the premise that the epistemological diversity of the world is immense, as immense as its cultural diversity and that the recognition of such diversity must be at the core of the global resistance against capitalism and of the formulation of alternative forms of sociability (Santos, 2006b).[1]

Over the last decades, there has been a growing recognition of the cultural diversity of the world, with current controversies focusing on the terms of such recognition. But the same cannot be said of the recognition of the epistemological diversity of the world, that is, of the diversity of knowledge systems underlying the practices of different social groups across the globe. However, from an anti-capitalist perspective such recognition is crucial. The epistemological privilege granted to modern science from the seventeenth century onwards, which made possible the technological revolutions that consolidated Western supremacy, was also instrumental in suppressing other, non-scientific forms of knowledges and, at the same time, the subaltern social groups whose social practices were informed by such knowledges. In the case of the indigenous peoples of the Americas and of the African slaves, this suppression of knowledge, a form of epistemicide (Santos, 1998), was the other side of genocide. There is, thus, an epistemological foundation to the capitalist and imperial order that the global North has been imposing on the global South. This book aims at elucidating some of the destructive consequences of this epistemology and at proposing an alternative epistemology that, far from refusing science, places the latter in the context of the diversity of knowledges existing in contemporary societies. Starting from the assumption that cultural diversity and epistemological diversity are reciprocally embedded, this book is intent to show that the reinvention of social emancipation is premised upon replacing the "monoculture of scientific knowledge" by an "ecology of knowledges" (Santos, 2003b; 2004a). The ecology of knowledges is an invitation to the promotion of non-relativistic dialogues among knowledges, granting "equality of opportunities" to the different kinds of knowledge engaged in ever broader epistemological disputes aimed both at maximizing their respective contributions to build a more democratic and just society and at decolonizing knowledge and power.

THE DIVERSITY OF CULTURES
AND THE DIVERSITY OF KNOWLEDGES

Many non-Western (indigenous, rural, etc.) populations of the world conceive of the community and the relationship with nature, knowledge, historical experience, memory, time, and space as configuring ways of life that cannot be reduced to Eurocentric conceptions and cultures. For instance, the definition of the identity of peoples in the non-Western world and of their collective rights tends to be strictly bound to a notion of "territoriality" associated with responsibilities in relation to a territory, which is defined as a collective of spaces, human groups (including both the living and their ancestors), rivers, forests, animals, and plants. Differences between worldviews become explicit and turn into sites of struggle when the integrity of these collectives is threatened by alternative notions of relationships to territory and knowledges—such as those that are based on the right to property—or when the distinction between the respect for culture and the imperative of development is used to justify the exploitation of "natural resources" by outside forces. The struggle of the U'wa in Colombia against a petroleum multinational (this volume), or of the peasants and rural communities in India against the appropriation by multinational companies of the biological resources of the territories they inhabit and in defense of a balanced environment and a way of life that respects and preserves this environment (this volume), provide examples of how confrontations between different worldviews can take the form of cultural, legal, and political conflicts on national and international levels.

The adoption of allegedly universally valid, Eurocentric legal and political models, such as the neoliberal economic order, representative democracy, individualism, or the equation between state and law often rests, as the different case studies in this book show, on forms of domination based on class, ethnic, territorial, racial, or sexual differences and on the denial of collective identities and rights considered incompatible with Eurocentric definitions of the modern social order. Yet, even within Eurocentric normative frameworks, there is still scope for the right to difference to be affirmed, through conceptions of normality, nature, and morality that are alternative to the dominant ones.

Conceptions of knowledge, of what it means to know, of what counts as knowledge, and how that knowledge is produced are as diverse as the cosmologies and normative frameworks alluded to above. All social practices involve knowledge. The production of knowledge is, in itself, a social practice and what distinguishes it from other social practices is its self-reflexivity, which productively reshapes the context of practices in motive and engine of actions.

Self-reflexivity, viewed as the discovery of hetero-referentiality, is the first step towards the recognition of the epistemological diversity of the world. The latter, in turn, is inseparable from the diversity of cosmologies that divide and organize the world in ways that differ from Western cosmology and its offshoot, modern science. Both the proposals for radicalizing democracy—which point towards post-capitalist horizons—and the proposals for de-colonizing knowledge and power—which point towards post-colonial horizons—will be feasible only if the dominant epistemology is subject to a critique allowing for the emergence of epistemological options that give credibility to the forms of knowledge that underlie those proposals.

These different expressions of diversity are often subsumed under the term "multiculturalism," a term that, like many others that have emerged from the critical discourses in/of modernity, has become a contested word with a variety of meanings and uses.

Multiculturalism: a contested concept

Especially after the 1980s, the humanities and the social sciences converged on the transdisciplinary area of cultural studies, considering culture as a phenomenon associated with repertoires of meaning or signification shared by members of a society, and also with differentiation and hierarchy within national societies, local contexts, and transnational spaces. Culture therefore became a central strategic concept in the definition of identities and alterity in the contemporary world, a resource for the affirmation of difference and the demand for its recognition, as well as a field of struggle and contradiction (McClintock, 1995; Werbner and Ranger, 1996; Spivak, 1999; Mosquera, Pardo, and Hoffman, 2002). As a consequence, the concept of multi-culturalism became equally controversial and riddled with tensions. It stands, either simultaneously or alternatively, both for a *description* and a *project* (Stam, 1997). As a description, it may refer to: 1) the existence of a multiplicity of cultures in the world; 2) the coexistence of diverse cultures within the same political space; 3) the existence of cultures that influence each other, both within and outside the geo-political space of the nation-state.[2]

Inasmuch as multiculturalism, as a description of cultural differences and the ways in which they interrelate, has superimposed itself on multiculturalism as a political project that celebrates or recognizes these differences, it has given rise to criticisms and controversies, both from conservative sectors and from different progressive and left-wing currents. Conservative critiques have resonated in the USA and Western Europe as responses to a complex set of social, cultural, and political transformations, such as: changes in the ethnic composition of their populations as a result of the increased presence of immigrants, especially the large contingents of illegal immigrants from Latin America, in the case of the USA, and from Africa, in the case of Europe; social programs of affirmative action aimed at excluded or marginalized groups, such as African Americans, Native Americans or Hispanics in the USA; the development of cultural studies and women's studies programs within the university and the subsequent transformations of the curricula of traditional fields such as literature, aimed at giving a presence and a voice to women and to minorities; some public policies supporting the cultural production of minorities; the diversity of social critiques of the hegemonic role of Western science; and, finally, the emergence, in the public space, of movements promoting a politics of identity based on the recognition of difference. Stam (1997) summarizes these conservative critiques under the following four points: a) multiculturalism is anti-European, since it seeks to replace the values and achievements of Western civilization with an uncritical promotion of "inferior" achievements; b) multiculturalism promotes disunity and division, thus fragmenting society and threatening the cohesion and unity of national goals; c) multiculturalism is a "therapy for minorities," aimed at promoting their self-esteem in the face of their manifest inability to perform adequately within the educational system and within society as a whole; d) multiculturalism represents a kind of "new Puritanism" supported by the policing of language and the totalitarian imposition of "politically correct" speech.

Some progressive responses to this picture underline the anti-Eurocentric (but not anti-European) nature of multicultural projects that promote the recognition and visibility of cultures that have been marginalized or excluded from Western modernity. Such projects recognize cultural differences, historical experiences, and intercultural dialogue in order to forge political alliances and coalitions supporting subaltern cultures and groups; they promote historical and cultural counter-perspectives in order to produce a relational history that includes subaltern groups; they also argue that examples of political correctness occur in all sectors of society and all shades of the political spectrum but that they are only attacked when they are associated with the defense of equality or the recognition of difference.

However, the response of the progressive sectors to multiculturalism is neither unanimous nor peaceful. The reason for this lies in the diversity of the cultural and political projects that describe themselves as multicultural, and in the different geopolitical and spatial environments in which they operate (whether North or South, local, national, global, etc.). The main progressive criticisms of multiculturalism may be grouped as follows:

1. The concept of multiculturalism is Eurocentric, created to describe cultural diversity within the framework of the nation-states of the Northern hemisphere and to deal with situations resulting from the flow of immigrants from the South into a European space without internal borders, the ethnic diversity and affirmation of the identity of minorities in the USA and the specific problems of countries like Canada, with territorially differentiated linguistic or ethnic communities. The North has sought to impose this concept on the countries of the South as a means of defining their historical condition and identity. This entails the "exporting" or "traveling" of concepts or analytical frameworks that remain bound to Eurocentric intellectual domination. In the South, the concept is associated with the rhetoric and political agenda of states, often with the aim or result of legitimizing oppressive or exclusionary forms of communalism, sometimes linked to religious fundamentalism (as in India). The multiplicity of adjectives employed in relation to multiculturalism, which has been variously described as "liberal," "authoritarian," "corporate," "insurgent," "boutique," "critical," "aggregate," "universalist," "essentialist," "paradigmatic," and "modular" points to the fact that it is a concept that has no precise content and is not necessarily associated with emancipatory perspectives or projects (Bharucha, 2000: 10).

2. Multiculturalism is the prime expression of the cultural logic of multinational or global capitalism (a capitalism "without a homeland," at last) and of a new form of racism,

> which empties its own position of all positive content (the multiculturalist is not a direct racist, he doesn't oppose to the Other the *particular* values of his own culture), but nonetheless retains his position as the privileged *empty point of universality* from which one is able to appreciate (and depreciate) properly other particular cultures—the multiculturalist respect for the Other's specificity is the very form of asserting one's own superiority. (Zizek, 1997: 44)

3. Multiculturalism tends to be "descriptive" and "apolitical," thus suppressing the problem of power relations, exploitation, inequality, and exclusion (the "United Colours of Benetton" model). The notion of "tolerance" does

not demand any active involvement with others and reinforces feelings of superiority among those who speak from a self-defined site of universality.

4. In the cases where it does occur, the politicization of multicultural projects takes place within the framework of the nation-state as a special status conferred on certain regions or peoples whose collective existence and collective rights are recognized only as subordinate to the hegemony of the constitutional order of the nation-state (and only while compatible with established notions of sovereignty associated rights, especially with property rights, such being the case of the conflicts surrounding the access to and the privatization of natural resources in Africa, Asia, and Latin America). In this context, Gunew stresses the need to differentiate between *"state multi-culturalism, dealing with the management of diversity, and critical multiculturalism, used by minorities as leverage to argue for participation, grounded in their differences, in the public sphere"* (Gunew, 2004: 16). In this latter sense, multiculturalism contributes towards a post-colonial analysis of cultural encounters.[3]

5. Within cultural and post-colonial studies, the concept of multiculturalism tends to be dealt with through a focus on mobility and migration, with an emphasis on intellectuals, while ignoring forced or subordinate mobility (refugees, migrant workers, or returned emigrants) or those who have not moved but have been subjected to the effects and consequences of translocal cultural, economic, and political dynamics. This focus is evident both in the post-colonial theories of hybridization (Bhabha, 1994) and in the emphasis placed on the use of literature and other "expressive" cultural forms that can be studied drawing on Eurocentric academic disciplines. This privilege awarded the "migrant condition" denies the specific histories of migrations and, furthermore, ignores the "individuals and communities that resist migrancy on the basis of other loyalties and bonds to family, tradition, community, language, and religion that are not always translatable within the norms of liberal individualism" (Bharucha, 2000: 7).[4]

6. Finally, it is possible to question the relevance of terms such as culture or multiculturalism in describing and characterizing specific contexts and experiences that involve distinct ways of viewing and dividing up the world and for which the notion of culture or the division between the cultural, the economic, the social, and the political is not relevant. This criticism raises the problem of the "strategic" use of hegemonic concepts, which may often have the effect of reaffirming the very colonial imposition it opposes.

The tensions and criticisms presented above stress the importance of specifying the conditions under which multiculturalism as a project can take an emancipatory content and direction. Emancipatory versions of multiculturalism are based on the recognition of difference, and of the right to difference and the coexistence or construction of a common way of life that extends beyond the various types of differences. These conceptions of multiculturalism are linked, in general, as Edward Said has noted (1994), to "overlapping territories" and "intertwined histories," the products of the dynamics of imperialism, colonialism, and post-colonialism, which have put metropoles and dominated territories in contact with each other (Memmi, 1965), and which have created the historical conditions of diaspora and other forms of mobility (Anderson, 1983; Clifford, 1997). The idea of movement, the articulation of difference, and the emergence of cultural configurations based on contributions from specific experiences and histories have led to the exploration of the emancipatory possibilities of multiculturalism, thus fuelling debates and initiatives involving new definitions of rights, identities, justice, and citizenship. However, the relationship between the conditions that make these forms of mobility and hybridization possible and the dynamics of the capitalist world-system that produce, reproduce and increase inequality, marginalization and the exclusion of important sections of the world's population, in the North as well as in the South, are not always made explicit. For some proponents of emancipatory versions of multiculturalism, the relevance of culture lies in the fact that, in the era of global capitalism, it is the privileged arena for the articulation of the reproduction of capitalist social relationships and antagonism towards them, "the field on which economic and political contradictions are articulated" (Lowe and Lloyd, 1997: 32).

The viability of an emancipatory cosmopolitan politics calls for adequate responses to two kinds of problems which the transformations of global capitalism have brought to emancipatory struggles and to the production of knowledge relating to them. First, the multidimensionality of forms of domination and oppression gives rise, in turn, to forms of resistance and struggle that mobilize different collective actors and (not always mutually intelligible) vocabularies and resources, and this can place serious limitations on attempts to redefine the political arena. Second, since the majority of these struggles are local in origin, their legitimacy and effectiveness depend on the ability of collective actors and social movements to forge translocal and global alliances, which presuppose mutual intelligibility. The answer to these two problems cannot be accounted for by any general theory of society or of social transformation, as the latter tends to be situated in and respond to a particular social and cultural context. A politics of cultural diversity and mutual intelligibility calls for a complex procedure of reciprocal and horizontal translation rather than for a general theory. According to Boaventura de Sousa Santos, because there is no single principle of social transformation, it is not possible to determine, in abstract, the articulations or hierarchies among the different social experiences and their conceptions of social transformation. Only by means of the mutual intelligibility of practices is it possible to evaluate them and identify possible alliances among them. (2004a: 182).

This theory of translation allows common ground to be identified in an indigenous struggle, a feminist struggle, an ecological struggle, etc., without erasing the autonomy and difference of each of them. Translation is also fundamental to the articulation between the diverse and specific intellectual and cognitive resources that are expressed through the various modes of producing knowledge about counter-hegemonic initiatives and experiences, aimed at redistribution and recognition and the construction of new configurations of knowledge anchored in local, situated forms of experience and struggle. To achieve these aims, it is crucial to mobilize and prioritize concepts or forms of knowledge—such as the modern sciences, including the social sciences, and the humanities—that were originally elaborated in an Eurocentric context. This allows the biases associated with these concepts to be exposed and alternative concepts based on strategies such as diatopical hermeneutics or reconfigurations of knowledges based on the mutual recognition of their partiality and incompleteness to be proposed (Santos, this volume). Their adequateness in different situations, experiences, and struggles has to be evaluated pragmatically; it is not possible to determine the "intrinsic" superiority of any one strategy over another. Taken as a whole, these responses represent a set of critical or emancipatory versions of multicultural projects, opposed to the apolitical nature of celebratory multiculturalisms. We shall encounter different uses of these in the case studies included in this volume.

The procedures of translation, articulated with what Boaventura de Sousa Santos (2004a) calls "the sociology of absences," are important resources for preventing the reconstruction of emancipatory discourses and practices from falling into the trap of reproducing, in a wider form, Eurocentric concepts and concerns. As in the debate on human rights, it is important here as well to identify the concerns and concepts that correspond to those that, in the West, endow notions such as "culture," "multiculturalism," "rights," "citizenship," "science," or "knowledge" with an emancipatory content. The strategic and emancipatory use of these concepts depends on the recognition of the variety of situated knowledges that have often been marginalized, silenced, or destroyed by the hegemony of Western science and technology (see Visvanathan, Meneses, and Xaba in this volume).

The idea of "multicultural citizenship" acquires a more exact meaning as the privileged site of struggles for the mutual articulation and activation of recognition and redistribution.[5] This is the path to the proliferation of local public spheres that are, at the same time, able to establish translocal connections, sometimes with and sometimes against the national states, as nodes of counter-hegemonic forms of globalization, emancipatory global subpolitics, and genuinely cosmopolitan citizenships. The chapters by Shalini Randeria, Carlos Marés, Lino Neves, and Luis Carlos Arenas illustrate from different perspectives the difficult paths towards the recognition of both the principle of equality and the principle of recognition of cultural difference and its translation into a politics of multicultural collective rights, particularly when the control over natural resources, such as those existing in indigenous peoples' territories, is at stake. In the African context, the question is also raised in the chapter by Borges Coelho when he discusses the role of knowledge in the process of shaping local, ethnic identities.

The debate on the universality or multiculturalism of human rights illustrates a more general problem: that of knowing how to make commensurate demands for human dignity, formulated in different languages of rights and justice. The wider the circle of reciprocity, as defined by a given conception of rights and justice, the better it will be able to include diverse actors, dialogues, and conceptions. The successes of the indigenous movements in Brazil and of the U'wa in Colombia in mobilizing translocal and transnational solidarity provide exemplary illustrations of the importance of broad circles of reciprocity. The language of culture and multiculturalism is mobilized, in these situations, as a fundamental strategic resource and as a means of making claims for difference mutually intelligible and shared.

As the case studies in this volume show, policies to integrate the indigenous populations of Brazil and Colombia within liberal citizenship, as autonomous individuals "free" of collective bonds, have signified in practice the denial of their collective rights, the right to their territory, to their way of life, and to their cosmologies. For the case of Brazil and Colombia these collective rights have come to be recognized and affirmed through their struggles to inscribe a multicultural constitutional order in the 1988 and 1991 Constitutions, respectively. As the case of India suggests, the legal pluralism that results from the intersecting dynamics of the global, the national, and the local can create spaces for the recognition of alternative forms of normativity, but these can only effectively result in emancipatory dynamics in articulation with alternative conceptions of justice and redistribution policies aimed at the most vulnerable and subaltern groups in the population. The demand for the recognition of local identity can be mobilized in order to demand equal treatment for citizens within the same country. In other contexts, such as the case of the U'wa in Colombia, the affirmation of identity is a resource for demanding recognition of collective rights, associated with an effective guarantee of control over a territory and its resources. However, identity discourses can also be used to impose repressive orders, based on a precarious peace enforced by arms, invoking the so-called harmony of a pre-modern past. The answer to these tensions and dilemmas proposed by Boaventura de Sousa Santos (this volume) is to defend equality whenever difference generates inferiority and to defend difference whenever a call for equality implies a threat to or a loss of identity.

The struggles of the indigenous peoples of Latin America have drawn attention to a crucial point: these struggles owe their success and their endurance to their ability to forge alliances between different peoples and ethnic groups, other social movements, non-governmental organizations (NGOs), and international solidarity movements. The consolidation of struggles for collective rights and for justice on a local scale depends, on the one hand, on mobilizing the national state as a guarantor of these rights and, on the other hand, on transnational solidarity. In many circumstances, alliances with sectors of the state (exploiting its tensions and internal contradictions) or the mobilization of judicial power may make all the difference between a successful and an unsuccessful struggle. To the extent that the processes of globalization generate definitions of rights on varying scales that affect the local definition of rights, resorting to international legal instances may be highly relevant to the success of local emancipatory alliances.

Alternative, counter-hegemonic globalization is based on the construction of emancipatory citizenships that articulate the local and the global through networks and polycentric coalitions. If the safeguard of the emancipatory nature of the struggles carried out at a local level requires that the direction and coordination of these struggles remain in the hands of local actors, then translocal and transnational alliances and the creation of international networks of information and active solidarity are an indispensable condition for preventing these struggles from becoming too localized and particularistic.

THE CRITIQUES OF SCIENCE
AND THE PLURALITY OF KNOWLEDGES

Some of the recent epistemological and political debates that have cut across the sciences and the transdisciplinary field known as "science studies" have displayed concerns that intersect or parallel many of the themes mentioned above. The questioning of the hegemonic conception of modern scientific knowledge, especially from the South and, in particular, during the last decades of the twentieth century, had ·significant consequences for all disciplines, not least for the social sciences (Santos, 1995, 2004a; Guha and Martinez-Alier, 1997; Visvanathan, 1997; Prakash, 1999; Escobar, 1999; Masolo, 2003). In the North, the debate drew as well upon Western traditions of philosophy and history of science and developed in two directions: one, which we could describe as "internal," questions the monolithical character of the epistemological canon and asks for the epistemological, sociological, and political relevance of the internal diversity of scientific practices and of the different ways of doing science; the other direction questions the epistemological exclusivism of science and focuses on the relationships between science and other knowledges, what we shall call the external plurality of science. Feminist and post-colonial critiques of conventional epistemologies have played a central role in both debates.

The internal and external plurality of modern science

The question of the *internal plurality of science* was raised, in the West, primarily by feminist epistemologies,[6] by social and cultural studies of science and by the currents in the history and philosophy of science influenced by the latter.[7] These approaches displayed the dependence of scientific research as an activity on the selection of topics, problems, theoretical models, methodologies, languages, and images and forms of argument; they studied, through historical and ethnographic research, the material cultures of the sciences,[8] the different ways in which scientists related to institutional contexts, to their peers, to the state, to funding agencies and entities, and to economic interests or to public interest; they highlighted the central significance of the conception of knowledge as a construction, as the interaction, through socially organized practices, of human actors, materials, instruments, ways of doing things, and skills, in order to create something that did not exist before, with new attributes, not reducible to the sum of the heterogeneous elements mobilized for its creation; and, finally, they scrutinized the conditions and limits of the autonomy of scientific activities, displaying their connections to the social and cultural context where they are carried out. Through their analyses of the heterogeneity of practices and of scientific narratives, these approaches exploded the presumed epistemological and praxiological unity of science and turned the opposition of the "two cultures" (of the sciences and of the humanities), as a structuring feature of the field of knowledge, into a rather unstable plurality of scientific and epistemic cultures and configurations of knowledges.[9] The recent episodes of the so-called "science wars" can be understood, according to this view, as an attempt at reasserting that divide and re-establishing and policing the boundaries of different domains of knowledge and their hierarchy.[10]

As the aforementioned studies have shown, the differentiation and specialization of the sciences are the outcome of historical changes associated with two processes. The first is the drawing of boundaries between science and technology, which often is still used to claim the intrinsic neutrality of science and locate the consequences of scientific research—be such consequences desirable or undesirable, good or bad, constructive or destructive—on its applications. The changes undergone over the last decades by the organization of scientific knowledge and its relationship to technological innovation and development have led, though, to significant reassessments of the historical record of that divide, which showed evidence of many situations in the past in which technological innovation and development were inseparable from the activity of scientific research itself. The widely used expression "technoscience" was proposed as a way of describing the impossibility of a radical differentiation of science and technology, stressing their mutual implication, as Laymert Garcia dos Santos points out in his chapter.[11]

The second process consists of the demarcation of science from other modes of relating to the world, taken to be non-scientific or irrational, including the arts, humanities, religion, and different versions of that relationship to the world which, paraphrasing Marx, confounds essence and appearance or, as Durkheim would say, allows collective life to rest upon "well-founded illusions," known as common sense. The assertion of the discontinuities of science and its "others" requires, as Gieryn (1999) has shown, a permanent commitment to boundary work, a ceaseless policing of borders and a persistent epistemological vigilance, in order to contain and repel the always allegedly imminent assaults of irrationality. This boundary work, however, had to face a number of obstacles, namely the very difficulty of dividing scientific knowledge and the objects of science from those that "belonged" to other domains of culture or to the vaguely defined territory of "opinion." The latter always had an ambiguous status in the history of the sciences, being regarded either as the "other" of science, which had to be denounced, demystified, and defeated in the name of rigor and reason, or as the "natural" ally of science, the obligatory point of passage for a transformation of the world according to the principles of reason and the Enlightenment.

But the sciences are themselves internally "disunified" (Galison and Stump, 1996). The attempt at reducing science to a single epistemological model inspired by Newtonian mechanics and based on mathematization as the ideal of scientificity was belied by a diversification of situated practices coexisting and/or intertwined in an "ecology of practices," hosting distinctive epistemological models, and which has been the object of social studies of science for the last three decades. The recognition of the principles that legitimated the different practices constituted as sciences led not only to the claim of a diversity of models of scientificity but to tensions between these models within the sciences themselves. The different ways in which that constitutive distinction of modern science, of subject and object, is enacted within different disciplines and scientific domains is another marker of the "disunity" of the sciences. The particular circumstances and conditions of the production of knowledge are crucial for assessing the difference that knowledge makes and how boundaries and demarcations work as modes of making autonomous and legitimating distinctive fields of practices, without their submission to "foreign" epistemological models, or, conversely, how the transgression of boundaries allows the emergence of new disciplines or research domains, as illustrated by the history of the life sciences or of the environmental sciences.[12]

Epistemological diversity is neither the simple reflection or epiphenome-non of ontological diversity or heterogeneity nor a range of culturally specific ways of expressing a fundamentally unified world. There is no essential or definitive way of describing, ordering, and classifying processes, entities, and relationships in the world. The very action of knowing, as pragmatist philosophers have repeatedly reminded us, is an intervention in the world, which places us within it as active contributors to its making. Different modes of knowing, being irremediably partial and situated, will have different consequences and effects on the world. The very capacity of the modern sciences to create new entities and in this way to enact an ontological politics (Mol, 2002)—with the effect, intentional or not, of increasing the hetero-geneity of the world—seems to support this conception. It gives shape to a robust realism and to a strong objectivity, a clear awareness of the need to accurately and precisely identify the conditions in which knowledge is produced and its assessment on the basis of its observed or expected consequences. This allows a rigorous account of the situatedness, partiality, and constructedness of all knowledges, while rejecting relativism as an epistemological and moral stance.[13]

That which exists—knowledge, technological objects, buildings, roads, cultural objects—exists *because* it is constructed through situated practices. The relevant distinction, as Latour reminds us, is not between the real and the constructed, but between that which is well constructed, which successfully resists the situations in which its consistency, solidity, and robustness are put to the test, and that which is badly constructed, and hence vulnerable to criticism or erosion. This is the difference that allows a distinction to be made between facts (well constructed) and artifacts (badly constructed).[14]

To produce knowledge is to accept the risk of putting to the test our beliefs and our ignorance without reducing what we do not know to what we already know and without dismissing as irrelevant what we cannot describe because we ignore it, but it is also to exercise prudence and precaution when dealing with the unknown or with the possible conse-quences of our actions.

This quick expedition into the "disunity" of the sciences suggests that the opposition of the two cultures, of the humanities and the sciences, is inadequate to account for the differentiation of the practices of knowledge-production and for the organization of knowledges, even in the context of modern Western societies. The emergence of post-colonial epistemological discourses showed how that opposition was constituted as an artifact of Western academic tradition, an outcome of the specific parameters that bounded the process of acculturation of science and the differentiation and hierarchization of knowledges (Alvares, 1992; Santos, 2004a).

Feminist criticism, in turn, has provided some of the most powerful resources for the criticism of the monoculture of knowledge based on modern science and, in particular, of the way it has historically excluded or marginalized certain subjects, such as women. The influence of women's movements and of the different currents of feminism on the growth of the participation of women in the academic world and in the worlds of science is well established.[15] There is less agreement on how this influence made itself felt. Schiebinger (1999) proposes a critical scrutiny of three paths to that influence: the participation of women in the production of science and in scientific institutions, including their access to advanced training, to jobs, and to career advancement; the changes in the culture of the sciences associated with that participation and with feminist critique, namely in shaping the organization of careers and of daily work, of the interactions between colleagues and between teachers and students, or the reorganization of the relationships between family life and occupational life; the change in the contents of knowledge itself in different disciplines and areas, in the definition of research topics, languages, images, research procedures, inter-pretation of results, and in the very definition of the boundaries between science and other forms of knowledge, allowing the recognition of practices associated, for instance, with local economic life, or with the local manage-ment of environment and health, usually performed by women, in a variety of social contexts.[16]

From the extensive body of literature on this subject, it is obvious that the consequences of feminist critique and of the debates over the science-gender link are, first, the denaturalization of the male dominance of modern science, sustained by a range of institutions, practices, and occupational ideologies; and second, the identification of the conditions associated with the constitution of knowledge subjects—not only gender, but ethnicity, class, nationality, or religion, to name only a few—and the consequent development of "strong" forms of objectivity, linked to the idea of the "positioned" or "situated" subject. Thus, feminist critique aims not to create a "separate" science but rather to contribute to changes in existing science, extending and renewing the critical horizon at the origins of modern science, incorporating new questions, perspectives, topics, and practices, in renewed institutional and occupational contexts, towards what Schiebinger (1999) describes as "sustainable science."[17]

Intercultural comparisons of Western science and other knowledge systems that have become localized (as traditional, native forms of knowledge) by the hegemonic force of Western science have brought new contributions to the debate, displaying continuities and disjunctions (Apfel-Marglin, and Marglin, 1990; Eze, 1997; Visvanathan, 2003; Escobar and Pardo; and Visvanathan, Meneses, and Xaba in this volume). This is where the discussion of the external plurality of knowledge, of the ways in which modern sciences have opened themselves to confrontation and dialogue with other forms of knowledge, has found an anchor.[18] In the light of this cultural critique of science it does not come as a surprise that Sarah Franklin (1995) defends *"science as culture,"* or that Sandra Harding (1998) regards modern science itself as an ethnoscience, with a deep imprint of particular conventions, boundary work procedures, and values.

THE COLONIALITY OF POWER AND KNOWLEDGE

Post-colonial criticism has conceived the hegemony of Western science, after the end of the colonial era, as a form of "coloniality of knowledge and power" (Shiva, 1993; Ela, 1998; Quijano 2000; Lander, 2000). From the fifteenth century onwards, the constitution of the "modern/colonial world-system" (Wallerstein, 1979; Mudimbe, 1988; Dussel, 1994, 1995; Chakrabarty, 2000; Quijano, 2000; Mignolo, 2000; Mbembe, 2001) rested upon multiple "creative destructions," often carried out on behalf of "civilizing," liberating, or emancipatory projects, which aimed at reducing the understandings of the world to the logic of Western epistemology. Examples of this were the conversion of the knowledges of colonized peoples and of the diversity of their cultures and cosmologies to expressions of irrationality, of superstition, or, at best, to practical and local forms of knowledge whose relevance was dependent on their subordination to modern science, perceived as the sole source of true knowledge, or to religious conversion or acculturation; the subordination of their customs to the law of the modern state and of their practices to the capitalist economy; and the reduction of the variety of their forms of social organization to the state/civil society dichotomy (Meneses, 2005). This multifaceted reduction, despite its arbitrary origin, became a conceptual orthodoxy and was responsible for the subordination of the peripheral and semi-peripheral regions and countries of the world system, which were to be called, at a later historical moment, the Third World, and which we shall refer to as the global South (Santos, 1995: 506–519).[19] This denial of diversity is a constitutive and persistent feature of colonialism. While the political dimension of colonial intervention has been widely criticized, the burden of the colonial epistemic monoculture is still accepted nowadays as a symbol of development and modernity (Alvarez,

1992; Escobar, 1995; Visvanathan, 1997; Meneses, 2003). Post-colonial studies may be regarded as a means to deal with this burden and its consequences. They will be defined, for our purposes, as

> a set of theoretical and analytical currents, firmly rooted in cultural studies but also present today in all the social sciences, sharing an important feature: in their understanding of the contemporary world, they all privilege, at the theoretical and political level, the unequal relations between the North and the South. Such relations were historically constituted by colonialism, and the end of colonialism as a political relation did not carry with itself the end of colonialism as a social relation, that is to say, as an authoritarian and discriminatory mentality and form of sociability. (Santos, 2004b)[20]

The post-colonial critique of the epistemic foundations of Western academic discourse has triggered and nourished discussions on the possibilities of construction of an alternative to capitalism. Post-colonialism, as some critics argued, is hostile to the possibility of such an alternative, due to its criticism of unified and homogeneous categories such as class, gender, and nation-state. Because post-colonialism does not contemplate the possibility of a politics of emancipation, they argue, it transforms resistance into an individual act. Much of this debate rests on the meanings of post-colonialism, as well as on the ambiguities that distinct visions of history place upon this concept. Although the "post" in post-colonialism is indicative of the end of colonialism and imperialism as direct political dominance, it does not imply the demise of imperialism as a global system of hegemonic power. Not surprisingly, Homi Bhabha, following Nkrumah, regards the condition of post-coloniality as "a salutary reminder of the persistent 'neo-colonial' relations within the 'new' world order and the multi-national division of labour" (1994: 6). As McClintock argues (1995: 10), the "post" in post-colonialism seeks to capture the continuities, ruptures, and complexities of specific historical periods, and attempts to go beyond the strict unilinear chronological and dichotomous conceptions that dominate contemporary social and political thinking. In our view, a post-colonial perspective draws on the idea that the structures of power and knowledge are more visible from the margins. Hence its interest in the geopolitics of knowledge, its eagerness to problematize the equation of who produces knowledge, in what context, and for whom. In this context, the reflections of Ghandi (2000), Nkrumah (1965), Césaire (2000), Fanon (1963), or Memmi (1965), which laid the foundations of the history of violence and misunderstanding produced by capitalism and of a vibrant indictment of colonialism, are still of great relevance for the debate over the knowledge–power relation. As the studies in this volume illustrate in detail, the end of political colonialism did not mean the end of colonialism as a social relationship associated with specific forms of knowledge and power, the coloniality of power and knowledge. It is clear, nowadays, that beyond its economic and political dimensions colonialism had a strong epistemological dimension.[21] And when one considers the resilience of such dichotomies as nature/society, savage/civilized, developed/underdeveloped one must ask how much of the colonial past remains in the post-colonial present.

The production of the West as hegemonic knowledge required the creation of an Other, constituted as an intrinsically disqualified being, a collection of characteristics that were markers of inferiority towards the power and knowledge of the West and, thus, available for use and appropriation by the latter.[22] Colonial alterity as a space of inferiority took various shapes that reconfigured the already existing processes of manufacturing inferiority, based on sex, race, or tradition (Ranger, 1988; Schiebinger, 1989; Santos, 1995; McClintock, 1995). As a result, three resilient subaltern figures are still with us: the woman, the savage, and nature.[23]

Many alternative forms of knowledge were destroyed and the social groups that relied on them to pursue their own and autonomous paths of development were humiliated, all in the name of modern science (Dussel, 2000: 49–50). Whatever the epistemological merits of modern science and their admittedly positive or, at least, benign effects, the self-constitution of science as a universal form of knowledge that claims the right to legislate over all other forms of knowledge leads to it being frequently regarded in the non-Western world as a Western particularism whose specificity consists of holding the power to define as particular, local, contextual, and situational all knowledges that are its rivals.

One of the most important events of the colonial intervention from the late seventeenth century to the early twentieth century was the invention of the "savage" as an inferior being and the promotion of the idea of scientific and technological progress as imperative to achieve the highest stage of development—Western civilization. This creation of the other as a being devoid of knowledge and culture—"*Historically, Africa is not part of the world; it cannot show evidence of any movement or development. The historic movements it displays—on the Northern region of the continent—belong to the Asian and European world*" (Hegel, 1970: 193)—was the counterpoint of the colonial requirement of transporting civilization and wisdom to peoples who lived in the dark recesses of ignorance. The segmentation of colonial society into the "civilized" and the "indigenous" endowed the whole colonial system with consistency by means of the reduction of the natives to the category of natural objects.

If the savage represents the ultimate locus of inferiority, nature is the ultimate locus of exteriority (Santos, 1999). But since what is exterior does not belong and what does not belong is not recognized as equal, the locus of exteriority is a locus of inferiority as well. The civilizing violence enacted upon the "savages" via the destruction of native knowledges and the imprinting of "true," civilized knowledge is performed, in the case of nature, through its transformation into an unconditionally available natural resource. In both cases, though, knowledge strategies are basically strategies of power and domination. In the case of the construction of "nature," knowledge and power went hand in hand; this is not to say that knowledge was produced in advance as an instrument to justify the subordination of nature to society, but that the latter is an effect of the joining of power and knowledge. The savage and nature are, in fact, the two sides of the same purpose: to domesticate "savage nature," turning it into a natural resource. This unique will to domestication makes the distinction between natural and human resources as ambiguous and fragile in the sixteenth century as it is today.

To be persuasive and effective, this account of the discovery of nature cannot question the nature of the discovery. Over time, what cannot be questioned ceases to be a question. Nature, turned into a resource, has no logic but that of being exploited to its exhaustion. Once nature is separated from human beings and from society, there is no way of conceiving of how they feed back into each other. This concealment prevents the formulation of balances and of limits, and that is why ecology can assert itself only through ecological crises.[24]

This construction of nature as external to society and as a resource—something alien to the peoples the Europeans came in contact with—was one of the core foundations of the capitalistic civilizational model. It followed the requirements of the constitution of the new world economic system based on the intensive exploitation of resources. The deterministic script resting upon the divisions of nature and society, of subject and object, and the central role of mathematical language turned nature into an interlocutor as unintelligible and alien as the "savages" dwelling in the territories occupied and conquered by Westerners: nature could not be understood; it could only be explained, and explaining it was the mission of modern science; it was there to be used, exploited and appropriated (Santos, 1999).

The building of colonial empires implied the export to the colonies of the ways of living of the so-called "civilized," a process that persists today, disguised as aid to the poor and underdeveloped (Diawara, 2000; Meneses, 2003; Pithouse, 2003). Colonialism, devised as an epistemic concept during imperial times, is still a synonym of the impoverishment of "local" knowledges in so far as it promotes the ghettoization of those knowledges and the obliteration of other forms of knowing, that is, of producing and passing on experiences. The latter came to be confined to the condition of artifacts to be displayed in museums, as examples of an earlier, obscure, so-called "traditional" knowledge (Nygren, 1999; Lander, 2000). As a consequence, the plural landscape of knowledges existing in the world was rapidly overshadowed by the rise of modern science—a means of adjudicating supremacy and unicity.

In Africa and Asia, as had happened earlier in Latin America, the emergence of nationalist movements in the twentieth century would revive the debates over science and its function, the politics of knowledge, and the entitlement to existence of other forms of knowledge (Mondlane, 1969; Cabral, 1979; Apffel-Marglin and Marglin, 1990; Alvares, 1992; Diouf, 1993; Dussel, 1995; Visvanathan, 1998; Prakash, 1999; Mora-Osejo and Fals Borda, 2003; Meneses, 2003).But these debates would soon wither away with the independence of colonial territories. "Defeating underdevelopment" became the new rallying call.[25] The application of scientific results regarded as relevant and already achieved by other countries became a central aim. Efforts were thus directed towards the application and diffusion of scientific results and resources transferred from the North, both in the main front of the "battle for production" and in the training of qualified experts and technicians. Science was restored to its place of domination, this time as part of state-centered and deterministic schemes, stuffed with a rootless positivism that dismissed doubt, as was the case with the decision to build the big dams in India (Alvares, 1992). The buzzword was technological transfer and the associated concepts of invention, innovation, and diffusion. Invention was the experimental field of the expert, the scientist. Innovation was the world of technique, subject to local applications; and diffusion appeared as the very embodiment of democracy: the knowledges that had been at the root of the progress and prosperity of others were now made available for the common good (Visvanathan, 2003). During this period, science moved from a recurrent reflection on its social role to science as an object of popularization, of consumption: science as a marketable good.

By the time feminist criticism, science studies, and post-colonial studies relaunched debates over the legitimacy of different knowledges and their intercultural comparison, the influence of Western notions of rationality and scientificity had already transformed modern science into a central reference for assessing "other" local cultures and knowledge systems (Hountondji, 1994; Wiredu, 1996). This capacity to reproduce the Other *ad aeternum* through the epistemic and cultural dichotomy opposing scientific knowledge and alternative, rival knowledges has guaranteed the self-renewal, to the present, of the notion of underdevelopment. Having been stripped of experience, the South can regain it only through the accumulated experiences of the North, exported under the form of "the transfer of scientific knowledge and technology." International agencies still operate on the premise that the South has problems and the North has the solutions to them. The global South, underdeveloped, illiterate, sick, becomes an object of intervention, and normalizes the right of the North to intervene and control, adapt, and reshape structures, practices, and ways of life. The argument of "development" thus helps legitimize interventions in the South, in order to accommodate it to Western norms of progress, governance, and efficiency. The idea of development encapsulates the notion that it is the North that possesses "good" knowledge and ensures that science will overcome superstition and ignorance and benefit the needy, namely those who lack any suitable environmental ethics and long-term sustainable planning, are unable to carry out experiments, etc. (Crewe and Harrison, 2002).

In most countries of the South, the political changes of the 1980s and 1990s took shape in the application of neoliberal reforms, many of them imposed by international agencies such as the World Bank and the International Monetary Fund, for whom technical support and the imposition of scientific knowledge produced in the North are key areas of intervention (Stiglitz, 1999; Mehta, 2001; Santos, 2006b). As Cox and Schechter argue (2002: 76), "*globalisation is a struggle over knowledge of world affairs,*" reminding us that science-as-commodity remains the central vector of subordination of South to North. Asymmetries between North and South are expressed in a broad range of dichotomies: donor/recipient; developed/underdeveloped; knowledge/ignorance; teaching/learning; thinking/acting; recommending/following; designing/implementing. The reconceptualization of power is useful here not only to broaden our understanding of colonial relations, but also for generating a powerful criticism of current political structures, institutions and practices of power.

A common element in different development discourses is the emphasis on the difference between specialist knowledge and local forms of knowledge and the deepening of oppositions such as rational/magical (religious), universal/particular, theoretical/practical, and modern/traditional. These powerful dichotomies influence the way in which arguments are constructed and favor one form of knowledge at the expense of another (or others). If scientific, modern knowledge is portrayed as holding a dynamic, neutral, and objective authority, this image contrasts with a static and particularistic vision of other systems of knowledge found in the world (Masolo, 2003; Meneses, 2003).

Within the context of contemporary interactions between modern science and other "local" knowledges, the latter are regarded as valid only when they serve the projects of capitalist modernity; such is currently the case with traditional medical and agricultural knowledge, as discussed in the chapters by Laymert Garcia dos Santos, Flórez Alonso, Shiva, Meneses, Xaba, and Egziabher.

However, if the expressions "local knowledge," "indigenous knowledge," "traditional knowledge," or even "ethnoscience" have become part of academic discourse throughout the last two decades, their use in the North and the South is associated with distinct meanings. Until recently, social scientists did not recognize local forms of knowledge as being central to the process of development (Agrawal, 1995; Warren *et al.*, 1995; Battiste and Youngblood, 2000), nor were forms of so-called "lay" knowledge or experience regarded, in the North, as relevant sources and resources for the construction of epistemically and socially "robust" configurations of scientific knowledge (Irwin and Michael, 2003; Callon, Lascoumes, and Barthe, 2001).

It is increasingly acknowledged that current scientific knowledge imposes as the only true or adequate interpretation of reality a worldview conceived as a global explanation of the world, thereby eliminating the possibility of a complementarity or articulation of knowledges (Santos, 1995: 25 ff; 2004b). But if we take scientific knowledge as a form of globalized localism,[26] we may recognize that one of the aspects of the crisis of modern knowledge rests upon the fact that it perpetuates the relations of colonial inequality, giving shape to a monoculture of knowledge.[27]

Over the last two decades, the struggle of "alternative" knowledges has vigorously challenged this conception of other knowledges as "merely" local or indigenous by demonstrating that knowledges are hybrid and situated constructions (Nygren, 1999; Masolo, 2003; Derman, 2003). They are the outcomes of socially organized practices involving the mobilization of different types of material and intellectual resources, bound to specific situations and contexts. The call for the democratization of knowledges is equated with the multifarious capacity of science for interaction with other knowledges and practices, contesting the ideals of the "unity of science" (Dupré, 1993; Galison and Stump, 1996; Nader, 1996).

Towards new configurations of knowledges

A critical front that resonates strongly with the multiculturalism debates and pursues themes that are common to post-colonial, feminist, and science studies has allowed the recognition of plural systems of knowledges, alternative to modern science or entering into articulations with the latter and creating new configurations of knowledges. This process has been achieved, with productive results, especially in the more peripheral areas of the modern world system, where the meeting of hegemonic and non-hegemonic knowledges is more unequal and violent. It is precisely in these areas that non-hegemonic knowledges and their carriers are more in need of founding their resistance in processes of self-knowledge that mobilize the broader social, cultural, and historical context that breeds and sustains inequality, while generating energies that resist it (see Meneses, Xaba, Escobar and Pardo, in this volume).[28]

These "local" resistances open up a window towards a broader critical evaluation of knowledge as situated and socially constructed, a perspective that allows for a more comprehensive "translation" and comparison among all knowledges (including scientific knowledge) on the basis of their capacities for the fulfillment of certain tasks in social contexts drawn by particular processes (including those that are associated with scientific knowledge). The work of translation, as we conceive of it, seeks to turn incommensurability into difference, a difference enabling mutual intelligibility among the different projects of social emancipation. The goal is to construct an ethical and political position without grounding it on any absolute principle, be it human nature or progress, since, historically, it was in their names that many emancipatory aspirations turned into forms of violence and atrocity, especially in the South. This stance is anti-relativistic. From the point of view of the pragmatics of social emancipation, relativism, as an absence of criteria for hierarchies of validity among different forms of knowledge, is an untenable position. If anything is equally valid as knowledge, all projects of social emancipation are equally valid or, which amounts to the same, equally invalid (Santos, 2004b). Dialogues between knowledges may lead to regional or sectoral universalisms constructed from below, that is, to counter-hegemonic global public spheres—what we refer to in this introduction as "subaltern cosmopolitism." Cosmopolitan approaches start from the recognition of the presence of a plurality of knowledges and of distinctive conceptions of human dignity and of the world. The merit or the validity of the different knowledges and conceptions must obviously be assessed, but not on the basis of the mere disqualification of some. The future is not in going back to old traditions, since no technology is neutral: each technology carries with it the weight of its mode of seeing and being in nature and with other human beings. The future can thus be found at the crossroads of knowledges and technologies.

The epistemic diversity of the world is open, since all knowledges are situated. There are neither pure nor complete knowledges; there are constellations of knowledges. The claim of the universal character of modern science is increasingly displayed as just one form of particularism, whose specificity consists of having the power to define all the knowledges that are its rivals as particularistic, local, contextual, and situational. The recognition of epistemological diversity is a highly contested terrain because in it converge not only contradictory epistemological and cultural conceptions but also contradictory political and economic interests. A domain in which this has become most evident in recent times is biodiversity, which appears as an exemplary instance of the issues dealt with in this introduction.

CONTENTIOUS AREAS: THE CASE OF BIODIVERSITY

There is enough evidence today of how capitalism has appropriated the human body, turning cells into microfactories, revolutionizing the concept of social work, and eroding even more the thin line that separates the reproduction of life from the production of life, as is shown, in this volume, by Laymert Garcia dos Santos. When human nature is conceived as a potential or actual commodity and is used as technology—specifically in the case of reproduction and genetic research—the belief in scientific progress is inscribed in the human body itself. Biological and human integrity thus become vulnerable to the demands of the market. Studies of biodiversity and the projects related to the human genome have shown that the emerging markets for genetic information are new areas for both the accumulation of capital and the construction of new meanings and contexts for nature, both human and non-human (Wilkie, 1996; Haraway, 1997; Flinter, 1998; Hayden, 1998; Reardon, 2005).[29]

These issues have fostered a proliferation of controversial themes at the intersection of the internal debates within scientific knowledge, of the tensions and confrontations between rival forms of knowledge, and of the contradictions and conflicts that weave together the scientific-technical, the political, the cultural, and the economic that the critics of colonialism and of coloniality have brought to the fore. The controversies over biodiversity condense in an exemplary way these different dimensions of contention.

The concept of biodiversity emerged in the late 1980s and early 1990s (Takacs, 1996), and was rapidly integrated into the discourse on the environmental situation of the world, namely in international fora such as the 1992 Rio Summit. It has tight connections to the conception of the South as the world reservoir of biological diversity (Shiva, 1993; and in this volume). Biodiversity or biological diversity is understood, according to the United Nations Convention on Biological Diversity (CBD), in its article 2, as the "*variability among living organisms of all origins, including, inter alia, the terrestrial, marine and other aquatic ecosystems and the ecological complexes they are part of. It includes the internal diversity of species, between species and of ecosystems.*"[30] The World Resources Institute proposed a broadening of this definition, including genetic diversity, the variations among individuals and populations within the same species, and the diversity of species and ecosystems (WRI, 1994: 147). The term "biodiversity" in fact refers to the diversity of organisms, genotypes, species, and ecosystems, but also to the knowledges about that diversity.

The actually existing knowledge of ecosystems and of living species and organisms is a lot broader than that "officially" registered in databases constructed by scientific institutions.[31] Not surprisingly, as Laymert Garcia dos Santos analyzes in his contribution, the construction of what is currently a network—or, more precisely, a set of networks—of knowledges on biodiversity has not been the outcome of a hegemonic conception and of the "stabilization" of that concept, as happened in other instances of technoscience when it met other knowledges. The alternative discourses produced by subaltern actors are themselves part of that network, and they circulate within it with great visibility and impact. The discourse on biodiversity is, in fact, a set of discourses where different knowledges, cultures, and political strategies intersect. In spite of being dominated by institutions from the North (NGOs, botanical gardens, universities and research institutions, pharmaceutical multinational corporations, etc.), the knowledges produced by these networks have been used as well in "subversive" ways, through their appropriation by social movements of the South and their allies and through their reinscription in other constellations of power–knowledge. Escobar (1999) thus identifies four main positions within the biodiversity network:

1. A "globalocentric" view, focused on the management of the resources of biodiversity, sustained mainly by global institutions, including the World Bank, G8 and several NGOs based in the North, such as the World Conservation Union, the World Resources Institute or the World Wildlife Fund. The focus of this view is the response to what it defines as the threats to biodiversity, including the loss of habitats, the introduction of species in foreign environments, the fragmentation of habitats following their reduction, etc. Responses consist of a set of measures articulated at different levels (local, regional, global), including scientific research, inventories, *in situ* conservation, national planning of the management of biodiversity and the creation of economic mechanisms to promote the conservation of resources, such as intellectual property rights and others. The CBD itself draws on dominant views of science, capital, and management practices, and is at the origin of the current dominant discourse on biodiversity. A role is acknowledged, under this perspective, for knowledges alternative to the dominant ones, usually described as "traditional," but the position that governs is that which endows science with a central role in designing strategies of conservation, insertion in programs for sustainable development,

or the creation of a variety of schemes for sharing benefits between national governments, corporations, research institutions, and communities. It is mostly in relation to so-called bioprospecting that these schemes have been proposed over the last two decades.[32]

2. A national perspective, in countries of the South, that, without putting into question the main features of the previous position and the "globalo-centric" discourse, seeks to negotiate the terms of treaties and strategies for biodiversity following what they define as the national interest. According to Escobar (1999: 59), the topic of genetic resources has given a renewed vigor to the interest of governments in these negotiations. Included among the most lively discussed themes of these negotiations are conservation *in situ* and access to collections *ex situ*, sovereignty over genetic resources, ecological debt, and technology transfers. Some of the studies included in this volume, such as those by Escobar and Pardo and Borges Coelho, provide a record and analysis of these negotiations.

3. A conception sustained by the progressive NGOs of the South that may be described as biodemocracy: through a reinterpretation of "threats to biodi-versity"—emphasizing the destruction of habitats through megaprojects of development, the monocultures of the mind, agriculture promoted by capital and the reductionist science and habits of consumption of the North promoted by narrowly conceived economic models—biodemocracy advo-cates the displacement of attention from South to North as the origin of the biodiversity crisis. At the same time, it suggests a radical redefinition of production and productivity, moving away from a logic of uniformity towards a logic of diversity. The latter assumes the local control of natural resources, the suspension of developmental megaprojects, support for pro-jects promoting the logic of diversity, and the recognition of a cultural basis associated with biological diversity.[33] Those who advocate this approach oppose the use of biotechnology as a means for maintaining diversity[34] and of intellectual property rights (IPR) as a tool for the protection of local knowledges and resources, proposing as an alternative the defense of collective rights. The articulation of forms of local activism connected through networks at the transnational and global scales appears here as an effective means of defending local knowledges.

4. Finally, the perspective of cultural autonomy starts form a critique of the concept of "biodiversity" as a hegemonic construction to search for the opening up of spaces within the biodiversity network. This enables the construction of forms of development based on culture and on livelihood projects associated with places, in order to counter ethnocentric or, as

Escobar describes them, "extractivist" orientations towards biological diversity. This position is upheld by the movements of the Pacific coast of Colombia studied by Escobar and Pardo, in this volume.[35]

The controversies and conflicts over biodiversity raise new questions concerning the foundational overlap of the discovery of the savage and the discovery of nature. It is hardly by chance that a good deal of the biodiversity of the planet is present in territories inhabited by indigenous peoples, for whom nature never was a natural resource, as the West understands this notion. For these peoples, nature cannot be dissociated from society, within the frame of cosmologies that divide and classify the world in ways that are different from the one enshrined by modern, Western cosmology. Colonialism and, at a later stage, the forms of subalternization that are characteristic of post-colonialism are associated with attempts to destroy these cosmologies and their worlds. Nowadays, as happened in the dawn of the world capitalist system, the multinational corporations of the pharmaceutical industry and of biotechnology seek to turn the indigenous peoples themselves into resources, no longer labor resources, but genetic resources and tools for accessing, through traditional knowledges, plants and other living beings, including human biology itself, in the form of biodiversity.[36] The IPRs that allow and legitimate these forms of appropriation of indigenous and local knowledge and the private appropriation of goods that are vital, for instance, for the safeguard and promotion of public health rest upon conceptions of private property rooted in the legal order of capitalism.[37] This is a central concern associated with the application of TRIPS.[38] Its article 27.3b requires from member countries of the World Trade Organization that they award patents over living matter, with the exception of plants and animals, although the obligation is still pending on offering an effective *sui generis* protection of the varieties of plants (Flórez and Rojas, 2001). If for some this offer appears as a solution to strengthen the collective rights of indigenous peoples and farming communities within the narrow space for maneuver allowed by this legal Western codification,[39] there are many who oppose any form of legal compromise on protection. For them, any global legal imposition is seen as a threat to the survival of communities, as an attack on their cultures and on their rights. Ultimately, what is at stake is the sovereignty of each culture, of each community, since the imposition of TRIPS—and consequently the rise of monopolies over seed banks, for instance—threatens the possibility of protecting the world's genetic diversity (Cullet, 2001), enforcing a regime of monocultures of knowledge and increasing the risk of contamination with genetically modified plants of the places where greatest biological diversity is found (Simpson, 1997).

The process—typical of dominant approaches in the fields of technos-cientific knowledge involved in the prospection of biodiversity, of decomposing and reducing the phenomena of life and of the diversity of the living, and appropriating them as knowledge and as commodities—has been denounced as biopiracy (Shiva, 1997; Mooney, 2000; Laymert Garcia dos Santos, in this volume). There have been, however, attempts at defining alternative frameworks for legislation and the regulation of the appropriation of local and community knowledges, and in particular of knowledges of biodiversity. The Model Proposal of Law of the Organization for African Unity, proposed by the government of Ethiopia in 1998, seeks to promote legislative initiatives based on the cooperation of African states with a view to the protection of the resources of biodiversity and local forms of social organization and to ensure food sovereignty, through the defense and active mobilization of what we describe as rival knowledges.[40]

The wide circulation, reinterpretation and redefinition of the concept of biodiversity, despite all its problems and limitations, has thus given rise to new possibilities of articulating different cosmologies and languages from a variety of critical perspectives that seek to redefine the articulations between—or the mutual constitution or co-production of—objects, beings, and the qualities that used to be attributed either to nature or to culture (Descola and Palsson, 1996; Haraway, 1997).

CONCLUSION: TOWARDS AN EMANCIPATORY, NON-RELATIVISTIC, COSMOPOLITAN ECOLOGY OF KNOWLEDGES

The case studies included in this volume articulate the different themes dealt with in the previous sections, and go one step further by exemplifying the promises, possibilities, and difficulties of bringing together and staging dialogues and alliances between diverse forms of knowledge, cultures, and cosmologies in response to different forms of oppression that enact the coloniality of knowledge and power. Boaventura de Sousa Santos's appeal for "learning from the South" (1995: 508) indicates precisely that the aim to reinvent social emancipation goes beyond the critical theory produced in the North and the social and political praxis to which it has subscribed. As a contribution to the "opening" of the canon of knowledge, we have formulated a set of theses on the ongoing debates and initiatives on diversity and recognition.

1) *Different human communities produce diverse forms of viewing and dividing up the world, which do not necessarily conform to Eurocentric distinctions. The latter include, for example, those that divide up social practice between the economy, society, the state, and culture, or that drastically separate nature from society. A re-evaluation of the relationship between these different conceptions of the world and their repercussions on law and justice is currently in progress.*

Differences between worldviews become explicit and turn into sites of struggle when the integrity of the communities is threatened by alternative notions of relationships to territory—such as those that are based on the individual right to property—or when the distinction between respect for culture and the imperative of development is drawn upon to justify the exploitation of "natural resources" by external forces (be they national or multinational institutions).

The adoption of Eurocentric legal and political models, and claims of their allegedly universal validity, such as the neoliberal economic order, representative liberal democracy, or the supremacy of liberal law, often rest upon forms of domination based on class, ethnic, territorial, racial, or sexual difference and on the denial of collective identities and rights deemed incompatible with Eurocentric definitions of the modern social order. Yet, there is scope for the right to difference to be affirmed, as several examples discussed here demonstrate, by creating conceptions of normality, law, nature, and morality alternative to dominant conceptions.

2) Different forms of oppression or domination generate equally distinct forms of collective resistance, mobilization, subjectivity, and identity, which invoke differentiated notions of justice and dignity. In these types of resistance and their local/global articulation through procedures of intercultural translation resides the impulse towards counter-hegemonic globalization.

It is by resisting assimilation that indigenous populations have come to impose on the Latin American states recognition of their identity as a people and of their collective rights. The rural populations in various regions of India are struggling against the multinationals, international organizations, and the state itself for the right to their own environment, way of life, and natural resources. Human rights activists are fighting for human dignity and against suffering in different parts of the world.

The collective identities associated with these different forms of struggle are the emerging result of the struggles themselves, even when based on pre-existing conditions or collectives. The ability to widen, sustain, and win the struggles depends on the transition of these communities from local to imagined and invented communities, created through a "voracity of scales" that enlarges the struggles from the local to the national and transnational. The successes of the indigenous movements in Brazil and in Colombia in mobilizing translocal and transnational solidarity provide exemplary illustrations of the importance of broad circles of reciprocity. The language of culture and multiculturalism is mobilized, in these situations, as a fundamental strategic resource and as a means of making claims for difference that are mutually intelligible and shared.

3) Emancipatory politics and the invention of new citizenships are played out within the tensions between equality and difference, that is, between the need for redistribution and the demand for recognition.

Equality and difference are not, in themselves, sufficient conditions for a politics of emancipation. The debate on human rights and their reinvention as multicultural rights, as well as the struggles of indigenous peoples show that the affirmation of equality based on universalistic presuppositions, such as those that prevail in Western individualistic conceptions of human rights, lead to the decharacterization and denial of differentiated identities, cultures, and historical experiences, particularly through the refusal to recognize collective rights. Yet the affirmation of difference, in itself, can serve to justify discrimination, exclusion, or subordination in the name of collective rights and cultural specificity. The collective rights of the indigenous populations of Brazil and Colombia have come to be recognized and affirmed through their struggles in the 1988 and 1991 Constitutions, respectively, thus giving rise to a multicultural constitutional order. As the case of India suggests, the legal pluralism that results from the intersecting dynamics of the global, the national, and the local can create spaces for the recognition of alternative forms of normativity, but these can only effectively result in emancipatory dynamics in articulation with alternative conceptions of justice and redistribution policies directed towards the most vulnerable and subaltern groups in the population. In the case of the U'wa or the Afro-Colombians of the Pacific coast, the affirmation of identity is a resource for demanding recognition of their collective rights, associated with an effective guarantee of control over a territory and its resources. In other cases, as with natural disasters in Mozambique, identity enacted on the basis of local knowledges can also be used to contrast external, national solutions. In order to address these tensions and dilemmas Boaventura de Sousa Santos (this volume) proposes the following meta-right: we have the right to be equal when difference breeds inferiority and the right to be different when claims of equality threaten our right to identity based on shared experiences and histories.

4) The epistemic diversity of the world is potentially infinite. There is no ignorance or knowledge in general. All ignorance is ignorant of a certain knowledge, and all knowledge is the overcoming of a particular ignorance. There are no complete knowledges.

As the concrete experiences discussed here show, the epistemological diversity of the world is immense. The production of knowledge is, in itself, a social practice and what distinguishes it from other social practices is the thinking or reflecting on actors, actions and their consequences in the contexts where they take place. Every form of knowledge thus involves self-reflexivity, which productively reshapes the context of practices into the motive and engine of actions that do not simply repeat their contexts. This self-reflexivity is the same as the discovery of hetero-referentiality. It is the first step towards·the recognition of the epistemological diversity of the world. The latter, in turn, is inseparable from the diversity of cosmologies that divide and organize the world in ways that are different from that of Western cosmology and modern science. A cosmopolitan epistemology must start from the recognition of the presence of a plurality of knowledges and of different conceptions of human dignity, nature, and the world itself, as the cases from South Africa, Mozambique, Brazil, India, and Colombia suggest. The principle of incompleteness of knowledges is a basic condition for the possibility of epistemological dialogue and debate among knowledges.

5) *In practice, knowledges operate as constellations of knowledges. The relativity of knowledges is not synonymous with relativism.*

Constellations of knowledges always involve hierarchies among the forms of knowledge that constitute them. The practical knowledge and good sense of the scientist in the laboratory are very important, but, of course, scientists are at the service of the scientific knowledge he or she starts from and seeks to advance. In other words, from a pragmatist point of view, relativism is a non-issue. No human practice could be carried out in a consistent way if all the different types of knowledge that intervene in it had the same weight. As an epistemological problem, relativism is less about criteria of validation than about the criteria for establishing hierarchies of validation or their absence. From the point of view of the pragmatics of social emancipation that is at the center of the research project out of which came the studies in this volume, relativism, as long as it is regarded as an absence of criteria for the hierarchies of validation, is an untenable position, since it makes impossible the very conception of a meaningful relation between knowledge and social change. If everything is equally valid, and equally valid as knowledge, all projects of social change are equally valid or (which is the same) equally lacking in validity.

6) *The epistemological privilege of modern science is a complex phenomenon that cannot be explained in exclusively epistemological terms. The claim of the universal character of modern science is just one form of particularism, whose specificity is the power to define all the knowledges that are its rivals as particularistic, local, contextual, and situational. Global cognitive justice will be possible by substituting a monoculture of scientific knowledge by an ecology of knowledges.*

The differences among knowledges imposed by modern science are the result of what counts as relevant knowledge, differences in identifying, validating, or hierarchizing the relations between Western-based scientific knowledge and other knowledges derived from other practices, rationalities, or cultural universes.

After centuries of mutual implication between epistemological models and models for social change, it is not possible to think and even less enact alternatives for emancipatory social change without epistemological changes. The challenge of an ecology of knowledges (Santos, 2004a: 168–171) is the epistemological stance from which it is possible to start thinking about the decolonization of science and, thus, the creation of a new type of relationship between scientific knowledge and other knowledges. The ecology of knowledges represents the possibility of opening up the dominant canon of knowledge and recognition, by bringing into the picture other, alternative, non-scientific knowledges. This new relationship lies in granting an "equality of opportunities" to the different kinds of knowledge engaged in ever broader epistemological disputes aimed at maximizing their respective contributions to build a more democratic and just society, and the decolonization of knowledge and power. The point is not to ascribe equal validity to all kinds of knowledge but rather to allow for a pragmatic discussion of alternative criteria of validity, which does not straightforwardly disqualify whatever does not fit the epistemological canon of modern science.

It is not so much a matter of opposing modern science to other knowledges as of creating dialogues, both within science and between different conceptions and practices of knowledge that the ruling epistemology is unable to identify. What is at stake in the epistemological change we propose is not the validity of science, but its exclusive validity. The proposed pluralism of knowledges will facilitate radical democratization and the decolonization of knowledge and power.

7) *The decolonization of science is based on the idea that there is no global social justice without global cognitive justice. The logic of the monoculture of scientific knowledge and rigor must be confronted with the identification of other knowledges and criteria of rigor that operate credibly in other social practices regarded as subaltern.*

The coloniality of power and knowledge plays a central role in providing the conditions and resources for multiple forms of domination and discrimination. Colonialism has come to an end as a political relationship, but not as a social relationship, persisting in the shape of the coloniality of power. In dealing with the relations between North and South, between core and periphery of the world-system, the coloniality of power is, nowadays more than ever, inextricable from the coloniality of knowledge. Neoliberal globalization and the strict recipes of economic science and the type of technological development they promote have brought to a peak the destruction of other knowledges and practices, worldviews, symbolic worlds, and the modes of living they legitimate and make credible. This massive attack on the diversity of knowledges in the world promotes an unprecedented impoverishment of social and cultural experience.

8) *The recognition of the diversity and plurality of knowledges requires the internal democratization of science itself.*

There are two sides to this. The first concerns the recognition of the internal plurality of science, not only the plurality that follows from disciplinary divisions but also that emerging from the different theoretical, analytical, and conceptual traditions and of their modes and processes of constructing knowledge, and the ways in which controversy and methodological transgression are dealt with. The process of paradigm construction is neither linear nor irreversible and even after its consolidation rival paradigms persist with more or less visibility. The persistent signs of the existence of the latter, even if repressed by the mechanisms Kuhn identified, are not just residues of the past; they may well be the embryos of new paradigms. Their insertion in the process of making science is related to their multi-situatedness. In other words, science is produced in different social contexts and these are not external to science; rather, science and context interpenetrate to co-produce practices and styles of scientific activity. This does not make scientific knowledge less valid in general. But it is upon these features that the always provisional and relative validity of scientific statements, their recurrently contestable "warranted assertibility," as John Dewey put it, rest. The recognition of this internal plurality expands the scope of theoretical, analytical, and epistemological debates and makes science more pliable and open to the epistemological diversity of the world. In other words, recognition of internal plurality is a condition for the recognition of external plurality.

The other side of the democratization of science concerns the relationships and mutual engagements of scientific communities and citizens, of scientific knowledge and the cognitive skills required for active citizenship, both individual and collective, in societies that conceive of their welfare as increasingly inseparable from their multicultural character and as dependent on the quantity and quality of the knowledges circulating within them. From laboratory practices to ritual practices, every human activity with a minimal degree of complexity mobilizes a plurality of types of knowledge, even if one of these comes to be dominant in configuring the practice in question and the way in which it relates to the context it operates in and transforms. In pragmatist terms, there are only constellations of knowledges and the most decisive epistemological question is that which asks for the hierarchies of the different types of knowledge within these constellations, for the reasons for those hierarchies, for their effectiveness, and for their consequences.

9) *The transition from a monoculture of scientific knowledge to an ecology of knowledges will make possible the replacement of knowledge-as-regulation with knowledge-as-emancipation.*

The ecology of knowledges is the principle of consistency underlying constellations of knowledges. The transition from the monoculture of scientific knowledge to the ecology of knowledges will be difficult since its success is concurrent with that of other transitions pointing towards post-capitalist horizons of radical democracy and the decolonization of power and knowledge. One way of describing this process is as the replacement of knowledge-as-regulation by knowledge-as-emancipation. Knowledge-as-regulation knows through a trajectory that goes from ignorance, regarded as disorder, to knowledge, described as order, while knowledge-as-emancipation knows through a trajectory that leads from ignorance, conceived of as colonialism, to knowledge conceived of as solidarity (Santos, 1995: 25–27; 2002). The possibility of modern science contributing to the construction of knowledge-emancipation was historically frustrated by the self-assigned epistemological exclusiveness of modern science, a process "required," historically, by the increasing connections of science to the objectives of social change associated with capitalism and colonialism. The recovery of the emancipatory potential of science is possible through the democratization and decolonization of science. But this requires that science cease to be a metonymy of knowledge and become one of its constituents, an important one for sure, within the constellations of knowledges aiming at social emancipation.

BIBLIOGRAPHY

Abrahamsen, R. (2003), "African Studies and the Postcolonial Challenge," *African Affairs,* 102, 189–202.

Afzal-Khan, F.; Sheshadri-Crooks, K. (2000), *The Pre-occupation of Postcolonial Studies.* Durham, NC: Duke University Press.

Agrawal, A. (1995), "Dismantling the Divide between Indigenous and Scientific Knowledge," *Development and Change,* 26(3), 413–439.

Ahmad, A. (1992), *In Theory: Classes, Nations, and Literatures.* London: Verso.

Alvares, C. (1992), *Science, Development and Violence: The Revolt against Modernity.* Delhi: Oxford University Press.

Anderson, B. (1983), *Imagined Communities: Reflections on the Origin and Spread of Nationalism.* London: Verso.

Apffel-Marglin, F.; Marglin, S. A. (eds.) (1990), *Dominating Knowledge: development, culture and resistance.* Oxford: Clarendon Press.

Asad, T. (1991), "Afterword: From the History of Colonial Anthropology to the Anthropology of Western Hegemony," *in* G. Stocking (ed.), *Colonial Situations: Essays on the Contextualization of Ethnographic Knowledge.* Madison: University of Wisconsin Press.

Balick, M.; Elisabetsky, E.; Laird, S. (eds.) (1996), *Medicinal Resources of the Tropical Forests*. New York: Columbia University Press.

Battiste, M.; Youngblood Henderson, J. (2000), *Protecting Indigenous Knowledge and Heritage*. Saskatoon: Purich Publishing Ltd.

Bebbington, A. (1993), "Modernization from Below: an Alternative Indigenous Development?," *Economic Geography*, 69(3), 274–292.

Bennett, D. (1998), *Multicultural States: Rethinking Difference and Identity*. London: Routledge.

Bhabha, H. K. (1994), *The Location of Culture*. London: Routledge.

Bharucha, R. (2000), *The Politics of Cultural Practice: Thinking Through Theatre in an Age of Globalisation*. London: The Athlone Press.

Cabral, A. (1979), *Unity and Struggle: Speeches and Writings of Amilcar Cabral*. New York: Monthly Review Press.

Callon, M.; Lascoumes, P.; Barthe, Y. (2001), *Agir dans un Monde Incertain: Essai sur la Démocratie Technique*. Paris: Éditions du Seuil.

Caporale, L. H. (1996), "The Merck/INBio Agreement: A Pharmaceutical Company Perspective,", *in* M. J. Balick, E. Elisabetsky and S. Laird (eds.), *Medicinal Resources of the Tropical Forest*. New York: Columbia University Press, 137–141.

Césaire, A. (2000), *Discourse on Colonialism*. New York: New York University Press

Chabal, P. (ed.) (2002), *A History of Postcolonial Lusophone Africa*. Bloomington: Indiana University Press.

Chakrabarty, D. (2000). *Provincializing Europe*. Princeton, NJ: Princeton University Press.

Clifford, J. (1997), *Routes: Travel and Translation in the late twentieth century*. Cambridge, MA: Harvard University Press.

Cox, R.; Schechter, M. (2002). *The Political Economy of a Plural World: Critical Reflections on Power, Morals and Civilization*. London: Routledge.

Creager, A. N. H.; Lunbeck, E.; Schiebinger, L. (eds.) (2001), *Feminism in Twentieth-Century Science, Technology, and Medicine*. Chicago: University of Chicago Press.

Crewe, E.; Harrison, E. (2002). *Whose Development? An Ethnography of Aid*. London: Zed Books.

Cullet, P. (2001), "Plant Variety Protection in Africa: Towards Compliance with TRIPs Agreement," *Biopolicy International*, 23.

Dean, B.; Levi, J. M. (eds.) (2003). *At the Risk of Being Heard: Identity, Indigenous Rights, and Postcolonial States*. Ann Arbor: University of Michigan Press.

Derman, W. (2003), "Cultures of Development and Indigenous Knowledge: the Erosion of Traditional Boundaries," *Africa Today*, 50(2), 67–85.

Descola, P.; Palsson, G. (eds.) (1996), *Nature and Society: Anthropological Perspectives*. London: Routledge.

Diawara, M. (2000), "Globalization, Development Politics and Local Knowledge," *International Sociology*, 15(2), 361–371.

Diouf, M. (1993), "Les Intellectuels Africains face à l'Entreprise Démocratique," *Politique Africaine*, 51, 35–47.

Dirlik, A. (1994), "The Postcolonial Aura: Third World Criticism in the Age of Global Capitalism," *Critical Inquiry*, 20, 328–356.

Dupré, J. (1993), *The Disorder of Things: Metaphysical Foundations of the Disunity of Science*. Cambridge, MA: Harvard University Press.

Dupré, J. (2003), *Darwin's Legacy: What Evolution means Today*. Oxford: Oxford University Press.

Dussel, E. D. (1994), *1492: El Encubrimiento del Otro, hacia el Origen del "Mito de la Modernida."* La Paz: Plural Editores y Universidad Mayor de San Andrés.

Dussel, E. D. (1995), *The Invention of the Americas: Eclipse of "The Other" and the Myth of Modernity*. New York: Continuum.

Dussel, E. D. (2000), "Europa, Modernidad y Eurocentrismo," in E. Lander (ed.), *La colonialidad del Saber: Eurocentrismo y Ciencias Sociales—Perspectivas Latinoamericanas*. Buenos Aires: CLACSO, 41–53.

Egziabher, T. (1999), "The TRIPs Agreement of the WTO and the Convention on Biological Diversity: the Need for Coordinated Action by the South," *Third World Resurgence*, 106. Access in October 2001 at http://www.twnside.org.sg/.

Ekpere, J.A. (2000), *The OAU's Model Law—The Protection of the Rights of Local Communities, Farmers and Breeders, and for the Regulation of Access to Biological Resources* (an explanatory booklet). Lagos: Organization of African Unity, Scientific, Technical and Research Commission.

Ela, J.-M. (1998), *Innovations Sociales et Renaissance de l'Afrique Noire: les Défis du "Monde d'en bas"*. Paris: L'Harmattan.

Escobar, A. (1995), *Encountering Development: the Making and Unmaking of the Third World*. Princeton, NJ: Princeton University Press.

Escobar, A. (1999), "After Nature: Steps to an Anti-essentialist Political Ecology," *Current Anthropology*, 40(1), 1–30.

Escobar, A. (2003), "Actores, Redes e Novos Produtores de Conhecimento: os Movimentos Sociais e a Transição Paradigmática nas Ciências," in B. S. Santos (ed.), *Conhecimento Prudente para uma Vida Decente: 'Um Discurso sobre as Ciências' Revisitado*. Oporto: Afrontamento, 605–630.

ETC Group (2002), "Conquering Nature! . . . and Sidestepping the Debate over Biotech and Biodiversity." *ETC News Release, April 4th 2002*. Acessed on April 2002, at http://www.rafi.org/documents/.

Eze, E. C. (ed.) (1997). *Postcolonial African Philosophy: a Critical Reader*. Oxford: Blackwell Publishers.

Fanon, F. (1963), *The Wretched of the Earth*. Pref. by Jean-Paul Sartre. New York: Grove Press.

Fausto-Sterling, A. (2000), *Sexing the Body: Gender Politics and the Construction of Sexuality*. New York: Basic Books.

Flinter, M. (1998), "Biodiversity: of Local Commons and Global Commodities," in M. Goldman (ed.), *Privatizing Nature: Political Struggles for the Global Commons*. New Brunswick, NJ: Rutgers University Press, 144–161.

Floréz, M.; Rojas, I. (2001), "Conflicto entre Comercio global y Biodiversidad," Fundación Gaia/GRAIN, 6.

Franklin, S. (1995), "Science as Culture, Cultures of Science," *Annual Review of Anthropology*, 24, 163–184.

Fujimura, J. H. (1997), *Crafting Science: a Sociohistory of the Quest for the Genetics of Cancer*. Cambridge, MA: Harvard University Press.

Galison, P. (1997), *Image and Logic: A Material Culture of Microphysics*. Chicago: University of Chicago Press.

Galison, P.; Stump, D.J. (eds.) (1996), *The Disunity of Science: Boundaries, Contexts, and Power*. Stanford, CA: Stanford University Press.

Gandhi, M. K. (2001). *The Selected Works of Mahatma Gandhi*. Vols. II, III. Ahmedabad, Navajivan Publishing House.

Gardey, D.; Löwy, I. (eds.) (2000), *L'Invention du Naturel. Les Sciences et la Fabrication du Féminin et du Masculin*. Paris: Éditions des Archives Contemporaines.

Gieryn, T. F. (1999), *Cultural Boundaries of Science: Credibility on the Line*. Chicago: University of Chicago Press.

Gould, S. J. (2002), *The Hedgehog, the Fox, and the Magister's Pox: Mending the Gap between Science and the Humanities*. New York: Three Rivers Press.

Guha, R.; Martínez-Allier, J. (1997), *Varieties of Environmentalism: Essays North and South*. London: Earthscan.

Gunew, S. (2004), *Haunted Nations: The Colonial Dimensions of Multiculturalisms*. London: Routledge.

Haraway, D. J. (1992), *Primate Visions: Gender, Race, and Nature in the World of Modern Science*. London: Verso.

Haraway, D. J. (1997), *Modest_Witness@Second_Millenium. FemaleMan_ Meets_Oncomouse: Feminism and Technoscience*. New York: Routledge.

Harding, S. (1986), *The Science Question in Feminism*. Ithaca, NY: Cornell University Press.

Harding, S. (1998), *Is Science Multicultural? Postcolonialisms, Feminisms, and Epistemologies*. Bloomington: Indiana University Press.

Harding, S. (ed.) (2003), *The Feminist Standpoint Theory Reader: Intellectual and Political Controversies*. New York: Routledge.

Hayden, C. P. (1998), "A Biodiversity Sampler for the Millenium", in S. Franklin, H. Ragoné (eds.), *Reproducing Reproduction: Kinship, Power, and Technological Innovation*. Philadelphia: University of Pennsylvania Press, 173–206.

Hegel, G. W. F. (1970), *Vorlesungen über die Philosophie der Geschichte*. Moldenhauer, E.; Michel, K.M. (eds.), Frankfurt am Main, Suhrkamp.

Hobart, M. (1993), "Introduction: the Growth of Ignorance?", in M. Hobart (org.), *An Anthropological Critique of Development: The Growth of Ignorance*. London: Routledge, 1–30.

Hountondji, P. J. (ed.) (1994), *Les Savoirs Endogènes: Pistes pour une Recherche*. Dakar: CODESRIA.

Hountondji, P. J. (2002). *The Struggle for Meaning: Reflections on Philosophy, Culture, and Democracy in Africa*. Athens: Ohio University Center for International Studies.

Irwin, A.; Michael, M. (2003), *Science, Social Theory and Public Knowledge*. Maidenhead: Open University Press/McGraw-Hill Education.

Jasanoff, S.; Markley, G. E.; Peterson, J. C.; Pinch, T. (eds.) (1995), *Handbook of Science and Technology Studies*. Thousand Oaks, CA: Sage.

Jewitt, S. (2000), "Unequal Knowledges in Jharkhand, India: De-Romanticizing Women's Agroecological Expertise", *Development and Change*, 31(4), 961–985.

Keating, P.; Cambrosio, A. (2003), *Biomedical Platforms: Realigning the Normal and the Pathological in Late twentieth-century medicine*. Cambridge, MA: MIT Press.

Keller, E. F. (1985), *Reflections on Gender and Science*. New Haven, CT: Yale University Press.

Keller, E. F. (1995), *Refiguring Life: Metaphors of Twentieth-Century Biology*. New York: Columbia University Press.

Keller, E. F. (2002), *Making Sense of Life: explaining Biological Development with Models, Metaphors, and Machines.* Cambridge, MA: Harvard University Press.

King, S. R.; Carlson, T. J. S.; Moran, K. (1996), "Biological Diversity, Indigenous Knowledge, Drug Discovery, and Intellectual Property Rights," in S. King; D. Stabinsky (eds.), *Valuing Local Knowledge.* Washington: Island Press, 167–185.

Kleinman, D. L. (ed.) (2000), *Science, Technology and Democracy.* New York: State University of New York Press.

Kleinman, D. L.; Kloppenburg, J. (1991), "Aiming for Discursive High Ground: Monsanto and the Biotechnology Controversy," *Social Forum*, 6, 422–447.

Klug, H. (2005). "Campaigning for Life: building a New Transnational Solidarity in the face of HIV-AIDS and TRIPS," in B. S. Santos; C. Rodriguez Gavarito (eds.), *Law and Globalization from Below: Towards a Cosmopolitan Legality.* Cambridge, Cambridge University Press, 118–139.

Kohler, R. E. (2002), *Landscapes and Labscapes: Exploring the Lab-Field Border in Biology.* Chicago: University of Chicago Press.

Kymlicka, W. (1995), *Multicultural Citizenship.* Oxford: Oxford University Press.

Lacey, H. (2002), *Alternatives to Technoscience and the Values of Forum Social Mundial.* Paper delivered at the II World Social Forum (Workshop on technoscience, ecology and capitalism), Porto Alegre, January–February 2002.

Lander, E. (org.) (2000), *La colonialidad del saber: eurocentrismo y ciencias sociales—perspectivas latinoamericanas.* Buenos Aires: CLACSO.

Latour, B. (1987), *Science in Action.* Milton Keynes: Open University Press.

Latour, B. (1999a), *Pandora's Hope: Essays on the Reality of Science Studies.* Cambridge, MA: Harvard University Press.

Latour, B. (1999b), *Politiques de la Nature: Comment Faire entrer les Sciences en Démocratie.* Paris: La Découverte.

Leach, M. (1992), "Gender and the Environment: Traps and Opportunities," *Development in Practice*, 2(2), 12–22.

Leff, E. (2004), *Saber Ambiental: Sustentabilidad, Racionalidad, Complejidad, Poder.* México: Siglo VeintiUno Editores.

Loomba, A. (1998), *Colonialism/Postcolonialism: the new Critical Idiom.* London: Routledge.

Lowe, L.; Lloyd, D. (1997), "Introduction", *The Politics of Culture in the Shadow of Capital.* Durham, NC: Duke University Press, 1–32.

Lynch, M. (1993), *Scientific Practice and Ordinary Action: Ethnomethodology and Social Studies of Science.* Cambridge: Cambridge University Press.

Mama, A. (2001), "Challenging Subjects: Gender, Power and Identity in African Contexts," *South African Journal of Sociology*, 5(2), 63–73.

Masolo, D. A. (2003), "Philosophy and Indigenous Knowledge: an African perspective," *Africa Today*, 50(2), 21–38.

Mbembe, A. (2001), *On the Postcoloniality.* Berkeley: University of California Press.

McClintock, A. (1995), *Imperial Leather: race, gender and sexuality in the colonial conquest.* New York: Routledge.

Mehta, M. (1996), "Our Lives Are no Different from That of our Buffaloes," in D. Rocheleau, B. Thomas-Slayter and E. Wangari (orgs.), *Feminist Political Ecology, Global Issues and Local Experiences.* New York: Routledge, 180–210.

Memmi, A. (1965), *The Colonizer and the Colonized*. New York: The Orion Press.

Meneses, M. P. G. (2003), "Agentes do Conhecimento? A Consultoria e a Podução do Cnhecimento em Moçambique," *in* B. S. Santos (ed.), *Conhecimento Pudente para uma Vida Decente: 'Um Discurso sobre as Ciências'*, Revisitado. Oporto: Afrontamento, 683–715.

Meneses, M. P. G. (2005), "Traditional Authorities in Mozambique: between Legitimisation and Legitimacy", *Oficina do CES*, 231.

Mignolo, W. (2000), *Local Histories/Global Designs: Coloniality, Subaltern Knowledges and Border Thinking*. Princeton, NJ: Princeton University Press.

Mignolo, W. (2003), "Os Esplendores e as Misérias da 'Ciência': Colonialidade, Geopolítica do Conhecimento e Pluri-versalidade Epistémica," *in* B. S. Santos, (ed.), *Conhecimento Prudente para uma Vida Decente: 'Um Discurso sobre as Ciências' Revisitado*. Oporto: Afrontamento, 631–671.

Mondlane, E.C. (1969), *Struggle for Mozambique*. Harmondsworth: Penguin.

Mooney, P.R. (2000), "Why We Call it Biopiracy", in H. Svarstad e S. Dhillion (eds.), *Bioprospecting: From Biodiversity in the South to Medicines in the North*. Oslo: Spartacus Forlag as: 37–44.

Mora-Osejo, L.E.; Fals Borda, O. (2003), "A Superação do Eurocentrismo: Enriquecimento do Saber Sistémico e Endógeno sobre o nosso Contexto Tropical", in Santos, B. S. (ed.). *Conhecimento Prudente para uma Vida Decente: 'Um Discurso sobre as Ciências' Revisitado*. Oporto, Afrontamento, 673–681.

Mosquera, C.; Pardo, M.; Hoffman, O. (eds.) (2002), *Afrodescendientes en las Americas*. Bogotá, ILSA.

Mudimbe, V. Y. (1988), *The Invention of Africa: Gnosis, Philosophy, and the Order of Knowledge*. Bloomington: Indiana University Press.

Nader, L. (ed.) (1996), *Naked Science: Anthropological Inquiry into Boundaries, Power, and Knowledge*. London: Routledge.

Nanda, M. (1991), "Is Modern Science a Western Patriarchal Myth? A Critique of the Populist Orthodoxy", *South Asia Bulletin*, 11, 36–61.

Nanda, M. (1997), "The Science Wars in India," *Dissent*, 44(1).

Nandy, A. (1982), *The Intimate Enemy: Loss and Recovery of Self under Colonialism*. Delhi, Oxford University Press.

Nandy, A. (1999), *Traditions, Tyranny and Utopias: Essays in the Politics of Awareness*. New Delhi: Oxford University Press.

Narayan, K. (1993), "How Native is a 'Native' Anthropologist?" *American Anthropologist*, 95(3), 671–686.

Nkrumah, K. (1965), *Neo-Colonialism: The Last Stage of Imperialism*. New York: International Publishers.

Nunes, J. A. (1998/99), "Para além das 'Duas Culturas': Tecnociências, Tecnoculturas e Teoria Crítica," *Revista Crítica de Ciências Sociais*, 52/53, 15–59.

Nunes, J. A.; Gonçalves, M.E. (eds.) (2001), *Enteados de Galileu? A semiperiferia no sistema mundial da ciência*. Oporto: Afrontamento.

Nygren, A. (1999), "Local Knowledge in the Environment—Development Discourse: from Dichotomies to Situated Knowledges," *Critique of Anthropology*, 19(3), 267–288.

Oyama, S.; Griffiths, P. E.; Gray, Russell D. (orgs.) (2001), *Cycles of Contingency: Developmental Systems and Evolution*. Cambridge, MA: MIT Press.

Petitjean, P.; Jami, C.; Moulin, A. M. (eds.) (1992), *Science and Empires: Historical Studies about Scientific Development and European Expansion*. Dordrecht: Kluwer.

Pickering, A. (ed.) (1992), *Science as Practice and Culture*. Chicago: University of Chicago Press.

Pithouse, R. (2003), "Producing the Poor: the World Bank's New Discourse of Domination," *African Sociological Review*, 7(2), 118–147.

Prakash, G. (1999), *Another Reason: Science and Imagination of Modern India*. Princeton, NJ: Princeton University Press.

Quijano, A. (2000), "Colonialidad del Poder y Classificacion Social", *Journal of World-Systems Research*, 6(2), 342–386.

Raju, S. (2002), "We are Different, but Can We Talk?" *Gender, Place and Culture*, 9(2), 173–177.

Ramalho Santos, J. (2003), "Sobre as Fronteiras," in B. S. Santos (ed.), *Conhecimento Prudente para uma Vida Decente: 'Um Discurso sobre as Ciências' Revisitado*. Oporto: Afrontamento, 511–528.

Ranger, T. (1988), "The Invention of Tradition in Colonial Africa," in E. Hobsbawm; T. Ranger (orgs.), *The Invention of Tradition*. Cambridge: Cambridge University Press, 211–262.

Ranger, T. (1996), "Postscript: Colonial and Postcolonial Identities", in R. Werbner; T. Ranger (eds.), *Postcolonial Identities in Africa*. London: Zed Books, 271–281.

Reardon, J. (2005), *Race to the Finish: Identity and Governance in the Age of Genomics*. Princeton, NJ: Princeton University Press.

Reid, W. V.; Laird, S.; Meyer, C. A.; Gamez, R.; Sittenfeld, A.; Janzen, D. H.; Gollin, M. A.; Juma, C. (1993), *Biodiversity Prospecting: using Genetic Resources for Sustainable Development*. New York: WRI.

Robert, J. S. (2004), *Embryology, Epigenesis, and Evolution: Taking Development Seriously*. Cambridge: Cambridge University Press.

Said, E. W. (1994), *Culture and Imperialism*. London: Vintage.

Santos, B. Sousa (1987), *Um Discurso sobre as Ciências*. Oporto: Afrontamento.

Santos, B. Sousa (1989), *Introdução a uma Ciência Pós-moderna*. Oporto: Afrontamento.

Santos, B. Sousa (1995), *Toward a New Common Sense: Law, Science and Politics in the Paradigmatic Transition*. New York: Routledge.

Santos, B. Sousa (1998), "The Fall of the Angelus Novus: beyond the Modern Game of Roots and Options," *Current Sociology*, 46(2), 81–118.

Santos, B. Sousa (1999), "O Oriente entre Diferenças e Desencontros," *Notícias do Milénio, Diário de Notícias*, 08.07.1999, 44–51.

Santos, B. Sousa (2000), *A Crítica da Razão Indolente: Contra o Desperdício da Experiência*. Oporto: Afrontamento.

Santos, B. Sousa (2001a), "Nuestra America: Reinventing a Subaltern Paradigm of Recognition and Redistribution", *Theory, Culture and Society*, 18 (2/3), 185–217.

Santos, B. Sousa (2001b), "Entre Próspero e Caliban: colonialismo, pós-colonialismo e inter-identidade", in M. I. Ramalho; A. Sousa Ribeiro (eds.), *Entre Ser e Estar: raízes, percursos e discursos da identidade*. Oporto: Afrontamento, 23–85.

Santos, B. Sousa (2001c), "Os processos da globalização", in B. S. Santos (ed.), *Globalização: Fatalidade ou Utopia?*. Oporto: Afrontamento, 31–106.

Santos, B. Sousa (2002), *Toward a New Legal Common Sense*. London: Butterworths.

Santos, B. Sousa (ed.) (2003a), *Conhecimento prudente para uma vida decente: 'Um discurso sobre as Ciências' revisitado.* Oporto: Afrontamento.

Santos, B. Sousa (2003b), "Para uma Sociologia das Ausências e uma Sociologia das Emergências", in B. S. Santos (org.), *Conhecimento Prudente para uma Vida Decente: 'Um Discurso sobre as Ciências' Revisitado.* Oporto: Afrontamento, 735–775.

Santos, B. Sousa (2004a), "A Critique of Lazy Reason: against the Waste of Experience," in I. Wallerstein (ed.), *The Modern World-System in the Longue Durée.* Boulder, CO: Paradigm Publishers, 2004, 157–197.

Santos, B. Sousa (2004b), *Do Pós-moderno ao Pós-colonial. E para além de um e outro.* Opening lecture at the VIII Congresso Luso-Afro-Brasileiro de Ciências Sociais, held in Coimbra, Portugal. Accessed on November 2005, at http://www.ces.uc.pt/misc/Do_pos-moderno_ao_pos-colonial.pdf.

Santos, B. Sousa (ed.) (2005), *Democratizing Democracy: beyond the Liberal Democratic Canon.* London: Verso.

Santos, B. Sousa (ed.) (2006a), *Another Production is Possible: Beyond the Capitalist Canon.* London: Verso.

Santos, B. Sousa (2006b), *The Rise of the Global Left: The World Social Forum and beyond.* London: Zed Books.

Santos, B. Sousa; Rodríguez Garavito, C. (2006), "Introduction: Expanding the Economic Canon and Searching for Alternatives to Neoliberal Globalisation," in B. S. Santos (ed.), *Another Production is Possible: Beyond the Capitalist Canon.* London: Verso.

Schiebinger, L. (1989), *The Mind has No Sex: Women in the Origins of Modern Science.* Cambridge, MA: Harvard University Press.

Schiebinger, L. (1999), *Has Feminism Changed Science?* Cambridge, MA: Harvard University Press.

Shiva, V. (1989), *Staying Alive: Women, Ecology and Development.* London: Zed Books.

Shiva, V. (1993), *Monocultures of the Mind. Perspectives on Biodiversity and Biotechnology.* London: Zed Books.

Shiva, V. (1997), *Biopiracy.* Boston, MA: South End Press.

Simpson, T. (1997), *Indigenous Heritage and Self-determination: the Cultural and Intellectual Property Rights of Indigenous Peoples.* Copenhagen: IWGIA.

Singh, R. S.; Krimbas, C. B.; Paul, D. B.; Beatty, J. (orgs.) (2001), *Thinking About Evolution: Historical, Philosophical, and Political Perspectives.* Cambridge: Cambridge University Press.

Soper, K. (1995), *What Is Nature? Culture, Politics and the Non-Human.* Cambridge: Cambridge University Press.

Spivak, G. C. (1999), *A Critique of Postcolonial Reason: Toward a History of the Vanishing Present.* Cambridge, MA: Harvard University Press.

Stam, R. (1997), "Multiculturalism and the Neoconservatives," in A. McClintock, A. Mufti, E. Shohat (eds.), *Dangerous Liaisons: Gender, Nation, and Postcolonial Perspectives.* Minneapolis: University of Minnesota Press, 188–203.

Stengers, I. (2003), "Para Além da Grande Separação, Tornarmo-nos Civilizados?" in B. S. Santos (ed.), *Conhecimento Prudente para uma Vida Decente: 'Um Discurso sobre as Ciências' Revisitado.* Oporto: Afrontamento, 125–142.

Stiglitz, J. (1999), *Public Policy for a Knowledge Economy. Remarks at the Department for Trade and Industry and Center for Economic Policy Research.* London. Accessed in January 1999 at http://www.worldbank.org/html/extdr/extme/ jssp01799a.htm.

Svarstad, H.; Dhillon, S. S. (2000), "Responding to Bioprospecting: Rejection or Regulation?", in H. Svarstad, S. Dhillion (eds.), *Bioprospecting: from Biodiversity in the South to Medicines in the North*. Oslo: Spartacus Forlag as, 9–15.

Takacs, D. (1996), *The Idea of Biodiversity: Philosophies of Paradise*. Baltimore, MD: Johns Hopkins University Press.

Taylor, P. (2005), *Unruly Complexity: Ecology, Interpretation, Engagement*. Chicago: University of Chicago Press.

Visvanathan, S. (1997), *A Carnival for Science: Essays on Science, Technology and Development*. Oxford: Oxford University Press.

Visvanathan, S. (1998), "A Celebration of Difference: Science and Democracy in India," *Science*, 280, 42–43.

Visvanathan, S. (2003), "Convite para uma Guerra da Ciência", in B. S. Santos, (ed.), *Conhecimento Prudente para uma Vida Decente: 'Um Discurso sobre as Ciências' Revisitado*. Oporto: Afrontamento, 717–734.

Wagner, P. (2003), "Sobre Guerras e Revoluções", in B. S. Santos (ed.), *Conhecimento Prudente para uma Vida Decente: 'Um Discurso sobre as Ciências' Revisitado*. Oporto: Afrontamento, 99–116.

Wallerstein, I. M. (1979), *The Capitalist World-Economy*. Cambridge: Cambridge University Press.

Wallerstein, I. M. (2003), "As Estruturas do Conhecimento ou Quantas Formas temos nós de Conhecer?", in B. S. Santos (ed.), *Conhecimento Prudente para uma Vida Decente: 'Um Discurso sobre as Ciências' Revisitado*. Oporto: Afrontamento, 117–123.

Warren, D.M.; Slikkerveer, J.; Brokhensa, D. (eds.) (1995), *The Cultural Dimension of Development: Indigenous Knowledge Systems*. London: Intermediate Technology Publications.

Werbner R.; Ranger, T. (eds.) (1996), *Postcolonial Identities in Africa*. London: Zed Books.

Wilkie, T. (1996), "Genes 'R' Us," in G. Robertson; M. Mash; L. Tickner; J. Bard; B. Curtis (eds.), *Future Natural: Nature/Science/Culture*. New York: Routledge, 133–145.

Wiredu, K. (1996), *Cultural Universals and Particulars: An African Perspective*. Bloomington: Indiana University Press.

WRI (1994), *World Resources 1994–95: People and the Environment*. Washington, DC: World Resources Institute, in collaboration with PNUD.

Zerbe, N. (2002), "Contested ownership: TRIPs, CBD, and Implications for Southern African Biodiversity," *Perspectives on Global Development and Technology*, 1(3–4), 294–321.

Zizek, S. (1997), "Multiculturalism, or the Cultural Logic of Multinational Capitalism", *New Left Review*, 225, 28–51.

Notes

1 While the first two volumes of this collection focused on the political (Santos, 2005) and economic (Santos, 2006a) aspects of the reinvention of social emancipation, the current volume focuses on its cultural and epistemological aspects.

2 The "nation-state" is a concept intensely scrutinized by post-colonial approaches in the light of the political realities prevailing in the global South.

3 Several authors regard post-colonialism as reflecting the condition of Third World intellectuals joining the First World academia (e.g., Dirlik, 1994: 356).

4 Another line of criticism refers to the privileging, in post-colonial studies, of the experience of the territories and populations colonized by England and France, and the relative marginalization of other experiences, such as those of Latin America and the African regions colonized by Portugal and Spain (Dussel, 1995; Mignolo, 2000; Santos, 2001a, 2001b; Chabal, 2002). Scarce attention has been given as well to the colonial condition from a pan-African and pan-Asian ethical critique (Mudimbe, 1988; Nandy, 1999). Despite the limitations noted, see Spivak's critical reflection on the field of post-colonial studies (1999). See also Afzal-Khan and Sheshadri-Crooks' criticism of the "(pre)occupation of postcolonial analysis" (2000).

5 Will Kymlicka has produced important work on multicultural citizenship (e.g., Kymlicka, 1995), although within the framework of Western liberalism. For a broader analysis of this question, see Bennett, 1998; Santos, 2002; Dean and Levi, 2003; and Ghai in this volume.

6 Feminist epistemologies—the plural is meant to address the diversity of positions on this matter within feminism—have been central to the critique of the "classical" dualisms of modernity, such as nature/culture, subject/object, human/non-human and the naturalization of hierarchies of class, sex/gender, and race (Soper, 1995).

7 See, for instances of a still growing literature, Santos, 1987, 1995, 2000, 2003a; Pickering, 1992; Lynch, 1993; Jasanoff *et al.*, 1995; Galison and Stump, 1996; Latour, 1999a; Kleinman, 2000; Nunes and Gonçalves, 2001; Stengers, 2003.

8 For recent exemplars, see Galison, 1997; Kohler, 2002; Keating and Cambrosio, 2003.

9 For different approaches to this topic, see Galison and Stump, 1996; Nunes, 1998/99, 2001; Wallerstein, 2003; Wagner, 2003; Stengers, 2003.

10 For different discussions of the "science wars," see Santos, 2003a, 2003b; Gould, 2002. On cultural authority as a stake in this episode, see Nanda, 1997; Fujimura, 1997.

11 On this topic, see Latour, 1987, as well as several of the contributions to Santos, 2003a.

12 On this, see, for example, Oyama, Griffiths, and Gray, 2001; Keller, 2002; Singh *et al.*, 2001; Ramalho Santos, 2003; Robert, 2004.

13 See, on this, Duprés proposal of a "promiscuous realism" (1993, 2003), which has strong affinities with pragmatist approaches (that of John Dewey in particular) earlier explored by Santos (1989).

14 On construction see, for instance, Latour, 1999a, and the contributions to Santos, 2003a.

15 For some relevant contributions to feminist critiques of science, see Keller, 1985; Harding, 1986, 1998, 2003; Schiebinger, 1989, 1999; Haraway, 1992, 1997; and Fausto-Sterling, 2000. Gardey and Lowy, 2000; and Creager, Lunbeck, and Schiebinger, 2001 offer useful overviews, even if focused on the North.

16 There is a wide body of literature revealing the complexity of the crossroads of feminist epistemologies in the South, a subject that is beyond the scope of

this Introduction. See, for example, Shiva, 1989; Nanda, 1991; Leach, 1992; McClintock, 1995; Harding, 1998; Jewitt, 2000; Mama, 2001; Raju, 2002.

17 On these debates, see the contributions to Harding, 2003.

18 However, the precise terms of these relationships must be scrutinized, as modern science tends to cannibalize other knowledges, appropriating them as raw materials and turning them into commodities, as Laymert Garcia dos Santos, Vandana Shiva, and Margarita Flórez Alonso discuss in their chapters.

19 On the eve of World War II, colonies and ex-colonies covered about 85 percent of the land surface of the globe. Colonialism played a key role in the transformative encounter for both colonizers and colonized (Loomba, 1998: xiii).

20 Two main sources of criticism of post-colonialism can be identified (Abrahamsen, 2003: 191): a critique that reacts to post-colonialism's rejection of metanarratives and categories such as class, race, and nation; and a critique that objects to its theoretical language and to the focus on text and discourses. By stressing the discontinuities of the colonial and post-colonial periods and emphasizing inquiry into the colonial encounter, post-colonial studies are perceived as a successor of Eurocentric social science. See Ahmad (1992) and Ranger (1996: 273) for instances of this critique.

21 On the implications of the epistemological consequences of the "colonial encounter" see Nandy, 1982; Apffel-Marglin and Marglin, 1990; Asad, 1991; Petitjean et al., 1992; McClintock, 1995; Santos, 1995; Dussel, 1995; Ela, 1998; Mignolo, 2000; and Mbembe, 2001.

22 In the words of Mbembe, the understanding of the "West" emerged simultaneously with the notion of "the rest," where Africa "still constitutes one of the metaphors through which the West represents the origins of its own norms, develops a self-image, and interprets this image into the set of signifiers asserting what is supposed to be its identity" (2001: 2).

23 On the meanings of "alterity from below" (from a broader perspective, including gender, race, and colonial subjectivities) see Narayan, 1993; Raju, 2002; and Masolo, 2003.

24 For different discussions of the epistemological and political implications of ecological approaches to the world, see Latour, 1999b; Leff, 2004; Taylor, 2005.

25 On the critiques of development, see Hobart, 1993; Escobar, 1995; Visvanathan, 1997; Crewe and Harrison, 2002; as well as the introduction to volume 2 of this series, by Boaventura de Sousa Santos and César Rodríguez-Garavito, 2006.

26 Santos (2001c: 71) defines globalized localism as "the process through which a given local phenomenon is successfully globalized." In this sense, the opposition tradition/modernity expresses the outcome of hegemonic globalization, which carried with it the projection of Western science as the sole valid form of knowledge, thus localizing all other knowledges. But "local" refers, here, not to a mere space of reaction to modernity but to spaces of emergence of diverse historical paths, of different modernities, including those that are alternative to the hegemonic one.

27 Describing modern science as a monoculture of knowledge does not mean that it is not internally diverse, as has been shown earlier, but that it takes on this "monocultural" quality in its relations to the range of forms of knowl-

edge and experience regarded as "non-scientific," "local," "lay," "traditional," etc.

28 On this subject, see also Mudimbe, 1988; Alvares, 1992; Bebbington, 1993; Hountondji, 1994, 2002; Dussel, 1995; Santos, 1995, 2002, 2004b, 2006b; Visvanathan, 1997, 2003; Ela, 1998; Mignolo, 2000, 2003; Chakrabarty, 2000; Lander, 2000; Lacey, 2002.

29 Access to these new reproduction strategies and the definition of who provides the "raw materials" for the trade in cells, tissues, and organs are further sources of conflict. These incursions, often in indigenous communities and ecosystems, tend to perpetuate the inequalities associated with the persistence of colonial situations.

30 For the full text, see http://www.biodiv.org.

31 Estimates of the number of actually existing living species tend to vary between 5 and 30 million, with some suggesting up to 80 million. The number of species that have been the object of inventory and inclusion in databases following international scientific conventions, however, is less than 2 million.

32 See, *inter alia*, Reid *et al.*, 1993; Caporale, 1996; Balick *et al.*, 1996; King *et al.*, 1996; Svarstad and Dhillion, 2000; Zerbe, 2002.

33 Vandana Shiva is one of the best-known advocates of this position. See her contribution to this volume.

34 Some promoters and supporters of biotechnology confuse the promotion of biological diversity with the heterogeneity of living beings through biotechnological manipulation, allowing the creation of hybrids, such as transgenic organisms, which did not exist before that manipulation was performed. But biotechnological manipulation is associated, more generally, with a search for the optimization of productivity or of resistance to certain kinds of threats (pests) through techniques such as genetic recombination. This leads to a selection of certain characteristics of organisms and to the dismissal or rejection of others which are not compatible with that search for optimization. The increase in the heterogeneity of living beings tends, thus, to promote the reduction of the diversity of organisms, species, and ecosystems, not their increase. On this controversy, see Kleinman and Kloppenburg, 1991; Shiva, 1993; ETC, 2002; Lacey, 2002.

35 See also Escobar, 2003.

36 On the prospecting of human biodiversity, namely within the Human Genome Diversity Project, see the "Declaration of Indigenous People of the Western Hemisphere Regarding the Human Genome Diversity Project" (in *Cultural Survival Quarterly* 63 [1996]); for discussions, see Hayden, 1998, and Reardon, 2005.

37 On the issue of patents and the fight against HIV-AIDS, see also Klug, 2005.

38 TRIPS—Trade-Related Aspects of Intellectual Property Rights—is the World Trade Organization agreement on matters related to intellectual property rights.

39 In June 2003, the African Group of WTO member countries drafted a proposal for opening TRIPS to traditional knowledge systems, and is seeking its approval by other WTO member states.

40 See Ekpere, 2000, and Egziabher 1999, and in this volume.

Part I

MULTICULTURAL CITIZENSHIP
AND HUMAN RIGHTS

1

Human Rights as an Emancipatory Script? Cultural and Political Conditions

Boaventura de Sousa Santos

INTRODUCTION

For the past fifteen years I have been puzzled by the extent to which human rights have become the language of progressive politics. Indeed, for many years after the Second World War human rights were very much part and parcel of Cold War politics, and were so regarded by the Left. Double standards, complacency towards friendly dictators, the defense of tradeoffs between human rights and development—all this made human rights suspect as an emancipatory script. Whether in core countries or in the developing world, the progressive forces preferred the language of revolution and socialism to formulate an emancipatory politics. However, with the seemingly irreversible crisis of these blueprints for emancipation, those same progressive forces find themselves today resorting to human rights in order to reconstitute the language of emancipation. It is as if human rights were called upon to fill the void left by socialist politics. Can in fact the concept of human rights fill such a void? Only if a politics of human rights radically different from the hegemonic liberal one is adopted and only if such a politics is conceived as part of a broader constellation of struggles and discourses of resistance and emancipation rather than as the sole politics of resistance against oppression. Accordingly, my analytical objective here is to specify the conditions under which human rights can be placed at the service of a progressive, emancipatory politics.

The specification of such conditions leads us to unravel some of the dialectical tensions that lie at the core of Western modernity.[1] The crisis now affecting these tensions signals better than anything else the problems facing Western modernity today. In my view, human rights politics at the beginning of the century is a key factor to understanding such a crisis.

I identify three such tensions. The first one occurs between social regulation and social emancipation. I have been claiming that the paradigm of modernity is based on the idea of a creative dialectical tension between social regulation and social emancipation that can still be heard, even if but dimly, in the positivist motto of "order and progress." At the beginning of the twenty-first century this tension seems to have vanished. The tension between social regulation and social emancipation was based on the discrepancy between social experiences (the present) and social expectations (the future), between an unjust, difficult, and precarious current social and personal life and a better, more just, and, in sum, more positive future. However, since, in the mid 1980s, neoliberalism began to impose itself globally as the new version of *laissez-faire* capitalism, the relation between experiences and expectations among ever larger bodies of population worldwide was reversed. No matter how difficult the present looks, the future looks even more difficult. In a social and political context of negative expectations, emancipation has ceased to be the opposite of regulation in order to become the double of regulation. Herein lie the deep roots of the crisis of modern left politics. The latter has always been based on a critique of the status quo in the name of a better future, that is, in the name of positive expectations. The differences within the left have, accordingly, derived from the measure of the discrepancy between experiences and expectations: a wider gap sustaining a revolutionary politics and a narrower one, a reformistic politics. In a context of negative social expectations, the left often sees itself in a position of having to defend the status quo, a political task for which it was not historically tailored. While until the mid-1970s any given crisis of social regulation was met by the strengthening of emancipatory politics, today we witness a double social crisis. The crisis of social regulation, symbolized by the crisis of the regulatory state, and the crisis of social emancipation, symbolized by the double crisis of social revolution and social reformism. Human rights politics, which has been predominantly used to manage and to keep the tension between social regulation and social emancipation under control, is trapped in this double crisis while attempting, at the same time, to overcome it.

The second dialectical tension occurs between the state and civil society. As Dicey perceptively noted in the nineteenth century (1948: 306), the modern state, although initially a minimalist state, is potentially a maximalist state, to the extent that civil society, as the other of the state, reproduces itself through laws and regulations that emanate from the state and for which there seems to be no limit, as long as the democratic rules of lawmaking are respected. Human rights are at the core of this tension; while the first generation of human rights was designed as a struggle of civil society against the state as the sole violator of human rights, the second and third generations of human rights resort to the state as the guarantor of human rights. As a result

of this historical process, the state came to be seen as the :
problems confronting civil society. Indeed, civil society came
inherently problematic and in need of an ever more interv
Accordingly, a strong civil society could only be the mirror
tically strong state. For reasons that I cannot go into here, all
from the 1980s onwards with the rise of neoliberalism. The state turned from
a source of infinite solutions into a source of infinite problems, civil society
ceased to be the mirror of the state and became the opposite of the state and,
accordingly, a strong civil society came to demand a weak state. Human
rights politics, both in its hegemonic and counter-hegemonic versions, was
caught in this fast turn of conceptions and has not as of yet recovered from it.

Finally, the third tension occurs between the nation-state and what we
call globalization. The political model of Western modernity is one of
sovereign nation-states coexisting in an international system of equally
sovereign states: the interstate system. The privileged unit and scale both of
social regulation and social emancipation is the nation-state. The interstate
system has always been conceived of as a more or less anarchic society, run
by a very soft legality, and even working-class internationalism has always
been more an aspiration than a reality. Today, the selective erosion of the
nation-state due to the intensification of neoliberal globalization raises the
question of whether both social regulation and social emancipation are to
be displaced to the global level. We have started to speak of global civil
society, global governance, global equity. The worldwide recognition of
human rights politics is at the forefront of this process. At this point
however this displacement raises many more problems than it provides
solutions. To begin with, most enforceable human rights are still enforced
(and violated) at the state level and, therefore, the weakening of the state
may bring with it the erosion of enforceability. Second, as from the 1990s
onwards neoliberal globalization began to be confronted by social movements and progressive NGOs, leading to a counter-hegemonic globalization, a globalization from below,[2] new conceptions of human rights
emerged offering radical alternatives to the liberal North-centric conceptions that until then had dominated with unquestioned supremacy. According to the latter conceptions, the global South was in general
problematic concerning its respect for human rights, while the Global
North, considered to be immensely more respectful of human rights,
offered its example and its international aid to help improve the situation
of human rights in the global South. With the emergence of counter-
hegemonic globalization, the global South began to question these conceptions by showing, in striking ways, that the global North and its imperial
domination over the South—now intensified by neoliberal global capitalism—was indeed the root source of the most massive violations of human

ts: millions and millions of people condemned to famine and malnutrition, pandemics and the ecological degradation of their livelihoods. With such contradictory conceptions of human rights and human rights violations being played out on a global scale, the whole field of human rights politics has become rather contentious. The third problem haunting human right politics is also related to the emergence of conflicting globalizations. It has to do with the fact that in very crucial aspects human rights politics is a cultural politics, so much so that we can even think of human rights as symbolizing the return of the cultural and even of the religious at the end of the twentieth century and at the beginning of the twenty-first century. But to speak of culture and religion is to speak of difference, boundaries, particularity. How can human rights be both a cultural and a global politics?

My purpose in this chapter is to develop an analytical framework that will serve to highlight and support the emancipatory potential of human rights politics in the double context of competing globalizations, on the one hand, and cultural fragmentation and identity politics, on the other. My aim is to establish both global competence and local legitimacy for a progressive politics of human rights.

ON GLOBALIZATIONS

I shall begin by specifying what I mean by globalization. Globalization is very hard to define. Most definitions focus on the economy, that is to say, on the new world economy that has emerged in the last two decades as a consequence of the globalization of the production of goods and services and financial markets. This is a process through which transnational corporations have risen to a new and unprecedented preeminence as international actors.

For my analytical purposes I prefer a definition of globalization that is more sensitive to social, political, and cultural dimensions. I start from the assumption that what we usually call globalization consists of sets of social relations; as these sets of social relations change, so does globalization. There is, strictly speaking, no single entity called globalization; there are, rather, globalizations, and we should use the term only in the plural. Any comprehensive concept should always be procedural, rather than substantive. On the other hand, if globalizations are bundles of social relations, the latter are bound to involve conflicts, hence, both winners and losers. More often than not, the discourse on globalization is the story of the winners as told by the winners. In actuality, the victory is apparently so absolute that the defeated end up vanishing from the picture altogether.

Here is my definition of globalization: it is the process by which a given local condition or entity succeeds in extending its reach over the globe and, by doing so, develops the capacity to designate a rival social condition or entity as local. The most important implications of this definition are the following. First, under the conditions of the Western capitalist world system there is no genuine globalization. What we call globalization is always the successful globalization of a given localism. In other words, there is no global condition for which we cannot find a local root, a specific cultural embeddedness. The second implication is that globalization entails localization. In fact, we live in a world of localization as much as we live in a world of globalization. Therefore, it would be equally correct in analytical terms if we were to define the current situation and our research topics in terms of localization rather than globalization. The reason why we prefer the latter term is basically because hegemonic scientific discourse tends to prefer the story of the world as told by the winners. Many examples of how globalization entails localization can be given. The English language, as *lingua franca*, is one such example. Its expansion as a global language has entailed the localization of other potentially global languages, in particular the French language. Therefore, once a given process of globalization is identified, its full meaning and explanation may not be obtained without considering adjacent processes of relocalization occurring in tandem and intertwined with it. The French or Italian actors of the 1960s—from Brigitte Bardot to Alain Delon, from Marcello Mastroiani to Sophia Loren—who at the time symbolized the universal technique of acting, seem today, when we see their movies again, as rather ethnic or parochially European. Between then and now, the Hollywoodesque manner of acting has managed to globalize itself.

One of the transformations most commonly associated with globalization is time–space compression, that is to say, the social process by which phenomena speed up and spread out across the globe. Though apparently monolithic, this process does combine highly differentiated situations and conditions and for this reason it cannot be analyzed independently of the power relations that account for the different forms of time and space mobility. On the one hand, there is the transnational capitalist class that is in fact in charge of the time–space compression and capable of turning it to its advantage. On the other hand, the subordinate classes and groups, such as migrant workers and refugees, which are also involved in a lot of physical moving, are not at all in control of the time–space compression. Between corporate executives and immigrants and refugees, tourists represent a third mode of production of time–space compression.

There are also those who heavily contribute to globalization but who, nonetheless, remain prisoners of their local time–space. The peasants of Bolivia, Peru, and Colombia, by growing coca, contribute decisively to a world drug culture, but they themselves remain as "localized" as ever, just like the residents of Rio's favelas, who remain prisoners of the squatter settlement life, while their songs and dances are today part of a globalized musical culture.

Finally, and still from another perspective, global competence sometimes requires the accentuation of local specificity. Most tourist sites today must be highly exotic, vernacular, and traditional in order to become competent enough to enter the market of global tourism.

In order to account for these asymmetries, globalization, as I have suggested, should always be referred to in the plural. In a rather loose sense, we could speak of different modes of the production of globalization to account for this diversity. I distinguish two main modes of the production of globalization, which, I argue, give rise to two forms of globalization. The first mode consists of a twin process of *globalized localisms/localized globalisms*. Globalized localism is the process by which a particular phenomenon is successfully globalized, whether it be the worldwide activities of a multi-national corporation, the transformation of the English language into a *lingua franca*, the globalization of American fast food or popular music, or the worldwide adoption of the same laws of intellectual property, patents or telecommunications and, most recently, anti-terrorism, all of them aggressively promoted by the USA. In this mode of the production of globalization, what is globalized is the winner of a struggle for the appropriation or valorization of resources, for the hegemonic recognition of a given cultural, racial, sexual, ethnic, religious, or regional difference, or for the imposition of a given international (dis)order. This victory translates into the capacity to dictate the terms of integration, competition/negotiation and inclusion/exclusion. The second process of globalization is localized globalism. It consists of the specific impact on local conditions produced by transnational practices and imperatives that arise from globalized localisms. To respond to these transnational imperatives, local conditions are disintegrated, oppressed, excluded, destructured, and, eventually, restructured as subordinate inclusion. Such localized globalisms include: the elimination of traditional commerce and subsistence agriculture; the creation of free-trade enclaves or zones; the deforestation and massive destruction of natural resources in order to pay off external debt; the use of historic treasures, religious ceremonies, or places, craftsmanship and wildlife for the purposes of the global tourism industry; ecological dumping (the "purchase" by Third World countries of toxic waste produced in the core capitalist countries in order to pay for the foreign debt); the conversion of subsistence agriculture into agriculture for export as part of "structural adjustment"; the ethnicization of the workplace (the devaluing of salaries because the workers belong to an ethnic group considered "inferior").

These two processes operate in conjunction and constitute the hegemonic globalization that is also called neoliberal, top-down globalization or globalization from above, in sum, the most recent version of global capitalism and imperialism. The sustained production of globalized localisms and localized globalisms is increasingly determining or conditioning the different hierarchies that constitute the global capitalist world, converging in the global North/Global South divide. The international division of the production of globalization tends to assume the following pattern: core countries specialize in globalized localisms while peripheral countries only have the choice of localized globalisms.

There is, however, a second mode of the production of globalization. I call it *insurgent cosmopolitanism*, a counter-hegemonic globalization, or globalization from below. It consists of the transnationally organized resistance against the unequal exchanges produced or intensified by globalized localisms and localized globalisms. This resistance is organized through local/global linkages among social organizations and movements representing those classes and social groups victimized by hegemonic globalization and united in concrete struggles against exclusion, subordinate inclusion, the destruction of livelihoods and ecological destruction, political oppression, cultural suppression, etc. They take advantage of the new possibilities for transnational interaction made possible by the revolution in information and communications technologies and by the reduction of international travel costs. Insurgent cosmopolitan activities include, among many others: egalitarian transnational North/South and South/South networks of solidarity among social movements and progressive NGOs; the new working-class internationalism (dialogues among workers' organizations in the different regional blocs; transnational coalitions among workers of the same multinational corporation operating in different countries; workers' and citizenship groups' coalitions in the struggle against sweatshops, discriminatory labor practices, and slave labor); international networks of alternative legal aid; transnational human rights organizations; worldwide networks of feminist, indigenous, ecological or alternative development movements and associations; and literary, artistic and scientific movements on the periphery of the world system in search of alternative non-imperialist, counter-hegemonic cultural values emerging from post-colonial perspectives.

The confrontations surrounding the World Trade Organization meeting in Seattle on 30 November 1999 was a first eloquent demonstration of insurgent cosmopolitanism and the World Social Forum is today its most accomplished manifestation. The use of the term "cosmopolitanism" to describe the global resistance against the unequal exchanges produced by hegemonic globalization may seem inadequate in the face of its modernist or Western ascendancy. The idea of cosmopolitanism, like universalism, world citizenship and the rejection of political and territorial borders, has indeed a long tradition in Western culture, from the cosmic law of Pythagoras and the philallelia of Democritus to the "*Homo sum, humani nihil a me alienum puto*" of Terence, from the medieval *res publica christiana* to the Renaissance humanists, and from Voltaire, for whom "to be a good patriot, it is necessary to become an enemy of the rest of the world," to working-class internationalism. This ideological tradition has often been put at the service of European expansionism, colonialism, and imperialism, the same historical processes that today generate globalized localisms and localized globalisms. Insurgent cosmopolitanism, on the contrary, refers to the aspiration of oppressed groups to organize their resistance and consolidate political coalitions on the same scale as the one used by the oppressors to victimize them, that is, the global scale. Insurgent cosmopolitanism is also different from that invoked by Marx as meaning the universality of those who, under capitalism, have nothing to lose but their chains—the working class. In addition to the working class described by Marx, the oppressed classes in the world today cannot be encompassed by the "class-which-has-only-its-chains-to-lose" category. Insurgent cosmopolitanism includes vast populations in the world that are not sufficiently useful or skilled enough to "have chains," that is, to be directly exploited by capital. It aims at uniting social groups on both a class and a non-class basis, the victims of exploitation as well as the victims of social exclusion, of sexual, ethnic, racist and religious discrimination. For this reason, insurgent cosmopolitanism does not imply uniformity, a general theory of social emancipation and the collapse of differences, autonomies and local identities. Giving equal weight to the principle of equality and to the principle of the recognition of difference, insurgent cosmopolitanism is no more than a global emergence resulting from the fusion of local, progressive struggles with the aim of maximizing their emancipatory potential *in loco* (however defined) through translocal/local linkages.

This character is both the strength and the weakness of insurgent cosmopolitanism. The progressive or counter-hegemonic character of the cosmopolitan coalitions cannot be taken for granted. On the contrary, it is intrinsically unstable and problematic. It demands constant self-reflection on the part of those who share its objectives. Cosmopolitan initiatives conceived of and created with a counter-hegemonic character can later come to assume hegemonic characteristics, even running the risk of becoming converted into globalized localisms. It is enough to think of the local initiatives in participatory democracy, which had to fight for years against authoritarian populism, the "absolutism" of representative democracy, and the mistrust of the conservative political elites, and which nowadays are beginning to be recognized and even adopted by the World Bank, seduced by their efficiency and lack of corruption in managing funds and development loans. Self-reflexive vigilance is essential in order to distinguish between the technocratic concept of participatory democracy sanctioned by the World Bank and the democratic and progressive concept of participatory democracy as an embryo of counter-hegemonic globalization.

The instability of the progressive or counter-hegemonic character is derived from another factor as well: the different concepts of emancipatory resistance held by cosmopolitan initiatives in different regions of the world system. For example, the struggle for minimum standards in working conditions (the *international labor standards*)—a struggle led by trade unions and human rights organizations in the more developed countries to prevent products produced by labor that does not reach these required minimum standards from circulating freely in the world market—is certainly seen by the organizations that promote it as counter-hegemonic and emancipatory since it aims to improve the conditions of the workers' lives. However, it can be seen by similar organizations in peripheral countries as yet another hegemonic strategy of the North to create one more form of protectionism that favors the rich countries and harms the poor ones.

In spite of all these difficulties, insurgent cosmopolitanism has succeeded in credibly demonstrating that there is an alternative to hegemonic, neoliberal, top-down globalization, and that is counter-hegemonic, solidary, bottom-up globalization. From now on, what we call global and globalization cannot but be conceived of as the provisory, partial and reversible result of a permanent struggle between two modes of production of globalization, indeed, between two globalizations. The conflicting conceptions and politics of human rights, far from being above such a struggle, are an important feature of it.

INTERCULTURAL RECONSTRUCTION OF HUMAN RIGHTS

The complexity of human rights is that they may be conceived of either as a form of globalized localism or as a form of insurgent cosmopolitanism, that is, in other words, as a globalization from above or as a globalization from below. My purpose is to specify the conditions under which human rights may be conceived of as a globalization of the latter kind. In this chapter I will not cover all the necessary conditions but rather only the cultural ones. My argument is that so long as human rights are conceived of as universal human rights they will tend to operate as a globalized localism, a form of globaliza-tion from above. To be able to operate as a cosmopolitan, counter-hegemonic form of globalization human rights must be reconceptualized as multicultural. Conceived of, as they have been, as universal, human rights will always be an instrument of Samuel Huntington's "clash of civilizations," that is to say, of the struggle of the West against the rest, of Western imperial cosmopolitanism against any alternative conceptions of human dignity that are socially accepted elsewhere. Thus conceived, the global competence of universal human rights will be obtained at the cost of their local legitimacy. On the contrary, progressive multiculturalism, as I understand it, is a precondition for a balanced and mutually reinforcing relationship between global competence and local legitimacy, the two attributes of a counter-hegemonic human rights politics in our time.

We know, of course, that human rights are not universal in their application. Four international regimes of human rights are consensually distinguished in the world in our time: the European, the Inter-American, the African and the Asian regimes.[3] One of the most heated human rights debates is indeed whether human rights are a universal or rather a Western concept and, concomitantly, whether they are universally valid or not. Though closely related, these two questions are nonetheless autonomous. The first one deals with the historical and cultural origins of the concept of human rights, the second with their claims to validity at a given point in history. The genesis of a moral claim may condition its validity but it certainly does not determine it. The Western origin of human rights may be made congruent with their universality if, hypothetically, at a given point in history they are universally accepted as ideal standards of political and moral life. The two questions are, however, interrelated, because the mobilizing energy that can be generated to make the acceptance of human rights concrete and effective depends, in part, upon the cultural identification with the pre-suppositions that ground human rights as a moral claim. From a sociological and political perspective, the elucidation of this linkage is by far more important than the abstract discussion of either the question of cultural anchorage or of philosophical validity.

Are human rights universal, a cultural invariant, that is to say, part of a global culture? I would assert that the only transcultural fact is that all cultures are relative. Cultural relativity (not relativism) also means cultural diversity and incompleteness. It means that all cultures tend to define as universal the values that they consider ultimate. What is highest is also most widespread. Thus, the specific question about the conditions of universality in a given culture is itself not universal. The question about the universality of human rights is a Western cultural question. Hence, human rights are universal only when they are viewed from a Western standpoint. The question of the universality of human rights betrays the universality of what it questions by the way it questions it. In other words, the question of universality is a particular question, a Western cultural question. The extent to which this standpoint can be shared, rejected, appropriated or modified by other cultures depends on the cross-cultural dialogues made possible by the concrete political and sociological power relations among the different countries involved.

Because the question of universality is the answer to an aspiration of completeness, and because each culture "situates" such an aspiration around ultimate values and universal validity, different aspirations to different ultimate values in different cultures will lead to isomorphic concerns that, given the adequate hermeneutical procedures, may become mutually intelligible and mutually translatable. At best it is even possible to achieve a mixture and interpenetration of concerns and concepts. The more equal the power relations among cultures, the more probable it is that such *mestizaje* might occur.

We may then conclude that, once posed, the question of universality betrays the universality of what it questions, no matter what the answer may be. Other strategies to establish the universality of human rights have, however, been designed. This is the case of those authors for whom human rights are universal because they are held by all human beings *as* human beings, that is, because independently of explicit recognition they are inherent to human nature.[4] This line of thought begs the question by dislocating its object. Since human beings do not hold human rights because they are beings—most beings do not hold rights—but because they are human, the universality of human nature becomes the unanswered question that makes possible the fictive answer to the question of the universality of human rights. There is no culturally invariant concept of human nature.

The concept of human rights is based on a well-known set of presuppositions, all of which are distinctly Western, namely: there is a universal human nature that can be known by rational means; human nature is essentially different from and higher than the rest of reality; the individual has an absolute and irreducible dignity that must be defended against society or the state; the autonomy of the individual requires that society be organized in a non-hierarchical way, as a sum of free individuals (Panikkar, 1984: 30). Since all these presuppositions are clearly Western and liberal, and easily distinguishable from other conceptions of human dignity in other cultures, one might ask why the question of the universality of human rights has become so hotly debated, why, in other words, the sociological universality of this question has outgrown its philosophical universality.

If we look at the history of human rights in the post-war period, it is not difficult to conclude that human rights policies have been by and large at the service of the economic and geo-political interests of the hegemonic capitalist states. The generous and seductive discourse on human rights has allowed for unspeakable atrocities, and such atrocities have been evaluated and dealt with according to revolting double standards (Falk, 1981). But the Western and indeed the Western liberal mark in the dominant human rights discourse could be traced in many other instances: in the Universal Declaration of 1948, which was drafted without the participation of the majority of the peoples of the world; in the exclusive recognition of individual rights, with the sole exception of the collective right to self-determination (which, however, was restricted to the peoples subjected to European colonialism); in the priority given to civil and political rights over economic, social, and cultural rights; and in the recognition of the right to property as the first and, for many years, the sole economic right.

But this is not the whole story. Throughout the world, millions of people and thousands of non-governmental organizations have been struggling for human rights, often at great risk, in defense of oppressed social classes and groups that in many instances have been victimized by authoritarian capitalistic states. The political agendas of such struggles are often either explicitly or implicitly anti-capitalist. For instance, counter-hegemonic discourse and the practice of human rights has been developing, non-Western conceptions of human rights have been proposed, cross-cultural dialogues on human rights have been organized. The central task of emancipatory politics in our time, in this domain, consists in transforming the conceptualization and practice of human rights from a globalized localism into an insurgent cosmopolitan project.[5]

What are the premises for such a transformation?[6] The first premise is that it is imperative to transcend the debate on universalism and cultural relativism. The debate is an inherently false debate, the polar concepts of which are both equally detrimental to an emancipatory conception of human rights. All cultures are relative, but cultural relativism, as a philosophical posture, is wrong.[7] All cultures aspire to ultimate concerns and values, but cultural universalism, as a philosophical posture, is wrong. Against universalism, we must propose cross-cultural dialogues on isomorphic concerns. Against relativism, we must develop cross-cultural procedural criteria to distinguish progressive politics from regressive politics, empowerment from disempowerment, emancipation from regulation. To the extent that the debate sparked by human rights might evolve into a competitive dialogue among different cultures on principles of human dignity, it is imperative that such competition induce the transnational coalitions to race to the top rather than to the bottom (What are the absolute minimum standards? The most basic human rights? The lowest common denominator?) The often-voiced cautionary comment against overloading human rights politics with new, more advanced rights or with different and broader conceptions of human rights (Donnelly, 1989: 109–24) is a latter-day manifestation of the reduction of the emancipatory claims of Western modernity to the low degree of emancipation made possible or tolerated by world capitalism: low-intensity human rights as the other side of low-intensity democracy.

The second premise is that all cultures have conceptions of human dignity but that not all of them conceive of human dignity as equivalent to human rights. It is therefore important to look for isomorphic concerns among different cultures. Different names, concepts and *Weltanschaungen* may convey similar or mutually intelligible concerns or aspirations.

The third premise is that all cultures are incomplete and problematic in their conceptions of human dignity. Such incompleteness derives from the very fact that there is a plurality of cultures. If each culture were as complete as it claims to be, there would be just one single culture. The idea of completeness is at the source of an excess of meaning that seems to plague all cultures. Incompleteness is thus best visible from the outside, from the perspective of another culture. To raise the consciousness of cultural incompleteness to its possible maximum is one of the most crucial tasks in the construction of an emancipatory multicultural conception of human rights.[8]

The fourth premise is that no major culture is monolithic. Cultures have different versions of human dignity, some broader than others, some with a wider circle of reciprocity than others, some more open to other cultures than others. For instance, Western modernity has unfolded into two highly divergent conceptions and practices of human rights—the liberal and the Marxist—one prioritizing civil and political rights, the other prioritizing social and economic rights.[9]

Finally, the fifth premise is that all cultures tend to distribute people and social groups among two competing principles of hierarchical belongingness. One operates through hierarchies among homogeneous units. The other operates through separation among unique identities and differences. The two principles do not necessarily overlap and for that reason not all equalities are identical and not all differences are unequal.

These are the premises of a cross-cultural dialogue on human dignity that may eventually lead to a *mestizo* conception of human rights, a conception that instead of resorting to false universalisms organizes itself as a constellation of local and mutually intelligible meanings, networks of empowering normative references. But this is only a starting point. In the case of a cross-cultural dialogue the exchange is not only between different knowledges but also between different cultures, that is to say, between different and, in a strong sense, incommensurable universes of meaning. These universes of meaning consist of constellations of strong *topoi*. *Topoi* are the overarching rhetorical commonplaces of a given culture, self-evident, and, therefore, not an object of debate. They function as premises for argumentation, thus making possible the production and exchange of arguments. Strong *topoi* become highly vulnerable and problematic whenever "used" in a different culture. The best that can happen to them is to be moved "down" from premises of argumentation into arguments. To understand a given culture from another culture's *topoi* may thus prove to be very difficult, if not impossible. I shall therefore propose a *diatopical hermeneutics*. In the area of human rights and dignity, the mobilization of social support for the emancipatory claims they potentially contain is only achievable if such claims have been appropriated in the local cultural context. Appropriation, in this sense, cannot be obtained through cultural cannibalization. It requires cross-cultural dialogue and diatopical hermeneutics.

Diatopical hermeneutics is based on the idea that the *topoi* of an individual culture, no matter how strong they may be, are as incomplete as the culture itself. Such incompleteness is not visible from inside the culture itself, since the aspiration to totality induces taking *pars pro toto*. The objective of diatopical hermeneutics is, therefore, not to achieve completeness—that being an unachievable goal—but, on the contrary, to raise the consciousness of reciprocal incompleteness to its possible maximum by engaging in the dialogue, as it were, with one foot in one culture and the other in another. Herein lies its *dia-topical* character.[10]

A diatopical hermeneutics can be conducted between the *topos* of human rights in Western culture, the *topos* of *dharma* in Hindu culture, and the *topos* of *umma* in Islamic culture. According to Panikkar, *dharma*

is that which maintains, gives cohesion and thus strength to any given thing, to reality, and ultimately to the three worlds (triloka). Justice keeps human relations together; morality keeps oneself in harmony; law is the binding principle for human relations; religion is what maintains the universe in existence; destiny is that which links us with future; truth is the internal cohesion of a thing [. . .]. Now a world in which the notion of Dharma is central and nearly all-pervasive is not concerned with finding the "right" of one individual against another or of the individual vis-à-vis society but rather with assaying the dharmic (right, true, consistent) or adharmic character of a thing or an action within the entire theantropocosmic complex of reality. (1984: 39)[11]

Seen from the *topos* of *dharma*, human rights are incomplete in that they fail to establish the link between the part (the individual) and the whole (reality), or, even more strongly, in that they focus on what is merely derivative, on rights, rather than on the primordial imperative, the duty of individuals to find their place in the order of the entire society and of the entire cosmos. Seen from *dharma* and, indeed, from *umma* also, the Western conception of human rights is plagued by a very simplistic and mechanistic symmetry between rights and duties. It grants rights only to those from whom it can demand duties. This explains why, according to the Western concept of human rights, nature has no rights: it cannot be imposed any duties. For the same reason, it is impossible to grant rights to future generations; they have no rights because they have no duties.

On the other hand, seen from the *topos* of human rights, *dharma* is also incomplete due to its strong undialectical bias in favor of harmony, thereby occulting injustices and totally neglecting the value of conflict as a way toward a richer harmony. Moreover, *dharma* is unconcerned with the principles of democratic order, with freedom and autonomy, and it neglects the fact that, without primordial rights, the individual is too fragile an entity to avoid being run over by whatever transcends him or her. Lastly, *dharma* tends to forget that human suffering has an irreducible individual dimension: societies do not suffer, but individuals do.

At another conceptual level, the same diatopical hermeneutics can be attempted between the *topos* of human rights and the *topos* of *umma* in Islamic culture. The passages in the Qur'an in which the word *umma* occurs are so varied that its meaning cannot be rigidly defined. This much, however, seems to be certain: it always refers to ethnical, linguistic or religious bodies of people who are the objects of the divine plan of salvation. As the prophetic activity of Muhammad progressed, the religious foundations of *umma* became increasingly apparent and, consequently, the *umma* of the Arabs was transformed into the *umma* of the Muslims. Seen from the *topos* of *umma*, the incompleteness of individual human rights lies in the fact that on its basis alone it is impossible to ground the collective linkages and solidarities without which no society can survive, much less flourish. Herein lies the difficulty for the Western conception of human rights to accept the collective rights of social groups or peoples, be they ethnic minorities, women, or indigenous peoples. This is in fact a specific instance of a much broader difficulty, the difficulty of defining the community as an arena of concrete solidarity and as a horizontal political obligation. Central to Rousseau, this idea of community was flushed away in the liberal dichotomy that set asunder the state and civil society.

Conversely, from the *topos* of individual human rights, *umma* overemphasizes duties to the detriment of rights and, for that reason, is bound to condone otherwise unjust inequalities, such as the inequality between men and women and between Muslims and non-Muslims. As unveiled by diatopical hermeneutics, the fundamental weakness of Western culture consists in dichotomizing too strictly between the individual and society, thus becoming vulnerable to possessive individualism, narcissism, alienation, and anomie. On the other hand, the fundamental weakness of Hindu and Islamic cultures consists in that they both fail to recognize that human suffering has an irreducible individual dimension that can only be adequately addressed in a society not hierarchically organized.

The recognition of reciprocal incompletenesses and weaknesses is a *condition-sine-qua-non* of any cross-cultural dialogue. Diatopical hermeneutics builds both on the local identification of incompleteness and weakness and on its translocal intelligibility. As mentioned above, in the area of human rights and dignity, the mobilization of social support for the emancipatory claims that they potentially contain is only achievable if such claims have been appropriated in the local cultural context and if a cross-cultural dialogue and diatopical hermeneutics are possible. Many highly differentiated exercises in diatopical hermeneutics between Islamic and Western cultures in the field of human rights have been tried in recent times. Some of the most notable cases are provided by Abdullahi Ahmed An-na'im (1990; 1992), Tariq Ramadan (2000, 2003), and Ebrahim Moosa (2004).

There is a longstanding debate on the relationships between Islamism and human rights and the possibility of an Islamic conception of human rights.[12] This debate covers a wide range of positions and its impact reaches far beyond the Islamic world. Running the risk of excessive simplification, two extreme positions can be identified in this debate. One, absolutist or fundamentalist, is held by those for whom the religious legal system of Islam, the Shari'a, must be fully applied as the law of the Islamic state. According to this position, there are irreconcilable inconsistencies between the Shari'a and the Western conception of human rights, and the Shari'a must prevail. For instance, regarding the status of non-Muslims, the Shari'a dictates the creation of a state for Muslims as the sole citizens, non-Muslims having no political rights; peace between Muslims and non-Muslims is always problematic and confrontations may be unavoidable. Concerning women, there is no question of equality; the Shari'a commands the segregation of women and, according to some even stricter interpretations, excludes them from public life altogether.

At the other extreme, there are the secularists or modernists who believe that Muslims should organize themselves in secular states. Islam is a religious and spiritual movement, not a political one and, as such, modern Muslim societies are free to organize their government in whatever manner they deem fit and appropriate to their circumstances. The acceptance of international human rights is a matter for political decision unencumbered by religious considerations. Just one example, among many: a Tunisian law of 1956 prohibited polygamy altogether on the grounds that it was no longer acceptable and that the Qur'anic requirement of justice among co-wives was impossible for any man, except the Prophet, to achieve in practice.

An-na'im criticizes both extreme positions. The via per mezzo he proposes aims at establishing a cross-cultural foundation for human rights, identifying the areas of conflict between Shari'a and "the standards of human rights" and seeking a reconciliation and positive relationship between the two systems. For example, the problem with historical Shari'a is that it excludes women and non-Muslims from the application of this principle. Thus, a reform or reconstruction of Shari'a is needed. The method proposed for such an "Islamic Reformation" is based on an evolutionary approach to Islamic sources that looks into the specific historical context within which Shari'a was created from the original sources of Islam by the founding jurists of the eighth and ninth centuries. In the light of such a context, a restricted construction of the other was probably justified. But this is no longer so. On the contrary, there is in the present, different context within Islam full justification for a more enlightened view.

Following the teachings of *Ustadh* Mahmoud, An-na'im shows that a close examination of the content of the Qur'an and Sunna reveals two levels or stages in the message of Islam, one of the earlier Mecca period and the other of the subsequent Medina stage. The earlier message of Mecca is the eternal and fundamental message of Islam and it emphasizes the inherent dignity of all human beings, regardless of gender, religious belief, or race. Under the historical conditions of the seventh century (the Medina stage) this message was considered too advanced, was suspended, and its implementation postponed until appropriate circumstances might emerge in the future. The time and context, says An-na'im, are now ripe for it.

It is not for me to evaluate the specific validity of this proposal within Islamic culture. This is precisely what distinguishes diatopical hermeneutics from Orientalism. What I want to emphasize in An-na'im's approach is the attempt to transform the Western conception of human rights into a cross-cultural one that vindicates Islamic legitimacy rather than relinquishing it. In the abstract and from the outside, it is difficult to judge whether a religious or a secularist approach is more likely to succeed in an Islamic based cross-cultural dialogue on human rights. However, bearing in mind that Western human rights are the expression of a profound, albeit incomplete process of secularization that is not comparable to anything in Islamic culture, one would be inclined to suggest that, in the Muslim context, the mobilizing energy needed for a cosmopolitan project of human rights will be more easily generated within an enlightened religious framework. If so, An-na'im's approach is very promising.

But he does not stand alone and, indeed, Islam scholars and activists have been contributing in recent years to intercultural translation and diatopical hermeneutics in new and important ways. This is most notable in the case of Tariq Ramadan. Addressing himself to the Muslims living in the West and to their socio-economic conditions (most of them being immigrants), he encourages them to join forces with all the other oppressed social groups, independent of their cultural or religious background, with the following rationale:

The one who has already worked on the ground with grassroots communities, developing at the local level, social and economic strategies, can only be surprised with their similarities to the experience of Muslim forces. The reference points are certainly different as are the grounds and application, but

the spirit is one and the same in the sense that it is nourished from the same source of resistance to the blind interest of the great superpowers and the multinationals. We have already said it: it is not a matter of affirming the reality of a beatific Islamic third-worldism, which would echo the one that we have known for a long time in our part of the world. The truth is that Islam, by the fact that it is the reference point for many active Muslims, results in the same demand for dignity, justice and pluralism as those ideas which shape the mobilization of the Christian or humanistic community. Thus in this respect, the relations should be multiplied and the exchanges of experience made permanent (2003: 14).

For Tariq Ramadan, the impulse for intercultural translation lies in the overriding need to build broad coalitions to fight against neoliberal globalization: "it is necessary to be both a friend and a partner of those, in the West, who denounce the global oppression and invite us all to bring such change" (2003: 10).

In India, a similar way of combining cultural integrity with broader struggles for social justice is being pursued by some human rights groups and, particularly, by untouchables' social reformers. It consists in grounding the struggle of the untouchables for justice and equality in the Hindu notions of *karma* and *dharma*, revising and reinterpreting them or even subverting them selectively in such a way as to turn them into sources of legitimacy and strength for contestations and protests. An illustration of such revisions is the increasing emphasis given to "*common dharma*" (*sadharana dharma*) in contrast to the "*specialized dharma*" (*visesa dharma*) of caste rules, rituals and duties. According to Khare, the "*common dharma*,"

> based on the spiritual sameness of all creatures, traditionally promotes a shared sense of mutual care, avoidance of violence and injury, and a pursuit of fairness. It traditionally promotes activities for public welfare and attracts progressive reformers. Human rights advocates might locate here a convergent indigenous Indian impulse. The *common dharma* ethic also eminently suits untouchable social reformers (1998: 204).

The "Indian impulse" of the "*common dharma*" provides human rights with cultural embeddedness and local legitimacy whereby they cease to be a globalized localism. The revision of the Hindu tradition not only creates an opening for human rights claims, it also invites a revision of the human rights tradition to include claims formulated following other cultural premises. By getting involved in reciprocal revisions, both traditions act as guest cultures and as host cultures. These are the paths necessary for the demanding exercises of intercultural translation (diatopical hermeneutics). The outcome is a culturally hybrid claim for human dignity, a *mestiza* conception of human rights. Herein lies the alternative to an all-encompassing general theory, the peculiar version of universalism that conceives as particularity whatever does not fit in its narrow confines.[13]

Diatopical hermeneutics is not a task for a single person writing within a single culture. It is, therefore, not surprising that, for example, An-na'im's approach, though a true *exemplar* of diatopical hermeneutics, is conducted with uneven consistency. In my view, An-na'im accepts the idea of universal human rights too readily and acritically.[14] Even though he subscribes to an evolutionary approach and is quite attentive to the historical context of Islamic tradition, he becomes surprisingly ahistorical and naively universalist as far the Universal Declaration goes. Diatopical hermeneutics requires not only a different kind of knowledge but also a different process of knowledge creation. It requires a production of knowledge that is collective, interactive, inter-subjective, and networked.[15] It must be pursued in the full awareness that there will be black spots, zones of irredeemable mutual unintelligibility, which, in order not to lead to paralysis or factionalism, must be relativized by overriding common interests in the struggles against social injustice. This much is emphasized by Tariq Ramadan:

> The West is neither monolithic nor diabolic, and the phenomenal assets in terms of its rights, knowledge, culture and civilization are too important to simply minimize and reject. [However, t]o be a Western citizen from a Muslim background and to maintain these truths is to, almost systematically, undertake the risk of being regarded as someone who is not successfully "integrated." Thus the suspicion remains on such a person's true allegiance. Everything proceeds as if our "integration" has to be bought with our silence. One needs to refuse this kind of intellectual blackmail (2003: 10–11).

The diatopical hermeneutics conducted from the perspective of Islamic culture must be matched by a diatopical hermeneutics conducted from the perspective of other cultures, most notably from the perspective of Western culture. This is probably the only way to embed in Western culture the ideas of collective rights, of the rights of nature and of future generations, and of the duties and responsibilities *vis-à-vis* collective entities, be they the community, the world, or even the cosmos.

CULTURAL IMPERIALISM AND
THE POSSIBILITY OF COUNTER-HEGEMONY

Given the historically intimate connection between Western human rights and colonialism, submitting them to a diatopical hermeneutics is definitely the most difficult translational task. Learning from the South is only a starting point, and it may actually be a false starting point if it is not borne in mind that the North has been actively unlearning the South all along. As Said has frequently pointed out, the imperial context brutalizes both the victim and the victimizer and induces in the dominant as well as in the dominated culture "not just assent and loyalty but an unusually rarified sense of the sources from which the culture really springs and in what complicating circumstances its monuments derive" (1993: 37).[16] Monuments have, indeed, messy origins. Viewing the pyramids, Ali Shariati once observed:

> I felt so much hatred toward the great monuments of civilization which throughout history were praised upon the bones of my predecessors! My predecessors also built the great wall [sic] of China. Those who could not carry the loads were crushed under the heavy stones and put into the walls with the stones. This was how all the great monuments of civilization were constructed—at the expense of the flesh and blood of my predecessors (1982: 19).

In my view, the same could be said about human rights as one of the greatest monuments of Western civilization. The clean, clear-cut, ahistorical formulations to which they have lent themselves hide their messy origins, ranging from the genocides of European expansion to the Thermidor and the Holocaust. But this rarification of cultures occurs in the subordinate cultures as well, as Said has shown:

> Young Arabs and Muslims today are taught to venerate the classics of their religion and thought, not to be critical, not to view what they read of, say, Abbasid or *nahda* literature as alloyed with all kinds of political contests. Only very occasionally does a critic and a poet like Adonis, the brilliant contemporary Syrian writer, come along and say openly that readings of *turath* in the Arab world today enforce a rigid authoritarianism and literalism which have the effect of killing the spirit and obliterating criticism (1993: 38).

As became evident in the analysis of diatopical hermeneutics above, to recognize the reciprocal impoverishment of victim and victimizer alike, however asymmetrical, is the most basic condition for a cross-cultural dialogue. Only the knowledge of history permits us to act independently of history. Scrutiny of the relationships between victim and victimizer cautions us against too strict distinctions among cultures, a caution that is particularly relevant in the case of the dominant culture. According to Pieterse, Western culture is neither what it seems, nor what Westerners tend to think it is: "What is held to be European culture or civilization is genealogically not necessarily or strictly European" (Pieterse, 1989: 369). It is a cultural synthesis of many elements and currents, many of them non-European. Bernal has undertaken a deconstruction of the concepts of "classical civilization" to show its non-European foundations, the contributions of Egypt and Africa, Semitic and Phoenician civilizations, Mesopotamia and Persia, India and China, regarding language, art, knowledge, religion, and material culture. He also shows how these Afro-Asiatic roots of Ancient Greece were denied by nineteenth-century European racism and anti-Semitism (Bernal, 1987).

In line with this inquiry, the messy origins of human rights, as a monument of Western culture, can be seen not only in the imperial and domestic domination that they once justified, but also in their original composite character as cultural artifacts. The presuppositions of human rights, which were indicated above in their clear-cut, Enlightenment, rational formulations, echo the vibrations of other cultures, and their historical roots reach far beyond Europe. A cross-cultural dialogue must start from the assumption that cultures have always been cross-cultural, but also with the understanding that exchanges and interpenetrations have always been very unequal and inherently hostile to the cosmopolitan dialogue that is here being argued for. Ultimately, the question is whether it is possible to construct a post-imperial conception of human rights. Put differently, the question is whether the vocabulary or the script of human rights is so crowded with hegemonic meanings as to exclude the possibility of counter-hegemonic meanings. Although I am fully aware of the almost insurmountable barriers, I give a positive answer to my basic question. In the following I try to specify the conditions under which the possibility of counter-hegemony can be actualized. I will start by addressing the conditions for the multicultural conception of human rights laid out above and will then present an outline of a counter-hegemonic, emancipatory conception of human rights.

Difficulties of an intercultural reconstruction of human rights

Diatopical hermeneutics offers a wide field of possibilities for the debates going on in the different cultural regions of the world system, on the general issues of universalism, relativism, cultural frames of social transformation, traditionalism, and cultural revival.[17] However, an idealistic conception of cross-cultural dialogue will easily forget that such a dialogue is only made possible by the temporary simultaneity of two or more different contemporaneities. The partners in the dialogue are unequally contemporaneous; indeed, each of them feels himself or herself only contemporaneous with the historical tradition of his or her respective culture. This is most likely the case when the different cultures involved in the dialogue share a past of interlocked and unequal exchanges. What are the possibilities for a cross-cultural dialogue when one of the cultures *in presence* has been itself molded by massive and longlasting violations of human rights perpetrated in the name of the other culture? When cultures share such a past, the present that they share at the moment of initiating the dialogue is at best a *quid pro quo* and, at worst, a fraud. The cultural dilemma is the following: since in the past the dominant culture rendered unpronounceable some of the subordinate culture's aspirations to human dignity, is it now possible to pronounce them in the cross-cultural dialogue without thereby further justifying and even reinforcing their unpronounceability?

Cultural imperialism and epistemicide are part of the historical trajectory of Western modernity. After centuries of unequal cultural exchanges, is the equal treatment of cultures fair? Is it necessary to render some aspirations of Western culture unpronounceable in order to make room for the pronounceability of other aspirations of other cultures? Paradoxically—and contrary to hegemonic discourse—it is precisely in the field of human rights that Western culture must learn from the South[18] if the false universality that is attributed to human rights in the imperial context is to be converted into the new universality of cosmopolitanism in a cross-cultural dialogue. The emancipatory character of diatopical hermeneutics is not guaranteed *a priori* and, indeed, multiculturalism may be the new mark of a reactionary politics. Suffice it to mention the multiculturalism of the Prime Minister of Malaysia or of the Chinese gerontocracy when they speak of the "Asian conception of human rights" (Rajagopal, 2004: 212–216).

One of the most problematic presuppositions of diatopical hermeneutics is the conception of cultures as incomplete entities. It may be argued that, on the contrary, only complete cultures can enter into an intercultural dialogue without risking being run over by and ultimately dissolved into other, more powerful cultures. A variation of this argument states that only a powerful and historically victorious culture, such as Western culture, can grant itself the privilege of proclaiming its own incompleteness without risking dissolution. Indeed, cultural incompleteness may be, in this case, the ultimate tool of cultural hegemony. None of the non-Western cultures are allowed today such a privilege.

This line of argumentation is particularly convincing when applied to those non-Western cultures that endured in the past the most destructive "encounters" with Western culture. Indeed, so destructive were they that they led in many cases to utter cultural extinction. This is the case of the indigenous peoples and cultures in the Americas, in Australia, New Zealand, India, etc. These cultures have been so aggressively *incompleted* by Western culture that the demand for incompleteness, as a precondition for a diatopical hermeneutics is, at least, a ludicrous exercise.[19]

The problem with this line of argumentation is that it leads, logically, to two alternative outcomes, both of them quite disturbing: cultural closure or conquest as the sole realistic alternative to intercultural dialogues. In a time of intensified transnational social and cultural practices, cultural closure is, at best, a pious aspiration that occults and implicitly condones chaotic and uncontrollable processes of destructuring, contamination, and hybridization. Such processes reside in unequal power relations and in unequal cultural exchanges, so much so that cultural closure becomes the other side of cultural conquest. The question is then whether cultural conquest can be replaced by intercultural dialogues based on mutually agreed conditions and, if so, on what conditions.

The dilemma of cultural completeness, as I would call it, may be formulated as follows: if a given culture considers itself complete, it sees no interest in entertaining intercultural dialogues; if, on the contrary, it enters into such a dialogue out of a sense of its own incompleteness, it makes itself vulnerable and, ultimately, offers itself to cultural conquest. There is no easy way out of this dilemma. Bearing in mind that cultural closure is self-defeating, I do not see any other way out but that of raising the standards for intercultural dialogue to a threshold high enough to minimize the possibility of cultural conquest, though not so high as to preclude the possibility of dialogues altogether (in which case it would revert into cultural closure and, hence, into cultural conquest).

Conditions for an intercultural reconstruction of human rights

The conditions for a progressive multiculturalism vary widely across time and space and primarily according to the specific cultures involved and the power relations among them. However, I venture to say that the following contextual procedural orientations and transcultural imperatives must be accepted by all social groups interested in intercultural dialogues.

From completeness to incompleteness. As I said above, cultural completeness is the starting point, not the point of arrival. Indeed, cultural completeness is the condition prevailing before the intercultural dialogue starts. The true starting point of this dialogue is a moment of discontent with one's culture, a diffuse sense that one's culture does not provide satisfying answers to some of one's queries, perplexities or expectations. This diffuse sensibility is linked to a vague knowledge of and an inarticulate curiosity about other possible cultures and their answers. The moment of discontent involves a pre-understanding of the existence and possible relevance of other cultures and translates itself into an unreflective consciousness of cultural incompleteness. The individual or collective impulse for intercultural dialogue and thus for diatopical hermeneutics starts from here.

Far from turning cultural incompleteness into cultural completeness, diatopical hermeneutics deepens, as it progresses, the cultural incompleteness and transforms the vague and largely unreflective consciousness of it into a self-reflective consciousness. The objective of diatopical hermeneutics is thus to create a self-reflective consciousness of cultural incompleteness. In this case, self-reflectivity means the recognition of the cultural incompleteness of one's culture as seen in the mirror of the cultural incompleteness of the other culture in the dialogue. It is very much in this spirit that Makau Mutua, after arguing that "[t]he relentless efforts to universalize an essentially European corpus of human rights through Western crusades cannot succeed," states that

> [t]he critiques of the corpus from Africans, Asians, Muslims, Hindus, and a host of critical thinkers from around the world are the one avenue through which human rights can be redeemed and truly universalized. This multi-culturalization of the corpus could be attempted in a number of areas: balancing between individual and group rights, giving more substance to social and economic rights, relating rights to duties, and addressing the relationship between the corpus and economic systems (2001:243).

From narrow to wide versions of cultures. As I mentioned above, far from being monolithic entities, cultures comprise rich internal variety. The consciousness of such variety increases as the diatopical hermeneutics progresses. Of the different versions of a given culture, one must choose that which represents the widest circle of reciprocity within that culture, the version that goes farthest in the recognition of the other. As we have seen, of two different interpretations of the Qur'an, An-na'im chooses the one with the wider circle of reciprocity, the one that involves Muslims and non-Muslims, men and women alike. From a different perspective, Tariq Ramadan assumes a contextual conception of cultural and religious differences with the objective of putting them at the service of cross-cultural coalitions in the struggle against global capitalism. In the same way and for similar reasons, the untouchables' social reformers emphasize "*common dharma*," to the detriment of "*specialized dharma*." I think the same must be done within Western culture as well. Of the two versions of human rights existing in Western culture—the liberal and the social-democratic or Marxist—the social-democratic or Marxist one must be adopted because it extends to the economic and social realms the equality that the liberal version only considers legitimate in the political realm.

From unilateral to shared times. The time for intercultural dialogue cannot be established unilaterally. Each culture and therefore the community or communities that sustain it must decide if and when they are ready for intercultural dialogue. Because of the fallacy of completeness, when one given culture starts feeling the need for intercultural dialogue it tends to believe that the other cultures feel an equal need and are equally eager to engage in dialogue. This is probably most characteristically the case of Western culture, which for centuries felt no need for mutually accepted intercultural dialogues. Now, as the unreflective consciousness of incompleteness sets in in the West, Western culture tends to believe that all the other cultures should or indeed must recognize their own incompleteness and be ready and eager to enter intercultural dialogues with it.

If the time to enter an intercultural dialogue must be agreed upon by the cultures and social groups involved, the time to end it provisionally or permanently must be left to the unilateral decision of each culture and social group involved. There should be nothing irreversible about diatopical hermeneutics. A given culture may need a pause before entering a new stage of the dialogue, or feel that the dialogue has brought it more damage than advantage and, accordingly, that it should be ended indefinitely. The reversibility of the dialogue is indeed crucial to defend the latter from perverting itself into unassumed reciprocal cultural closure or unilateral cultural conquest. The possibility of reversion is what makes the intercultural dialogue into an open and explicit political process. The political meaning of a unilateral decision to terminate the intercultural dialogue is different when the decision is taken by a dominant culture or by a dominated culture. While in the latter case it may be an act of self-defense, in the former case it will be most probably an act of aggressive chauvinism. It is up to the politically progressive forces inside a given culture and across cultures—what I have called above "insurgent cosmopolitanism"—to defend the emancipatory politics of diatopical hermeneutics from reactionary deviations.

From unilaterally imposed to mutually chosen partners and issues. No culture will possibly enter a dialogue with any other possible culture on any possible issue. The intercultural dialogue is always selective both in terms of partners and of issues. The requirement that both partners and issues cannot unilaterally be imposed and must rather be mutually agreed upon is probably the most demanding condition of diatopical hermeneutics. The specific historical, cultural, and political processes by which the otherness of a given culture becomes significant for another culture at a given point in time varies widely. But, in general, colonialism, liberation struggles, post-colonialism, and anti-capitalism have been the most decisive processes behind the emergence of significant otherness. In this vein, Tariq Ramadan encourages the Muslims in the West, "however in the heart of industrialized societies, [to] remain the conscience of the Sotuh and of the destitute" (2003: 10). Concerning issues, the agreement is inherently problematic not only because issues in a given culture are not easily translatable into another culture but also because in every culture there are always non-negotiable or even unspoken issues, taboos being a paradigmatic example. As I discussed above, diatopical hermeneutics has to focus on isomorphic concerns, rather than on "same" issues, on common perplexities and uneasinesses from which the sense of incompleteness emerges.

From equality or difference to equality and difference. Probably all cultures tend to distribute people and groups according to two competing principles of hierarchical belongingness—unequal exchanges among equals, such as exploitation (by capitalists over workers) and the unequal recognition of difference, such as racism or sexism—and thus according to competing conceptions of equality and difference. Under such circumstances, neither the recognition of equality nor the recognition of difference will suffice to found an emancipatory multicultural politics. The following transcultural imperative must thus be accepted by all partners in the dialogue if diatopical hermeneutics is to succeed: people have the right to be equal whenever difference makes them inferior, but they also have the right to be different whenever equality jeopardizes their identity.

INTERCULTURAL POST-IMPERIAL HUMAN RIGHTS

A new politics of rights is needed, a fresh approach to the task of empowering the popular classes and coalitions in their struggles for emancipatory solutions beyond Western modernity and global capitalism. A new architecture of human rights based on a new foundation and with a new justification is called for. Since it is not my purpose in this chapter to go beyond proposing a new research agenda, I will limit myself to some exploratory remarks and general guiding principles. The new architecture of human rights must go to the roots of modernity, both to the roots that it recognized as its own and to the roots that it rejected as it colonial exteriority. In this sense, to go to the roots involves going beyond the roots. This inquiry and building plan is a genealogy, in that it looks for the hidden transcript of the origins, of inclusions as well as exclusions, of legitimate as well as bastard ancestors; it is also a geology because it is interested in layers of sedimentation, gaps and faultlines (that cause both social and personal earthquakes); it is finally an archaeology as well in that it is interested in knowing what was once legitimate, proper, and just, and which was then discarded as anachronistic, suppressed as deviant, or hidden as shameful. While for centuries modernity was taken to be universal from an assumedly Western point of view, from the nineteenth century onwards it was reconceptualized as a universal, from a supposedly universal point of view. Universal Western human rights became, then, universal human rights. From then on, a totalizing relationship between victimizers and victims evolved that, however unequal in its effects, brutalized both of them, forcing them both to share a common culture of domination in their acceptance of rarified and impoverished versions of their own respective cultures. Modern social sciences are the most sophisticated epistemology of such rarification and impoverishment.

Under these conditions, building a cross-cultural post-imperial conception of human rights is first and foremost an epistemological task. At this level, the founding, underground rights must be designed—I call them *ur-rights*— which the Western colonialist and capitalist modernity suppressed in order to build, upon their ruins, the monumental cathedral of fundamental human rights. Conceiving of ur-rights is an exercise in retrospective radical imagination. It means to establish and denounce an abyssal act of negativity at the core of colonial expansion, an abyssal negativity upon which Western modernity built its glaring epistemological, political, economic and cultural constructions. As conceived here, ur-rights are therefore not natural rights in the Western idealist tradition; they are rights that exist only in the process of being negated and as negations. Indeed, they are not *ur*-rights but rather *ur*-wrongs; they are ur-rights that only exist to signal the perpetration of ur-wrongs. To vindicate them is to open the time-space for a post-colonial and post-imperial conception of human rights.

The right to knowledge. The suppression of this ur-right was responsible for the massive epistemicide upon which Western modernity built its monumental imperial knowledge. In a period of paradigmatic transition,[20] the vindication of this ur-right involves of necessity a right to alternative knowledges. Such alternative knowledges must be grounded on a new epistemology from the South, from the non-imperial South. Since the abovementioned tension between social regulation and social emancipation is also an epistemological tension, the right to alternative knowledges is a right to move away from knowledge-as-regulation in the direction of knowledge-as-emancipation,[21] from a form of knowledge that proceeds from chaos to order toward a form of knowledge that proceeds from colonialism to solidarity. Such a knowledge is the epistemological precondition to break the vicious circle of a reciprocal manufacturing of victims and victimizers. When from this perspective we analyze the institutional and organizational knowledges that underlie the practices of state governments and international agencies, we can easily observe how their exclusive emphases on order render unthinkable the passage from colonialism to solidarity. Since no distinction is made between the two categories, victims and victimizers are equal before the liberal conception of human rights.

The right to bring historical capitalism to trial in a world tribunal. The suppression of the second ur-right grounded the conversion of capitalism into an irreversible and unconditional manifestation of progress. The vindication of this ur-right demands that capitalism, as represented by core capitalist actors (states, multilateral financial agencies, and and transnational corporations [TNCs]), be made accountable for its crucial quota of responsibility for massive violations of human rights, occurring in the form of mass immiseration, cultural impoverishment, and ecological destruction. As this ur-right emerges from the archaeological excavation of Western capitalist and colonialist modernity, the history of world capitalism and Western modernity will gradually evolve into a tragic history of ethical degradation.

Whatever happened in history did not just happen; it also prevented other pasts (and thus other presents) from happening. Lacunae in the present are therefore seen to have their source in suppressed pasts. By the same token, no confrontation between facts and non-facts can be adjudicated factually: the debate over facts and non-facts becomes a debate over rights and wrongs. The tribunal and the trial, though modern forms in themselves, will be put to a trans-modern use. As a world tribunal, the institutional setting will be a transnational time-space of its own, a counter-hegemonic globalization, or globalization from below. The proceedings will be guided by an overarching principle of global responsibility, the idea of global *Sorge,* an expanded version of the idea formulated by Hans Jonas.[22] Rather than looking for narrowly defined disputes over short-range responsibilities and for well-delimited courses of action and consequences, this ur-trial will conceive of the world system as a single collective dispute, leaving nobody out, either as a victim or as a victimizer. Since many parties will be both victims and victimizers, the relative weight of each partial identity will be at the core of legal-political argumentation. The adjudication of responsibility will be determined in light of long-range, intergenerational courses of action occurring both in society and in nature. The decisions, always provisional and reversible, will be the result of rhetorical capital accumulation either around the arguments of emancipatory coalitions, those of the victims and their allies, or around the arguments of regulatory coalitions, those of the victimizers and their allies. The verdict will be enforceable through the type of collective action being undertaken by the social actors involved in bringing about counter-hegemonic globalization and will constitute an ongoing, neverending project, the project of a socialist society.

The right to a solidarity-oriented transformation of the right to property. The ways by which the third ur-right has been historically suppressed bears witness to the inherently colonial character of Western modernity. As an ur-right, it is not a right to property precisely because it did not exist as such before colonial usurpation. Again, it is negativity that founds the colonial land occupation. Conceived as an individual right in the Western conception of human rights, the right to property is at the core of the global North/ global South divide. It develops historically through a series of transformative legal questions: from the general question of the legitimacy of the European land occupation in the New World (sixteenth century), to the question of the public relation of *imperium* or jurisdiction grounding individual claims to land by individual states (seventeenth century), and, finally, to the question of the nature of land as a thing, an object of private property (seventeenth and eighteenth centuries). While in the first two questions property implied the control over people, in the third it expresses merely control over things. The bourgeois property theory is wholly contained in this move. A concept ridden by political connotations, such as the concept of occupation, is followed by a neutral concept of physical possession involving the right of property over a thing. This thing, at the moment that property theory is created, is basically the land, the concept of property itself designating now in the common language the thing itself, i.e., land as property. Locke (1952) [1689] is the great creator of this conception.[23] With great forethought, Rousseau saw, in the right to property conceived as an individual right, the seeds of war and of all human suffering, as well as the destruction of community and nature; the problem rested, as Rousseau clearly saw, in the dialectics between the consequences of individual and collective hold- ings. This dialectics has reached a climax in recent decades with the rise of the TNCs to world economic prominence. Though constituted by large collectivities of stockholders and managers, with resources exceeding those of many nation-states, operating worldwide and controlling the provision of public services that are essential to the survival of large bodies of population, TNCs are nevertheless considered right-holder individuals and are dealt with as such by both domestic and international law. An insurgent cosmopolitan politics of human rights must confront head-on the possessive individualism of the liberal conception of property. Beyond the state and the market, a third social domain must be reinvented: a collective, but not state-centered, private, but not profit-oriented, a social domain in which the right to a solidarity-oriented transformation of property rights will be socially and politically anchored.

The right to grant rights to entities incapable of bearing duties, namely nature and future generations. The suppression of the fourth ur-right grounds the symmetry between right-holders and duty-bearers that is at the core of the Western conception of rights. According to this conception, only those susceptible of being duty-bearers are entitled to be right-holders. This symmetry narrowed the scope of the principle of reciprocity such that it left out women, children, slaves, indigenous peoples, nature, and future generations. Once removed from the reciprocity circle, these were included as things in economic and political rationales and calculations. The progressive transformations of the last two centuries have been too timid to neutralize the tragic result of these arbitrary exclusions. The broad principle of responsibility mentioned above provides the normative orientation for the enlarged scope of reciprocity within which rights held by non-bearers of duties will be recognized as paramount.

The right to democratic self-determination. With a long tradition in Western modernity, the suppression of this right legitimated the popular defeats in the wake of the revolutions of the eighteenth and nineteenth centuries, as well as of the elitist independence of Latin American colonies throughout the nineteenth century. The same suppression could be traced in the almost simultaneous proclamation of the right of nations to self-determination by both Woodrow Wilson and Lenin (Wallerstein, 1991: 5). In the postwar period, the vindication of this ur-right has been present in the process of decolonization and is now being invoked by indigenous peoples in their struggle for social, political, and cultural identity. Though the strength of this tradition is undoubtedly a progressive historical fact, it may also become a serious barrier to the further vindication of the ur-right to the democratic self-determination called for by an insurgent cosmopolitan practice of human rights.

The trajectory of the right to self-determination during the past fifty years shows how much is still to be done in this area. The moderate and relatively ambiguous formulation of this right in the United Nations Charter was soon superseded by the strength of the anti-colonialist movement (the Bandung Conference was held in 1955) and the predominance of the socialist doctrine of self-determination over that of the Western world (Cassese, 1979: 139). While expanding the concept of self-determination to mean liberation from colonialism, racist domination (for instance, South Africa and Southern Rhodesia), and foreign occupation (such as the Arab territories occupied by Israel), socialist countries, together with Arab and African countries, restricted its use to external self-determination; for sovereign independent states, self-determination was tantamount to the right to nonintervention. On the contrary, Western countries maintained that self-determination should also be understood as internal self-determination, that is to say, as the right of peoples against sovereign states that massively violated human rights—meaning the totalitarian regimes of the Communist bloc. Normative developments in the United Nations system, particularly after the International Covenants of 1966, show that the UN has been one-sidedly concentrated on "external"—to the detriment of "internal"—self-determination. In my analysis of indigenous peoples' struggles (Santos, 2002: 237–257), I have tried to lay bare the almost insurmountable barriers raised by the principle of sovereignty against the recognition of "internal" self-determination. Although the priority given to "external" self-determination may have been justified during the anti-colonialist process, it has since lost all justification.[24]

From the perspective of a non-imperial conception of self-determination, a special reference must be made to a non-governmental document that has gained worldwide moral authority and in which the right to self-determination of peoples receives the fullest recognition. I am referring to the Algiers Declaration of the Rights of Peoples of 1976, and, specifically, to its Articles 5, 6 and 7.

Article 5
Every people has an imprescriptible and unalienable right to self-determination. It shall determine its political status freely and without foreign interference.

Article 6
Every people has the right to break free from any colonial or foreign domination, whether direct or indirect, and from any racist regime.

Article 7
Every people has the right to have a democratic government representing all the citizens without distinction as to race, sex, belief or color, and capable of ensuring effective respect for the human rights and fundamental freedoms of all.

The Algiers Declaration comes closest to the full vindication of the ur-right to democratic self-determination. It provides, in my judgment, an adequate foundation for a broader and deeper conception of the right to self-determination insofar as it acts as a guiding principle in the struggles for a counter-hegemonic globalization. Shivji has proposed the right of people to self-determination as one of the core rights in the African context, a collective right "embodying the principal contradiction between imperialism and its compradorial allies vis-a-vis [sic] people on the one hand, and oppressor vis-a-vis [sic] oppressed nations, on the other" (1989: 80). According to him, the right-holders of this right are dominated/exploited people and oppressed nations, nationalities, national groups, and minorities, while the duty-bearers are states, oppressor nations and nationalities, and imperialist countries. Although basically in agreement with Shivji, I would like to stress that, in my conception, the right to self-determination can be exercised both as a collective *and* as an individual right: at the core of any collective right is the right to opt out of the collectivity. Furthermore, I put an equal emphasis on the political outcome of self-determination and on the participatory democratic processes towards self-determination. Peoples are political entities and not idealized abstractions: they do not speak with one voice and, when they do speak, it is imperative to establish participatory democracy as the criterion for the legitimacy of the positions voiced.[25]

The right to organize and participate in the creation of rights. The suppression of the sixth ur-right has been the foundation of capitalist rule and domination. Without such suppression, minorities would never have been able to govern over majorities in a political field consisting of free and equal citizens. By relying on radical conceptions of democracy, the emancipatory struggles converging in the counter-hegemonic globalization of our time vindicate this ur-right as their guiding political principle. The conflict between neoliberal globalization and anti-capitalist counter-hegemonic globalization is a relatively unmapped social field characterized by relatively and totally uninsurable risks of oppression, human suffering and destruction, as well as by new, unsuspected possibilities and opportunities for emancipatory politics. The risks feed on the atomization, depoliticization, and *apartheidization* of people that derives from the downward spiraling of old forms of resistance and organization: the vicious circle between declining mobilizing energies and increasingly pointless organizations. Far from being an "organic" process, such spiraling down is actively provoked by repressive measures and ideological manipulation.[26] On the other hand, the opportunities for emancipatory politics depend, according to the circumstances, either on the invention of new forms of organization specifically targeted to meet the new risks or on the defense of old forms of organization, which are then reinvented to measure up to the new challenges, new agenda, and new potential coalitions.

The right to organize is a primordial right, without which none of the other rights can be minimally achievable. It is an ur-right in the strictest sense since its suppression is at the core of the modern conception that the most fundamental rights do not have to be created: they are already there as natural rights, as a "given." Without the denunciation of this abyssal suppression it will be impossible to organize all necessary solidarities against all existing colonialisms. Upon this ur-right the indigenous peoples are founding their struggles to win the right to follow their own rights.

The right to organize and the right to create rights are thus two inseparable dimensions of the same right.[27] According to the vulnerabilities of specific social groups, the repression of human rights is targeted against either the creation of rights or the organization to defend or to create rights. The morally repugnant divide between the global North and the global South and, related to it, the growing interiorization of the Third World in the global North (the poor, the permanently unemployed, the homeless, the undocumented migrant workers, the asylum-seekers, the prisoners, as well as women, ethnic minorities, children, gays, and lesbians), clearly show the extent to which an emancipatory politics of rights is deeply interlocked with the politics of participatory democracy, and calls for the theoretical reconstruction of democratic theory.

CONCLUSION

As it is conventionally understood, human rights politics is based on a massive suppression of constitutive rights, or ur-rights, as I have called them. Such a politics is a child of colonialism and imagines no future beyond capitalism. It is also a kind of Esperanto, which can hardly become the everyday language of human dignity across the globe. In this chapter I have laid the grounds for an intercultural conception of emancipatory human rights politics. Such politics must be based on two radical reconstructions. On the one hand, one has an intercultural reconstruction by means of translational diatopical hermeneutics, whereby the networking of mutually intelligible and translatable native languages of emancipation finds its way into an insurgent cosmopolitan politics. On the other hand, there must be a post-imperial reconstruction of human rights centered on undoing the massive acts of constitutive suppression—the ur-rights—upon which Western modernity was able to transform victors' rights into universal rights.

This project may sound rather utopian. But, as Sartre once said, before it is realized an idea has a strange resemblance with utopia. Be that as it may, the important fact is not to reduce realism to what exists.

BIBLIOGRAPHY

Afkhami, Mahnaz, ed. (1995). *Faith and Freedom: Women's Human Rights in the Muslim World.* Syracuse, NY: Syracuse UP.

Al Faruqi, Isma'il R. (1983). "Islam and Human Rights," *The Islamic Quarterly* 27(1):12–30.

An-na'im, Abdullahi A. (1990). *Toward an Islamic Reformation.* Syracuse, NY: Syracuse UP.

——————, ed. (1992). *Human Rights in Cross-Cultural Perspectives. A Quest for Consensus.* Philadelphia: U. of Pennsylvania P.

Arendt, Hannah (1951). *The Origins of Totalitarianism.* New York: Harcourt, Brace.

Bernal, Martin (1987). *Black Athena: The Afroasiatic Roots of Classical Civilization.* Vol. 1. *The Fabrication of Ancient Greece, 1785–1885.* London: Free Association Books.

Bhargava, Rajeev, ed. (1998). *Secularism and Its Critics*. New Delhi: Oxford UP.

Bhargava, Rajeev, Amiya Bagchi, and R. Sudarshan, eds. (1999). *Multiculturalism, Liberalism and Democracy*. New Delhi: Oxford UP.

Buergenthal, Thomas (1991). "The CSCE Rights System," *George Washington Journal of International Law and Economics* 25: 333–386.

Cassese, Antonio, ed. (1979). *UN Law Fundamental Rights: Two Topics in International Law*. Alphen aan den Rijn, The Netherlands: Sijthoff and Noordhoff.

———————— (1979). "Political Self-Determination—Old Concepts and New Developments," in Cassese (ed.): 137–173.

Chatterjee, Partha (1984). "Gandhi and the Critique of Civil Society," in Guha (ed.): 153–195.

Coetzee, P. H., A. P. J. Roux (2003). *The African Philosophy Reader: A Text With Readings*. New York: Routledge.

Dicey, Albert Vern (1948). *Law and Public Opinion in England*. London: Macmillan.

Donnelly, Jack (1989). *Universal Human Rights in Theory and Practice*. Ithaca, NY: Cornell UP.

Dwyer, Kevin (1991). *Arab Voices. The Human Rights Debate in the Middle East*. Berkeley: U. of California P.

Falk, Richard (1981). *Human Rights and State Sovereignty*. New York: Holmes and Meier.

Galtung, Johan (1981). "Western Civilization: Anatomy and Pathology," *Alternatives* 7: 145–169.

Gilroy, Paul (1993). *The Black Atlantic. Modernity and Double Consciousness*. Cambridge, MA: Harvard UP.

Guha, Ranajit, ed. (1984). *Subaltern Studies III: Writings on South Asian History and Society*. Delhi: Oxford UP.

Hassan, Riffat (1982). "On Human Rights and the Qur'anic Perspective," *Journal of Ecumenical Studies* 19(3): 51–65.

Hountondji, Paulin J., ed. (1983). *African Philosophy: Myth and Reality*. Bloomington: Indiana UP.

——————————, ed. (1994). *Les Savoirs Endogènes: Pistes pour une Recherche*. Paris: Karthala.

———————— (2002). *Struggle For Meaning: Reflections on Philosophy, Culture, and Democracy in Africa*. Athens: Ohio UP.

Horton, Robin (1990). *Patterns of Thought in Africa and the West: Essays on Magic, Religion and Science*. Cambridge: Cambridge UP.

———————— *et al.* (1990). *La Pensée Métisse*. Paris: Presses Universitaires de France.

Inada, Kenneth K. (1990). "A Buddhist Response to the Nature of Human Rights" in Welch, Jr. and Leary (eds.): 91–101.

Jonas, Hans (1985). *Das Prinzip der Verantwortung*. 5th ed. Frankfurt: Insel Verlag.

Khare, R. S. (1998). *Cultural Diversity and Social Discontent. Anthropological Studies on Contemporary India*. London: Sage.

Leites, Justin (1991). "Modernist Jurisprudence as a Vehicle for Gender Role Reform in the Islamic World," *Columbia Human Rights Law Review* 22: 251–330.

Locke, John (1952) [1689]. *The Second Treatise of Government*. New York: Liberal Arts Press.

Mayer, Ann Elizabeth (1991). *Islam and Human Rights: Tradition and Politics.* Boulder, CO: Westview.

Mitra, Kana (1982). "Human Rights in Hinduism," *Journal of Ecumenical Studies* 19(3): 77–84.

Moosa, Ebrahim (2004). "The Dilemma of Islamic Rights Schemes," *Worlds and Knowledges Otherwise* Fall: 1–25.

Mutua, Makau (1996). "The Ideology of Human Rights," *Virginia Journal of International Law* 36: 589–657.

———————— (2001). "Savages, Victims, and Saviors: The Metaphor of Human Rights," *Harvard International Law Journal* 42: 201–245.

Nandy, Ashis (1987a). "Cultural Frames for Social Transformation: A Credo," *Alternatives* XII: 113–123.

———————— (1987b). *Traditions, Tyranny and Utopias. Essays in the Politics of Awareness.* Oxford: Oxford UP.

———————— (1988). "The Politics of Secularism and the Recovery of Religious Tolerance," *Alternatives* XIII: 177–194.

Obiora, L. Amwede (1997). "Bridges and Barricades: Rethinking Polemics and Intransigence in the Campaign against Female Circumcision," *Case Western Reserve Law Review* 47: 275–378.

Oladipo, Olusegun (1989). "Towards a Philosophical Study of African Culture: A Critique of Traditionalism," *Quest* 3(2): 31–50.

Oruka, H. Odera (1990). "Cultural Fundamentals in Philosophy," *Quest* 4(2): 21–37.

Pannikar, Raimundo (1984). "Is the Notion of Human Rights a Western Concept?" *Cahier* 81: 28–47.

Pantham, Thomas (1988). "On Modernity, Rationality and Morality: Habermas and Gandhi," *The Indian Journal of Social Science* 1(2): 187–208.

Pieterse, Jan N. (1989). *Empire and Emancipation. Power and Liberation on a World Scale.* London: Pluto.

Pollis, Adamantia (1982). "Liberal, Socialist and Third World Perspectives of Human Rights," in Pollis and Schwab (eds.): 1–26.

Pollis, Adamantia; P. Schwab (1979). "Human Rights: A Western Construct with Limited Applicability," in Pollis and Schwab (eds.): 1–18.

Pollis, Adamantia, and P. Schwab, eds. (1979). *Human Rights: Cultural and Ideological Perspectives.* New York: Prager.

Procee, Henk (1992). "Beyond Universalism and Relativism," *Quest* 6(1): 45–55.

Rajagopal, Balakrishnan (2004). *International Law from Below: Development, Social Movements and Third World Resistance.* Cambridge: Cambridge UP.

Ramadan, Tariq (2000). *Islam, the West and the Challenges of Modernity.* Leicester (UK): The Islamic Foundation.

———————— (2003). *Globalization Muslim Resistances.* Geneva: Editions Tawhid Oxford: Oxford UP.

Ramose, Mogobe B. (1992). "African Democratic Traditions: Oneness, Consensus and Openness," *Quest* 6(1): 63–83.

Rousseau, Jean-Jacques (1973). *The Social Contract and Discourses.* London: J. M. Dent and Sons.

Said, Edward (1993). "Nationalism, Human Rights and Interpretation," *Raritan* 12(3): 26–51.

Santos, Boaventura de Sousa (1995). *Toward a New Common Sense. Law, Science and Politics in the Paradigmatic Transition*. New York: Routledge.
—————— (1997). "Pluralismo Jurídico y Jurisdicción Especial Indígena," in VV. AA. *"Del Olvido Surgimos Para Traer Nuevas Esperanzas"— La Jurisdicción Especial Indígena*. Bogotá: Ministerio de Justicia y Derecho, Consejo Regional Indígena del Cauca and Ministerio del Interior, Dirección General de Asuntos Indígenas: 201–211.
Santos, Boaventura de Sousa, and Mauricio García Villegas (2001). *El Caleidoscopio de las Justicias en Colombia*. Bogotá: Ediciones Uniandes, Siglo del Hombre.
Santos, Boaventura de Sousa (2002). *Toward a New Legal Common Sense: Law, Globalization, and Emancipation*. London: Butterworths.
——————, ed. (2006). *Democratizing Democracy: Beyond the Liberal Democratic Canon*. London: Verso.
Sharabi, Hisham (1992). "Modernity and Islamic Revival: The Critical Tasks of Arab Intellectuals," *Contention* 2(1): 127–147.
Shariati, Ali (1982). "Reflection of a Concerned Muslim: On the Plight of Oppressed Peoples," in Falk, Kim and Mendlovitz (eds.): 18–24.
—————— (1986). *What is to be Done: the Enlightened Thinkers and an Islamic Renaissance*. Edited by Farhang Rajaee. Houston: The Institute for Research and Islamic Studies.
Shivji, Issa (1989). *The Concept of Human Rights in Africa*. London: Codesria Book Series.
Thapar, Romila (1966). "The Hindu and Buddhist Traditions," *International Social Science Journal* 18(1): 31–40.
Wallerstein, Immanuel (1991). *Geopolitics and Geoculture*. Cambridge: Cambridge UP.
Wamba dia Wamba, Ernest (1991a). "Some Remarks on Culture Development and Revolution in Africa," *Journal of Historical Sociology* 4: 219–235.
—————— (1991b). "Beyond Elite Politics of Democracy in Africa," *Quest* 6(1): 28–42.
Welsh, Jr., Claude, and Virginia Leary, eds. (1990). *Asian Perspectives on Human Rights*. Boulder, CO. Westview.
Wiredu, Kwasi (1990). "Are there Cultural Universals?" *Quest* 4(2): 5–19.

Notes

1 Elsewhere, I deal at length with the dialectical tensions in Western modernity (Santos, 1995).
2 On the nature of globalization, see the following section.
3 For an extended analysis of the four regimes, see Santos, 1995: 330–337; 2002: 280–311, and the bibliographies cited there.
4 For two contrasting views, see Donnelly, 1989 and Renteln, 1990. See also Schwab and Pohs, 1982; K. Thompson, 1980; A. Henkm, 1979; A. Diemer, 1986; Ghai, 2000b; Mutua, 2001. See also Ghai's commentary at the end of this volume.
5 As I said above, to be emancipatory a politics of human rights must always be conceived of and practiced as part of a broader politics of resistance and emancipation.

6 I will say more on the premises in the following section.
7 For a recent review of the debate on universalism versus relativism, see Rajagopal, 2004: 209–216. See also Mutua, 1996.
8 See, for instance, Mutua, 2001; Obiora, 1997.
9 See, for instance, Pollis and Schwab, 1979; Pollis, 1982; Shivji, 1989; Anna'im, 1992; Mutua, 1996.
10 See also Panikkar, 1984: 28.
11 See also K. Inada, 1990; K. Mitra, 1982; R. Thapar, 1966.
12 Besides An-na'im (1990; 1992), see Dwyer, 1991; Mayer, 1991; Leites, 1991; Afkhami, 1995. See also Hassan, 1982; Al Faruqi, 1983. On the broader issue of the relationship between modernity and Islamic revival, see, for instance, Sharabi, 1992; Shariati, 1986; Ramadan, 2000; and Moosa, 2004.
13 Volume 5 of this collection will develop in great detail the work of translation as an alternative to the idea of a general theory.
14 The same cannot be said of Tariq Ramadan.
15 A more sophisticated formulation of the relations between universal human rights and Islam can be found in Moosa (2004).
16 Gilroy criticizes the "overintegrated conceptions of pure and homogeneous cultures which mean that black political struggles are construed as somehow automatically *expressive* of the national or ethnic differences with which they are associated" (1993: 31).
17 For the African debate, see P. Hountondji, 1983, 1994, 2002; O. Oladipo, 1989; O. Oruka, 1990; K. Wiredu, 1990; Wamba dia Wamba, 1991a, 1991b; H. Procee, 1992; M. B. Ramose, 1992; R. Horton et al. 1990; R. Horton, 1993; P. H. Coetzee and A. P. J. Roux, 2003. A sample of the rich debate in India is in A. Nandy, 1987a, 1987b, 1988; P. Chatterjee, 1984; T. Pantham, 1988; Bhargava, 1998; Bhargava, Bagchi, and Sudarshan, 1999. A bird's-eye view of cultural differences can be found in Galtung, 1981.
18 Elsewhere, I deal in detail with the idea of "learning from the South" (Santos, 1995: 475–519).
19 In this chapter I concentrate on the diatopical hermeneutics between Western culture and the "great Oriental cultures" (Hinduism and Islamism). I am aware that a diatopical hermeneutics involving indigenous peoples' cultures raises other analytical issues and demands specific preconditions. Focusing on the indigenous peoples of Latin America, I deal with this topic in Santos (1997) and in Santos and Villegas (2001).
20 On the paradigmatic transition, see Santos, 1995 and 2002.
21 On the distinction between these two forms of knowledge, see Santos, 1995: 7–55. In Volume 5 I will defend that knowledge-as-emancipation is a mere starting point and that it is necessary to go beyond it. See also the introduction to this volume.
22 Jonas, 1985. See also Santos, 1995: 50.
23 On the debate over the evolution of Locke's thought on property, see Santos, 1995: 68–71.
24 As Cassesse puts it, "new forms of oppression are developing and spreading (neo-colonialism, hegemonical oppression, domination by multinational corporations and transnational repressive organizations) and minorities are awakening from secular oppression to a more vital sense of freedom and

independence" (Cassese, 1979: 148). See also Ghai's commentary at the end of this volume.

25 See Volume 1 of this collection (Santos, 2006).

26 For instance, in the core countries, particularly in the US (but also in Europe and Japan), the right of workers to organize in labor unions has been undermined by union-bashing, while at the same time their interests have been ideologically miniaturized as "special interests" and, as such, equated with any other special interests (for instance, those of the National Rifle Association).

27 The right to organize, conceived as an *ur*-right, is a politically grounded formulation of the more abstract "right to have rights" proposed by Hannah Arendt (1951). It is the denunciation of concrete *ur*-wrong suppressions of organized resistance.

2

Legal Pluralism, Social Movements and the Post-Colonial State in India: Fractured Sovereignty and Differential Citizenship Rights

Shalini Randeria

INTRODUCTION

In contrast to the predominant preoccupation of recent studies of transnational legal pluralism that have focused on *lex mercatoria* and the autonomous and spontaneous production of law by a small elite of international commercial arbitrators and mega corporate law firms (Garth, 1995; Teubner, 1996, 1997), this chapter delineates the role of international institutions, NGOs and social movements in their complex interactions with the state as actors in a heterogeneous legal landscape. The dynamics and trajectories of legal pluralism and the transnationalization of law are analyzed using empirical material from India. In considering how law enters into the making of the neoliberal order, the chapter attempts to unravel the working of power in the domestication of neo-liberal discipline and the resistance to it. It examines the resistance by the subaltern state to global institutions but also the struggles by people's movements against the Indian state. Three brief case studies are used to discuss the ambivalence of movement-groups towards the state, which is needed as an ally against multinational corporations in order to protect farmers' rights to seeds, yet which is initially bypassed in the Narmada struggle to target the World Bank directly only to seek judicial remedy later in the federal Indian Supreme Court against administrative malpractices and the highhandedness of the state government. Nevertheless, in the conflict over ecodiversity in the Gir Forest, human rights groups and the World Bank are allied together to use project law to protect the traditional rights of pastoralists against the state government and the World Wildlife Fund, who are keen to protect the habitat of lions using federal environmental law.

The changing contours of governance both within and beyond the nation-state are discussed with a view to exploring some of the ambivalences of law as both a tool of domination but also of empowerment. The chapter argues that unpacking the politics of social movements and NGOs is to understand them not merely as local entities subsumed in larger national and global structures (like a Russian doll, with each larger entity encompassing and containing the one smaller) but as fragmented sites that have multiple national and supranational linkages. Social movements and NGOs in India assume salience as mediators of national and international laws at the local level but also as channels for the assertion of customary law and traditional collective rights of local communities in the national arena and in international fora. NGOs linked to grassroots movements are equally important in mobilizing dissenting knowledge in order to formulate alternative people's laws and policies by using a variety of norms from different sources. Their contribution to the reassertion of customary law, to the development of national and transnational law as well as their role as mediators, translators, and interfaces between local communities, nation-states, and international organizations thus deserves careful analysis.

Many of these developments toward the emergence of a global civil society in a "post-Westphalian world order," to use Richard Falk's term (1999), are ambivalent. On the one hand, they widen the spectrum of the possibilities of democratic participation in the age of the "post-sovereign state," as Scholte (2000) argues, in that citizens bypass their governments and enter into direct interaction with those institutions that are responsible for the new supranational governance. On the other hand, some of the actions of the social movements and NGOs paradoxically lend the WTO, the IMF, and the World Bank a greater authority and legitimacy contributing indirectly to a further weakening of the sovereignty of subaltern states.

LEGAL PLURALISM AND SUBALTERN STATES

The idea of legal pluralism, pivotal to legal anthropology in the 1960s and 1970s, calls into question the basic assumptions of liberal political theory and jurisprudence, namely the congruence of territory, state, and law. By foregrounding the coexistence of a plurality of legal orders within a single political unit (Upendra Baxi, 1999, speaks, for example, of state law vs. people's law/non-state legal systems), particularly of community/customary laws and religious laws along with metropolitan law, as well as law created specifically in and for the colonies in (post-)colonial societies, legal pluralism interrogates the centrality of state-made law and its exclusive claim to the normative ordering of social life. National legal landscapes have always been complex, variegated, and multi-layered, shaped more or less by diverse external influences through processes of borrowing, diffusion and imposition. But the growing prominence of international law, supranational legal orders and regimes, the transnationalization of state law and, finally, the direct intervention of multilateral institutions, international donors and transnational NGOs have all lent a new dimension to legal pluralism. These changes affect the very nature of the law's regulatory and protective functions, transform the conditions for legitimation, and increase the direct involvement of global actors in the national legal arena.

Transnationalization and legal pluralism in the sense of a multiplicity of actors, arenas, methods, and forms of law production are also changing the very nature and concept of law as a coherent and unitary body of knowledge and a principled practice of decision-making (Cotterrell, 1995). As a plurality of supra-state and infra-state governance regimes with public and private actors replace government, decentralized and micrological law coexists, more or less uneasily, with the monumental law that used to be the monopoly of states. The domain of law is being expanded in the process to include conventions, treaties, bilateral and multilateral agreements, as well as protocols that have a legal effect, although they cannot be understood as laws in the strict sense of having a legislative basis. Moreover, the dividing line between private and public law, between law and policy, is being redrawn due to norm production by actors such as corporate law firms, private arbitrators and NGOs. Law creation increasingly becomes an open-ended process, as administrative as legislative in origin, with rules, regulations, and prescriptions being produced from a diversity of sources and sites with shifting boundaries.

But the state itself is being decentered and reconfigured in the process of the transnationalization of law and the supranational legal pluralism accompanying it. However, the widely prevalent diagnosis of the erosion of state sovereignty by the forces of globalization overlooks the continued salience of the state, albeit as a contested terrain in an increasingly plural legal landscape, a terrain in which various infra-state and supra-state legal orders interact and compete with one another (Santos, 1995). Since (post-)colonial states never had an absolute monopoly over law production, the specificities of their contemporary trajectories of economic and legal globalization can only be analyzed against the background of historical continuities, which are often represented as processes of recolonization (Randeria, 1999). Fractured sovereignty, the fragmentation of state action and legal plurality are not specific to the South, yet the ambivalent effects and contradictory character of these developments are felt most strongly in these weak states.

I use the term "weak states" in three senses: 1) (post-)colonial states with fragile structures and a relatively short history of state formation; 2) states that are subaltern in the international system, dependent on external aid and the dictates of international agencies; and 3) states that have not colonized completely the imaginary of their populations. How much space is available for weak states to adopt policies to protect the interests of vulnerable sections of their own populations within the framework set by the neoliberal dogma enshrined in the "Washington Consensus" and the WTO regime, which privileges the interests of powerful states and global players? If subaltern states cannot set or change the rules of the game, do they at least have choices with regard to the extent, timing, and sequencing of economic reforms and concomitant legal changes, of the implementation of the WTO agreements, or of structural adjustment conditionalities?

It may be useful to distinguish here between failed states such as Somalia or Rwanda, weak states like Benin or Bangladesh, and cunning states such as India or Russia.[1] Cunning states, usually corrupt, short-change as middlemen both their citizens and international institutions and donors. While a weak state is unable to discharge its obligations to justice, lacks the capabilities to successfully discipline and regulate state and non-state actors and to negotiate the terms on which it will share sovereignty with sub-national and supranational actors, semi-peripheral cunning states use their weakness to legitimate their non-accountability to their citizens and to international institutions. Faced with popular discontent over their policies, they plead an inability to withstand external donor pressure for reforms. But they also use their weakness *vis-à-vis* domestic constituencies in order to justify their partial and selective implementation of reforms to international institutions.

Cunning states are autonomous enough to strategically select the reforms they introduce; they postpone some changes, drag their feet on others, implement certain policies half-heartedly, comply with credit conditionalities partially, and sequence reforms (e.g., privatization before de-monopolization). Though a weapon of the weak, such a strategy of cunning can be used to reap huge profits for sections of the ruling elites in these states. These may, of course, be seen as signs of a soft state, but in my view such a reading misrecognizes these strategies of resistance. For proponents of economic globalization, the Indian state is not strong enough to deregulate, privatize, and liberalize as necessary. They feel that reforms have been too late, too slow, and not far-reaching enough, whereas for opponents of neoliberal prescriptions it is a weak Indian state that has given in to the dictates of the Bretton Woods Institutions without adequate social policy measures to soften the impact of radical reforms on the poor. The former argue that the Indian state has been soft on labor while for the latter it is soft on capital but harsh against the laboring poor (Randeria, 1999).

It could be argued that some forms of legal plurality in India evince a continuity with traditional norms and institutions and that yet others reflect colonial design as well as post-colonial compromises, whereas recent forms of legal pluralism have been thrust on the country in the wake of neoliberal restructuring and resistance to it. Traditionally, legal pluralists, who have studied infra-state pluralism, have always been advocates of community law and more or less explicit anti-statists. But, faced with globalization, the transnationalization of law, and supra-state legal plurality under the dominance of international institutions that champion the interests of global capital, legal pluralists, like many movement-groups in India, are beginning to discover the virtues of regulation by the state, its sovereignty and autonomy.

Legal pluralism was never a purely descriptive category but always also an evaluative one. Earlier, the idea of legal pluralism was part of a binary conceptualization of the world that distinguished non-Western societies that were characterized by a plurality of competing and overlapping legal orders from Western societies that were not. If anthropology, with its hostility, or at least its indifference, toward the state tended to celebrate legal pluralism, liberal political theory viewed such heterogeneity as a sign of backwardness, of immature state formation. It was assumed that modernization would lead to the establishment of the monopoly of the state over the production, implementation, and interpretation of law, along with the idea of abstract citizenship involving a single set of laws for all citizens. With the growing recognition among sociologists of law that all societies are legally plural, the existence of a variety of sources of legal norms and institutional arenas ceased to be a marker of difference and achieved the status of a universal.

But, by insisting on the "legal polycentricity" (Petersen and Zahle, 1995) of all societies, such an approach collapsed the different historical trajectories and temporalities of state formation in various regions of the world into a single conceptual category. Moreover, it overlooked the specific articulation of supranational and sub-national legal orders with lawyer's law within the rich and complex legal landscapes of most non-Western societies. Intended to counter the attribution of a deficient modernity to societies with legal pluralism by turning legal heterogeneity and hybridity into the norm, such a perspective ended up losing sight of the specificities of that plurality in different societies. So that even if all societies are legally plural, they are legally plural in different ways. depending on the reach and effectiveness of state law, the coexistence or interpenetration of state and non-state legal orders—whether the latter are traditional community structures parallel to state law or consist of (revolutionary) popular justice challenging state law—the extent of explicit recognition of non-state law by the state or its mere tolerance due to the weakness of the state *vis-à-vis* external actors or its inability to compete against private militias, religious authorities or local community councils. The careless homogenization and the spurious universalization involved in considering all societies to be legally plural begs the question of whether legal pluralism in India is the same as in Canada or in Kenya. Is India legally plural in the same sense as South Africa or Colombia?

Should the term be applied in common to Portugal, Brazil and Mozambique?

I shall discuss four different kinds of legal plurality in India, or rather routes by which it is introduced into the national legal field as a result of transnational actors and processes: 1) international or supranational law competes as one among several legal orders that operate at the local level, or are invoked by different actors; 2) changes are introduced into national rules, regulations and policies by the national legislature or administration either under external pressure of aid conditionalities or in order to bring state law into consonance with international regimes, protocols, etc., which lead to a pluralization "within" state law; 3) rules, contracts, procedures of international organizations and donor agencies operate directly within the nation-state;[2] 4) NGOs contribute to legal plurality by either framing alternative treaties or people's policies having a national or supranational character using a variety of traditional community based, or national or international norms. The extensity, intensity, velocity, and impact of these processes of legal transnationalization is not uniform within the national space, so that we can speak of uneven gradients of globalization depending on the area of regulation involved and the local context.

DOMESTICATING NEOLIBERAL DISCIPLINE: THE DANCE OF DONORS WITH DEPENDENT STATES[3]

The World Bank's *World Development Report: The State in a Changing World* redefines the role of the state as an "enabling state" in terms of the "reliability of its institutional framework" and the "predictability of its rules and policies, and the consistency with which they are applied" (World Bank, 1997: 4–5) as the key issues for ensuring the credibility of governments. The new role envisaged for the state in this neoliberal script is the attracting of foreign capital, securing the protection of its rights and of investor freedoms. Much of the rhetoric of globalization theories to the contrary, the state is not being rolled back as a rule-making or enforcing agency. Rather, it should be restructured as one arena of regulatory practice among others in order to facilitate the highest profits for capital.

The establishment of a new legal framework conducive to trade, investment and global capital is central to the "Washington consensus," which advocates a universally valid and applicable policy mix (privatization, deregulation, trade liberalization, free capital movement, demonopolization, flexible labor markets tight monetary and fiscal policy, the protection of investor's rights and of intellectual property rights) irrespective of regional context and the specificities of the country's economy. This also necessitates the creation of rule-making bodies and enforcement agencies within the state (hence the emphasis on the rule of law and institutional, legal, and judicial reform) as well as those that transcend the boundaries of the nation-state. The WTO document, "Ten benefits of the WTO trading system," lists "good government" as one of them. What is meant by the term is that by restricting the options available in domestic regulatory and distributive policies and constraining special interest groups from lobbying for options at variance with the neoliberal prescription, the WTO contributes to the successful implementation of the Bretton Woods policy package.

Multilateral investment agreements, trade treaties, and the adjudicative powers of the WTO are all part of this new architecture of global governance, both "within" and "beyond" the nation-state. Their critics in India contend that these new constitutional and quasi-constitutional legal frameworks seek to anchor in the long run the power of capital with respect to the state and the operation of macroeconomic and social policy within a narrow understanding of democracy as multi-party elections and a selective interpretation of the rule of law. A major consequence of such strategies is to insulate many economic fields from the political arena of parliamentary control (Gill, 2000) and thus to limit democratic decision-making and accountability with regard to them. Keywords in development discourse, such as participation, empowerment, and civil society involvement, do not apply, for example, to macroeconomic policy, governance aspects of IMF structural adjustment programs, or the acceptance of trade and investment disciplines including the extension and institutionalization of intellectual property rights and contract law under the WTO. Attempts are made to ground its claims to legitimacy in the universal validity of its prescriptions because they derive from economics science and are used to plead for a need to insulate this expert knowledge from the exercise of political choice. The case for the WTO trade and investment liberalization rules is made, for example, in terms of the need to insulate them from the vagaries of democratic politics, which renders them domestically non-negotiable. By removing the relevant laws and policies from decision-making in the domestic political and legal sphere and diluting the jurisdiction of the national legislature these processes exacerbate the democratic deficit and weak legitimacy of semi-peripheral and peripheral states.

The issue of the legitimacy of international institutions such as the WTO, IMF or the World Bank is entangled with the issue of power. Critics in India point to the detrimental effects on state sovereignty of policy prescriptions and conditionalities—which are offers dependent states cannot refuse—and of the secrecy of negotiations leading to agreements between national bureaucrats and international organizations without parliamentary scrutiny and public debate. IMF and World Bank agreements with governments are negotiated similarly with the administration and are not subject to discussion in and approval by domestic democratic institutions. WTO rules have to be ratified by parliament, which cannot amend them but only accept or reject the treaty *in toto*. The secrecy surrounding the prior negotiations, which civil society organizations have no access to and voice in,[4] means that no information on the process itself, the positions of various members, and the alternatives available or considered is available to politicians or citizens (Howse, 2001). Interestingly, when confronted with the democracy deficit and problems of legitimacy of the IMF, WTO or the World Bank, bureaucrats working for these institutions insist that they are powerless advisors, merely serving their member governments but without the means to ensure political compliance.[5]

The necessity for not only formal but also "social legitimacy," to use Weiler's (1999) term of law in the domestic context, is underscored by the public debates on credit conditionalities in all countries of the South. As Sally Falk Moore (2000) points out, conditionalities have a law-like character and are an operational dimension of international relations practiced by donors *vis-à-vis* dependent states. Ordinary legal categories may be inadequate to classify conditionalities and capture their complexities. Does acceptance of these imposed conditions make it a contract-like arrangement? Or does the fact of a profound asymmetry of power turn the laying down of conditionalities into a quasi-legislative act?

Conditions coupled with credits are an offer that subaltern states can hardly refuse. But the formal acceptance of the terms of an agreement is one thing, compliance with them another. Non-compliance, partial or delayed compliance, and selective enforcement belong to the art of resistance by subaltern states in the international order.[6] Often both donors and recipients know at the outset that absolute compliance is either impossible or politically unfeasible. Yet neither can afford to say this publicly. Thus, at the inception of each new policy initiative, some conditions are rescheduled, others overlooked as long as at least nominal compliance on a few terms can be taken as a symbolic reaffirmation of the unequal power of the two sides in "the dance of donors and their dependents," to use Moore's phrase (2000).

The Indian state has, for example, privatized only some public sector enterprises and even those rather slowly; it has enthusiastically embraced some parts of the WTO regime but asked for a five-year moratorium on others; although it complied willingly with most conditionalities coupled with the 1991 IMF loan. The government was asked to abolish statutory controls on foreign exchange flows, sharply cut public spending, and devalue the rupee by 18 percent against the dollar. The World Bank required in return for its loan the abolition of industrial licensing and a rise in the statutory ceiling on foreign equity ownership to 51 per cent. In return for another loan in 1993 it followed IMF and World Bank directives to speed up finance sector reforms, remove unproductive farm subsidies, and liberalize consumer imports yet argued that the demand for the deregulation of the labor market (which would allow employers a free hand to hire and fire employees) could only be met gradually given the political sensitivity of the issues.

However, an "exit policy" that will permit the retrenchment of workers in the public and private sector as well as the closure, liquidation or restructuring of unviable enterprises is yet to be legislated. Labor market deregulation as required by the World Bank will require federal legislation repealing or diluting the Industrial Disputes Act of 1947 and the Indian Trade Unions Act of 1926. Studies by the ILO have already shown that the social costs of market reforms in India have been substantial and systematically underestimated. But retrenchments without a proper safety-net scheme violate important economic, social and cultural rights recognized by the International Covenant on Economic and Social Rights (ICESCR) and granted protection by the Indian constitution. The reform of the tax system as desired by the donors remains incomplete, and the Indian government also has resisted the pressure by the World Bank and the IMF to introduce full convertibility of the rupee on the capital account, whereas it has been extremely pliable and accommodating of donor demands with regard to population policy and programs.

In the 1990s, for example, USAID was allowed not only to make its comeback in India in order to implement its largest and most expensive population control project in the world (State Innovations in Family Planning) in the state of Uttar Pradesh, but also permitted to help formulate state-level population policies for different states of the Indian Union. Interestingly, the central government did not accede to the USAID demand that the 350 million dollar project be administered by an independent agency and instead set up an organization under its own control but staffed primarily by bureaucrats of the state government of Uttar Pradesh. It also rejected the longstanding demand by USAID to introduce injectables into the public health system through the program. Instead of using the argument of the prohibitive costs of injectables to the public exchequer, it legitimized the refusal by pointing to the strong opposition by women's groups in the country to long-acting contraceptives viewed as health hazards. It pointed out that a case in the Supreme Court by women's groups against the testing of the injectable contraceptive Depo-Provera in public health programs has been pending since 1994 but that the interim injunction of the court banning such tests was in force (Randeria, 1999).

The state is usually presumed to be a unified set of institutions, but social movements in India have often sought and received judicial support against bureaucratic power, as in the case against shrimp farms on the southern coast.

Swaminathan (1998) has suggested that the Final Report to the ECOSOC's Commission of Human Rights (Türk, 1992) opens up an interesting and novel possibility of judicial remedy at the national level against Structural Adjustment Programs (SAPs). In a situation where governments are more accountable for their policies to international institutions, legal remedy against the violation of personal rights could render a cunning state accountable to its citizens. The Special Rapporteur of the ECOSOC Commission notes that SAPs impinge upon the right to an adequate standard of living, especially as it is related to basic subsistence rights. Thus these have a profoundly negative impact on a number of economic and social rights guaranteed in the International Covenant on Economic, Social and Cultural Rights (ICESCR). Since the statutory language in question is relatively vague, it is difficult to show that the SAPs definitely violate these rights. Besides the Covenant lacks effective means of enforcement insofar as it is dependent on state action.

The ECOSOC's Committee on Economic, Social and Cultural Rights, set up in 1987, indicated that their violation should be remedied in accordance with the national legal system without either specifying the extent to which the rights should be justiciable or laying down the appropriate remedies. For example, the introduction of user fees in schools and hospitals as well as the cutting or redirection of expenditure in these areas restricts access to health and education, especially for the poor, just as the deregulation of labor markets and the privatization of public sector enterprises adversely affect the basic right to work and dilute the benefits of social legislation and wages while increasing working hours. Certain economic reform policies could, therefore, be argued to implicate constitutionally guaranteed economic and social rights to an adequate means of livelihood, living wages, and just and humane working conditions. Also, the procedural innovations in the framework of Public Interest Litigation could well be used for this purpose (Randeria, 2001a).

CIVIC ALLIANCES, PROJECT LAW AND STATE LAW: THE RIGHTS OF PASTORAL COMMUNITIES VS. THE RIGHTS OF LIONS[7]

International agencies are important sources for legal pluralism through the introduction of new norms into the national and local arena. Often they are also responsible for concretizing and implementing law either directly or through governments or NGOs. This may be international law or "project law" (Benda-Beckmann, 2000), i.e., rules and procedures used by bilateral and multilateral agencies, which they either have evolved on their own or derived from their respective national legal systems. By introducing their own formal procedures and substantive rules for the implementation of projects, bilateral, and multilateral aid agencies have become a significant new factor in transnational legal pluralism.

As Benda-Beckmann (2000) has argued, international organizations also introduce into the national legal arena concepts and principles that may be seen as "proto-law" since they do not yet have the formal status of law but in practice often obtain the same degree of obligation. Moreover, through their loan and credit agreements with the state they also introduce what may be described as "project law" as an additional set of norms. Similarly, concepts like "good governance," "co-management," "sustainability," etc. have all been elaborated in various international treaties, conventions, and protocols, though they are neither fully developed principles nor show internal coherence. At the national and local levels, various sets of actors invoke them as competing with, or overriding, national laws, or use them to ground the legitimacy of claims against traditional rights and customary law. In the process, strange coalitions sometimes are forged, which might be described as "odd bedfellows.com."

Some of the paradoxes and contradictions of the possibilities of the co-existence of multiple and overlapping normative orders are evident, for example, in a clash between environmentalist NGOs and the human rights movement in India, which at times have been at odds with one another. The controversy surrounding a national park in Gujarat, in western India, illustrates such a conflict involving the use of different sets of legal norms at the local level with two different groups of NGOs, each with its own transnational networks representing opposing interests. Whereas the environmentalists champion the protection of wildlife in the Gir Forest, the human rights NGOs have been concerned with securing the livelihood and cultural continuity of the pastoral community in the area. Environmental groups, including the powerful transnational NGO World Wide Fund for Native-India (WWF-India), draw their moral legitimation from their status as representatives of global stakeholders. The lions, due to the financial resources and media connections of the WWF-India, received better national and international press than the pastoralists. The environmentalists invoke and apply norms laid down in national and international environmental laws in order to campaign for the protection of biodiversity, and especially of the lions, of the Gir Forest. Local human rights NGOs, supported by a South Asian and Southeast Asian network, advocate the protection of traditional rights of access to natural resources based on the customary law of the pastoral group. But they also invoke the doctrine of public trust that would require the state to uphold these rights (Randeria, 2001a).

The traditional rights of the pastoralists to forest products, grazing land, and water resources are sought to be overridden in the name of the greater common good by WWF-India, with which the state government of the province of Gujarat is aligned in this conflict. They argue that both the local ecological system and the lions are endangered by the traditional grazing methods of the large herds of livestock of the pastoral community as well as by its increasing demands for the provision of modern infrastructure and other facilities in the area (such as tarred roads, electricity, schools, and health centers) (Ganguly, 2000). The World Bank is at present financing several biodiversity programs in India under its eco-development project, both in the Gir Forest and in six other regions of the country (Randeria 2001a, 2001b). For the limited duration of the project and within the project areas, World Bank policies favoring the protection of indigenous peoples prevail over state laws and actions, in terms of the overriding commitments accepted by the government of India in its agreement with the World Bank (World Bank, 1996). However, it is far from clear whether the conditionalities in this agreement will continue beyond that, or will have any permanent or pervasive impact on national policy or law.

The background to the conflict is the national legislation in the form of the Wildlife Protection Act drafted with the expert advice of the Smithsonian Institute (USA) in the 1970s and adopted by the Indian Parliament. This Act has provisions for declaring certain areas as "protected areas" for the purposes of setting up national parks or wildlife sanctuaries. Aimed at environmental conservation, it also contains procedures that work in practice to the detriment of the rights of local communities in these areas. More specifically, action taken by the state government of Gujarat under these provisions would have resulted in further forced displacement of pastoral communities from the "protected areas." WWF-India has sided with the government in the interest of environmental protection, whereas human rights groups have found an ally in the World Bank, whose operational directives and policies seek to protect project-affected persons from forced eviction and guarantee the traditional rights of tribals. These provide for a participatory resettlement and rehabilitation policy that at least protects the living standards, earning capacity, and production potential of those affected by a project, and stipulates that these not deteriorate as a result of it. Thus, ironically, the displacement envisaged by the Gujarat government in consonance with national law has been temporarily averted with the help of the courts, not because it would violate the traditional rights of the local communities but because it contravenes not only this new policy of the World Bank but also the conditionalities accepted by the government of India as signatory to the agreement with the World Bank.

But the human rights NGOs present a case that goes much beyond the highly limited protective approach outlined in the World Bank policy. In fact, they have recently challenged the very basis both of such a policy and of national laws, which recognize only individual rights for purposes of compensation while disregarding the collective rights of communities to access natural resources (Randeria 2001a, 2001b). They are at present forming a larger nationwide coalition in order to reassert and protect the collective rights of local communities to common, customary rights (e.g., the rights of pastoralists, fisher folk, marginal and poor farmers, landless laborers and indigenous peoples to land, water, and forests), which they have enjoyed for centuries. Apart from court battles, the NGOs have been involved in local struggles on this issue for several years. But the entire issue has acquired salience due to an exacerbation of the situation under the liberalization and privatization policy of the Indian state in the era of "predatory globalization," to use Richard Falk's term. Increasingly, "wasteland," forest areas, and coastal areas under special environmental protection through the Coastal Area Zonal Plan are being acquired by the state and made over to industries at nominal prices. The Indian Supreme Court has ruled such acquisition of land by the state for the benefit of private industry to be permissible because it constitutes a "public purpose" irrespective of the fact that it is destructive of the lives and livelihoods of the local communities who lose their customary rights, and who may be forcibly displaced and impoverished as a result. Here we see how the "enabling state" comes increasingly into conflict with its citizens, especially those who are marginalized and underprivileged and dependent on common property resources of land, water, and forests for their survival. Hence, voluminous new national and supranational environmental law, as well as an increasing juridification of social life, goes hand in hand with the erosion of the collective rights of communities and their cultural autonomy (Randeria, 2001b).

The human rights and grassroots movement NGOs have in this context questioned the very concept of "eminent domain" in Anglo-Saxon jurisprudence, under which all natural resources vest in the state. As such, the British Crown and the colonial state and now the post-colonial Indian state have claimed unfettered ownership rights over all natural resources in its domain. Human rights NGOs see this understanding introduced through British law as contrary to, and unable to accommodate, the customary rights of local communities to commons. Moreover, they are advocating its replacement by the doctrine of "public trustee," which is now being increasingly recognized by the Indian Supreme Court following US interpretation and judgments, and which challenges the absolute nature of the "eminent domain" concept by viewing the state as a trustee rather than an owner of natural resources within its territory.

These are processes of the particularization of Western law and its creolization in which Western law is given a distinct accent and style through its local translation within the context of specific political struggles. They caution us against the search for presumably authentic alternatives to modern Western legal concepts and norms in pre-colonial Indian traditions by pointing to the highly creative processes of what Merry (1997) has called the "vernacularisation of law." The specificity of the current processes of the transnationalization of law with their divergent dynamics, uneven trajectories, and dissimilar effects in different cultural contexts can, however, be adequately analyzed only against the background of the colonial importation, imposition, and reconstitution of law in the non-Western world (Randeria, 2001).

Two pieces of colonial legislation that remain valid even today in India are the Land Acquisition Act of 1894 and the Forest Act of 1927, both of which are based on the premise of "eminent domain." Actions taken by local authorities under these Acts in the name of "public interest," a concept not defined in the law, have been challenged by the NGOs invoking human rights, collective customary rights, and, most recently, the doctrine of the state as "public trustee." Several social movements and developmental NGOs have waged a long struggle for the revision of the laws that would adversely affect indigenous people as well as other marginalized and poor communities. Thus far they have succeeded in preventing repeated attempts by the government to enact a new Forest Bill that would further dilute, or abolish altogether, the traditional rights of access to natural resources enjoyed by these communities. As part of their campaign, the NGO coalition has formulated its own alternative draft of a People's Forest Policy together with a draft Bill. They have also sought to anchor the customary collective rights of communities to land, water, and forests in the constitutional right to life and livelihood (Article 21).

The Indian state has an inconsistent approach to the issue of collective rights. It recognizes the rights of some groups but not of others to their own religiously based family law (e.g., Hindus, Muslims, Christians, and Parsis have separate personal laws but not Sikhs, Buddhists, or Jains). Lower courts tolerate the decisions of semi-autonomous caste, tribal and jamat councils in family law matters. Groups that are recognized as legal entities for this purpose are different from those to whom reservations apply. The recognition of collective rights is in part a legacy of British colonial policy and of post-colonial compromises for the protection of religious minorities and the redressing of injustices to marginalized communities, yet it is also driven by present electoral pressures and political expediency. Once the British colonial state institutionalized both caste-based quotas and separate family laws for different religious groups, the identities of all these communities was colored by and forged in the context of these policies. The Indian constitution reflects this tension between accommodating collective rights of various kinds and a basic framework committed to the liberal principle of individual rights. The legal pluralism both within state law (the recognition of differential rights or laws for various groups) and at the level of infra-state law (the tolerance of the parallel jurisdiction semi-autonomous community councils) is an index of uneven modernities rather than a remnant of traditional institutions and practices.

Though highly reluctant to accept any collective rights of local communities to natural resources, the state does confer group rights in various other contexts. One of the few exceptions to the former principle is the granting of special rights to some indigenous groups over the land and forests used by them collectively in order to protect these from alienation by non-tribals (Schedule V of the Indian Constitution). However, in addition to indigenous communities, several religious communities are recognized as legal entities to which separate sets of personal laws apply, just as group rights are conferred on Dalits (Scheduled Castes), indigenous peoples (Scheduled Tribes), and a heterogeneous category of castes including some Muslim groups (the so-called Socially and Educationally Backward Classes) for the purpose of quotas proportionate to the respective population of these groups.

The quotas, or reservations, as these measures of "positive/compensatory discrimination" are known, include provisions for political representation in legislative bodies as well as preferential treatment in admissions to institutions of higher learning and for jobs in the state bureaucracy and in public enterprises. Unlike the collective rights for local communities over natural resources that are being claimed in order to protect their right to life and livelihood and to preserve their own distinctive way of life, and which would thus be permanent, the group rights recognized by the Indian constitution are temporary measures. The policy of caste-based quotas was from the beginning introduced as a short-term measure designed to ensure political representation and remove educational and employment disabilities. Similarly, separate personal religious laws were envisaged to be of temporary duration until the uniform civil code for all citizens recommended in the non-justiciable Directive Principles of State Policy in the constitution could be legislated.

Both the policy of quotas for the underprivileged communities and separate religion-based family laws for minorities have been under massive attack in recent years from the predominantly Hindu middle classes. Both these policies of legal pluralism within state law have been represented as being detrimental to Indian society because they are seen as cementing and perpetuating particularistic identities at the expense of the integration of minorities into the "national mainstream." But that is a different story.

THE NARMADA STRUGGLE REFORMS THE WORLD BANK BUT LOSES THE LEGAL BATTLE IN INDIA

Given the fact that more and more citizens are now directly affected in their daily lives by the working of international institutions and their policies, it is not surprising that they choose to address these institutions directly with their protests, bypassing the national political arena and transnationalizing the issues. Many of the ambivalences of the new transnational arena of "global sub-politics," as Ulrich Beck (1998) terms it, are illustrated by the long drawn out though ultimately successful struggle of the local Narmada Bachao Andolan (Save Narmada Movement), together with a network of national NGOs and transnational NGOs in India, Europe, and the USA, against the building of the Sardar Sarovar project on the river Narmada in western India. The project comprised thirty large dams, 133 medium dams and 3000 small dams along with a 1200-megawatt powerhouse. The World Bank was eventually forced to withdraw its financial support to this environmentally damaging project, which would have ended up forcibly displacing between 100,000 and 200,000 people, and without adequate rehabilitation. Some of the complexities and contradictions of the campaign, which involved several Indian NGOs, environmental rights groups in the USA, and development aid groups in Europe, Japan, and Australia are explored in Jai Sen's (1999) excellent ethnography. It traces the emergence of a new modality of transnational social action—the "transnational advocacy network" (Keck and Sekknik, 1998) and also delineates how the dynamics of local resistance came increasingly to be shaped by the choice of the arenas of negotiation and the structures of the international institutions used as levers of power.

As the campaign against the Narmada Dam reminds us, transnational politics takes place within the national political arena of several countries of the North simultaneously, rather than outside the national political sphere. For example, public support on the issue was mobilized, and a domestic constituency built by various European NGOs in their respective countries, in order to lobby development ministries, parliamentarians and each country's executives director on the board of the World Bank. But, as social movements and NGOs in the South linked up with powerful US NGOs to use US congressional hearings as a forum to put pressure on multilateral development banks in general (and on the World Bank in particular) in order to change their policies and reform their structures, they not only reinforced existing asymmetries in power between the North and the South but also lent greater legitimacy to these institutions by leapfrogging the national political arena in order to address them directly, and thereby further diminished the legitimacy of their own government (Sen, 1999).

However, it is also in Washington that the Indian movement and the transnational campaign supporting it resulted in several unintended and unexpected long-term structural changes. The strategy to target executive directors from Europe and the USA on the board of the World Bank led to the directors taking the unprecedented step of challenging the authority of the bank's staff and taking a direct interest in the negotiation of projects. Jai Sen argues that, paradoxically, the campaign thus reduced democratic control over the structures of the World Bank by increasing the control of the US Congress and the concentration of power of the major share-holding states of the North (G-7 members control about 60 per cent of the vote) over the staff of the World Bank. However, the campaign also resulted in the setting up of the Global Panel on Large Dams, as well as internal changes of control and review mechanisms at the World Bank. Among the significant changes introduced as a result of the Sardar Sarovar Dam experience is an information disclosure policy that lays down that specific project information pertaining to the environment and resettlement be made known to those affected by the project prior to its appraisal. Bank manage-ment, therefore, is required to obtain this information from the borrowing government and make it publicly available (Udall, 1998).

GOVERNANCE BEYOND AND WITHIN THE STATE: THE WORLD BANK INSPECTION PANEL AND THE SUPREME COURT OF INDIA[8]

A major achievement of the campaign against the Narmada Dam was the establishment of an independent inspection panel at the World Bank in 1993 in response both to pressure from NGOs for more transparency and accountability and to threats from influential members of the US House of Representatives to block further US contributions to the International Development Association (Udall, 1998). The panel is by no means a full-fledged body for adjudication yet still provides a forum for an appeal by any party adversely affected by a World Bank-funded project (Kingsbury, 1999). The primary purpose of the Inspection Panel, however, is to examine whether the Bank's staff has complied with its own rules and procedures.

Among the seventeen requests entertained by the panel until mid 1999, two were related to projects in India: the National Thermal Power Cor-poration (NTPC) power generation project in Singrauli in 1997, and the eco-development project (of which the Gir project discussed above is a part) in the Nagarhole National park in Karnataka in 1998. In both cases it was alleged that the Bank's management had failed to comply with its own policies on environmental assessment, indigenous people, and involuntary resettlement. The request regarding serious flaws in the design and im-plementation of the eco-development project was submitted by an Indian NGO representing indigenous people living in the Nagarhole National Park.

It submitted that no development plans had been prepared with their participation as stipulated in the Bank's guidelines because the project had simply not recognized the fact that they resided within the core project area. The forced displacement of these Adivasi communities from their forest habitat would not only disrupt their socio-cultural life but also destroy their means of livelihood. Although the bank staff denied any breach of policies and procedures, the panel, after studying the written documents and a field visit, recommended that the World Bank's board authorize an investigation. The panel felt that "a significant potential for serious harm existed" (Shihata, 2000: 135), because key premises in the design of the project appeared to be flawed. In view of the meager information available to the bank staff, the panel felt that it could not have been able to foresee during project appraisal how the project could harm the Adivasi population in the park. Rather than consultations with them prior to the project, as was required, bank management stated that it was envisaged to ensure their participation in the implementation stage. Shihata points out that the more flexible and innovative "process design" of the project, as opposed to a "blueprint project" meant that ongoing planning mechanisms are established parallel to project implementation. Thus, as Shihata, who at the time was the counsel to the World Bank, points out, the very approach chosen surprisingly involves the risk of non-compliance with the World Bank's policy of consultation and participatory planning: a "feature, though apparent, was not explained at the time the project was presented to the Board for approval" (2000: 134).

The panel noted that, in violation of the guidelines on involuntary resettlement, no separate indigenous people's development plan was prepared at the appraisal stage and that no "micro plans," through which individual families and groups in the protected area can express their needs and get financial support, were under preparation for the Adivasi families, 97 per cent of whom wished to remain in the national park. Despite these findings and the potential of the serious negative impact of the project on the indigenous communities in the area, the Bank's board, bowing to pressure from the government in India, decided not to authorize any investigation in 1998. Instead, it merely asked the management, together with the regional government of the state of Karnataka and the affected people, to address the issues raised in the panel's report and to intensify the implementation and micro-planning of the project. Given the long history of non-compliance with bank guidelines, both by its own staff and by the government of Gujarat (as amply documented in the Morse Commission report on the Narmada Dam), the board's decision is a cause for concern. It reflects the refusal of the executive directors from borrowing countries on the World Bank's Board (including India) to permit Panel investigations that, in their view, might infringe on their national sovereignty.

A decade after the World Bank's and the government of India's serious violations of environmental and resettlement policies led to the withdrawal of the bank from the Sardar Sarovar project, one is surprised by the poor institutional memory of the bank; by its lack of responsibility, even in the absence of legal liability, towards those affected adversely by its projects; by its faith in the borrowing government's political will and capacity to implement environmental and human rights conditionalities; by the lack of bank supervision of this implementation and, more generally, the bank's continued insensitivity to the social and ecological costs of the kind of development it advocates and finances. Despite the decades-long failure of the government of India to issue a national resettlement and rehabilitation policy, the World Bank surprisingly continues to advance credits to it for development projects involving forced displacement. It is a poor consolation for those forcibly evicted by bank projects that the bank has an information disclosure policy absent in their own national context. An Inspection Panel with very limited powers hardly seems a solution to their problems of survival in the wake of forced displacement, especially so long as there exists neither an independent appeals commission with the authority to modify, suspend or cancel World Bank projects nor any appropriate judicial remedy against illegal state practices. NGOs critical of these half-hearted reform measures by the bank point out that the debt incurred by borrower governments is not cancelled even in the event of the discontinuance of a project, and that the bank continues to enjoy immunity from legal liability for the adverse social and ecological impacts of its projects.

If the experience of Indian citizens before the Inspection Panel has been disappointing so far, the bitter experience of the Narmada Bachao Andolan's attempts to seek judicial remedy against a state that has constantly flouted its own laws and policies shows equally some of the limitations of the use of national courts by social movements as an arena for social justice. Recourse to the judiciary helps publicize an issue in the press but also may lead to its depoliticization during an expensive, long-winded, and unpredictable court battle in which legal technicalities, and not moral claims, count. Despite a controversial and protracted public debate in India, and the extensive use of the Indian Supreme Court by the Narmada movement after the withdrawal of the World Bank from the project, the issue has yet to be seriously debated in the national parliament. The campaign has not been able to affect legal or policy changes in India with respect to mega-dams, land acquisition, involuntary displacement, or resettlement and rehabilitation. The movement in the Narmada valley, which sought to radicalize the "damn-the-dams" agenda into a critique of the ideology and practice of gigantism in developmental practice as well as to broaden policy to include models of an alternative future, relying on small local autonomous projects, has been caught up for years in the Supreme Court in negotiating technicalities such as the height of the dam. Further, the government has justified its inaction with respect to policy changes for several years by pointing to the sub-judice status of all the issues before the court. In retrospect, the withdrawal of the World Bank from the project may seem like a mixed blessing since under pressure from NGOs in Gujarat, some of the bank's staff and missions had sought to enforce rehabilitation policies and their implementation. The relative improvement of the policies and their enforcement in Gujarat, as compared to Madhya Pradesh and Maharashtra, can be traced to this donor pressure.

The judges of the Indian Supreme Court pronounced their verdict on 18 October 2000, and the severe blow to people's movements and the grave denial of justice raises fundamental questions about the very limitations of the use of law courts by social movements in their struggle for social justice. For it has taken the apex court six-and-a-half years to come to the conclusion that the judiciary should have no role in such decisions! The majority judgment, by Chief Justice Anand and Justice Kirpal, dismissed all the objections regarding environmental and rehabilitation issues, relying entirely on the affidavits given by the state governments. It merely asked the Narmada Control Authority to draw up an action plan on relief and rehabilitation within four weeks. As critics of the judgment pointed out, it was hardly likely that the state government would do in four weeks what it had failed to do in thirteen years. The majority judgment, which praised large dams and their benefits for the nation, permits not merely the construction of the Narmada Dam but, by questioning the *locus standi* of social movements as public interest petitioners, it also limits the future legal options for collective action by citizens against the state.

In its writ petition filed by the Narmada Bachao Andolan (NBA) against the union government in 1994, the movement had asked for a ban on the construction of the dam. It sought this judicial remedy under Article 32 of the Indian Constitution, which guarantees every citizen the right to petition the Supreme Court in defense of the enforcement of his or her fundamental rights. The NBA contended that the magnitude of displacement caused by the dam was such that a total rehabilitation of those whose land was to be submerged by the project was impossible. Since no adequate provision for resettlement and rehabilitation had been made by the state governments, or could even be possibly made, it asked for a ban on the construction for violating the award of the inter-state tribunal, which required this condition to be met prior to the building of the dam. More fundamentally, the NBA raised the question of who has the right to define the greater common good and according to which criteria. Whose interest may be defined as the national interest when the interests of the displaced collide with those of future beneficiaries? Can a merely utilitarian calculus of a larger number of beneficiaries as compared to victims be used to deny poor and vulnerable communities their rights to life and livelihood? Is it legitimate for the state to declare one set of partial interests, those of the wealthy farmer lobby, industrialists, and contractors, to be synonymous with the public good? The NBA thus challenged the very assumption that the state by definition acts in the public interest and asked for an independent judicial review of the entire project, its environmental, economic and human costs. Apart from raising the issue of the illegality of state practices (e.g., the absence of environmental studies that should have been conducted prior to the construction process as mandated by the Ministry of Environment), the NBA also argued that the adverse human and ecological costs of large dams in general far outweigh their benefits.

In response to the petition, the Supreme Court stayed further construction on the dam from 1995 to 1999 while asking for reports from the three state governments on the progress of the rehabilitation of the "oustees," as well as on the future provisions for them along with expeditious environmental surveys and plans to overcome hazards. In the hearings in 1999, the counsels for the state government of Gujarat had asked the court to give a clear signal in favor of the dam so that foreign investors would be encouraged to invest in it (Sathe, 2000). It is difficult to judge how much weight the argument carried in the court's decision to allow construction to be resumed although not much progress had been made on either rehabilitation or environmental assessment. But the argument reflects the priorities and concerns of the government of Gujarat, which chose to privilege the right to security of foreign investment over the fundamental rights of its own citizens. Interestingly, the Narmada project, which has since been propounded by the state government to be the "life-line of Gujarat" in so far as it would provide drinking water and irrigation facilities to the drought prone areas of Saurashtra and Kachch,[9] has now been revealed to follow completely different aims. In 1996 it was announced that water from the dam would be sold to private industries at market prices, an offer that several large fertilizer, cement, petrochemical, and chemical companies may accept as a cheaper alternative to desalinating sea water.

It is also worrying that the court refused to consider the general question of the utility of big dams on the grounds that policy matters were best left to the legislature and administration, while at the same time declaring them to be essential for economic progress. Premised on the doctrine of the separation of powers, this advocacy of judicial restraint with regards to not going into policy issues in order not to trespass on administrative competence, came as a surprise and a disappointment, after more than a decade of judicial activism in general and five years after the admission of the plea by the NBA in particular. However, the Narmada judgment does not mark an anomaly in the apex court's history of judicial restraint in the context of public interest petitions challenging large developmental and infrastructure projects in the last decade. Rather, as Upadhyay (2000) points out, it is consonant with the inclination of the judiciary to insist on the executive taking decisions correctly as opposed to taking correct decisions. The Supreme Court has often left it up to the government to decide on the nature of public projects for an improvement in living standards of citizens and to resolve conflicts of interest arising from contrary perspectives on development. Here it sees its own role as examining whether all relevant aspects have been taken into consideration and if the laws of the land have been followed, but not whether the decision is right or wrong. Interestingly, in cases of environmental protection, the court has taken a very different view. Neither technical expertise nor policy issues have led it to apply judicial restraint when it has sought to reconcile development with ecological considerations. It has sought to develop a rich environmental jurisprudence to compensate for administrative indifference but has preferred a defensive approach of non-interference into administrative decisions on infrastructure projects (Upadhyay, 2000).

Decades of resistance by the victims of development in the Narmada valley, who have borne the brunt of state repression and violence, have not led to any rethinking on the basic issues raised by the movement: forced displacement, ecological destruction in the interest of industrial development, as well as the search for more environmentally sustainable and socially just alternative models of development that respect cultural diversity and the right of communities to determine their own ways of life and livelihoods. After the World Bank pulled out of the financing of the Sardar Sarovar Dam on the Narmada River, the government of Gujarat floated bonds to raise capital for it within the country and abroad. Attempts to attract multinational finance, which are removed from democratic control in any of the countries concerned, have continued for the Maheshwar Dam on the Narmada.

THE INDIAN NEEM TREE ON TRIAL IN MUNICH

The story of the struggle around the Indian neem tree serves to illustrate seven theses on supranational and sub-national legal pluralism, the role of the state as both an architect but also as a victim of the transnationalization of law, and the contribution of NGOs both in mobilizing resistance as well as in creating alternative law.

On 9 and 10 May 2000, the fate of the Indian neem tree hung in balance in Room 3468 of the European Patent Office in Munich. At issue was the legitimacy of a patent for a method of preparing an oil from the seeds of the tree to be used as a pesticide, one of fourteen patents on products of the

Indian neem tree granted by the Munich authority. The American transnational corporation W. R. Grace and the US Department of Agriculture, joint owners of six of these patents, were represented by a legal firm from Hamburg. Ranged against them was a transnational coalition of petitioners asking for the patent to be revoked: Vandana Shiva, Director of the Research Foundation for Science, Technology and Ecology; Linda Bullard, President of the International Federation of Organic Agricultural Movements; and Magda Alvoet, currently the Belgian Health and Environment Minister. They were represented by a Swiss Professor of Law from the University of Basel.

The representatives of the US chemical concern remained silent throughout the two days of the hearing. It was the silence of the powerful, of those who knew that time, money, and the government of the USA were on the side of US corporate interests. The European Patent Office heard the eloquent political arguments of Vandana Shiva on biopiracy and intellectual colonialism as well as the testimony of a Sri Lankan farmer, Ranjith de Silva, on the moral illegitimacy of a patent that disregards centuries of traditional local knowledge. But what ultimately counted for the Opposition Division Bench hearing the case were measurements of centrifugation, filtration, and evaporation in the testimony of Abhay Phadke, an Indian factory owner. His firm near Delhi has been using since 1985 a process very similar to the one patented by the American multinational corporation and the US Department of Agriculture to manufacture the same product in India. At the end of a five-year legal battle, on 10 May 2000 the European Patent Office revoked the patent on the grounds that the process patented by the Americans lacked novelty.

The struggle over the patents relating to the neem tree may be used to illustrate seven theses on the transnationalization of law and legal pluralism which delineate the constrained yet central role of the state and the significance of NGOs and social movements in this process:

1. *Hegemonic vs. counter-hegemonic globalization.* Contrary to the view expressed in the *Frankfurter Allgemeine Zeitung*, the European Patent Office in Munich was not the scene of a conflict between the East and the West but between two visions of globalization and over the future direction of the process. The battle lines were drawn here, as in Seattle, between proponents of a neoliberal globalization for profit and its globally networked civil-society opponents. As actors in an emerging global civil society, transnationally networked farmers' movements and environmental NGOs in India are among the most ardent opponents of a new international legal regime of "intellectual property rights" that enables transnational corporations (TNCs) in the North cheap and easy access to the natural resources of the South,

turning common heritage into commodities, jeopardizing the biodiversity of agricultural crops, threatening the livelihood of poor primary producers, and forcing consumers of seeds and medicines in the South into dependency and often destitution. They point out that the capitalist countries of the North industrialized without the constraints of the patent regime that they have now imposed on the developing world (Shiva *et al.*, 2000). Central to their struggles in the local, national and transnational legal and political arena is the question: who sets the rules for the processes of globalization and according to which norms? These movements are raising issues of food security and farmer's rights, but also and more generally issues of social justice, the democratization of global governance, and the legitimacy of international institutions and legal regimes.

For example the transnational "seed tribunal" on September 24 and 25 in Bangalore, organized by several NGOs, women's groups, agricultural worker's unions, and farmer's movements heard testimonies from Indian farmers about: the sale of kidneys by family members to meet the rising expenses of agricultural inputs; suicides by farmers caught in a debt trap due to the high price of seeds from multinational corporations and subsequent crop failure; the inadequate and poor quality of the public distribution of seeds, which facilitates the entry of foreign multinationals; increased market dependency of small peasants; as well as the destruction of biodiversity in their regions. The farmer's organizations passed a resolution calling on multinationals like Monsanto to "Quit India," echoing Mahatma Gandhi's slogan coined in 1942 at the height of the national movement against British domination. They called for a boycott of seeds from the Indian subsidiaries of multinationals unless the former became independent of these foreign firms. They also vowed to maintain the food sovereignty and seed sovereignty of farmers and to protect it from multinational companies while declaring that they would not obey any patent law or plant variety protection law under the WTO regime that considered seeds to be the private property of these corporations. They demanded that seeds and food be excluded from the TRIPs (Trade Related Intellectual Property Rights) regime of the WTO and advocated for the reintroduction of the quantitative restrictions on agricultural imports that had been removed recently by the government of India in consonance with WTO provisions for trade liberalization, a point to which I shall return below.

2. *Cunning rather than weak states? Contesting the limits to state autonomy.* The jury at the "seeds tribunal" envisaged a central and active role for the state in the protection of the livelihoods of farmers in India. It recommended making improvements in the public distribution of seeds, the setting up of regulatory bodies to ensure good quality agricultural inputs, a ten-year moratorium on

the introduction of genetic engineering in food and farming, representation for farmers on the agricultural prices commission, and ensuring minimum support prices. But the jury's diagnosis of the "silence of the state" on the issue of farmer's rights coexists uneasily with the state's own demands in recent legislation for changes to protect the interests of farmers. For the state has been anything but silent, as testified to by the Patents (Second) Amendments Act of 1999, the Protection of Plant Varieties and Farmer's Rights Bill of 1999, and the Biological Diversity Bill of 200 currently before parliament. A harsh critique of the state, coupled with an appeal to it for the protection of national food security and sovereignty and the rights of poor primary producers, reflects some of the ambivalence of civil society actors with respect to the state, which is seen both as an opponent but also as an ally. Under the conditions of economic and legal globalization the state is simultaneously seen as being in collusion with multinational corporate interests and as the protector of national sovereignty. But can the Indian state be relied on to reform its policies in favor of its vulnerable citizens rather than in favor of global capital? This depends on whether we have oftentimes tended to misrecognize cunning states as weak ones. Weak states cannot protect their citizens, whereas cunning states do not care even to afford them the limited security they could.

The global harmonization of differing national systems of patent law illustrates some of the complexities of legal globalization and the contra-dictory role of the state in it. There is no global patent law; the field is still regulated on the national level, with the exception of the EU. But the WTO's TRIPS regime imposes powerful constraints on the sovereignty of nation-states both with regard to the content and the timing of national laws that have to conform to the new WTO regime. The extent of national autonomy under the *sui generis* system available as an option under TRIPs, which NGOs would like their governments to exploit, remains highly contested, with mounting pressure against it from genetic technology exporting nations like the US and Argentina. However, despite legal transnationalization and the growing importance of the WTO, the state remains an important arena of law production. Despite the fact that India has an elaborate legal framework in this area, it has had to amend its patent laws, which earlier permitted only process patents to include product patents, as well as to introduce laws on plant varieties and breeder's rights in order to permit for the first time the patenting of agricultural and pharmaceutical products. Given the necessary political will, it could enact and implement laws within the WTO framework that would protect the interests of farmers, consumers, and Indian producers.

The Gene Campaign in India has pointed out, for example, that the GATT/WTO requires member states to provide either a patent regime or an effective *sui generis* system to protect newly developed plant varieties. It does not enjoin states to follow the UPOV model. Thus, the Indian state has a choice to opt for a *sui generis* system more suitable to the Indian context. The UPOV system is based on the needs of industrialized countries in which agriculture is a commercial activity, unlike in India, which has a large majority of small and marginal farmers. It protects the rights of seed companies, who are the major producers of seed in an environment where seed research is conducted in private institutions for profit. It is thus at odds with Indian realities, where farmers are breeders who have individually and collectively conserved genetic resources and produced seeds, and where most research in the area is done in public institutions. The Gene Campaign, therefore, advocates *sui generis* legislation by the Indian state to protect the rights of farmers as producers and consumers of seed.

Was it a lack of technical expertise, an ignorance of the options available within the WTO agreement, an indifference towards the needs of poor primary producers, a conscious perusal of policies to their detriment due to pressure from powerful national and international lobbies, or some mixture of all of these, that led the Indian government to remove the quantitative restrictions (QR) on the importation of 714 items, including 229 agricultural commodities in March 2000, after having lost the legal battle against the USA in the WTO? The government claimed that its new Exim policy met its WTO obligations and benefited consumers by allowing imports of cheap foreign goods. But under the WTO agreement, India was bound neither to remove the QRs in 2000 nor to select the specific items that it did. In fact, had it argued for retaining QRs on the grounds of food security as well as the negative impact of their removal on employment and on the livelihoods of poor primary producers, it may have been able to continue most QRs. That the government chose to argue for a continuation of QRs in view of its balance of payments problems undermined its own case, given that it no longer has a foreign exchange deficit. It is difficult to say if this was a strategy deliberately intended to fail. The contrast to the policies of highly industrialized nations, however, could not be greater. The USA, Japan, and most European governments increased subsidies to their own farmers, thus seriously distorting agricultural prices and making calculations of measures of productivity or competitiveness based on relative prices spurious. For example, imposing an 80 per cent tariff on rice imports into India, in conformity with WTO prescriptions, after lifting the QR on rice imports is unlikely to afford Indian rice producers adequate protection. Along with rice, one can now freely import tea, coffee, rubber, spices, milk, vegetables, fish, and more than sixty fishery products. The National Fishworker's Forum, in its strong protest against the lifting of QRs, has warned that fish prices are likely to crash as a result of large-scale imports. It views this latest move by the government in the context of a long history of attempts to liberalize the deep-sea fishing policy regime.

Moreover, as many critics in India of the Uruguay Round have pointed out, contrary to the rhetoric of creating a level playing field, many WTO rules tilt the balance further against countries of the South (Khor, 2000a; 2000b). Theoretically, it may be the case that the latter, who are net losers from the TRIPs regime, could offset such losses by gains from textile or agricultural trade liberalization. However, most countries of the North, which have been very slow to comply with their commitments in this regard, can take recourse to the very extensive safeguards provision for agricultural and textile trade. The TRIPs agreement lacks any such provision that would permit countries to reimpose tariffs temporarily in case losses to domestic producers are heavier than expected (Howse, 2001). So, though the costs of implementing the TRIPs regime has turned out to be much higher than anticipated for most developing countries, the agreement merely allows for a certain grace period for implementation. Many of them, including India, therefore, would like to reopen for negotiation the compromises that they made in the GATT Uruguay Round under the sway of imperfect informa-tion and the threat of unilateralism by the USA (Khor, 2000a; 2000b).

3. *A plurality of conflicting supranational legal regimes.* Two of the strategies that have been adopted by subaltern states faced with structural adjustment conditionalities and several supranational legal regimes are to delay imple-mentation at the national level and to exploit the existence of a plurality of international laws and treaties, which often contravene one another. India, along with African and five Central and Latin American countries, has called for a review and an amendment of the TRIPs Agreement of the WTO as well as a five-year moratorium on its implementation. The Organization of African Unity and India have demanded that the TRIPs regime be brought into consonance with the Convention on Biological Diversity and the International Undertaking on Plant Genetic Resources, which would result in the exclusion of life forms from patentability and the protection of innovations by local farming communities. The Indian government has pointed out that its obligations under TRIPs run counter to some of its obligations under the Convention on Biological Diversity. However, the sanctions under the former, which permit, e.g., cross retaliation in any area of trade, are much stronger compared to the weak enforcement mechanisms of international environmental laws. Indian NGOs, along with transnational advocacy networks like GRAIN and RAFI, for example, have been using this plurality of transnational legal regimes to question the legitimacy of the WTO TRIPs regime, which contravenes provisions of both the Biodiversity Convention and the Protocol on Biosafety on genetically modified life forms

and does not conform to the earlier International Undertaking of the FAO, which explicitly recognizes Farmer's Rights to seeds.

4. *NGOs as mediators and creators of laws.* The protracted struggle against the Dunkel Draft and the TRIPs Agreement shows the variety of vital contributions to legal globalization made by transnationally linked NGOs and social movements in India. Just as they have represented the interests of Indian farmers in international and transnational fora, they have also disseminated information on the legal complexities to the national press and local communities. Not only have their campaigns created public awareness of the issues involved, mobilized farmers, and put pressure on the state but they have also challenged in US and European courts the granting of patents to TNCs from the North over agricultural and pharmaceutical products and genetic resources in the South. But, in addition to mediating between the local level and national as well as supranational fora, and contesting new legal regimes in various political and legal arenas, NGOs and advocacy groups are also engaged in the production of alternative norms by weaving together norms from different sources. In 1998, as an alternative treaty to UPOV, the Gene Campaign drafted a "Convention of Farmers and Breeders" (COFaB) that recognizes the collective community rights as well as individual rights of farmers as breeders; recognizes their common knowledge from oral or documented sources; stipulates that a breeder will forfeit his right if the "productivity potential" claimed in the application is no longer valid or if he fails to meet the demands of farmers, leading to a scarcity of planting material, increased market price, and monopolies; and grants each contracting state the right to independent evaluation of the performance of the variety before allowing protection. The UNDP Human Development Report of 1999 commends it as a

> strong and coordinated international proposal [that] offers developing countries an alternative to following European legislation on needs to protect farmers' rights to save and reuse seeds and to fulfil the food and nutritional security goals of their peoples. (74)[10]

5. *Fragmentation of state law and fractured sovereignty.* The transnationalization of law is accompanied by an increasing fragmentation of law and a fracturing of state sovereignty. State action becomes increasingly heterogeneous with state law losing its unitary and coherent character. For example, Indian patent laws have to be brought into conformity with several supranational legal regimes that may contravene one another, such as the WTO TRIPs regime and the Convention on Biological Diversity. Or Indian population policy, which is strongly influenced by the UNFPA and the USAID, has to be in tune both

with the UN Cairo Conference Action Program, with its emphasis on reproductive rights, and with the Tirhat Amendment in the US Congress, which prohibits US financial assistance to any national population program that permits abortion. The IMF and the World Bank loan conditionalities in the 1990s required far-reaching changes in Indian tax laws, industrial licensing laws, and trade liberalization. The dilution of labor laws demanded by them would contravene constitutional guarantees but would also collide with ILO agreements and ICESCR provisions, as I discuss below. The coexistence of these different logics of regulation by different institutions of the state, or in different areas of regulation (and sometimes even within the same area of regulation), results in a new kind of legal pluralism, a pluralism within state law linked, on the one hand, to the transnationalization of law (see Santos, 1995: 118) and, on the other, the simultaneous operation of multiple transnational norms without their incorporation into domestic law.

For example, the plurality of transnational laws on biodiversity regimes is duplicated at the national level as well. The Indian Parliament's Biodiversity Bill of 2000 provides for the setting up of a new regulatory body, the National Biodiversity Authority (NBA). But the NBA may not be the sole authority to deal with bioresources or claims on rights over bioresources, a fact that the bill does not make provision for, or even recognize. It specifies neither the jurisdiction of the NBA *vis-à-vis* other competing bodies nor the applicability of other laws regulating intellectual property rights and access to bioresources. Its provisions may not be in harmony with the much older Drug and Cosmetics Act, the new Geographical Indicators Bill, or the Plant Varieties Protection and Farmer's Rights Bill. The Biodiversity bill refers to the Convention on Biodiversity of 1992 yet fails to utilize its provisions in order to recognize the claims of indigenous peoples or to allow benefit claimants to assert their traditional rights. By vesting regulatory authority solely in the NBA, it in effect may end up denying communities the right to defend their traditional rights and make claims independently of the state body, especially one without an adequate database to protect such claims and rights. Given the record of the Indian state, such a centralization of all regulatory power in a bureaucratic body, with little civil society participation, may or may not be effective against the biopiracy of multinational corporations. However, it is likely to be to the detriment of local communities and indigenous peoples, despite lip-service to the establishment of local biodiversity committees.

6. *Legal plurality and the emergence of the cunning citizen?* The existence of multiple and overlapping transnational legal orders within a particular field may also present a third option for states with a political will and strong democratic institutions, an option between the unrealistic hope of restoring

national legal autonomy and the equally utopian dream of all-encompassing global regulation. National norms could be supplemented and strengthened through a multi-layered approach that envisaged various public and private actors acting within and beyond national borders in order to establish multi-level public and private regulatory regimes. Rather than pinning one's hopes on the state as a unitary source of normative order, it is important to include the role of transnationally networked movements and advocacy networks, which, as private actors, create, mobilize, mediate, and weave together norms from different systems into new regulatory webs (Trubek *et al.*, 2000). Instead of posing the problem in terms of a stark binary choice between national or global legal regulation, or between state law as opposed to community law, this chapter has tried to sketch the contours of an emerging new landscape of legal pluralism, a mosaic of supranational regulation, national legislation, alternative people's treaties and policies, project law, traditional rights, and international laws.

In such a context the protection of the rights, lives, and livelihoods of most citizens in the South will need shifting alliances with states and international institutions. The World Bank, for example, and the Indian state are both cast in a neoliberal globalization script, like in Hindi films, in the double role of ally and adversary. Faced by cunning states and non-accountable international organizations, citizens and civic alliances in the twenty-first century may well be in the same position as the British government in the nineteenth century. They have neither permanent friends nor permanent enemies but only permanent interests.

7. *Post-colonial continuities?* Let us return for a moment to the Sri Lankan farmer Ranjith de Silva, who appeared as a witness for the transnational coalition of petitioners in the European Patent Office in Munich to challenge the US patent on a product of the neem tree. His grandparents would certainly have been astonished that products of a tree in their backyard could become—with the stroke of a European pen—the intellectual property of a US corporation and the US Department of Agriculture. But neither legal pluralism nor transnationalization jurisdiction would have been unfamiliar to South Asians of his grandparents' generation. The Privy Council in London, for example, had the ultimate authority to decide over their property disputes, due to the fact that they were subjects of the British Empire. And personal law for Muslims and Christians in South Asia always has had a transnational dimension. The family law that applied to the de Silva's as members of the Catholic community in Sri Lanka was a hybrid mixture of the prescriptions of the Roman Catholic Church with a variety of local practices codified by the colonial state into a homogeneous Christian personal law. In disputes concerning the control of land, British ideas of

individual property or of "eminent domain," depending on how their land had been classified, would have collided with traditional norms of community access to natural resources and collective usufructory rights, a point to which I shall return below.

Sensitivity to the history of colonialism could be an important corrective to the presentism and Eurocentrism of most analyses of (legal) globalization, with their propensity to overstate the singularity of the present and to posit a radical discontinuity between contemporary social life and that of the recent past. For example, in the literature on globalization, when references are made to the erosion of the sovereignty of the nation-state, or to an increasing legal pluralism (both supranational and sub-national), or to hybridity of laws in the wake of their transnational export, transplantation, and domestication in different cultural contexts, these may represent new developments for societies in the West. From the perspective of the non-Western world, however, it may seem to be an irony of history that, turning Marx on his head, one could argue that today the former colonies mirror in many ways the legal future of Europe. This is especially striking with regard to phenomena such as transnational jurisdiction, supranational and sub-national legal pluralism, the role of private actors in legal diffusion, as well as the emergence of multiple and shared sovereignties. Like the transnational corporations of the contemporary world, the British East India Company, which began the process of introducing British law into India prior to its becoming a Crown colony, was a private trading company. The relationship between the state and private trading companies in European countries has been unclearly delineated in the past and present. Powerful, partly autonomous from the state and seeking to escape from government control and metropolitan law, private trading companies in the nineteenth and twentieth centuries, like their transnational counterparts today, always relied on their respective governments to further their interests abroad. The "post-sovereign states" (Scholte, 2000) of the industrialized world increasingly resemble (post-)colonial ones in which the state has never enjoyed a monopoly over the production of law and has always had to contend with competition from within and beyond its borders. That Western social theory misses this convergence and represents overlapping sovereignties as a re-feudalization of Europe may have to do with its parochialism as well as with its tendency to see the West as both unique and universal.

BIBLIOGRAPHY

Baxi, Upendra; Jacob, Alice; Singh, Tarlok (1999), *Reconstructing the Republic*. New Delhi: Har-Anand Publications.
Beck, Ulrich (ed.) (1998), *Politik der Globalisierung*. Frankfurt: Suhrkamp.

Benda-Beckmann, Keebet von (2000),"Transnational Dimension of Legal Pluralism" (*mimeo*).

Cotterrell, Roger (1995), *Laws Community. Legal Theory in Sociological Perspective.* Oxford: Clarendon Press.

Falk, Richard (1999), *Predatoy Globalization. A Critique.* Cambridge: Polity Press.

Ganguly, Varsha (2000), 'Displacement and quality of life of women: a case study of pastoral women of gir forest'. Phd. thesis, South Gujarat University, Surat.

Garth, Bryant (1995), "Merchants of Law as Moral Entrepreneurs: Constructing International Justice from the Competition for Transnational Business Disputes," *Law and Society Review,* 29(1), 27–64.

Gill, Stephen (2000), "Toward a Postmodern Prince? The Battle in Seattle as a Movement in the New Politics of Globalisation," *Millenium: Journal of International Studies,* 29(1), 131–140.

Günther, Klaus; Randeria, Shalini (2001), "Recht, Kultur und Gesellschaft im Prozeß der Globalisierung," Heft Nr. 4, Werner Reimers Konferenzen, Bad Homburg.

Howse, Robert (2001), "Eyes Wide Shut in Seattle: The Legitimacy of the World Trade Organization," Veijo Heiskanen and Jean-Marc Coicaud (eds.), *The Legitimacy of International Institutions.* UN: United Nations University Press.

Keck, Margaret E.; Sekknik, Kathryn (1998), *Activist beyond Borders. Advocacy Networks in International Politics.* Ithaca NY and London: Cornell University Press.

Khor, Martin (2000a), "Globalization and the South: Some Critical Issues," United Nations Conference on Trade and Development, Discussion Papers Nr. 147, Geneva: UNCTAD.

Khor, Martin (2000b), "Rethinking Liberalisation and Reforming the WTO: Presentation at Davos (28th January 2000)," Third World Network, Trade and Development Series (http://www.twnside.org.sg /title/davos2-cn.htm).

Kingsbury, B. (1999), "Operation Policies of International Institutes as Part of the Law-Making Process: The World Bank and Indigenous People," G. S. Goodwin-Gill and S. Talmon (eds.), *The Reality of International Law: Essays in Honour of Ian Brownlie.* Oxford: Clarendon Press, 323–342.

Merry, Sally Engle (1997), "Legal Pluralism and Transnational Culture: The Ka Ho'okolokolonui Kanaka Maoli Tribunal," Hawai'i,1993, in Richard Wilson (ed.) (1997), *Human Rights, Culture & Context: Anthropological Perspectives.* Chicago: Pluto Press, 28–48.

Moore, Sally Falk (2000), "An international legal regime and the context of conditionality," unpublished manuscript, Harvard University.

Morse, Bradford; Berger, Thomas (1992), *Sardar Sarovar. Report of the independent review.* Canada: Resource Futures International Inc.

Petersen, Hanne; Zahle, Henrik (ed.) (1995), *Legal Polycentricity: Consequences of Pluralism in Law.* Aldershot: Dartmouth.

Randeria, Shalini (1999), "Through the Prism of Population: The Post-Colonial State and Body Politic(s) in India," paper for the AGORA 2000 project at the Institute for Advanced Studies, Berlin.

Randeria, Shalini (2001), "Domesticating Neoliberal Discipline: Transnationalisation of Law, Fractured States and Legal Pluralism in the South," in Wolf

Lepenies (ed.), *Shared Histories and Negotiated Universals*. Frankfurt/New York: Campus Verlag.

Randeria, Shalini (2001a), "Local Refractions of Global Governance: Legal Plurality, International Institutions, NGOs and the Post-Colonial State in India," Habilitation, Faculty of Political and Social Sciences, Free University of Berlin.

Randeria, Shalini (2001b) "Globalising Gujarat: Environmental Action in the Legal Arena — World Bank, NGOs and the State," Mario Rutten and Ghanshyam Shah (eds.): Festschrift for Professor Jan Breman, Amsterdam/ Delhi.

Santos, Boaventura de Sousa (1995), *Toward a New Common Sence, Law, Sciences and Politics in the Paradigmatic Transition*. New York: Routledge.

Sathe, S P (2000), "Supreme Court and NBA," *Economic and Political Weekly*, 35(46), November 11, 2000, 3990–3994.

Sen, Jai (1999), "A World to win — But Whose World is it, anyway? Civil Society and the World Bank, the view from the 'front': Case Studies," John W. Foster and Anita Anand (eds.), *Whose World is it Anyway? Civil Society, the United Nations and the Multilateral Future*. Ottawa: The United Nations Association in Canada.

Shihata, Ibrahim F.I. (2000), *The World Bank Inspection Panel: In Practice*. Washington: Oxford University Press.

Shiva, Vandana; Jafri, Afsar H.; Emani, Ashok; Bhutani, Shalini; Antony, Margaret; Prasad, Urvashi (2000), *Licence to Kill. How the Unholy Trinity— the World Bank, the International Monetary Fund and the World Trade Organisation—are Killing Livelihoods, Environment and Democracy in India*. New Delhi: Research Foundation for Science, Technology and Ecology.

Scholte, Jan Aart (2000), *Globalisation: A Critical Introduction*. London: Macmillan.

Swaminathan, Rajesh (1998), "Regulating Development: Structural Adjustment and the Case for National Enforcement of Economic and Social Rights," *Columbia Journal of Transnational Law*, 37, 161–214.

Teubner, Gunther (1997), *Global Law Without a State*. Aldershot: Dartmouth.

Teubner, Gunther (1996), "Globale Bukowina. Zur Emergenz eines transnationalen Rechtspluralismus," *Rechtshistorisches Journal*, 15, 255–290.

Trubek, David M.; Mosher, Jim; Rothenstein, Jeffrey S. (2000), "Transnationalism in the Regulation of Labor Relations: International Regimes and Transnational Advocacy Networks," *Journal of Law and Social Inquiry*, 25 (4).

Udall, Lori (1998) "The World Bank and Public Accountability: Has Anything Changed?," Jonathan Fox and L. David Brown (eds.), *The Struggle for Accountability: The World Bank, NGOs and Grassroots Movements*. Cambridge, MA: MIT Press, 391–435.

United Nations Development (UNDP) (1999), *Human Development Report 1999*. New York; Oxford: Oxford UP.

Upadhyay, Videh (2000), "Changing judicial power: courts on infrastructure projects and environment," *Economic and Political Weekly*, 35(43–44), 3789–3792.

Türk, Danillo (1992), *The realisation of Economic, Social and Cultural Rights: Final Report of the Special Rapporteur*. United Nations Economic and Social Council, Commission on Human Rights, Subcommission on Prevention of Discrimination and Protection of Minorities, 14. U.N. Doc. E/CN/Sub.2/1992/16.

Weiler, Joseph (1999), "The transformation of Europe," *The Constitution of Europe*. Cambridge: Cambridge UP.
World Bank (1996), "Staff Appraisal Report: India. Ecodevelopment Project," *Report* No.14914-IN, August 3.
World Bank (1997), *World Development Report: The State in a Changing World.* Oxford UP.

Notes

1 Many thanks to Ivan Krastev for suggesting the term "cunning state" in the course of several stimulating discussions around the issues developed in this chapter.

2 See K. von Benda-Beckmann (2000) for a detailed discussion of this point.

3 This section draws on many of the issues dealt with at length in Günther and Randeria (2001) and summarizes several arguments elaborated in Randeria (2001).

4 When the WTO declares that it has been consulting with NGOs, these are more likely to be chambers of industry and commerce (see the list of NGOs with whom the WTO consults on its website) rather than advocacy networks or grassroots development groups, since the negatively defined umbrella term, non-governmental organizations, encompasses a heterogeneity of organizations with little in common except that they are neither government nor profit-making firms.

5 The representative of the WTO, at a recent conference at the Institute for Advanced Studies in Berlin on "Governance Beyond the State" (May 2000), when questioned about the legitimacy of the power exercised by the organization reiterated the standard WTO defense that "the WTO Secretariat simply provides administrative and technical support for the WTO and its members," a formulation found on the organization's website "10 Common Misunderstandings about the WTO," the first among them being "The WTO Dictates Government's Policies."

6 In my interviews with them, IMF and World Bank lawyers underscored their helplessness in the face of foot-dragging and non-compliance by member states with the terms of the loan agreements with them.

7 I am grateful to Achyut Yagnik (SETU, Ahmadabad) for discussions relating to the issues raised in this section of the chapter. My thanks to him, Varsha Ganguly, and Ashok Shrimal for sharing with me their experiences of the World Bank project and the campaign for the rights of pastoral communities, as well as for giving me access to their material on the subject.

8 For a detailed critical study of the World Bank Inspection Panel, and especially of the two Indian cases that have come up before it, see Randeria (2001a).

9 The Independent Review mission of the World Bank (Morse and Berger, 1992) cast grave doubts on these claims because it found little evidence of any serious planning towards this end.

3

Multiculturalism and Collective Rights

Carlos Frederico Marés de Souza Filho

INTRODUCTION

The survival of multiculturalism in a world in which the state recognizes, protects, and seeks to transform all rights into individual rights is practically impossible. In fact, the construction of the contemporary state and its law was characterized either by legal individualism or by the transformation of each person with rights into an individual. This was done with businesses, societies and with the state itself. The fiction was created that each entity was a person, a legal or moral individual. Similarly, indigenous peoples came to be seen as individuals with protected rights. This transformed the essentially collective rights of peoples into individual rights.

Contemporary law, apart from being individualistic, is also dichotomous. People—individuals with rights—are made to correspond to one thing: a protected legal title. The legitimacy of this relation is established by a contract, an agreement between two people. It is obvious that this legal model would not serve the interests of the indigenous peoples of Latin America because, even if each people was considered a legal individual, the protected property (i.e., the property that the peoples need to protect) and its legitimacy bear no relation to either individual availability or contractual origin.[1] It is because of this that Latin American countries always seek to separate the individual native from his/her people, assimilating the individual into the "national society" in such a profound way that his/her native identity is lost. The system has always believed that such an assimilation would be possible via labor yet has never understood that labor that produces property is not a part of the indigenous cultures of America.

So much did these peoples struggle, and so slight was the possibility of assimilation that the developing societies exerted on them, that the system ended up recognizing collective rights, which opened a new horizon of recognition of the peoples, enabling countries to consider themselves multi-cultural and multi-ethnic. These collective rights moved the indigenous peoples to other social segments, in such a way that they ended up being liberating.

The trajectory of this transformation, its potential and difficulties are the theme of this chapter. The following stories, though extremely representative, must be understood as examples of a much vaster and more complex reality that points always in the same direction, towards a type of renaissance of native peoples or a renaissance of hopes (Souza Filho, 1988).

THE FORMATION OF STATES IN LATIN AMERICA

The mercantile colonialism that began with the discovery of the Americas and the sea route to India led to a profound exploitation of the indigenous peoples of those lands, easily culminating in contempt and genocide. The wars that Portugal and Spain engaged in against the resistance of the peoples of America were marked by the inequality of conditions and cruelty. The Europeans had gunpowder, and did not hesitate to abuse it. The so-called Indians were hunted down in the jungles, mountains, and plains, forced into the interior and sold or trained in captivity to serve as slaves, made Christians and transformed into a workforce for the mercantile capitalists, who ironically in Europe constructed the theory of the independent worker as a basis of private property. No Native American people was immune to the arrival of the Europeans. The war waged on the coastal peoples rapidly spread to the interior. The native people either surrendered or fled. Those who fled did not find unoccupied territories, but groups of other natives with whom they had to fight for control of the land. Trapped between two enemies, every native group was constantly forced to choose between fighting and surrendering. If we could picture the routes taken by each native people on a map of America, we would undoubtedly see paths covered in blood throughout the vast forests, enclosures, fields, and mountains.

As if this was not enough, the Europeans brought slaves with them, who intended to free themselves of their chains, become reunited with members of their people, and find a place in which to live, hidden from the Indians fighting the fierce persecution of "the captains of the forest."[2] Clearly, they sought a refuge, a place of difficult access, a hiding place in which to settle. Such places, which in Brazil came to be known as "quilombos," existed and indeed still do in many countries of America. The blacks who escaped did not know the local terrain as well as the Indians, and thus were generally at a disadvantage when it came to fighting. The fact that America was organized into nation-states at a very early date (the same time as Europe) did not help to change the lot of the native inhabitants. The wars of independence at the beginning of the nineteenth century did not have a liberating effect, despite the efforts of men like Tiradentes, Bolívar, and Artigas. The struggles, supported militarily and logistically by the indigenous peoples, did not manage to build free and truly independent states led by the will of the various peoples of which they were constituted. Quite simply, Iberian colonialism was replaced by an English version.[3] The new colonialism had to be adapted to the new contexts of Africa and Asia, where the establishment of nation-states was abandoned, probably due to the fact that local leaders there did not exercise the same level of control over the people as did the far more Europeanized American leaders.

The exception is Paraguay. Francia, along with the indigenous people, promoted a real independence, evicting the landowners and the representatives of Spanish and English interests. Benefiting from freely accepted labor and a policy of inhibiting primitive and predatory capitalist accumulation, he industrialized the country, securing an excellent standard of living for the literate, well nourished and profoundly nationalist people. This experiment in freedom lasted four decades. Not resigned to the Paraguayan example, England encouraged and subsidized Argentina, Brazil, and Uruguay to wage a war of destruction to kill every Paraguayan man.[4] Nowadays, Paraguayans, decimated in the last century, speak Guarani in informal situations in order to keep alive the experience of freedom.

Once the nation-states had been established, the indigenous peoples forgotten, and foreign interests always served, the governments took to expanding the agricultural borders and seeking new and interesting riches in the interior, treating the local peoples as a hindrance and obstruction to progress. Under these policies, their lands, lives, and societies were once again violated. The immigration of the nineteenth and twentieth centuries, on the other hand, also brought various other peoples, exiled from their homelands and deceived by false propaganda. The immigrants, who were independent workers, were treated in an equally inhuman fashion. Having no right to land in the nineteenth century, arriving as workers in an agricultural enterprise, they found themselves already in debt. There are innumerable examples of bad treatment, slavery, and misery. In the search for land and freedom, they ended up either accepting their fate or having to struggle for land in the already densely populated indigenous territories.

The nation-state and its individualist law denied all these groups any collective rights, and merely recognized their individual rights, crystallized in property. Thus, whoever benefited from economizing to establish a property was integrated into the system, while all the others would never become integrated—Indians, fugitive slaves, fishermen, riverside dwellers, rubber extractors, and small leaseholders living by gathering, hunting, fishing, and subsistence farming, maintaining strong relations with the community in order to live, and, not infrequently, while far from contact with civilization, living lives of abundance and happiness. However, they were always threatened, because if they found themselves living on land rich in plants or minerals, they were envied, cheated, and split up.

THE FALLACIOUS INTEGRATIONIST POLICY

The colonialist policy in America was characterized by the subjugation and integration of the peoples encountered. The cultural and economic subjugation consisted in forced religious and economic integration. There were two choices: either accept such a policy or be wiped out. The policy varied according to the violence and ambition of its maker. In the Prata basin, the Jesuits were sincere and concerned about the salvation of the souls of the Guarani people, while among the Incas and Aztecs, Pizarro and Cortés were violent and arrogant. There were cases of alarming ambition and aggression. Great peoples with access to technology and gold, such as the Chibchas (Muíscas) were utterly wiped out in a careful and efficient act of genocide during the conquest of Colombia.

Those who survived were able to serve the kingdom as workers, semi-slaves, or participants in the missions of "pacification" of other native peoples. It is probably for this reason that so many native peoples participated in the wars of independence in Latin America, always led by the Spanish or their descendants. In Brazil, which was a special case, independence was achieved without bloodshed by the heir to the throne of Portugal. It was a choice of the organization and division of the state and not an attempt to gain freedom.

The creation of Latin American nation-states, following the European model, led to the establishment of a constitution that set out a list of individual rights and guarantees. This meant forgetting their Indians and omitting all rights apart from the possibility of individual patrimonial acquisition. However, the Indians maintained the possibility of integration as individuals, as citizens, or, in legal terms, as individual subjects with legal rights. Gaining individual rights meant losing their rights as a people. Despite this, the peoples are still peoples. This attempt to integrate individual Indians was established in the Carta Régia of 1808 that declared war on the Botucudo Indians of Paraná, and stipulated that the prisoners would be obliged to serve the militia or residents who captured them for fifteen years. To those who put down their weapons, became subjects of the realm, and populated villages would be given the opportunity to enjoy the permanent benefits of a peaceful and lenient society living under just and humane laws (Souza Filho, 1988: 56).

Nevertheless, the public policies and laws for many years proposed to satisfy this will of the nation-states to integrate the peoples as citizens, legal subjects, able to negotiate legally, without recognizing their collective rights. From this perspective, the genocide continued, and each attempt at integrating these people meant the continuation of the state of war imposed when the Europeans arrived. Not only were the native people made invisible, but they also lost their very lives.

When the nation-states wrote their constitutions guaranteeing rights, they inaugurated a new system of justice with a number of dichotomies, such as the public and the private, the subject and the object of rights, based on private property, the legal security of freely established contracts, and the judicial solution of legal conflicts. This benefited property owners and those who held contracts, especially contracting parties, while the various native peoples, those living in communities, did not benefit from this system. In Latin America, the policies in relation to the indigenous peoples were those of integration. In other words, being indigenous was provisional. Many decades after the national constitutions were written, judicial protection of some indigenous rights began to appear, but this was always of a provisional character. In Brazil, in the twentieth century, indigenous laws stated that their goal was the integration of the Indians into the national community, and while this has not come about, some rights would have been granted. The first article of the present Indigenous Law in Brazil states that "it regulates the legal situation of the Indians or aborigines and of the indigenous communities, with the purpose of preserving their culture and integrating them progressively and harmoniously into the national community."[5]

It was not so in other parts of the world. Colonialism in Asia and Africa did not treat the local peoples in the same way, but maintained the colonies under policies of apartheid, the level of violence of which was in proportion to the resistance of the indigenous people. This meant that individual integration would only occur in exceptional cases. The consequence of this difference is that native peoples in America found it more difficult to continue living their lives according to their habits, customs, and traditions. The solution of their internal conflicts depended on the laws of the respective nation-states. Integration, in the case of Latin America, was proposed on the level of the individual. This meant the extinction of the native people.

In Brazil, each native people suffered differently from this policy; however, two fundamental methods can be easily observed. On the one hand, there was a policy of total omission, as if the native peoples did not exist and were merely a group of people who would be integrated sooner or later, while, on the other hand, there was a policy of consistent protection by creating remote refuges for the native peoples. Their traditional territories were not respected. This policy was especially applied in the Amazon. These two methods will be analyzed next, with historical examples to demonstrate the wide diversity of official policy.

THE INVISIBLE PEOPLES

The first method is the application of a classical assimilationist culture, in which there is no place for collectives that are situated between the citizen and the state. The invisibility with which the native peoples of the coast and the south of Brazil were treated is comparable to the lack of consideration given to the Peruvian indigenous people, as immortalized by the hero Garabombo the invisible (Scorza, n.d.).

To exemplify this situation of invisibility and the return to existence or rebirth (Souza Filho, 1998) I have chosen three cases: the Xetá people to the west of Paraná; the Guarani people, who occupy practically the whole southern region, and the people of the northeast, represented by the Pataxó Hãhãhãe. I have chose these three cases because the state totally ignored them in their public policies, and insisted on denying their existence for a considerable length of time. Those who survived resisted with such force that today their struggles have become the main land conflicts in Brazil, supported now in the collective laws recognized in the Constitution of 1988.

The Xetá people: chronology of a genocide

The Xetá people have not survived. Today there are about ten individuals living separately, some in villages loaned to them by the Kaigangues, others in cities of the region. But before they were wiped out by the merciless advance of the agricultural border, the Xetá controlled the jungle of the Serra de Douradas. With the arrival of the colonization company Suemitsu Miyamura & Co., the forests were burnt down, as the wood was of no interest. The plots of land were sold off to new occupiers. The history of the Xetá Indians is very recent, yet it is so similar to the accounts of Bartolomé de Las Casas in the sixteenth century that it makes one doubt the passage of time. In 1952 the new large landholders captured an 8-year-old boy by the name of Tikuein. The confirmation that the territory was occupied by a "primitive" people came in the following year with the capture of another boy who became a servant for the whites.

In December of 1954, six naked and unarmed men came across some landholders. They spoke and gesticulated in such a calm and peaceful way that the whites did not react, and let them leave. What these Xetá said has never been translated. It was never known whether it was an appeal for clemency or a threat, but it is certain that if it was a threat, nothing came of it, and if it was a plea for clemency, it was unheeded.

In 1955, the Federal University of Paraná and the national indigenous organ organized an expedition that found villages and objects that today can be seen in the Museum of Paraná. However, no Indians were located.

Perhaps what they wanted to say in the previous year was that they intended to leave. In the following year the expedition went further and located two peaceful groups who allowed photographs to be taken and film to be shot. They joked around and laughed, but did not accompany the expedition, who had wanted to accommodate them temporarily at the nearest ranch; they stayed in the forest. A few months later, one of the groups was massacred. The crime was never completely explained nor were the perpetrators brought to trial. Members of Parliament pressed for the creation of the national Park of Sete Quedas (the Seven Waterfalls),[6] inside of which was to be an area for the Xetá. The Xetá "reserve" was never created and a few years later this people was deemed extinct, removing any obstruction to the legitimization of private property in the region. The new colonialization firm, the Companhia Brasileira de Colonização e Imigração (Cobrinco), continued the devastating work, leaving not a single tree standing, and with the last copse of the forest died the hope of finding a member of the Xetá alive. The massacre had ended. Still, today a few Xetá survive outside their culture and the forest, which had sheltered them. Indeed, the forest itself has been transformed into vast plantations of cotton and soy and is riddled with textile factories. Not even the beauty of the Sete Quedas remains, flooded by the Itaipu reservoir, as if nature remains silent in homage to the death of the people who were always so close to it.

In 2000, FUNAI, the Brazilian indigenous organization, organized a study group to create a Xetá area, with the idea of accommodating the last dozen individuals who still survive, and maintaining the memory and the history of a people destined to die.[7]

The Guarani's long road in search of a land of freedom

If the history of contact with the Xetá was fulminant, the relationship of the Guarani with "civilization" has been very different. The Guarani appear in the texts written by the first Spanish chroniclers who went up the Paraná and Paraguay rivers. They were used as domestic slaves and were present in the cities of Buenos Aires and Asunción from the sixteenth century on. Throughout these five hundred years, they became so visible that a conflict broke out between Portugal and Spain, based on the Society of Jesus. They were once deemed practically extinct, and then once again became, in more recent times, the most populous indigenous people in Brazil. The Guarani gave Paraguay a national language, the toponymy of almost all of its geographical features, especially the rivers and mountains, and the names of innumerable cities in the south of Brazil. Nowadays it is common to see Guaranis in the streets of coastal cities in discreet conversations conducted in their native tongue.

The trajectory of contact with the Guarani is curious. In 1607, the Jesuits chose the region in which today stands the city of Asunción, the capital of Paraguay, as their headquarters in the south. The idea of converting the Indians was linked to that of building, based on the Guarani's social organization and the Jesuit concept of state and law, an independent model of organization that was known as "Jesuit missionary returns." Persecuted by "bandeirante" violence[8] in Portuguese territory and by representatives of the king in Spanish lands, the Guarani finally embraced not only Christianity but also life in the new villages, a life that was a blend of Guarani tradition and Jesuit social organization, with significant alterations in the division of labor. Apart from this, they maintained their beliefs, traditions, and customs, including their language. With the defeat of the Jesuits and their expulsion from South America, the Guarani also were dispersed throughout the territory. They accepted the encroachment of the agricultural boundary, and were not particularly concerned about the non-Indians who arrived in the region.

Traditionally, the Guarani shared their territory with other native peoples, and managed to live in relative harmony. They were great travelers and sought the land of freedom they knew lay to the east. The official policy of the Brazilian government in relation to them was one of total omission. They are for that reason an invisible people. In the states of Rio Grande do Sul, Santa Catarina, Paraná and São Paulo, they were deemed extinct and had practically no designated or reserved land for their exclusive use. In Mato Grosso do Sul, at the beginning of the century, their lands were occupied and given over in development programs to white immigrants. The Indians, who were seen as a labor force for the businesses, apparently accepted employment on the ranches given access to their sacred lands.

They always accepted sharing their territory with other peoples. In their cosmology, the gods created the earth for them. Thus, its use by other peoples was of secondary concern. They knew, however, that somewhere there existed a land of freedom, which they sought incessantly. They did not imagine that the new inhabitants had such different habits from the Kaingangues, Charruas, and Xoclengs with whom they had shared their territory from time immemorial. They neither knew nor believed that the use of the land by the new inhabitants was devastating and implied the death of local flora and fauna in order to facilitate the introduction of new plants and tame animals, all of which were raised by men. In order to survive, and while not integrated individually as independent workers in the local society, the Guarani collectively were given small plots of land to which they were dramatically confined. Nevertheless, they were never integrated.

In this way, the Guarani, lords of a vast territory and culture, came to live in the three southern states, on land lent to them in the territories of other peoples and in Mato Grosso, where they were confined. Despite this situation, they continued to search for the land of freedom. On this journey, keeping themselves half hidden, they left the destroyed forests in search of other forests they might inhabit. They established themselves in more and more remote places, untouched by private property. Nowadays, important Guarani areas are located in places considered "untouchable" by civilization, parks, and other conservation groups. Perplexed, then, they ask themselves where they should go. They are aware that the whole of the immense territory that they have forever thought of as only theirs is not and never was. However, those with whom they share it treat it strangely. They kill the rivers, destroy the forests, kill the animals, and make criminals of the Guarani for living in the last areas of virgin forest. Thus, a conflict of rights clearly occurs. On the one hand, one has the Guarani living, or trying to live, in the last areas of rainforest held sacred by them and, on the other hand, environmentalists who, with the best intentions, are concerned about saving the last forests, or "sanctuaries," which implies that they should be completely uninhabited.

The recognition of collective, native rights and the rights of everyone to an ecologically balanced environment, as laid down in the Brazilian Constitution of 1988, provoked an apparent conflict between the Guarani and the collective rights of all the parks and other conservation groups. As we shall see, this contradiction is only apparent, because there is a solution; however, it goes against the old system of the individual rights of landowners. The Guarani are not only extremely knowledgeable about the earth, its plant and animal life, but also about the sky and the stars. This great people, shy and reserved, are an example of invisibility. Their cause is not just about land, about a territory, but essentially about collective rights to its development, which includes the land, but goes beyond that. The acceptance of collective rights by the system has helped this people to become visible.

The renaissance of the Pataxó Hãhãhãe

The most striking example, however, of the renaissance of indigenous collective will is located in the northeast of Brazil. It was there that under five hundred years of European occupation the majority of the native peoples were wiped out or forced into exile. The native peoples contacted in the 1950s in Matogrosso, almost 2,000 kilometers in the interior, proved to be from the northeast coast.[9] The history of the Pataxó Hãhãhãe stands out. In the 1930s, their territorial rights having been recognized, the Pataxó Hãhãhãe were granted an area of approximately 50,000 hectares in the southern part of the state of Bahia. Twenty years later, the region was transformed into a great cocoa producing area, which brought the region to the attention of other interested parties. The Brazilian state took measures to ensure the integration of the Pataxó Hãhãhãe Indians, that is, it provided them with education and work in far-off places, relocating the few remaining families to other indigenous areas, including one that served as a prison, called, ironically, the Guarani Ranch. The Pataxó Hãhãhãe were deemed extinct and their lands went to ranchers.

Less than thirty years later, in the 1980s, the individual members of the Pataxó Hãhãhãe, believed to be integrated and content in their lives as Brazilian citizens and as independent workers, gradually began to regroup. In a daring symbolic act, they reclaimed and occupied one of the ranches that had been set up on their lands. This sparked a conflict, which has lasted twenty years and claimed many lives. The first group was joined by other groups, new families who recognized themselves and were recognized as Pataxó Hãhãhãe, who, rejoicing, remembered their common ancestors and reaffirmed their status as Indians, as a people, as a collective. The state and the local elite denied them this status, and do so to this day. This has forced them to appeal to the law in order to have their rights recognized.

There are a number of legal cases that have to do with indigenous rights in the region currently being judged. The most important one, which defines the indigenous character of the whole area, is so well constructed and proven that technically it is impossible to rule against the Pataxó Hãhãhãe. At present, a decision by the Supreme Court is expected. In the meantime, taking action as spectacular as it is efficient, this native people are reconquering their former land. After the first ranch was retaken in 1982, many others went the same way. The Indians have regained something in the region of 5000 hectares of that which was attributed to them in the 1930s (Ricardo, 1996; 2000).

In 1988, when the constitution was passed, further progress was made in their rights, but the process was still very slow. In 1997, the murder of Hãhãhãe Galdino dos Santos in Brasilia, mistaken for a beggar and burned alive as a macabre joke by children of the local elite, unexpectedly made visible the question of their rights that for almost ten years had been recognized by the constitution but had not yet been implemented.[10] In 1999, the Pataxó Hãhãhãe were subjected to further violence when they were subdued by the military police of the state of Bahia. Two police officers died in an unexplained operation and the Indians were accused of causing the deaths. Throughout the trial nothing was proven, but the impression was given that the police had died at the hands of their own colleagues.

The Pataxó Hãhãhãe have mobilized on two fronts: 1) legally, in the Federal Supreme Court for the recognition of all of their land; and 2) by direct action, by reoccupying ranches and further regrouping as a people. They have become visible and today are recognized and present. However, they still have a long way to go before all their rights are recognized.[11]

The history of the Hãhãhãe resembles that of other native peoples who managed to survive in the northeast. Ignored by the state, they continued to exist. Their language was mutilated, their dignity slighted, and frequently were they split up, recruited as integrated individuals into the developing society. Like the Hãhãhãe, many other native peoples of the northeast began to regroup and reconquer small areas of land. With the advent of the Constitution of 1988, their claims were anchored in the collective rights therein guaranteed.

THE EQUIVOCATIONS OF
THE CONTACT POLICIES IN THE AMAZON

In none of the above examples did the state organize expeditions to make contact with the native peoples before the arrival of the agricultural border. On the contrary, expeditions of a scientific nature or later official studies could do nothing to limit the violent, disorganized, and crushing shock caused by the colonizing companies.

Sometimes, however, especially in the Amazon, the Brazilian state sought to protect native peoples in certain circumstances, favoring the widening of the agricultural borders and the concentration of native peoples in certain places, like the Indigenous National Park of Xingú, even if it was not their original land. At other times, the state felt itself obliged to keep the native people on their traditional land; still, though in the guise of protector, it seriously interfered with their culture. This brought about new situations, which it was and still is not prepared to resolve. It can be said then that while the Brazilian state in its public policies ignored the indigenous peoples beyond the Amazon, being not in the slightest bit concerned about the resulting ethnic destruction, in the Amazon itself there was an effort to make contact. This contact preceded the expansion of the agricultural boundary, after which came roads, much construction work, adventurers looking for gold and precious stones, and merchants and migrants from other areas in search of their fortune or simply the place of their dreams. On the contact fronts, as they were called, there was no agreement on what should be done once contact had been made, apart from the general idea, stemming from colonial times, of offering the Indians the gentle laws of the empire, that is, integration into the national community.

As there was, and still is, no agreement on how to deal with contacted natives, some initiatives became particularly relevant, such as the Indigenous Park of Xingú, where the contacted natives could maintain their traditions. For that reason, the policy of transferring Indians from their traditional lands to other areas came to be the accepted norm, albeit an illegal norm according to current legislation, dated from 1973, which prohibits the transference of native peoples. After the Constitution of 1988, this policy changed. There are no longer concerted efforts to make contact with new native peoples, despite the fact that many are still unknown in the Amazon.

The Constitution of 1988 made it possible for the native peoples who had been victims of this abandoned policy to reclaim their rights. Such is the case of the Panará, which will be presented next. Other native peoples of the Amazon, who were not transferred, had their lands recognized, but the lack of public policy and disorganized action led to profound social changes, as exemplified by the indigenous cities of the Amazon.

Capitulation and the return of the "giant Indians"

The Panará were renowned as great warriors and were feared in the whole region. They lived on the left bank of the river that has the Western name of Peixoto de Azevedo. Just before 1970, the civilized world knew that there was gold at the mouth of the river and precious stones further upstream. But they also knew that exploration would mean having to put down Panará resistance. As not even their name was known, strange names were given to them, borrowed from other languages of the region and from the reports of their traditional enemies, the Krenacarore, Kranhacãrore and Keen Akarore. Alternatively, they were simply referred to as the giant Indians, as one of the first to be captured was 2.06m tall (Panará, 1988).

The Brazilian government, which did not expound the merits of development, decided to build a road linking Cuiabá to Santarém, crossing the full length of the eastern Amazon and passing right through Panará land. The machines, and behind them the adventurers, pioneers, representatives, and businessmen, came right up to the territory on the banks of the river Peixoto de Azevedo. Facing them were the dreaded giant Indians.

To convince the Indians not to be hostile towards the construction of the road and, naturally, those who would follow, an expedition was organized, led by the Villas-Bôas brothers.[12] After five years of intense work, a few deaths and many stories, the giant Indians were "appeased" and allowed the road through, which brought those in search of wood, gold and precious stones, and also influenza, measles, diarrhea and hunger. The survivors tell of not being strong enough even to bury the dead strewn along the path, let alone hunt or open a clearing. They have ended up living on the charity of those passing through.

Very soon, the giant Indians were no more than a pale caricature of the noble people who appeared in photographs in the national press for the first time on 10 February 1973. The statistics are daunting: of a population estimated to have been between 300 and 600 before contact was made by the Villas-Bôas brothers' expedition, as of 1975, when they were transferred from their lands, there were merely 79.

Moribund, their dignity as a people wounded, humiliated, begging for a crust of bread, they were taken from their fertile lands to a village in the middle of the Indigenous Park of Xingú.[13] Either by irony or the cruel turns of history, the village lent to them as their new home belonged to a traditional enemy, the Caiapó, to whom in the past they had shown only minimal respect, a situation brought about by wars and mutual aggression. The Panará lived humiliated in the house of their enemies for twenty years, hoping to return one day to their territory, reconquer their land, their home and once again live among the animals, plants, and rivers so close to them.

Twenty years later, in 1995, the Panará began to struggle in earnest to return home. Encouraged by the victories of other native peoples who had been brought to live in the Xingú, and of others, such as those in the northeast, who hoped to recover the lands that had once been theirs, the Panará undertook a journey to what was their region and found that a fifth of the original territory had been preserved. Organized with the help of non-governmental organizations such as the Socioenvironmental Institute (O Instituto Socioambiental, or ISA), they brought two cases against the Brazilian state and FUNAI (The National Foundation for Indians [Fundação Nacional do Índio]).[14] The first asserted a legal claim over the land, and the second compensation for damages. In the first case an agreement was reached in which the state recognized native rights over a part of the original territory that was yet preserved (the remainder was already occupied, and even had cities). The second case, also supported by the ISA, claimed damages from the Brazilian state and those responsible for indigenous affairs for ill treatment at the moment of contact. The court recognized the illegal character of the contact and of the relocation of the Indians to the Indigenous Park of Xingú, and awarded damages to the surviving Indians. As of this writing, the ruling had not yet been issued, due to formal questions, but the case has been tried and will be settled shortly.

This ruling indicates a change in the behavior of the judicial system because the case was based on collective rights established in the Constitution of 1988, even though the events took place before it came into being.

Villages surrounding cities: a new threat to native rights

When the arrival of the agricultural frontier did not mean extermination or relocation, the native peoples basically continued living normally on their lands, which had been demarcated after legal disputes or direct appeals to the constitution. This is true of many native peoples in the Amazon, among them the Ticuna. Despite having appealed to the law for recognition of their territories, the Ticuna had no problem in seeing them demarcated by the Brazilian government. Their lands were demarcated in the 1990s, that is, with the constitution in full force, the indigenous policy already changed, and with collective rights respected.

The Ticuna are one of the most numerous of the indigenous peoples of the Amazon and inhabited a vast territory that included the three borders of Brazil, Colombia, and Peru. The agricultural frontier had not advanced much into this region, despite the fact that navigation was open, due to the proximity of the port of Rio Solimões. Nevertheless, the Ticuna were obliged to appeal to the law in order to have their main lands recognized.

The territories are extensive, but the agency responsible for indigenous affairs and religious missions concentrated their efforts on small villages on the banks of the great river. In the course of the last few years the small village ports have grown in an unprecedented way. The concentration, however, did not lead to the arrival of farmers or outsiders, but to the strengthening of the will of the people to join together where it was easier to receive the benefits of contact. These villages grew at such an alarming rate that some had as many as one, two, or even four thousand inhabitants.[15] In fact, the so-called Belém do Solimões is a real city, with four thousand people living on badly planned roads and with no urban infrastructure whatsoever: no sanitation, paving, water, or other services.

The cities of the Ticuna are clearly visible because they are located on the banks of a large navigable river, but it is not this that determines the phenomenon. Indigenous urbanization in the Amazon began to spread and reached far distant and almost inaccessible regions. In the region of the upper river Negro, near the border between Brazil and Colombia, Iauareté is a city of two thousand multi-ethnic inhabitants living with no infrastructure.[16] The city grew so much that a number of small businesses were set up. Immediately after the demarcation of the area (in 1998), the Indians expelled the whites and took over control of the city.

In the region of Raposa Serra do Sol, on the border with Venezuela and Guyana, at least two other indigenous cities are growing and facing very serious problems. In these cities there is a non-indigenous local population, even if small, and the government of the state of Roraima has turned one of them into the seat of the municipality. The indigenous territory where these cities are found has not been demarcated and the anti-indigenous, local politicians are struggling to prevent demarcation by using, of course, the existence of the cities as an argument.

All of these peoples still live in their traditional ways, with barely any consumer goods, and yet with unthought-of urban problems. Brazilian legislation offers no solution. There is no political organization, no representation, not even tax collection. These are new situations from which the indigenous populations are looking for an exit. It is interesting to note that in the argument in Raposa Serra do Sol, where the territory has not yet been demarcated, there are those who defend the present organization of the state with the exclusion of non-indigenous use.

All of the examples cited here and in the previous section serve only to give some indication of the cultural diversity of Brazil, with its more than two hundred different peoples and more than 170 spoken languages, but it is enough to begin a socio-legal reflection on the successes and failures of the state, on sovereignty, citizenship, and international relations, including the consequences of globalization in these areas of the world that insist on the local.

THE NEW LAWS IN LATIN AMERICA

The nation-states of Latin America, with their history of extreme shifts, of dictatorships alternating with formal democracies, are very similar to one another. Portuguese and Spanish colonialism were linked in time and by violence. The historic moment of the outbreak of the wars of independence was more or less synchronized, those involved were similar and the same hopes were frustrated. Founded at the beginning of the nineteenth century, the relation of these states with the native peoples in their territories is also similar. They inherited a common colonial past, used the native peoples in the wars of independence, and believed they would be able to integrate them as citizens, guaranteeing them individual rights, including land ownership, while commonly ignoring their customs, traditions, languages, beliefs, and territory. When in conflict, these states dragged the native peoples into sordid wars or subjected them to direct repression. The rights of the indigenous people, because collective, were omitted from written legislation.

During the Cold War, the majority of the states in Latin America became military dictatorships in order to put down popular movements. Thus, the 1960s and 1970s are characterized by military states, and the indigenous question also became a military one. In the 1980s, a long period of tension began. Many arguments occurred and the countries were led to rewrite their constitutions. Indigenous organizations and civil society took part in discussions on the new constitutions, defending collective rights, founded in a recognized manner on the cultural diversity of each country. The threat of environmental devastation led to the native peoples returning to their lands, and groups organized by environmentalists joined with indigenous organizations and indigenous supporters in collective claims. The new constitutions began to emerge. They were clearly concerned about multiculturalism and multi-ethnicity and the preservation of the environment. Alongside the homogenizing individualism was a pluralism of great social, cultural, and natural diversity, in a perspective that could be called socio-environmental.

Thus, each constitution established collective rights alongside absolute and exclusive individual rights. The local populations discussed the range of this new phenomenon that came to contradict the growing hegemonic perception of post-Berlin Wall capitalism, which put forward the end of local cultures.[17]

Once again, the Latin American nation-states reaffirmed their similarities. The constitutional legal systems, having refused in the past to recognize multiculturalism and multi-ethnicity, now one by one began to accept that the countries of the continent were made up of a variety of ethnicities and cultures and that each group was organized according to its culture and was living according to its traditions, in harmony with nature, of which each is a part, and that each has the right to choose their own development.

The main characteristic of these new rights is the fact that they were not individual. They did not stem from a legal relation, but merely from a fundamental guarantee that had to be honored and that, in doing so, would end up determining the exercise of individual rights. This means that collective rights do not spring from a specific legal relation but from a reality—how to belong to a people or form a group that needs or wants clean air, water, forests, and the traces of their culture preserved, or even a guarantee of life in society, a job, a house, and the guarantee of the quality of goods bought.

This characteristic distances them from the concept of individual rights conceived in its entirety in the contractualist or constitutionalist culture of the nineteenth century, because it is a law without a subject. Or, put in terms that might seem even more confusing to individualist thought, it is a law to which everyone is subjected. If everyone is subjected to the same law, everyone can appeal to it, but at the same time nobody can benefit from it, since a benefit to one party would be an infringement of the rights of others.

If we were to analyze each of the constitutions rewritten in the 1980s we would see that they are very similar, although they might use different terminologies. Paraguay's, for example, apart from recognizing the existence of the indigenous peoples, declared that the country was multicultural and bilingual, and considered the remaining languages to be the cultural heritage of the nation (Paraguay, 1992, Art. 140). The Colombian constitution established that "The Colombian state recognizes and protects the ethnic and cultural diversity of the Colombian nation" (Colombia, 1991, Art. 7). As a sign of the times, the new American constitutions recognized social diversity more and more. Mexico (in 1992) assumed that it has a "multicultural makeup"; Peru in its constitution approved in 1993 did not go so far and merely accepted Quechua, Aimara, and other "aboriginal" languages as official alongside Castilian. Finally, in 1995, Bolivia, with its prominent indigenous majority, broke the silent integrationist tradition and defined itself as multi-ethnic and multicultural, while Argentina ordered its Congress to recognize the pre-existence of the indigenous peoples. Other constitutions, such as that of Brazil (1988) and Nicaragua (1987), although steering clear of the words "diversity" or "pluralism," define the rights of indigenous peoples and protect them.

This same recognition is apparent in international agreements, such as Convention 169 of the International Labor Organization (A Organização Internacional do Trabalho, or OIT), dated 26 June 1989. Both the United Nations and the Organization of American States (A Organização dos Estados Americanos, or OEA) have debated declarations along the same lines. This agreement does not mean that Latin American countries have accepted international norms, which proves the insincerity of the local elites who always imagine that their constitutions can be invalidated for legal reasons (by failing to pass regulatory laws demanded by the Constitution). For this reason, they allow the inclusion of progressive changes in their constitutions only because they control the regulatory process that will restrict the ambit of application of such changes. If accepted in real terms, the international norms, especially Convention 169, would provoke a revolutionary transformation of both the constitutions and the regulatory legislation. These rights, however, are not exclusively indigenous. The constitutions of Colombia and Brazil go out of their way to recognize the rights of traditional black communities, and all those who recognize collective rights fundamentally admit that other communities can claim them. The collapse of the individualist paradigm is set in the constitution and its coming into effect is the question put to local communities, movements, and groups.[18]

APPLYING THE LAW, AND ITS DIFFICULTIES

Apart from the fact that a decade has gone by since the recognition of these collective rights, it cannot be said that there has been significant progress in their application. There is no doubt that indigenous territorial rights in the region beyond the agricultural boundary, especially in the Amazon, came to be more readily recognized than in the previous period. The example of the Panará is evidence of this. Apart from being forced to appeal to the law, the Panará gained rights over the territory from which they had previously been removed. There are other examples, like that of the Indigenous Area's Yanomami and the territory of the native peoples of the Upper Negro river, among many others.[19]

In the regions where there is political pressure and stronger economic interests, progress has not been so significant. An important factor in the application of judicial protectionist norms has been the international visibility of the indigenous peoples. That is, those native people who succeed in drawing international attention to their local problems have had more success in bringing protectionist rules into effect.

The judiciary has had a prevalent role in the application of these new rights, but has maintained a conservative position most of the time. The judicial tools are reasonably well constructed in Latin America and are an addition to instruments that serve other collective rights fundamentally recognized by the population, such as the right to an ecologically balanced environment and to one's cultural heritage. Despite this, indigenous populations have gained little directly from the public administration. Generally, to obtain rights it has been necessary to appeal to the law, as in the case of the Panará. This limits the scope of action of the indigenous peoples, who need to create organizations along Western parameters rather than traditional ones in order to achieve recognition of their rights, even in the Amazon.

Outside the Amazon, the situation is even more difficult. Some native peoples of the northeast have had their existence recognized, that is, they have come to be treated as indigenous peoples, a status that they had lost to the national state due to their apparent integration into the regional population. Upon recognizing their existence, the state allocated to them a small and insufficient territory, which was not sufficient to allow their culture to flourish. It was not even enough on which to survive. The expansion of their rights, however, brought new possibilities. The judicial action that is holding back the Pataxó Hãhãhãe, which as described earlier is being decided in the Federal Supreme Court, has gained new impetus, but is taking an exaggeratedly slow path. From a technical point of view, it is impossible for the Pataxó Hãhãhãe to lose the case. The question is when it will be resolved. They live in a region of strong political opposition and have powerful enemies among the local elite.

In light of the 1988 Constitution, the Federal Supreme Court has already passed judgment on a number of other cases with the same characteristics as that of the Pataxó Hãhãhãe. One of them was the Krenak case, in Vale do Rio Doce, in Minas. This became prominent historically when indigenous lands (which were similar to those of the Pataxó Hãhãhãe) that had been distributed to farmers in the 1950s were returned to the Krenak. All that is lacking is political will in the highest authority of the country to make the decision and confront the regional political situation. It is true that in the Vale do Rio Doce those whose interests were at stake were small ranch owners, who at most had influence in local municipal governments, while in the case of the Pataxó Hãhãhãe in Bahia, a cocoa-producing region, political influence is on a national level.

Apart from the political circumstances, the judicial disputes over land in Brazil are still strongly influenced by individual rights established in the nineteenth century, with their preferential option for individual ownership of the land. The individualist and absolute character of ownership of land has been a distinctive feature of Western law and the basis of Latin American civil law. The peoples of this continent tried, in the twentieth century, to make laws which would promote a change in this absolute character: from the remarkable Mexican Constitution of 1917, on through various laws of agrarian reform, including the powerful Bolivian Law of 1952, to the Chilean experiment of Salvador Allende in the 1970s, whose tragic and violent end appalled America.

With the exception of Cuba, no other country can seriously put land ownership in question. Laws originating in the Bolivian revolution of 1952, and subsequent Colombian and Venezuelan laws could offer theoretical interpretations that led to the structuring of a new concept of land ownership, characterized by the idea of its social function. However, even this concept came to be absorbed by the elites to the point of identifying social function with capitalist productivity. In other words, the social function of all land was to provide revenue for production. Social function, as such, is beyond this idea. There is no sense of its role as an integrator of cultures and a protector of the ecologically balanced environment, guaranteeing the life of the planet.

With the advent of collective rights, it became more and more clear that the land would have to fulfill this social role, or socio-environmental role, as the protector of the environment and the cultures associated with it. But a territory controlled by a single group is a characteristic of the judicial culture of Latin America, whether from the point of view of public or private law, disputing absolute and meticulously demarcated sovereignties, including unknown regions, or transforming all the land into private lots. For this reason, apart from the legal changes introduced by the constitutions, it is still very difficult for judges to interpret the law against the interests of private property.

This position of the judges explains the greater tendency towards decisions in favor of the Indians in areas not of predominantly private property, such as the Amazon. Inside the agricultural boundaries, private enterprise culture has already been established, creating greater difficulty. The indigenous organizations and peoples face restrictive interpretations of their rights. The question is put in such a way that in the Amazon, most of the time, conflict occurs between traditional populations, with guaranteed collective rights, and trespassers, adventurers, drug dealers, prospectors, and others with no rights whatsoever. Inside the agricultural boundary, however, confrontations spring up between traditional populations who were stripped of their rights by the government and the people who received these same tracts as returned land.[20] Thus, confrontation breaks out between traditional populations and individual landowners considered legitimate by the system.

Moreover, this conflict is at the very heart of the new decree that controls the administrative procedure for the demarcation of indigenous lands, because the Federal government decided that, once a particular land was deemed indigenous, all those with claims would have to be called by edict to determine whether there was anybody with individual rights over it.[21] The reinterpretation given by the federal government made the process of demarcation difficult and also made all the previous demarcations dubious. The publication of the decree was a victory for anti-indigenous property interests, but the mobilization of the Indians, their organizations and the organizations that support them saw to it that, in practical terms, the rulings against the Indians did not have the feared impact. Perhaps the clearest example of the difficulty in regulating the collective rights established in the constitution is that of the general law concerning the indigenous peoples of Brazil. The old Indian Act (Estatuto do Índio) of 1973, still in place, has an individualist, integrationist, and legally civil profile, and for that very reason attributed to the legal institutions of protection a provisional character; that is, it was relevant only until the Indians individually became integrated in the national community as citizens without qualification and without ethnic distinction, in other words, until they stopped being Indians.

Since the publication of the new constitution, the indigenous organizations and their allies have begun to mobilize by rewriting the general law, which today should be called the Indigenous Peoples' Act, and with its contents including collective rights. Many versions were written and much discussion took place. A version was approved by a Commission of the National Congress, but by direct order of the President of the Republic, Fernando Henrique Cardoso, just elected for a first term, it was removed from the list before he took office in December 1994. Since then, due to a strange and unacknowledged government interest, the Act has remained in a kind of legislative "freeze."

There have been a number of polemic issues, such as the use of the natural resources of the forest, the mineral wealth, and the protection of traditional knowledge having to do with biodiversity. However, it does not seem to be these issues that are complicating the approval of the project. It was only in 1999 that legislative discussion of the statute was reopened, and it became clear then that the main obstacle to its approval, on the part of the government, was the old and already resolved integrationist question. Prior to the Constitution of 1988, the government wanted to maintain a conservative position and keep the indigenous cultures provisional. The immediate advisors to the President of the Republic defended an individualist concept dealing with personal integration and the loss of indigenous identity. This concept clearly was formed prior to the Statute of 1973.[22]

The President of the Republic had to intervene directly, and convened a meeting with the main indigenous leaders of the country in April 2000 so that the advisory committee might renounce its position and allow the legislative process for the writing of a statute that put constitutional rules into practice to begin again.[23]

This fact demonstrates the extreme difficulty in applying current principles upon which a new relation between the indigenous peoples and the Brazilian state is to be based. Conservative sectors hold on to the fixed idea that the Indians are a nuisance to the process of development, and use all of their power to diminish, restrain, and limit, not only the possibility of demarcating the land, but its use according to the customs and traditions of each people. Alongside the conservative sectors stand the military and those with interests in the local economy, who are often protected by judges, courts of law, and important civil servants, such as the President's group of advisors.

On the other hand, the right to be recognized as a people has been steadily gaining momentum among indigenous groups. During these years under the new constitution, there have been large-scale mobilizations of indigenous peoples and of groups of indigenous people seeking the application of collective rights. To the examples already cited, among them the case of the Panará, can be added many others, such as the indigenous organizations of the peoples of the Amazon, of the northwest, the Guarani, etc.

The current organizations and indigenous movements with claims are significantly different from those before 1988. The present movements claim rights that can be understood by the system, given that they always defend collective rights. Before the constitution, these were utopian demands, dreams that now have achieved the status of claims. These dreams became law and are an element in what lawyers refer to as the catalogue of fundamental rights recognized by the constitution. Thus, these claims can be put forward not merely as a political hope but as a judicial fact; without ever leaving the streets they can reach the chambers of the courts; they must be recognized by the public administration, and yet when they are not, they can be guaranteed in judicial rulings. This has led to the indigenous and also the popular movement gaining another important dimension—the legal dimension.

SHARED TERRITORIALITY

The names that Brazilian law has given throughout time to indigenous territories reveal the content attributed to sanctioned rights. "Reserve" was the word used in the Land Law of 1850, Law no. 601. It maintained the idea both of reserving a territorial space for the indigenous peoples who were found during colonization and of distributing the land, referred to as "the organization of the land," to those with capital to invest. Indians had to stay on the reserved lands until they had learned to perform a "civilized" job and could be integrated into national life. Although reserved, the rights were provisional, though always linked to a territorial space.

The word "area" was also used, before finally arriving at "indigenous land." The word "territory" was never used; on the contrary, it was deliberately avoided. "Land" is the legal term to describe individual property, public or private; "territory" is the legal term used to describe a jurisdictional space. Thus, "territory" is a collective space that belongs to an indigenous people. The same ideology, which denies the existence of the indigenous people, as we shall later see, denies the use of the term "territory." Apart from this, indigenous rights in Latin America are always linked to a territorial space, however it is referred to.

The idea of a provisional reserve to be used while individuals learn a job that will allow them to be integrated into the Brazilian national community (which in most instances transforms indigenous peoples into peasants) is now outdated. The new constitution is characterized by the recognition of collective rights, which include the right to determine individual courses of development and the right to a territory. This collective right does not go so far, however, as to allow self-determination to become a state. The fear of the conservative sectors, especially the military, is that struggles for indigenous rights may become struggles for freedom or independence. From this stems the real fear of referring to them as "indigenous peoples," of using the word "territory" and the category of "self-determination."

The Bolivian Constitution recognizes all the rights of the indigenous groups as rights given to peoples, but does not refer to them as such. It guarantees that the natural authorities of the indigenous communities are responsible for the administration and application of their own rules, including alternative solutions to conflicts, but refers to their territories as "original common land" (Bolivia, 1995, Art. 171). Moreover, in 1994, the Law of Popular Participation was passed,[24] the intent of which was to "recognize, promote, and consolidate the process of popular participation, articulating the indigenous communities, both rural and urban, in the legal, political, and economic life of the country." To this end, citizens were tied to a specific, territorial space on the basis of popular participation. As a result, they became politically organized. The entity of popular participation thus came to be called OTB—Organizaciones Territoriales de Base.

The struggle for participation, for the recognition of collective rights, is common to practically every Latin American state, which have reinvented the legal system in order to recognize these collective guarantees and make possible new perspectives of local life. However, in Latin American law, the local is always linked to a territorial space. Native peoples and the rights inferred by a particular territorial space are beyond the system. The recognition of the collective rights of indigenous peoples is, thus, defined by a territory, and it is necessary to situate it in a territory in order to comply with the system.

Precisely this relation of collective rights with territory is at the root of the limited rights attributed to the populations of African origin, which as much in Brazil as in Colombia have rights recognized in demarcated spaces, as remnants of the old communities that lived hidden from the slave system. This right does not extend to other descendants.

Territoriality is just as important in the protection of environmental collective rights, another recently created category. The judicial system came to protect territorial spaces that can be referred to as "conservation units." Such territorial spaces are defined by the function they fulfill, or can fulfill, such as border forests, or because they contain preserved biotas. Generally, the preserved areas, for whatever reason, are either inaccessible or still beyond the agricultural boundary. Among the causes of this inaccessibility is the presence of indigenous people who are struggling for their legal title to the land, as is the case with large stretches of the Amazon.[25] Thus, when the native people and their rights are determined by a territory, apart from the difficulties already referred to, it has been possible to recognize them and guarantee them. A major problem arises when there are no territorial limits laid down, as in the case of the Gypsies, or when the limitation is not clear, as in the case of the Guarani.

In fact, there are native peoples who have always accepted the possibility of sharing their territory with others, of different cultures living together with great respect. Many demarcated indigenous lands are homes to more than one people, such as the Indigenous Land of the Upper Negro river with its twenty different ethnic groups. The problem of sharing the territory is exclusively that of the native peoples who live there, as long as it is demarcated and recognized by the respective national state (Ricardo, 2000: 243).

In the Guarani territory, as has already been noted, this does not apply. Other peoples, such as the Kaingang and the Xocleng, lived in the space that the Guarani thought of as their own. For this reason, it was not so serious when whites also arrived and occupied a part of these lands. The difference is that the whites did not only occupy, but profoundly changed the biota, altering the nature of the lands. Plants and animals were substituted, accidents of geography were altered, forests were destroyed, hills were flattened, lakes were built, and marshes were dried out.

The Guarani, who, because of their rights, shared the territories, began to feel more and more evicted from their own land since they could no longer recognize the places where the spirits of their ancestors appeared and where they received advice and punishment from the gods. The land was not what it used to be, and with its disappearance there was no longer any sense in sharing the territory. The Guarani, travelers in time and space, sought the right to continue living in areas of their territory where they were familiar with the animals and plants and the accidents of geography, a place they could understand and in which they could be understood. These places, though, are those that civilization or current law considers as property subject to collective rights, the property of all. An ecologically balanced environment is here under protection. And so, as the interpreters of the law have it, human beings are not accepted. The areas of conservation, or the spaces that have survived devastation, must remain untouched.

Two collective rights, here, are in conflict. But it is a false conflict because both sides seek to protect and preserve a territory against the devastation of private property and the individual right to accumulate property, including forests. It is a false conflict because the Indians are not only protecting the forest but also protecting the knowledge that springs from it, including the secrets of its rebirth. The Guarani know every plant and how it relates to animals and soils and, by reinforcing this or that collective right and confronting individual rights and their strange privileges, it is possible to dream of another law being passed. From the dryness of the old individual right, a rose might grow.

By accepting the collective rights of native peoples, the possibility of claiming rights that are not territorial appears on the horizon, even though sometimes they appear linked to an area of land, such as the Guarani's. A typical example is that of the area of the Pankararu people, originally from the northeast of Brazil, but who immigrated to the southeast, living finally in the shantytowns of São Paulo. This group's claim is not to return to their traditional territory, where the majority of their relations live, but to obtain a rural, cultural space in São Paulo, where sacred plants can be grown and rituals practiced far from the prying eyes of fearful and often violent neighbors.[26] Another people who have never claimed exclusive territory but who have begun to claim rights, given that a less secret, because less dangerous, life is clearly possible, is the gypsies.

On the other hand, the problem does not end once the land has been demarcated, even if it is an area large enough for its inhabitants, as was shown by the disorganized urbanization and the unforeseen creation of indigenous cities in the Amazon.

ECONOMIC, SOCIAL, CULTURAL, AND ENVIRONMENTAL RIGHTS

Clearly, collective rights, especially those of indigenous peoples, are not limited to the question of territory. They go beyond, indeed, to the very heart of the right to development, to human, economic, social, cultural, and environmental rights. The difference between these rights and those established in international agreements on human rights is in the collective character that they acquire. For that reason, they represent something new to the judicial system and makes its emancipatory role possible.

As much in the International Agreement on Economic, Social and Cultural Rights as in the International Agreement on Civil and Political Rights, both dated 16 December 1966, the idea is to guarantee individual rights. The first article of the two agreements is the same and deals with the rights of native peoples. They state that native peoples have the right to settle their own affairs and to determine their political status, freely promoting their economic, social, and cultural development. In this sense, both agreements recognize the native people's power to employ freely their natural riches and resources—never again would they be deprived of their means of subsistence.

The concept of "a people," according to the UN and international law that is employed in the Agreements and other official documents, is limited to the human base of a nation-state, with no internal differentiation. "A people," then, means the simple sum of all the citizens seen individually who live in a specific, national territory, under the law of a state. The national constitution must recognize the rights of every individual citizen as equal. From this perspective, minorities, those who are excluded, organically structured local populations, the overlooked, previous occupiers, and those living far away and do not have a role in the running of the state have their civil, political, economic, social, cultural, and environmental rights established by the state, or by the ruling class of the state, and not by their own organization.

In this concept of a "people" the trap of self-determination is clear. Native peoples are free to determine whether they are a state, as long as they are not under the jurisdiction of an already constituted state. The organization of a state, the self-determination, and the free arrangement of themselves as a people means following the established, legal, rules of the state itself. The recognition of the right to self-determination of native peoples according to international law is, then, the right to self-determination of the state that guarantees individual rights, among which are rights to property.

However, the concept of a "people" used in the agreements is not that which is used in this paper, nor is it appropriate to native peoples. Moreover, this is clear in international law. The International Organization of Labor produced two conventions on indigenous peoples: Convention 107, dated 5 July 1957 and, more recently, Convention 169, dated 27 June 1989. The former dealt with "the protection and integration of tribal and semi-tribal populations of independent countries" and anticipated what was presented in the Agreement on Civil and Political Rights almost ten years later. There, article 27 prohibited states from denying people who belonged to ethnic, religious or linguistic minorities their right to social organization and their right of access to their culture, religion, and language.

These rights were characteristically individual because the catalogue of rights, as it was referred to, recognized only individual rights. Any collective idea was understood as meta-juridical; in other words, it was a political or social claim, often prohibited, that attained the category of the anti-juridical.

In contrast, Convention 169 in its introduction recognizes the desire of the "indigenous peoples and tribes to control their own institutions, ways of life, and economic development compatible with their cultural, linguistic, and religious identity," within the legal limits of the state in which they live. Thus, it was established that the convention applied to "tribal peoples in independent countries" (Gomez, 1991).

The convention changed the character of the right, recognizing it as collective right. The nation-states did not allow the term "people," even with the adjective "tribal," to refer to indigenous populations. To progress beyond the impasse, the convention established that its use of the word "people" did not have the same meaning as it did in international law.[27] In light of this, the states thought that an interpretation that gave indigenous people the right to self-determination, that is, to the constitution of the states themselves, would be out of the question.

The indigenous peoples of Latin America, despite their participation in the wars of independence, never sought to establish their own states. They always fought for their own rights in shared territory, respecting the way of life of each person. This is very clear today in the eastern indigenous areas of Chiapas, Mexico, and in the struggles of the Mapuche in Chile, both of whom are undergoing difficult confrontations with their respective nation-states. In the case of the former, the confrontation is armed. Apart from this, the local elites are concerned that native peoples, or at least some of them, will fight for local independence, which would weaken national sovereignty.

Ironically, the weakening of national sovereignty is occurring because of globalization, while the local peoples need—precisely in the struggle against globalization that yet again is trying to integrate them, no longer as citizens, but as consumers or providers of knowledge—are strong national sovereignties that will manage to guarantee their collective rights of survival.

For this reason, the minorities, those excluded, organically structured local populations, the forgotten, the previous inhabitants, those far from the centers, those with no capital, need a strong state to protect them from individual rights, from property owners, from global capital and power. They need to reinvent the state, substituting the logic of capital with the logic of the indigenous peoples.

BIBLIOGRAPHY

Andrello, Geraldo, and Marta Azevedo (n.d.). 'Iauretê'. Unpublished text.
Boletim Informativo da Fundação Cultural de Curitiba (1996). Curitiba: FCC, 23(114). Dec. 1996.
Chiavenatto, Julio José (1981). *Genocídio Americano: a guerra do Paraguai*. São Paulo: Brasiliense.
Gómez, Magdalena (1991). *Lectura comentada del Convenio 169 de la OIT*. Mexico City: INI.
Ladeira, Maria Inês; Azanha, Gilberto (1988). *Os índios da serra do mar*. São Paulo: Nova Stella.
Marés, Carlos Frederico (1996). "El nuevo constitucionalismo latinoamericano y los derechos de los pueblos indígenas," in *Derechos de los pueblos indígenas en las constituciones de América Latina: Bolivia, Brasil, Colombia, Ecuador, Guatemala, México, Nicaragua, Panamá, Paraguay, Peru e Venezuela*, Enrique Sanchez (ed.). Santafé de Bogotá: Disloque.
Paraná (1998). *Panará a volta dos índios gigantes*. São Paulo: Instituto Socioambiental.
Quem são os xetá? (2000). Curitiba: Secretaria do Estado da Cultura/Museu Paranaense. CD-ROM.
Ricardo, Carlos Alberto, ed. (1996). *Povos indígenas no Brasil: 1991–1995*. São Paulo: Instituto Socioambiental.
———— (2000). *Povos indígenas no Brasil: 1996–2000*. São Paulo: Instituto Socioambiental.
Scorza, Manuel (n.d.). *Garabombo, o invisível*. São Paulo: Círculo do Livro.
Souza Filho, Carlos Frederico Marés de (1998). *O renascer dos povos indígenas para o direito*. Curitiba: Juruá.

Notes

1 No judicial system in Latin America has resolved this question. Some laws did recognize in the end the legal character of native peoples, but only after the recognition of collective rights, that is to say, in the 1990s.
2 During slavery, "Capitão do mato" was the name given to those who hunted down runaway slaves. Normally, they were not employed by a single slave owner; whenever they caught a runaway slave, they would hand him over for a reward. However, when they did not manage to find the "legitimate" owner, they acquired the property and could sell the slave for their own profit.
3 Tiradentes, Bolívar, and Artigas are examples of leaders who brought freedom to their countries. However, no sooner had they constituted their respective states than they were ostracized and denied any practical influence in the organization of the nation. Tiradentes was hanged as a traitor; Bolívar, away from political life, died in exile in Colombia, after seeing the country he liberated divided up by local elites; Artigas lived out the last 30 years of his life in exile in Paraguay, where he died without ever returning to his homeland, Uruguay, which he had freed from Spanish oppression.
4 Before the war, the population of Paraguay was approximately 800,000. Afterwards it fell to 194,000, of which a mere 14,000 were men, half of them under 20 years of age (Chiavento, 1981).

5 Law No. 6001, 19 December 1973.

6 Sete Quedas was a remarkable group of waterfalls on the Paraná River. Its incomparable beauty was destroyed to build the electricity-producing Itaipu dam.

7 Most of the information on the Xetá is based on the CD-Rom "Quem são os Xetá" ["Who are the Xetá?"] produced by the Paranaense Museum in 2000.

8 Those involved in armed expeditions that left from São Paulo for the interior in search of Indians and precious minerals were referred to as "bandeirantes." These expeditions, which were generally very aggressive, sought to reduce the number of runaway slaves, known as "quilombos."

9 The well-known Xavante people, contacted at the end of the 1950s, covered upwards of 2000 kilometers, crossed at least three great rivers, the São Francisco, Tocantins, and Araguaia—a journey on foot that lasted 200 years or more, which implies difficult periods of adaptation and confrontations with renewed enemies.

10 Galdino had gone to Brasilia, with other members of his people, to claim their rights to the land and spent the night on a public bench. Mistaking him for a beggar, a group of youths decided upon a violent joke, pouring gasoline over him and setting him alight. He died as a result of the burns.

11 The Pataxó Hãhãhãe, numbering approximately 2000, is grouped in the area known as Paraguaçu-Caramuru.

12 Cláudio and Orlando Villas-Bôas are the two most famous Brazilian supporters of the indigenous peoples. They promoted contact with many native peoples and for a long time ran the experiment of the Indigenous Park of Xingú.

13 The Indigenous Park of Xingú, centered on the river Xingú, was created in 1961. On the one hand, it left out important territories occupied by indigenous peoples and, on the other, did not include the rivers that flowed into the Xingú. Today, the effects of these mistakes are seriously detrimental to the Park, which now has polluted waters as a result of the predatory actions of those living in the surrounding areas and of the increase in the number of its inhabitants. For further information, see the two books entitled *Povos Indígenas no Brasil* by Carlos Alberto Ricardo (1996; 2000).

14 FUNAI was responsible for the contact and the dislocation.

15 Nowadays, it is estimated that the Ticuna number 20,000.

16 Geraldo Andrello and Marta Azevedo, anthropologists at the Instituto Socioambiental (Socio-Environmental Institute), in unpublished research describe more than ten ethnic groups living in Iauraeté.

17 In 1988, the Macuxi, inhabiting the extreme north of Brazil, on the border with Venezuela and Guyana, met, as they do every year, in January, and invited me to participate. During the meeting, someone asked me the meaning of the words "constituinte" [constituent] and "constituição" [constitution]. I explained as best I could, and not only did they understand but thought that they too should have a local constitution to define both their territory and who should have rights within it. This account is described in two books: *O renascer dos povos indígenas para o direito* (Souza Filho, 1998) and *Derechos de los pueblos indígenas en las constituciones de América Latina* (Marés, 1996).

18 Even before the Brazilian constitution of 1988, in the period immediately preceding what was referred to as "redemocratization" (1983), the city of Curitiba was the setting for an experiment that was the catalyst that increased the status of local urban cultures. At its heart was a circus that served as an itinerant cultural center, and this instigated the flowering of various demonstrations of local urban culture. The experiment is described in a text I wrote, which was published in the Boletim Informativo da Fundação Cultural de Curitiba in December 1996, in the period presided over by the Fundação Cultural de Curitiba (Cultural Foundation of Curitiba). The most durable and striking example, however, is that of the MST (Movimento do Trabalhadores Rurais Sem Terra, or, the Movement of Landless Rural Workers) that claimed and occupied lands, exercising a right that directly challenged property rights. However, the collective right of the MST exists in the social function of the land as recognized in the constitution, yet it has not been easy to get the system to recognize it, apart from a number of rather timid initiatives by the Brazilian Judiciary.

19 After more than twenty years of claims, the Indigenous Area of Yanomami of 9.4 million hectares, located on the border with Venezuela, was officially recognized on 25 May 1992. The 8.15 million hectare territory of the peoples of the Upper Negro River was recognized on 15 April 1998.

20 Uninhabited lands are those that neither belong to any private landowner nor are for public use. They have belonged to the member states of the Federation since 1981 and can be transferred to private individuals according to regional legislation. The unrecognized indigenous lands were considered uninhabited and as such were transferred to private individuals who became the legitimate owners.

21 In January 1996, the President of the Republic signed Decree 1775, which redefined the procedural rules for the recognition and demarcation of indigenous lands. In this decree, which broke with tradition, there was introduced the possibility of interested third parties (including states and municipalities) in disagreement with the demarcation to manifest their discontent in order to claim rights, compensation, or to denounce unfair dealings.

22 I had the opportunity of participating personally in these discussions as the President of FUNAI (the Fundação Nacional do Índio, or the National Indian Foundation). Restarting the discussion, moreover, led to direct pressure by FUNAI and the Indians.

23 As of June 2001, the new statute still had not been approved. Personally, as President of FUNAI, I delivered a copy of the statute to the indigenous leaders in April 2000, at the same time as it was delivered to the person responsible in the National Congress. Discussions were restarted and the text is ready to be voted on.

24 This is Law No. 1551, 20 April 1994, referred to in Spanish as "La Ley de Participación Popular."

25 Aerial photographs of the Amazon clearly show the limits of the indigenous areas. When taken during the day, the process of deforestation is visible in the surrounding areas; when taken at night, dots of artificial light precisely describe the indigenous areas.

26 The Pankaru are from Pernambuco and have, since 1988, managed to obtain an area of demarcated land in the state. The land is too small to support the

4000 Indians who survive on their traditional territory and the 1000 Indian inhabitants of the shantytowns of São Paulo who have returned. Even if it were sufficient, they still would not want to return and constitute a group with claims of their own. Those from Pernambuco still make claims for the expansion of their lands because of the difficulty of practicing their sacred rituals far from prying eyes.

27 Article 1, Number 3 clearly establishes the meaning of the word "people," or, rather, what the word does *not* mean: "The use of the term 'pueblos' in this Convention must not be interpreted in the sense of having anything to do with the rights that could be conferred in international law" (Gómez, 1991).

4

The Struggles for Land Demarcation by the Indigenous Peoples of Brazil

Lino João de Oliveira Neves

This chapter focuses on the initiatives and struggles of the indigenous people in Brazil that have aimed at gaining official recognition of their lands and reclaiming control of their territories and of the natural resources within them.

"SELF-DEMARCATION"

The new federal constitution, which entered into effect in 1988, brought a new aspect to the native question, namely the issue of original rights to land. That is to say, the notion of "homeland" was no longer understood as an option of the state but as a right due to all native peoples. Previously, the state had recognized land, and, in truth, for Brazilian society as a whole this meant that the state would concede those lands to the Indians. After the constitution, given that the Indians had a right to land, it was up to the state to officially recognize and legalize that right. For the Indians, before the constitution, the question of land was perceived as a historical right to be claimed; with the constitution, it became a constitutional right in recognition of the historical right. It was the constitution that opened up the possibility of official recognition of Indian participation in the demarcation of their own territories. Previously, the Indians were considered to be a people in transition, a social group that was in the process of being integrated into the national fabric, of losing their "nationhood" in order to become "citizens." Article 231 of the new constitution granted the native peoples "the primitive and collective right to the lands that they occupy, while recognizing an individual, therefore public, right of property over those lands, handing over ownership to the Federal Union" (Marés, 2000: 14). As it is a "collective right," ownership of the homelands is not individualized. Thus, all the members of a native community are subject to the same rights over the land to which they historically and constitutionally belong; all may dispose of the land but at the same time no one may dispose of it individually because to do so "would infringe the rights of all the others" (Marés, 2000: 7). As there was no possibility of relating the native lands "to a single title-holder, or person, in traditional terms, this is apparently not a right, but a simple interest" (Marés, 2000: 7), which means that, even today, the homelands are considered most of the time to be a "no man's land," both for the people concerned and for the politicians and authorities. This opens up the possibility that the demarcation of the homelands will be contested by outsiders and other parties with claims to ownership. It was this legal ambiguity that enabled the federal government in January 1996 to impose Decree No. 1775 from the Ministry of Justice, which "disposes of the administrative procedure of demarcation of the native lands," as well as FUNAI's statute No. 14, which "establishes norms for the elaboration of a circumstantial report on the identification and delimitation of the home-lands." Thus, the political stalemate concerning territorial boundaries was transformed into a legal matter, according to which the occupation of land was perceived not as a historical right but as subject to a decree that could concede to the Indians the right to remain on the lands that had always been theirs (Neves, 1999: 120).

In a situation similar to that described by José Manuel Pureza (2000), the only argument that the Brazilian state could evoke to legitimize its claim of control over the Indian lands, and consequently over the demarcation process, was that of "effectively consummated facts."[1] In the light of international principles defending the self-determination of all peoples, the native question in Brazil is a "clear black and white case of a manifesto that does not respect the basic principles of international law" (Pureza, 2000: 11). Through FUNAI and other state agencies set up to deal with native demands, the Brazilian state continues to claim the right to administer the lives of the indigenous populations by means of the control that it exercises over sectoral policy and, more incisively, through processes of legal recogni-tion of the lands occupied by the indigenous peoples.

The land demarcation process involves a succession of sequenced and prioritized stages, from the situation in which the land does not have any official recognition, to the extreme situation in which its agrarian situation is regulated by means of a register in the Union Heritage Department and in real estate registry offices. For the objectives of this chapter, it is enough to mention four phases of this process: identification and delimitation; demar-cation; legal ratification, and agrarian regulation. To simplify, the entire process of the official recognition of native lands is commonly called the "demarcation process."

After the wave of European colonization, which extended to all parts of

Brazil, the "homelands" today cover less territory than they did before. The total number of indigenous lands varies in accordance with the criteria used by each agency to manipulate the data. According to figures provided by the Native People's Missionary Council (CIMI),[2] updated in March 2000, Brazil contains 739 native homelands, of which 179 (more than 24 per cent of the total) are lands claimed by indigenous peoples but for which no provision has yet been made. Of the 560 lands recognized officially by FUNAI, only 231 (around 31 per cent) have their agrarian situation regulated according to official norms, while the other 220 (almost 40 per cent) have suffered invasions and pressures from non-indigenous interests (*Reportagem*, 1999).

Given the legal ambiguities and ineffectiveness of the state as regards the fulfilling of its constitutional obligation to undertake the demarcation of indigenous lands, the Indians took into their own hands the task of demarcating and protecting their lands. One of the first of these initiatives was carried out by the Kulina Indians of the Upper Purus river region in the state of Acre, on the frontier between Brazil and Peru. They undertook the physical demarcation of their land by opening up pathways in the forest and fixing improvised markers and wooden plaques that they had constructed themselves.[3] Although these plaques and markers were totally unofficial, they served to assert the territorial rights of the Kulina within the region; as a result, the area was not subject to trespass as it had been before (Monteiro, 1999: 156).

To the Kulina Indians, their initiative constitutes a *de facto* demarcation, defining the boundaries of the lands that were historically and mythically identified as their "homeland," although the state does not recognize that procedure as a legal demarcation. In an assembly of the Kulina in 1990, the Indians of the Upper Purus river, used their own experience to encourage their relatives to open up tracks on the limits of the Kulina Homeland of the Middle Juruá river. This had been delimited in 1988 by FUNAI but had never been demarcated, and thus was constantly being invaded by lumber-jacks, fishermen, rubber-tappers and, in particular, *seringalistas*,[4] who refused to accept that the land was native territory.

Having decided to take action themselves, "the Kulina, in the same assembly, planned to extend the *roçados* in order to sustain the arduous work of demarcation"[5] (Monteiro, 1999: 156). As the time for the work to begin drew near, the population of the region reacted against the Kulina's initiative in the Middle Juruá river. In order to dissipate tensions, a seminar was held,[6] in which members of the indigenous teams supporting the Kulina and representatives of UNI-Acre and South Amazonas[7] explained to the population and local authorities the nature of and reasons for their activities. From that moment, it became clear to all that the initiative was designed exclusively to attend to native rights and that "the Kulina would undertake this work with the aim of marking the limits of their homeland in order to put an end to conflicts, precisely because the federal government had omitted to do this and had not fulfilled their obligations" (Monteiro, 1999: 157).

In the first phase, the work followed a well-tested methodology developed in the short topography courses given at the villages for the training of the Indians. Based upon the use of compasses, boundary posts, and even fireworks and smoke signals in order to guide the direction of the tracks that were being opened up in the forest, there were at first many mistakes and a great deal of imprecision that was later corrected. In addition to technical matters, another obstacle that the Kulina confronted was the supply of food, because, as the paths advanced, the workers drew further and further away from the villages that supplied them with manioc flour, game, and salted fish, their staple diet. This situation persisted during the first two years of operations. In the second stage, the work scheme was modified on the basis of support from an international aid agency called "Bread for the World" ("Pão para o Mundo," or PPM)[8] and, mainly, because of an agreement between the Brazilian state and the Indians granting legal recognition of the demarcation carried out by the Kulina.[9] Following the signing of the agreement, the orientation of the paths and the implantation of markers and plaques was done using sophisticated measuring equipment, such as theodolites and GPS,[10] which permitted greater technical precision. However, the need to follow the standards and technical norms demanded by the accord meant that the work became even more laborious than it had been in the first phase. In addition, the dependence of the technical team on the administrative and bureaucratic procedures of the organs of government for funding not only reduced the efficiency of the work but also contributed to the "dejection and disappointment suffered by the Kulina" (Monteiro, 1999: 159).

The shift teams that carried out the work in the forest consisted essentially of adult men, generally accompanied by the village chief. The women made a decisive contribution by supplying the necessary food and, in some cases, helping their husbands to fell trees for the opening-up of the tracks. It is worth pointing out that all the villages situated in the Kulina Homeland of Middle Juruá took part in the demarcation, although some contributed more intensely than others.

The physical demarcation lasted from 1991 until the beginning of 1998, a period that brought great achievements for the Kulina. They saw the strengthening of their political organizations, got to know their lands in a more detailed way, and underwent a technical apprenticeship that enabled them to work with maps, geographical coordinates, boundary markers, satellite pictures, etc. (Monteiro, 1999: 163). As "the demarcation of an indigenous territory is carried out within a web of social relations, both internal to the community and external, with the surrounding population, it requires more than the simple application of technical and legal know-how to be long-lasting" (Monteiro, 1999: 163); consequently, the Kulina demarcation functioned at the same time as a procedure, as an assertion of rights over the occupied lands, and as a process of affirmation of Kulina self-esteem in the context of inter-ethnic relations. Undoubtedly, "respect for the indigenous people grew significantly among the urban and rural population of the region as a result of the Kulina's courage and skill in taking the responsibility to demarcate their own lands" (Monteiro, 1999: 162).

Therefore, "self-demarcation" began to be seen as an important issue within the indigenous struggle. It was taken the furthest by the Kulina, who not only asserted their territorial rights but also generated and consolidated a methodology of demarcation involving the effective participation of local groups in the work of the physical demarcation of the lands that they occupied in the Middle Juruá river region in Amazonas, which came to be legally recognized as indigenous land through the agreement between FUNAI and the Indians.

The "self-demarcation" model, as a strategy for forcing the Brazilian state to officially recognize the lands, spread throughout the country and was adopted by many indigenous peoples. On the same River Juruá, for example, two neighbors of the Kulina, the Kanamari and the Deni, used the system of placing wooden markers and opening paths in the forest to mark the divisions of the lands they had traditionally occupied, having waited many years for official recognition. Although devoid of any formal legality, the Kanamari initiative, carried out in 1991, was very important as an assertion of the right of this people over its lands, and it helped to put an end to trespassing on their territory. While the move was initially contested by regional estate-owners, the precarious and improvised system of markers was adopted by a technical work group that identified and delimited the Mawetek Homeland, the anthropological report of which (Neves, 1998) recognized indigenous rights and validated the boundaries that had been established using the "self-demarcation" process practiced by the Kanamari.[11]

As regards the Deni, their lands had been identified and delimited in 1985, but they had waited sixteen years for the demarcation process to pass through the interminable administrative bureaucracies of FUNAI. Tired of waiting for solutions that never appeared, the Deni Indians themselves, supported by native organizations and environmentalists[12] recently began (in September 2001) the process of demarcating their own lands following the Kulina model. It is interesting that, after an initial negative reaction, in which the president of FUNAI demanded that the Deni's work of opening and marking boundaries in the forest be stopped, a government decree granted the Deni rights of possession of their lands and established a short period for the beginning of the technical work of demarcation.

Through FUNAI and other agents dealing with native questions, the Brazilian state made use of the actions and procedures generated by the indigenous peoples, incorporating them into their public policies. The Kulina "self-demarcation" was no exception. On the basis of initiatives taken between the state, indigenous NGOs, and native organizations, the methodology and organizational form of "self-demarcation" lost its emancipatory dimension and was subjected to an "abbreviating interpretation" (Santos, 1998), reduced by PPTAL/FUNAI/GTZ[13] to a model of physical land demarcation. As a model, the strategies and systems created and refined by the Kulina Indians during the "self-demarcation" process were isolated from the political, historical, geographical, and inter-ethnic contexts of the region of Middle Juruá river, and instead were converted into a new type of institutional knowledge, renamed "participative demarcation" and extended by the PPTAL, as a demarcation model, to the 119 native lands located in Brazilian Amazonia.[14] In accordance with its initial proposal, the PPTAL "proposed the identification of 55 areas, the demarcation and regulation of 58, and the revision of six more" (Arruda, 1998: 6). Thus, the PPTAL assumed the role of the regulator of a successful counter-hegemonic experiment by replicating it in different indigenous contexts, while what was really required were different procedures and treatments adequate for the different realities involved.

Following this replicated institutional dynamic, the PPTAL promoted two experimental demarcation processes aimed at technically refining the "participative demarcation" model,[15] after which the demarcation of the Javari Valley homeland (the largest in Brazil and located on the border between Brazil and Peru) got under way. The Vale do Javari homeland was

demarcated during 2000 and ratified in April 2001. Demarcation was carried out by a topography company (SETAG) contracted by FUNAI via public bid. FUNAI, through PPTAL, contracted CIVAJA,[16] which mobilized the Indians to accompany the demarcation process, divulge it and present a plan for the security of the border after the demarcation was concluded (Mendes, 2001).

The anthropologist Gilberto Azanha, an employee of FUNAI, who accompanied the work in the Javari Valley, stated in a personal interview that the demarcation of this homeland was indeed limited to "bureaucratic self-demarcation" (Azanha, 2000). The Indians were little more than observers, with no active role to play in the process of demarcation of their own land, which was nevertheless presented as a "self-demarcation" based on the model created by the Kulina. Although PPTAL recognized that "partnerships" with indigenous NGOs and Indians had been functionally quite successful in the demarcation of the homelands of the Waiãpi of the Upper Negro river and the Javari Valley,[17] their analysis of the development of the regulation process indicated that, both qualitatively and quantitatively, their commitment "left something to be desired" (Arruda, 1998: 7).

According to the description given by the coordinator of PPTAL, "participative demarcation" carried out in partnership

> consisted basically in contracting with a topography firm for the geodesic survey, the opening of tracks, and placement of markers," while the Indians were mobilized "directly by the local indigenous organization or indirectly by some NGO indicated by them to accompany the work on all fronts, place signposts, and divulge to their villages and surrounding areas what this implied in terms of territorial rights (Mendes, 1999: 19).

Explained in this way, the difference between "participative demarcation" and "self-demarcation" becomes obvious. The latter becomes the process by which the Indians who reside in the homeland take upon themselves all the activities directly or indirectly related with the physical construction and legal consolidation of their territory according to the norms of the Brazilian state.

While, "demarcation," as an external initiative undertaken by the state, has connotations of outlining spaces for the confinement, reduction, social enclosure, and exclusion from relations with the world outside, "self-demarcation," as an indigenous movement for the construction of territory, suggests the exercise of internal organization that extends the political possibilities of native organization, thus strengthening the ethnic group in its relations with the state and the surrounding society. Although "self-demarcation" and "participative demarcation" have the same goal of achieving the agrarian regulation of indigenous lands and often make use of similar methods and procedures, they are substantially different as regards native participation. While "self-demarcation" is the means *par excellence* of exercising political mobilization for the formulation of proposals and ethnic emancipation, in "participative demarcation" the indigenous presence is no more than an accessory or support for the fieldwork, and is regulated by technical rules, schedules, and administrative plans that are totally alien to the indigenous universe.

As regards the "participative demarcation" model diffused by PPTAL, we may even question whether there are really any differences in relation to the inefficient model of "demarcations by bid," the model traditionally used by FUNAI, since the dynamics involved are very similar. We could also ask to what extent "partnerships" of this type ensure the long-term sustainability of counter-hegemonic indigenous initiatives, given the risks of the institutionalization of the indigenous movement and of the administrative bureaucratization of its organizations and formalization of its actions and movements. Indications of this loss of counter-hegemonic sustainability may be detected in the "bureaucratization" of the demarcation of the Javari Valley as well as in the growing process of institutionalization and formalism that the Federation of Indigenous Organizations of the Negro River (FOIRN) and CIVAJA have imprinted onto the indigenous movements of the Negro river and Javari Valley respectively. The most frightening aspect is the way in which the counter-hegemonic dimension of the indigenous organizations has been weakened by the incorporation of the "abbreviation interpretation" by the native movement itself, which sanitizes the process and leads to the stagnation of indigenous initiatives, reducing their efficiency as "emerging realities." The drawing-up of agreements in order to form "partnerships" represents the incorporation of the indigenous "mobilization routine" by the state, to be then sanitized and converted by state rationale into "routine mobilization," which is transferred back to the organized indigenous movement or indigenous organizations as a way of doing politics.

"Participative demarcation," formulated by the PPTAL on the basis of the Kulina "self-demarcation," is a new institutional idea that adapts the indigenous creativity of "self-demarcation" to the obsolete institutional bureaucracy of Brazil's native question. It is a model in which the participation of the Indians is once more relegated to the work of accompanying and regulating technical work, and is taken as cooperation in the process of the political construction of indigenous territory through demarcation.

The analysis of the emancipatory dimension of the new dynamics of demarcation inspired in the "self-demarcation" invented by the Kulina during their mobilization in defense of their lands means that

> participative demarcations are not a possible utopia, nor are they the artificial products of undefined routes that need to be measured to be displayed in showcases. They do not correspond to façades of government policy but rather are experiments with great density and social consistency. They are not the invention of PPTAL, nor do they result from the pure and simple application of a model of social engineering; they are constructions of the natives themselves, culturally distinct with distinct historical backgrounds and heterogeneous political projects (Oliveira, 2001: 32).

The demarcation of indigenous lands should not be seen as a simple application of measurement techniques for the delimitation of terrains, or as an exercise in environmental division; the demarcation of the native lands is a much more complex political fact than the

> construction of a new socio-political reality, in which a historical subject, an ethnic group that perceives itself as descendents of the original occupiers of

that land, becomes involved in a process of territorialization and becomes recognized under a model of citizenship as an effective participant in the Brazilian nation (Oliveira, 2001: 34).

For this reason, "self-demarcation" may not be seen merely as the Indians doing the work that the state should have done. If it were this, "self-demarcation" would have been stripped of its myth of having an innovative political potential. It is much more than the Indians merely taking on the job in the state's absence; it is the safest way for an indigenous people to establish the base for the reinforcement of their ethnic identity. It is the beginning of the process of reorientation of inter-ethnic relations, a step in the direction of a "process of social construction by the inhabitants of a territory, which impels them to search for solutions to their problems and needs through the self-diagnosis of their own world" (Fundación Gaia Amazonas, 2000: 236). Understood in this way, "self-demarcation" becomes similar to the process of "territorial planning" conceived by the indigenous communities of Colombian Amazonia as a cluster of relations that have implications for the life of the population of a given territory, as the "backbone that regulates the principles of the governments themselves, and of all cultural, political, economic, and social relations, both internally and externally" (Sánchez, 2000: 102).

The Kulina "self-demarcation" was not an institutional idea; on the contrary; it was a concrete practice constructed with indigenous protagonists within the whole process of political construction of territory, an initiative that revolutionized the institutional way of demarcating indigenous lands, taking on the shape of an "emerging reality." "Self-demarcation" rapidly spread throughout the country, less as a method of demarcation developed empirically by the Kulina than as a way of asserting rights over occupied lands, and today it forms a part of the political agenda of all the indigenous peoples.

With the demarcation of the Kulina homeland of the Middle Juruá river, officially recognized by the agreement between FUNAI and the Kulina, "self-demarcation" asserted itself definitively as the most important and innovative political mobilization of the indigenous peoples, revolutionizing the whole process and system of land demarcation. These three examples of "self-demarcation" in Amazonas—the case of the Kulina, whose technical work was recognized by an accord between FUNAI and the Indians; that of the Kanamari, whose limits on the land were validated as the limits of the native land; and that of the Deni, which obliged the state to take the attitude that it had long delayed—demonstrate the emancipatory dimension of "self-demarcation." This does not reside only in its capacity to mobilize local populations with the objective of achieving one-off conquests, but also in its ability to construct a new system of relations between the indigenous peoples and the state.

WINDING TRAILS IN THE RIGHT DIRECTION[18]

Long before the organized indigenous movement was formed, there were land conflicts in the history of the contact between the indigenous peoples and European society. The struggle for the defense of land is a common mark in the lives of all the indigenous peoples of Latin America; the struggle for the demarcation of those lands is at the root of the indigenous movement.

For the Indian, land is not merely a means of production; "it is a totalizing concept to which all other aspects belong, such as culture, Indianness, history, religion, politics, economics, etc." (Barre, 1983: 162). The claim for "demarcation" should not be confused with the concept of "territoriality," which emerged from the native struggle together with the concept of "property," which reduces the land to a mere means of production, according to the economic perspective. In this sense, the struggle for the demarcation of land has a clearly emancipatory dimension, since it questions the whole cluster of western presuppositions and values at the service of a "northern" hegemony. The emancipatory, revolutionary, and subversive potential of the indigenous peoples offers the Western world "prospects of change that are both cultural and civilizational, and which will signify the recuperation and development of communities, cultures and civilizations that could naturally 'modernize' in a different way" (Barre, 1983: 239).

The indigenous movement represents a decisive break with the exclusion to which the Indians were historically subjected by colonization; it is a break with the imperial South, the South in the image of the North, a South that reproduces, confirms, and reifies the North–South dichotomy in which it is subordinated.[19] It is a "paradigmatic political struggle" that has on its horizon the construction of new social relationships, the configuration of a new alternative paradigm of inter-ethnic democratic sociability (Santos, 2000: 314). The tenuous line between emancipation and regulation oscillates according to the ambiguity of the "partnerships," which, for tactical reasons, may combine the emancipatory initiatives of the struggle with instruments of social regulation (Santos, 2000: 319).

The demarcation of lands, the issue at the center of the native claims, is the most explicit and objective way of breaking with the regulatory order that the nation-states impose upon ethnic minorities. Therefore, the demarcation of the land is not the final objective of the indigenous movement; it is merely the first step in the affirmation of territoriality as the basis of an ethnic project for the future. For the Indians,

> demarcation is less a topographical, cartographical or legal activity than the creation of conditions for the emergence of a form of political organization, within this territorialized ethnic group, that is able not only to adequately

administer its agrarian and environmental resources, but which also modernizes its own culture, enriching it with new experiences, without harming the reproduction of its cognitive heritage or the maintenance of those values considered central by the present members (Oliveira, 2001: 34).

These teachings are dictated by the model of "self-demarcation" invented by the Indians in the historical process of defending their lands. "Self-demarcation" opened up the way, traced the outline, taught the steps, indicated the direction in which the construction of a multi-ethnic, multicultural social system ought to head, in which equality and difference are the orienting principles of relations between peoples.

However, despite representing processes of assertion of distinct sociocultural particularities in the scenario of inter-ethnic relations, some initiatives may not realize their emancipatory potential and may lose their counter-hegemonic dimension, becoming "globalized localisms," in the process of "hegemonic globalization." In the case of indigenous groups, the true counter-hegemonic dimension of the initiatives, originating in local groups or indigenous organizations, rests in the distinction between ethnic affirmation and subordination to nation-states.

For the Brazilian state, only two possibilities were reserved for the Indians: 1) "isolation from civilization," like societies paralyzed in time; or 2) "integration into civilization," as societies on the margins of national society. It is against this limitation that the Indians are mobilizing. The indigenous initiatives, whether they are labeled as "emerging," "counter-hegemonic," or something else, demonstrate that another possibility exists, namely that the indigenous peoples assume themselves as active subjects in the process of inter-ethnic relations.

Indian mobilization has not been impelled by the international solidarity of NGO networks; rather, it is "emancipatory commonsense," a "subversive order" (Santos, 2000: 254), a multiple proposal of a multi-ethnic and multicultural society (Patzi Paco, 1999: 13), which subverts democracy, constructing a plural democracy. The indigenous movement is not only "anti"; it is above all a movement that proposes a model of society different from the Western model and which manifests itself as anti-Western by its refusal of western thought in accepting diversity, the possibility of the coexistence of difference. In this, the power of indigenous mobilizations "reveals itself to be non-accepting of the democratic character" (Almeida, 1994: 531).

In the field of the indigenous struggles in Brazil, self-determination is focused on the historical right to the land and its natural resources, based on an autonomous social organization compatible with the principles of national sovereignty reclaimed by the Brazilian state; an "internal self-determination" that claims ethnic equality as an alternative to homogenization (Santos, 1995: 321). "Self-determination" and "emancipation," understood as the reconquest of immemorial rights, bring together a group of local issues and specific problems experienced by the different indigenous peoples, while "land demarcation" represents the immediate mechanism for the access of rights and the basic presupposition for achieving the required self-determination and emancipation, that is, autonomy.

The proposal for "autonomy" put forward by the indigenous movement of Brazil is a way of overcoming exclusion, which, in the field of inter-ethnic relations, shaped the "exclusive/defensive communities" closed in upon themselves in defense against the domination (social, cultural, environmental, agrarian, political, epistemological, etc.) of the state as an "exclusive-aggressive community" (Santos, 2000: 314). With its objective of constructing a plural, multicultural, and multi-ethnic country, the indigenous movement is close to the paradigm of the "amoeba communities" associated with the "principle of internal self-determination" that is a component of the new emerging paradigm of "democratic sustainability and dispersed sovereignty" (Santos, 2000: 317).

For the indigenous movement in Brazil, "emancipation" expresses a meaning close to "autonomy" without, however, containing the connotations of "national liberation" or "regional autonomy" so frequently employed by other indigenous movements of Latin America.[20] The key word for the indigenous peoples of Brazil has always been "self-determination." Recently, as a result of the involvement of indigenous movements and the state in activities and programs designed to attend to immediate demands, "self-determination" has given way in political discourse to other terms such as "partnership," "alliance," and "collaboration," which, though not new, have gained a force that they previously had only in the field of Brazilian native politics. From the theoretical point of view, the question is whether it is possible to reconcile the "emancipatory" interest of the indigenous movement with the western bureaucratic paradigm into which the indigenous organizations are inserted, by means of such "partnerships," "alliances," and "collaborations."

A careful assessment of the state of the indigenous movement in Brazil suggests that today the Indians have lost some of the political force and power that they had in the 1980s for the winning of support and solidarity from other segments of society. However, the native question continues to be a potential source of social emancipation. This resides in two facts. First, it lies in the inheritance of a recent past in which the indigenous movement represented a great, organized force (maybe the only organized force) of resistance to the military dictatorship's "project of national integration" that unleashed a process of cultural and social homogenization imposed upon the country. Second, and more importantly, the indigenous movement, given its intrinsic nature, opposes the national model of society, and from this "rivalry" of different forms of knowledge, values, principles, political systems, and social organization, there emerges a "social rivalry." Despite the anticipated risks and alternatives already confronted, the struggles of the indigenous peoples of Brazil cannot be called a failure. Counter-hegemonic initiatives and the capacity of the indigenous peoples to generate counter-hegemonic initiatives demonstrate that the struggles of the 1970s have not been forgotten, only that they are sometimes put on hold in a *varadouro*[21] in order to be resumed at the most opportune moment. Thus, this may be seen as a strategic maneuver on the part of the movement, local organizations, or indigenous peoples in their constantly renewed counter-hegemonic struggle against colonization, subordination, and the exclusion of 500 years.

BIBLIOGRAPHY

Almeida, Alfredo Wagner Berno de (1994). "Universalização e localismo: movimentos sociais e crises dos padrões tradicionais de relação política na Amazônia," in Maria Ângela D'Incao and Isolda Maciel da Silveira (eds.), *Amazônia e a Crise da Modernização*. Belém: Museu Paraense Emílio Goeldi, 521–537.

Arruda, Rinaldo Sérgio Vieira (1998). *Avaliação de Meio Termo—Texto preliminar.* São Paulo: PPTAL.

Azanha, Gilberto (2000). Personal interview. 20 September.

Barre, Marie-Chantal (1983). *Ideologias Indigenistas y Movimientos Indios.* México: Siglo Veintiuno.

Fundación Gaia Amazonas (2000). "Ordenamiento territorial indígena: clave para el futuro del Amazonas," in Juan José Vieco, Carlos Eduardo Franky and Juan Álvaro Echeverri (eds.), *Territorialidad Indígena y Ordenamiento en la Amazonia.* Santafé de Bogotá: Universidad Nacional de Colombia, 235–249.

Marés, Carlos Frederico (2000). "Os Direitos Coletivos." Paper presented at the symposium: "Reinvenção da Emancipação Social," Coimbra: CES, MacArthur Foundation, Calouste Gulbenkian Foundation, 23 to 26 November.

Mendes, Artur Nobre (1999). "A demarcação das terras indígenas no âmbito do PPTAL," in Carola Kasburg and Márcia Maria Gramkow (eds.), *Demarcando Terras Indígenas: Experiências e Desafios de um Projeto de Parceria.* Brasília: FUNAI, PPTAL, GTZ, 15–19.

——————— (2001). E-mail to the author. 11 June.

Merz, Martin (1997). *Auto-demarcação Madijá: um exemplo de iniciativa e competência dos povos indígenas da Amazônia.* Rio Branco: UNI.

Monteiro, Rosa Maria (1999). "Vamos acabar nosso trabalho!: A demarcação da área indígena Kulina do mério Juruá," in Carola Kasburg and Márcia Maria Gramkow (eds.), *Demarcando Terras Indígenas: Experiências e Desafios de um Projeto de Parceria.* Brasília: FUNAI, PPTAL, GTZ, 155–165.

Neves, Lino João de Oliveira (1998). *Relatório de Identificação e Delimitação da Terra Indígena Mawetek.* Brasília: FUNAI.

——————— (1999). "Juridificação do processo de demarcação das terras indígenas no Brasil (ou Antropologia/Direito: grandes esperanças ou aliados perigosos na regulação social do movimento indígena no Brasil," *Revista Crítica de Ciências Sociais* 55 (November): 113–129.

Oliveira, João Pacheco (2001). *As Demarcações Participativas e o Fortalecimento das Organizações Indígenas*. Rio de Janeiro: Museu Nacional.

Patzi Paco, Felix (1999). *Insurgencia y sumisión: Movimentos indígeno-campesinos (1983–1998)*. La Paz: Muela del Diablo.

Pureza, José Manuel (2000). *Quem Salvou Timor Leste? Novas Referências para o Internacionalismo Solidário*. Paper presented at the symposium: "Reinvenção da Emancipação Social," Coimbra: CES, MacArthur Foundation, Calouste Gulbenkian Foundation, 23–26 November.

Ramos, Alcida Rita (1997). "The Indigenous Movement in Brazil: A Quarter Century of Ups and Downs," *Cultural Survival Quarterly* (Summer): 50–53.

Reportagem (1999). I: 1

Sánchez, Tomás Román (2000). "Experiencia de ordenamiento territorial del Medio Caquetá," in Juan José Vieco, Carlos Eduardo Franky, and Juan Álvaro Echeverri (eds.), *Territorialidad Indígena y Ordenamiento en la Amazonia*. Santafé de Bogotá: Universidad Nacional de Colombia, 99–106.

Santos, Boaventura de Sousa (1995). "Ancient Grievances and New Solidarities: The Law of Indigenous Peoples," in *Toward a New Common Sense: law, science and politics in the paradigmatic transition*. London: Routledge. 313–327.

————— (1998). *Reinventing Social Emancipation: Exploring the Possibilities of Counter-Hegemonic Globalization*. Research Proposal presented to the MacArthur Foundation. Coimbra: CES.

————— (2000). *A crítica da razão indolente: contra o desperdício da experiência*. Oporto: Afrontamento.

Schröder, Peter (1999). "Os índios são 'participativos'? As bases sócio-culturais e política de participação de comunidades indígenas em projetos e programas," in Carola Kasburg and Márcia Maria Gramkow (eds.), *Demarcando Terras Indígenas: Experiências e Desafios de um Projeto de Parceria*. Brasília: FUNAI, PPTAL, GTZ, 233–263.

Notes

1 An argument used by Indonesia to impose its sovereignty upon East Timor.

2 CIMI, the indigenous organ of the Catholic Church, set up in 1972, is connected to the National Conference of Brazilian Bishops (CNBB), which is oriented towards liberation theology.

3 Not recognizing this initiative as legal, FUNAI refused to supply the official markers and plaques used to indicate the limits of the indigenous lands.

4 "*Seringalistas*": "owners" of rubber plantations, which control the commercialization of natural rubber of Amazonia.

5 "*Roçados*": fields of manioc/cassava, the staple vegetable of all the indigenous peoples of Amazonia. In the region of the River Juruá, manioc is eaten mainly in the form of flour.

6 Seminar held in Eirunepé, the small city that acts as the political center of the River Juruá region.

7 At first, UNI-Acre was a representative of UNI for the state of Acre. With the disappearance of UNI as a national organization, UNI-Acre asserted itself as the local organization, extending its action to South Amazonas and taking

over the historic initials of UNI (National Union of Indigenous Peoples).
8 "'Bread for the World' (PPM) is a cooperative project of the Evangelical/ Lutheran churches. In supporting the Madijá project, PPM implements its principle of 'helping to self-help,' that is, by helping the Indians to become responsible for their own development" (Merz, 1997: 9). The word "Madijá" is the self-denomination of the Kulina people.
9 Accord No. 004/93, between FUNAI, as the representative of the Brazilian state, UNI-Acre, and South Amazonas, and the Kulina Indigenous Community of Middle Juruá, which represented Kulina interests.
10 Theodolites are precision surveying equipment. GPS: global positioning system for the scanning of geodesic points by satellite.
11 The physical demarcation of the Mawetek Homeland was carried out during the year 2000, in accordance with boundaries initially defined by the Kanamari.
12 The Deni "self-demarcation" had the support of CIMI, the Native Amazonia Operation (OPAN), the Coordination of the Indigenous Organizations of the Amazon Basin (COIAB), and of Greenpeace.
13 The Integrated Project for the Protection of Indigenous Populations of Legal Amazonia (PPTAL) is a sub-project of the Pilot Program for the Protection of Tropical Forests in Brazil (PPG7), implemented by FUNAI with the technical cooperation of Deutsche Gesellshaft für Tetchnishe (GTZ). Hereafter, the abbreviation PPTAL will be used when referring to this partnership.
14 The PPTAL action affected 81 different indigenous peoples, of which eight were groups that did not have regular contact with Brazilian society (Schröder, 1999: 235).
15 The first, with the demarcation of the Waiãpi Homeland on the Brazil–Guyana border, was carried out between January 1994 and February 1996; the second, involving the demarcation of five indigenous homelands located in the region of Upper River Negro, on the Brazil–Columbia–Venezuela border, was undertaken between April 1997 and April 1998.
16 CIVAJA: the Indigenous Council of the Javari Valley, an organization representing the peoples of the Javari Valley.
17 In addition to these, the PPTAL has promoted other "demarcation operations through bidding, the traditional model used by FUNAI" (Mendes, 1999: 18). This chapter is limited to these three indigenous homelands, where the "participative demarcation" model was put into practice.
18 "It is necessary to remember that the indigenous peoples have had a long experience of following winding trails. While it might appear to the Western mind that they are losing their way, this may in truth represent the shortest path between two points, which could teach us some unexpected lessons about productivity" (Ramos, 1997: 53).
19 "As a product of the Empire, the South is the house where the South does not feel at home," so "seeing itself only through the lens of the imperial North, the periphery cannot but recognize itself in the imperial South" (Santos, 2000: 345).
20 Whatever it may be, the issue of "autonomy" has not until now been raised by the Indians of Brazil, at least not in the form in which it appears with other peoples in Latin America and Canada.
21 "Varadouro": a secondary path opened in the forest to shorten distances.

5

The U'wa Community's Battle against the Oil Companies: A Local Struggle Turned Global

Luis Carlos Arenas[1]

INTRODUCTION

Since 1993, the U'wa people, a small indigenous community in Colombia, have been waging a battle against the American oil company Occidental Petroleum Corporation and, more recently against the Colombian state-owned oil company, ECOPETROL, in order to keep them from drilling for oil on their ancestral lands. The conflict surrounding the oil issue began in 1991, when Occidental and other associated companies acquired exploration and drilling rights for what is known as the "Samoré Block," a large tract of land that cuts across a portion of the U'wa's ancestral lands in the foothills of Colombia's eastern mountain range, the home of this people for countless generations. The oil companies started moving into U'wa territory in late 1992, and the U'wa staged their first public protests sometime in 1993. However, their opposition to the drilling did not receive national attention until 1995, when the recently created Ombudsman's Office took their case against the oil companies to the highest court in the land. Since that time, not only has publicity on the case increased, it has gained surprising force, spilling over the national borders. In fact, for several reasons I will address later, the U'wa case has been at the international forefront since 1997, during which time it has provided unexpected revelations as to the current dimensions, potential, and limits of contemporary globalization processes.

Two decisive legal changes—one national and one international—affecting indigenous peoples' rights have played a major role in the conflict between the oil companies, the Colombian government, and the U'wa community: 1) International Labor Organization (ILO) Convention #169, which established a new international framework of regulation for indigenous peoples; and 2) the 1991 changes framed in the Political Constitution of Colombia, one of which provided for ample protection of indigenous peoples. As we will see, these two key legal instruments will be a continuous reference for the issue of oil found on the U'wa's territory.

The "U'wa case" has now become the symbol for a broad range of struggles currently being waged inside and outside of Colombia's borders by indigenous peoples, environmental and human rights movements, and in the mobilizations against multinational companies. How could an indigenous community that has been insulated and forgotten for such a long time become the center of worldwide attention? Why has the U'wa case been so attractive to very different kinds of activists and the mass media? What can we learn of this process of local struggle which has become global? How did it become a symbol in the struggle against hegemonic globalization? These are some of the questions that this chapter will try to address.

SOCIAL STRUGGLES BEYOND NATIONAL BORDERS

Although the study of forms of collective action beyond national borders is a new academic field, in the last years some very influential texts have been published on this subject (Smith *et al.*, 1997; Keck and Sikking, 1998; Brysk, 2000; Tarrow, 1998; Evans, 2000; Smith, 2000). However, this bibliography usually perpetuates the confusion regarding the role and interaction of grassroots movements and international NGOs in building up collective forms of transnational struggles. International NGOs have undoubtedly been the most visible actors and have played an important role in the globalization of these social struggles. However, they are not the only actors, and in many cases are not even the leading players. There are many varied and rich experiences in local struggles, which, for different reasons, have managed to establish international ties, thus changing the balance of power in their specific fights. In order to fully appreciate these local struggles, we must look beyond the international NGOs. By no means am I suggesting that the two are in opposition; in fact, the most sucessful cases of social struggle are those with dynamic local–national–global interactions and ties. In this sense, as emphasized by Boaventura de Sousa Santos, the U'wa case is paradigmatic (Santos, 2001: 201). The international NGOs facilitate the transnationaliza-tion of social struggles, but they cannot assist in all of them and certainly cannot take the place of local efforts (Evans, 2000). Nevertheless, as we will see in the U'wa case study, the success and emancipatory potential of transnationalized social struggles depend to a great extent on the local organizations, working day to day and serving as the grounding force for a specific social effort.

One of the paradoxes faced by any social movement that transcends national borders is the continuous temptation for international NGOs and their allies to usurp the role of local groups and for analysts to fail to recognize the importance of local battles. Any solidary-emancipatory perspective should always seek to increase the success potential of local struggles through transnational actions, while attempting to ensure that any decision-making power as to the direction of the struggle remains in the hands of local organizations. The emancipatory potential of these struggles also lies in creating horizontal solidarity ties, be these North–South or South–South, and working to avoid falling back on traditional forms of interaction based on imposed conditions, subordination, and vertical relationships. Otherwise, their emancipatory potential will be greatly reduced. As we will see, the U'wa case is a good example of the success that can be achieved through a high degree of cooperation among international NGOs, social organizations, and in this case the traditional authorities of the U'wa community, who undoubtedly still hold decision-making power as to the direction in which they wish to take their fight, despite its marked transnationality.

Another argument in favor of the importance of taking a closer look at local developments in social conflicts that manage to establish transnational ties is related to the fact that the current hegemonic globalization process is bringing about major institutional transformations on both global and national levels. These changes have led to the creation of new institutions or have transformed existing ones, as witnessed by the current reforms in justice systems, the creation of Ombudsman's Offices, and the adoption of "multicultural constitutionalism" in Latin America (Van Cott, 2000), as well as the adoption of ILO Convention #169.

Within the framework of contemporary globalization processes, any social struggle now has the potential to take its case beyond national borders. The U'wa case provides examples of the specific forms these efforts can take. Nevertheless, I propose to focus on the different situations that favor the creation of collective actions outside national borders. Social struggles are generally efforts to influence decision-makers and so change social conditions seen as unjust or damaging (or potentially unjust or damaging) by those who are subject to, or concerned by, such conditions (or who fear being subjected to them in the future). Below I cite at least two different situations in which social struggles have the potential to generate collective transnational actions.

First, there is the case when the power to make a decision depends on a national government or a state institution. However, sometimes social mobilization or actions at the national level do not succeed in changing the situation, or the state institutions do not work (for example, judicial institutions). These kinds of situations can open a set of possibilities for collective action beyond national borders for the following reasons:

(a) Countries are signatories of international conventions. There are some international institutions in the field of human rights which were created to enforce those conventions when national institutions are not working. For example, actions before the human rights system of the United Nations, or before the regional systems of human rights, such as the Inter-American System of Human Rights.

(b) Countries have a scheme of international relations (commercial, political) with other countries. Some countries react when they know that other countries are concerned about a specific issue.

Second, there is when the power of decision-makers is to a considerable extent outside the control of the national government.[2] This kind of situation could be generated for at least three main reasons:

(a) The power of decision is in the hands of an international institution. International financial institutions in most cases are the institutions that have this power, such as the World Bank, the International Monetary Fund, regional development banks, etc. One of the classic examples is the case study that Margaret Keck analyzed (1998) about the project *Planafloro*, funded by the World Bank in Brazil.

(b) The power of decision is in the hands of a multinational corporation. The U'wa case is a good example of this type of situation.

(c) The power of decision is in the hands of a hegemonic country, such as the United States. One has, as an example, decisions about the forced eradication of illegal crops in Colombia and Bolivia.

The changing of the place in which the power of decision about more general matters resides is one of the main characteristics of the current process of hegemonic globalization. National sovereignty is not diluted, but transformed. The power that national states are losing is displaced to international financial institutions, multinational corporations, or hegemonic powers. Transnational social struggles undoubtedly make a contribution to the reversal of this process.

AN APPROACH TO THE U'WA PEOPLE

The U'wa currently inhabit northeastern Colombia, close to the border with Venezuela. Their ancestral territory, however, extended from the territory around the Sierra Nevada del Cocuy, in the department of Boyacá, Colombia, to the Sierra de Mérida in Venezuela (Osborn, 1985). Traditionally, the U'wa have lived and moved inside their territory between three different altitudinal spaces: the low areas, the foothills, and the mountains of the eastern range of the Colombian Andes (Osborn, 1995). For more than three centuries they were known as *Tunebos*, a nickname that was introduced by the Spanish conquerors, and which was abandoned only ten years ago. Since that time, in a process of growing cultural affirmation, they have been using their real name, U'wa, which means "people that think, people that can speak."

The U'wa are a very ceremonial people, who relate and recreate their own system of thinking through song.[3] Songs are complemented by their own system of rituals and the structure of social relations (Osborn, 1985: 18). The U'wa society is "very flexible and decentralized" (Osborn, 1985: 27). According to their mythical texts, it was divided formally into eight groups, but some of these have disappeared (Osborn, 1985: 27). The most traditional group is the Kubaru'wa. All U'wa groups speak the same language, *Uw'aka*, which means "the soul of the people" (Osborn, 1985: 26). Their language is very flexible and each group has its own variations, and additional variations exist in each group between the spoken language and the ceremonial language (Osborn, 1985: 26).

The modern process of social organization among the U'wa has followed a path parallel to that of the modern Colombian indigenous movement, which in the early 1970s started to create social organizations to fight for indigenous peoples' rights. At the beginning of the 1980s, some U'wa leaders decided to create *cabildos*, the kind of indigenous organization promoted by the most important indigenous organization at that moment, the CRIC (Consejo Regional Indigena del Cauca—Cauca Regional Indigenous Council). In 1984, representatives of the majority of the U'wa communities created the *Cabildo Tunebo*. Between 1987 and 1989, with the aid and guidance of the National Indigenous Organization of Colombia (ONIC), the U'wa founded the Tunebo Indigenous Organization of Eastern Colombia (Organización Indígena Tunebo del Oriente de Colombia—OITOC).[4]

Prior to this, the traditional U'wa authorities had never been represented in any of the organizations founded from the late 1970s on. For this reason, the U'wa community initiated an internal dialogue with its traditional authorities to determine what name would best represent their entire community. In 1990, after extensive internal debate, a consensus was finally reached to call themselves U'wa, and to rename the organization. The final consensus was the name "Asociación de Cabildos y Autoridades Tradicio- nales U'wa," or "Cabildo Mayor U'wa," which became the legal name in 1994.

Beginning in the 1940s, the U'wa began to lose their land to peasants who wanted to settle the Sarare region, which was the last frontier of the ancestral U'wa territory. The settlement process slowly ate away at the U'wa territory.

Even so, relations between the U'wa and the peasants never became violent (Rucinque, 1972: 46). In the early 1970s, the U'wa began to claim their land and to call for a reservation to be created (Osborn, 1982: 8). From the mid seventies to the mid eighties the Colombian Institute for Agricultural Reform (INCORA) granted 61,115 hectares of land to the U'wa.

In 1992, ONIC and the U'wa put together a territorial reorganization team whose mission was to reconstruct the historical borders of the U'wa territory and to create a territorial entity in the future, as had been established in the 1991 Colombian Constitution. This effort led to the idea of building the *Resguardo Único U'wa* (IDEADE, 1996: 8). At the beginning of 1993, the U'wa made a request to INCORA asking for the creation of this reserve, which would bring together the U'wa communities living in the departments of Boyacá, Santander, and Norte de Santander. The petition coincided with the beginning of the search for oil by Occidental Petroleum through its contracted companies. With the passage of time, the U'wa community began to perceive that the oil issue could become an obstacle to the success of their territorial claims.

THE U'WA OPPOSITION TO THE OIL DRILLING:
THE NATIONAL SCENARIO

In late 1991, Colombia's state-owned petroleum company, ECOPETROL, began signing equal partnership contracts (50/50) with the transnational oil companies Occidental Petroleum and Shell. From that time on, Occidental and Shell each held 25 per cent of the shares, while ECOPETROL held the remaining 50 percent.

On 14 May 1992, Occidental applied to INDERENA, Colombia's National Institute for Renewable Natural Resources, for an environmental license to start drilling for oil in the Samoré Block zone. At around the same time, Occidental used one of its subcontractors to begin geological testing on the U'wa territory (Project Underground, 1998: 27). It appears that the first public complaint by the U'wa was filed on 31 March 1993, against a company called Grand Tensor for unauthorized seismic activities as part of oil-related exploration in its territory (Mesa Cuadros, 1996: 174). On this date the U'wa issued the following communiqué:

> The company Grand Tensor commenced oil exploration on a portion of the Traditional U'wa Territory, despite the fact that, in January 1993, this same company held a meeting in which it agreed to respect the borders of the duly constituted Indigenous Reserve and Reservation. We, the U'wa people, hereby restate our opposition to any type of study or tampering with the natural resources of our land [. . .]. We are against exploration because: The

land has a head, arms, and legs, and the U'wa territory is its heart, it is the wing that sustains the Universe; if it is bled dry, it cannot continue to give life to the rest of the body. Oil and other natural resources are its blood, and for this reason we must take care of them. (U'wa Communiqué, 31 March 1993).

Between 1993 and 1995, Occidental developed public relations programs geared towards the U'wa community, highlighting the benefits of the company's investment in the area, such as health and education programs, roads, etc. (Project Underground, 1998: 27). Occidental took advantage of the absence of government institutions and attempted through numerous strategies to convince the members of the U'wa community to sign documents approving and accepting the oil exploration project on their lands.[5] At the same time, the company managed to divide the community: on one side stood a few members in favor of Occidental's position, and on the other the U'wa authorities and the majority of the community who were opposed to it.

THE CONFLICT REGARDING THE PROCESS OF PREVIOUS CONSULTATION IN ADMINISTRATIVE AND LEGAL JURISDICTIONS: THE FIRST ROUND

On 1 November 1994, the Cabildo Mayor U'wa sent a letter to the General Directorate of Indigenous Affairs (DGAI) expressing their opposition to the oil project and asking for a meeting (Jimeno Santoyo, 1995: 8). After consulting with the Ministers of the Environment and of Mining, as well as with ECOPETROL (Jimeno Santoyo, 1995: 7), the DGAI wrote up a document that included general criteria for the dialogue with the U'wa, and scheduled a meeting for early January 1995 in Arauca, a city in the department of the same name. In this document, the DGAI emphasized that Occidental and the Colombian government had to provide the U'wa with "ample information and effective intercultural communication" (DGAI, 1994). The DGAI further pointed out that the U'wa "should independently consider the different aspects of the project proposed, and inform the national government of their conclusions through the pertinent institutions [the Ministry of Government, DGAI] which would then issue an opinion on the consultation and make the pertinent recommendations" (DGAI, 1994). The DGAI emphasized two main concerns with respect to the project. One was the absence of a study on the possible social and cultural impacts of the project, and the other was the severe impact that other previous national projects had had on the life of the U'wa (DGAI, 1994).

A few days prior to the meeting in Arauca, the U'wa held the Third U'wa

Congress in el Chuscal, Boyacá. In the course of the Congress, the U'wa representatives repeated that Occidental had never attended its group assemblies or congresses and stated that "we, the indigenous U'wa ethnic communities, had no knowledge of the existence of this project." The assembly added that "in our territory there have been assemblies and congresses and Oxy was never present. They always talk with some U'wa members, but the majority of the population does not know them" (Centro de Bienestar Indigena, 1995).

The meeting in Arauca was held with the participation of the Ministry of Mines and Energy and the Ministry of the Environment, the DGAI, ECOPETROL, Occidental, and the U'wa. The minutes of the meeting stated: "There is a unanimity for beginning to study the modifications to the seismic project of Samoré with the participation of the U'wa authorities." The meeting concluded that an intercultural commission composed of the Cabildo Mayor U'wa, the DGAI, and Occidental would be created, with the purpose of reconnoitering the lands in which the project would take place, as well as those where the *resguardos* and indigenous reservations are located (DGAI, 1995). However, on 3 February 1995, the Ministry of the Environment (through Resolution #110) granted an environmental license to Occidental, a decision that took everyone by surprise.

The second meeting scheduled to continue talks was held on 21 February 1995. The U'wa representatives at this meeting protested because the license had been given without the due process of consultation (Corte Constitucional, 1997). "Some representatives of the indigenous communities expressed the necessity of not committing themselves to any kind of agreement before consulting their respective communities" (Ministerio de Medio Ambiente, 2000). After consultations, the U'wa made public a communiqué that had a strong impact at the national and international level:

> Facing certain death as a result of the loss of our lands, the extermination of our natural resources, the invasion of our sacred places, the disintegration of our families and communities, the forced silence of our songs and the lack of recognition of our history, we prefer a death with dignity: THE COLLECTIVE SUICIDE OF THE U'WA COMMUNITIES. This type of death corresponds with the pride of our ancestors who challenged the domination of the conquerors and missionaries (U'wa Communiqué, 1995).[6]

The DGAI took the threat of collective suicide seriously, and strongly emphasized that the conditions agreed in the meeting of Arauca had not yet been accomplished, and therefore it "considered that currently there is no legal basis to act in the U'wa territory" (DGAI, 1995).

On 22 August 1995, the ombudsman filed two different legal suits on behalf of the U'wa against the environmental license granted by the Ministry of the Environment. As the decision to grant this license had been an administrative decision, the regular legal path for this kind of suit was a petition of nullification before the Council of State (*Consejo de Estado*), the highest administrative court in Colombia. However, since the main purpose of the suit was to avoid irreparable damage to the U'wa people, the ombudsman also resorted to an extraordinary measure, a *tutela* action (writ of protection), as a rapid, temporary protective mechanism. This meant that the U'wa's legal dispute entered the court system through two different legal routes.

The *tutela* was filed with the Bogotá Superior Court. Twenty days later, the court ruled in favor of the petitioners. In fact, the court concluded that the administrative decision of the Ministry of the Environment was an attempt against the right to live of the U'wa, because "it did not take into account their own will" and was "precipitate" because it took everyone by surprise, including the officials of the DGAI. Therefore, the court decided to declare inapplicable the administrative decision of the Ministry of the Environment until the "the process of consultation is accomplished in a proper and legal manner" (Tribunal Superior de Bogotá, 1995).

The specific outcome of the Bogotá Superior Court's decision was that all seismic activities within U'wa territory be suspended until a true consultation process had been completed. Then, two days later, there was news regarding the suit filed with administrative authorities. The Council of State issued its initial decision, admitting the claims made by the ombudsman, but it also ruled that the seismic testing could not be suspended while the case was under consideration, effectively blocking the main legal consequences of the Bogotá Superior Court decision.

Occidental and ECOPETROL contested the unfavorable decision of the Bogotá Superior Court. Thus, the *tutela* action went before the Supreme Court on appeal. A month later, the Supreme Court ruled that the competent judicial authority to make a decision on the case was the Council of State. The Supreme Court reversed the Bogotá Superior Court decision without considering the case in depth. According to the Supreme Court, the differences in the interpretation of how the consultation process was to be managed did not constitute a violation of any constitutional right (Corte Suprema de Justicia, 1995).

In early 1996, the Constitutional Court, exercising its discretional powers of review, selected the U'wa *tutela* case for review. This meant that two of the highest courts in Colombia were simultaneously studying the U'wa case in different jurisdictions.[7] Finally, on 3 February 1997, a year after it began considering the case, the Constitutional Court reached a decision. As we will see, the Council of State made its decision almost immediately afterward, only one month later.

The Constitutional Court framed the constitutional discussion of the case as a conflict "created as a result of the exploration of natural resources in indigenous territories," and referred to "the special protection that the state should provide to the indigenous communities to preserve their ethnic, cultural, social, and economic identity and integrity" (Corte Constitucional, 1997). Thus, the court concluded that the right of the indigenous communities to preserve their cultural integrity is a fundamental right, as it is their right to participate in the decisions that affect them "through the mechanism of consultation." Effective participation in decisions is ensured by consultation. To the Constitutional Court, the right of participation established in Article 40(2) of the Colombian Constitution and ILO Convention #169 (approved by Colombia through Law 21 from 1991) represents a group of norms that "tend to secure and make effective that participation" (Corte Constitucional, 1997). With respect to this concrete case, the Constitutional Court found that the meeting of 10 and 11 January 1995, did not fulfill the requirements of a consultation. In conclusion, the court considered that the granting of the environmental license was accomplished in an irregular manner, and ruled that a new consultation process take place within the next 30 days.

After awaiting the Constitutional Court's decision for more than a year, the U'wa were very critical about it:

> The U'wa have learned through the media of the verdict of the Constitutional Court. [. . .] It is said that this verdict is favorable to us, that it recognizes that the government did not consult us about the project, and that they will now have to do this within a month. [. . .] However, we are also aware that the verdict authorizes the government to make the final decision, even if it is not in agreement with our way of thinking, or our life. If this is true, we are sorry that those judges have not been able to defend our fundamental rights: the integrity of our territory, our culture, and, in general, our lives. Rights which, besides being recognized by the constitution and both national and international norms presently in force, are also ancestral rights. [. . .] We do not understand why they will call us to a consultation if they already know what we have to say, which is what we have been saying since the beginning. (U'wa Communiqué, 10 February 1997)

As I said before, the Council of State's decision was issued a month later than that of the Constitutional Court. The Council of State concluded that the license had been granted in accordance with the legal requirements, and that a new process of consultation was not necessary. It emphasized that its decision would be final regarding this case. The main issue the Council of State analyzed to arrive to this conclusion was the indigenous communities' right of participation through the process of consultation, which, although not mandatory, was an ideal that the state should strive to achieve. The power to decide pertains to the Ministry of the Environment, not to the indigenous community. The Council of State added that, since the norms regulating the consultation do not specify the way to accomplish it, it is not possible to require the environmental authority to follow a specific procedure. It is only necessary that a representative of the state and the multinational company make a presentation of the project to the indigenous community, and that the latter expresses its opinions about the issue. As a result, the Arauca meeting in January 1995 was deemed a valid "consultation" (Consejo de Estado, 1997).

THE U'WA–OXY CONFLICT ARRIVES
ON THE INTERNATIONAL SCENE

In the first half of 1997, the U'wa–Oxy conflict entered the international scene through two different and simultaneous paths. In early May 1997, U'wa leader Berito Kubaru'wa and some members of ONIC were invited to the United States by the environmental group Amazon Coalition. Berito and the other indigenous leaders initially visited the cities of Washington, DC, New York, Los Angeles, and San Francisco. The meetings with Berito Kubaru'wa made a great impression on the US environmental, human rights, and indigenous organizations. In Washington, DC, Berito and the chairman of ONIC presented the case of the U'wa people before the Inter-American Human Rights Commission, with the legal assistance of the Earth Justice Legal Defense Fund, CEJIL, and the Colombian Judiciary Commission. Later, Berito traveled to New York, Los Angeles, and San Francisco.[8]

The success of the first visit to the US led to another invitation extended to Berito five months later, in October 1997. During the second visit, Berito Kubaru'wa went to Washington, DC, New York, Cambridge, Los Angeles, San Francisco, and Berkeley. In the course of that visit, he sent an open letter to the chairmen of Occidental and Shell, in which he stated:

> I am writing to ask you to hear my people's request and suspend your oil drilling project on the U'wa ancestral land. It is our hope that you will comply with the request of the U'wa people contained in this letter, you have no other choice. [. . .] You speak of negotiation and consultation with the U'wa. My people say that they cannot negotiate. Our Father has not authorized it. We cannot sell oil, the blood of our Mother Earth. Mother Earth is sacred. It is not for negotiation, so please do not try to confuse us and

others with offers. Please hear our request, a request that comes from our ancestral right by virtue of being born on our territory: Halt your oil project on U'wa ancestral land. The U'wa people need your sign of respect (U'wa Communiqué, 20 October 1997).

At the same time that the U'wa began traveling to the US, the Colombian government officially asked the Organization of American States (OAS) to intervene in the case (Arenas, 2001). In fact, in May 1997, the Colombian Minister of Foreign Affairs formally asked the OAS Secretary-General, headed by a former Colombian President, to conduct a research project about the dispute between the U'wa and Occidental, taking into account that the U'wa had a petition before the IACHR (Inter-American Commission on Human Rights). Former Colombian Minister of Defense, Rafael Pardo, working at that moment with the OAS, suggested the participation of Harvard University's PONSACS group in the mediation process (Arenas, 2001). As a result, the Secretary-General created the OAS/Harvard ad hoc project under the responsibility of the Unit for the Promotion of Democracy and indirectly funded by Occidental through Harvard University. The OAS/Harvard team visited Colombia a couple of times, and elaborated a document with recommendations that were presented to the Colombian government in September 1997 (Arenas, 2001).

The OAS/Harvard team made eight recommendations (Macdonald, Anaya, and Soto, 1998a), among them the following:

—An immediate and unconditional public statement by Oxy and Shell, "in which they commit to suspending the execution of plans for oil exploration or exploitation in the Samoré Block as a first step toward creating better conditions for any future resumption of oil development activities."
—The "normalization of the process to expand the U'wa *Resguardo*," as a way to eliminate the perception that it had been stopped "as a means of exerting pressure on them."
—"A moderation of the public rhetoric," especially "in statements that link those who have opposed the oil companies to the guerrilla movement or drug traffickers."
—"Recognition of and respect for the U'wa system of leadership and authority." As a result, if there are internal differences among the U'wa, "they must be allowed to resolve their differences using their own system of authority."
—"Establishment of a consultation process under the responsibility of the Government of Colombia" that should be divided into two phases, the first to occur in the near future, and the second later. The purposes of the first consultation would be "to reach an agreement with the U'wa on the

geographical limits of their territory, which should also serve to identify the area outside of which the suspension of oil operations could be lifted." The purposes of the second phase would be "to develop measures to prevent harm to the U'wa that might result from renewed operations in the Samoré Block."

The conclusions and recommendations from the OAS/Harvard team were widely publicized in the Colombian mass media and presented as a big success for the U'wa claim. The Colombian government and the oil companies sent letters to the OAS accepting the recommendations and showing their interest in the continuation of the process (Avila, 2000). However, the U'wa and ONIC reacted with caution. Both were worried that the recommendations might open the door to future oil exploration within U'wa territory. In a communiqué, ONIC stated its agreement with some of the conclusions, but was very critical of the entire framework of the ad hoc project:

> A dialogue in which only one party is expected to persuade the other is not a dialogue, but an imposition. [. . .] These recommendations seem to pre-figure a result, and there is no space for deliberation. As a result, the procedure that is recommended and the temporary suspension of the project will benefit the oil companies and the government, and will prolong the anxiety of the U'wa people (ONIC Communiqué, October 1997).

The continuation of the OAS/Harvard project was made dependent on a written answer from the U'wa expressing their interest in continuing with the process. The U'wa verbally said that they were interested, but never sent a letter (Avila, 2000).[9] As a result, the second phase of the work of the OAS/Harvard team could not be developed.[10]

THE NEW DYNAMICS OF THE NATIONAL AND INTERNATIONAL SCENARIOS

The U'wa–Oxy conflict has not been the same since it became an inter-national story. Now, it is more complex, more public. Perhaps that is why the U'wa struggle is quite exceptional within the context of contemporary Colombia, where the majority of social struggles, including those of other indigenous peoples, have been harshly and bloodily repressed by paramilitary groups, with close collaboration from the Colombian army representing the interests of landowners, drug traffickers, and local and national politicians.

Occidental has tried to take the main decisions relating to the conflict back to the national scenario. For this reason, it has not been very active in promoting a second stage of the OAS/Harvard project.[11] The publicity received by the case changed the balance of power between the oil company and the U'wa, and the first result of this was Shell's decision to withdraw and sell its shares to Occidental in 1998 (Avila, 2000).

It is clear that the Colombian government changed its strategy regarding the U'wa conflict, and took into account some of the ideas contained in the OAS/Harvard report (Arenas, 2001). President Samper's government (1994–1998) began the process by designing a new legal framework that would change the reference points of the U'wa–Oxy conflict; President Pastrana's government (1998–2002) maintained and reinforced these changes. Legislation regarding the consultation process with indigenous communities, the requirements for granting environmental licenses to oil companies, and the status of oil territories changed, in ways that are undoubtedly more favorable to multinational companies. At the same time, in an apparently contradictory measure, the government increased the size of the U'wa territory, and issued an environmental license to Oxy, allowing it to begin oil exploration on U'wa land.

As we saw before, the expansion of the U'wa *resguardo* was an old aspiration of the U'wa people. As part of the new strategy of the government, the Minister of the Environment decided to push that petition before INCORA. For this purpose, the Minister began to approach the U'wa community. The discussion about the expansion of U'wa territory started formally on 23 January 1999 in Samoré. By July 1999 the work of delimitation was completed. One of the last minutes of the meetings between the Ministry of Environment and the U'wa stated that "the U'wa highlighted the accomplishment of the activities accorded by the Minister and involved institutions, expressing their satisfaction about the advance of their territorial aspirations" (Mayr and Pérez, 1999b). In fact, it only took six months to resolve an issue that had been raised more that ten years previously.

On 23 August 1999, the Colombian government formally gave the U'wa community the title of the expansion of their territory, and promised 150 million dollars to clear the area and buy the land from the settlers who lived there. The Ministry and the Cabildo Mayor U'wa signed a joint statement to the following effect:

> Today, we complete the process agreed to between the Minister of the Environment, the INCORA, and the Cabildo Mayor U'wa to define the limits of the *Resguardo Unido U'wa*, which are protected through Resolution #56 of August 6, 1999 elaborated by INCORA (Mayr and Pérez, 1999b).

In this same communiqué, the U'wa added: "The U'wa hereby state [. . .] that the process that was just completed in no way compromises their position of disagreement regarding oil exploration either on or off their land"

(Mayr and Pérez, 1999b). The Cabildo Mayor U'wa also sent a letter to President Pastrana stating:

> Today you have shown a willingness to recognize a part of our struggle in the defense of life. Although today you are formally turning over to us a portion of our territory, we request unconditional respect for the position that we the U'wa maintain of not permitting any type of OIL EXPLORATION AND DRILLING ON OR OFF THE LAND you have legally recognized as ours (U'wa Comuniqué, 23 August 1999).

At the same time that the reserve's boundaries were being expanded (in October 1999), Occidental applied for a new environmental license under the new regulations mentioned earlier. This was denounced by the U'wa and ONIC in February 1999 in the following terms:

> [T]he national government, through the Ministry of the Environment and with the support of the General Directorate of Indigenous Affairs of the Ministry of the Internal Affairs, is about to issue a new license for exploratory drilling in the U'wa territory behind the U'wa people's back [. . .]. It is almost certain that in the next few days the Ministry of the Environment will grant Oxy a new environmental license inside the U'wa territory (U'wa Communiqué, 4 February 1999).

However, the environmental license was granted only after the process of extension of the U'wa territory was finished. On 21 September 1999, the Minister of the Environment authorized Oxy to explore the Gibraltar I well, in the department of Norte de Santander. The well is located just 500 meters outside of the new *resguardo*, but is still part of the U'wa's ancestral territory. The decision caused indignation among the U'wa, who said that the government had deceived them:

> In an ironic move that injures our most highly esteemed historic and ancestral rights, the Minister of the Environment, Juan Mayr, has issued an environmental license that will allow the multinational company Occidental of Colombia (Oxy) to begin drilling activities [. . .].
> Furthermore, we would like to make it known that, through a shady process that was conducted without full consultation, we were called to negotiate the terms of our territory, which historical circumstances wrested from our community. With good faith, we attempted to secure a part of our legitimate rights, but on a parallel path, the Minister of the Environment and his closest aids have shown that economic interests will pilfer and destroy our Mother Earth (U'wa Communiqué, 21 September 1999).

The growing support for
the U'wa at the local level

Support for the U'wa among the social organizations from the Arauca Department started before the U'wa Hearing for Life, in 1996. However, it was only after August 1998 that the U'wa and the social organizations in Arauca started to work together. In that month, the social organizations of the Sarare region, in the departments of Arauca, Norte de Santander and Boyacá, organized a two-week civic protest. The protest involved the towns of Arauquita, Saravena, Fortul, and Tame (Arauca), Cubará (Boyacá), as well as Toledo and Labateca (Norte de Santander), and mobilized almost 20,000 peasants. The main objective of the protesters was to paralyze the commercial activities in all the towns in the region. The novelties were the participation of the U'wa and the inclusion of a list of claims against oil exploration throughout the region, especially inside U'wa territory, as well as the demand for the expansion of their *resguardo*.

The U'wa feel that the Arauca people have been their main ally in this struggle. They have mobilized the Araucas to work with them "because they already had the experience of the Caño Limón catastrophe, brought about by Occidental in their own department."[12] ONIC and indigenous Senator Lorenzo Muelas have also been very important allies of the U'wa. ONIC has given priority to the U'wa case, as well as to another very complex and tragic case: the struggle of the Emberá Katio people against a dam that was built in their territory with funds from Canadian and Swedish corporations. The Emberá Katio have been regularly attacked and massacred by paramilitary groups as punishment for their opposition to the dam. Without a doubt, after the U'wa case, the Emberá Katio case is the Colombian social struggle that has attracted the most global attention.

The mobilization of the Colombian indigenous movement in support of the U'wa and Emberá Katio peoples started at the national level in September 1999, when ONIC, the movement Autoridades Indigenas de Colombia [Colombian Indigenous Authorities] (AICO), and the Coordinadora Indigena de la Cuenca Amazonica [Indigenous Coordinating Committee of the Amazon Basin] (COICA), stated that the Pastrana government had declared a war of extermination against Colombian indigenous peoples because it was not complying with the constitutional and legal measures that protect indigenous people and had introduced changes to the law to benefit multinational corporations (ONIC Communiqué, 23 September 1999). ONIC stated that "a long process is beginning, a process of legal developments and regulations that openly clash with the recognition of the country's multiculturalism" (ONIC Communiqué, 21 October 1999). On 25 February 2000, ONIC and environmental groups mobilized in Bogotá in support of the U'wa and Emberá Katio people. On 4 April 2000, ONIC announced the beginning of a national mobilization in defense of their fundamental rights, after President Pastrana expressed interest in being part of the North American Free Trade Agreement (NAFTA). ONIC stated: "We are facing the imminent possibility of a constitutional counter-reform that will eliminate our rights [. . .]. Our future depends on the struggle of the U'wa and Emberá Katio peoples. This struggle will define what will happen concerning agrarian reform, territorial organization, cultural diversity, autonomy, and life" (ONIC Communiqué, 4 April 2000).

The U'wa advocacy network in the United States, Europe, and Latin America

As stated previously, the group Amazon Coalition invited the U'wa to the United States in May 1997. The news about the U'wa's threat to commit mass suicide in 1995 attracted the attention of many environmental groups to their dispute, but it was the U'wa's first trip to the United States that represented the main impulse in the construction of networks and the high public profile of the case in the US. As a result of this visit, the activist Terry Freitas from the United States became one of the most active supporters of the U'wa (Arenas, 2001). Two years later, in circumstances that remain unclear, Freitas and two North American pro-indigenous leaders working in support of the case against Oxy were murdered by leftist FARC guerrillas on U'wa lands in Colombia.

The U'wa have been traveling to the United States regularly since 1997, visiting cities such as Washington DC, New York, Boston, Cambridge, Los Angeles, San Francisco, Berkeley, Chicago, and Madison. The most active groups supporting the U'wa in the United States have been the Rain Forest Action Network (RAN), Amazon Watch, Amazon Coalition, and the U'wa Defense Project. The first two organizations have the most complete and updated web sites about the U'wa case (www.ran.org and www.amazonwatch.org). One of the first strategies used by the coalition of US environmentalist, human rights, and indigenous groups supporting the U'wa cause was to take out advertisements in the *New York Times*.

Former Vice-President Al Gore and the investment fund giant Fidelity Investment were favorite targets of the US environmental movement supporting the U'wa people. Their mobilization against these targets got the attention of the most important newspapers in the United States. The main US-based U'wa support groups were in constant communication with the U'wa people in Bogotá and Cubará, where the Cabildo Mayor's headquarters is located.

One of most interesting outcomes of the U'wa support networks in the

United States was the fact that their cause became linked to the new and growing movement against multinational companies. For many individuals involved in this movement, the U'wa case has been a source of inspiration. In April 2000, the Rain Forest Action Network (RAN) organized public protests in Washington, DC as part of the demonstrations against the World Bank, and a more ambitious action was organized in Los Angeles during the August 2000 Democratic Convention, when nearly 3000 people took to the streets to express their support for the U'wa.

The U'wa made their first trip to Europe in March 1998 when they went to England. Between this date and June 2000, the U'wa made seven different tours of Europe, visiting at least nine countries: England, Spain, Finland, Russia, Belgium, Germany, Switzerland, Holland, and Italy. The first group to support the U'wa in Europe was probably the one created in Madrid, Spain, in 1997. The publicity of the U'wa case in Spain resulted in the selection of Berito Kubaru'wa as the recipient of the prestigious Bartolomé de las Casas Prize, awarded by the Spanish government in April 1998.

Many of the solidarity actions in Europe and Latin America originated from the actions of the main Ecuadorian environmental group, Acción Ecológica. They were the only non-Colombian organization that was present at the U'wa Hearing for Life, in August 1996, representing Oilwatch. Acción Ecológica is the umbrella organization of Friends of the Earth-Ecuador and one of the most active members of the coalition of environmental groups in Friends of the Earth International (FoEI). This coalition created Oilwatch in 1996, a global network of activist groups campaigning against the oil industry. Oilwatch's International Secretariat is located in Ecuador, under the responsibility of Acción Ecológica.

In an interview, one of the members of the Oilwatch Secretariat stated that the organization's strategy is to work directly with local people (Melsher, 1999).[13] In keeping with this philosophy, in February 1999, Oilwatch Africa organized a trip to Nigeria for Colombian indigenous leader and senator Lorenzo Muelas, to get a firsthand impression of the effects of oil drilling on the Niger River delta. The Oilwatch International Secretariat also organized the July 1999 visit of Lorenzo Muelas, Berito Kubaru'wa, and two other U'wa leaders to Ecuador, to visit the Secoya, a small indigenous community on whose lands Occidental Petroleum is conducting drilling.[14] In late 1999, the Oilwatch Secretariat stated: "the U'wa are now at the head of the environmental movement because they are bringing new arguments to the table. This brings hope to other peoples in their efforts to resist the onslaught of the oil industry" (Melsher, 1999).

The Colombian Minister of the Environment's initiative to organize a conference in Brussels in the summer of 2000, entitled "Colombian-European Environmental Alliance," was hailed by many U'wa support groups as a unique lobbying opportunity (Van der Hoek, 1999). For this reason, Oilwatch organized a European tour for U'wa and Emberá Katio spokespersons. Although the event itself was cancelled at the last minute due to growing opposition and criticism of the Colombian government in many Brussels diplomatic circles (Dupret, 2000: 13), the U'wa and Emberá Katio spokespersons made successful visits to six European countries, including a presentation before the European Parliament, meetings with representatives from the International Labor Organization responsible for Convention #169, and a meeting with the Secretariat of the UN Working Group on Indigenous Peoples.

The U'wa have been connected to indigenous organizations throughout Latin America, some of which have invited them to events in Mexico, in 1998, and in Chile, in June 2000. Paradoxically, the interest of the U'wa in maintaining control over their struggle at the national level, and thus avoiding manipulation, has caused a demobilization of many environmental and human rights NGOs in Colombia. Despite the fact that these NGOs are supportive of the U'wa cause, they have taken a passive role in the last couple of years. This tendency slowly began to be changed from the outside, through Friends of the Earth International, which has been encouraging the environmental NGO Censat-Agua Viva to have a more active role in the U'wa case and inside the Oilwatch group.[15] As a result, Censat-Agua Viva has became the main local point of support for many international initiatives related to the U'wa struggle.

THE CONFLICT REGARDING THE PROCESS OF PREVIOUS CONSULTATION IN ADMINISTRATIVE AND LEGAL JURISDICTIONS: THE SECOND ROUND

After the environmental license was granted to Occidental in September 1999, the President of ONIC appealed against this administrative decision. Responding to the appeal, the Minister of the Environment stated that "based on the information contained in the socioeconomic study of environmental impact, it was possible to establish with certainty that there are no indigenous or black communities in the region of the well, or within the area of interest to the drilling, or in the areas where it can have a direct or indirect influence" (Ministerio de Medio Ambiente, 1999).

He added that, in compliance with Decree #1320 of 1998, he had consulted the Ministry of Internal Affairs and INCORA, the institutions responsible for certifying the presence of indigenous peoples in areas of oil exploration. The Office of Indigenous Affairs (Ministry of Internal Affairs), using only maps, concluded and certified that there was no permanent presence of indigenous peoples in the area of the project. INCORA, also using only maps, certified that no indigenous territory had been legally established in that area. As a result, the Minister of the Environment washed his hands of the issue and concluded:

> Thus, the Ministry of the Environment has strictly and diligently complied with the legal provisions that require that certifications from the competent authorities must document the facts related with the presence of indigenous communities in the territory and that an adequate consultation takes place (Ministerio de Medio Ambiente, 1999).

There is no doubt that Minister Mayr knew that what the DGAI was certifying was patently false. He had personally visited the U'wa territory several times, but the civil servants who wrote the certification based their information only on maps. Perhaps for this reason, Mayr added the following to his response:

> [T]he Honorable Council of State declared that Decree #1320 of 1998 [. . .] conforms to the law [. . .]. In this case, the Ministry of the Environment has made a strict application of Decree #1320 of 1998 [. . .]. Taking this into account, the Ministry of the Environment cannot order the realization of a previous consultation with the U'wa indigenous community, because it would be violating the juridical order of the country (Ministerio de Medio Ambiente, 1999).

Although the Ombudsman's Office continued supporting the U'wa, especially through the delegate for indigenous affairs, it did not present a new complaint against the Ministry of the Environment's decision to grant an environmental license to Oxy. This time, the U'wa had the legal support of MINGA, a Colombian human rights NGO.[16] The U'wa's lawyer filed a *tutela* action (writ of protection) against the Minister of the Environment, the Minister of Internal Affairs, and Occidental Petroleum for violation of the fundamental right of the indigenous communities to be consulted.

In the first hearing, the judge concluded that the legal problem was to determine if in the process of granting an environmental license to Occidental the administration had failed to comply with the fundamental right of consultation to the indigenous communities established in ILO Convention #169. Basing her arguments on the constitution, previous rulings from the Constitutional Court, ILO Convention #169, and especially on the fact that Decree #1320 had not been applied, the Judge of the 11th Circuit Court of Bogotá concluded that the license had been granted without previous consultation. Additionally, the judge found "serious doubts" and contradictions in the process concerning the possible existence of indigenous peoples and *resguardos* in the area of the environmental license. The judge concluded that the plaintiff should carry the case before the administrative jurisdiction, which should decide the matter. However, at the same time, she accepted the *tutela* as a transitory mechanism of protection until the administrative jurisdiction made a decision. Finally, the judge decided to order the suspension of activities in the Gibraltar I well to avoid any irreparable harm to the indigenous community.

The decision of the 11th Circuit Court of Bogotá was impugned by the Ministry of the Environment, the Ministry of Internal Affairs, and Occidental Petroleum. Occidental argued that the decision ignored the current norms relating to the process of previous consultation to indigenous communities, and that the order for suspension of activities would bring serious damage to the country.

The Bogotá Superior Court studied the petition in its second hearing, and centered its analysis on two main issues. The first was the protection of fundamental rights invoked by the plaintiff. The court concluded that, because Occidental Petroleum had annexed a study of environmental impact and a study of the ethnography of the region to their petition for an environmental license, the Minister of the Environment had arrived at the conclusion that the life of the U'wa community was not in danger, and neither was the natural and cultural wealth in the area of influence of the project. The court added that "the area of exploratory interest of the Gibraltar I Well is completely outside the new U'wa *resguardo*" (Tribunal Superior de Bogotá, 2000).

The second issue that the court analyzed was the legal path taken by the plaintiff. In this respect, the court concluded that the *tutela* was not the way to decide these matters, but the administrative jurisdiction was, because the impugnation of a study on the social and anthropological reality of an indigenous community takes time and requires the advice of experts. The court added that the ancestral territories are not recognized by the constitution or by ILO Convention #169. As a result, it revoked the decision of the 11th Circuit Court of Bogotá.

THE LATEST DEVELOPMENTS IN
THE AREA OF OIL EXPLORATION

After the Ministry of the Environment approved Oxy's new environmental license in 1999, the U'wa launched a series of direct actions that they termed civil disobedience. Those actions included a peaceful occupation of the drilling site, a general strike in the Sarare region, and the blockade of regional routes, among other actions. The Colombian government initially responded to those actions with violence, taking back the Gibraltar I Well by force,[17] and violently dispersing the indigenous people involved in the blockades, resulting in the death of three U'wa children.[18] Days later, about 1200 U'wa and 4000 peasants from the region staged a demonstration at the Gibraltar site, in the municipality of Toledo, Norte de Santander.[19] The Colombian government chose to completely ignore most of the direct actions taken by the U'wa. In late June 2000, the social organizations of the region launched a new popular strike by blocking the Saravena-Pamplona road.[20] A week later, the blockade was called off after a partial agreement was reached with the government, which promised to start negotiations to seek a solution to the conflict.

However, at the beginning of September 2000, after increased incidents and rising tension with the police and the army, the U'wa community issued the following statement:

> The U'wa people reject the despotic attitude of the Andres Pastrana government, the lies and the deceit that he attempts to legalize by means of informing national and international citizens of a process of alleged respect for our rights that in reality does not exist. While national talks are taking place, the machinery is arriving at the drilling site and the process of violence is growing stronger. (U'wa Communiqué, 11 September 2000).

Consequently, days later the U'wa community decided to walk out on the negotiations with the government. Through mass militarization of the zone, the Colombian government managed to allow Occidental to start exploration by the end of that year. The mobilizations of the year 2000 basically closed out another cycle of direct local struggle.

Given the intense militarization to which the zone was subjected, and the repression of all peaceful protest, the U'wa community intensified its actions on an international level. However, in an unexpected turn of events, on 3 May 2001 Occidental announced that it had not found oil in the area; as a result, it returned oil concesessions on U'wa land to the Colombian government. Transnational NGOs supporting the U'wa announced their victory and celebrated the episode as the culmination of the international campaign (Reinsborough, 2004). With Occidental's withdrawal, therefore, the cycle of contentious transnational mobilization that began in 1997 with the first visit of the U'wa to the US came to an end.

After witnessing many tactics by their opponents, the U'wa were most skeptical about Occidental's withdrawal, and declared that "a battle has been won, the war to defend the earth and our territories is on."[21] In fact, in early 2002, ECOPETROL resumed seismic prospecting in U'wa land, now renamed Siriri and Catleya blocks. Since then, the U'wa have tried to reignite international solidarity, but the response has not been as enthusiastic as before, despite several trips to the US by some of their leaders. It is clear that it is always harder for international supporters to fight against local actors such as ECOPETROL.

The oil exploration on U'wa territory has advanced very slowly during the last few years, allowing the U'wa to concentrate on strengthening their own community, including starting some projects on education and health with the support of some international NGOs. Violence continues to be a permanent threat to the U'wa as a result of the unresolved Colombian armed conflict. Anticipating the possibility of future drilling inside the U'wa territory, for the last three years ECOPETROL has tried to reach an agreement with the U'wa for a new consultation process. If oil is found inside the U'wa territory, ECOPETROL would apply for a new environmental license from the environmental authorities, which could restart a third wave of conflict at administrative and judicial scenarios at both national and international levels. In May 2005, the U'wa categorically rejected any possibility for a new consultation process proposed by the Colombian government. Instead, they asserted that their territorial aspirations had not yet been accomplished, even though INCORA had ordered in 1999 that the area granted to the U'wa be cleared. Additionally, they asserted that they do not have knowledge about the state of the investigation for the killings of the three Americans killed inside U'wa territory in 1998 nor the killing of three U'wa children during the repression of their protest in 2000.[22] Whatever the results of the exploration now underway, the outcome of the U'wa-oil companies conflict remain uncertain.

CONCLUSIONS

If any one trait can be used to describe Latin American indigenous communities, it is their tenacity, their refusal to disappear as a people. In recent decades this trait, combined with their ability to adapt their struggles to the historical moment, have once again demonstrated the originality and wealth of ideas of the cause they defend. In an era of transationalization, indigenous movements have achieved one of the most dynamic and original linkages among local, national, and transnational efforts seen to date. As Boaventura de Sousa Santos points out, even when an initially local struggle becomes national, it remains local, and the same occurs when it becomes transnational. But at the same time, when a struggle is taken up outside national borders, it becomes deterritorialized, and new national and local dynamics are created (Santos, 2001: 211); in turn, these new local dynamics transform and influence transnational actors and spaces.

Some have suggested that solidarity with the U'wa was aroused due to their dramatic strategy of threatening mass suicide, which elicited an unexpected international response. The truth is that the suicide threat did initially help attract both national and international attention to the U'wa community's cause. However, as I have attempted to show, all individuals and organizations who have come into direct contact with the U'wa people have been struck by the richness of their culture, the charisma of many of their spokespersons, and by the originality, exemplarity, and emancipatory potential of their discourse and struggle. For the great majority of their supporters, it is the preservation of the U'wa culture and their very special relationship with nature that has motivated their solidarity. It should be noted that as time goes on, the issue of group suicide is less and less frequently cited in news about the U'wa struggle, but solidarity with their cause has continued to grow.[23]

The U'wa case contains a series of special circumstances that have led to its successful transnationalization: 1) the strong cultural heritage of the U'wa people; 2) their collective pride and incredible ability to speak for themselves, as well as their talent for adapting the presentation of their arguments to many different scenarios; 3) the extensive use the U'wa made of public communiqués and open letters, which helped to keep their allies informed as well as to provide an ongoing update on the facts regarding their case; 4) the existence of a national and international human rights movement focused on Colombia (with headquarters in large cities like Washington, DC, Madison, and Brussels), possessed of extensive experience in legal work and lobbying, plus national and international contacts and resources that have helped support and build promotional networks for the U'wa cause in Europe and the United States; 5) the fact that Occidental Petroleum's headquarters is located in the US, a hegemonic global power and principal player in Colombia's economic and political affairs.

In this chapter I have attempted to illustrate the social and institutional complexity underlying a specific social struggle before it became an issue taken up by a "transnational promotional network." I have offered a detailed analysis of the process the U'wa community was involved in before the issue of oil exploration placed them in the national and international spotlight. The oil conflict arose at a time when the U'wa were immersed in a positive process of reconstructing their culture and identity as a people, which was linked to consolidating their social organization, to a willingness to fight to recover a large portion of their ancestral lands, and to the growing national prestige of the indigenous movement. I have also described the complex institutional, administrative, and legal developments that can be activated in cases such as this, which serve to mobilize and test such institutions. Many of the national institutions involved in the case, such as the Ombudsman's Office and the Constitutional Court, were newly created under the 1991 Constitution. Some of the legal concepts and regulations are also new, such as the concept of the *tutela* action, and ILO Convention #169.

I have attemped to pay attention to all processes: local (the U'wa's development of a process of modern social organization, their fight for their lands), regional (the social struggles in the Arauca Department), national (the responses of administrative and legal institutions to the conflict between the U'wa and Oxy, the national solidarity in the Colombian indigenous movement and others), and transnational (the construction of solidarity networks and promotion of the U'wa cause). I have also described how transnationalization has created new dynamics and fostered new relationships among local, national, and transnational spheres.

BIBLIOGRAPHY

Arenas, Luis Carlos (2001). "Postscriptum: sobre el caso U'wa," Boaventura de Sousa Santos and Mauricio Garcia-Villegas (eds.), *El Caleidoscopio de las Justicias en Colombia. Análisis sociojurídico*. Vol. II. Bogotá: Colciencias. 143–157.

Avila, Ricardo (2000). "El Caso de la Comunidad U'wa: Territorio y Petróleo," (mimeo).

Berichá (1992). *Tengo los Pies en la Cabeza*. Bogotá: Los Cuatro Elementos.

Brysk, Alison (2000). *From Tribal Village to Global Village. Indian Rights and International Relations in Latin America*. Stanford, CA: Stanford UP.

Centro de Bienestar Indigena (1995). *Tercer Congreso Indigena U'wa*. 7 January.

Corte Constitucional (1997). Sentencia T-652/97. Bogotá, 10 November.

Corte Suprema de Justicia (1997). Sentencia *SU-039/97*. Bogotá, 3 February.

Defensoría del Pueblo (1996). "Audiencia U'wa por la Vida. Intervención de la Defensoría del Pueblo" (mimeo), 17 August.

DGAI (1994). "Criterios generales sobre la consulta al pueblo U'was en relación con el proyecto Samoré" (mimeo).

——————— (1995). "Comunicado de Prensa" (mimeo), 4 May.

Dupret, Paul-Emile (2000). "Conferencia 'Tierra, derechos humanos y paz en Colombia,'" *Boletin Informativo de la Coordinación Colombia-Europa-Estados Unidos* 8 July: 13–14.

Evans, Peter (2000). "Fighting Marginalization with Transnational Networks. Counter-Hegemonic Globalization," *Contemporary Sociology* 29(1): 231–241.

IDEADE—Instituto de Estudios Ambientales para el Desarrollo, *et al.* (1996). "Estudio Socioeconómico, Ambiental, Jurídico y de Tenencia de Tierras para la Constitución del Resguardo Único U'wa. Resumen Ejecutivo" (mimeo), Bogotá.

Jimeno Santoyo, Gladys (1995). Letter to Judge Aida Rangel Quintero, Magistrate of the Bogotá Superior Court (mimeo), 7 September.

Keck, Margaret E. (1998). "Planafloro in Rodania: The Limits of Leverage?" Jonathan A. Fox and L. David Brown (eds.), *The Struggle for Accountability. The World Bank, NGOs, and Grassroots Movements*. Cambridge, MA: MIT Press.

——————————, and Kathryn Sikkink (1998). *Activists Beyond Borders. Advocacy Networks in International Politics*. Ithaca, NY: Cornell UP.

Macdonald, Theodore (1998). "Environment, Indians, and Oil, 'Preventive Diplomacy,'" *DRCLAS News* Fall.

———————————, James Anaya, and Yadira Soto (1998a). *The Samore Case:*

Observations and Recomendations. Organization of American States/Harvard University. Washington, DC. Accessed on 10 October 1999.

——————— (1998b). Letter to Roberto Cobaria and Abadio Green, (mimeo), Washington, DC, 16 June.

Mayr, Juan, and Roberto Pérez Gutierrez (1999a). "Comunicado" (mimeo), Tamaría, 23 August.

——————— (1999b). "Acta de Acuerdo del Consenso entre el Ministerio del Medio Ambiente y el Cabildo Mayor U'wa" (mimeo). Cubará, 19 July.

Melsher, Elisa (1999). "A Year of Oil Resistance. An Interview with FoE Ecuador's Esperanza Martinez," *Link* 91, October/December. Friends of the Earth.

Mesa Cuadros, Gregorio (1996). "Los U'wa: Pueblo Indigena Ancestral del Norte de Boyacá," *Memorias Ambientales de las Provincias de Norte y Gutierrez, Boyacá (1990–1996).* Bogotá: Pontificia Universidad Javeriana—IDEADE.

Ministerio de Medio Ambiente (1999). *Resolución Número 0997. Por Medio de la Cual se Resuelve un Recurso de Reposición Interpuesto contra la Resolución # 0788 del 21 de Septiembre de 1999 y se Toman Otras Determinaciones.* Bogotá, 23 November.

——————— (2000). "U'wa" Accessed on 7 July 2000.

ONIC (1997). "U'wa: Defensa del Destino Indigena. El Presente y Futuro de un Pueblo y el Petróleo," *Utopias* 5(42), March.

——————— (1999). "Defendiendo la Sangre de Kerachikará. Breve Resumen del Caso del Pueblo U'wa," (mimeo), Oficina jurídica de la ONIC.

Organizaciones Sociales Departamento de Arauca y Cubará (1998). "Pliego de Exigencias del Paro Cívico por el Derecho a la Vida, Soberania y Medio Ambiente—Contra la Explotación y Exploración Petrolera y el Fenómeno Paramilitar en Arauca" (mimeo), Saravena, August.

Osborn, Ann (1985). *El Vuelo de las Tijeretas.* Bogotá: Fundación de Investigaciones Arqueológicas Nacionales, Banco de la República.

——————— (1995). *Las Cuatro Estaciones. Mitologia y Estructura Social entre los U'wa.* Bogotá: Banco de la República.

Project Underground (1998). *Blood of Our Mother. The U'wa People, Occidental Petroleum and the Colombian Oil Industry.* Berkeley. http://www.moles.org/ProjectUnderground/uwa_index.html.

Reinsborough, Patrick (2004). "How the U'wa and People's Globalization Beat Big Oil," David Solnit (ed.), *Globalize Liberation. How to Uproot the System and Build a Better World.* San Francisco: City Lights.

Rucinque, Hector F. (1972). *Colonization of the Sarare Region of Eastern Colombia.* PhD dissertation. University of Wisconsin-Madison.

Santos, Boaventura de Sousa (2001). "El significado politico y jurídico de la jurisdicción indígena," Boaventura de Sousa Santos and Mauricio Garcia Villegas (eds.), *El Caleidoscopio de las Justicias en Colombia.* Bogotá: Colciencias.

Smith, Jackie (2000). "Globalizing Resistance. The Battle of Seattle and the Future of Social Movements," paper presented at the seminar "Contentious Politics," Lazersfeld Center for Social Movements, Columbia University.

———————, Charles Chatfield, and Ron Pagnuco, eds. (1997). *Transnational Social Movements and Global Politics. Solidarity beyond the State.* Syracuse, NY: Syracuse UP.

Tarrow, Sidney (1998). *Power in Movement. Social Movements and Contentious Politics.* Cambridge: Cambridge UP.

Tribunal Superior de Bogotá (1995). Sentencia de Tutela. Magistrado ponente
Aída Rangel Quintero, Bogotá, 12 September (mimeo).
——————— (2000). Sentencia de Tutela. Sala Penal. Magistrado ponente
Marco Elias Arevalo Rozo. Bogotá, 15 May (mimeo).
Tribunal Superior de Pamplona (2000). Sentencia de Tutela. Magistrado
ponente Victor Hugo Ballen. Pamplona, 10 July (mimeo).
U'wa Defense Working Group (2000). "U'wa Leaders Present the Colombian
Government with Proof of Royal Land Titles Granted by the King of Spain."
E-mail from the U'wa Defense Working Group, 15 September.
Van der Hoek, Aart (1999). "At the Cliff's Edge. Demonstrating with the U'wa
in Colombia," Link 91 (Oct/Dec). Friends of the Earth.

Notes

1 My thanks to U'wa leaders Berito Kubaru'wa, Gilberto Kubaru'wa, and
Ebaristo Tegria. For their generous collaboration, I would like to thank Carlos
Gomez of ONIC, the National Indigenous Organization of Colombia;
Tatiana Roa of Censat-Agua Viva; Leslie Wirpsa, Amanda Hammatt, Esther
Sanchez, and Yesenia Pumarada. Obviously, the author assumes sole respon-
sibility for all statements, interpretations, and omissions in the text.

2 There are multiple reasons that can explain why the decision could be out of
the hands of a national government (in the case of agreements, contracts,
different kinds of conditions or restrictions, fear of economic sanctions, etc.).

3 "Our university is the song," stated Berito Kubaru'wa to the students of the
University of Wisconsin-Madison (transcript of the public presentation of
Berito and Gilberto Kubaru'wa at the University of Wisconsin-Madison, 20
July 2000).

4 Interview with Gilberto Kubaru'wa (Madison WI, 20 July 2000).

5 The company stated that during this period it held 33 meetings with
members of the U'wa community (Corte Constitucional, 1997).

6 This important communiqué was probably made public between late
February and the end of April, 1995.

7 This situation has arisen on several occasions in Colombia due to a lack of clarity
in the constitution regarding which court has the broadest jurisdiction over the
others. This has led to serious differences among Colombia's highest judicial
authorities. Both courts' lengthy deliberation processes (over one year) led to a
great deal of speculation in Colombia, since it appeared that the last court that
issued its ruling would have the power to determine the final decision.

8 Interview with Berito Kubaru'wa (Madison, WI, 20 July 2000).

9 Telephone interview with Yadira Soto, OAS (22 July 2000).

10 Theodore Macdonald, from the OAS/Harvard team, is more optimistic
about the project. He wrote: "The U'wa have not yet responded, nor,
however, have they indicated that they will not do so sometime in the
future. Moreover, they still have a 'complaint' before the Inter-American
Commission on Human Rights. As such, they still retain the right to respond
to the OAS, and have not indicated that they consider the matter closed.
Therefore the issue remains open, even though, as you can see, there has
been no action in three years" (Personal e-mail message from Theodore
Macdonald to the author. 28 August 2000).

11 According to OAS sources, the Ministry of the Environment and Oxy wanted to avoid further internationalization of the case. Occidental was tired of the patience shown by the OEA/Harvard team, and pressured the Ministry of Mining to put the problem back into the hands of Colombia, to be dealt with by Colombians.

12 Gilberto Kubaru'wa, press conference (Madison, WI, 19 July 2000).

13 "If we play a strong role locally, increasing information flows, exchanging experiences, providing arguments, including legal strategies, and preparing ways to confront corporations, we open up a unique pathway for waging a sustainable battle" (Melsher, 1999).

14 During the visit, Lorenzo Muelas said: "I am very pleased to be on Secoya land. First I want to say that we have come to speak honestly to you about the consequences of oil. We haven't come to help you negotiate better. Our sole interest is for you to continue to live here, on your land. I am sure that when Oxy finds out that the U'wa or I have been here, they will try to make up something to derail our efforts. Sometimes they call us guerrillas, or communists, because we oppose the type of development they impose on us. This is why I want to warn you of the consequences" (http://www.oil-watch.org.ec/intercambio/uwa.htm, consulted on 12 July 2000).

15 Censat-Agua Viva has also worked for several years in the municipality of Cerrito, Santander, where some U'wa people live (interview with Tatiana Roa and Hildebrando Velez of Censat-Agua Viva; Bogotá, 1 June 2000).

16 Interview with Tito Gaitán from MINGA, the lawyer of the U'wa community in this process (Bogotá, 15 June 2000).

17 U'wa communiqué, 25 January 2000

18 U'wa communiqué, 11 February 2000.

19 U'wa communiqué, 21 February 2000. After two months of protest, the U'wa issued a statement, saying: "the goals of our mobilization are so important that they have gained international awareness and support. Among those who have publicly supported our cause are the European Parliament, environmental and human rights NGOs in Sweden, Canada, Germany, France, China, Spain, Belgium, as well as US ethnic groups. All have recommended and then demanded that the Colombian government and the multinational company respect the agreements signed by the Colombian government with the ILO (Indigenous Legislation, Convention #169)" (U'wa communiqué, 3 April 2000).

20 U'wa communiqué, 29 June 2000.

21 U'wa communiqué, 31 July 2001.

22 U'wa Communiqué, 5 May 2005.

23 For the U'wa people, the possibility of suicide was always taken very seriously and had a major impact inside the community. The U'wa asked themselves and their traditional leaders what was going to happen. The traditional authorities have reinterpreted their original message, in yet another demonstration of cultural adaptability, stating that the U'wa will not commit mass suicide but that they may well be murdered by the Colombian government and Occidental Petroleum because they are willing to give up their lives in order to protect their sacred territory (interview with Gilberto Kubaru'wa; Bogotá, 15 June 2000).

Part II

THE WORLD'S LOCAL KNOWLEDGES

6

High-Tech Plundering, Biodiversity, and Cultural Erosion: The Case of Brazil

Laymert Garcia dos Santos

For Ana Valério Araújo and Sérgio Leitão,
untiring defenders of native rights

THE CULTURAL TURN AND THE CYBERNETIC TURN

In the past three decades there has been increasing support for the theory that capitalism is changing by incorporating culture into the production process or even by turning culture into the motor of accumulation. In a way, all discussions in the area of social science concerning the question of post-modernity revolve around what Frederic Jameson has called "the cultural turn." In Jameson's view, if we wish to understand contemporary society, we must first understand how culture has been colonized by capital, and what devastating effects such colonization has on politics, resistance movements, and the quest for emancipation.

Following in the footsteps of Jameson and other authors, Jeremy Rifkin, a shrewd detector of contemporary economic trends, ends his book *The Age of Access* with the argument that global capitalism is not only "knowledge-based" but that, more importantly, by cannibalizing cultures—*all* cultures— it threatens the very foundation of society because it dissolves the planet's cultural diversity through an increasingly intense and rapid instrumentaliza-tion (Rifkin, 2000). Rifkin's analysis of the relations between global capitalism and cultural diversity evokes Vandana Shiva's critique of the way "agribusiness" and transnational pharmaceutical and food corporations treat biodiversity (Shiva, 1993). This parallel is not fortuitous: it would seem as if Rifkin had discovered that contemporary economic dynamics lead to cultural erosion, whereas Shiva discovered that the same dynamics lead to biological erosion. From this point of view, economic production takes on a destructive, not to say suicidal, character, and begins to produce destruction.

However, what Rifkin and Shiva see as an eminently negative process is entirely positive to those who support the development in progress. In their view, there is no erosion, only transformation; there is no loss, only gain; and instead of destruction, there is construction. This raises the question: How can erosion mean positive transformation? From what point of view? Based on what criteria? One could argue that Shiva's and Rifkin's world is not the same one referred to by the promoters of global capitalism; it is as if the former were referring to the world that exists, and the latter to a world yet to come. But such worlds are not separate and opposite realities—as if the construction of this new world depended on the erosion of the existing world or, at the very least, its shrinkage.

To understand the world yet to come, one must do more than just understand the "cultural turn" of contemporary capitalism, i.e., the full incorporation of culture into the market system. It would seem that what is much more important than the transformation of culture into commodity is the "cybernetic turn," which sealed the alliance between capital and science and technology, and provided technoscience with the role of a motor of accumulation that will turn the entire existing world into raw material at the disposal of technoscientific work.

"Cybernetic turn" is the term used by Catherine Waldby to refer to the change that occurred in the logic of technology, based on Donna Haraway's description of the reciprocity of information between different organisms, and between organisms and technology:

> Communication sciences and modern biologies are constructed by a common move—the translation of the world into a problem of coding, a search for a common language in which all resistance to instrumental control disappears and all heterogeneity can be submitted to disassembly, reassembly, investment and exchange. [. . .] The world is subdivided by boundaries differentially permeable to information. Information is just that kind of quantifiable element (unity, basis of unity) which allows universal translation, and so unhindered instrumental power (Haraway, 1994, qtd. by Waldby, 2000: 45).

Waldby therefore perceives the cybernetic turn to be this "common move" that occurs in the field of science and technology and that provides the possibility of totally opening up the world to instrumental control through information. But it is obvious that this possibility brought about within laboratories is not limited only to laboratories. The cybernetic turn is not only a change in the logic of technology: it is a change in socio-technical logic.

The concept of information

Scott Lash observes that sociologists (particularly Daniel Bell, Alain Touraine, and Manuel Castells) have viewed the information society as a society in which there is intensive production of knowledge and of a range of post-industrial goods and services. But he thinks that this characterization is insufficient:

> What is key in how we should understand the information society [. . .] is a focus on the primary qualities of information itself. Here information must be understood sharply in contradistinction from other, earlier socio-cultural categories such as narrative or discourse or monument or institution. The primary qualities of information are flow, disembeddedness, spatial compression, temporal compression, real time relations. It is not exclusively, but mainly, in this sense that we live in an information age. Some people have called some of such qualities late-modern (Giddens, 1990), others post-modern (Harvey, 1989), but these concepts seem to me to be too amorphous. Information is not (Lash, 2001).

Lash's merit in expressing his dissatisfaction lies in pointing out the centrality of the concept of information and, above all, its primary qualities. In his view, the key question is to understand what is produced by information production not as goods and services rich in information, but rather as greater or fewer bytes of information out of control. His concern is directed, therefore, at the collateral effects of the systems for conveying messages and the growing impact of these effects on the economy, on politics, on power relations and, last but not least, on theoretical thinking about society. But, although his characterization of the primary qualities of information is based on the cybernetic concept of information, he does not discuss how this concept, developed in the field of science and technology, can be transplanted to the field of the social sciences.

After all, what information is this that is capable of bringing about a radical change in the logic of technology and, at the same time, have such a tremendous impact on contemporary society that one is justified in talking about an information era and an information society?

In his short introduction to Norbert Wiener's paper presented at the conference on "Le concept d'information dans la science contemporaine," the philosopher Gilbert Simondon noted, in regard to the importance of the publication of *Cybernetics, Theory of Control and Communications in the Animal and the Machine*:

> We soon realized that this was something new that would provide the starting point for a new era of reflection. Some thought it was the renewal of

Cartesianism, others realized that there was the desire to constitute a unity in the sciences, whereas throughout the beginning of the 20th century there had been an increasingly greater separation between scientific specializations; it so happened that after World War II, the *no man's land* between the sciences, the *boundary regions* [. . .] were regarded as extremely fertile fields; and whereas scientific specialization stood in the way of communication, if only because of the different languages used among specialists of different sciences, cybernetics, on the other hand, was the result of several men working as a team and trying to understand each other's language. [. . .] The presence of eminent doctors, physicists and mathematicians on this team revealed that, without a doubt, something was being produced in the sciences that had not existed since Newton, for, as you said, Newton can be considered the last man of science to have covered the entire field of objective reflection. [. . .] In fact, historically, cybernetics arose as something new, with the aim of bringing about a synthesis (Wiener, 1965: 99–100; my italics).

Simondon's words are important because they provide a measure of the relevance of cybernetics not only for the progress of scientific activity but also, mainly, for the field of reflection as a whole. The development of a common language beyond the specificities of the different branches of scientific knowledge and the establishment of a new synthesis, comparable only to the Newtonian revolution, indicated that information theory seemed to take on a central role in contemporary human thought. And this is what we can glean from Simondon's own work. However, Simondon could not simply adopt the notion of information exactly as it had been developed by Norbert Wiener, because this only concerns the transmission of a signal through energy modulation. The information signal is not only what should be transmitted, but also *what should be received*; in other words, it acquires a meaning, it has some efficacy for a whole that has its own way of operating. But such a meaning cannot be found at either the point of exit or the point of entry: information only exists when the emitter and the receiver of the signal form a system; information exists *between* the two halves of a system that had had no sense until then. Information is this aptitude for establishing a relationship that provides a solution, integration; it is the real singularity through which potential energy becomes actual, through which an incompatibility is overcome; information is the establishment of communication, containing an energetic quantity and a structural quality; "it is that through which the incompatibility of an unresolved system becomes the organizing dimension of the solution" (Simondon, 1964: 15).

The technological paradigm and the notion of information made it possible for the ontogenesis of individuation to be pondered in the fields of physics, biology, and technology, based on a single theoretical reference. In each of these fields, invention comes about when information acts in this pre-individual, intermediate reality, which the philosopher terms "the consistent centre of being." This natural reality, as pre-vital as it is pre-physical, is witness to a certain continuity between the living being and inert matter and it also acts in technical operations. As Simondon states:

> The technical being can only be defined in terms of information and transformation of the different types of energy or information, in other words, on the one hand as a vehicle for action that stems from man to the universe, and on the other hand as a vehicle for information that stems from the universe to man (Simondon, 1989: 283).

Simondon's analysis establishes information as a real singularity that provides consistency to inert matter, to the living being (plant, animal, man), and to the technical object. And it would not be out of place to liken the philosopher's formulation to the brilliant statement by Gregory Bateson, who defined information as "a difference which makes all the difference" (Bateson, 1987: 40–41). The possibility of conceiving a common substratum to inert matter, to the living being, and to the technical object progressively erases the frontiers established between nature and culture by modern society. What is more, everything takes place as if there was a plane of reality in which matter and human spirit could meet and communicate, not as external realities placed in contact with one another but as systems that have become a part of a solution process that is immanent in the plane itself. If technology is the vehicle for an action that stems from man to the universe, as well as of information that stems from the universe to man, it is the solution factor of an intense dialogue in which what counts is interaction, the productive character of agency, and not the pre-existing parts. The basis of the cybernetic turn is therefore man's capacity to "speak" the language of the "consistent centre of being," to gain access to the molecular plane of the unlimited finite in which, according to Gilles Deleuze, a finite number of components produces a practically unlimited diversity of combinations (Deleuze, 1986: 140).

It so happens that the exercise of this intense dialogue of man with nature, this mutual involvement in a common becoming, is still understood, even by scientists themselves, in Baconian terms, in other words, in terms of the unrestricted domination of nature (including human nature) by man, which also means, we should point out, that it is understood in terms of an extreme extension and intensification of instrumental control. This converts dialogue into an exercise of power still propelled by a kind of thinking that Simondon characterizes as the autocratic philosophy of technology, which uses the machine only as a means to conquer nature and aims at domesticating the forces of nature through primary subjection: the machine as a slave used to enslave others (Simondon, 1969: 126–127).

From this perspective, the cybernetic turn becomes the quintessence of control and domination by converting the means of access to the molecular plane of the unlimited finite and to the digital and genetic information plan into a weapon against nature and cultures—*all* cultures—with the exception of technoscientific culture. This obviously causes a reaction of alarm against the "state of cybernetic nature" and the "state of cybernetic culture," about which Hermínio Martins, in the footsteps of Serge Moscovici, tells us:

> If we are already living within the horizon of the "state of cybernetic nature," which can be adequately summarized as "nature-as-information," we can also say that we are moulding and being moulded, increasingly so, by that which we can call by analogy the "state of cybernetic culture," when culture becomes culture-as-information. This is particularly obvious in the case of the paradigmatic cognitive culture, natural science or technoscience, although it should be noted that, for several decades, this cybernization of science was almost completely confined to military science (during the Cold War). [. . .] Nowadays, it is said that, as a result of increasingly numerous roles [. . .], a lot more has been done than joining an additional techno-logical front to the *instrumentarium* of scientific investigation, at least in the physical and life sciences. Instead, it would seem more appropriate to speak of nothing less than the emergence of a third form of science, as has been suggested by some researchers (Martins, 2000: 25).

The cybernetic turn, as it is occurring now, therefore disqualifies all cultures, including modern culture, in favor of technoscientific culture because the reductionism of the Baconian model prevails. But would there have to be opposition and conflict between contemporary technoscientific culture and other cultures? The entire work of Gilbert Simondon revolves around demonstrating the need to rethink the technological paradigm and the concept of information beyond the autocratic philosophy of technology. But as there does not seem to be much support for this effort, it may be worth our while to take a longer look at what technoscientific practice has valorized.

Technoscientific knowledge and the value of control

In a study of the relationship between science and technology, the philo-sopher of science Hugh Lacey observed that scientific understanding involves representing phenomena as products of an underlying order, and, therefore, the abstraction of phenomena as objects of experience, value, and practice. "Scientific understanding is gained through practices that involve both observation of and active interventions into the phenomena, practices that are conducted under what I call the *materialist constraint/selection strategies*" (Lacey, 1999: 15). Why—inquires Lacey—undertake an investigation conducted according to materialist constraint/selection strategies? Among the three possible answers, that which stands out is the one that meets the interests of Baconian utility: the understanding obtained through materialist strategies increases the human capacity to control nature. The philosopher recognizes that it is part of human nature to control nature, but notes that in modernity control has taken on such proportions, pre-eminence, and centrality that it has become a superior and virtually unsubordinate value.

In the modern value scheme of control, Lacey continues, the expansion of the human ability to control nature, the exercise of control, and the implementation of new forms of control are valued above all else, and all projects and institutions that express rival values should be subjected and adapted to them. On the other hand, social values that tend to reveal themselves in the same institutions in which control is manifest, such as private property for example, are reinforced by this association. So much so that the modern value scheme of control seems to have no limits in either the natural world or the social world.

Lacey sees an elective affinity between the materialist strategies of scientific research and the modern perspective of control. He writes:

> The modern value scheme of control cannot be manifested unless the world is amenable to be controlled by human action. [. . .] So if things are or can become like the way they are represented under the materialist strategies, they can become objects of control—*provided that* we can directly manipulate the relevant initiating events and ensure that the relevant boundary conditions remain in place. [. . .] I do not know whether or not the control schemata of traditional knowledge can all be re-articulated within materialist understanding. Whatever the case may be, materialist understanding leads us to schemata that far transcend traditional constraints, so much so that in modern practical life it is virtually uncontested that possible objects of control are considered as objects of materialist understanding. Materialistic understanding grasps objects in the way they need to be grasped so as to become objects of control (Lacey, 1999: 21–22; my italics).

Lacey's analysis is relevant because it allows us to understand how a relationship is forged in which the world is *for* control, in other words, how the phenomena that are objects of materialist understanding are virtually identical to objects of control. In addition, it is obvious that traditional knowledge remains on the sidelines of this relationship and is not even acknowledged. Finally, it is worth pointing out that this identification between the materialist strategies of science and the world they seek to control feeds the dialectics between theoretical and technological development within research institutions. In fact, in the eyes of this philosopher, this dialectic can only unfold in societies whose institutions and policies recognize and sanction the modern value scheme of control—which has become particularly marked with the ascent of neoliberalism.

But the picture would not be complete if the relevance of materialist metaphysics were left out. According to Lacey,

> This metaphysics affirms that the world "really is" such that all the objects in it (including human beings) are fully characterizable by materialist (perhaps ultimately physicalist) properties and relations [. . .]; all phenomena in terms of being generated in accordance with underlying structure, process and law; and the possibilities of things are exhausted by their material possibilities. [. . .] In principle, all other options seem to be ruled out, for materialist metaphysics implies that our interactions with the world cannot be understood in any other way. It also supports that, where practices of control bring with them undesirable or unexpected side-effects, in principle they can be dealt with through further controlling interventions (Lacey, 1999: 25–26).

The circle closes. It would seem that there is no alternative to modern technical and scientific knowledge, that there is no option outside metaphysics and materialist strategies, much less outside the value scheme of control. As Lacey himself points out, his explanation binds materialist understanding to the latter internally. And yet, it is widely held that science has no values, that it is value-free. How then can we reconcile such an apparent contradiction?

The strong point of Lacey's work is that he confronts modern science with values. He reminds us that the conception of science as value-free consists of three components: impartiality, neutrality, and autonomy. His thorough demonstration establishes that science, although impartial, is not neutral. This is not the place to follow his arguments step-by-step. But we do need to highlight the exact moment at which he captures the way in which the movement of scientific research itself breaks with neutrality and makes the value of control stand out against other values.

The whole question revolves around the relationship between social values and cognitive values. As Lacey observes, it is important to keep the roles played by both separate, since they occur at different logical moments. Thus, when we ask why a certain theory is accepted, we know that the answer involves taking into account cognitive values and data, but not social values. Conversely, when we ask why the scientific community privileges theories aligned with certain strategies of selection and constraint, we know that the answer includes reference to social values. This leads Lacey to emphasize the need to keep the roles played by social values and cognitive values separate. Lacey takes up the question of human flourishing, which usually legitimizes all scientific practice and research. From a modern point of view, the value scheme of control proposes to intensify human flourishing. However, this is contested by feminist and environmentalist perspectives, and particularly by popular movements in underdeveloped countries. Lacey's focus is precisely on the latter.

In summary, the value of control, the pillar of scientific theory and practice, is not universal; there is no consensus about its supremacy. This means that the option to develop modern science and technology as an option for increasingly greater control of nature, seen from other perspectives, becomes the object of controversy. Science chooses what to study objectively, according to cognitive values, but this choice always already presupposes that the value of control is undeniable as a form of human flourishing.

Biodiversity, technoscientific culture and traditional cultures

After undermining the neutrality of science and questioning the value of control, Hugh Lacey goes even further in his discussion by examining the relations between science and development in order to inquire into the possibility of an alternative. He takes as an example the case of agriculture, as conceived by the Green Revolution and the biotechnological revolution on the one hand, and by agro-ecology on the other (Lacey, 1998: 141–151; Lacey, 2000, 2001). This problematic finds a strong echo in the analyses of Shiv Visvanathan.

In a stimulating text, the Indian sociologist conceives science as a mode of violence carried out by the "Laboratory State," the project for which was contrived by the trio of Bacon–Descartes–Hobbes, and which is based on four hypotheses:

1. *The Hobbesian project*, which is the conception of a society based on the scientific method;

2. *The imperatives of progress*, which legitimize the use of social engineering on all those objects defined as backward or retarded;

3. The *vivisectional mandate*, where the "Other" becomes the object of experiment which, in essence, is violence and in which pain is inflicted in the name of science;

4. The *idea of triage*, combining the concepts of rational experiment, obsolescence, and vivisection—whereby a society, a subculture or a species is labelled as obsolete and condemned to death because rational judgement has deemed it incurable (Visvanathan, 1997: 17; my italics).

In Visvanathan's understanding, the combination of these four theses makes the project of the Laboratory State a project of genocide (Visvanathan, 1997: 17), and makes modern development "development-as-terrorism" (Visvanathan, 1997: 46). Let us take as an example the question of agriculture, the author's object of research in another essay in the same book. How does modern technoscientific culture deal with biodiversity and traditional cultures that have been developing methods and practices of cultivation for millennia? Visvanathan explores the destructive character of the Green Revolution, with its ferocious dedication to disrespecting the rhythms of nature and disqualifying the knowledge, practices, and innovations of traditional cultures. But what really attracts attention in his analysis is the way he reads modern biologists, including the great "defender" of biodiversity, Edward Wilson. Take, for example, the forest in Wilson's *Biophilia*. Visvanathan writes:

> The forest is not a "dwelling," in the Heideggerian or even tribal sense. Wilson inhabits the forest but does not dwell in it, nurturing it, preserving it or merely watching it unfold: he inhabits it as a field biologist. The forest as a whole does not exist. One senses that before he has even entered it, it has already been resolved into a cluster of research programmes.
>
> In *Biophilia*, there is a split-level sense about the loss of the forest. There is, first, the danger to man's biological need for the forest, and there is also the threat of the constant advance of science. To scientists like Wilson, the forest is literally a magic well from which science can draw endlessly. The forest is information (Visvanathan, 1997: 54).

Wilson feels that the extinction of species and the loss of genetic variability are the worst things that could happen to us, since evolution would take millions of years to correct them. And yet, Visvanathan observes, science seems not to lament this daily death; it seems to have no ritual for this kind of mourning: the scientific conception of time would not allow science to deal with the different temporalities of ecology, which in turn would require the unraveling of the notions of time contained in concepts such as extinction, death, obsolescence, and memory; in short, a clarification of how science relates to nature and to other cultures. Conceived as a system of information from a reductionist viewpoint, the forest is only of interest as long as it has not yet been abstracted, classified, and fully known. What is not clear is how this same conception facilitates the process of extinction.

THE STRUGGLE FOR ACCESS
TO BIODIVERSITY AND KNOWLEDGE

The first part of this text has sought to characterize the importance of the cybernetic turn in contemporary society and how the concept of information has become central in the relations that technoscience establishes, not only with nature, but also with other cultures. This second part aims to show how, throughout the 1990s, the conflict unfolded between the different conceptions regarding the access to and the use of biodiversity and the traditional knowledges associated with it.

As everyone knows, in the mid-1980s deforestation propelled the Amazon Forest into the center of the world ecological debate, and actually led to the emergence of the very concept of biodiversity, posing a new question. All of a sudden, the entire world discovered that tropical forests are the richest habitats in terms of species on the planet, while it also discovered that these same species run the greatest risk of extinction. At the same time, the advances of technoscience, and of biotechnology in particular, began to explain the important roles that genetic resources were meant to play in the economy of the future. Thus, even before Rio-92, the question of access had already been brought up.

In a paper written in 1993, in which I tried to demonstrate why Brazilian environmental policy was at a crossroads, I noted that the so-called "war of genes" had already made an appearance in the preparatory meetings for the Rio conference (Santos, 1994a: 152 ff.). At the time, the developed countries supported the thesis of free access to genetic resources, arguing that plants and animals are *res nullius* and that biodiversity is *res communis*, that, in other words, since they belong to everyone, they are not the property of anyone. Brazil defended, obviously, the thesis that access should be regulated by agreement, at the discretion of the country that has biodiversity, based on the principle of the sovereign right of the state over the natural resources located within its territory. According to the Brazilian diplomats, if genetic resources were a "global patrimony," so too should be the products deriving from the very existence and transformation of the genetic patrimony. In short, access to genetic resources should correspond to the transfer of biotechnology and other types of technology that take part in conservation.

As everyone also knows, the Convention on Biological Diversity established, at Rio-92, the sovereignty of countries over their genetic resources. Meanwhile, the day after the conference ended, the same President Collor who had signed the multilateral agreement sent Congress a bill for patents that sought to open access to biodiversity without any corresponding compensation. The bill was widely criticized by the opposition, non-governmental organizations, the scientific community, the national pharmaceutical industry, the unions, the Catholic Church, and even by some state research institutions. In February 1992, organized civil society had established the Forum for Freedom of the Use of Knowledge, which conceived the issue as a trade war and tried to block the adoption of a law that would authorize the patenting of food, medicine, and especially living beings. In turn, Brazilian exporters, transnational corporations, a large segment of the media, and a considerable number of high-ranking federal officials supported a permissive law, while the United States exerted heavy pressure and threatened to impose new sanctions on the entrance of Brazilian products into the US market. Finally, on 6 May 1993, within the context of opening up the Brazilian market to globalization, the House of Representatives (Câmara dos Deputados) approved a new industrial property law, which, although it prohibited patenting plants and animals, allowed the patenting of microorganisms, "providing they are to be used solely for a specific process that generates a specific product." This became known as a "virtual patent." Later sanctioned by the Federal Senate, the patent law instituted the protection of access to the processes and products generated by technoscience, and by the biotechnology industry in particular (Santos, 1998: 29). Access to genetic resources was yet to be regulated.

David Hathaway, from the non-governmental organization AS-PTA (Consultancy and Services for Projects in Alternative Agriculture), who followed the entire process in the legislature, notes that the Brazilian authorities and the government politicians steadfastly refused to discuss the implications of patenting biotechnological processes used to research, develop, and use genetic resources—they were more concerned about satisfying the interests of transnational corporations. He adds that, furthermore, the government had no plans to regulate such access (Hathaway, 1993: 2–3). This negligence went on for years, which is curious to say the least, if we consider that Brazil is the number 1 country in mega-diversity! Meanwhile, some sectors of the environmentalist movement (such as the Socio-Environmental Institute [Instituto Socio-Ambiental] and AS-PTA) did not feel the same way, and tried to awaken Brazilian civil society to the importance of the matters of socio- and biodiversity. It seems to me that, among the several initiatives of the time, the fact that David Hathaway and myself took part in the "International Conference on Redefining the Life Sciences," organized by The Third World Network in Penang, Malaysia, from 5 to 12 July 1994, took on some relevance.

The conference invited the participants to shift the center of discussion on the loss of biodiversity by moving the focus from the South to the North—in other words, to shift from the relationship between genetic erosion and underdevelopment to the relationship between erosion and development; furthermore, it replaced the discussion of the old causes of unsustainable exploitation of natural resources (lumbering, panning, extensive farming, and cattle raising) with a look at the new predatory force. The change in focus showed that the new predators were "high-tech," since they used science, whose development is based on the extremely operative systematization of knowledge about life; biotechnology, whose performance involves the project of transforming living beings into raw material; and intellectual property rights, the legal system of which seeks to grant legitimacy to the economic appropriation of the active principles of living beings. Thus, the change in focus meant having to admit that it was more important to prepare to fight high-tech violence than to simply fight against the old extraction practices, since the predatory force now seemed to feed directly off the diversity of life forms in order to keep expanding and evolving (Santos, 1994b).

Within environmental circles the need to resist the patenting of life was obvious. But this did not appear to be enough. In Brazil, the prestige of science and biotechnology remained intact, and it was disturbing to see that most of those who fought against the patent system claimed that the country should have the right to exploit biodiversity according to the same criteria. In other words, in Brazil the new intellectual property law was being contested in the name of the very same modern project for exploiting nature, which ignored the value of the traditional knowledge of indigenous peoples and their right to preserve, use, and develop biodiversity. Now, this was precisely the issue that several participants at the conference, especially Vandana Shiva, from India, Tewolde Egziabher, from Ethiopia, and Gurdial Singh Nijar, from Malaysia, wished to debate.

In his presentation at the conference in Penang, the lawyer Gurdial Nijar took up the central issues of the paper he had prepared for the Second Session of the Intra-governmental Committee of the Convention on Biological Diversity, held in Nairobi at the end of June of the same year (Nijar, 1994). His presentation brilliantly articulated: 1) the relationships between the systems of knowledge of indigenous peoples and communities and the protection of biodiversity; 2) the progress of discussions in international forums that concerned the recognition of the rights of nations, farmers, and indigenous peoples in regard to biodiversity; 3) the search for a legal framework that would allow access to genetic resources and relevant traditional knowledge to be regulated; 4) the struggle against the patenting of life forms; 5) the issue of biosecurity. For many participants, this was the first time the matter had been laid bare with its main implications at the local, national, and international levels. But the Third World Network's lawyer had more than just a deep understanding of the matter; his analysis led to a proposal he was interested in discussing with the participants from countries rich in biodiversity.

Nijar started off with the observation that throughout history biodiversity has been shared as a common good among local communities, which freely exchange both the resources and their knowledge of them. In his view, biodiversity and the different local systems of knowledge have a symbiotic relationship: people live off nature while at the same time helping it to develop, which can be seen both in the management of forests and in traditional agriculture. This relationship is broken by modern commercial agriculture, which favors monoculture, uniformity, and productivity—symbiosis gives way to erosion, both of biological diversity and of knowledge. It is therefore crucial to understand the link between the preservation of biodiversity and the knowledge and practices of local populations, i.e., their understanding of and their ethics concerning conservation. Since it is impossible to protect the former without defending the latter, Nijar proposes that both be considered together for the purposes of legislation.

In recognizing the sovereign rights of states over their natural resources, article 15 of the Convention on Biological Diversity discarded the principle of "common patrimony," while at the same time determining that the states should try to create conditions "to facilitate access to genetic resources for environmentally sound uses," while upholding the three objectives of the convention: the conservation of biodiversity, the sustainable use of its components, and fair and equitable sharing of the benefits derived from the use of genetic resources. Finally, the convention recognized that both the access to and the transfer of technology are essential to attaining these objectives. But, after a closer look at article 16, Nijar concluded that its wording "is far from clear. It is therefore open to interpretation and definition" (Nijar, 1994: 9). Article 16 deals with the matter of intellectual property. Article 16.2 establishes a distinction between patented and non-patented technology. "In the case of technology subject to patents and other intellectual property rights, such access and transfer shall be provided on terms which recognize and are consistent with the adequate and effective protection of intellectual property rights." But non-patented technology does not have the same protection. In the well-known article 8(j), the convention recommends that each contracting party "should, as far as possible and as appropriate," in keeping with national laws, "respect, preserve and maintain knowledge, innovations and practices of indigenous and local communities embodying traditional lifestyles relevant for the conservation and sustainable use of biological diversity and promote their wider application with the approval and involvement of the holders of such knowledge, innovations and practices and encourage the equitable sharing of the benefits arising from the utilization of such knowledge, innovations and practices." Where, then, does that leave the protection of non-patented technology? According to Nijar,

What emerges from a review of the international developments and debates is that there is an acknowledgement that farmers' and indigenous peoples' rights are essential for the conservation and protection of biological diversity, and that this emanates from the recognition of their diverse systems of knowledge and innovation in biological resource improvement and utilization; and that equity demands a sharing of benefits. However, *what emerges equally clearly is that the existing international mechanisms are not entirely supportive of this understanding*. The search for a coherent legal framework advancing this understanding is therefore of crucial importance for the preservation and protection of these critical values (Nijar, 1994: 9; my italics).

Exploring the gaps in international mechanisms that in one way or another concern the issue of access to genetic resources and its associated knowledge, Nijar then proposed the adoption of a *sui generis* protection regime, which, in contrast to intellectual property rights, would take into account the intellectual rights of indigenous peoples and local communities. Nijar recalled that the TRIPs agreements required the member countries of the World Trade Organization to ensure the protection of plant varieties through a system of patents or an effective *sui generis* system, or a combination of the two. The question that arises is this: How should we interpret the term "effective"? If we look at the term as it appears in Section 301 of the United States Trade and Competitiveness Act, it reinforces the protection of patents; but "effective" can also mean coherent and consistent with the spirit and terms of the Convention on Biological Diversity, which strongly encourages the parties to create "conditions to facilitate access to genetic resources for environmentally sound uses" (art. 15.2), to respect, preserve, and maintain the knowledge, innovations, and practices of the indigenous peoples and local communities (art. 8[j]), and to promote the development and use of indigenous and traditional technologies (art. 18.4).

Working within the parameters of the World Trade Organization and the Convention on Biological Diversity, Nijar suggests that a *sui generis* regime for protecting "community intellectual rights" should do the following:

—allow an alternative definition of knowledge systems, capable of recognising the system of informal, collective and cumulative innovation of indigenous peoples and local communities;
—define innovation in such a way that it would include not only the technologically improved final product but also knowledge about the use of properties, values and processes of any biological resource, as well as any plant variety or any plant (or part of it). Such a definition should also be broad enough to include any alteration, modification, improvement or obtaining of by-products that use the knowledge of indigenous groups or

communities in the marketing of any product, and should also include any more sophisticated process for extracting, isolating and synthesizing chemical agents in biological extracts and in the compounds used by indigenous peoples;

—turn the indigenous peoples and local communities into the guardians of these innovations, defining such rights as "non-exclusive" and "non-monopolistic" and encouraging their free and non-commercial use and exchange;

—allow such rights to be guaranteed in conjunction with other indigenous peoples and communities (Nijar, 1994: 16).

Nijar justified the adoption of the *sui generis* regime thus:

> The evolutionary process was in fact used in the service of industrial capitalism. The intellectual property system of the 19th century was a product of the industrial revolution and the inability of normal property law to protect the ideas of mechanical inventors. Plant breeders' rights is a product of the 20th century development of Mendelian genetics and the inability of intellectual property systems to protect the idea of breeders. So, too, community rights [. . .] is a product of the era of biotechnology and the inability of other systems, in the context of new biotechnologies, to protect the ideas of informal innovators (Nijar, 1994: 17).

Nijar pointed out that the main objective of his proposal was to prevent the privatization and usurpation of community rights and knowledge through the existing definitions of innovation. In my view, his lucid conception of the predatory relationship that technoscience had been establishing with traditional knowledge helped him to understand that everything revolved around the terms "property" and "innovation." For this very reason, his proposal of a *sui generis* regime ruled out the possibility of traditional knowledge being exclusively appropriated, and he redefined the concept of innovation so that it would reflect the unique character of knowledge production on the part of indigenous peoples and local communities.

The radical opposition to the patenting of life and the defense of the genetic resources of the indigenous peoples and the local communities that had assimilated traditional knowledge, innovations, and practices found an echo in all of those who saw high-tech predation as a kind of ultimate plunder, not only because of the critical content of Nijar's proposal, but primarily because he put forward arguments and a positive agenda that went against the legal interests and traps formulated by state officials and by corporate lawyers to regulate the matter of access to genetic resources in national law. In addition, the fact that his *sui generis* regime interlinked protection and access gave a precise content to the exercise of national sovereignty over biological resources. Sovereignty would no longer be a merely rhetorical aspiration, given that the national state would be the entity that would ensure the conditions required for the preservation and sustainable use of resources, the equitable distribution of the benefits provided by their use in industry, and, above all, would make it impossible for such resources to be exclusively appropriated and monopolized, as this would harm both the communities and the country. By protecting the communities against biopiracy and by regulating the access to biological resources, the state would be limiting the attempt to appropriate life, which, as mentioned before, would accelerate the erosion of biodiversity. For this very reason, the Third World Network's proposal as a whole was embraced with much interest in several Third World regions, and began to be discussed in all of the Latin American countries that have a large amount of biodiversity: Colombia, Ecuador, Venezuela, Peru, Bolivia, and, last but not least, Brazil.

The concern over the socio-environmental dimension of access

Vandana Shiva, Tewolde Egziabher, and Gurdial Nijar put together the proposal concerning collective intellectual rights because they felt that the trend in international forums was to favor the intellectual property regime, and also because they realized that countries rich in biodiversity should not wait for an international legal framework to be developed and then try to fit into it; quite the opposite, they thought that it was up to the southern countries to come up with new solutions in their national laws in order to defend their biological and cultural wealth.

The idea of legislation that would protect collective intellectual rights by means of a *sui generis* regime spread to some groups in Latin America. After discussing the regime in a broad process of consultation with indigenous and black communities as well as with NGOs, the Ad Hoc Biodiversity Group of Colombia (Grupo Ad Hoc de Biodiversidad da Colombia) drafted a bill on biodiversity (Holguín, 1996: 118–176). Taking up the matter in the Brazilian context, Senator Marina Silva submitted bill 306/95 to the Federal Senate, which included contributions from Brazilian NGOs and the Colombian discussion.

Both in Colombia and in Brazil, the starting point for the debate about collective intellectual rights was the acknowledgement of the differences among cultures. In fact, such rights are only conceivable if the state and national societies legally recognize the unique character of traditional peoples. This is the case of the Colombian Constitution of 1991, which recognized the nation's pluri-ethnic and pluri-cultural character, and of the Brazilian Constitution of 1988, which recognized as "collective rights," among others, the right to socio-diversity (art. 215.1), the right to cultural heritage (art. 216), the right to an ecologically balanced environment (art. 225), and the right to biodiversity (art. 225).

The jurist Carlos F. Marés de Souza Filho defines collective rights as those

> whose principal characteristic is the fact that their ownership is not individualized and is not certain or cannot be ascertained. [. . .] [T]his characteristic sets them apart from the concept of individual rights as conceived by the contractualist or constitutionalist culture of the nineteenth century because these are rights without a subject! Or, to put it in an even more confusing manner for individualist thinking, everyone is a subject of these rights. If all are entitled to the same rights, all have access to them, but, at the same time, nobody can have access to them, because one person's access would be a violation of the rights of all (Souza Filho, 1999: 176).

Marés notes that as of 1988 this new class of rights was included in the constitution, even though doctrine and jurisprudence are still reluctant to call them by this name. This means that although there is already a formal framework in which collective rights are included, there is still a long way to go before the legal existence of these rights becomes a reality. On the other hand, this same constitution established something of great import for the formulation of collective intellectual rights, namely article 231 of Chapter VII, which recognizes the "original rights" of indigenous societies to the land they have traditionally occupied. Original rights have two extremely important characteristics in regard to the matter at hand: first of all, they are collective rights, which concern communities and/or societies; second, these rights do not regard land as the property of Indians: the land belongs to the Union, but its permanent, inalienable, and irrevocable use belongs to the communities and/or societies. It would be a good idea to explore the articulation between collective intellectual rights and the original rights of indigenous societies to the land, as a way of binding land, knowledge, and innovation in a legal and coherent whole. If it were a case of really protecting biodiversity and its resources, as well as of actually respecting the right to socio-diversity, then this might be the best alternative. However, this articulation has not been investigated.

In the mid-1990s, when Senator Marina Silva presented her bill, whoever wished to fight for a law to protect biodiversity and its associated knowledge needed to discuss whether to opt for intellectual property rights or for collective intellectual rights; in addition, one also had to face, in a critical and inventive manner, the relationship of this law with a permissive patent law, with a government bill on cultivated varieties that sought to extend similar rights to those of patents (as indeed later became the case), and with the bill on the status of indigenous societies, which was to replace that concerning the status of Indians, which was obsolete in the context of the 1988 Constitution, and which provided for the recognition of collective intellectual property and even guaranteed the right of the communities to request a patent for invention based on their collective traditional knowledge. The centrality of the conflict between intellectual property rights vs. collective intellectual rights was, therefore, evident. But at the time, as is still the case today, there was very little clarity in this respect.

Let us take a look at Marina Silva's proposal. First of all, I would like to point out that it was a woman, from the state of Acre, a senator for the Workers' Party, a militant from the social and environmental Amazon movements, and Chico Mendes' companion in the *empates* (those daring actions in which the men and women of the forest tied themselves to rubber trees to prevent deforestation), who introduced the issue of the importance of the protection of biodiversity and traditional knowledge to the Brazilian Parliament. Presented to the Senate on 26 October 1995, bill 306/95 officially opened the debate on a subject that had until then been a resounding non-issue. In presenting the motives that explained her initiative, Marina Silva went straight to the point: "biodiversity is power. Do not forget the heated controversies that currently influence international relations (a paradigmatic example is the legal regulation of genetic patenting) and which pertain to the field of biodiversity" (Silva, 1996: 15).

Senator Marina Silva's project was an invitation for civil society to participate, and, accordingly, public audiences on the matter were held in Brasília, São Paulo and Manaus. Article 1 of the bill takes up the constitutional provision to preserve the diversity and the integrity of the country's genetic patrimony, and states that such preservation should abide by eight principles: 1) sovereignty over resources; 2) the participation of the local communities and indigenous peoples in the decisions; 3) national and local participation in the benefits derived from access; 4) priority for undertakings carried out within the country; 5) the promotion of and support for the different forms of generating knowledge and technology; 6) protection of and incentive to cultural diversity, valorizing the knowledge, innovation, and practices of local communities; 7) biosecurity; 8) the guarantee of individual and collective rights to the knowledge associated with biodiversity. The bill, therefore, revealed a strong socio-environmental concern. It subordinated economic interests to the three basic points stated in the preamble of the Convention on Biological Diversity: the conservation of biodiversity, the sustainable use of its components, and the fair and equitable distribution of benefits. Linking bio- and socio-diversity, Marina Silva dedicated the whole of Chapter IV to the protection of knowledge. But she did so using the notion of collective rights of intellectual property, to be regulated later by law. The bill stated the need for specific protection that took into account the knowledge of indigenous peoples and local communities, but the form such protection should take was left for society to discuss. And at the time it seemed that collective intellectual property was the most that could be envisioned within the Brazilian context: I myself, in a letter to the senator on 8 November 1995, commented on the different articles and suggested that the law establish "*sui generis* intellectual property rights" (?!), which reflected my still precarious and confused understanding of the Third World Network's proposal.

This equivocation persisted. In October 1997, the state of Acre approved a bill on access to genetic resources inspired by the one submitted by Senator Silva, which, in its article 41, recognizes and protects "the rights of local communities to collectively benefit from their traditions and knowledge and to be compensated for the preservation of biological and genetic resources, either through intellectual property rights or other mechanisms." The law does not recognize individual intellectual property rights regarding genetic resources when the collective knowledge of local communities is used; but the notion of collective intellectual property rights exists side by side with collective intellectual rights (Bill 15/97 of the State of Acre). In its turn, the Amapá law (the only Brazilian state with a government plan for sustainable development), approved on 29 October 1997, ensures "remuneration for access to the collective intellectual rights" (*sic*) of traditional and indigenous communities, among others (Bill 0039/97 of the State of Amapá). Also at the end of 1997, Senator Osmar Dias's amendment substantially reformulated bill 306/95, shifting the emphasis from the local to the national plane, depleting its socio-environmental dimension and giving primacy to the economic, not to say purely commercial, sense of access to genetic resources and relevant knowledge. From the start, in article 2, the amendment considers genetic resources and their by-products as *public goods of special usage*, which caused great controversy among jurists, environmentalists, and indigenous activists because the ownership of the goods, as defined here, would seem to entitle the Union to a right that would go against the Indians' exclusive use of their natural resources as established by the constitution. This shift in emphasis also occurred in several other articles, to the point of changing the spirit of the law: the amendment seemed more intent on stipulating the conditions of access (and contract) than on affirming rights. In addition, the protection of traditional knowledge seemed to boil down to a question of "fair and equitable" compensation for benefits, which is the same as saying that the right to knowledge can be negotiated.

Oblivious to the *sui generis* regime, the amendment showed a lack of awareness about the fact that the Gordian knot of access lay, not in access as such, but in the limitation of what industry can do with what is accessed.

Article 5.V states that the rights to traditional knowledge held by the local community or indigenous population are inalienable, unseizable, and irrevocable, but that they may be used, provided that prior, justified permission is obtained and that just and equitable compensation is given. Everything would therefore seem to indicate that traditional knowledge cannot be patented. However, article 41 contains a contradiction: those applying for intellectual property that is based on genetic resources or on the traditional knowledge of local communities or indigenous populations should obtain prior and informed consent. In addition to this, the amendment stated that the intellectual property rights for products or processes pertaining to traditional knowledge associated with genetic resources or their by-products would only be recognized if the access were legal!

The same ambiguities appear in bill 4579/98, presented to the House of Representatives the following year by representative Jacques Wagner of the Workers' Party. The new version contained some important positive differences, since it defined the ownership of genetic resources as *goods of public interest*, reaffirmed the exclusive use by the indigenous communities of the natural wealth located on their lands, and recognized the right of the indigenous and local communities to deny access to resources and knowledge whenever they felt it would threaten the integrity of their heritage. In short, as noted by Juliana Santilli in her evaluation of the bills, "such initiatives are still tentative and imprecise"; a *sui generis* regime for protecting collective intellectual rights should be based on several premises, which include:

> 1) the express provision that any patents or any other intellectual property rights [. . .] granted for processes or products resulting directly or indirectly from the use of the knowledge of indigenous or traditional communities are null and void, as a way of preventing an exclusive monopoly on the same. [. . .] 3) the express provision that traditional knowledge may not be patented would allow the free exchange of information among different communities, which is essential to the very generation of such knowledge (Santilli, 2001: 58).

The concern over the marketing of resources and knowledge

While some sectors of the opposition and civil society debated the matter, the Federal Government, through the Inter-Ministerial Group for Access to Genetic Resources (GIARG), formulated a bill of its own, which was sent to the House of Representatives on 20 August 1998. Coordinated by a representative of the Ministry of the Environment and supervised by the Civil Office of the Presidency of the Republic, the GIARG was composed of members of the Ministries of Industry and Trade, Foreign Affairs, Justice,

Health, Agriculture, Science and Technology, the Navy, and Public Administration, as well as by members of the Oswaldo Cruz Foundation, the National Indian Foundation, the Brazilian Institute of the Environment, the National Institute of Industrial Property, and the Brazilian Company of Agricultural Research. Its mission was to analyze and submit a proposal for the improvement of Senate bill 306/95.

GIARG stated that it decided to work on a new bill "mainly by reason of the need to make the Executive responsible for defining the responsibilities of its organs, something which could not be done by the Legislature" (Message no. 98, 1998: 2). The statement is surprising in the aggressiveness with which it dismisses the prerogatives and responsibilities of the parliament, by claiming a right to legislate, which would later be carried out by a provisional measure. But the government's arrogance did not end there: its project went against the initiatives already presented, not only because it was discussed behind closed doors, but also because it ignored the socio-environmental aspect, one of the main concerns of the sectors of civil society involved in the process. In fact, the emphasis was now being placed on the economic, technical, and scientific aspects, incorporating the dominant logic in developed countries and in the industry of biotechnology.

The government's access project was accompanied by the proposal of a constitutional amendment that intended to include genetic patrimony among the goods of the Union, "in order to allow the state to preserve its diversity and integrity and to oversee the entities dedicated to the research and manipulation of genetic matter" (Message no. 977, 1998: 1). This would, therefore, in keeping with the text of the Convention on Biological Diversity that establishes national sovereignty over biological resources, put genetic patrimony on the same standing as wealth found in the subsoil; in other words, it would make it a national good. As Carlos Marés rightly noted at a meeting of the Socio-Environmental Institute (Instituto Socio-Ambiental), which discussed the first version of the government's bill in September 1999, the objective of the proposed amendment was to open up the possibility of economic access and exploitation of genetic patrimony, something that had hitherto been hampered by the very same article 225 that requires the preservation of its integrity! The amendment would therefore solve the problem of a law that ran the risk of clashing with the constitution. But the matter does not end here: the inclusion of genetic patrimony in article 20 is justified by the intention to preserve it; however, when one reads the accompanying government bill, it is obvious that it deals not with the patrimony but with its components. As Carlos Marés commented at the time, the problem to be solved is the legal access to the components, in other words, the need to guarantee the use of something that falls outside the protection of the law. The intention, he concluded, is to create a new right.

The proposed constitutional amendment intended to turn biodiversity into the genetic patrimony of the Union. But one has to understand that biological beings would not become goods in the hands of the state: the very justification of the reasons behind the amendment highlights the fact that care must be taken "not to confuse them with the rights already established by Brazilian legislation regarding the material and immaterial property of biological resources, which are commonly used in the activities that involve their economic exploitation, such as agriculture and animal husbandry, the agricultural industry or agribusiness in general." Basically, the Union would "only" hold rights over the genetic patrimony. But what exactly is genetic patrimony?

The chapter on definitions reads:

> I.—Genetic patrimony: information of genetic origin, contained in all or part of a vegetable specimen, including those that are domesticated or semi-domesticated, microbial or animal, in substances to be found in the metabolism of these living beings and in extracts obtained from these living or dead organisms, found *in situ* or kept in *ex situ* collections, provided they have been retrieved *in situ*, within the national borders, on the continental shelf, within territorial waters or within the exclusive economic zone.

This definition deserves comment. First of all, we should highlight the fact that all biodiversity has been reduced to its molecular dimension—genetic patrimony is considered to be a stock of information. Second, such a reduction implies the total absence of the notion of a living being; in addition, matter is exclusively understood as raw material, as a means for biotechnological transformation. Lastly, if genetic patrimony is a stock of information, of discrete units, this means that the Union owns a virtual good! But why would the Brazilian government want to claim ownership of such a good? If we recall that genetic information is made equivalent to the minerals found below ground we soon find the answer. The patrimony is only in the hands of the nation until it is appropriated; as Carlos Marés argued, "national patrimony is the idea of it in nature." Once its ownership has been passed on to someone else, that person can access the virtual information, modify it, patent it, and sell it on the global market.

The access bill was therefore a legal formulation that left out the value of the use of genetic resources and opened up the possibility for technoscience and corporations to exploit their informational value. By regulating something that was not yet available and creating a new right, the law would deal with a good that could not be mistaken for any other regulated good, tangible or intangible. Because it dealt with access to virtual components that could be valorized, the bill could afford to state that the material or immaterial property rights that applied to the component accessed or to the place in which it was found would be respected. By regulating the ownership of the information, the law would be perverse: apparently all the goods and all the rights acquired would remain untouched; in practice, however, the goods will be devalued and the rights diminished, but this will only become evident when the valorization of the biotechnological processes and products reveals that the exchange value and informational value have become synonymous, and when the right to intellectual property has made explicit the way in which it interferes in the exercise of other rights.

The bill also stated that the benefits from the economic exploitation of the product or process developed from a sample of the component of the genetic patrimony would be fairly and equitably shared with the Union. In fact, no one knows what the bill considers to be "fair and equitable," since it merely says that the division will be based on a "percentage to be defined in later legislation," when the genetic component is collected on indigenous lands. The state is therefore responsible for defining the value of the informational raw material that will be "transferred" with the property right.

Thus, a close look at the government bill reveals that the state interpreted the exercise of sovereignty over the genetic resources as the prerogative to decide on its own how and under what conditions to sell the virtual information it would own. By equating genetic resources with mineral resources, the government bill attempts to place the animals, plants, and microorganisms found on indigenous lands outside the sphere of the 1988 Constitution. As we have seen, the bill states that the exclusive use by the indigenous communities of the natural wealth to be found on their land will be respected, because the constitution so stipulates. But since these are not considered natural wealth, but rather something to be found virtually within it, the approval of the bill would mean that genetic components would be excluded from exclusive use.

Virtualization of resources and fragmentation of knowledge

In October 1999, two months after the approval of the amendment to bill 306/95 in the senate, the government proposed a merger of the three bills into one amendment. Chapter V of this version is dedicated to the protection of the traditional knowledges associated with the genetic patrimony. All three articles and the many paragraphs of this chapter echo all of the important questions raised by the renowned article 8(j) of the text of the Convention on Biological Diversity: exclusive rights of the indigenous and local communities to their traditional knowledge; access preceded by prior, informed consent; sharing of benefits; and the right to deny access. The crowning glory of all this, article 24, chapter VII, reads: "Processes or products obtained from access to the traditional knowledge associated with the genetic patrimony may not be patented."

Apparently, therefore, this bill was a major step forward, despite the fact that it discarded the possibility of a *sui generis* regime. But a less daring examination of the matter shows that the mentality governing the thinking of government officials has not changed that much. Obviously, the prohibition of patenting contained in article 24 is commendable in that it prevents the exclusive appropriation of the genetic components obtained through traditional knowledge. However, it is worth asking if the inclusion of this paragraph was actually to serve some purpose. What is the use of holding exclusive rights over traditional knowledge if article 9, paragraph 8, states that ingress into lands belonging to indigenous or local communities for access to genetic resources in the event of relevant public interest to the nation will not require prior permission from those communities? Article 9 allows for access irrespective of the will of Indians and traditional communities; this, as we well know, clears the way for making the proclaimed right and freedom of choice devoid of meaning.

However, none of the aspects referred to above is the most serious. In my view, the greatest violence lies in the very definition of associated traditional knowledge: "individual or collective information or practice of the indigenous community or local community, with real or potential value, associated to the genetic patrimony." As if the knowledge of these peoples could be translated into discrete units, into bits of information, and still remain traditional knowledge! As if the definition was not, in itself, a testimonial to the predatory appropriation of one culture by another.

Trampling the legislature and civil society: the "Novartis Provisional Measure"

The bills dragged on for years in Congress. Finally, at the end of May 2000, the scandal of the bio-prospecting agreement between the Swiss multi-national Novartis and the social organization BioAmazônia broke out. BioAmazônia had been created by the Brazilian state to implement the Molecular Ecology Program for the Sustainable Use of Biodiversity of Amazonia (PROBEM), in other words, to foment the development of bio-industry.

The scandal broke out and grew as the terms of the partnership were revealed, which were considered harmful by the opposition, by the better part of the Brazilian scientific community, and by the press. Criticized even by members of the BioAmazônia Board, who were unaware of the content of the negotiations, the agreement also had its validity questioned by the Minister of the Environment himself: in his view, BioAmazônia was not authorized to sign bio-prospecting agreements or contracts.

The "agreement for cooperation" dealt with the collection and supply of stocks and extracts for a period of three years, and provided for a supplementary project regarding the isolation of purified natural compounds of plants, fungi, or microorganisms. In a far-reaching article, the President of the Butantan Foundation summarized the reasons for such a negative reaction. After pointing out that the greatest value of biodiversity lies in microorganisms, Isaías Raw expressed his amazement at the fact that BioAmazônia thinks it reasonable to isolate, characterize, and sell stocks of Brazilian bacteria at 100 Swiss francs, up to a maximum limit of 1 million Brazilian reais, figures he feels are lower than the cost of upkeep for the association's office in São Paulo. He adds:

> BioAmazônia signs an agreement giving Novartis the exclusive right to request and maintain the protection of a patent to make, produce, use and sell direct compounds and derivatives within the territory (which the contract defines as the world!). In exchange Novartis offers, and BioAmazônia accepts, 500 thousand Swiss francs, while Novartis announces that it is conducting a clinical study with a product derived from Brazilian biodiversity, and another 2,250,000 Swiss francs before the product is launched. In the meantime, Novartis will teach us to be its technicians, collecting microorganisms and fermenting and analyzing the presence of products of interest. We would then have the important task of sending the isolated extracts and compounds, and later sending the stocks. For only 100 Swiss francs per stock, BioAmazônia will have to set up a machine to send 10 thousand cultures to Novartis! (Raw, 2000)

There are many more controversial items to be pointed out in this agreement for cooperation, which essentially boils down to the cheap sale of access to genetic raw material for the biotechnological industry. For this very reason, several voices echoed the harsh words of Isaías Raw, who ended his article by calling the partnership a "spurious agreement that turns the Amazon into a backyard for multinational companies."

Opposition to the agreement grew. In mid-June, Senator Marina Silva asked the Attorney General to investigate its legality. Other bio-prospecting agreements also came to light, including the agreement between Glaxo Wellcome and Extracta, in July 1999. The House set up a committee to speed up the voting on the law of access, and the government pondered the creation of a code of conduct to regulate such contracts. But, at the same time, despite all the fuss regarding the reaction of the Ministry of the Environment, signs began to appear that the government intended to validate the agreement made with Novartis by issuing a provisional measure prepared by the Civil Office of the Presidency and inspired by the government bill.

The news that the "Novartis Provisional Measure," as the regulation of access became known, was to be passed, caused protests from the NGOs, which pointed out the anti-democratic character of the initiative, the disregard of the legislature and civil society, which were being run over in the process, and the legal insecurity the text would bring about, since the provisional measures could be changed every time they were reissued, and could therefore be influenced by specific interests. With a governmental decision imminent, 32 entities and forums of environmental organizations sent an appeal to the President of Brazil, with legal arguments against the issuing of the provisional measure and requesting that the matter be dealt with through a bill.

This was all to no avail: on 30 June 2000, the government passed Provisional Measure no. 2052, conceived in the Civil Office of the Presidency. An attentive look at this measure reveals that it is simply a revised version of the government bill. Article 1 reads:

> This Provisional Measure regulates the goods, rights and obligations pertaining to the access to components of genetic patrimony [. . .], to traditional knowledge associated with it [. . .], to the integrity of the country's genetic patrimony, to the use of its components and the fair and equitable distribution of the benefits derived from its exploitation, as well as the access to technology and the transfer of technology for the preservation and use of biological diversity.

The text does not clearly state that the Union holds the title to genetic patrimony; it only recognizes this tacitly and avoids dealing with the controversial question of the legal nature of this patrimony. However, in article 2 the text confers the exclusive right to exercise sovereignty over these resources to the Union. It also retains the definitions that allow the virtualization of biodiversity so that it can later be objectified as a private good, and confirms the possibility of patenting life, thanks to the distinction between genetic resource and biological resource. But worst of all is the violation of the rights of the indigenous peoples guaranteed by the constitution.

In an attempt to appear to respect and uphold the principles of the Convention on Biological Diversity in regard to the protection of traditional knowledge, the provisional measure dedicates its entire chapter III to this matter. In this chapter the state recognizes the rights of indigenous and local communities to decide on the use of their traditional knowledge associated with the country's genetic patrimony. However, in article 8, this right begins to be undermined: paragraph 4 states that protection cannot be interpreted in such a way as to prevent the use of this traditional knowledge, and paragraph

5 states that protection cannot affect, damage, or limit any other type of right to intellectual property. Article 10 grants pardon to biopirates by establishing that "any person of good faith who, up until 30 June 2000, used or economically exploited any of the country's traditional knowledge, will be entitled to continue to use or exploit such knowledge." Lastly, article 9 concerns the ability of indigenous and local communities to prevent the unauthorized use of their traditional knowledge; however, since this article does not specify how they can prevent the action of third parties, and since paragraph 5 protects intellectual property, the entire chapter dedicated to the protection of traditional knowledge is devoid of meaning.

As if that was not enough, other articles of the provisional measure go even further. Article 14 reiterates that in cases of relevant public interest, so defined by the competent authority, the entry into indigenous land to gain access to genetic resources does not require prior consent from the indigenous and local communities. Carlos Marés and the Attorney General, Aurélio Rios, point out that this article ignores the need for prior and informed consent. Furthermore, this article is unconstitutional on two counts. In the first place, it would violate article 231 of the constitution, which establishes the Indians' entitlement to the exclusive use of the natural resources located on their lands (we have already seen that such an interpretation can be contested if we take into account that we are not dealing with natural resources, but virtualities to be found in them). Second, the constitution determines that the public interest should be regulated by a complementary law, but article 14 of the provisional measure describes what constitutes an abuse. The allegation of exemption in cases of relevant public interest is absurd because in principle there is no such thing as irrelevant public interest; moreover, since neither relevant cases nor the authority competent to define such relevance are specified, any entity will do—or, seemingly rather, an Inter-Ministerial Committee made up of members of the Civil Office of the Presidency, far removed from the sectors of civil society and the entities directly involved in the matter. Lastly, article 14 of the provisional measure completely depletes the negotiating conditions of the indigenous peoples as to the distribution of the benefits referred to in article 21: if the Indians are not "reasonable" during negotiations, the state representative can always invoke "relevant public interest" in order to fit them in—or to exclude them.

In truth, the authorities, who appear so liberal when negotiating with Novartis, harden when it comes to the purveyors of resources. Article 28 puts an end to the issue of the rights of indigenous peoples to their resources and knowledge by making these freely patentable, since in order to gain the right to the industrial property of a process or product obtained from a sample of the genetic patrimony all one has to do is provide information as to the origin of the material and the traditional knowledge collected.

INCONCLUSION

Since June 2000, the provisional measure has been reissued by the government and challenged wherever and whenever possible. In August, the National Confederation of Agricultural Workers (Confederação Nacional dos Trabalhadores na Agricultura—CONTAG) filed a Direct Suit of Unconstitutionality (ADIN no. 2289/00) put together by the lawyers of the Socio-Environmental Institute, questioning the constitutionality of articles 10 and 14. Realizing the legal fragility of these articles, the Civil Office of the Presidency altered them in the revised version of the provisional measure on 27 April 2001, suspending the general amnesty granted to those who already had exploited traditional knowledge, and revoking the free entry into indigenous lands in cases of relevant public interest. This latter question should now be regulated by a complementary law and not entrusted to the Management Council for Genetic Patrimony (Conselho de Gestão do Patrimônio Genético).

This retreat shows that the government only pays attention to the point of view of the communities as a last resort. For this very reason, the struggle continues within Congress to approve one of the bills. In any case, even with the provisional measure, the question of access to genetic resources and associated knowledge remains unresolved: since it was passed, bio-prospecting has been legally paralyzed in Brazil because the management council has not yet been created; at the same time, the governing bodies are divided over whether the genetic patrimony should be considered a good of the Union through the proposed constitutional amendment—some sectors interpret this as a limitation of the right to property. That is why it has not yet been possible to vote on the amendment and transform the provisional measure into law, as the executive branch would like[1].

BIBLIOGRAPHY

Bateson, G. (1987). "Men Are Grass—Metaphor and the World of Mental Process," W. I. Thompson (ed.), *Gaia: a Way of Knowing—Political Implications of the New Biology*. Great Barrington, MA: Lindisfarne. 37–47.

Câmara dos Deputados (1998). *Projeto-de-Lei n. 4579/98*, http://www.socioambiental.org/website/noticias/naintegra/docs/rtf/4579_98.rtf, accessed on 28 June 2001.

——————— (1998). *Projeto-de-Lei n. 4751/98*. Câmara dos Deputados http://www.socioambiental.org/website/noticias/naintegra/docs/rtf/regulame.rtf, accessed on 28 June 2001.

Comissão Especial, "Proposta de Emenda à Constituição 618-A/98—Patrimônio Genético," http://www.camara.gov.br/Intranet/Comissao?index/esp/pec61898nt171000.pdf, accessed on 19 December 2000.

Conselho Indigenista Missionário, (n.d.). "Medida Provisória para recursos genéticos é mais uma afronta aos direitos indígenas," cimi@embratel.net.br, accessed on 7 July 2000.

CONTAG, (n.d.). "Contag contesta MP de acesso a patrimônio genético," agenciacontag@contag.com.br, accessed on 17 August 2000.

Deleuze, G. (1986). *Foucault*. Paris: Editions de Minuit.

Estado do Acre (1997). *Lei n. 15/97 de Acesso aos Recursos Genéticos*.

Estado do Amapá (1997). *Lei n. 0388 de 10/12/1997*, http://www.socioambiental.org/ website/noticias/naintegra/docs/rtf/0388.rtf, accessed on 28 June 2001.

Gonçalves, M. (2000). "ONGS condenam regulação do acesso aos recursos genéticos por MP," marco@socioambiental.org, accessed on 29 June 2000.

———— (2000). "Governo federal insiste em regulamentar acesso aos recursos genéticos por MP," marco@socioambiental.org, accessed on 11 August 2000.

Haraway, D. (1994). "Um manifesto para os *cyborgs*: ciência, tecnologia e feminismo socialista na década de 80," H. B. Hollanda (ed.), *Tendências e Impasses—O Feminismo como Crítica da Cultura*. Rio de Janeiro: Rocco. 243–288.

Hathaway, D. (1993). "Some Biodiversity Issues in Brazil." Paper presented at Journée d'Etudes "L'Accès aux Resources Génétiques: Un Enjeu du Développement." Paris: Solagral-FPH-IUCN-CFCF.

Holguín, D. P. (1996). "The Civil Society of Colombia Proposes a Legal Framework to Protect Their Biological Resources," S. Tilahun and S. Edwards (eds.), *The Movement for Collective Intellectual Rights*. Addis-Ababa: Institute for Sustainable Development; London: Gaia Foundation. 118–176.

Jameson, F. (1991). *Postmodernism, or The Cultural Logic of Late Capitalism*. Durham, NC: Duke UP.

———— (1998). *The Cultural Turn*. London: Verso.

Lacey, H. (1998). *Valores e Atividade Científica*. São Paulo: Fapesp/Discurso Editorial.

———— (1999). "Scientific Understanding and the Control of Nature," *Science and Education* 8: 13–35.

———— (2000). *The Social Location of Scientific Practices*. Swarthmore, PA: n.p.

———— (2001). "As Sementes e o Conhecimento que elas Incorporam," *São Paulo em Perspectiva* 14(3):53–59. [São Paulo: Revista da Fundação Seade].

———— (2001). "Informationcritique," http://www.goldsmiths.ac.uk/cultural-studies/html/inform.html, accessed on 30 November 2000.

Martins, H. (2000). "Tecnociência e Arte," C. Leone (ed.), *Rumo ao Cibermundo?* Oeiras: Celta Editora. 11–35.

Medida Provisória n. 2.052–1, de 28 de Junho de 2000. Brasília: Diário Oficial, n. 145-B, Seção 1 (30 July 2000): 49.

Medida Provisória n. 2.126–13, de 26 de Junho de 2001. Casa Civil da Presidência da República—Subchefia de Assuntos Jurídicos, http://www.planalto.gov.br/ccivil_03/MPV/2126–13.htm, accessed on 28 June 2001.

Nijar, G. S. (1994). "Towards a Legal Framework for Protecting Biological Diversity and Community Intellectual Rights—A Third World Perspective." Third World Network Discussion Paper. Nairobi: Second Session of the Intergovernmental Committee on the Convention on Biological Diversity.

Presidência da República (1998). *Mensagem n. 977 ao Congresso Nacional*, 20 August.

——————— (1998). *Mensagem n. 978 ao Congresso Nacional*, 20 August.
Raw, I. (2000). "BioAmazônia, Novartis e o Brasil," *Jornal da Ciência E-Mail* 8 June 2000.
Rifkin, J. (2000). *The Age of Access*. New York: Jeremy P. Tarcher/Putnam.
Santilli, J. (2001). "A Proteção Legal aos Conhecimentos Tradicionais Associados à Biodiversidade," C. M. Azevedo and F. N. Furriela (eds.), *Biodiversidade e Propriedade Intelectual*. São Paulo: Secretaria do Meio Ambiente. 51–68.
Santos, L. G. dos (1994a). "A Encruzilhada da Política Ambiental Brasileira." M. D'Incao and I. M. Silveira (eds.), *A Amazônia e a Crise da Modernização*. Belém, Pará: Museu Paraense Emílio Goeldi. 135–1454.
——————— (1994b). "Shifting the Focus on the North-South Debate." Paper presented to the International Conference on Redefining the Life Sciences. Penang: Third World Network.
——————— (1995). Letter to Senator Marina Silva, 8 November.
——————— (1998). "Tecnologia, natureza e a 'redescoberta' do Brasil," H. R. Araújo (ed.), *Tecnociência and Cultura—Ensaios sobre o Tempo Presente*. São Paulo: Estação Liberdade. 23–46.
———————, and G. Muzio (1996). "Collective Intellectual Rights and Control of Access to Biological Resources," S. Tilahun and S. Edwards (eds.), *The Movement for Collective Intellectual Rights*. Addis-Ababa: Institute for Sustainable Development; London: Gaia Foundation. 177–198.
Shiva, V. (1993). *Monocultures of the Mind*. London: Zed Books. Penang: Third World Network.
Silva, M. (1996). *Lei de Acesso à Biodiversidade Brasileira*. Brasília: Senado Federal.
Simondon, G. (1964). *L'Individu et la Génèse Physico-Biologique*. Épiméthée. Paris: Presses Universitaires de France.
——————— (1969). *Du Mode d'Existence des Objets Techniques*. Coll. Analyses et Raisons. Paris: Aubier/Montaigne.
——————— (1989). *L'Individuation Psychique et Collective*. Coll. Res. Paris: Aubier.
Souza Filho, C. M. (1999). *O Renascer dos Povos Indígenas para o Direito*. Curitiba: Juruá Editora.
Visvanathan, S. (1997). *A Carnival for Science—Essays on Science, Technology and Development*. Delhi: Oxford UP.
Waldby, C. (2000). *The Visible Human Project—Informatic Bodies and Posthuman Medicine*. London: Routledge.
Wiener, N. (1965). "L'Homme et la Machine," *Le Concept d'Information dans la Science Contemporaine*. Cahiers de Royaumont—Philosophie No. V. Paris: Editions de Minuit.

Note

1 By the end of 2005, the question remains an open one — even though Marina Silva becomes then the Minister of Environment of President Lula's government, she is fiercely opposed by the Ministers of Agriculture, Industry and Commerce, and Science and Technology.

7

Between Cosmology and System: The Heuristics of a Dissenting Imagination[1]

Shiv Visvanathan

INTRODUCTION

The history of the debates between tradition and modernity in India is a story that has been told twice. The first fable centers on the archives of the national movement;[2] the second springs from the debates on science and technology enacted during the grassroots struggles of the last two decades. These debates in India, both in the colonial and post-colonial eras, have been marked by three qualities.

First, the notion of hospitality. The national movement sought to overthrow colonial rule yet was confident enough to invite the British to participate in the debates on modernity. Some of the most fascinating contributions to the understanding of traditional systems came from these dissenting Englishmen. "The other colonialisms," as I call this genre of discourse, saw in India a set of possibilities that the West had either out or rendered recessive. These Englishmen were particularly interested in creating a more humane transition to modern industrialism. One can cite the works of Patrick Geddes, Albert Howard, and Alfred Chatterton in this context (Visvanathan, 2001a).

Second, the Indian national movement also saw the West as a possibility. We fought the West but the West, like the Orient, was not just out there but something within ourselves. It became an experimental site for the free play of the nationalist imagination, which sought to liberate the other Wests that England had suppressed within itself.

Third, while the concerns and experiments in science, technology, medicine, and education were local, there was a feeling that the neighborhood must reflect the interests of the cosmos. Furthermore, the debate did not reify the dualism of tradition and modernity, especially in the domain of knowledge, but sought an encounter that was both confrontational and dialogic. Tradition and modernity were not only self-critical sites but were also what might be called a complicity of opposites. Unfortunately the pluralist archives of the nationalist movement became partially submerged in the 1950s and 1960s. They appeared more in the form of eclectic quotes used instrumentally to make less fascinating arguments.

These debates were however re-invented during the spate, the epidemic, of experiments in science and technology that arose in the early 1970s, triggered by several phenomena. One must emphasize in particular the famines of Bihar, the Emergency (which was the declaration of a dictatorship by Indira Gandhi), and the abortive Marxist movements that began at Naxalbari. This chapter begins with the backdrop of these events. In the domains of science and technology, what one saw was an encounter between transfer-of-technology models and social movements like those concerned with forestry (Chipko), anti-dam struggles (Narmada, Koel Karo), anti-nuclear protests (Kaiga), and scientific movements like that of the Kerala Shastra Sahitya Parishad (KSSP). Many of these groups spun off their own critiques of science and knowledge, and these I believe can be mapped in terms of their positions vis-à-vis the transfer-of-technology model (TOT) (Visvanathan, 2001b).

The TOT model is the genetic code of the Third World nation-states. The nation-state is a modern creation. It represents a social contract between the state and modern Western science to pursue the twin projects of security and development. The battle between traditional knowledges and modern Western science was fought in this political context. Simplistically put, the TOT model is an innovation chain, and it consists of three phases: invention, innovation, and diffusion. The invention stage represents the conceptualization of a scientific idea and its possible translation into a small sample or a product. Innovation is the upscaling, the commercialization of the idea, from pilot plant to market. Diffusion represents the wider extension of the product into society. The three stages of the chain are not monotonic.

The science movements, the experiments in science and technology that arose in the last two decades, can be mapped in terms of the critique of the TOT model. It represents, as it were, a quick semaphore of the politics of knowledge in the last two decades. The movements in science that were inspired by the left "black-boxed" modern Western science as a cosmology. Their dream was to diffuse Western science. India, they felt, would be more democratic as it became more scientific. Science, modern Western science, was to be a liberating Brechtian force that was to be the domain of every citizen. So democracy in science became analytically reduced to two acts: First, diffusion and second, participation. The lingo of the World Bank and left groups like the KSSP, the Delhi Science Forum (DSF), and the Bharatiya Gyan Vigyan Samiti (BGVS) often sounded similar.

Outstanding among this genre of movements was the KSSP and the Hoshiangabad experiment in Madhya Pradesh. The latter was a superbly conceived exercise in pedagogy, of taking science to the villages. The preoccupation was with science books, science kits, weaving the environment into the child's imagination. The KSSP, like the Hoshiangabad experiment, was generally leftist and modernist. It was conceived as a giant tutorial college, a popularized cram course in science, replete with quizzes. It was a populist drama of science with Desmond Bernal, Albert Einstein, and C. V. Raman as heroes. Its greatest achievement was to help save one of the last great tropical tracts of land, the Silent Valley in Kerala, from the impact of development. The KSSP used traditional forms of theater like the *Jatra* for diffusing science, although in this case tradition was more a costume ball within which the modern script of science was enacted. Its attitude to traditional knowledge verged on the illiterate and its theory of science was desperately positivist. The DSF and the BGVS were all lesser clones of this same imagination and worked at the diffusion end of the map. As a result, they often became extension counters of the regime. Their attitude to traditional systems was patronizing or hostile.

The innovation phase was the preoccupation of many Gandhians and scientists working on technologies. This pluralism of experiments, ranging from the Khadi Village Industries Corporation (KVIC) to the Application of Science and Technology to Rural Areas (ASTRA) at the Indian Institute of Science at Bangalore has often been grouped under the Schumacherian idea of intermediate technology. Schumacher himself was a consultant to the Indian Planning Commission. Outstanding among these experiments was Amulya Kumar Reddy's ASTRA at Bangalore. Its contributions to energetics, to biogas plants, and to the conceptualization of biomass are classic. For ASTRA, traditional technology was both rational and ecologically sound but it was a text disrupted by new contexts. This group worked with the basic belief that science was universal but that technology was local and adaptable. *Local* knowledges, *local* materials came into play in this context. Ashok Khosla's Development Alternatives (Delhi), now playing the scripts of sustainable development, is another example of this genre. Within this discourse local knowledge was welcome, but epistemology was noise or taboo.

A more critical focus came from a fascinating group that had christened itself with a terrible name: the Patriotic and People Oriented Science and Technology Group (PPST). Basically a group of scientists and technologists from the Indian Institute of Technology and the universities, it sought its inspiration in the historiography of the maverick nationalist Dharampal (Dharampal, 1971). The group claimed that colonialism destroyed not only the political economy but the epistemological basis of Indian society, namely agriculture. The *PPST Bulletin* chronicled the strengths, the imagination, and the rationality of traditional systems of agriculture, medicine, and water management. It was fascinatingly orientalist in some ways but it also provided a devastating critique of the scientific antics of the Indian nation-state. Its annual conference, part fair (*mela*), part science congress replete with papers, reflects both its statist policy inclinations and a touch of the carnivalesque.

The one set of movements not generally included within this frame is that of the farmers' movement, the anti-dam struggles, and forest movements like the Chipko. Each of these titanic struggles produced their own hermeneutics of science. The work of Vandana Shiva (1988), Claude Alvares (1995), and Sunil Sahasrabuddhey (1991) are outgrowths of this struggle. The writings of Jit Uberoi and Ashis Nandy are more rarefied academic reflections in this genre. Chipko has been hyphenated with a feminist critique of science. The farmers' struggle is addressing the issue of genetic diversity where the question of traditional knowledges is central. To this we must add one organization, a science laboratory that has fought a lonely, exuberant, maverick struggle to create a different dream of science, inspired by the intellectual exuberance of the chemist C. V. Seshadri (Seshadri, 1993).

His laboratory became the site for a beautiful set of experiments, an encounter between tradition and modernity that was playful, elliptical, plural, and utterly unfundamentalist. It was a critique of modern scientific knowledge conducted by a practicing scientist. The Indian adage that good scientists do science, but that bad ones do science policy does not apply to Seshadri. But Seshadri argued that the scientist must be his own anthropologist and philosopher. The work of the Murgappa Chettiar Research Group produces as it were a frame for the debate between traditional and modern knowledge. It begins with three suggestions.

One, the work of the science movements produced its own historiography of science. The grassroots groups in various forms were the dissenting academics of the university and the national laboratories in India. Plotted across the TOT model we get a new critique. Science as a black box is opened up. The work of the movements can be visualized in terms of two oppositions: first, the opposition of internalist and externalist approaches to science, and second the opposition between exoteric and esoteric approaches. Science becomes not only a political economy à la Marx but a cosmology.

Two, the challenge arises of how other religions and cosmologies can introduce life-giving hypotheses into science. The classic example is the work of J. C. Bose, the Indian botanist.[3] While the first step opens the black box called invention, the second introduces knowledge as a problem in democratic theory. Questions of cognitive justice and methodologies of assessment all become crucial. How does one relate the question of energy and justice? Seshadri's theory of energetics and biomass becomes central to this debate.

Three, the debate between tradition and modernity is not one of preservation or conservation. In an everyday sense, it emphasizes the importance of invention, of heuristics. We need neither a rigid theory of the modern nor an ossification, an orientalizing, or a museumification of tradition. In Seshadri's laboratory, tradition and modernity meet in the theater called the laboratory. Science becomes an inventive morality play around the dreams of energy in India and neither tradition nor modernity is privileged in this agonal struggle.

This chapter begins with some biographical reflections which could also be considered as reflections on biography. It then moves to a more impersonal phase and describes the conceptualization of energy in India and Seshadri's critique of thermodynamics. The next section deals with the politics of a biomass society and Seshadri's experiments to develop quality markers for projects in science. The final section deals with Seshadri's efforts to link science and democracy. The whole effort is presented as a thought experiment, a site for the heuristics of a debate. One hopes that more such dramas are enacted in the years to come.

BIOGRAPHICAL REFLECTIONS

C. V. Seshadri was a scientist, an engineer trained at Bombay and Carnegie Mellon University. He taught at the Indian Institute of Technology (IIT), Kanpur, where he wrote a standard book on fluid dynamics. He left IIT to establish India's first yeast factory. The last two decades of his life were spent at the Murgappa Chettiar Research Centre at Chennai.

C. V. Seshadri was more than a scientist. He used to growl, "I am not a sociologist of science. I am a scientist and I want my science to do the talking." And talk it did, in many voices. I can still remember the day he drove in late, stood in front of the car glaring at the tire as if it was a new exotic species. He looked like a huge little-boy-lost and said, "Gender was the first diversity and we muffed it." I asked him wickedly, "Did you quarrel with your wife today?" and he said, "Yes," as if "yes" was an affirmation of life in all its complications. For him everything was autobiographical and everything was cosmological. He loved life in its grand patterns and loved life in its little particulars. I remember his student V. Balaji once told me, "for Doc, science was not about policy and populations. Science was about particular persons. He wanted to know what troubled Rajathi and he turned her complaints into scientific problems." For Seshadri, an autobiography could not be an act of bookkeeping, and he hated the chartered accountants of life. He made mistakes and he hurt people. Some of his decisions were disastrous, particularly the choice of his successor. Yet he could reflect on his mistakes. He was a hundred unfinished hypotheses. He was fascinated by death, was himself quite a hypochondriac, but saw hypochondria as a collection of redeemable hypotheses.

He felt Indians were cosmologists except when it came to modern western science, and he missed this cosmic daydreaming and this thinking with the hands. He wanted science to be a life-giving myth and he read and reread Descartes, Poincaré, and Feynman in order to envision the possibilities of one. He saw the Cartesian meditations as an ethical exercise. His was an anthropological, even a religious sense of science as a mode of thought and a code of conduct. A Confucian science. An ethics of possibility. Not method but ritual and, beyond method, lifestyles. He loved Paul Feyerabend but saw his epistemological anarchism as a truncated critique, a Dadaism that never really challenged method because it failed as a cosmology.

He loved words, their magic, and their etymology. He was obsessed with dictionaries as a form of life and always wanted to write one. An Ambrose Bierce on science, a philosophical dictionary, a "don't use me" dictionary.[4] He had even scribbled the beginnings of one. For him everything was a sign to be read. Landscapes, buildings, and bodies. Even chemistry was an almost semiotic discipline, an alchemy where matter, meaning, sign, symbol, and symptom could combine and yet be read separately. In that sense, the history of science was a part of science and not separate from it, as De Solla Price and other historians had argued.

The socialist leader Ram Manohar Lohia once wrote a fascinating piece on the two models for modern India, Mohandas Gandhi and Visvesvaraya. He saw them as ideal citizens and emphasized the competitive complementarity between them. One was the author of *Industrialise or Perish*, the other of *Industrialise and Perish*. Seshadri's ideas pushed this perspective even further. He saw in each the idea of the autobiography as an experiment. Gandhi wrote of his life as an experiment on truth while Visvesvaraya wrote everything as if it were a scientific report. The autobiography with the body as vessel and the self as experiment itself becomes a laboratory, a thought experiment. Seshadri wanted to see each life as a set of unfinished hypotheses. It is only when a life is incomplete that it is a part of the whole. Seshadri felt that autobiography as experiment prevents it from being an iconography or a hagiography. Otherwise India becomes a demographic anomaly, a population that makes no mistakes from Shivaji to G. Parthasar-athi. Science allows for that confident open-ended humility.

When the self becomes an experiment, the standard dualisms of western science are broken or rethreaded in interesting ways. Bruno Latour once made a fascinating Archimedean statement: "Give me a laboratory and I will change the world." In this sentence, subject and object are still estranged, the observer and observed still distant. The experiment as an existential act is still on the other. To this the Seshadrian reply would have been, "Give me a laboratory and I will change myself." One could respond similarly to the ethics of the Cartesian meditation: "I think therefore I am." It becomes "I think of the other, therefore I am."

The "I" of science is a denatured I. But there is the I of evolution, of cosmology, of genealogy, of civilization, and of citizenship. The reductionism of science and its power begins with the impoverishment of the I, of the self in science. For Seshadri, an autobiography begins an experiment in the construction of the self and the self he wants to unravel is the Brahminic, scientific self. In an everyday sense Seshadri knew his laboratory was called "Iyer and Company." He was deeply aware of his Brahminism and deeply critical of it. He wanted to sustain it, reinvent it, and exorcise it. He realized the deep affinity between Brahminism and science, an affiliation as deep as that between Protestantism and science as immortalized in the essays of Max Weber. In both, there is an effort to look at that devastating combination of repression and creativity that we dub as science.

Seshadri and I used to talk about Brahmin Madras for hours. I didn't interview him. We gossiped, compared notes, talked of intellectual pregnancies and philosophical corns.[5] There was an aloneness in each that the other recognized. I remember a line in Bar-Olman's book on physics where there was an inexplicable statement, about science as a solace, a balm for grief. It had been underlined almost tentatively, almost shyly. We were both preoccupied with genealogies, felt generations of time and multiplicities of time within us. We were Brahmins. There is a crudity to the fact, even an obscenity that we recognized. To be a Brahmin is almost unforgivable in Marudur Gopalamenon Ramachandran's Madras. I remember a colleague of mine, a Lohiaite Socialist, fat, in his forties, raving against Brahmin hegemony. Seshadri listened quietly and then asked "How many generations of public service will exonerate me for being a Brahmin?" An ethical self was confronting a political cut-out. Yet Seshadri knew he was a double anachronism, someone who didn't fit in the ghettoized world of Brahmin Madras. He was fascinated by elite Brahmins, who were the scientific hawks of the nation-state, and who were also perpetual émigrés of the mind, who saw San Francisco and Princeton as an annex, an upmarket extension of Adyar, Madras. He also knew that in a deep and fundamental way that we were the last Victorians.

He knew that any critique of Tamil Brahmin science must begin with the grandfathers. He saw grandfathers as a heuristic, a halfway house between genealogy and autobiography. He used to make me talk about my family and about Bengali scientists. We used to chuckle wickedly about a photograph of the Calcutta School of Science, which included Raman, Ramanathan,

Venkatesvaran, Ganesan, Krishnan, Ramdas and, yes, there were a Bannerji and a Ghosh thrown in. Talking about science at that time we classified scientists in terms of two musical metaphors—the piano and the violin. The piano was classically Western. It stands outside Indian culture and yet has a niche in it. Popular culture captures it best. When there is something everyday but Western the piano is all there. Think of all the "happy birthdays to you" and "I love you" in Hindi films—which desperately need a piano. Yet it remains Western. The violin is a hybrid. It is something Carnatic, music absorbed and imbibed creatively.[6] The violin represents the west we had taken and domesticated.

For Seshadri, Westernization was not just the three-piece suit. It was the violin. In the idiom of science, Homi Bhabha was the piano; C. V. Raman was the violin. Yet neither actually produced a grammar for a modern Indian science, and this is what Seshadri sought. There was something distressing, even authoritarian about science. It was a combination of the authoritarian and the authoritative. It was a kind of repressive masculinity. Let me emphasize science in Brahmin India was not a theory of method. It was more of what Richard Rorty once called a collection of virtues. Live life in a certain way and the scientific becomes possible. It was a domestic civics, a grammar, a hygiene, a ritual for living.

Science in Tamil Brahmin India was definitely male. What marked it off was that ghastly invention called home science. Physics was male, home science was female. My aunts practiced home science or social work and worshipped physics. Home science and social work were the *oikos* and *polis* of a woman's life. Home science was to physics as female was to male. The women of that generation were talented, driven, close to science, and deeply voyeuristic about it. Science was like their husbands, contiguous and strangely distant. Science in Tamil Brahmin India produced the bureaucratic ascetic. It was a *service* in that double sense Indians gave the English word. Science, especially physics was a sublimated field, a non-erotic domain. It was not so much truth but certainty, predictability, and correctness that mattered. There was an imperious intolerance about it, an authoritarianism articulated in linear time. In this world, "Be scientific" and "be good" were synonymous statements, but what bothered one were the qualities of goodness and science. Let me cite some of the stories Seshadri and I collected.

The first was about my grandfather. I remember my father had brought me an electric train from Germany. I was about 7 then. I wrote to my grandfather about it, claimed it ran at 500 miles an hour. Pat came the reply: "Your electric train could not possibly run at that speed. Please check and let me know the correct speed." I think my disgust with science began that day with grandfathers who calibrated fantasies.

I secretly dreamt my grandfather and other scientists were clocks, or at least timetables. There was an arid precision to life that bothered me. In fact, science was like table manners, a ritual correctness in life where morality yielded to routine. Clock time was central to their lives. When they went to their office they put on their science, when they came home they put on their caste and their ritual clericalism. Time and honesty were the two spokes of their lives. In fact, the presentation of the watch was as important a ritual into manhood as the sacred thread. The clock was aridly male and it didn't menstruate. The clock was secular and utterly indifferent to all other times. In constructing the civics for the scientist and of his surrogates the clerk and the accountant, we swallowed the variety of times. The Republic of Brahminic Science was constructed on clock time, like the plan, the laboratory, and the calendar. In fact, Seshadri and I believed that the national movement was all about clocks. Remember Gandhi's clock, his punctuality, and Nehru's obsession with plans. I remember a cousin of mine who went to meet S. Chandrasekhar. He rushed in full of expectation to meet his uncle and was stunned to find the latter upset that he had not made an appointment.

What I want to emphasize is the link between this disciplinary body, its time and its honesty, and science as it was constructed by Brahmin-Brahmo India. I remember the psychologist Ashis Nandy's lovely story about the statistician Prasanta Mahalanobis's father.

The father of Indian planning was then only a child. He was travelling with his father to Burdwan. In those days, like today, you could travel on a half-ticket if you were under 12. The train was chugging happily when Mahalanobis senior suddenly pulled the chain and demanded that his son get down immediately. The fellow passengers were flabbergasted and asked the father what the son had done. He replied that Prasanta was 12 a few minutes ago and was travelling under false pretences. Fortunately, common sense came to the rescue. The passengers suggested that the father should pay the other half and the journey proceeded happily.

What fascinated Seshadri and me was the strange stiffness of this generation, a definition of the body and the mind that it projected on to public space. It was a generation that dealt with love out of pipettes and loved the Emergency because the trains ran on time. It is a question we must ask. "Why did so many Tamil Brahmin scientists love the Emergency, the imposition of dictatorship in the 1970s?" We formulated the question in a different way. Science, we felt, was based on the impoverished body, on an impoverishment of time, and an aridness of sexuality. Seshadri felt he wanted to create a science that was muscular, not machismo, a science that thought with its hands, a science that was more sexual and sensual, a science that was sensitive to suffering.

He felt that there was a connection between the autobiography as experiment and the nation-state as one. One remembers the old idea of

Visvesveraya about nation-building, character-building, and dam-building as isomorphic activities, and Seshadri hinted that something had gone wrong with all three. Seshadri felt that the roots and the theater for such an examination lay in science. He also added that the laboratory as theater must reflect the rules of dialogue. He realized that this was less of a set-piece battle that Tagore dreamt of between the city university and the forest university (Visvanathan, 2001a). This was a more fluid movement of ideas across osmotic categories.

To systematize this, one must begin with a genealogy of words. For Seshadri, contemporary constitutions like modern Western science were Judeo-Christian documents. One must not allow for the immaculate innocence of words and instead realize that there is more violence tucked into words like "health," "poverty," and "energy" than in the worst annals of crime. Once you introduce words such as "history," "development," and "progress" into poverty and suffering, you economize and scienticize it on Judeo-Christian time. For Seshadri it was the Judeo-Christian nature of modern texts that was a bit unsettling. Whether it is thermodynamics or the detective novel, one had to realize the Christian nature of the exercise. Consider the classic detective novel. It is a scientific text built on a Judeo-Christian frame. Murder is a violation of order and the detective restores it. The detective in the text plays God. Remember the last chapters. All the characters are assembled around the table with the detective at the head. The whole act is modeled on the Last Supper. Seshadri's work is not an attack on Christianity but a critique of those who fail to explore the tacit knowledges underlying their life worlds. He said that Einstein was fond of saying that scientists imbibed their concepts with mother's milk. One sometimes feels that scientists are more critical of mother's milk than they are of science at the everyday level.

Seshadri also added that dialogicity in Western science was difficult because science was caught between the dualisms of state and Church and science and religion. Here science was a public role and religion a private space. Encounters between religion and science were either conflict-ridden, as in the evolution debates, or weak-kneed and sentimental, as in the writings of John Barrow, Stephen Gould, and Fritjof Capra. One needed to improvise a more agonal space for such dialogues, where one is critical and avoids the fundamental of both extremes. Seshadri did not develop a strict grammar but did develop a set of exercises for such a critique, especially through his examination of the axiomatics of energy.

THE CONCEPTUALIZATION OF ENERGY IN INDIA

Jawaharlal Nehru's often quoted statement, "Dams and laboratories are the temples of new India," was an idiotic combination of Comte and Fabian socialism. These temples of energy, these creations of science were indices of modernity. Reified, dams became the health of the nation. A threat to a dam or nuclear reactor was a threat to the state. When Medha Patkar and the anti-Narmada activists protested, the state prohibited such acts under the Defense of India Rules. A threat to the dam was a threat to the security of India. When journalists and scholars like Praful Bidwai or a Dhirendra Sharma criticized nuclear energy, they were seen as both anti-scientific and anti-national. Today grassroots groups realize that they must begin by breaking this social contract between state-science-economic development. Under-lying all three is the metaphor of energy. Jawaharlal Nehru's statement on dams as the temples of modern India is only another variant of Lenin's celebrated and more genocidal dictum, "Soviets + Electrification = Com-munism." The man who bridged Lenin and Nehru was the Indian physicist Meghnad Saha (Visvanathan, 1985).

Meghnad Saha was one of the legendary scientists of India, a poor boy who became one of the fathers of Indian planning, a scientist whose work on ionospheric research earned him a nomination for the Nobel. Meghnad Saha was born and brought up in the Brahmaputra valley, where floods were a frequent event. Both in 1913 and 1923 Saha participated in flood relief operations. After the 1923 flood, Saha was obsessed with the idea of flood control. His early efforts were published in *Modern Review* and in the festschrift to the great botanist J. C. Bose. By 1938, as President of the National Institute of Sciences, Saha had convened a seminar on river valley civilizations where he echoed the words of the British engineer Francis Spring, that "the establishment of a River Commission for the organized study of the alluvial rivers would be an act worthy of the state." It was the result of Saha's efforts that Voordiun, an expert from the TVA, was invited to India and it was the latter's report that provided the basis for the Indian equivalent of the TVA—the Damodar Valley Corporation.

Saha wanted to move to a more total vision of planning and his encounters with Congressional politicians left him irritated. These agitators had little conception of modern science or economics. In 1936, Meghnad Saha the astrophysicist decided to turn economist. He began by consulting the yearbooks of the League of Nations in order to generate a comparative index of income. He started with the production of various commodities but failed to generate an appropriate index. He then felt that the wealth of a country was proportionate to the energy it consumed. He calculated the per capita output of every country. The energy index of the UK was 2000, of the USA, 2500. Statistics on India were unreliable but Saha estimated that the average energy consumption was 90 units per year. "It was equal to that of Europe in the middle ages." Saha went out in search of a model of a high energy society and found it in Lenin's Russia. He was enchanted by the

GOELRO plan and particularly in the relation between Lenin and Krzhiz-hanovsky. Krzhizhanovsky, a colleague of Lenin from his undergraduate days, was an electrical engineer. He saw in the October Revolution a prelude to the technological revolution. He shared with Lenin a belief in a society based on the efficient use of energy and even coined a term for it, the *Energetika*. By 1921, Lenin had made electrification the second program of the party. Krzhizhanovsky's commission for electrification became Russia's first planning body. Saha went out in search of his Lenin, and found it in Subash Chandra Bose. While Bose was president of the Indian Congress, he established the Indian planning committees. What is interesting about this is the role of energy in linking science to economics.[7]

Energy provides not only a rationale for the state but a grid of discipline. Energy is potentially an organizational metaphor. It is a polyvalent term, at once work, power, potential, vigor, and effect; it is occult, spiritual, and kinetic. What the advocates of planning scientists and economists did was to desemanticize the term, break its varied meanings into one politically correct word, transforming an icon into an index, a multivalent possibility into one univalent quantitative concept. Simultaneously it became a disciplinary term; energy had to be measured, planned, and channeled. What threatened excess or uncontrolled flow was now a controlled grid. Dam, reactor, and labora-tory were the pilgrimages of this new geography. Discipline and energy became deeply linked and stratified. So energy became transformed into what the state and the plan considered it to be, and petroleum, nuclear, hydel and electric now constituted the alphabet of the energy of the new state. Expert energy was official energy. Energy generated by the people, the traditional world of dung and fuelwood was not considered immaculate and scientific. Within this view, all forms of energy were seen as standardized and convertible, disembedded from the knowledge systems that they were implicated in.

Mahatma Gandhi realized in a deep and fundamental way the danger of such a preoccupation with energy as an index of material progress. He warned that "the control over the hidden forces of nature enables every American to have 33 slaves. Repeat the process in India and every Indian will be 33 times a slave," and he was right. Energy has been the Trojan horse through which development has completed its bloodless conquest. In the late seventies, when scientists like Hussein Zaheer and Adinath Lahiri requested Indira Gandhi to move away from the petroleum base of industrialization, we find the first recognitions of this impasse. But this was more reactive and desperate than systematically epistemic. To exorcise the modern dreams of energy we must shatter the term and this can only begin if we re-examine the steam engine and the laws of thermodynamics.

SHESHADRI'S CRITIQUE OF THERMODYNAMICS

The steam engine is the basis of the industrial revolution. The role of the steam engine is captured in Marx and Engel's statement that if the windmill gave us feudalism the steam engine gave us industrial society. This statement in *The Communist Manifesto*, even if reductionist, emphasizes the importance of the steam engine. The steam engine is popularly seen as the basis of the mechanical world, of industrialism. Yet it is around steam that the laws of thermodynamics were developed. These were the most polemically contentious laws of physics and even today scientists grumble about some aspects of them. We shall provide two glimpses of the steam engine, first through the brilliant exegesis of Georgesceau-Roegen and then through the lenses of C. V. Seshadri. What we wish to show is that the physics of the steam engine carries along with it its anthropology of modernity.

Imagine an old-fashioned railway steam engine. Heat from the burning coal flows into the boiler and escapes as steam into the atmosphere. As a result of this the engine has moved from point A to point B. Yet, following the laws of conservation, the overall quantity of matter and energy has remained constant. What has occurred is a qualitative change. Coal has been converted to ash. Heat has moved from the hotter to the colder part of the machine. Physics, which has so far dealt with the laws of locomotion, has encountered a qualitative change. The nature of this "conversion" experience is described brilliantly by Nicholas Georgesceau-Roegen (1971). The steam engine startled the world of Newtonian mechanics. Classical mechanics could not deal with unidirectional movement, for mechanical time dealt with qualityless movement and was reversible. The fundamental metaphor was that of a swing of a pendulum and mechanics as a science was indifferent to its directionality. But thermodynamic phenomena conformed to a picture of an hourglass that could not be inverted, that is, they were basically irreversible.

The concept of entropy was coined by Rudolf Clausius while formulating the two laws of thermodynamics. It was used to differentiate between bound and free energy available for work in the system. For example, the coal used to run the engine when burnt turns into ash, becoming bound energy. Entropy is the measure of this bound or unavailable energy in a system. Scientists were in general ambivalent to the notion of entropy. The ambivalence stemmed from several reasons. First, they felt that entropy was a subjective concept, that it introduced the taint of anthropomorphism into physics. Only the human mind can make a distinction between free and bound energy and this distinction pertains to what human beings find *useful*. As Jaynes has remarked, "entropy is an anthropomorphic concept for it is the property not of the system but of the experiments you and I choose to make of it."

Second, the notion of time it introduces becomes problematic for Newtonian mechanics. Entropy introduces the arrow of time, the notion of irreversibility into physics. Weyl has remarked that "in the world of exact laws, time is reversible." For example, the film of a mechanical phenomenon, such as the bouncing of a perfectly elastic ball, can run either way without the observer noticing the difference. But anyone would notice the difference if the film of a plant growing from a germinating seed and in the end dying is run in the reverse. The second law of thermodynamics is the most important example of an evolutionary law.

Third, by emphasizing qualitative change like degradation rather than quality-less locomotion, entropy emphasized *waste*. Work and waste became central parts of any production system. As Georgesceau-Roegen noted, *had* economics recognized the entropic nature of the economic process, it would have realized that bigger and better washing machines, automobiles, and superjets mean bigger and better pollution.For Nicholas Georgesceau-Roegen, economics is still mechanistic and does not realize that thermodynamics itself creates a physics of limits to the world. As a result, the myth of the perpetual machine rather than being a valuable heuristic has become one of the reified pursuits of both economics and science. As late as 1972, the Nobel Laureate Glenn Seaborg could claim that "ultimately we will be able to recycle any waste, to extract, transport and return to nature when necessary materials in an acceptable form, in an acceptable amount and in an acceptable place so that the natural environment will remain natural." By showing that the energy cost of recycling is high, the idea of entropy forecloses the possibility of bootlegging energy through the continuous recycling of coal or uranium. It is this theology of *limits*, popularized through the eschatological notion of "heat death" that has irritated scientists and economists. But it is precisely by doing this that entropy becomes so fundamentally ecological. In fact the liminality of the entropy concept increases because it mediates the world of economics and physics. Entropy deals with the physics of economic value.

In 1983, C. V. Seshadri worked as a fellow at MIT under the auspices of the United Nations University. During that period he wrote his monograph *Development and Thermodynamics*, a theoretical reflection of the work at Murugappa Chettiar Research Center (MCRG). For Seshadri, the theology of limits that physics as thermodynamics provides is forceful but not life-enhancing enough precisely because it is theological. Science is replete with Judeo-Christian concepts and it is precisely as theology that entropy fails.

Let us reread the liturgy of the steam engine. If one reads the records of the steam engine, whether it is Crosbie Smith on energy or Cardwell's life of Joule, one realizes that there is something Christian about the discourse. Push your mind a bit. One wished one had a Roland Barthes to help; Barthes with a touch of Umberto Eco. The ritual of the engine constitutes the equivalent of the Christian mass. The boiler is the vessel, the coal the literal equivalent of sacred bread. The nature of the act and its meaning constitutes one of the great theological problems of Western society. It raises questions about quality, of time, of transubstantiation, of the liturgy of work, and of the notion of death and apocalypse. One often hears the claim that science owes more to the steam engine than the steam engine to science. One must elaborate on the nature of the debt.

First, the steam engine obviously did as much for the nature of work as the Christian monastery. The economic notion of "work" or "duty" becomes central to this physical concept. Pierre Duhem's complaint of the factory mentality of nineteenth-century English physicists is well known. While fair to Britain, it is also equally true for thermodynamics in general. It is this that led the American physicist Percy Bridgman to complain that these laws "had an unblushing economic tinge." The preoccupation with energy, as Crosbie Smith points out, replaces the concept of force with the concept of *work*. Work remained the central measure of energy throughout this period, appearing under various names such as mechanical power (John Smeaton) or simply "effect" (James Watt) or "duty." It was the basic measure of engine achievement and derived from the practical work of early engineers, who required a useful comparison of the relative performances of water, wind, animal, and steam power. The work of Joule, Carnot, Mayer, and Thompson sought to provide a measure of work and efficiency.[8]

But what sort of work? The work that thermodynamics is talking about involves work done at high temperature gradients. Consider the statement of the American Physical Society on energy quality. It states that "from the perspective of the second law, organized coherent motion is most precious, very high and very low temperature energy is next most precious and heat at a temperature near ambient (lukewarm cool) is degraded energy." Apart from the mechanistic bias present, this holds that 1) the higher the temperature, the lesser the entropy production, and the more useful the work produced; 2) ambient temperature processes are degraded energy processes. Such descriptions, says Seshadri, are unfortunate.

Consider the following examples. A monsoon over Africa and Asia carries billions of tons of water across continents, performing countless gigawatts of work, but work as defined by physics deems this a work of low quality since it is done across small gradients at ambient temperatures; also, living creatures work and live at ambient conditions but that energy is seen as degraded. The American Physics Society (APS) sets strange standards of energy quality, strictly related to economics. Thermodynamics sensitizes one to the limits of natural resources but not fully to the fact that nature works. Given its preoccupation with gradients it provides the rationale for the factory and synthetic fertilizer processes rather than traditional farming. In terms of the APS statement, composting is a low-quality activity!

Thermodynamics is anthropomorphic but one often misses the fact that the anthropomorphism is of two kinds. "One by virtue of being *human* and the other by virtue of being *western*. The poorer countries, ignorant of the latter kind of anthropomorphism, apply it to end up with gross misapplication and enhancement of existing disparities." Seshadri was the first to point out it was not just that thermodynamics had an unblushing economic tinge. Applied as a scale of value it increases disparities or warps priorities. Since energy is inseparable from use, it becomes a criterion for prioritizing the use of resources. Consider, for example, a forest. A forest had a multiplicity of uses. Forest wood, for instance, was used as fuel for smelting iron, boiling sugar, and as household fuel. Wood provides the fuel for cooking in many households in India today. Considerations of energy indicate that the forest should be primarily used as a raw material for industry. Forests are marked more and more for the paper and pulp industry. Forest people in fact are deprived of their traditional rights to fuel, and the forest becomes the preserve for the paper pulp industry. So when we apply the modern criteria of efficiency embodied in the Second Law, tribal people lose access to the forest that provides food, fuel, fodder, and medicine, this diversity of uses losing out to the paper industry, which soon converts the forest into a monocultural plantation of fast growing eucalyptuses. Seshadri shows that the logic of thermodynamics sets loose a chain reaction that works against the tribes and peasants of the Third World. So the tribes and peasants are confronted not just with nation-states and the multinationals but also with the logic of modern science, which works against them. Within this view, Chipko and the anti-dam movement are complete only when the laws of energy are rewritten.

There is a final point. The notions of time, of heat death, and of the apocalyptic ending of the world, all rhyme with the Judeo-Christian ideas of eschatology. In fact whether it is thermodynamic laws or the modern detective story, both are constructed out of the scaffolding of Christianity.[9] Thermodynamics coincides with the doomsday view of knowledge that has become such a powerful feature of modernity. It is just such a narrow scaffolding of religious belief that Seshadri objects to. He makes two separate points. First that the scientific method is not neutral. It is a part of the Judeo-Christian consciousness. It is based on cultural roots that are not universal, and consequently "they become very difficult to stream into the consciousness of a practicing engineer who does not share the tradition. Dreaming and creativity require native categories." Otherwise one loses one's sources in the archetypal and the primordial. Second, our civilizational notions of time are different. "We should teach our people that our own lives and deaths are not synonymous with the deluge, that they are a part of much larger enmeshed cycles, helices, spirals of time which give the earth substance and civilization."

For Seshadri, the debate between traditional knowledge and modern science required a reconstruction not only of the categories of science and economics but of the myths at its core. We do not seem to be able to escape the myths of Faust, Prometheus, or the Schumpeterian entrepreneur. Even someone as sensitive as Nicholas Georgesceau-Roegen lapses back to Prometheus. In his *Energy, Matter and Economic Evaluation* he divides history into three Promethean phases, the wood age, the mineral age, and the third uncertain phase where one is waiting for Prometheus III. Nicholas Georgesceau-Roegen is clear that the market will not provide him with this but he is equally committed to the caloric power of the Promethean myth. We are looking for a world that modulates both Prometheus and the price system. In that sense thermodynamics is still an incomplete mythopoesis-cum-science of limits. The inadequacies of such a view become clearer when we conceptualize the idea of biomass economics.

THE POLITICS OF A BIOMASS SOCIETY

For Seshadri, the idea of a biomass society was not anchored on a second-rate science for a second-rate society. He evaded many of the political traps associated with the intermediate technology movement. He repeatedly emphasized that the idea of biomass demanded a new epistemology and a reinvention of citizenship. He also added that the concern with biomass societies is not only a Third World discourse but that it emerged at two levels. There was first the northern discourse that began with the oil crisis and the discussion of the *Limits to Growth* model, as well as with the discussion of the need for soft energy paths in a nuclear world. There was a radicalism to the discourse, a critique of industrialism where, to paraphrase Patrick Geddes, "the economics of the leaf and the economics of metals were in opposition." But sadly the radical edge of such a discourse became co-opted into the technocratic and ecocratic discourse called sustainability.

In the Third World biomass as a discourse arose primarily as a challenge to the surreal science of elites who worshipped electricity. It was a crisis of wood and cooking. But the biomass discourse began as a radical critique of industrialism at two levels. A theory of limits became a praxis of creative possibilities. We realize today that oil, the Green Revolution and modern medicine cannot deliver. Given this—the local, the traditional, and the futuristic—all become sites of innovation.

The radical possibilities of biomass as an epistemology can be easily suppressed. For example, in anthologies of energy, biomass is categorized as a way of life, of societies outside the pale of industrialism. It usually appears in chapter 10 or 12 of a textbook on energy, a sidebar following the preoccupations with nuclear, oil, hydel, or even wind energy. It is seen as residual. There is simultaneously a split in the construction of the globalization regime. Oil and nuclear are for the industrial what biomass is for the societies of Africa and Asia that may be triaged out of history. Biomass then becomes the discourse of the defeated, the Third World, and the third rate. Consider how the regime of biomass appears in the spy thrillers that Seshadri was so fond of. Into the happy life of Western industrialism appear the oil sheikhs, the OPEC cartels, and the urban guerrilla. Constructed simultaneously with the oil crisis is the wood crisis. The pictures of the woman carrying wood, the guerrilla in the forest, and the oil sheikh become the three archetypal figures of the crisis. Yet we should not succumb to such a reading because it not only predetermines narratives but also creates pre-emptive futures. We have to remember that the Vietnam War represents the victory and resistance of a biomass society over an industrial high-calorie regime. Seshadri repeatedly emphasized that biomass is the conversation of the leaf with its ancient friends coal and oil, establishing similarities and differences in their common genealogy in their relation to the sun.

One must emphasize some dangers here. The first is the sheer economism of discourse and the danger of conventional economic categories and thought. The sun is not a conventional factory. It is not too keen to subject itself to man-made time and organization. Second, biomass should not be reduced to the language of scarcity and crisis. There are shortages, there is poverty, but biomass need not be reduced to a discourse on scarcity. Nicholas Xenos's comments are apt in this context. In his Scarcity and Modernity (1989), Xenos observes that the European eighteenth century saw the invention of both the steam engine and of scarcity. Scarcity, as anthropologists have pointed out, is seen as episodic in most societies. It first signified a period of insufficiency or dearth. This remained the principal usage until the late nineteenth century, when neoclassical economics made the scarcity postulate its foundation. The notion of scarcity also opens up a Pandora's Box of technological fixes, where biomass problems need biotechnology and then the entire spectrum of biotechnology gets reduced to genetic engineering. Seshadri explained that biomass is a word for people. It smacks "of the ordinary and the non-mechanical. Compare the tree to a factory, or a cow to a reactor. Like the people it is not amenable to efficiency and control in a factory sense. You can't boss over the science of photosynthesis." The state thus has problems with biomass in a way that it does not have with electricity. Electricity is a disciplinary grid but biomass offers little ground for collectivization to "turn the stinking pastry of the ordinary people into a tasty pie by trainers, educators, the masters." You can't say Soviets + Electrification = Communism in a biomass society. Unless, you are a Pol Pot.

It is around biomass that the resistance to the state can come into being. Biomass reopens the debate in a tremendous way. First, energy forms such as oil, nuclear, or large dams are state-oriented, while biomass speaks the language of civil society. Second, by linking life and death in the idea of the cycle, it brackets the idea of obsolescence, preventing it from being read as a universalizing process. Biomass brackets the idea of progress in its linear form by offering the multiplicity of times that democracy so desperately needs. Biomass also recalls the idea of the commons and particularly the idea of cognitive justice. The two concepts are closely interlinked. The idea of the commons is not just an amalgamation, a mapping of physical and natural resources. It is also the diversity of skills required to understand, access, and dwell within it. Seshadri dubbed it "a commons of the mind." It is in this context that we must emphasize that rights often speak the economistic language of access. Speaking a language of rights in a biomass society only leads to conceptual inflation, to a proliferation of rights, including the rights to food, fuel, and employment without tying or connecting them at a moral or epistemic level. The language of rights, particularly in its individualistic-economistic language, becomes partly alien to a biomass society, creating in fact the tragedy of the commons. One does not seek to abandon it but to translate it into the language of community and cosmos.

In this sense, the politics of a biomass society go beyond the standard discourses of the French revolution, of the *Communist Manifesto*, or the *Rights of Man*. First, it goes beyond the discourses of liberty and equality towards an emphasis on fraternity, not merely between communities but between man and nature. But it should not be seen only as an ecolacy of nature but of technology. It reads liberty, equality, and fraternity as the first triangle of modern politics. But it counterposes to it a second triangle of pollution, waste, and obsolescence, which it reads in terms of a community of multiple times. The notion of the cycle becomes fundamental here. As Balaji observed, "When Seshadri introduced the centrality of food, he knew that food chains exist in cycles. Through food you can see the interrelationship between a wide variety of complex systems. Terrestrial. Aquatic. Cosmic. A variety of cycles interface and Doc wanted to track the process through energy."

It is around the idea of cycles that the discourse on waste, pollution and obsolescence is constructed. Seshadri's idea of *shakthi* was an attempt to develop quality markers for creating a grammar for this discourse. Seshadri, the early Seshadri, talked in aphorisms and epigrams. I remember him grinning and observing that "pollution is someone else's profit," or that "one man's waste is another man's resource." But these were not just pretty little proverbs. Consider the popular idea of recycling. He said, "You can't recycle waste without violating the second law of thermodynamics. The question of recycling has to be looked at in this perspective for all waste is useful in some context." For Seshadri it was more fruitful to recycle ideas instead of things. He provided the example of sheet metal stamping.

Circular blanks of metal are stamped out of metal sheets leaving behind perforated sheets that the manufacturers characterize as waste. But one man's waste is another man's resource. The perforated sheets are used by many poor people as fencing, structural elements in housing, tracks for paths, etc. What has been recycled is neither material nor energy. *Only the idea.* A waste has been turned into a resource by perceiving it differently. A low-value high-entropy perforated sheet becomes a high-value low-entropy fence, tracks, and such through the recycling of ideas. The process also adds value locally.

"The classic recycling option would be to melt down the perforated sheets and then re-roll them. The material is recycled at tremendous cost. Idea recycling is far less energy intensive than material recycling." Recycling ideas is the forte of the squatter and scavenger. The Indian slum becomes the great laboratory for recycling ideas. "For the wasted people of our states, wastes and nature are the only resources left for them to build on. Only these resources are available outside the commercial mainstream."

The idea of cycles substitutes and goes beyond the alchemical limits of the perpetual machine. In fact, the idea of cycles is disappearing in modern agriculture. As one Japanese scientist noted, "modern agriculture has replaced most of the cycles in nature by products of manufacturing, especially with chemical fertilizers and petroleum products. These are not compatible with the cycles of nature."

Seshadri's still incomplete idea of *shakthi* was developed as a quality marker to understand such processes. V. Balaji observed that "it helped one redesign processes, identify the real wastes in the system like the amount of pure water used in flush toilets in western countries, or the consumption of processed water in chemical industrial processes. Viewed this way the efficiency of the thermal plants may be scaled down by 50 percent."

"The notion of *shakthi* is scale invariant. It can range from the depth of the ocean to the upper atmosphere. It can look at the interaction of two microbes in a bio-gas digester." Balaji added that it is an engineer's understanding of thermodynamics.

It is like a *Thanedar's* understanding of thermodynamics rather than a commissioner's. It sensitizes you to the real costs of water and nutrients in, say, an agricultural process, as for instance the over-application of water and fertilizers in hybrid seed technology. *Shakthi* would give you a knowledge-intensive rather than an input-intensive approach to agriculture. You apply that many grams of fertilizer at *that* time on *that* place. A *vaidyar's* approach rather than that of agri-business.

But biomass is not merely a discourse on nature and the environment; it is a plea for a new pedagogy of citizenship. Seshadri felt that the state was not going to wither away or that it was something easily compostible. The more interesting challenge for lateral thinking in politics was to reinvent nature, citizenship, and civil society. In this context, he and Joe Thomas would often talk of the *Juliflora* almost as a fable. I remember one of the first times Joe and I were having tea outside the gate of the Murgappa Chettiar Research Group (MCRG). Joe showed me a beautiful garden fence, exquisitely green, trimmed and beautiful. "The prosopis Juliflora,"[10] he announced. No compère could have been prouder and more delighted.

The Juliflora, a mesquite, provides 40 per cent of Madras firewood. The irony is that it is not a creation of state forest policy but an inadvertent introduction that grew in spite of the state. One felt that Seshadri wanted the Julifloras of citizenship.

Once we accept Arthur Koestler's statement that "the greatest superstition of our time is the belief in the ethical neutrality of science," we have to look again at biomass economics. In a vernacular world, technology is not a solution; it is a means to an end. Love is a solution, and if technology is to be an act of love, like cooking or prayer, we have to go beyond the political economy of biomass. This sees only poverty and hunger. We have to look beyond the scientific epistemology of biomass, which sees poverty as hunger, hunger as nutrition, and nutrition as so many kilo-calories. The moral economy of resistance and reciprocity worked out by James Scott needs an epistemic sense that the knowledge system itself may create immiseration. The politics of knowledge must combine all three: ethics, politics, and science. This marriage of Gandhi and self-critical thermodynamics can be illustrated through the calculus of sugar. It is a search for quality markers that can also alter the level of debate. Otherwise you are caught in contradictions. It is no use criticizing the Green Revolution and accepting a petroleum economy. For this you need a different notion of economics. One can examine the need for a different, more holistic quality marker other than price by means of the problem of the sugar-food-alcohol nexus.

UNITING SCIENCE AND DEMOCRACY

The sugar-food-alcohol nexus

Consider the use of a carbohydrate resource such as sugar cane or cassava. Sugar cane in a tropical country is one of the highest-yielding photosynthetic organisms. India is not only the largest sugar cane producing country but has the largest area under cane cultivation. The decision that one faces is whether cane should be used for the manufacture of white sugar and alcohol or as food. Alcohol always appears profitable as an end product not only because of taxability but as a substitute for imported petroleum. The question is what are the quality markers used in such a decisional calculus. "Assuming once again that purely economic criteria should not be allowed to be the method of choice, how should we grow a proper mix of food and fuel; how do we balance food and fuel calories?" Seshadri calls this search for a comparative standard the search for *shakthi*. He describes it as an attempt to link Gandhi's objection to prohibition to the world of thermodynamics.

The cane industry produces a variety of products from sugar, alcohol, *gur*, bagasse, *khandsari*, etc. In optimizing the welfare of the people we have to decide how much importance to give to each of these products. India has been the traditional home of sugar or *sarkara*. There are two ways to refine cane to make a sweet product. We could make open pan sugar or *khandsari*, or make jaggery or *gur*, which is solidified cane juice. Today these traditional processes are disappearing, giving way to modern sugar factories with their huge evaporators and crushers. In fact, today the sugar industry is one of the largest in the country, second only in scale to cement, steel, and petroleum. In 1977 the percentage of traditional sugar was 56 percent, today it has decreased to 35–40 per cent or less. This change is usually justified in terms of "efficiency," science, progress, or the laws of scale, all of which appear objective and value-neutral, justifying the downgrading of *gur*.

There are generally three ways of downgrading a traditional product. First, you imprint a traditional product as impure, dirty, and unhygienic. Unlike *gur*, sugar carries all the moral semantics of white. It is something produced by a man in a white coat, as clean, cool, and hygienic as Listers antiseptic. Gur smacks of dirt and soil, it is "muddy" and in need of refinement. It carries all the ambiguity of a mixed product. Second, you downgrade traditional products through the laws of scale and finally through the laws of science. "In general, energy that is consumed for metabolic purposes is supposed to be of low quality since the temperatures at which humans and animals live is at ambient temperatures. On the other hand, according to the Carnot principle, energy is of high quality, the higher the temperature of its availability." This logic is implicit in the market value of sugar.

Large scale crushers are seen as more efficient using less steam per kilogram of sugar. It is also attested that white sugar is stored and transported easily. While the last point is to be conceded no one bothers to calculate the respective energy cost of making sugar and *gur* including the capital costs of machines. It is a paradox of modern science that the more reductionist and refined the practice, the more it justifies its extravagance. Thus a 10,000 tonnes per day crusher is supposed to be more efficient than a 1000 tonnes per day crusher regardless of how much entropy and waste it adds to the surroundings.

What is worse, within such calculations no one examines the nutritional value of these commodities. *Gur* has more naturally occurring iron, calcium, and phosphorus than refined white sugar. Even molasses is richer in vitamins. *Gur* is a natural supplement for the iron deficiency of our populations, especially women and children. In fact the government is planning to spend huge sums to combat anemia. Finally, the negative effects of white sugar should also be considered. Combating dental and diabetic problems is a multibillion dollar industry. Viewed this way the real value of sugar is far less than its calorific value as obtained from a bomb calorimeter.

The tragedy of white sugar is further compounded by the alcohol industry. "Only if you make white sugar, do you make large amounts of molasses, gigantic amounts of which are used for drinking; thanks to official policies. The constitution of India has a moral commitment, yet successive governments have seen alcohol as a profit maker."

Seshadri itemizes the questions of choice as follows:

1) Do we wish to live with the white sugar problem?
2) If the answer is yes, do we want to get the best out of molasses?
3) If the answer is yes, do we want to supplement the food situation?

The question of a quality marker becomes absolutely necessary in this context. Assuming the answer to the first question is affirmative, despite all the negative effects of white sugar, we can still ask for all the uses of molasses, which include feedstock/cattle, fertilizers, substrates for yeast, as well as alcohol; we have to produce an energy accounting that balances "molasses for food" against alcohol, despite it being one of the most energy profligate processes. Alcohol is the choice if economics as profit were the only criteria. Here economics dictates energetics. But once we search for new quality markers, the question can be readdressed. Given a piece of land, given knowledge of the constraints, what is the best mix of food-fuel we can obtain? Consider the following facts:

—1 sq km of cane gives 20,000 children all their vitamins from yeast at 10 gm per day.
—On land used for growing 60×10^6 liters of alcohol, we can produce 21,000 tonnes of paddy.
—India's 50×10^7 palm trees can yield 10×10^6 tonnes of sugar per year, releasing all cane land for other crops.

Viewed in this way, sugar cane can only be grown to make yeast for people's welfare. In this, prohibition is a technological necessity. Yet current technological imperatives lead one to emphasize the wrong value system, where alcohol and profit triumph over well-being.

This question of quality markers, the search for what Seshadri dubs *shakthi*, is a recurrent theme of any effort to liberate energetics from economics. It leads to an examination of another of the great sources of fermentation technology, the *idli*. The *idli*, south India's exquisitely fermented rice cake, is a ubiquitous cereal food. Seshadri reports that a survey in Madras showed that in one street "10,000 *idlis* were sold per linear kilometer everyday." Yet the government is the greatest propagator of white bread. In his paper to the Seventh GIAM Congress, Seshadri compares the nutritive value of *idlis* and white bread, each made respectively from 1 kg of *idli* batter and white wheat flour dough.[11]

	Protein mg/kg	Minerals gm/kg	ß-Carotene ug/kg	Fe mg/kg	Thiamine mg/kg
1 kg *idli* batter 42 *idlis*	83.3	3.05	5.5	13.3	0.07
Bread 1 kg dough 45 slices	67.6	0.35	14.7	15.29	0.7

In reading the table we must remember that all the vitamins in commercial bread are added synthetically while in *idlis* they are synthesized naturally by the microbiota. It is also well known that white bread contains neither fiber nor roughage. The question we must ask is why does the government promote white bread and what are its consequences? White bread displaces *idli* in a deliberate policy of "commerciogenic" malnutrition. It encourages the introduction of food habits that cannot be sustained by local production, such as wheat and wheat products. In addition, large bread factories are energy intensive and cannot provide the employment that the world of the *idli* provides. It is the absence of a new quality marker that creates this litany of malnutrition, whether it is polished rice, white bread, or white sugar. Such a notion of *shakthi* has to be built into conventional economics and energetics.

Murgappa Chettiar Research Group (MCRG) and its FADs

If the first set of instances show how to interrogate modern Western science from an eccentric or marginal perspective, the second set of efforts deals with MCRG efforts to preserve traditional forms of life. One shall focus in this context on the making of fish aggregation devices (FADs) and the refashioning of the catamaran.

India has a 7517 km-long coastline that is farmed by three kinds of boats. It is important to realize that even now large trawlers only contribute one percent of the total marine fish production and that another 33 percent comes from mechanized boats. Roughly 66 percent of India's sea fish come from the 1.8 million traditional fishermen using country crafts.

Over the last decade fish production in India has stagnated at about 1.6 million tonnes a year. There were several reasons for this, including the lack of effective harvesting technology and the inability to diversify fishing techniques. Compounding this was the depredation of fishing pirates from Taiwan, Thailand, and Pakistan, who, using giant trawler nets and modern fishing vessels, are robbing India of valuable fish.

MCRG's constituency was the traditional fishermen. In 1985, MCRG began a project on fish aggregation devices.

Our fishermen, who do not have motors and things like that, will spend about six hours going into the ocean and about six hours coming back and three to four hours fishing. They spend a long time searching for fish. To save the search time for a fish you make a fish aggregating device. A fish aggregating device is an ancient technology in this country. What they do is to cut a big palm tree, drag it out and anchor it in the middle of the ocean. The fish in the open ocean like the shade and the little shell fish like to hang on to the leaves of the palm tree and lay their eggs. The big fish come in search of the smaller fish and so on. Therefore a fish aggregating device is something in the middle of the ocean that collects fish together.

In nature, the coral reef is the ideal FAD and thus MCRG fashioned an equivalent. Between 1985 and 1986, MCRG built three types of FAD, using different types of attractants—replicas of shore drilling pipes, of coral reefs, and of coconut fronds—and installed them on an experimental basis in the Bay of Bengal. The results were encouraging but these floating rafts were towed away by mechanized boat operators. The scientists of MCRG had long discussions with the fishermen and the group decided to submerge the structure, creating sunken FADs. The idea worked and MCRG was besieged by fishing cooperatives for more of these devices. There was something ecologically efficient about FADs. It was discovered that FADs attracted and concentrated fish from far away waters. In fact, nineteen varieties of fish not generally found within the 5-km zone were attracted to these structures. Given such concentrations it was also possible to engage in line fishing. By harvesting bigger fish with lines, with single and multiple hooks, juvenile fish were spared. This helped in the conservation of fish in the long run. FADs, it was obvious, were increasing the average income of the fishermen.

But a scientific solution has to be seen within the politics of resource conflicts. FADs became a threat to mechanized boats, which attempted to destroy them or tow them away. One realizes that one begins with a community and sees the community as a solution. MCRG felt the solution was not just the improvement of traditional technology but the revival of the fishing panchayats.[12] A cluster of villages around the FADs would discover not only an improvement in technology but new possibilities of resistance. In this sense, MCRG's work on FADs illustrates one of its basic principles. To the MCRG scientists there are two kinds of innovation, the innovation of the virus and the innovation of the organism. The virus enters the body and replicates itself, thus destroying the body. An organism lives in symbiosis, engaging in reciprocity and conversation. Sustainability for the MCRG requires the symbiosis of laboratory and society. In fact, a laboratory seen as alien to a society becomes a virus. A scientist's relation to a society is that of dwelling. You begin not with poverty but with the poor and the people in a particular community. Poverty is not a state to be eradicated but a site for invention. Seshadri illustrated it with an example from housing.

> When we go to an architect to decide how to build a house in the city, he will throw phrases like metabolic comfort, temperature control, humidity control, comfort index, etc. We don't want any of these considerations for houses to be built for poor people. Why don't we introduce metabolic comfort for the poor people as the first criteria of low-cost housing? It can be done easily by sloping the roof in such a way that solar energy coming into the house is minimized. We are so busy eradicating poverty that we never think of comfort for the poor. It needs a change in framework from thinking of a slum as a threat to the slum as a warm living human organism that can invent its way out of poverty.

One of the most fascinating attempts at working out the interface between traditional forms of life and knowledge and modern science is the laboratory's work on the *Katumaram*. It also involves the elaboration of a style of thinking. Consider a tree. A tree can either be an icon or an index. Iconographically, a tree becomes a cosmology of connections. For instance, the coconut is a little cosmology, a network of connections linking myth, religion, economics, ritual, food, and agriculture. A coconut is a celebration of over a hundred different uses. It is also a micro-climate creating its own minor ecology of plants. Seshadri suggests science must think like the coconut, link cosmology and system, and it is precisely this that the monocultural effects of modernity abandon. Monoculture is not only thinking of one kind of plant or tree. It is reducing it to a single one of its uses. When we reduce the forest to pulp, the answer is eucalyptus. But once we understand the trophicity of even a tree we realize that one man's waste is another woman's life material. It is precisely this kind of iconic thinking that Seshadri suggests. One captures an idea of this in his work on the catamarans, an imagination that links the forest and the sea.

The *Katumaram*, or the catamaran as they call it in English, is a great achievement. Seshadri describes it as a superb hunting steed for what are perhaps the last great hunter-gatherers—our fishermen. Seshadri points out that these fishermen are great "predators" in one context, but that in another, that of land, they are at the lowest trophic level of the market-economic system. The question that faces our country is how long we can support our fishermen with boats, given that the wood they use is now subject to competing demands. Almost all the trees used for the catamaran—the Bombax, the *shorea robusta* (*sal*), the mango—have competing industrial uses. Further, *sal* is used by tribals as food, for oil, and for its leaves. The Bombax is used for making matchsticks and fodder. Mango trees are used for housing, packaging and mangoes. So any competition for the forest is likely to hit the fisherman hardest. Yet the catch of fish from the catamarans supplies most of the animal protein of cities like Vizakapatnam, Madras, Pondichery, Tuticorin, Trivandrum, and Bombay. Yet we face the fact that over 5000 boats have to be replaced annually in Tamil Nadu alone.

Seshadri realized that the industrial uses of forestry are so predominant in even social forestry programs that the small users of forests, the traditional fishermen, may be given little consideration.The solution that Seshadri devised was a polyethylene boat made from biomass products. Polyethylene is a polymer made from alcohol or ethanol. Since ethanol is a product made from cellulose biomass, polyethylene may be looked at in some sense as a renewable resource. Seshadri suggests that only a small portion of the alcohol obtained from molasses can supply all the fishermen with boats. He cites the following figures:

22.5 km of Bombax forest supply 5000 *marams*.

70 sq km of sugarcane can supply 5000 *vastis*, which can last over 25 years instead of the usual five.

Such rafts can also be used for river hydroponics. The *vastis* developed by the MCRG are an example of how science can keep traditional crafts alive.

I will consider one other attempt at thinking about the forest and mediating between traditional ways and modernity. An experiment still in progress, it deals with MCRG's experiments with paper.

The Energetics of Paper
The MCRG as an institute is full of thought experiments, outrageous hypotheses that become the basis of scientific programs. Scientists like Seshadri

often contend that political rhetoric without numeracy is romanticism. They point out that there is repeated talk of the commitment to education but few translate the requirements of that commitment into the question of the number of students, the quality of paper, the acreage of forests or the energetics of paper. Seshadri performs what Hans Jonas calls a heuristics of fear: mental exercises to find out the future of various resources like paper. Heuristics of fear then need technologies of hope where innovative answers are worked out. The paper industry is a protected industry attracting enormous subsidies in terms of power, materials, and forest land. However, by the turn of the century, the consumption of paper per capita is likely to be only 4.5 kg. Yet, even at the current demand of 3 kg per capita per year, India will need 150,000 to 600,000 tonnes per annum if 50 to 200 million people are going to be literate. One faces the possibility that a literate India is a deforested India. Seshadri adds that "even if the present illiterate population cannot be taught using paper, future children will need about 10–15,000,000 tonnes per year at the rate of 1 kg/child/year, assuming an annual birth rate of two percent. The demand for innovative techniques in education and materials are needed." The problem is further compounded by the nature of the paper industry in the Third World. The Indian paper industry has an installed capacity of 25 lakhs of tonnes[13] spread over roughly 250 units. Production of hand paper is about 7000 to 10,000 tonnes a year. An examination of the paper industry reveals that it is wasteful at almost every stage. Discounting the wastage of leaves and twigs, only 20 per cent of a tree crop ends up as paper. For this, enormous forest areas have been taken over.

The energetics of paper in India is even more disheartening. Paper manufactured from wood pulp is even more energy intensive than steel manufactured at 67 MJ/per kg of paper.[14] Roughly "24–25 percent of the total energy is wasted irreversibly, the maximum loss of high quality energy (39.8 percent) occurs in the soda recovery process, followed by another 30 percent in the steam production unit. The annual fuel energy cost of paper manufacture is approximately 21.9 percent of the annual turnover of the industry." Not only is the industry highly energy intensive, it is excessively polluting. "Waste water is regarded as the biggest hazard to the environment from the paper industry. Chemical compounds that contain chlorine have been identified as the major source of pollution. Conventional pulp bleaching which includes chlorination will produce 6000–9000 gm of chlorinated organic material per tonne of bleached pulp prior to effluent treatment."

The MCRG developed a two-pronged strategy that embodied what Seshadri calls its philosophy of holistic invention:

1) The choice of the appropriate technology with its accompanying energetics.
2) Reconceptualizing the tree.

The strategy of energetics begins with the fact that "under Indian conditions wastes or residues become a resource for energy generation and the manufacture of useful products." Rice straw, for instance, is considered waste in Punjab but is deemed valuable in other parts of India. Similarly, distillery effluents, which are valuable carbohydrate resources, are discarded after minimal treatment. All these are what we might call renewable wastes from renewable materials.

Cellulose, which has a worldwide production of 50 billion tons, is one such resource, particularly in countries short of petroleum. Cellulose raw materials or wastes could be the raw material for paper. Cellulose degradation through biotechnology seemed the optimal choice because the process eliminated the requirement of caustic soda and steam for paper and thus effected drastic cuts in the energy budget. "Given that in India over 1.7 million tonnes of cotton lint are required to be disposed of annually, such a process could result in the control of hazardous pollution with the simultaneous production of paper."

The MCRG also felt treating forests as pulp was violence. The diversity of tropical forest soon gives way to the monoculture of pulpwood species. Instead of using trees as raw material, they decided to use tree usufructs to harvest the raw material for pulp. Silk cotton, obtained from the Cuba *pintandra* or S. Malabarica, contains 64–70 per cent cellulose and is used for papermaking. The cotton that is to be degraded to pulp is treated with ash, or with bacteria and solar energy. Less energy is spent and there are no harmful chemicals used.

These silk cotton trees are available generally all over India. Each tree gives 20 kg of cotton annually and is presently used for making mattresses and lifebelts. The plan is to cultivate these trees in wastelands. They need watering for the first two years. The trees start to yield from the second year and the maximum yield is from the sixth to the fiftieth year, although the trees live for a hundred years. Nor is the tree reduced to silk cotton. "Besides cotton, the trunk can be used for matchsticks and boats, and oil can be extracted from the seeds." Finally, since the harvesting is an annual one and is based on a crop rather than on timber, the problem of the depletion of forest cover is avoided. Work on the cellulose degradation process is still continuing. For the MCRG, this approach to paper reflects what American ecologists dub "green chemistry," which generates little waste, is resource conservative, and energy prudent.

Some axioms

The anthropologist in me can go on describing MCRG's efforts in algal technology, wind erosion, windmills, and biogas, but I will stop now by summing up how the scientists themselves conceptualize this experience. I must begin with a story.

While browsing through Seshadri's library I came across Harold Morowitz's beautiful essay on Willard Gibbs. Morowitz was asked to write an essay on the American bicentennial. Spurred on by the request, Morowitz remarks that the declaration of the thirteen colonies was historical, but that Gibbs's paper, his work on thermodynamics, was the second most historical document. It is this juxtaposition that tantalizes. A declaration of independence and an essay on entropy. It made me think of the sheer fascination of a scientific addendum to the constitution. There is talk of the scientific temper but reading it you would think that the scientific temper is some kind of extract that, once injected, provides immunity against some forms of imagination. This way, the scientific temper is little more than a bit of secular elitist moralizing. An appendix on science would make the constitution more alive, more real, more playful. You could begin to look at concepts like poverty and equity in a new way.

In the beginning was the "word." One must realize that scientific statements like the statements of the constitution are words. Words are not innocent. They have deep-rooted cultural meanings. Most of what we call science is 1) anthropomorphic and 2) Judeo-Christian. It posits the superiority of man in the universe, or at least a special place for him, as in the anthropomorphic principle. "This is by no means universally true and there are many examples of bird, insect, or animal communities excelling us in some attribute or other." It is this anthropic arrogance that led the biologist Lynn Margulis to demand a trade union to represent the role of bacteria.

If the first argues for the superiority of man, the second allows for the mastery and use of nature. Nature is made for man's use. Secularized, it is termed as a resource. The covenant with life is broken. This is important in a civilizational sense, for science must remind the constitution of the ecological matrix in which its society is embedded. Apart from the above, the addendum can include the following axioms.

Axiom I

1) Language is important in a second sense, for languages can be exploitative.

2) The language of science and technology is English. From English, if at all, we translate science and technology and development into our languages.

3) Thus the scientific temper is to be created in this country through this language.

4) But who is to temper the English language? England has the traditions of a small island that had to exploit the outside world for its benefit.

5) The semantics of western science and technology is by and large growth-oriented. This semantics is not helpful for resource conservation, or for resource distribution.

6) The technology, and therefore its semantics, is ultimately related to the market economy and the language of market forces. "How can such a language be used for the aid of a people who are completely outside the market economy? We think there is a need for a less exploitative linguistics."

Axiom II

Science and technology have always been and will always be the pursuit of exploitable knowledge with all the artifacts of such exploitation. All we can do is seek to minimize these effects.

Axiom III

A belief system should not be independent of lifestyle. Lifestyle is coeval with the technology that enables its practice. Violating this belief leads to the trauma of thermodynamics or Gandhian truth inconsistency. Science can no longer settle for observer participancy. It must be linked to questions of lifestyle. If not:
(a) Technology will become a substitute for ideology.
(b) Technology Imperatives may lead you to emphasize the wrong value system.

Axiom IV

1) "Indians should have a lifestyle that is evolved for Indian conditions. This includes resource constraints, disparities in society, overall lack of complex modern systems and the fact that the Third World does not have the fourth, fifth, and sixth worlds to exploit any more."
2) Science links lifestyle to ecolacy (ecological awareness). We must ask the question democratically and scientifically: "What level should we live at? Is it 5000 kilo calories a day or 10,000 kilo calories a day? This number must be arrived at by consensus."

Axiom V

Science must be linked to citizenship. A citizen is a person of knowledge. No science can be deskilling. Knowledge is a commons. Science must address itself to the question of diversity where life forms are disappearing, whether it is one variety of plant a day, or one language a week.

Paradigms must be linked to lifestyles to create ground rules for citizenship. Such ground rules should be seen as thought experiments that reveal the nature of choices, the knowledge base and their link to lifestyles. Such a greening may involve a coercive holism.

Three examples can illustrate this. One can think first of George Fernandes's directive that only mud *khullars* be used in railway stations, instead of paper or plastic cups for serving tea. Or Seshadri's suggestion that all school uniforms be made from *khadi*.

The "coercive holism" of Seshadri is only another variant of Gandhian Swadeshi, where locality provided the basis of lifestyle and self-reliance. You used local goods, local skills, and local raw materials to create a lifestyle that was self-reliant. Seshadri ends his essay with this dictum: "We can develop by developing new languages or remain underdeveloped forever. It is only through the creation of such thought experiments that science can link lifestyle to citizenship."

Axiom VI

Every citizen has to be a craftsman and an inventor. Gandhi was a master citizen and inventor. He was craftsman, cook, weaver, scavenger, lawyer, surveyor, drainage expert, psychologist, a theologian of Christianity, a practicing Hindu, as well as his own Havelock Ellis and Masters and Johnson. Inventiveness demands irony and humor. The industrialist Jamnalal Bajaj once donated a car to Gandhi's *ashram*, which refused to function after a while. It was pulled on occasions by a pair of bullocks. Gandhi called it his own Ox-FORD.

Citizenship as craftsmanship also needs ideas of numeracy and literacy.[15] Development like citizenship involves not only access, but competence and judgment. "Development involves vast transfers of knowledge. Before we undertake this, it is important to transmit the science of knowledge that underpins the knowledge we transfer." Seshadri emphasized that "by concentrating on lived concepts like numeracy, ecolacy, literacy, and democracy we evade the dualism of tradition and modernity."

Loosely, numeracy is the ability to see discrete entities in a connected whole or a continuum. Those lacking in numeracy usually possess two kinds of deficiency. The first is the inability to see discreteness in continuity. The second is to see only discreteness and not to perceive the continuum at all. Both deficiencies can create survival problems in a developing society.

Deficiencies of the first kind:

1) "This would include all tribals who gather fuelwood thinking it is a free good, unaware that energy has a value in the market place and that gradually they are being denied access to the traditional resource of fuelwood.

2) "All people who do not realize the difference between rearing five children and seven.

3) "All roads in South India are used as solar driers. However, roads do not belong to the village any more. They belong to the lorries, buses, and cars of a larger system. The enormous wastage of grain and cereals due to traffic is not accounted for—if it were, then people perhaps would arrange for a better drying system."

One must emphasize that innumeracy is not just a lack of arithmetic skill. It is a tacit knowledge, the awareness of resource limitation, a feel for quantity and its allocation that we need to inculcate in people.

Deficiencies of the second kind:

1) "These include all people who thought the forests of Silent Valley were equal to so many megawatts of hydel power.

2) "All people who do not realize that over 50 per cent of the total energy consumed in the country is consumed in the cooking stove.

3) "All the people who think that because non-commercial energy cannot be accounted for in our theories, it need not be accounted for. This is saying that the discretization of the money market is the only part of the continuum that exists."

4) "All people who consider development as increase in average per capita income." Numeracy is an absolute essential for survival in a developing society. It is also linked to time in a significant way. "Time is an essential constituent of numeracy, in fact time is the prime numeraire." This problem of time, science, and development constitutes one of the fundamental issues of exploitation.

Axiom VII

A constitution by itself does not complete the charter of modernity. To it one would add the other charters, each of which captures time in a particular way—the plan, the calendar, the metric system, the collection of standards, or even the schemes for the transfer of technology each exploits through a particular imposition of time.

Standardized time emasculates a series of vernacular times in a process called economic development. Seshadri observed that the Gregorian calendar is a measure of time. Peasant time is time. Confusing time with its measure is one of the greatest tragedies that have befallen the poor in the tropics. "The tax structure and collection, the education system, and the weekly and yearly holidays are all tied to an artificial system that bears no relation to the cycles of the peasant and those of husbandry. The 'oestrus window' of his cattle, the 'ploughing windows' of his fields, the synchrony of crop harvest and his earnings, have no place in printed calendars: the latter measure concepts of time far removed from nature befitting Roman emperors of bygone days." The East India Company used calendar time as the most potent tool to separate the farmer from his land.

The time of modernity is an attempt to impose Cartesian time on a basically a-Cartesian people. Concepts of time expressed independently of human existence fall into Cartesian categories. Peasant time is lived time, the time of the body, the time of nature's cycles. Modernity imposes a mind–body separation through time. The digital watch becomes an extreme example. Time is no longer a continuum here. It is discretized and attached to a number system.

Consider the negative discrimination that time imposes on the following people. The educational calendar is designed with the children of city office-goers in mind. The monsoon generally comes in June when school starts for the year. The question arises: should the farmer send his able-bodied children to school or should they assist him on the farm? It is not surprising that 8- to 10-year-old children have the highest dropout rates.

It is in the domain of time that the politics of affirmative action also needs to operate. Consider migrant communities. When one is talking of migrant shepherds or fishermen, one sees that not much effort is made to have mobile schools for them. Within a Western colonial heritage, education for the children must be separated from adults. Seshadri suggested that in tribal areas, all members of the family should have access to education simultaneously.

CONCLUSION

All knowledge systems (both traditional and modern) must embody principles of self-destruction.

These rules of impotence are limits, but limits should not be seen as constricting or puritanical. The analogy is to fasting. Fasting is not a calorific word, dieting is. When you fast, you don't lose weight; you live in harmony with your body.

1) Each knowledge system if it is to be democratic must realize it is iatrogenic in some context.

2) Each knowledge system must realize that in moments of dominance it may destroy life-giving alternatives available in the other. Each paradigm must sustain the otherness of other knowledge systems.

3) No knowledge system may "museumify" the other. No knowledge system should be overtly deskilling.

4) Each knowledge system must practice cognitive indifference to itself in some consciously chosen domains.

5) All major technical projects legitimized through dominant knowledge forms must be subject to referendum and recall.

I have presented this chapter as a set of fragments that I believe has the making of a heuristics. The laboratory is a critical site mediating between the policy-making agencies and the community. In this context, I must mention that Seshadri had a theory of the laboratory as an intrinsic part of his theory of knowledge. He felt that the science laboratory in India was a remote entity, an outpost of the western scientific establishment, but that it is unaware of its intellectual genealogies or its political contours. He felt that a laboratory must be as innovative and as embedded as the *gharanas*. In this context he saw the laboratory as a fourfold experiment. He felt it should be a *dharamshala*. This emphasizes the concept of refuge and hospitality to defeated and marginal ideas. The *dharamshala* is contra the museum, the repository of dead and traditional knowledges. The laboratory was to be also conceived as an *ashram*, appealing to an ascetic style of life, a science lean and sinuous in muscle. One adds to the other elements the notion of a *gurukul*, a transmission of the craft, the spirit and tradition of knowledge from generation to generation. And finally the laboratory was to be modelled on the kitchen, domestic, feminine, and open to the household, the farm, and society. It was a combination of four institutional elements setting a different style from official structures of science.

C. V. Seshadri did not complete his axiomatics of a compassionate science. He was deeply influenced by Sam Neillson's Nobel Symposium, "*The place of value in a world of facts*," particularly by Linus Pauling's argument that science must be based on an axiomatics of suffering. Yet it is necessary to emphasize that the text of suffering must remain polyvocal enough so that it is not reduced to innumerate indices of poverty or nutrition as calories. Yet he also emphasized that the constitution of India must guarantee a basic daily metabolic intake for all its citizens.

The Seshadrian experiment remains incomplete. The laboratory stands, but as an unhappy shell. The hypotheses and wishful thinking, the daydreams he conspired to construct with Joe, Jeejibhai, and Balaji are now memories. What we need today is to remember that he emphasized that memory is reinvention. We can turn him into a monument. We have to reinvent him and quarrel with his ideas in new and playful ways. He felt a sense of defeat in his last years, a sense of the embourgeoisement of radicalism, a feeling that NGOs had added to the overall sense of cynicism. He wanted more oddballs, eccentrics, dissenters, and classicists as citizens. I remember his comments during a seminar at the Max Mueller Bhawan in Madras. He was complaining there were not enough cranks in the room. "Have you read Schumacher's comments on the crank?" he asked. Schumacher said a crank is a simple everyday instrument and yet every time it is turned around it produces revolutions.

This chapter then, is a tribute to a classicist scientist, a crank who wanted to reinvent democracy, a crank who saw autobiography, the laboratory, and the constitution as thought experiments, a visionary who felt India could transform the current idiocies of globalization into something life-giving, and a crank who believed that Tamil Brahmin Madras had something radical and creative to contribute.

BIBLIOGRAPHY

Alvares, Claude (1995). *Science, Development and Violence*. Delhi: Oxford UP.
Dharampal (1971). *Indian Science and Technology in the Eighteenth Century*. Hyderabad: Academy of Gandhian Studies.
Elkana, Yehuda (1974). *The Discovery of the Conservation of Energy*. Cambridge, MA: Harvard UP.
Georgescu-Roegen, Nicholas (1971). *The Entropy Law and the Economic Process*. Cambridge: Harvard UP.
Hardin, Garret (1985). *Filters against Folly*. New York: Penguin.
Nandy, Ashis (1980). *Alternative Science*. New Delhi: Allied Publishers.
Sahasrabuddhey, Sunil (1991). *Science and Politics*. Delhi: Ashis Publishing House.
Seshadri, C. V. (1993). *Equity is Good Science*. Chennai: AMM Murgappa Chettiar Research Centre.
Shiva, Vandana (1988). *Staying Alive*. Delhi: Kali for Women.
Visvanathan, Shiv (1985). *Organizing for Science*. Delhi: Oxford UP.
——————— (2001a). "Ancestors and Epigones," *Seminar* 500 (April): 48–60.
——————— (2001b). "Technology Transfer," in *Encyclopedia of Social and Behavioural Sciences*, Oxford: Elsevier.
Xenos, Nicholas (1989). *Scarcity and Modernity*. New York: Routledge.

Notes

1 This chapter is based on fieldwork done for my forthcoming book on C. V. Seshadri. I wish to thank Jo Thomas and V. Balaji for their insights and conversations. All unreferenced quotations come from conversations with C. V. Seshadri.
2 See Visvanathan, 1985, especially chapters 1–3.
3 See Nandy, 1980.
4 *Editor's note:* North-American author of *The Cynic's Word Book* (1906) later published as *The Devil's Dictionary* (1911).
5 *Editor's note:* Indeed, throughout this chapter several citations occur which result from informal exchanges between the author and Seshadri.
6 *Editor's note:* Carnatic music is the classical music of Southern India. For more information go to http://www.carnatic.com/
7 See Visvanathan, 1985, chapter 3.
8 See Elkana, 1974.
9 See Sahasrabuddhey, 1991.
10 *Editor's note: Prosopis cineraria (Bot.)*, known in India as khejri, jand, sangri, jand, kandi, sami, or sumri, good for the arborization of desert land.

11 *Editor's note:* The VII Conference of GIAM tooks place in Helsinki on '12–16 de August' 1985.
12 *Editor's note: Panchayats* is the traditional form of communal government in India.
13 *Editor's note: Lakh* is a unit in the Indian numbering system. One lakh is equal to a hundred thousand.
14 *Editor's note:* MJ is the acronym for megajoule, a heat unit representing one million joules.
15 See also Hardin, 1985.

8

The State, the Community, and Natural Calamities in Rural Mozambique

João Paulo Borges Coelho

INTRODUCTION

Mozambique has been a particular victim of rapid climatic change, regularly enduring the scourge of drought, torrential rains, and floods, as well as tropical cyclones. In the twenty-five years since independence, the country has been hit by two severe droughts, both of more than two years duration, at least sixteen tropical cyclones and several floods, two of them of very wide scale. These phenomena are commonly called "natural calamities."

After independence, the term "calamities" acquired a wide meaning: it came to refer to all sorts of evils affecting society in a context of searching for the "enemy"forces hostile to the construction of the nation-state. Thus, parallel to the calamities caused by regional enemies (especially *apartheid*), there arose, by extension, a definition of nature as inimical when behaving abnormally. Later, "calamities" came also to describe, by association, goods donated by the international community to help victims of emergency situations created both by war as well as by natural calamities, with the Portuguese word *"calamidades"* referring to items such as clothing or maize flour (calamity clothing, calamity maize, and so on). In this text, natural calamities are considered as extreme climatic events—particularly, droughts, floods, and cyclones—characterized by accentuated and often very rapid changes in climatic behavior, with frequently catastrophic consequences for the economy and society. Such consequences consist of the threat to the security of communities, their culture and goods, whether suddenly and totally (cyclones, floods), or gradually, causing the scarcity of water and food (drought).

Mozambique is obviously not the only victim of extreme climatic events. Indeed, nowadays these have become a widespread global problem. Accentuated by various natural or man-made factors, their causes vary from industrialization to population growth and the intensive utilization of resources—in many cases, impeding their renovation. Some of these causes are identifiable, although not always consensually or definitively, and often have extremely negative effects at regional or even global levels. In general, the scientific identification of the factors causing extreme climatic events is carried out by the most developed countries, which have greater capacity for scientific research and more mechanisms to "enunciate" this identification. Normally, these two capacities—identification and enunciation—are found in the states of the North.[1] In contrast, the states of the peripheral South are, correspondingly, not only considered as important agents in the causal processes of "extreme climatic events" (above all as a result of the poor use of resources), but also find themselves deprived of the social and scientific capacity to identify the factors that give rise to such processes (to "perceive" them as global factors).

Whatever the causes, global or local, extreme climatic events manifest themselves in a concrete and local way. This text seeks to problematize the Mozambican response to the effects of these phenomena. What makes the Mozambican case special in this respect in the last few decades is that the intensification of the local effects of abnormal climatic events[2] took place in the context of a particularly long drawn out and destructive civil war. This combination generalized the misery of the rural areas and resulted in the policies adopted to respond to calamities being strongly affected and influenced by this context.

The Mozambican case shows clearly how policies adopted in response to emergency situations caused by natural calamities (as well as to prevent such situations) are far from being merely technical operations. On the contrary, they are established in specific historical contexts and depend on the nature of the state that formulates them and, therefore, on the relation between the state and society. The conflicted nature of this relation is rooted not only in diverse interests, but also in the very unequal conditions of production and legitimization of knowledge that structure the definition of those policies.

THE STATE AND NATURAL CALAMITIES

The construction of a formal response

The end of the colonial order in Mozambique in 1975 involved a profound rupture with the colonial state and the emergence of completely new structures. This resulted from a combination of factors, such as the massive exit of the Portuguese population (including the majority of civil servants), the extremely weak colonial heritage in respect of the education of the black population, and the posture of the liberation movement, FRELIMO, which advocated such a rupture.

Understandably, the new socialist-leaning[3] revolutionary state, weakened by the lack of cadres, resources, traditions, and procedures, was absorbed by efforts to prevent the collapse of the economy, to "control" both population and territory,[4] and to confront what was considered to be the main enemy—military aggression from the "white regimes" of Rhodesia and South Africa.[5] It did not pay much attention to questions of security in relation to natural calamities.

Surprised in 1977 by the first major floods of the Limpopo and, a little later, of the Zambezi, the state established commissions to provide aid to the affected populations. The experience of the Zambezi floods, to combat the effects of which the state established the Inter-Provincial Commission for Natural Calamities and Communal Villages (Comissão Inter-Provincial das Calamidades Naturais e Aldeias Comunais—CIPC-NAC), revealed the limitations of ad hoc institutions created in times of crisis. CIPCNAC had great difficulty in mobilizing resources and, above all, in coordination, composed as it was of personnel taken on an individual basis from other institutions. As a result, in September 1980, the government announced the creation of a more stable and institutio-nalized body, the Coordinating Council for the Prevention and Combat of Natural Calamities (Conselho Coordenador de Prevenção e Combate às Calamidades Naturais—CCPCCN), headed by the Prime-Minister and involving several ministers. Shortly afterwards, this body created its executive arm, the Department for the Prevention and Combat of Natural Calamities (Departamento de Prevenção e Combate às Calamidades Naturais—DPCCN), headed by a National Director under the authority of the Minister of Cooperation.[6]

The first years of the 1980s proved to be very difficult. In addition to the severe drought, which began to make itself felt towards the end of 1981 and which lasted until 1984, civil conflict, which had been latent for two years, now intensified rapidly, with the expansion of RENAMO guerrillas to almost the entire country. The combined effects of war and drought, aggravating the effects of rural socialization, resulted in the complete destabilization of rural Mozambique, creating a highly negative structural situation that came to last more than a decade. The consequences for the economy were naturally catastrophic, intensified as they were by the sharp deterioration in the international terms of trade.[7] As a result, from 1983, the country became for the first time an importer of foodstuffs as well an important recipient of food aid.[8]

Table 1: *Natural Calamities in Mozambique since Independence*

Data	Cyclones	Floods	Droughts
		Natural Calamity	
1976	Claudette, Dannae, Gladys, and Ella		
1977	Emille	Limpopo River	
1978	Angele	Zambezi River	
1979			
1980	Bettina		
1981	Benedette		Whole country
1982			Whole country
1983			Whole country
1984	Domoína		Whole country
1985	Center and South		
1986			
1987			South
1988	Filão		
1989		Center and South	
1990			
1991			Whole country
1992			Whole country
1993			
1994	Nádia		Whole country
1995			Whole country
1996	Bonita	Zambezi, Púnguè, and Búzi Rivers	
1997	Lisette		
1998		Sofala, Inhambane	
1999			
2000	Connie, Eline, Huddah, and Glória	Center and South	
2001		Zambezi valley	

As Mozambique could not receive significant help from socialist countries, the government sought aid from the West, particularly from the United States. The request for aid was accompanied by the necessary signals that the politics of the country was really changing, including the first steps toward a market economy and a formal request for membership of the World Bank and the International Monetary Fund. At the same time, these were paralleled at the political level by the first contacts for peace negotiations with South Africa, the main source of support for anti-government forces in the civil war.

The United States responded positively to the requests for food aid on certain conditions.[9] One of these was that consignments of food aid should reach beneficiaries without passing through state institutions considered suspect, namely the state commercial network and the DPCCN. The Mozambican government responded that the prevention and combat of natural calamities was a matter of national interest. In the end, an agreement was reached allowing the DPCCN to carry out the distribution of food aid in partnership with an American NGO, CARE (Concerned Americans for the Reconstruction of Europe). In this way, CARE International came to operate in Mozambique with central authorization and a very wide mandate, ranging from technical assistance to the training of personnel and organization of the DPCCN, as well as direct intervention in the system of transport of food aid.[10]

CARE International helped create a Logistical Support Unit (LSU) in the DPCCN. While the DPCCN defined intervention policy, the LSU functioned as a technical unit, equipped with radio communication means and a fleet of lorries for the transport of food consignments. The LSU had control over technical coordination, statistics, training of personnel, and the transport and storage of goods.

The negative impact of drought combined with war forced the DPCCN to widen its range of action. While initially it had focused its efforts only on Inhambane province, in 1984 it was operating in three, and in 1987 in all ten provinces of the country. At this juncture, the department created provincial branches to coordinate work at this level.

The CCPCCN thus became a weighty institution and, in May 1987, the government sought to transform it by creating in its place the National Emergency Executive Commission (Comissão Executiva Nacional de Emergência—CENE), headed by the Vice-Minister of Commerce. Following the appearance of CENE, Emergency Commissions (CPE) were created in all the provinces in what was intended to be a more decentralized system: CENE established its list of priority provinces in terms of action, while the CPE established their own priorities and coordinated emergency aid operations at the provincial level.

From this time on, there were two central coordinating organs in CENE. The first was the Emergency Technical Council (Conselho Técnico da Emergência—CTE), headed by the coordinator of CENE. The sectoral emergency units of the ministries involved—namely, those for health, education, agriculture, construction, and water, and for transport and commerce—participated in this body. The CTE was responsible for the identification, conception, implementation, and control of emergency projects. The other major coordinating structure was the Emergency Operations Committee (Comité das Operações de Emergência—COE), also headed by the coordinator of CENE. The aim of this body was to ensure effective relations with international bodies: it was constituted by representatives of individual donor countries, NGOs, UN agencies and governmental structures (Ratilal, 1989: 77–79; 110–122).

At the end of 1988, with Mozambique having joined the World Bank and showing clear signs of liberalizing its economy, the government invited its various partners to reflect upon the efficacy of state-based emergency logistics. At this time, USAID strongly advocated the involvement of private transport operators, while other partners, such as Canada, the Netherlands and the Nordic countries, indicated their reservations about such a decision, arguing that private operators operating on a commercial basis would not be inclined to take food aid to the areas considered most difficult.

From the end of the 1980s, the government sought to impede the development of parallel emergency structures that might add to the already very complex organizational situation. An effort was made to integrate existing structures into more permanent ones within such state bodies as the Ministries of Agriculture, and Commerce and Transport. At the same time, difficulties created by the war led the government to invite NGOs to involve themselves increasingly in the emergency effort. From this time, various tripartite agreements were made between the government, NGOs and United Nations agencies, particularly the World Food Program (WFP).

The drought of 1991–92, associated with the problems of food aid distribution caused by the war, created what was perhaps the most difficult situation of the post-independence period. At this time, the country requested emergency food aid of some 450,000 tons a year, a volume that the DPCCN was far from capable of handling. It was at this juncture that the WFP created its own logistical unit (UNILOG). At the same time, as a result of the talks preceding the Peace Agreement of 1992, the United Nations Humanitarian Assistance Coordination (UNOHAC) was created as the humanitarian component of the UN peace operation in Mozambique (ONUMOZ).

The severe drought of the early 1990s was also a very important factor behind the strong pressure exerted by external partners (particularly the NGOs) for the establishment of a peace accord between the government and RENAMO. Only an effective ceasefire would make possible the opening of corridors for emergency aid to reach hundreds of thousands of victims.

In the period of the implementation of the Peace Accord, from 1992 to 1994, there continued to be a vast array of emergency operations. Apart from support for the repatriation of 1.5 million refugees in neighboring countries and the resettlement of the more than 4.5 million internally displaced persons, the humanitarian structures were also involved in support for the victims of drought in 1991–2 and 1994–5 and of floods in 1996.

However, with the end of the war—without doubt the major cause of emergency situations—the falling away of the original justification for maintaining such a complex structure and the problems that it brought about, as well as international pressure, resulted in considerable restructuring. At the end of 1994, CENE ceased operating and, after a period of discussions with UN agencies, representatives of donor countries and of SADC, a new institutional model, implying an organization much smaller than the DPCCN but still capable of ensuring coordination, began to emerge. Finally, in June 1999, the National Institute for the Management of Calamities (Instituto Nacional de Gestão das Calamidades—INGC) was created to replace the DPCCN.[11] Besides ensuring the coordination of activities related to emergencies, it is the INGC's role to involve banks and insurance companies as partners, and to mobilize companies and civil society. Like the old DPCCN, the INGC is under the jurisdiction of the Ministry of Foreign Affairs and Cooperation.

The nature of the state response

The development of the response by the Mozambican state to natural calamities was informed by various contextual factors and also by a range of political options. Since independence, there have been two main periods: the socialist and the neoliberal. In the first, which lasted until the mid-1980s, the dominant context was, without a doubt, the extreme hostility with which Mozambique was viewed by its Rhodesian and South African neighbors, a context that made it extremely difficult, if not impossible, to implement a coherent and effective policy in the chosen direction. This was not only because it sidelined in the list of state priorities any policies designed to respond to the natural calamities (or it furnished the justification for such), but also because it impeded the development of regional perspectives for the resolution of problems that in large part were regional or global in origin. A clear example of this was the non-existence of agreements on the management of water resources: all of Mozambique's main rivers flow from the hinterland, where there are various storage dams, placing the country at the mercy of the management of these infrastructures upstream during times of drought or flood.

With respect to the initial political options behind the shaping of the response, clearly the most important was the tendency for highly centralized organization, given formal expression in the Third Congress of FRELIMO and developed in the following years. Apart from the need to guarantee control of the country—under attack by Rhodesians and threat from South Africans—authoritarian centralization was the result of several factors. These included the example of the socialist states during the Cold War, the authoritarian legacy of the colonial state—of which the new state, somewhat paradoxically, claimed to be the antithesis—and also, for some, the influence of the rigid hierarchy of "traditional" power.

In the economic sphere, this conception resulted in the emergence of a perspective in which progress was conceived in quantitative terms, in a dualistic scenario where the state was the prime "motor"[12] and the peasant masses were relegated to the marginal role of backward partner, which should nevertheless ensure their own reproduction. While the state took over the best land and the few installations left from the colonial period—apparently in order to modernize agriculture and sustain the accumulation that would provide the basis for development—the peasantry would be concentrated in communal villages—in reality labor reserves for state enterprises. In these first years of independence, 90 per cent of investment funds were attributed to the state sector, while the cooperative sector was awarded a mere 2 percent and peasant families completely neglected.[13]

In this context, the first responses of the independent state to the frequent natural calamities affecting the country were not specifically targeted, but rather subordinated to the objectives and efforts stemming from this developmental perspective, which gave great priority to political and administrative control of population and territory. Thus, the state pressured for and supported the creation of the first twenty-six communal villages in Gaza[14] in the aftermath of the floods affecting the Limpopo in 1977. Similarly, the state took advantage of the serious flooding of the Zambezi valley in 1977–8 to transfer the affected population and promote the creation of new communal villages.[15] For example, in the Mutarara district, one of the most heavily affected by floods in this period, in only a few days seven communal villages were created, on the basis of plans brought from Maputo of which the local population was totally ignorant. Despite authoritarian action in the shape of ideological pressure and what was described ambiguously as "intense persuasive effort" or "aggressive political mobilization," the project encountered resolute popular resistance. Clearly, there emerged two conceptions of security in the face of the risk of further floods: the state would impose massive population transfer to higher lands close to roads (thus associating political and administrative control to security from flooding); to ensure their own security, however, communities would only reluctantly leave the river margins where, despite the periodic risk of floods, the soils were much more productive, thus offering much greater security against hunger.

CIPCNAC, the state commission implementing this resettlement, displayed two of the most important tendencies that would come to typify state responses in subsequent years: on the one hand, the increasing centralization of action (mirroring the working of the state in other areas, particularly the economy) and, on the other, the search for the development of management capacity in calamity situations rather than their prevention. Rural communities were excluded from decision-making here, just as they were in the economic sphere.

In 1980, the creation of a more developed state structure—the CCPCCN, with its executive body, the DPCCN—was part of this "socialist conception" based on an all-powerful state, which the intensification of war and a severe period of drought in the early 1980s would only reinforce. In this the state sought the capability—here also "monopolistically"—of protecting society from natural calamities. The intensification of drought and war in the north-central and southern provinces in the following years reinforced this conception by gravely destabilizing the rural areas and multiplying the number of highly vulnerable refugees and displaced persons, thus giving space for the DPCCN's action as well as legitimization for its uncontrolled growth.[16] The resources were found thanks both to increased efforts of the state, which, despite obstacles, maintained social objectives, and to the intensification of international aid.

The adherence of Mozambique to the World Bank and International Monetary Fund, as a result of economic and social disarticulation affecting the country in the mid-1980s, signified the beginning of a process of profound transformation of the socialist state. It was a process that ended only in the 1990s, when, with the end of the war, the state assumed a clear position of submission to market dynamics. During the "grey" period of transition, the DPCCN resisted deeper American "penetration" through CARE International. As the state reluctantly opened up space for the humanitarian intervention of international agencies and non-governmental organizations, the DPCCN gradually changed into what would become its final shape: an immense and inefficient state body, riddled with corruption and discredited in the eyes of both Mozambicans and the international community.

In the second main period we have defined, after the changes that followed the peace accord of 1992 and the institution of formal multi-party democracy, the state took on the markedly neoliberal role of mediation between market and society. Consequently, the hitherto sustained "structural vocation" of social protection disappeared. In this period, the evolution of the response to natural calamities was also informed by factors of context and of political option. With regard to the former, there were indeed great changes. In the first place, a climate of regional and internal peace and security[17] was established, allowing policies related to emergency aid to victims of natural calamities to be clearly dissociated from the context of war. In the absence of a direct threat, the demilitarization of society went ahead rapidly, and the prime need of the state to constantly reassert its political and administrative control in the country fell away (the struggle for political control took other forms). In the second place, détente in southern Africa enabled the widening of regional and international cooperation, having an impact on meteorological forecasting and food security at the local level.[18]

This new dynamic, no doubt very positive, did not imply, however, a profound change of state attitude toward coping with calamities. In fact, research on forecasting continued to occupy a secondary place on the list of the state's priorities, which were confined more and more to the area of management.[19] Following the prevailing logic of the market, the state focused its action on the management of emergency situations. The INGC, created in 1999 to replace the DPCCN, mentions management in its title but omits any reference to prevention. Unlike prevention, management enables the collection of much more substantial funding, more direct commercialization of emergency action (set out in the guidelines of the INGC), besides creating the appearance of a more effective reply to calamity situations.[20]

Policies formulated in this new context have not substantially altered the relation between state and communities in the sense of enabling the greater participation of the latter.[21] On the contrary, in some ways they have exacerbated even further the marginalization of local communities, as the previous socialist state, in spite of everything, undoubtedly had more social concerns than its successor.

COMMUNITIES AND CALAMITIES

The knowledge of the community

After almost thirty years of independence, policies of response to natural calamities continue to limit rural communities to a very marginal role in the process.[22] This is not surprising in that it corresponds to the marginal position they occupy in other sectors of Mozambican life, despite the post-independence popular government having emerged from armed struggle. We can however indicate several reasons why the situation should be very different in this respect, particularly taking into account the fact that Mozambican rural communities constitute a clear majority of the population (around 80 per cent), and are perchance most exposed to the negative effects of extreme climatic events.

But there are also economic reasons in the sense that, as Mozambique is an eminently agricultural country, rural communities carry out as their main activity the domestic agriculture that produces most of the food crops.[23] Domestic agriculture is, in general terms, dryland agriculture reliant on burning, and uses the hoe as its main tool in a system of cultivated and fallow fields. Because it depends to a great extent on rainfall and soil fertility, it is an agriculture that maintains a delicate and vital equilibrium with the environment. Its viability depends, by definition, on the close attention its practitioners give to climatic variability.

We can consider local knowledge relating to climatic variability on two levels. The first includes a body of knowledge socially transmitted over time and constructed on the basis of observation, repetition, and the pattern of phenomena, in support of actions of local prevention. Historically, this knowledge structured criteria for the establishment of villages (above all, close to water) and the verification of natural conditions—not only the fertility of soils, but also the comportment of rivers, the threat or benefit presented by various types of rainfall, the hidden signs in, for example, the development of particular plagues of insects or particular types of winds—so as to construct forecasts (forecasting being the most effective form of guaranteeing security).

Upper Zambezian communities are exemplary in the construction and use of this knowledge of resource utilization and forecasting. The Tawara language, on the right bank of the river, distinguishes with great precision soil types such as those directly irrigated by the rivers (*gombe*, consequently the most disputed lands), and those of the interior lands (*kunja*), which are occupied when there is no room in the former. The choice of land depends also on knowledge of specific indications of fertility or suitability for particular cultures, such as the presence or absence of certain types of trees or grasses. Besides soil suitability, the choice of which crops to develop depends also on the always centrally important forecast of success of such cultures, particularly in relation to water. Thus, for example, in certain zones considered very suitable for the cultivation of sorghum, in years when drought is foreseen, this may be substituted by millet, which is much less demanding of moisture and has a shorter maturation cycle, or by maize, because experience shows that sorghum is much more vulnerable to certain local predatory birds (Oliveira, 1976: 32 ff).

Evidently, this store of knowledge is constructed and used in the context of concrete power relations, in which those possessing it maintain predominance over the majority who are supposed to benefit from it. In addition to "common" knowledge, there is also ritualized knowledge, the construction of which is also historical (through accumulation or adaptation), and whose availability and manipulation depend on specific rules and codes. The Tawara are part of a complex of Shona peoples whose structure of knowledge is based on the belief that, after death, the spirit of particular individuals is embodied in an animal, the most preponderant being that embodied in the lion (*m'phondoro*). The embodied spirit returns to contact the community through a medium, the *mvula*, whose exclusive status is socially recognized. It is through this medium of the *m'phondoro* that the dominant spirit advises the community on difficult decisions or those of vital importance, particularly where agricultural crops are concerned and in everything connected with water. It is not by chance that the term *mvula* signifies either the spirit medium or rain.

On the north bank of the river, peoples of the Marave complex hold regular propitiatory rain ceremonies at the end of the dry season, in a cosmogonic context where nature, society, and the cult form part of an indivisible triad. The ceremonies are performed in small village sanctuaries and in larger and more central shrines in times of serious drought. Here, the spirit may lie dormant for long periods, appearing through its medium only in situations of crisis caused by a natural calamity or by grave offences against the social order or against the cult itself (Schoffeleers, 1992: 61, 80). Rain is considered a common good that can only be obtained by a (political) territorial chief who, for that purpose, calls on the spirit medium. Thus, according to Schoffeleers (1997: 64–5), rain ceremonies include recognition of the powers of the chief and of the people's dependence on him. Only the chief and no one else can call for rain; if it does not fall, he (or one of his subjects) is to blame, and only he can remedy the problem.

In this way, a structure of knowledge (and its social organization), which is considered from the outside to be constituted by magic-religious elements of no material efficacy in terms of real action is, on the contrary, absolutely fundamental for upper Zambezi communities in their understanding of material reality and the maintenance of social order (Oliveira, 1976: 99). Also, the significance of this knowledge rests at a level, albeit relatively minimal, of efficacy, whether of objective knowledge gained from experience, or of ritualized knowledge in which the community objectively believes.[24]

It is also important to mention two central characteristics of this body of popular knowledge. One is its extreme diversity from region to region—corresponding, no doubt, to the adaptability resulting from the close attention invested in climatic phenomena that a material culture dependent on agriculture needs in order to reproduce itself. The second is its flexibility and adaptability in the face of change,[25] whether in "common" or ritualized knowledge.[26]

The confrontation between the state and communities

Without a doubt, the ability of these sets of knowledge to foresee natural calamities and to protect local communities from them is very relative. Their efficacy may have been much greater in the past, when ecological conditions were more favorable, population density was much lower, and when they could be deployed in their totality. However, in the last hundred years, various factors have contributed to limit the capacity of response of communities to natural calamities, most of them the result of the unequal confrontation of interests between the state and these communities, particularly during the period of submission to the colonial order, but also after independence in 1975.

In respect of the first, during the process of establishing its dominion, the colonial state promoted the political dismemberment of existing communities, removing their state of unity and radically altering relations of power and family ties, which regulated not only the norms of access to and management of natural resources but also structured all productive activity. In doing so, it determined not only what the communities could no longer be but also what they would have to become, in a dynamic in which dismemberment was accompanied by a double breach for rural communities: on the one hand, in respect of their land (knowing the behavior of the climate means knowing it on the basis of a specific territory and particular conditions) and, on the other, in respect of their internal organizational networks, eroding the corpus of community knowledge of the types already mentioned, empirical and ritualized knowledge.

The colonial state exerted this effect in various ways. In the first place, it implemented in a frequently violent way policies of political-administrative control and of integration of the rural labor force, which implied massive shifts of population that transferred entire villages to neighboring, but also frequently distant and unknown, territories.[27] Cotton concentrations, compounds for workers in the colonial agricultural undertakings, compulsory settlements in time of war or even migration to the poor suburbs on the periphery of the cities—all these processes consisted of the transfer and concentration of populations in larger units, which dismembered communities and deprived them of their most important strategic weapon in the response to climatic disaster: the relationship to the land and dispersed settlement.

The concentration of the population in larger agglomerations, located according to criteria external to the communities themselves, resulted in an induced syndrome of overpopulation, meaning that land was more scarce and access to it more difficult and distant (making more uniform, and reducing the size of, cultivation plots), making water supply more difficult, and reducing and overstocking the pastures. This phenomenon of concentration also resulted in larger numbers of victims a cyclone struck or when the level of a river rose suddenly.[28]

Regarding the vulnerabilities induced by the colonial order, it is also important to consider the various forms of forced labor and cultivation. The first because they systematically removed adult males from peasant families, disturbing the community at its roots and weakening its capacity for foresight in its response to climatic variabilities. The second accentuated this dynamic in a particularly perverse way, to the extent that, for example, the introduction of obligatory cotton cultivation removed in a very direct way the space and time for food crops, thus drastically reducing decentralized food reserves and paving the way for cyclical and chronic famine.[29] In a society still free from the model of accumulation, food reserves were important in guaranteeing security in times of insect plagues and drought. The generalized and structural reduction of these reserves made communities clearly much more vulnerable to natural calamities, particularly the most devastating of all—drought.

The rupture brought by independence did not alter the progressive and critical disarming of rural communities in coping with crisis situations caused by natural calamities. On the contrary, it aggravated the situation by introducing new elements, particularly the development of the new state's agrarian policy, which intensified the resettlement of the population (that is, its removal and concentration) in an unprecedented manner through its planning and its systematic application to the entire country, as well as the irruption of the civil war.

The new communal villages reproduced many of the difficulties that the colonial settlements had imposed on rural communities some years before,[30] making them worse as a result of new impositions. Apart from the intensification of concentration,[31] the most important without doubt was the introduction of collective forms of production by the state. Somewhat paradoxically—since they emanated from a state that called itself popular—these forms of production, which had a political-ideological rather than an economic meaning, signified powerful and unequal competition with the already weakened peasant agriculture, since they occupied the best land (marginalizing peasant production to poorer and more distant soils) and sought to withdraw labor from family cultivation for state agricultural enterprises.[32] Thus, the policies of the socialist state raised the levels of concentration of rural settlement (making such concentrations more vulnerable to floods) and made family agriculture still more difficult (reducing food reserves and thus making such settlements more vulnerable to drought).

Finally, both states—colonial and socialist—fought with equal energy and intolerance the ritualized knowledge of local communities. Because it constituted an obstacle to Christian penetration, the colonial made such knowledge illegal and criminal if there was any suspicion of consolidating or enabling forms of resistance to the colonial order, or simply neutralized it through its subsumption into the colonialist space reserved for folklore and the exotic. The attitude of the socialist state was based on positivist rationalism, which stigmatized as "obscurantist"—and therefore strongly criminalized and repressed—all forms of ritual explanation of natural phenomena that were locally based and that fell outside of the state's criteria. This attitude was reinforced by the identification the socialist state made between such knowledge and so-called traditional power, which was regarded with great suspicion owing to its history of close intimacy with the power of the colonial state at the grassroots level.[33]

Again, the Tawara communities of the southern bank of the Upper Zambezi River exemplify how this long process of confrontation between the logic of states and the logic of communities resulted in the critical weakening of the latter. Like many other communities, at the beginning of the twentieth century the Tawara began to migrate, particularly to southern Rhodesia, as a result of a combination of centrifugal factors within Mozambique[34] and of the attraction exercised by emergent agro-industries and mining in the neighboring territories. This tendency, intensified from the 1930s by Salazar's New State, transformed the region into a simple labor reserve, in which foreign interests competed with the plantation economy of the colony. Several decades later, with the beginning of the nationalist struggle for independence, the exhausted and impoverished region acquired high strategic value for its importance as a corridor for the passage of FRELIMO guerrillas to the south of the Zambezi (where the Cahora Bassa Dam was being built) and thus to the center of Mozambique, as well as a corridor for Zimbabwean guerrillas fighting the colonial order in Rhodesia. As a result, the Tawara communities were subjected to an intensive colonial program of resettlement in accordance with the strategic military precepts of counterinsurgency, but also linked to the filling of the shallow lake of the dam.

During the implementation of this program, there was great tension between the two major colonial agencies in charge. On the one hand, the Office of the Zambezi Plan (Gabinete do Plano do Zambeze—GPZ), concerned with the filling of the Cahora Bassa Dam, conducted studies with a view to resettling people whose lands would be submerged—detailed studies that included the identification of fertile areas with access to water and also cultural matters. On the other hand, given the proximity of the guerrillas, the Tete provincial government and the security and defense forces urgently needed to complete the establishment of defensible villages to impede contacts between the guerrillas and populations, and were not interested in the delays that the GPZ studies implied.[35] In the end, the second criterion prevailed, and the target population—between 15 and 25 thousand inhabitants—was resettled in villages whose location was decided solely on military considerations, a process that had the doubly negative effect of concentrating and marginalizing these communities, in a context of rapidly spreading, intense, and internationalized warfare.

The communities formed by the tens of thousands of people dislocated by the filling of the Cahora Bassa Dam were not interlocutors in this process, which occurred in 1974 and caused profound ecological alteration in the region. This alteration created an entirely new context, requiring a radical adaptation of the body of empirical knowledge.[36] Formerly, the regime of the river was "alive"; drought and flood followed one another in a pattern of relative regularity that successive generations of riverside communities learned to recognize and in their own way interpret and forecast. This

234 ANOTHER KNOWLEDGE IS POSSIBLE

was now followed by a dam and lake with a "dead" regime, without a regular pattern, in which the variations had no relation to the annual seasons, and in which the policy of maintenance of the water level had nothing to do with the inhabitants, but only with the needs of producing electricity. Consequently, there took place a progressive "unlearning" of behavior, particularly in relation to the small and periodic floods and to the community emergency precautions against unusual floods.[37] This erosion of empirical knowledge was accompanied by a corresponding erosion of ritualized knowledge, no doubt prefigured by Cahora Bassa's submergence of Kanyemba's grave in Malima, seriously affecting the cultic ceremonies and their practical impact on the forecasting of the weather.[38]

Finally, this process of degeneration of the capacity of the community to respond to natural calamities reached its highest point with the intensification of civil war, which spread to practically the entire country from the first half of the 1980s and lasted for more than a decade. It resulted in the most gigantic process of demographic dislocation seen in Mozambique, affecting about 40 per cent of the population, who became refugees inside the country—in cities or safer regions—or in neighboring countries, thus completing the estrangement of communities from their lands. As a result of the destructuring thus caused, popular knowledge (which does not long survive removal from context and absence of practice) was even further eroded and rural communities lost almost completely the capacity to act as interlocutors in national actions in response to natural calamities.

As a result of a transition process brought about by a combination of factors—international pressure, the ending of the civil war and also the critique within the former socialist state—the state radically changed in nature and policies, drastically reducing the domains of its intervention (as it began to privatize large sectors of its operations) and abandoning its former social vocation. Now it sought to assume a new vocation as a facilitator of the market, in a word, it assumed a new neoliberal character. In the countryside, this new order created a situation still far from stable, whose main dynamics are unequal competition for the occupation of land between commercial interests and rural communities, which are attempting to re-establish themselves after the immense upheaval of dislocation caused by the war.

Among the strategies of response to natural calamities, the present state dismantled the DPCCN, an apparatus that, owing to centralization, had grown beyond the "manageable" and was not only ineffective and costly but also riddled with corruption. In its place, in 1999, the INGC was created. This is an institution created from a combination of internal consensus[39] and the intervention of external agents (United Nations agencies, bilateral cooperation agencies such as USAID, and also non-governmental organizations).

However, this internal consensus was obtained within the state itself or sectors close to it. It was a consensus in which there was certainly no space at all for the tangible participation of rural communities. As a result, the INGC emerged as a structure that, far from seeking an original strategy for response to natural calamities based on partnerships between the state and the various organizations of civil society with rural communities, favors rather the combination of international management techniques in disaster situations—to the detriment of prevention—and residual elements of the previous strategy, that is, reliance on management still far too centralized.

Certainly, great steps have been taken in recent years in the development of regional cooperation relevant to systems of prevention, particularly with respect to meteorology and hydrometrics. However, the significance of such advances, translated into very frequent, detailed, and reliable forecasting, has been offset by the fragility of the Mozambican meteorological service, which is relatively marginal in the structure of the state apparatus, and which consequently lacks personnel and the means of participation in those systems.[40]

The difficulties that forecasting has in achieving a central place in strategy shows the lack of local assimilation of present-day perspectives: while forecasting requires relatively high levels of planned investment, with no direct return in financial terms, the management of disaster situations can be supported by a much easier international (and national—within civil society) recruitment of resources, since their greater visibility arouses humanitarian sentiments and a much stronger sense of urgency.[41]

TOWARD A NEW PARADIGM IN THE STRATEGY OF RESPONSE TO NATURAL CALAMITIES

Recent history has shown a consistent increase in the intensity and frequency of natural calamities in Mozambique, with a corresponding increase of loss of life and destruction of goods, to the point that it has seriously affected the country's economic, social, and cultural growth. There are two main causes of this situation: on the one hand, climatic alterations that are occurring at a global level and particularly in southern Africa; on the other, the marked weakening of the capacity of response of Mozambicans, particularly those living in the countryside, as a result of the negative effects of colonial and post-colonial policies.

Although originating in states apparently of contrary or radically different orientations (the colonial as opposed to the socialist state, or the latter as against the present neoliberal state), these policies have a common denominator based on the principle of extreme centralization, in which the state assesses and seeks to resolve problems, while the majority of the population fulfils the role of spectator and executor of the proposed lines of action.[42]

Centralization presupposes that the state is itself capable of confronting and resolving problems, which, in the case of the response to natural calamities, recent events have shown to be increasingly doubtful. In fact, despite the efforts to improve policies of state response (namely, the creation of the INGC as a result of the analysis of the errors of the DPCCN) and the greater effort at coordination, the floods of 2000 and 2001 have revealed the serious weaknesses of the state in this area. Indeed, it could not have been otherwise, considering that much more stable and older states, more powerful and better endowed with human and material resources, have also shown themselves incapable of handling catastrophes of these dimensions.

On the contrary, the improvement of the capacity for response can only emerge from an entirely new perspective, based on balanced principles of decentralization (as opposed to the tradition of centralization) and of prevention (as opposed to the tradition of concentrating on the capacity to react). The present government program dedicates two pages to the process of decentralization (Governo de Moçambique, 2000a: 91–3), in which decentralization appears confused with the construction of the state apparatus at the local level. Yet it is necessary to consider the concept at a broader level, which includes not only the construction of the state, at a local level and on the basis of local forces, but also the involvement of social sectors and forces outside the state.

In the first place, this is because such involvement creates conditions for the strengthening of a perspective of prevention, which does not depend simply on the mobilization of the formal knowledge circulating in official channels, but also relies on knowledge produced outside officialdom, including popular knowledge. This implies that the state has to create space for the integration of the former (produced by its own organs or channeled through regional or international networks) with the results produced in research centers, private universities, and other sectors, as well as with popular knowledge.[43] The incorporation of the latter, besides ensuring popular participation in prevention, complements formal academic knowledge, which, in the field of forecasting, is far from being infallible or absolute, and thus needs to move away from a positivist and exclusivist posture so as to be able to welcome new perspectives and interpretations.

But there is a further dimension to the importance of popular knowledge. Where it exists, its efficacy is based not only on the capacity to read and decode empirically the signs of nature and their social transmission, but also on the fact that, apart from daily experience, its re-utilization confers on it a very high level of credibility in the eyes of the community, which makes it a powerful element of popular mobilization for actions of prevention of calamity situations.

A mobilized community is not merely a repository of warnings of the imminence of calamity situations, but an entity that reacts as a subject in contexts requiring prevention, searching out refuge when it knows there are floods, or increasing food stocks in the face of approaching drought. The new position that communities should occupy in the strategy for responding to natural calamities implies the establishment of advance warning mechanisms and the management of crisis situations at the local level, including the establishment of local civil defense, controlled locally and coordinated vertically with provincial and national authorities. Such mechanisms, including systems for monitoring floods and the most secure escape routes, enable communities to carry out a more active role. They can thus become more effective partners of the state, perceiving warnings of imminent calamities issued from the center with greater clarity and, conversely, managing the stations installed locally to feed the meteorological forecasting system.[44]

The errors of the past show that population settlement imposed from above according to criteria and interests outside the target communities brings profoundly negative results. Apart from this, removing populations from richer and better watered areas in the name of security in the face of flood situations is impractical. The valley bottoms and other lowlands, economically more productive and capable of supporting concentrations of population, cannot be permanently abandoned owing to the episodic threat of floods. However, civil engineering construction guaranteeing the security of the population in these areas is also insupportable, owing to the dimensions required. The only solution, therefore, lies in an effective system of forewarning with full local participation.

It is also true that coordination does not only mean the exercise of good neighborliness or the interchange of information between departments at the highest level of the state apparatus. It includes, rather, the search for coherent functioning, which means, on the part of the state, the highest efficacy combined with an open and integrative vision. Thus, for example, the definition of agrarian policies and of land settlement must take into account, and seek to counter, the process that historically has made communities more vulnerable to calamity situations. Similarly, as the constitution stipulates that the security of citizens is part of defense policy and the concept of security can legitimately be extended to include all forms of threat—including the non-military—the mission of the armed forces should explicitly include the availability of its medical, logistical and engineering wings for the protection of the people in times of calamity, in coordination with the civil defense forces.[45]

The principles of decentralization and coordination constitute a great challenge to the nature of the existing state. This means that the state will have to abdicate important elements of its power of decision and restrict the range of its intervention, while correspondingly reinforcing the level of local power and intervention. At present, the neoliberal state seems to be doing so, not in favor of the majority of the population (which does not guarantee tangible returns except, potentially, in higher levels of legitimacy), but only when the space it concedes comes to be occupied by market forces. This means also that the state, although acceding to the elaboration of circumstantial management policies of crisis situations, will hardly be disposed to increase its level of coordination to the point of, for example, altering its agrarian policies so that communities can be protected from commercial interests that expel them from the best lands to marginal areas where they are more vulnerable to calamities.

The strengthening of local power presupposes the search for cohesive partnerships among local forces that, from below, can pressure the higher levels of the state in favor of these changes. It introduces a dimension that is much beyond the question of the search for a new strategy of response to natural calamities. There is perhaps here—in the tension and dialogue between communities, civil society, and the basic structures of the state—the beginning of the uphill path to what Sousa Santos (1998: 34) calls "the State as new social movement" (*Estado-novíssimo-movimento-social*), a construct that envisages the building of a state in which the present stress on the elitist accumulation of wealth and the lack of concern for the future will be substituted by preoccupations of solidarity, social welfare, and security for all Mozambicans, a security that will enable it to foresee with operational planning (to attenuate its effects) and manage with coherence and efficiency the so very often catastrophic results of natural calamities.

BIBLIOGRAPHY

Abrahamson, H., and A. Nilsson (1993). *Moçambique em Transição. Um estudo da história de desenvolvimento durante o período 1974–1992*. Gothenburg: PADRIGU—Peace and Development Research Institute.

Borges Coelho, J. P. (1987). "Historical notes on the conservation of soil and natural resources in Mozambique," SADCC (ed.), *History of Soil Conservation in the SADCC Region (Report no. 8)*. Maseru: SADCC Soil and Water Conservation and Land Utilization Programme.

——— (1993). 'Protected Villages and Communal Villages in the Mozambican Province of Tete (1968–1982): A history of state resettlement policies, development and war'. Bradford: University of Bradford, PhD thesis.

———, and P. Macaringue (1999). *From Negative Peace to Positive Peace: An Historical Approach to the Role of Mozambique's Armed Forces in a Changing Security Context*. Bonn: BICC/CCR.

———, and G. Littlejohn (2000). *Mozambique Case Study (The case of the 1997–98 El Niño)*. Boulder, CO: UNEP/NCAR.

Brito, Luís de (1991). 'Le Frelimo et la construction de l'état national au Mozambique: Le sens de la référence au marxisme (1962–1983)'. Paris: University of Paris VIII, PhD dissertation.

Carmo Vaz, Álvaro (1999). "Água, Desenvolvimento e Conflito (oração de sapiência por ocasião da abertura do ano lectivo de 1997–98)," Direcção Científica (ed.), *Oração de Sapiência*. Maputo: UEM. 37–51.

Casal, A. Y. (1988). "A crise da produção familiar e as aldeias comunais em Moçambique," *Revista Internacional de Estudos Africanos* 8/9: 157–191.

Chenje, M., and P. Johnson, eds. (1994). *The State of the Environment in Southern Africa: A Report by the Southern Africa Research and Documentation Centre.* Harare: SARDC.

——————, eds. (1996). *Water in Southern Africa.* Maseru and Harare: SADC/IUCN/SARDC.

Christie, F., and J. Hanlon (2001). *Mozambique and the Great Flood of 2000.* Bloomington: Indiana UP.

Governo de Moçambique (2000a). *Programa do Governo, 2000–2004.* Maputo: np.

—————— (2000b). *Programa de Reconstrução Pós-Emergência.* Maputo: República de Moçambique.

Hanlon, Joseph (1991). *Mozambique: Who Calls the Shots?* London: James Currey.

Isaacman, Allen (1992). "Coercion, Paternalism and the Labor Process: The Mozambican Cotton Regime, 1938–1961," *Journal of Southern African Studies* 18(3).

Medeiros, Eduardo (1991). "Formas de cooperação e ajuda mútua nas comunidades nyungwe de Tete," *Arquivo* 10.

Minter, William (1998). *Os Contras do Apartheid. As Raízes da Guerra em Angola e Moçambique.* Maputo: Arquivo Histórico de Moçambique.

Oliveira, Carlos Ramos de (1976). *Os Tauaras do Vale do Zambeze*, Lisbon: Junta de Investigações Científicas do Ultramar (Grupo de Missões Científicas do Zambeze).

Raikes, Philip (1988). *Modernising Hunger.* London: James Currey.

Ratilal, Prakash (1989). *Mozambique: Using Aid to End Emergency.* New York: UNDP, World Development.

Sachs, Wolfgang, ed. (1995). *The Development Dictionary: A Guide to Knowledge as Power.* London: Zed Books.

Schoffeleers, J. Matthew (1992). *River of Blood. The Genesis of a Martyr Cult in Southern Malawi, c. A.D. 1600.* Madison: U of Wisconsin P.

—————— (1997). *Religion and the Dramatisation of Life.* Blantyre: CLAIM.

Santos, Boaventura de Sousa (1998). "A reinvenção solidária e participativa do Estado." Paper presented at the conference *A Sociedade e a Reforma do Estado.* São Paulo.

Vellez Grilo (1972). *Aspectos Socio-Políticos do Distrito de Tete.* Lourenço Marques: Serviços de Centralização e Coordenação de Informações.

Wuyts, Marc (1978). *Peasants and Rural Economy in Mozambique.* Maputo: CEA.

—————— (1989). *Money and Planning for Socialist Transition: The Mozambican Experience.* Aldershot and Brookfield: Gower.

Notes

1 The construction of these global questions is recent and originates in the West. It is based on the principle that countries are not independent units in matters of the environment but are dependent on actions undertaken by others, thus giving rise to the concept of an interrelated world system, which forms the basis of what Sachs (1995: 35) calls the "ecocratic" discourse of the 1990s. In his view, this discourse has its cognitive basis in the theory of ecosystems and points towards new levels of administrative monitoring and control. The inability to reconsider the logic of competitive productivism has reduced ecology to a technical matter, a set of management strategies to increase the efficiency of resource use and to control risks.

2 Natural phenomena such as El Niño, La Niña, and global warming have contributed to this intensification. The influence that the first two may have on the Indian Ocean and the eastern coast of Africa has not yet been clarified definitively. The La Niña phenomenon apparently radically alters the "normal behavior" of tropical cyclones. Normally, these arise in the Indian Ocean and slowly move to the west toward Madagascar. Most bear to the south before reaching the island, while the rest move to the north, feeding Kenya's rainfall regime. Under La Niña's influence, the cyclones are impelled more to the west, passing through Madagascar to reach the Mozambican coast. Thus, the previous average of one cyclone every three years has suddenly changed to several cyclones a year. This alteration is exacerbated by global warming, which increases the area for the formation of cyclones in the Indian Ocean and, through increased air temperature, causes the cyclones to carry more water: the higher surface water temperature causes more numerous and stronger storms. See Borges Coelho and Littlejohn, 2000; Christie and Hanlon, 2001.

3 The formal option in favor of socialism was made two years later, in the 1977 FRELIMO Third Congress, which transformed the movement into a Marxist-Leninist party.

4 The nationalist struggle for independence had proceeded mainly from the outside (Tanzania and Zambia), owing to the extreme social control and repression imposed by the colonial state inside the country. Exceptions were the so-called liberated areas where guerrilla forces succeeded in establishing a presence and authority. Thus, when the colonial order collapsed following the coup of 25 April 1974, resulting in the sudden victory of the nationalists, the latter occupied the country, but had little confidence in the population until then living under colonial rule, whom they considered to be much under the influence of "enemy" values.

5 For the regional context in this period, see, for example, Minter, 1998. For the manner in which it was perceived by the new authorities and details of their military concerns, see Borges Coelho and Macaringue, 1999.

6 The inclusion of the national emergency apparatus in the cooperation sector, which would become a "tradition," was a clear sign of the fact that, in the absence of internal means, all forms of intervention depended principally on the mobilisation of foreign assistance.

7 According to Hanlon, "the unit value (or price per ton) of exports fell by 20 percent in just two years [. . .]. Thus, export earnings fell from a peak of $281 million dollars in 1981 to $132 million dollars in 1983" (1991: 23–4).

8 Hanlon (1991: 50, 61) considers the years 1981 to 1985 crucial to the degeneration of food security in Mozambique, and states that the position of the country in the list of countries receiving international aid rose from 51st in 1981 to 27th in 1985 (it became 12th in 1988). According to Raikes (1988: 189), Mozambique received 7.6 per cent of total international aid in cereals to tropical Africa in 1976, a percentage which rose to 10 per cent in 1983, and 13 per cent in 1986.

9 As an official of the US State Department explained in Washington some years later to Hanlon, "we made clear to the government of Mozambique that our food aid is political. There are always conditions on aid, although they are often not explicit [. . .]. To get better relations with us, Mozambique had to demonstrate a willingness to change its economic policies" (1991: 43).

10 See Abrahamsson and Nilsson, 1993: 92–93 and *passim*. According to the authors, the arrival of CARE in Mozambique was accompanied by rumors to the effect that the organization had close relations with United States information and security services. In a short time, CARE found itself in a privileged position in respect of information-gathering about the war situation at a district and even local level, as well as the planning of emergency operations, population movement, etc. Meanwhile, the strength of the American influence in the national food distribution system resulted in tensions with other donors, particularly the Nordic countries and United Nations agencies. The agreement was also the focus of intense debate in the US Congress, since it gave a still significant role to state agencies and thus did not conform to the usual patterns of non-governmental food distribution.

11 Silvano Langa, personal interview, 11 January 2000.

12 The monopoly role of the state in the development strategy was clear, for example, in the resolutions of the First National Seminar on Agriculture held in 1975: "The state will guarantee the acquisition of surpluses from collectively organized peasants; it is therefore advisable that the state take control of wholesale commerce. [. . .] Consequently, bank credits to commercial intermediaries such as shopkeepers, companies or industrial agents, will be restricted if not suspended. The state will be the only supplier to industry. Manufactured products will revert to the state, which, in turn, will supply these to the commercial networks." See Borges Coelho, 1993: 329.

13 According to Wuyts, "in the four years since the [Third] Congress, 3,000 tractors and 300 combined harvesters were imported amongst other machinery [. . .]. However, in the same period, not a single hoe was imported, despite the fact that the production of household hoes had fallen by more than a half" (1989: 60).

14 From this period (more precisely, in the aftermath of the decisions of the 8th Session of the FRELIMO Central Committee, held in February 1976), the state sought to promote the creation of villages with collective production and social life throughout the country. In 1982, five years after the beginning of the program, there were 1360 such villages, to which 1.8 million people had been transferred (about 20 per cent of the rural population), and the expectation was that the whole rural population would be placed in such villages by 1985. On this question, see Borges Coelho, 1993: 345, 361, and *passim*. On the policy of

communal villages as a means of reinforcing political-adminstrative control on the part of the new regime, see Brito, 1991.

15 See Borges Coelho, 1993: 333, 379, and *passim*. Particularly eloquent is the fact that CIPCNAC (Inter-Provincial Commission for Natural Calamities and Communal Villages), created to respond to the Zambezi floods, associates natural calamities with communal villages in its very title. CIPC-NAC was coordinated by the National Commission for Communal Villages (Comissão Nacional das Aldeias Comunais—CNAC), instituted to direct the installation of communal villages, and was headed by Lopes Tembe, deputy director of CNAC.

16 According to J. Macaringue (personal interview, 10 January 2000), the DPCCN began with a fleet of six lorries, which by 1992 had increased to 410, making it by far the largest single carrier in the country. Christie and Hanlon (2001) mention that the DPCCN had a staff of 3,000 and fleet of 400 vehicles in 1996.

17 In fact, the regional détente lasted less than initially foreseen, owing to the spreading of the Great Lakes conflict into southern Africa, where it led to the beginnings of the emergence of two main blocs and tension between them, apart from several instances of bilateral tension, mainly in disputes over natural resources. Internally, war was replaced by confrontations of a different order.

18 Regional cooperation in this area is already much advanced and is based on bodies such as the Southern African Climate Outlook Forum (SARCOF) and the Drought Monitoring Centre (DMC). Mozambique also has links with the Regional Centre for Tropical Cyclones in Réunion. Several regional cooperation programs in the ambit of the SADC Protocol on Systems of Common Water Courses, signed in 1995, are in operation, particularly that relating to the Zambezi (ZACPLAN), which in itself includes ten major projects. On this see Chenje and Johnson (1994, 1996).

19 The main forecasting body is the National System for Early Warning on Food Security (Sistema Nacional de Aviso Prévio para a Segurança Alimentar—SNAPSA), which involves the National Directorate of Agriculture (Direcção Nacional de Agricultura) and the National Institute for Agronomic Research (Instituto Nacional de Investigação Agronómica—INIA), both in the Ministry of Agriculture and Fisheries, and the National Meteorology Institute (Instituto Nacional de Meteorologia—INAM). SNAPSA has two main components, viz., agricultural statistics and agro-meteorological information. The National Directorate of Agriculture, as coordinator of SNAPSA, is represented on the INGC's technical committee. Other bodies taking part in forecasting are the Ministries of Environmental Coordination (Ministério da Coordenação da Acção Ambiental—MICOA), Health, Finance, and Commerce and Transport.

20 The lack of resources of INAM is significant in this respect. Its staff is composed of twelve officials in the Department of Weather Forecasting, who have bachelor's degrees from Eduardo Mondlane University. The director and the head of the monitoring network have BA (Honors) degrees; the heads of the Computer and Training Departments also have bachelor's degrees. INAM is also beset with a serious lack of equipment (Mussa Mustafa, personal interview, 15 December 1999).

21 This was in part as a result of the structural weakness of communities, as we shall see below, but mostly because of the nature of the state itself.

22 In this text, rural communities are taken to be population units in the countryside that depend on domestic agriculture as their main occupation, and on herding, fishing, hunting, and gathering as secondary activities. They are generally connected to the market and their economy is frequently complemented by male wage labor in neighboring countries, in the cities, or in local agro-industry. They vary between the small family village and larger units, such as the old communal villages.

23 In 1991, family agriculture was responsible for the production of 100 per cent of the groundnuts, 100 per cent of the sorghum, 98.5 per cent of the beans, 96.9 per cent of the cassava, 92.9 per cent of the maize, 40.3 per cent of the rice, etc., a contribution even more overwhelming than in colonial times owing to the collapse of the commercial and settler farming sectors after independence. For developments on this matter, see Wuyts, 1978.

24 Evidently, the distinction between empirical and ritual knowledge is not rigid, mainly because the latter is based to a considerable extent on the former.

25 This characteristic is often ignored by anthropology, which tends to "fix" societies in order to describe and analyze them.

26 In relation to the first, we may refer, for example, to the evolution of forms of mutual help and community cooperation with the introduction of money (for more on this, see Medeiros, 1991: 182–84), or the adoption of systems of ridge cultivation to offset the decrease in yields due to the diminution of cultivatable space in colonial villages. Among the second, we can include the various forms of syncretism that contradict the idea of the "purity" of traditional cults. An example of the m'phondoro, referred to above, occurred in 1820 in the case of Friar Pedro da Santíssima Trindade, a missionary of the Church of Our Lady of the Rosary in Zumbo, who was transformed after his death into a lion and re-baptized as Gomanhundo, and came to be regularly consulted by the community through a medium.

27 A classic example was the transfer of thousands of people from the old district of Angonia, in northeast Tete (whose population was considered well disciplined), to work in the sugar plantations of Sena Sugar Estates, in Zambézia, in the 1930s.

28 In Tete, for example, with the introduction of colonial villages at the end of the 1960s, a pattern of settlement of about fifty people per village was substituted in only five years by one of 1000 per village. Some years later, FRELIMO's rural policy resulted in the establishment of communal villages with an average population of 3000 inhabitants.

29 The dimension of this process is clear, for example, in the fact that, while in 1937 only 80,000 peasants in a total of four million grew cotton, three years later this number had grown 900 per cent to 720,000, without including, according to Isaacman (1992: 498), "the large, though indeterminate, number of children and elders who, although not formally registered, aided their parents or families." This situation was aggravated by numerous other factors, such as the marginalization of food crops to poorer soils or the introduction of less labor intensive food crops (to leave more time for cotton cultivation), such as cassava, which were manifestly much poorer in nutri-

tional terms. For the example of Mogovolas, in Nampula province, where an official report of the 1950s recognized that the policy of forced cultivation had resulted in the desertification of the entire district and in the famine and migration of thousands of its inhabitants, see Borges Coelho, 1987: 7–8.

30 Curiously, much FRELIMO propaganda during the armed struggle for national independence was based on the promise of doing away with the "concentration camps"—the colonial settlements—as soon as they came to power.

31 The communal villages, with an average of 3000 inhabitants (some had as many as 20,000), had the highest level of concentration attempted in the Mozambican countryside.

32 I have already referred to the exiguity of state investment in forms of collective production in the countryside in the first years of independence. Results were also exiguous. On the extremely negative impact of collective production on family cultivation in the communal villages, see, among others, Casal (1988) and Borges Coelho (1993). A further pressure not referred to here in detail consisted of a kind of political-ideological discrediting of family agriculture, at least until the self-critique made by FRELIMO at its 4th Congress, in 1982.

33 After the euphoria of affirming African values that followed independence, the socialist state began to criminalize and repress these forms of knowledge, which were considered counter-revolutionary precisely because they were based on an organizational structure outside the direct control of the party and the state.

34 In 1907, the Governor of Tete referred eloquently to one of these factors that made people from this region move out: "All this region is very poor in money or in any commodity that might produce it, and if it is relatively wealthy in foodstuffs, these have no market in which they might be sold. If the peasants go every year in large numbers to the mines in Rhodesia, it is simply to acquire the money to pay taxes, because, there being no market for foodstuffs, nor means of employing them in agricultural or other labor, the landholders find themselves obliged to collect taxes in money." See Borges Coelho, 1993: 95.

35 The government accused the GPZ of seeking to create "luxurious" conditions for the populations and of having a technocratic vision unrelated to the strategic urgency of the situation. The GPZ, on its side, was guided by theoretical precepts outlined in the international literature on the treatment of communities dislocated by this type of large engineering project. On this subject, see Borges Coelho, 1993: 251–257.

36 A concrete example of the changes provoked by the dam was the profound alteration in the classification of types of soils according to their fertility and suitability to the different cultures, namely the *gombe* (those directly irrigated by the Zambezi) and the *kunja* (those in the interior, used for dryland agriculture). The former, which were the most sought after, were submerged.

37 On the perverse collateral effect of dams, see Carmo Vaz, 1999. The day-to-day management of the Cahora Bassa Dam has been the object of recent controversy, with accusations that the floods of 2001 could have been minimized by a regime of water level control that had criteria other than the

production of electricity exclusively, that is, one also based on the security of the river populations. In the course of a journalistic debate, the absence of flood simulations—considered a normal procedure in the management of large dams and even provided for in law for South African dams, for example—was also criticized. See *Mail and Guardian*, 9–15 and 16–22 March, and 30 March–5 April 2001.

38 On the submergence, see Vellez Grilo, 1972: 70 ff.

39 Silvano Langa, personal interview, 11 January 2000. According to Langa, from 1995 there was a wide process of consultation among state departments on the nature and shape of the future institution.

40 For example, imaging from the METEOSAT satellite used by INAM in the monitoring and determination of the trajectory of cyclones has very weak temporal refreshing (every six hours) owing to the lack of the specific hardware required to enable clearer and faithful reception (every thirty minutes), and forewarning of up to two days. As is well known, much flooding is the result of the torrential rain caused by cyclones. In addition, a strong limitation on the climatic forecasting capabilities of INAM is the weak quality of information that feeds their models—it comes from only twenty-two stations in the entire country. See Governo de Moçambique, 2000b: 42–43.

41 Obviously, in absolute terms, the management of unforeseen disasters implies much higher real costs than those involved in the management of disasters minimized by adequate prevention. In the abstract, this difference is always greater than the value of investment in prevention.

42 In the colonial state this was due to its very nature; in the socialist state, centralization derived from the need of political-administrative control and from the strategy of the state as the motor of development. The present neoliberal state is still coping with the contradiction between decentralizing an important part of its power to market forces and maintaining centralized political power, in the context of a highly specific and dichotomous political struggle.

43 The research considered here is not limited to meteorology and agro-meteorology, but includes also historical and anthropological studies, particularly with respect to the recovery of popular knowledge and the social and political contexts in which it was and is produced.

44 Of the 836 stations that constituted the weather monitoring network in 1975 (whether synoptic stations or agro-meteorological, climatological, and rainfall measuring posts), there remain today only about fifty. Obviously, once reinstalled, their maintenance by state functionaries will be unaffordable and will therefore depend on local resources.

45 Borges Coelho and Macaringue, 1999: 23. The weak capability for intervention of the new armed forces in the floods affecting Inhambane province was evident. In contrast, the role of the South African armed forces on these two occasions was crucial. The present government program refers both to the creation of civil defense services and to the reinforcement of this role of the armed forces. See Governo de Moçambique, 2000a: 96, 100.

Part III

FROM BIODIVERSITY TO RIVAL
KNOWLEDGES

9

Can We Protect Traditional Knowledges?

Margarita Flórez Alonso

INTRODUCTION

In recent years, indigenous peoples, Afro-American communities, and ethnic groups demanding respect for their lifestyles and land for their respective peoples have gained recognition in the form of different regulations. But their interests have also been affected by the passage of other regulations in which they have had little or no voice, resulting in a fragmentation of the protectionist discourse and involving them in another emerging issue: the environment.

Hegemonic globalization is attempting to define the status of indigenous communities by placing them in a prominent position as individual subjects of rights comparable to Western subjects while ignoring the struggle of these communities to be recognized as societies that are different from national societies. In the eagerness to find owners for resources that formerly belonged to humanity, rights are being restricted and molded to fit the dominant logic, leading to distortions in group efforts and fragmenting the spaces of regulation. This chapter discusses how the concept of traditional knowledge and its relationship with biological diversity have evolved to date, and describes the responses of the indigenous and Afro-American movements to the new challenges they are facing.

Why so much interest in traditional knowledge? Traditional knowledge—seen as isolated from the society that produces it and as related to the environment, which, in turn, is understood as a biological and genetic resource, constituted by elements and ecosystems of biological diversity—became a significant issue at the beginning of the negotiation of the instruments and agreements that would be adopted in Rio de Janeiro in 1992, during the United Nations Conference on Environment and Development. Among the instruments negotiated there, the Convention on

Biological Diversity (CBD)—i.e., the regulation of the degree of variation in the species of given territories that have a high value in ecological, environmental, and (recently) economic terms—was the object of complex negotiations that patently demonstrated the gaping distance between the developed and the developing world. The higher value now assigned to areas of great biodiversity and the increased pressure they face are directly related to the serious destruction of the natural environment, to the categorization of these sites as heritage zones, to the existence of "hot spots," to indicate the danger they face, and to their need for protection.

From time immemorial, these biological and genetic resources have been considered the heritage of humanity, available for use by anyone. This changed in 1992, when developing nations in subtropical zones attempted to gain recognition for the high diversity of their national territories, demanding that, in the exercise of their sovereignty, access to biological and genetic resources be authorized by national states and that anyone desiring access to these resources should have to observe certain formalities and pay the duties set by national legislation.

One of the causes of this new attitude is the tremendous pressure placed on these areas by the world's food and drug industries, which require natural supplies to pursue their research and obtain a greater number of products. One of the reasons for this pressure is to safeguard the enormous investments made in the field of biotechnology. These companies attempted to make the intellectual property rights on the biotechnological innovations they developed using biological and genetic resources prevail over the sovereign rights held by nations over their own resources. The scenario they chose was that of the GATT (General Agreement on Tariffs and Trade) talks, which led to the creation of the WTO (World Trade Organization). It was here, in their area of influence, that multinational companies used their power to introduce the protection of intellectual property rights, by associating them with international trade (Shiva, 2003; Flórez, 1998; GRAIN, 1998: 1–12). At a time when there was an increasing investment in research on drugs and possible sources of foodstuffs for industry, finding out who would really hold title to the resources and was therefore entitled to compensation gained new importance.[1]

To obtain a clear idea of the importance of the bio-industry generated over the last three decades (when the boom of biotechnology integrated into industrial processes began) we will mention some indicators of the magnitude of the so-called life sciences industry and its influence in the global economy. The 1990s brought the consolidation of the sector of the global economy that produces bio-industrial products related to agriculture, foodstuffs, and health, which became concentrated in gigantic transnational corporations. The ten largest agrochemical companies control 91 per cent of the global market, valued at 31 billion dollars; the top ten seed companies control between one-fourth and one-third of the global market, valued at 30 billion dollars; the ten most powerful pharmaceutical companies have a share of 36 per cent of a global market estimated at 251 billion dollars (Crucible Group II, 2001: 15)

The issue of traditional knowledge associated with biological diversity was first included in the environmental instruments contained in the 1970 Stockholm Declaration, which recognized the role of indigenous peoples and peasant communities but failed to define specific protective measures. The debate on these would be opened during the 1992 Summit on the Environment and Sustainable Development in Rio. The Rio Declaration (Principle 22) specifically mentions the importance that traditional knowledge and practices have for environmental management and development. It is because of this special importance that states should recognize their identity, culture, and interests. Later, Agenda 21, Chapter 10 (Integrated approach to the planning and management of land resources), within the Basis for Action (Strengthening planning and management systems—10.7.d), recommends the inclusion of appropriate traditional and indigenous methods within the systems of land planning, such as the Hema reserves (traditional Islamic land reserves) and terraced agriculture. Chapter 15 of Program 21, on the conservation of biological diversity (15.4.g), urges the recognition and encouragement of the traditional methods and knowledge of indigenous peoples and their communities that are relevant to the conservation of biological diversity and the sustainable use of biological resources, emphasizing the special role of women. It also states that these groups should be guaranteed the opportunity to participate in "the economic and commercial benefits derived from the use of such traditional methods and knowledge." Likewise, within the management of biological diversity, it is considered strategic to extend the application of this knowledge, innovations, and practices in the management of ecosystems, and it is stated that the benefits derived from this preservation should be equitably distributed. All the references mentioned state the association of traditional knowledge and environmental conservation, and, in particular, biological diversity.

The issue of traditional knowledge and the importance of treating it as a whole was dealt with from a different perspective in the United Nations Draft Declaration on the Rights of Indigenous Peoples (E/CN.4/SUB.2/1994/2/Add.1: 1994), which mentions the right to full recognition of the ownership, control, and protection of the cultural and intellectual patrimony of indigenous peoples. It calls for special measures to be adopted in the control, development, and protection of their scientific, technological, and cultural manifestations, including human and genetic resources, seeds, medicine, knowledge of the properties of flora and fauna, oral traditions, literature, design, and visual and dramatic arts. The purpose is to guarantee the survival of whole ways of life, rather than only some of its elements.

Conversely, environmental legislation seeks to grant special status to this knowledge in order to achieve its legal utilization rather than to support the cultural survival of these peoples and communities. This is confirmed by the intent of some of the premises of the Convention on Biological Diversity, which are directly aimed at taking advantage of this potential in order to obtain better biological knowledge.[2] By recognizing the need for the conservation and enrichment of biological diversity, it maintains that traditional knowledge constitutes an incalculable contribution to the determination and supervision of the procedures required to do so. It states that, since the taxonomies of most of the world's species and ecosystems have yet to be completed and there is a lack of scientifically prepared taxonomists, the taxonomic classification systems maintained by these communities may add realms of new information and enhance our understanding of biological diversity and of the numerous factors affecting it.

The development of the traditional knowledge, innovation, and practices included in the CBD have been further dealt with by task groups formed by the Convention Secretariat. Article 8(j) of the CBD establishes the obligation to protect such knowledge. It challenges the communities and peoples possessing traditional knowledge, practices, and innovations (in the language of the convention) to enter unexplored areas, and presents them with two options: 1) to claim the protection of Western intellectual property rights developed for other types of individual innovations with industrial applications; or 2) establish systems to protect the context where this knowledge is produced, based on the internal laws of peoples and communities. This is the challenge faced by ethnic groups in many parts of the world: either to adhere to imposed legislation or to defend their right to self-determination and cultural foundations (Xaba, 2003).

But the real issue is the acceptance of the fact that the discourse on biological diversity should also include the cultural diversity of the groups of individuals who have adapted and enriched nature, as well as the recognition of the fact that the impact of attempts to impose any other legal order on diversity may endanger what we purportedly are trying to protect. For this reason, the representatives of some indigenous peoples argue that the philosophy that the market is the best incentive for conserving diversity flies in the face of indigenous cultural and practical values (Tauli Corpuz, 1998), and warn that no protection can be found in the texts of international instruments (Bastidas, 1999). The recognition of cultural diversity implies recognizing other alternative ways of life that have benefited biological diversity in the past, and that they are no less important now. They transcend the utilitarian dimension of this concept (Flórez, 1998).

During the negotiations of the Summit on the Environment, the Colombian government took a leading role among developing countries, the so-called G-77, to defend what were then seen as options for sustainable development. It insisted that, in the name of fairness, the country of origin should claim and exercise sovereign control over its natural resources. Also, in compliance with its 1991 constitutional reform, Colombia defended the rights of its traditional communities (the indigenous and Afro-Colombian peoples) and voiced its determination to move forward claims favoring ethnic groups. However, in the next decade, nothing came of this initiative. To date, no type of legal access to resources has yet been granted, nor has any system been established to protect such knowledge.

Colombia, like most developing countries, was also subject to compliance with trade legislation requiring reforms of its intellectual property laws. Before ratifying the Convention on Biological Diversity (1994), it proceeded to reform its industrial property system (Andean Decision 344 of 1993). In order to make environmental norms and those resulting from the agreements on economic integration compatible, Colombia began working on the promulgation of a Common Regime of Access to Genetic Resources (Pombo, 1998). This norm created an obligation, still unfulfilled, to establish a harmonized regime or a regime of special protection for traditional knowledge.[3]

SEEKING MULTIPLE ANSWERS

Protecting knowledge in isolation from its social and cultural contexts poses great difficulties, which have been recognized by the Conference of Parties of the CBD, which assumes final authority for its development. It emphatically pointed out (UNEP/CBD/COP/19) that there are no good instruments in place to fairly recognize the rights of indigenous and local communities, and also that the existing intellectual rights are insufficient to ensure benefits for these communities and peoples. It further mentions the need to find a proper regime, through a *sui generis* system.

In the early 1990s, regulatory developments within Colombia's constitutional, legal, and jurisprudential system that were related to indigenous peoples and Afro-American communities focused on their recognition as the essence of the nation's cultural diversity, their right to autonomy, to land, and their own forms of justice. However, no mention was made of the need to pass any kind of regulation on traditional knowledge (Roldán, 2000: xxiii).

The peoples and communities themselves pointed out the need to first resolve issues related to their territories and the use of resources before addressing the issue of isolating traditional knowledge in order to protect it (Semillas, 1996). They supported their claims using 1989 ILO Convention

254 ANOTHER KNOWLEDGE IS POSSIBLE

169 and the draft Declaration on Indigenous Peoples, both of which take an integral view of their social and cultural forms, highlighting their importance as peoples, as well as their values and culture, which are a source of strength and aid in their survival.

For the traditional communities of Colombia and the world, the task of defining regulations to protect their knowledge, innovations, and practices raises contradictions that are not easily reconciled. How can they possibly establish a regime separating their knowledge from the other components of their cultures? If the options now on offer are accepted, it would mean taking a part of the culture of these peoples and building a regime calling for respect and recognition of their rights based on only one part of their cultural heritage. This becomes even more complex in matters such as the effectiveness of internal controls in relation to positive regulations. If it is really possible to isolate traditional knowledge and protect it outside the culture in which it was produced, what type of norm is required to ensure sufficient protection of this knowledge? And to what degree?

ELEMENTS OF PROTECTION PROPOSALS

Facing the necessity imposed on them to define their position regarding the protection of knowledge and the problematic of traditional knowledge, Colombian indigenous peoples have resorted to the basic elements of cultural diversity. The existence of more than eighty indigenous peoples, of which sixty-four have maintained their own language, is highlighted by the indigenous peoples themselves as an element of the relation with biological diversity in the country. They claim that from the time of their ancestors their labor has been the adequate management of diversity, remarking however that this term was minted outside their culture. They maintain that, unlike the larger society, they have lived in harmony with nature and that their relation is not limited to living organisms but also includes the physical environment. The traditional knowledge that they possess involves medicinal properties of plants, varieties for planting, fishing, and hunting; the preservation of this knowledge is vital for these peoples. One of the causes of the cultural erosion that they are experiencing is the discrimination that they feel coming from the larger society for this kind of knowledge, which is both underestimated and at the same time substituted by other forms of knowledge considered to be of "better quality," forms of knowledge that are represented by western science and technology and sponsored by national and local governments (Bastidas, 1999).

Indigenous peoples possess a comprehensive and integrated conception of nature, which inter-relates and integrates flora, fauna, and human beings (Ulloa, Rubio, and Pardo, 1996). Thus, since their relation with the natural world is different, indigenous peoples also develop their own technologies, which involve possibilities and spaces that confront the dominant patterns (Mejía, 1993).

THE FOUNDATIONS OF TRADITIONAL KNOWLEDGE

One of the problems with isolated protection lies in defining traditional knowledge and how it is produced. It could be said that it is produced collectively, cumulatively, and is the result of responses to very different situations and motives. It is a complex whole based on tradition, observation, and the use of biological processes and resources. It has to do with a holistic conception of the relationship between society and nature, and is expressed and systematized in myths, rituals, oral narratives, and practices linked to the management of the environment, to health, to institutions, and to the rules established for the access to, use, apprehension, and transmission of such knowledge (Sánchez, Pardo, Ferreira, and Flórez, 2000). Nature is valued in different ways, depending on the conditions and situations interacting with it, and on ways of perceiving, representing, using, and relating it to non-human entities. (Ulloa, 2000). This aspect is disregarded by western science, which gives greater importance to the taxonomical categories of plants and animals than to their cultural significance.

The nature–culture relationship varies depending on the ethnic group in question. This means that any regulation of access to knowledge could not be uniformly applied but would have to be adapted depending on the community or people in question. For example, some groups believe that species are thinking beings, and so the traditional authorities consult them directly or through dreams. This occurs within a territory that is conceived as a whole, a unit, and determines the relationship among all living inhabitants of the territory.

Traditional knowledge is a legacy passed on by ancestors, and for this reason it belongs to the entire group, which assumes responsibility for how it is used. The relationship between human beings and nature must ensure the conservation of nature, since the balance of the universe might be negatively affected if care is not taken. The order of the cosmos must be ensured.

It is their belief that all species are useful and serve a given purpose. Moreover, they believe that each species is protected by a spiritual owner, who must be consulted before it is used or transformed in any way. This is extremely important, not only because it is completely different from the western concept that certain species are "non-essential or less valuable," but because the kind of permission required to use the knowledge associated with each species depends on the symbolic relations of each culture. One of the greatest contributions traditional knowledge has made to an understanding of nature is the systems they have established, their own taxonomies, which have led to a greater understanding of how nature and, particularly, species work. One example is the Muinane community of Amazonia, which uses categories comparable to the "kingdoms" of Western science (Sánchez, 1990).[4]

These beliefs greatly complicate the task of constructing rules concerning such knowledge, because it is not an "empirical" knowledge upon which another type of "superior" knowledge can be built, and then "protected." Rather, it has its own intrinsic value and its own protection mechanisms, the product of thousands of years of observation that has been handed down, structured, and organized by each social organization according to its own methodology.

This taxonomic knowledge allows them to make much more detailed identifications of the various species in a given location than scientists. For example, in one song about fishing, a community of the Colombian flatlands mentions over 250 types of fish, while scientific literature has identified only some 200 (Ortiz, 1991). The interconnection of different activities is characteristic of how different groups produce and maintain knowledge that is of enormous importance to their physical and spiritual survival. If the activity itself is lost to them, so is the possibility of increasing and consolidating the knowledge associated with it (Cobaleda, 1998).

Dynamism

Traditional communities and peoples believe that knowledge is dynamic and is generated over time through different means; it is acquired through repeated ancestral experiences and trials and is transmitted orally or in writing. According to the Izoceño people of Bolivia, traditional knowledge is the fruit of a long process, handed down from generation to generation. It is generated, developed, and transformed by the group, and is therefore considered a part of that group's identity.

Internal protection

Traditional communities develop their own institutions to deal with this knowledge and establish internal codes to protect it, commensurate with its scope and social significance. For example, in certain regions of the Colombian Chocó, the belief is that the life of each individual is linked to a specific plant. So, when a child is born, seeds are placed on his/her body to establish this connection. But in addition to this individual responsibility, the overall care of the world and its elements is entrusted to a spiritual owner. This is a deity from whom permission must be asked before using anything, and to whom an explanation is owed regarding the care of the world. Some communities have decided to share their knowledge as long as the use made of it is scientific and provided it is not for the economic benefit of only a few (Zurita, 1999: 153).

Classes of knowledge

The forms of knowledge that are the object of the revised regulations include a wide range of community practices and technologies relating to agriculture, forest management, fishing, crafts, medicine, and animal husbandry. Categories of knowledge are established according to type and field: there could be a specialized sacred or spiritual knowledge and a public knowledge. Access to these classes of knowledge would be determined by a greater or lesser restriction, which would be determined in turn by the degree of confidentiality and its significance for the life of the community in terms of spirituality (Valencia, 1998).

According to OREWA, the Regional Embera Wounan Organization of the Colombian Chocó, indigenous people see knowledge in an integral way, and knowledge belongs to the entire community. We cannot speak of one sole inventor or owner of knowledge, but rather of collective forms of knowledge that belong to the people as a whole. Thus, the idea of one individual innovator or inventor simply does not exist for them.

A part of this knowledge is available to each individual: some, like the *jaibaná*, have the ability to speak to and work with spirits; others, like the *tongueros*, can visualize problems through the power bestowed on them by the spirit; then there are the *yerbateros*, who understand and apply the different properties of plants. This they call the first spiral of knowledge, which is qualified knowledge kept within and safeguarded by the group. Certain fundamental aptitudes and attitudes are required of those who would learn it, one of which is having a good heart. A protective norm then should include the means of subsistence and practices against the erosion and degradation of the cultures as well as their destruction. It has even been thought that the question of the protection of cultures is a matter of national security, being one of the foundations of nationality. This is one of the broadest interpretations of the notion of pluri-ethnicity and multiculturalism, and which is enshrined in the Colombian Constitution (OREWA: 1996: 475).

Territorial bonds

Knowledge is territorial, and the territory is the material expression of the network of relationships that construct knowledge, including language and other cultural manifestations. Thus, intellectual rights are perceived as an extension of territorial rights. The indigenous peoples and the Afro-American communities in the Colombian case are the owners of some renewable natural resources within their territory, and that is the basic framework within which they have developed as peoples. The close relationship between the physical environment and the human being and, thus, their knowledge about the world that surrounds them, rejects the separation between biological resource and the knowledge associated with it and posits that the existence of resources implies the pre-existence of a knowledge that determines its valuation as such (Muelas, 1996; 1998). The availability of the resources in the Colombian Amazon depends on the interaction of energy flows and knowledge among three essential spaces: river, forest, and agricultural area (Velez, 1999).

Similarly, Afro-Colombian communities focus their claims on a defense of territory that is much more than the physical space, since it includes resources, rivers, and the forest (Flórez, 1998). This recent notion is probably due to their need to mark off the boundaries of what is still left to them, given the ongoing invasion and use made by economic agents who produce a new relationship among ecological, social, and territorial elements (Villa, 1998, as quoted in Escobar and Pardo, 2003).

These intimate and binding ties, among territory, natural resources, and traditional knowledge, could be interpreted as defense strategies, in keeping with the peoples' customs. The feeling in this regard is that the knowledge developed by the indigenous, Afro-American, and peasant communities is the product of thousands of years of observation, and it is considered to belong to present and future generations in a collective form. Traditional knowledge cannot be separated from biological diversity because it is a part of it, since the physical transformations correspond to the ancestors' management practices (Muelas, 1998).

To keep and enjoy their territory is a basic aspiration of the indigenous, Afro-American, and peasant communities. It is linked to the achievement of territorial rights and to self-determination. This territory should be the ancestral one, whether or not it coincides with what is legally recognized (Fundación Swiss Aid, 2000). Afro-Colombian communities begin from an ethnic demand that will allow them to continue to develop their life and culture as a people in peace (Flórez, 1998).

Some communities and leaders have begun to develop systems or draft proposals for the protection of traditional knowledge. These projects advocate the harmonized development of all the regulations on diversity based on a comprehensive reading of quite diverse instruments, such as environmental and human rights norms. Therefore, they aim to protect, develop, and buttress the notion of wholeness and the interconnection of all elements.

The regimes and proposals comprehend all the circumstances or forms of producing this knowledge, giving priority to spiritual, material, and cultural development in order to maintain the different paths to development. One of them even highlights as an element the attainment of happiness, an aspiration that expresses the different conceptualization of knowledge as a tool for living and not as something limited to an economic value. This presupposes the maintenance of physical conditions (territory), a respect for beliefs (strengthening of their worldview), and the encouragement of tradition (non-assimilation as regards their worldview).

Biological and genetic resources are conceived of as part of an ancestral patrimony that includes the previous, current, and future generations, taken in a kind of trust that generates individual and group responsibility. Therefore, the idea of an individual owner who could obtain economic benefits from this knowledge is inconceivable to them.

RIGHTS OF OPPOSITION

Indigenous peoples and traditional communities have tested different defense mechanisms to keep their knowledge from being appropriated by third parties or privatized without their consent. For this reason they refer to community rights as being inalienable and irrevocable. This means that they can never be ceded, sold, or appropriated, thus giving them the same characteristics they attribute to their territories. The Colombian reserves (*resguardos*) are one example: no commercial use can be made of them, and their use does not imply property rights.

Rights of opposition/Cultural objection

The power of the peoples and communities to oppose the use of their knowledge for cultural, religious, social, spiritual, or any other type of reason is recognized. Therefore, in principle these communities possess the right to block the use by third parties of their collective knowledge, and these parties would have to respect that right. Here is where the possibility of being supported through state action fits in.

One of the indigenous leaders who has spoken out in international forums to promote the idea that cultural objection is one of the rights of the peoples and that it is, for now, the only way, is Lorenzo Muelas, who has argued:

> And it is at this point that indigenous peoples, black communities, and peasants have to come down to earth; that is, we have to enter into our world if we do not want to disappear together with the rest of biodiversity. [. . .] And for the defense of those resources and that knowledge there is no

other way but the integral protection of our own societies, for nothing is separate and nothing can be preserved in an isolated manner. [. . .]

None of the protection mechanisms we are being told about is able to ensure the integral protection of our societies and our cultural identity. [. . .] It is possible that some of them may guarantee us a few pennies, though this is not easy to achieve either, but then we will have ceased to be the indigenous peoples we are, and the development systems that our peoples have used for millennia—the only ones that have managed to achieve "sustainable development"—will have ceased to exist.

For all the above reasons, and based on cultural objection, it is necessary to reject access activities, or at least reject them until our people understand what is at stake with either decision, while the rules with which we will participate are defined and made clear, and, if that is the decision, to declare a moratorium on all access activities to our resources and knowledge in our territories (Muelas, 1998).

Internal control

The defense of traditional knowledge as an integral part of the peoples' worldview implies the defense of the ancestral territory, the space where this same knowledge is reproduced and where present and future innovations are produced. All efforts to divide the nature–knowledge–territory trilogy are rejected, and full protection as the conceptual foundation of the proposals is required.

The social behavior of indigenous peoples and Afro-American communities is determined by unwritten rules that constitute real codes, sometimes of more importance than national laws. This regulatory regime has begun to be recognized as one of the elements of the right to self-determination by some national and international instruments.[5]

Internal regulations

In fact some indigenous peoples in Colombia and other countries have formulated internal regulations in which they define their position on the management of their territory and the norms that have to be followed by those who aim to carry out scientific research there. One of the ways of bioprospecting is to utilize scientific research as a way of obtaining information on diverse subjects, among them the data on knowledge and on the actual resources. This research is carried out without the informed consent of the communities, without an explanation of the importance of the tasks, the results obtained, and without recognizing the intellectual contribution of the community's members. Many of these regulations introduce normative categories typical of administrative proceedings, as well as a legalistic vocabulary, but the important aspect that concerns us here is their specific reference to traditional knowledge, the strengthening of the traditional authorities, and the aspiration that they express to reaffirm control over their territory.

The OREWA Regulation
Regulations are closely related with the environmental management of the territory. They draw boundaries for different areas depending on their final purpose or religious use. Thus, there are sacred areas, defined by the elders and wise men; conservation areas, in which the indigenous population must conserve animals like fish and wild birds; agricultural areas; hunting zones; fishing zones; and zones for raising farm animals. This was the basis used for organizing the territory, and an internal regulation was drawn up indicating the areas for the use of natural resources and those for fishing, hunting, etc., as well as ways to control these resources.

Research regulations
OREWA, made up of indigenous peoples from the northwestern part of the Chocó area, had previously issued an internal regulation covering scientific research in their territory, with particular emphasis on traditional knowledge, entitled "Regulations on territorial control, traditional resources, and traditional knowledge to guarantee the respect and valorization of traditional knowledge."[6] This document reaffirms the idea that knowledge is the ancestral patrimony of the community and has permitted the preservation of life and culture. It recognizes the importance of indigenous traditional authorities, among which are mentioned the jaibaná,[7] tongueros, herbalists, the elders, and heads of families. They also require that research be for the good of the communities. The basic point is that it is expressly prohibited to conduct research that involves collective knowledge and genetic resources. In other words, if internal regulations are complied with, they will allow scientific research on other subjects apart from those excluded, such as oral tradition, taxonomy, etc.

The Regulation of the Regional Indigenous Organization of Antioquia (OIA)
The OIA also adopted a regulation that defines the prerequisites needed to undertake research in their territory through the "Resolution by which are established the general requirements for the conduct of research in the indigenous communities of Antioquia." This is framed in a Plan of Ethno-Development, based on sustainable development, community welfare, and the training of leaders. It reaffirms the collective ownership of traditional knowledge and establishes the procedure that should be followed by those

interested in carrying out research within the territory. It allows the utilization of the resources and knowledge if and only if all of the community's decision-making bodies are consulted about the advisability of the research. The traditional authorities, representing the community, are responsible for granting permission for all types of research and should inform the entire community about the proposals as well as the results of each project. The regulation requires the participation of specialists from the community, and external researchers are prohibited from benefiting commercially or economically from the results of the research.

RESEARCH CONTRACTS

Research contracts signed between the communities and interested scientists or companies are now in use. These instruments require no further formality than being mandatory according to the internal laws of the communities that require them. The format is similar to that of an administrative contract for research in protected areas.

Parties

The parties involved are the community's legal representative and the interested party or parties, which means that those who do not apply as required are considered to be operating illegally. A request is made to community authorities, who must consult the community or the council, and only when an affirmative answer is received can the research begin. An agreement is signed with the researcher in order to ensure that community members take part in the project. The purpose is to train indigenous people to be "co-researchers" (assistants, guides, information providers) and so to train indigenous scientists, in order to ensure a true transfer of technology and knowledge. According to the annex to the Access Contract proposed by CIDOB, the co-researchers must take part in the entire research process and all its phases: design, selected techniques, methodology, and partial and final results. Similar manuals and codes have been elaborated elsewhere, such as those of the Kuna of Panama in 1988, which also requires that co-researchers be employed and paid for their work, and that the researchers provide the community with a copy of their reports (Zurita, 1999: 154).

In the case of Bolivia, the "Contract for the protection and recognition of the collective knowledge of the Izoceño people" was the initiative of the *Capitanía* (a territorial division) of the Upper and Lower Izozog (CABI). The community recognizes that in recent years there has been a growing interest from Bolivians and foreign nationals in conducting research that includes the collective knowledge of this people. So the CABI decided to elaborate this document, stating that it was "aware that this knowledge is of vital importance for its culture," but also recognizing that "it is of great importance for the general population because it represents a unique cultural contribution and offers, among other things, a model for conservation and the sustainable use of natural resources." According to this regulation, once the community has made a detailed study of the request (purpose, results, and source of financing), a procedure to concede or deny proposals begins, although the publication of results or the acquisition of traditional knowledge are not permitted. Whenever benefits are derived from the research, forms of compensation—either in cash or goods—will be established. This is based on the idea that the community's traditional knowledge is a contribution to society as a whole, which is why they maintain an open policy. They allow research, but only within limits that sufficiently protect their ancestral knowledge. To this end, they establish certain political lines, one being that the *capitanía* retains maximum authority to either grant or deny permission for all research applications submitted.

One of Colombia's Afro-American communities, the Organization for the Defense of the Interests of the Cajambre River (ODINCA), recognizes the importance of research on natural resources within its territory. Aware of the importance in all relations of the respect for differences and an attitude of transparency between the parties in what concerns the ways of interpreting knowledge (a fundamental requisite for the research and exchange of experiences), this organization, which aims to promote traditional practices, imposes certain conditions on researchers as regards their recognition that the community is the collective repository of traditional knowledge and, as such, can exercise cultural objection with respect to the information or materials that are the objects of research. The researchers are required to share all the information and this must be a vehicle for the interchange of knowledge with community members. They also have to guarantee the "ethical use of the information provided by the community, agreeing upon the procedures for and ways of disseminating such information, respecting the intellectual property rights of traditional knowledge."

AGREEMENTS BETWEEN COMPANIES AND COMMUNITIES

The knowledge of traditional peoples has been useful for pharmaceutical companies, which have found that biological prospecting is facilitated when, for example, three communities use a particular substance for medicinal purposes (RAFI, 1994). The companies themselves have undertaken the task of elaborating codes of conduct that aim to compensate the benefits derived from this activity. These codes are based on contractual terms of a commercial nature rather than on assumptions about the protection of cultures

(Laird, 1994; King, 1994; Moran, 1994). There is a typology in bio-prospection contracts, and there are a series of principles and rules that should be adopted in these agreements with the aim of guaranteeing a certain equity. One of the legal and political instruments already designed to foster conservation, development, and equitable distribution is the World Wildlife Fund manual, which advises that this type of agreement be submitted to ample consultation. The manual clearly distinguishes between information gatherers, bio-prospectors, and the companies that will eventually receive the final results of the research. While there appears to be a certain amount of control in relationships established directly between the researcher and the community, this may well be lost or get onto more slippery terrain once the researcher turns the product of his/her labors over to a biotechnology company, whose responsibility in relation to the community is tenuous. Therefore, in addition to designing research agreements that include prior consultation and informed prior consent, it is advised that these activities support the development of community institutions and public research facilities as well as seek ways to ensure greater added value to the products of diversity and greater benefits for the communities themselves (WWF, 1995).

Another type of agreement undervalues the contribution of indigenous communities, as is the case with the contract signed between the US National Cancer Institute and the AWA community. In this agreement, the commitments were very poorly defined. The community was obligated to provide the knowledge and physical resources, but the US institution failed to define its own obligations or how it planned to compensate the community's contribution to its efforts (Flórez, 1994).

The matter of seeking norms that adequately protect traditional communities is included under the right to exercise self-determination initially granted to indigenous peoples under ILO Convention 169, now applicable to all tribal peoples worldwide. One of the significant aspects in this quest has been the use traditional communities have made of international institutions, NGOs, and the networks of other international social movements.

In the case of Colombia, it has been mentioned that the construction of indigenous and Afro-American identities implies the claiming of their own territories and natural resources. By using concepts that go against modernity, in so far as they establish animistic relations between the human and the non-human, indigenous people have influenced and supported environmental thought (Ulloa, 2000).

The issue of the protection of biological and cultural diversity has generated alliances among environmental organizations and groups of indigenous people and traditional communities, all fighting to get their viewpoints on the table in international negotiations. The joint struggle of these social actors has been extremely important, and reinforces the idea that, to a certain extent, indigenous peoples and traditional communities represent the environmental aspirations to which western society must return, or at least which it should maintain. Another benefit is the experience garnered by these communities in working with NGOs, which have taught them how to make their voices heard before previously unresponsive organizations and institutions.

One particularly noteworthy joint effort is advocacy. Workshops have been organized on this issue, and numerous leaflets, books, journals, position papers, and letters to national and international authorities have been written. Lawsuits have been filed and moved forward, such as the case of COICA, the Confederation of Indigenous Organizations of the Amazon Basin, in a lawsuit against patents registered on *ahuasca* or *yagé*. The Third World Network is one of the best known networks and organizations in this fight. It sponsored *sui generis* regime models, later adopted as the basis for nearly all proposals drafted. Also, the Genetic Resources International Network, GRAIN, and the GAIA Foundation provide ongoing assistance and information through their Bio-IPR bulletins. In Latin America they sponsor a web page called *Biodiversidala*, which constantly updates information. The Ad Hoc Group for Biological Diversity in Colombia and the Latin American Institute for Alternative Legal Services also publishes a bulletin entitled *Alerta sobre Diversidad Biológica y Cultural* with the latest information available.

EMANCIPATORY POSSIBILITIES OFFERED BY A POLICY ON BIODIVERSITY AND THE PRODUCTION OF TRADITIONAL KNOWLEDGE

Despite the enormous disproportion between the hegemonic forces attempting to control life and its sources, there has been a reaction against the global demand for access to knowledge. The socialization process of this new threat has led to self-recognition among the indigenous peoples of the world, through joint actions undertaken with the support of other social actors, such as environmental and human rights organizations. The process of economic internationalization has led to the legalized appropriation of genetic resources and traditional knowledge, but it has also opened up possibilities for the transnationalization of the struggles of indigenous peoples (Santos, 1998: 152; Arenas, this volume).

Given the question of what emancipatory possibilities this offers to traditional communities, perhaps we should begin by mentioning what does not serve the interests of traditional peoples and communities: intellectual property rights (IPRs). These rights were defined and adopted to protect inventions of the Western world and were made using western methods that bear no resemblance to those of peasants, indigenous peoples, and traditional communities. Initially, IPRs were only applied to inanimate matter, and no changes were made prior to attempting to expand this to include animate matter. In other words, a mechanical application was made of these rights in order to protect the interests of large multinational food and drug companies.

But developing nations are the poor relations in the plant patent market and stand to gain very little; due to economic problems, investments in public research diminish yearly. If this situation does not change, the only recourse for developing nations is to take responsibility for due protection of those IPRs and force the multinational companies (and their shareholders) to pay for the benefits derived from using them.

So, what kinds of systems are available to protect genetic resources and biodiversity and to benefit traditional communities? This cannot be resolved using a *sui generis* or special regime, which would only serve to establish first-class and second-class rights. A combination of strategies is required. The first of these is to continue to oppose the privatization of life. This explains the position taken by the activists who submitted the draft of an instrument that takes up the idea that resources are the heritage of all humanity, and calls for a stop to the appropriation of life in a document called "A Treaty for Sharing Genetic Heritage." This draft, first presented in April 2001, recognizes that the genetic universe itself should takes precedence over its perceived commercial use and value, and therefore must be respected and protected by all political, commercial, and social institutions. This means that it cannot be appropriated by private agents or companies and that no intellectual property rights can be claimed over it. The genetic patrimony is a common legacy, a shared responsibility, and the human race must safeguard and conserve it, for the good of our species and all other creatures. This draft[8] will be presented at the Rio+10 UN Conference in 2002.

REINFORCEMENT OF UN MEASURES

It is necessary to support the Indigenous Peoples' Forum, an organization consisting of indigenous and ethnic leaders from all over the world, which works to achieve advances in harmonizing all the claims discussed by these peoples. Very different positions have been discussed within the forum, but it is recognized for generating transnational platforms that are gradually creating forms for articulating the highly diverse situations and interests imposed upon the participants, and for helping them express their opposition with a united front.

The strengthening of the forum is due not only to the importance the issue has received within the Draft Declaration on the Rights of Indigenous Peoples but also to the reaffirmation of the idea that traditional practices and knowledge have existed since the beginning of the human race and have been further enriched by exchanges among different peoples. In other words, this knowledge is not something that has suddenly appeared with the advent of its discussion in the legal sphere, but is rather a cumulative social and cultural product of humanity. Traditional peoples and communities have protected this knowledge to a greater or lesser extent, depending on their internal norms and mores. These should prevail over any legal construct of the Western world. We should reject this type of protection because it does not arise from any real need of traditional peoples and communities, but rather from Western society's desire to frame these social and cultural systems in different property rights' formats, and so define "owners" with whom to sign contracts or make deals.

Another type of protection might be to guarantee that indigenous peoples and traditional communities conserve and enrich the territorial, social, and cultural bases that have ensured their survival in the past. In order for these cultures to continue to develop and be preserved, they need proper land distribution so that full social reproduction can take place. Furthermore, once they own their own lands, no large-scale works, exploitation of renewable or non-renewable resources, or social or armed conflicts must deprive them of their right to that territory or displace them either internally or externally. Mechanisms should be sought to guarantee that any change in the legal status of traditional knowledge be submitted to a broad process of participation and consultation, respectful of their timeframes and with no pressure to adhere to Western "schedules."

There should be one sole law that recognizes their full rights to their land, culture, and different lifestyles as equal to the rights of transnational companies. Any type of protective measures to be adopted must guarantee that any access authorized be in accordance with their own needs, bearing in mind the state of their knowledge about their genetic and biological diversity. In other words, access to resources must be related to national, environmental, and social realities, rather than with possible obstacles to trade. A nation's resources should be used first to feed its people, and only after this fundamental right is guaranteed should they be ceded for bio-technological development.

The governments of developed nations should require biotechnology companies to explain to their respective parliaments the means used to access resources from developing nations, particularly if they make use of the knowledge of indigenous peoples and traditional communities. This is essential, since indigenous peoples and traditional communities are in no position to implement their own monitoring mechanisms to keep their resources from being plundered. Today, a great many resources are used *ex situ*, making it very difficult to determine when they were collected and virtually impossible for nations to exercise their sovereign rights over such resources.

Finally, for us, the citizens of developing nations, the patenting of animals, plants, or microorganisms is unacceptable, because they are part of our genetic and biological heritage. We cannot allow these resources to become—even temporarily—the monopoly of individuals or companies, since they are our heritage, our legacy, and have been given to us by physical, biological, social, and cultural conditions. They are to be used for our own benefit, and shared with others. We should valorize the knowledge of a culture with a lifestyle different from ours, and it is the lifestyle that should receive priority, rather than the culture's possible skills in conserving and maintaining biological diversity, or any use that is made of its knowledge. In short, we believe that only through open dialogue, through recognizing the inadvisability of continuing to pressure developing nations, of manacling indigenous peoples and traditional communities with legal formats, which, far from serving any need of theirs, serve only to increase inequalities, can any advances be made to guarantee an acceptable standard of living for all nations, not just a few.

BIBLIOGRAPHY

Arenas, Luis Carlos, (2004). "A luta contra a exploração petrolífera no território U'Wa: estudo de caso de uma luta local que se globalizou," Boaventura de Sousa Santos (ed.), *Reinventar a Emancipação Social: Para Novos Manifestos*, Vol. 3: *Reconhecer para Libertar: Os Caminhos do Cosmopolitismo Multicultural*. Porto: Afrontamento. 117–152. [Reprinted in this volume: Chapter 5: "The U'Wa Community's Battle against the Oil Companies: A Local Struggle Turned Global."]

Bastidas, Edith Magnolia (1999). *Proyecto de Capacitación y consulta a los pueblos indígenas de Colombia sobre el régimen de protección de sus derechos sobre el conocimiento tradicional y recursos genéticos (informe final)*. Organización Nacional Indígena de Colombia (ONIC); Organización Indígena de Antioquia (OIA) (mimeo).

Cobaleda (1998). *Proyecto Conocimientos Tradicionales*. Instituto Gestión Ambiental (internal document).

Crucible II Group (2000). *Seeding Solutions: Vol. 1. Policy Options for Genetic Resources (Peoples, Plants and Patents Revisited)*. Ottawa: International Development Research Centre (IDRC), the International Plant Genetic Resources Institute, and the Dag Hammarskjold Foundation.

Escobar, Arturo, and Mauricio Pardo (2004). "Movimentos sociais biodiversidade no Pacífico colombiano," Boaventura de Sousa Santos (ed.), *Reinventar a Emancipação Social: Para Novos Manifestos*, Vol. 4: *Semear Outras Soluções: Os Caminhos da Biodiversidade e dos Conhecimentos Rivais*. Porto: Afrontamento. 287–314. [Reprinted in this volume: Chapter 11: "Social Movements and Biodiversity on the Pacific Coast of Colombia."]

Floréz, Margarita (1994). "Manejo de la diversidad," *Derecho y medio ambiente*. Medellín: Corporación Penca de Sabila e Defensoría del Pueblo.

MARGARITA FLÓREZ ALONSO 269

Flórez, Margarita (1998). "Regulaciones, espacios, actores y dilemas en el tratamiento de la diversidad biológica y cultural," Grupo AD Hoc sobre diversidad biológica: Instituto Latinoamericano de Servicios Legales Alternativos (ILSA), Grupo Semillas, Instituto de Gestión Ambiental (IGEA), Proyecto Implementación Convenio sobre Diversidad Biológica (WWF) (eds.), *Diversidad biológica y cultural. Retos y propuestas desde América Latina.* Colombia: ILSA. 29–44.

Fundación Swiss Aid (2000). "Territorio, recursos naturales y gobierno entre los Embera," (*mimeo*).

GRAIN—Genetic Resources Action International (1998). "Patenting our food system. Patenting animals. Patenting health care systems. Patenting people," *Patenting, piracy and perverted promises. Patenting life: the last assault on the commons.* GRAIN, 1–12. http://www.grain.org/front/

King, R. Steven (1994). "Establishing Reciprocity: biodiversity, conservation and new models for cooperation between forest dwelling peoples and the pharmaceutical industry," Society for Applied Anthropology (eds.), *Intellectual Property Rights for Indigenous Peoples. A source book*, 69–80. http://www.sfaa.-net/

Laird, Sara (1994). "Natural products and the commercialization of traditional knowledge," Society for Applied Anthropology (eds.), *Intellectual Property Rights for Indigenous Peoples. A source book*, 152–155. http://www.sfaa.net/

Mejía Gutierrez, Mario (1993). *Amazonia colombiana. Historia del uso de la tierra.* Santa Fé de Bogotá: Corpes de la Amazonia.

Moran, Katy (1994). "Biocultural diversity conservation through the healing forest conservancy," Society for Applied Anthropology (eds.), *Intellectual Property Rights for Indigenous Peoples. A source book*, 99–109. http://www.sfaa.-net/

Muelas, Lorenzo (1998). "Acceso a los recursos de la biodiversidad y pueblos indígenas," Grupo AD Hoc sobre diversidad biológica: Instituto Latinoamericano de Servicios Legales Alternativos (ILSA), Grupo Semillas, Instituto de Gestión Ambiental (IGEA), Proyecto Implementación Convenio sobre Diversidad Biológica (WWF) (eds.), *Diversidad biológica y cultural. Retos y propuestas desde América Latina.* Colombia: ILSA. 171–180.

OREWA (1996). "Documento de trabajo: Unidad, Territorio, Cultura y Autonomía," (mimeo).

Pombo, Diana (1998). "Biodiversidad: una nueva lógica para la naturaleza," Grupo AD Hoc sobre diversidad biológica: Instituto Latinoamericano de Servicios Legales Alternativos (ILSA), Grupo Semillas, Instituto de Gestión Ambiental (IGEA), Proyecto Implementación Convenio sobre Diversidad Biológica (WWF) (eds.), *Diversidad biológica y cultural. Retos y propuestas desde América Latina.* Colombia: ILSA, 61–86.

Programa Semillas (1996). *Revista Semillas en la Economía Campesina* 6 (April).

RAFI (1994). *Conservación de Conocimientos autóctonos: integración de dos sistemas de conservación.* PNUD—RAFI.

Roldán, Ortega Roque (2000). *Pueblos Indígenas y leyes en Colombia. Aproximación crítica al estudio de su pasado y su presente.* Bogotá: Tercer Mundo.

Sánchez, Enrique (2000). "El caso de Colombia," Sánchez, Pardo, Flórez e Ferreira, *Protección del conocimiento tradicional. Elementos conceptuales para una propuesta de reglamentación—el caso de Colombia.* Santa Fé de Bogotá: Instituto de

Investigaciones de Recursos Biológicos Alexander von Humboldt.
————————, María del Pilar Pardo, Margarita Flórez, and Paola Ferreira (2000). *Protección del conocimiento tradicional: elementos conceptuales para una propuesta de reglamentación—el caso de Colombia.* Santa Fé de Bogotá: Instituto de Investigaciones de Recursos Biológicos Alexander von Humboldt.

Santos, Boaventura de Sousa (1998). *La globalización del derecho. Los nuevos caminos de la regulación y la emancipación.* Bogotá: *Universidad Nacional de Colombia, Instituto Latinoamericano de Servicios Legales Alternativos (ILSA).*

Shiva, Vandana (2003). "Biodiversidade, direitos de propriedade intellectual e globalização," Boaventura de Sousa Santos (ed.), *Reinventar a Emancipação Social: Para Novos Manifestos,* Vol. 4: *Semear Outras Soluções: Os Caminhos da Biodiversidade e dos Conhecimentos Rivais.* Porto: Afrontamento. 267–286. [Reprinted in this volume: Chapter 10: "Biodiversity, Intellectual Property Rights and Globalization."]

Society for Applied Anthropology, eds. (1994). *Intellectual Property Rights for Indigenous Peoples. A source book,* 69–80. http://www.sfaa.net/

Tauli-Corpuz, Victoria (1998). *State of Affairs in the UN Indigenous Peoples. Lobbying and advocacy in the international arena.* Tebtebba Foundation, Inc; Indigenous People's International Centre for Policy Research and Education, 81–88.

Ulloa, Astrid (2000). "De una naturaleza prístina a un ambiente politizado," ICAN (mimeo).
————————, Heidi Rubio-Torgler, and C. Campos (1996). Trua Wandra, Estrategias para el manejo de fauna con comunidades embera en el Parque Nacional Natural Utría, Chocó. Bogotá: Fundación Natura, OREWA, Unidad Administrativa Parques Nacionales, OEI.

Valencia, María del Pilar (1998). "Pluralismo jurídico: una premisa para los derechos intelectuales colectivos", Grupo AD Hoc sobre diversidad biológica: Instituto Latinoamericano de Servicios Legales Alternativos (ILSA), Grupo Semillas, Instituto de Gestión Ambiental (IGEA), Proyecto Implementación Convenio sobre Diversidad Biológica (WWF) (eds.), *Diversidad biológica y cultural. Retos y propuestas desde América Latina.* Colombia: ILSA, 45–58.

Vélez, Germán, and Antonio José Vélez (1999). *Sistema Agroforestal de las chagras del medio Caquetá.* Tropenbos Colombia, 83–138.

World Wildlife Fund (1995). "Acuerdos justos para la prospección de nuevos productos naturals" (mimeo).

Xaba, Thokozani (2003). "Prática médica marginalizada: a marginalização e transformação das medicinas indígenas na África do Sul," Boaventura de Sousa Santos (ed.), *Reinventar a Emancipação Social: Para Novos Manifestos,* Vol. 4: *Semear Outras Soluções: Os Caminhos da Biodiversidade e dos Conhecimentos Rivais.* Porto: Afrontamento. 317–353. [Reprinted in this volume: Chapter 12: "Marginalized Medical Practice. The Marginalization and Transformation of Indigenous Medicines in South Africa."]

Zurita (1999). "*Ni robo, ni limosna,*" Los pueblos indígenas y la propiedad intelectual. *IBIS, CABI, CEJIS and CIDOB.*

Notes

1 From the moment when this discussion began to develop, numerous books

and documents have brought to the fore the contradictions between, on the one hand, the interests involved in biological diversity and the ancestral knowledge of indigenous peoples and traditional communities and, on the other hand, the corporate interests of the multinational companies and the extension of intellectual property rights over their technologies and traditional knowledge. See Society for Applied Anthropology, *Intellectual Property Rights for Indigenous People. A sourcebook* (1994); Crucible II Group, *People, Plants, and Patents* (1994 [see below for revised edition]); RAFI, *Conservación de Conocimientos autóctonos: integración de dos sistemas de conservación* (1994); GRAIN and BIOTHAI, *Signpost to Sui Generis Rights* (1998 [available at: www.grain.org/briefings/?id=2]); Crucible II Group, *Seeding Solutions: Vol. 1. Policy Options for Genetic Resources (People, Plants, and Patents Revisited)* (2001), to mention only a few of the most salient works in the specialized literature.

2 Article 7.

3 Decision 391, Common Regime of Access to Genetic Resources, temporary provision 8 (www.can.org).

4 On the contributions made by traditional "taxonomies," see RAFI, 1994.

5 The Sub-Commission on Prevention of Discrimination and Protection of Minorities commissioned a "Study on the protection of the cultural and intellectual property of indigenous peoples" (E/CN.4/Sub.2/1993/28). In Resolution 1992/35/92, the Sub-Commission stated that, "in the laws and philosophy of indigenous peoples, there is a relation between cultural property and intellectual property," and that "the protection of both is fundamental to the survival and cultural and economic development of indigenous peoples."

6 Internal Document of the OREWA

7 The *jaibaná*, one of their highest authorities, should "utilize their force [so that] it serves to conserve the natural resources and the life and culture of the indigenous people."

8 The full text can be found at www.rafi.org.

10

Biodiversity, Intellectual Property Rights, and Globalization

Vandana Shiva

Biodiversity, the diversity of life forms—plants, animals, microbes—is the ecological basis of life. It is also the "natural capital" of the two-thirds of humanity that depends on biodiversity as its means of production—in farming, fisheries, healthcare, and crafts. This survival base of the poor is now being viewed as "raw material" for global business and industry, both because the older chemical technologies in agriculture and in health are failing and because continued capital accumulation is driving the launching of new technologies, like biotechnology, for enlarged control over markets and resources.

The manufacture of Sevin at the Union Carbide Plant in Bhopal led to the Bhopal gas leak disaster, which killed thousands and has disabled more than 400,000 people. Meanwhile, in recognition of the ecological failure of the chemical route to pest control, the use of plant-based pesticides is becoming popular in the industrialized world. Corporations that have promoted the use of chemicals are now looking for biological options. In the search for new markets and control over the biodiversity base for the production of biopesticides and chemicals, multinational corporations (MNCs) are claiming intellectual property rights (IPRs) on *neem*-based biopesticides.

This experience with agrochemicals is replicated in the field of drugs and medicines as well. Ironically, as a result of increasing public awareness of the side effects of hazardous drugs and the rise of strains resistant to antibiotics, the Western pharmaceutical industry is increasingly turning to the plant-based system of Indian and Chinese medicine. Indigenous medical systems are based on over 7000 species of medicinal plants and on 15,000 medicines of herbal formulations in different systems. The Ayurvedic texts refer to 1400 plants, Unani texts to 342, and the Siddha system to 328. Homoeopathy uses 570 plants, of which approximately 100 are Indian. The economic value of medicinal plants to 100 million rural households is immeasurable.

While biodiversity and indigenous systems of knowledge meet the needs of millions of people, new systems of patents and intellectual property rights are threatening to appropriate these vital resources and knowledge systems from the Third World and to convert them into the monopoly of northern corporate interests. Patents are therefore at the heart of the new colonialism.

PATENTS, TRIPS, AND THE SECOND COMING OF COLUMBUS

"Patents" originally referred to "letters patent" (a literal translation of the Latin *litterae patents*). *Litterae patents* began to be issued in Europe in the sixth century. The adjective "patent" means open and originally patents referred to the "letters patent," or "open letters" that were the official documents by which certain privileges, rights, ranks, or titles were conferred by sovereign rulers. They were "open" because they were publicly announced and had a seal of the sovereign grantor on the inside rather than on the outside. Charters and letters that were given by European monarchs to discover and conquer foreign lands on their behalf were referred to as "letters patent."

Patents have, through history, been associated with colonization. At the beginning of the colonization of the world by Europe, they were aimed at the conquest of territory; now they are aimed at the conquest of economies. The first such charter was granted on 17 April 1492 by Queen Isabel of Castille and King Ferdinand of Aragon to Christopher Columbus. As Djelal Kadir has stated, this charter was "The literal prototype, the paradigm and locus classicus of its genre. Columbus we might say, holds the patent on new world patents and licenses to conquer." The charter was finalized on 30 April at Santa Fé de la Vega, and was countersigned by Juan de Coloma, the State Secretary of Aragon, who had, a few days earlier, signed the order for the expulsion of the Jews from Spain. This included his own mother.

Letters, patents and charters created property rights to conquered lands. The most frequent phrase in Columbus's charter, the *Capitulaciones de Santa Fé*, was the dual verb "to discover and conquer." It was used seven times to assert the right to all "islands and mainlands" before their discovery. Five hundred years after Columbus, a more secular version of the same project of colonization continues through patents and intellectual property rights. The Trade Related Intellectual Property Rights (TRIPs) agreement of the WTO is a new version of the old patent charters and the Papal Bull. The freedom that TNCs are claiming through TRIPs is the same freedom that European colonies have claimed since 1942 as their natural right to the territories and wealth of non-European peoples. These patents for discovery and conquest provide the background for the contemporary conflicts over patents generated by GATT/WTO, which are often viewed by the Third World as tools of recolonization, while Western powers view them as a right that is as "natural" as conquest was during colonialism by western powers.

There are of course differences in yesterday's colonization and today's recolonization. Religion is not the ultimate justification for today's conquest. Recolonization is a "secular" project, but there is a new religion of the market that drives this so-called secular project. Territory, gold and minerals are no longer the objects of conquest. Markets and economic systems are what have to be controlled. Knowledge itself has to be converted into property, just as land was during colonization. This is why today "patents" have been covered by the broader label of "intellectual property," or property of the "products of the mind." Just as land was claimed to have been "discovered" and was treated as "*Terra Nullius*," or "Empty Land," because it was not inhabited by white Europeans, in spite of its being inhabited by indigenous people, knowledge that is claimed to have been "invented" and hence able to be "patented" and converted into "intellectual property" is often a pre-existing innovation in indigenous knowledge systems.

The claim to invention, like the claim to discovery in the patent charters of colonial conquest, is the justification for the takeover of market systems and economic systems through globalized patent regimes. The cloak of reward to inventiveness hides the real object—the control over the global economy. This secular conquest of diverse knowledge systems and economies is at the heart of the intense conflicts and controversies on patents.

Through patents and genetic engineering, new colonies are being carved out. The land, the forests, the rivers, the oceans, and the atmosphere have all been colonized, eroded, and polluted. Capital now has to look for new colonies to invade and exploit for its further accumulation. These new colonies are, in my view, the interior spaces of the bodies of women, plants, and animals. Resistance to biopiracy is a resistance to the ultimate colonization of life itself—of the future of evolution as well as the future of non-western traditions of relating to and knowing nature. It is a struggle to protect the freedom of diverse species to evolve. It is a struggle to conserve both cultural and animal diversity.

In this new colonization through patents, land has been replaced by life, the church has been replaced by the WTO, and the merchant adventurers like Columbus, Sir John Cabot, Sir Humphrey Gilbert, and Sir Walter Raleigh have been replaced by transnational corporations. In fact, the TRIPs agreement was drafted and introduced in the Uruguay Round of GATT by an industry coalition, the Intellectual Property Committee (IPC).

James Enyart of Monsanto, commenting on the IPC strategy, states:

> Since no existing trade group or association really filled the bill, we had to create one [. . .]. Once created, the first task of the IPC was to repeat the

missionary work we did in the US in the early days, this time with the industrial associations of Europe and Japan to convince them that a code was possible [. . .]. We consulted many interest groups during the whole process. It was not an easy task but our Trilateral Group was able to distill from the laws of the more advanced countries the fundamental principles for protecting all forms of intellectual property [. . .]. Besides selling our concepts at home, we went to Geneva where [we] presented [our] document to the staff at the GATT Secretariat. We also took the opportunity to present it to the Geneva based representatives of a large number of countries [. . .]. What I have described to you is absolutely unprecedented in GATT. Industry has identified a major problem for international trade. It crafted a solution, reduced it to a concrete proposal and sold it to our own and other governments [. . .]. The industries and traders of world commerce have played simultaneously the role of patients, the diagnosticians and the prescribing physicians (Enyart, 1990).

BIOPIRACY: COLONIALISM IN AN AGE OF BIOLOGY

Biopiracy is the patenting of biodiversity, its parts and products derived from it on the basis of indigenous knowledge. Patents are a right to exclude others from making, using, offering for sale, selling, or importing the patented product or products made from the patented process. Patents based on biopiracy therefore do not merely negate the collective, cumulative innovations and creativity of Third World societies, they become an instrument of enclosure of the intellectual and biological commons that make survival possible. If biopiracy is not challenged and stopped, Third World communities will have to buy their seeds and medicines at high costs from the global biotechnology and pharmaceutical giants, pushing them further into debt and poverty. The globalization of the seed industry and the spread of non-renewable hybrid seeds have already pushed thousands of Indian farmers to suicide (Shiva et al., 2000).

TRIPs globalizes the IPR regimes of Western industrialized societies and introduces patents and IPRs on seeds and plants, animals and microbes. Prior to the Uruguay Round, IPRs were not covered by GATT. Each country had its own national IPR laws to suit its ethical and socioeconomic conditions. The most significant change in IPRs through TRIPs was the expansion of the domain of the subject matter that is patentable. Article 27.1 of TRIPs on Patentable Subject Matter states that patents shall be available for any inventions, whether products or processes, in all fields of technology, provided that they are new, involve an inventive step, and are capable of industrial application.

The removal of all limits on patentability was a demand of the MNCs.

This undoes the exclusion in India's patent law, for example, which did not grant patents for food and medicine and allowed only process patents for medicine. The build-up of indigenous capacity, the self-reliance in medicine, the ability to control prices and keep them low, which had been made possible by the 1970 act, are all seen by MNCs as sources of profit loss.

TRIPs has also expanded the scope of patentability to cover life forms. Article 27.53(b) of the TRIPs agreement of the WTO refers to the patenting of life. This article enables the piracy of indigenous knowledge, while the same interests that see process innovation as involving no inventiveness attempt to claim patents on nature's processes and on indigenous knowledge as invention. The article states that

> Parties may exclude from patentability plants and animals other than micro-organisms, and essentially biological processes for the production of plants or animals other than non-biological and micro-biological processes. However, parties shall provide for the protection of plant varieties either by patents or by an effective *sui generis* system or by any combination thereof. This provision shall be reviewed four years after the entry into force of the Agreement.

This article forces countries to change patent laws in order to introduce patents for life forms and introduce plant variety legislation. The first part of the article addresses the patenting of life. On first reading, it appears that the article is about the exclusion of plants and animals from patentability. However, the words "other than micro-organisms" and plants and animals produced by "non-biological" and "micro-biological" processes make patenting of micro-organisms and genetically engineered plants and animals compulsory. Since micro-organisms are living organisms, making their patenting compulsory is the beginning of a journey down what has been called the slippery slope that leads to the patenting of all life.

The movement against biopiracy and against TRIPs has emerged as one of the core components of the anti-globalization struggle. It includes the movements of indigenous communities, movements of farmers, women's movements, health movements, and ecology movements. It is also among the few areas in which Third World states have resisted the hegemony of the North and made the review of TRIPs one of the most significant arenas of North–South conflicts.

Biopiracy and TRIPs have also pitted the WTO against other international agreements such as the Convention on Biological Diversity (CBD) and the International Undertaking on Plant Genetic Resources of the Food and Agriculture Organization. The Convention on Biological Diversity (CBD) is the international treaty that was signed at the first Earth Summit in Rio de

Janeiro, in 1992. Almost 200 countries are party to the CBD, although seven countries, including the US, have not yet ratified it. The TRIPs agreement, which has expanded patents to cover life forms, undermines the potential and promises of the Convention on Biological Diversity. Since individual countries that are members of both treaties have to implement both of them, the conflicts between CBD and TRIPs has serious problems for implementation.

TRIPS, PATENTS ON PLANTS, AND SEEDS AND FARMERS' RIGHTS

The entire structure of the patenting of seeds and plants in the US and in TRIPs is based on an arbitrary decision of the US Patent and Trademark Office in the Hibberd case in 1985. Prior to this 1985 decision, beginning in 1930, the US Congress had granted carefully crafted intellectual property protection for plants. But these laws included important exemptions for farmers and researchers.

The 1985 decision redefined plants as machines and other manufactures and since then thousands of patents on plants have been given in the US. The US has also pressured the rest of the world into implementing plant patents through TRIPs. The US IPR orthodoxy is based on the fallacious idea that people do not innovate or generate knowledge unless they can derive private profit. However, greed is not a "fundamental act of human nature" but a dominant tendency in societies that reward it. In the area of seeds and plant genetic resources, the innovation of both "formal" and "informal" systems has so far been guided by the larger human good.

THE UPOV CONVENTION, BREEDERS' RIGHTS, AND FARMERS' RIGHTS

The existing international agreement that covers plant breeders' rights is the International Convention for the Protection of New Varieties of Plants—the UPOV Convention. The UPOV Convention was adopted initially by five European countries, and membership was restricted to European countries until 1986. At that time the Convention was revised and membership opened to all countries. UPOV was signed in 1961 and came into force in 1968. Earlier, the applied version of this Convention was UPOV 1978. Then, a revised version, UPOV 1991, was negotiated, and it has since come into effect.

UPOV currently has twenty member states, including most EU countries, several European countries, Japan, the US, and some others. It has no developing country members. It has, therefore, evolved as legislation suitable to the socioeconomic context of industrialized countries where farmers do not form a large part of the population and do not have any control over plant breeding or seed supply. This situation is very different from contexts like ours in India, where the majority of the population continues to be engaged in farming and where farmers' seed production and supply system is still the main source of seed.

The objective of UPOV is to grant certain exclusive rights to plant breeders who develop new varieties of plants. Normally, farmers provide the source material to the breeders for the development of new varieties. They are also the users of the new varieties developed by the breeders. There is a need for a balance between breeders' rights and what has been called the farmer's privilege.

However, the UPOV Convention is rigid, requiring that members adopt its standards and scope of protection as national law. It has resulted in a high degree of standardization and goes against the reality of biological diversity and the socioeconomic diversity of different countries. It is therefore inappropriate as a *sui generis* system evolved to protect plants, people, and creativity in diverse realities.

The standardization is built into the manner in which plant varieties are defined. To be eligible for protection, a variety must be:

New—the variety must not have been exploited commercially.

Distinct—it must be clearly distinguishable from all other varieties known at the date of the application for protection.

Uniform—all plants of that particular variety must be sufficiently uniform in order to allow it to be distinguished from other varieties, taking into account the method of reproduction of the species.

Stable—it must be possible for the variety to be reproduced unchanged.

This definition by its very nature rules out farmers' varieties and destroys biodiversity while producing uniformity as a necessity. The reward under such a system of Plant Breeders' Rights (PBR) does not go towards breeding to maintain and enhance diversity and sustainability, but towards the destruction of biodiversity and the creation of a uniform and hence ecologically vulnerable agricultural system. Therefore, PBR legislation, like UPOV, is inherently incapable of protecting farmers' rights arising from the role of farmers as breeders who innovate and produce diverse farmers' varieties, which forms the basis for all other breeding systems.

Movements for farmers' rights have been based on the inalienable right of farmers to save and exchange seed freely and the recognition of farmers' breeding. In India, the farmers' rights movement has taken the shape of the *Bija Satyagraha*. This massive movement—the Seed *Satyagraha*—has emerged over the past few years in response to the threats of recolonization through GATT, especially its intellectual property rights clauses. According to Gandhi, no tyranny can enslave a people who consider it immoral to obey laws that are unjust. As he stated in *Hind Swaraj*: "As long as the superstition that people should obey unjust laws exists, so long will slavery exist. And a passive resister alone can remove such a superstition."

Satyagraha is the key to self-rule, or *swaraj*. The phrase that echoed most during India's freedom movement was *"Swaraj hamara janmasidh adhikar hai"* ("self-rule is our birthright"). For self-rule did not imply governance by a centralized state but by decentralized communities. *"Nate ne raj"* ("our rule in our village") is one slogan from India's grassroots environmental movement.

At a massive rally in Delhi in March 1993, a charter of farmers' rights was developed. One of the rights is local sovereignty. Local resources have to be managed on the principle of local sovereignty, wherein the natural resources of the village belong to that village. A farmer's right to produce, exchange, modify, and sell seed is also an expression of *swaraj*. Farmers' movements in India have declared they will violate the GATT treaty, if it is implemented, since it violates their birthright. The positive assertion of local control over local resources has emerged as the Jaiv Panchayat (Living Democracy) Movement.

The biodiversity movements are as diverse as the cultures and domains from which they emerge. However, beyond diversity and pluralism, two major strands can be observed. One strand is committed to challenging the commodification of life intrinsic to TRIPs and WTO and the erosion of cultural and biological diversity intrinsic to biopiracy. In this strand of the biodiversity movement, resistance to biopiracy is a resistance to the ultimate colonization of life itself—of the future of evolution as well as of the future of non-Western traditions of relating to and knowing nature. It is a struggle to protect the freedom of diverse species to evolve. It is a struggle to protect the freedom of diverse cultures to evolve. It is a struggle to conserve both cultural and biological diversity. The biodiversity movement is therefore a struggle over worldviews.

The second strand is more technocratic and seeks amelioration within the commercial and legal logic that seeks to rule the commoditization of life and monopolies on knowledge. The code words for this strand are "bio-prospecting" and "benefit-sharing."

A common proposal offered as a solution to biopiracy is that of bio-prospecting and benefit-sharing, i.e., those who claim patents on indigenous knowledge should share benefits from the profits of their commercial monopolies with the original innovators. Bio-prospecting is being promoted as the model for relationships between corporations that commercialize indigenous knowledge and indigenous communities that have collectively innovated and evolved the knowledge.

However, bio-prospecting is merely a sophisticated form of biopiracy. There are two basic problems with this model. First, if knowledge already exists, a patent based on it is totally unjustified since it violates the principles of novelty and non-obviousness. Granting patents for indigenous knowledge amounts to stating that the patent system is about power and control, not inventiveness and novelty. Second, the appropriation of indigenous knowledge vital for food and medicine, its conversion into an exclusive right through patents, and the establishment of an economic system in which people have to buy what they had produced for themselves is a system that denies benefits and creates impoverishment; it is not a process that promotes "benefit-sharing." It is the equivalent of stealing a loaf of bread and then sharing the crumbs.

THE VICTORY OF THE *NEEM* TREE

On 10 May 2000, the anniversary of the launching of the first Indian movement for independence, a major milestone was crossed in the contemporary movement for freedom from biocolonialism and biopiracy. The European Patent Office (EPO) struck down Patent No. 0436257 B1, jointly held by the US Government and the multinational W. R. Grace, finding that it was based on the pirating of existing knowledge and was lacking in novelty and inventiveness.

The patent had been filed by the USDA and W. R. Grace on 12 December 1990. On 14 September 1994, the European Patent Office granted a patent for "A method for controlling fungi on plants comprising contacting the fungi with a *neem* oil formulation containing 0.1 to 10 of a hydrophobic extracted *neem* oil which is substantially free of azadirachtin, 0.005 to 50% of emulsifying surfactant, and 0 to 99% water."

A patent challenge was filed on 5 June 1995 by me, as Director of the Research Foundation for Science, Technology and Ecology, along with Linda Bullard, President of the International Federation of Organic Agriculture Movements, and Magda Alvoet, currently Health and Environment Minister of Belgium. We filed a legal opposition because the use of *neem* extracts for fungicide and pesticide has been practiced for centuries and investigated scientifically and commercially for decades prior to the claim to invention in the USDA–Grace patent. Over five years, we brought every possible piece of evidence to bear on the case through affidavits from farmers and scientists, including Dr. Vijayalakshmi, Dr. Jyotsna, Dr. Phadke, and Dr. U. P. Singh. We also took Dr. Phadke and Dr. U.P. Singh as expert witnesses for the oral hearing on 9 and 10 March of 2000. Two days of very detailed cross-examination proved beyond any doubt to the Opposition Division bench chaired by Mr. D. Tzschoppe, and with Mr. A. Schmid and Dr. Rakshanda Faizi, that the patent was based on pirated knowledge. On the afternoon of May 10, Mr. Tzschoppe ruled that the "Patent is revoked."

The USDA and Grace attorneys tried every argument under the sun to dismiss the case and block the proceedings, including procedural arguments that as an Indian I could not bring a case to the EPO and that the Research Foundation had not separately paid a $2000 fee. However, our excellent lawyer, Dr. Dolder, who teaches IPR law at the University of Basel in Switzerland, pointed out to the bench that USDA and Grace were not European entities either, and had also not separately paid patent fees for their joint claim. In any case, the part of Indian systems and therefore Indians had a right to challenge the biopiracy-based European patent in European courts.

The work for the *neem* challenge started in 1994 when I first read about the *neem* patents in a journal. We launched the "*Neem* Campaign" in India, and formed the "*Neem* Team"—an international network of patent warriors to support our national campaign. For a decade before that, beginning after the Bhopal disaster in 1984, we had been advocating the use of *neem* in agriculture as an alternative to hazardous pesticides through a campaign— "No more Bhopals, plant a *neem*."

The *neem* tree, or *Azadirachta indica*, has been used for diverse purposes for centuries in India. It has been used in medicine and in agriculture. The *neem* is mentioned in Indian texts written over 2000 years ago as an air purifier and as a cure for almost all types of human and animal diseases because of its insect- and pest-repellent properties. It is used almost daily on every farm and in every house in India. Research has shown that *neem* extracts can influence nearly 200 species of insects, many of which are resistant to pesticides. A number of *neem*-based commercial products, including pesticides, medicines, and cosmetics have come on the Indian market in recent years, some of them produced in the small-scale sector, others by medium-sized laboratories. However, there has been no attempt to acquire proprietary ownership of the chemical formula since, under the 1970 Patent Act of India, agricultural and medicinal products are not patentable.

The combination of the *neem*'s cultural, medicinal, and agricultural values has contributed to its widespread distribution and propagation. More than 50,000 *neem* trees shelter pilgrims on the way to Mecca. Indians have given knowledge about *neem* to the entire world. The existence of diverse species and the freedom with which knowledge can be exchanged is best symbolized by the *neem*.

The *neem* is therefore referred to as the "free tree" of India. For centuries the Western world ignored the *neem* tree and its properties; the practices of Indian peasants and doctors were not deemed worthy of attention by the majority of British, French, and Portuguese colonialists. However, in the last few years, growing opposition to chemical products in the West, in particular to pesticides, has led to a sudden enthusiasm for the pharmaceutical properties of *neem*. In 1971, US timber importer Robert Larson observed the tree's usefulness in India and began importing *neem* seed to his company head-quarters in Wisconsin. Over the next decade, he conducted safety and performance tests upon a pesticidal *neem* extract called Margosan-O, and in 1985 received clearance for the product from the US Environmental Protection Agency (EPA). Three years later, he sold the patent for the product to the multinational chemical corporation W. R. Grace. Since 1985, over a dozen US patents have been taken out by US and Japanese firms on formulae for stable *neem*-based solutions and emulsions, and even for a *neem*-based toothpaste.

Having garnered their patents, and with the prospect of a license from the EPA, Grace has set about manufacturing and commercializing their product by establishing a base in India. The company approached several Indian manufacturers with proposals to buy up their technology or to convince them to stop producing value-added products and to instead supply the company with raw material. In many cases, W. R. Grace met with a rebuff. Eventually, it managed to arrange a joint venture with a firm called PJ Margo Pvt. Ltd. They have set up a plant in India that processes up to 20 tonnes of seed a day. They are also setting up a network of *neem* seed suppliers in order to ensure a constant supply of the seeds at a reliable price. Grace is likely to be followed by other patent-holding companies.

The company's demand for seed had had three primary effects:

1. The price of *neem* seed has risen beyond the reach of ordinary people; in fact, *neem* oil itself, used by local people to light lamps, is practically unavailable any more because local oil millers are not able to access the seed.
2. Almost all of the seed has been collected, which was freely available to the farmer and the company, because of its economic power.
3. Poor people have lost access to a resource vital for their survival—a resource that was once widely and cheaply available to them.

The victory of the *Neem* tree is a landmark victory that will arrest the flow of the rich biodiversity of the Third World to the rich of the North. It is a victory of people against power, of commons against monopolies, of freedom against slavery. It is significant that the *Neem*-Azad-Darakt, the "Free Tree," should be a symbol of this significant victory of the people.

THE TRIPS REVIEW

When TRIPs was forced on countries during the Uruguay Round, many issues of public concern were totally bypassed and the full ethical, ecological, and economic implications of patenting life were not discussed. Third World countries were coerced into accepting the Western-style IPR system. However, public interest groups showed that these systems were strong in establishing corporate monopolies globally but were weak in protecting indigenous knowledge and preventing biopiracy. Such systems were "advanced" means for taking away the resources of the poor and for stealing the knowledge of our grandmothers. But they were primitive when viewed from the perspective of justice, equality, and cross-cultural respect. As a result of sustained public pressure after the agreement came into force in 1995, many Third World countries made recommendations for changes in Article 27.3(b) to prevent biopiracy.

On the subject of patenting of life forms, India, in its discussion paper submitted to the TRIPs Council in Geneva prior to the WTO's Third Ministerial Conference in Seattle, stated:

> Patenting of life forms may have at least two dimensions. Firstly, there is the ethical question of the extent of private ownership that could be extended to life forms. The second dimension relates to the use of IPR's concept as understood in the industrialized world and its appropriateness in the face of the larger dimension of rights on knowledge, their ownership, use, transfer and dissemination. Informal systems, e.g. the "shrutis" and "smritis" in the Indian tradition and grandmother's potions all over the world, get scant recognition. To create systems that fail to address this issue can have severe adverse consequences on mankind, some say even leading to extinction.

Article 71.1 requires that in the year 2000 the implementation of TRIPs be reviewed and, if necessary, the TRIPs Agreement itself be amended in the light of any relevant new developments that might warrant its modification or amendment. African and Central American countries are consistently demanding a TRIPs review, a demand that is being delayed and denied by the US, which is instead putting pressure on the countries for the implementation of TRIPs. The African and Central American countries have also demanded, in their position paper to the WTO, a five-year delay in the implementation of TRIPs. In early 1999, the Research Foundation for Science, Technology and Ecology, a leading research group in India, has also demanded a five-year freeze of the TRIPs Agreement.

As a Third World country, India's interest lies in working with other developing countries to change the IPR systems being globalized through

TRIPs, which is biased in favor of the rich industrialized countries and global corporations. Since changing TRIPs is part of our right, there is absolutely no justification for implementing it in its present form.

TRIPS ADOPTS PATENTS ON LIFE AND MONOPOLIZES COMMUNITIES' KNOWLEDGE

A next major flaw with TRIPs, which is also rooted in using US Patent Law as its model, is the introduction of patents on life forms through Article 27.3(b). This article was supposed to be reviewed during the WTO Seattle Ministerial Conference.

Bolivia, Colombia, Ecuador, Nicaragua, and Peru have made a proposal regarding the protection of intellectual property rights relating to the traditional knowledge of local and indigenous communities. This paper states: "The entire modern evolution of intellectual property has been framed by principles and systems that have tended to leave aside a large sector of human creativity, namely the traditional knowledge possessed by local and indigenous communities." The group proposed that negotiations be initiated at the WTO Conference at Seattle, with the view to establishing a multilateral legal framework that will grant effective protection to the expressions and manifestations of tradition knowledge. The entire African group has also called for systems to protect traditional knowledge.

The African group, represented through the Organization of African Unity (OAU), has also proposed that a footnote be inserted in Article 27.3(b), stating that any *sui generis* law for plant variety protection can provide for the protection of the innovations of indigenous and local farming communities in developing countries, consistent with the Convention on Biological Diversity and the International Undertaking on Plant Genetic Resources.

Despite the fact that all of the countries of Africa, five countries in Central and Latin America as well as India have called for changes in 27.3(b) on the basis of their right to a review as built into the agreement, the US and Europe are determined to block the reform of TRIPs and any attempt to stop biopiracy. In a "green room" consultation (the undemocratic structure of decision-making in the WTO) the powerful industrialized countries told Mike Moore, the Director-General, that they rejected all the proposals for the reform of TRIPs.

The African group and India have also called for the exclusion of life forms from patentability and for the WTO to be subordinate to the Convention on Biological Diversity (CBD). In fact, India has pleaded in its discussion paper that neither the implementation of current obligations under the CBD nor a system that ensures the protection of the environment, promotes food and health security and also farmers' rights should be considered as a dilution of obligations under TRIPs.

The US and Europe have rejected the developing countries' proposals related to 27.3(b) on the grounds that the WTO cannot be subordinated to other international agreements, which confirms the belief of the environmental movement that in the WTO environmental issues are always sacrificed for trade. Northern countries have, however, been put on the defensive in TRIPs as a result of the health movement against patents.

Brazil is the country that has made the most progress in producing low-cost AIDS medicines, providing AIDS therapy for US$192 per month. Starting in 1994, the Brazilian government urged local companies to start making drugs to treat AIDS. The government invoked "national emergency" provisions in its patent laws to start manufacturing low-cost anti-retrovirals such as AZT. Brazil makes eight of the twelve drugs used in the so-called AIDS cocktail. As a result, prices have gone down by more than 70 per cent. The availability of cheaper drugs enabled the Brazilian government to provide anti-retrovirals to more than 80,000 citizens by the end of 1999, which has led to a more than 50 per cent drop in AIDS related mortality between 1996 and 1999. This has also allowed the government to save US$472 million in hospitalizations.

However, instead of applauding Brazil for its success in fighting AIDS through generic drug production supported under the 1997 Patent Law and making this kind of law a model, the US has taken Brazil to the WTO dispute panel in order to force Brazil to undo its patent laws. If as a result US patent monopolies are globalized through TRIPs, then millions of AIDS victims in the Third World will be denied affordable treatment and thus their right to life. Pressure from social movements and resistance from Third World governments forced the US to withdraw its dispute against Brazil.

For the first time, a number of developing countries, including the African Group, Barbados, Bolivia, Brazil, the Dominican Republic, Ecuador, Honduras, India, Indonesia, Jamaica, Pakistan, Paraguay, the Philippines, Peru, Sri Lanka, Thailand, and Venezuela, submitted a joint paper to the TRIPs Council on TRIPs and Health. TRIPs, which was aimed at undoing the sovereign national legislation of countries in order to create corporate monopolies over seeds and medicines, was now being jointly challenged. TRIPs had put profits before survival, corporations before citizens.

The citizens' movements against TRIPs empowered Third World governments to demand that the WTO take such action as would ensure that the TRIPs agreement did not in any way undermine the legitimate right of WTO members to formulate their own public health policies and implement them by adopting measures to protect public health (see the TRIPs Council discussion on access to medicines, IP/C/W/296 WTO). Where TRIPs interferes in ensuring public health, the developing country members have called for changes in the provisions. The reform and review of TRIPs can no longer be scuttled by the powerful.

THE EMANCIPATORY POTENTIAL OF
THE STRUGGLES TO DEFEND BIODIVERSITY

Food and health are basic to survival, and biodiversity and knowledge are central to both. The globalization agenda, driven solely by corporate interests, had attempted to use the TRIPs agreement of the WTO and Western-style IPR regimes to appropriate the vital biodiversity resources of the poor and to transform seeds, plants, and medicines from sources of sustenance for people into sources of limitless profits for global corporations.

However, a decade of movements and struggles against biopiracy and TRIPs have now begun to have an impact. These movements are about both the rights of communities to be producers of knowledge, food, and medicine, and the rights of citizens to have access to basic needs. They are, by their very nature, pluralistic in content and form, but they share some basic principles, which include:

1. The natural right of farmers to save and exchange seeds.
2. The right of Third World communities to use their resources and knowledge freely to meet their needs.
3. The right of diverse cultures to the integrity of their knowledge systems and cultural diversity.
4. The right of all peoples to affordable food and medicine.

The struggles over biodiversity and IPRs thus cut across issue-based movements and provide an integrating perspective for people's rights. These struggles also open a space in which to define a post-globalization agenda. Globalization was in effect a takeover of people's spaces by corporations with the participation of states.

The anti-biopiracy and anti-TRIPs movements have problematized the role of the state and destabilized the power of corporations. Through the right to seed and the right to medicine, the popular movements have forced states to push back the power of both the biotechnological agribusiness and pharmaceutical giants and the G-8 countries. The withdrawal of the case by pharmaceutical corporations against South Africa and the withdrawal of the US dispute against Brazil in the case of producing affordable AIDS medicines are new directions in the politics of IPRs.

The movements against biopiracy and against TRIPs have also shaped a new pluralistic politics, a rainbow politics, which has the generosity and inclusivity of place for indigenous struggles and the defense of local sovereignty as well as for movements for basic needs and the defense of national sovereignty. Where people can meet their own needs using local resources and indigenous resources, neither states nor corporations should interfere in their autonomy and freedom. Where people's capacity for the self-provisioning of food and medicine has been undermined by historical processes, national systems have an obligation to ensure that the rights to basic needs are protected and that access to affordable food and medicine is guaranteed. Global corporations and global institutions like the WTO cannot have the right to prevent states from fulfilling their obligations to their citizens or of recognizing the sovereignty of their local communities. National sovereignty is thus a derived concept and rests on local sovereignty. It does not give the national state the power to undermine local structures but only the duty to defend the freedom of peoples and the obligation to meet peoples' basic needs.

This pluralistic politics also implies that the diversity of species, the diversity of knowledge systems, and the diversity of economic systems can flourish side by side. In place of the hegemonic relationship of the North with the South, corporations with citizens, humans with other species, the global with the local, and the modern with the traditional, a politics emerging from the struggles over biodiversity creates a context of cooperation and mutuality, equality and ecological sustainability. In the final analysis, the biodiversity movement is a movement that recognizes the value of every species, every person, every culture, every community, and every country on its own terms, rather than on the hegemonic calculus of piracy, profits, and predation.

BIBLIOGRAPHY

Enyart, James (1990). "A GATT Intellectual Property Code," *Les Nouvelles* (June 1990): 54–56.
Kadir, Djelal (1992). *Columbus and the Ends of the Earth: Europe's Prophetic Rhetoric as Conquering Ideology*. Berkeley: U. of California P.
Shiva, Vandana, et al. (2000). *Seeds of Suicide. The ecological and human costs of globalization of agriculture*. New Delhi: Research Foundation for Science, Technology and Ecology.

11

Social Movements and Biodiversity on the Pacific Coast of Colombia

Arturo Escobar and Mauricio Pardo

INTRODUCTION

Tropical rainforests have become the scenes of intense disputes and renewed undertakings for both older and more recent forms of capitalist penetration. The encroachment of capitalist enterprises in the Colombian Pacific had until recently focused mainly on agro-industrial and extractive industries, as well as on transportation, energy, and port infrastructure projects. Now, however, multilateral agencies of natural resources and biotechnology multinationals have begun viewing the use and regulation of tropical rainforests' living species as potentially profitable. Hence, in different parts of the world, groups of local people who have traditionally inhabited these areas are organizing against the rapid advance of these powerful economic and political agents.

In the Colombian Pacific these facts have had strong manifestations. Black and indigenous organizations have challenged the government in order to obtain legal recognition of their lands and authority, to counter the actions of timber, mining, and palm oil industries, as well as government projects that aim to build roads, hydroelectric plants, and ports in the region. More recently, these organizations have begun to participate in discussions against the marketing and patenting of species traditionally used or contained in their territories. The control of their lands constitutes the focus of their struggle, which also includes respect for their cultural specificities, the autonomy to decide their future, and the protection of their traditional knowledge.

In order to strengthen their struggle, these local communities' organizations have resorted to networks of allies at local, national, and international levels. Thus, black and indigenous movements have designed cultural and ecological policies that articulate different aspects of their search for the well being of their peoples through a constructive use of natural resources. These movements participate in circles of groups with similar interests—other ethnic organizations, international groups, local NGOs, and academic sectors—to voice their demands and positions in both national and global venues. The actions of these social movements concerned with biodiversity and the right to maintain their traditional knowledge are part of a broader view of society and nature, and defend cultural policies that oppose the dominant views engendered by the agents of capitalism.

Indeed, these movements' struggles transcend a simple desire for reform. By demanding the recognition of their rights, by constructing internal forms of authority that are alternatives to the power of the state and of capital, and by stimulating alternative systems of knowledge, they display emancipatory aspects. However, the spreading of the Colombian internal war to the Pacific imperils the goals of ethnic movements and threatens their future.

In this chapter, we analyze these facts in light of contemporary debates on biodiversity, the emergence and dynamics of ethnic movements in the Pacific, and their positions regarding nature and biodiversity.

NEW APPROACHES TO THE TROPICAL FOREST: THE IRRUPTION OF BIODIVERSITY

The capitalist system has used diverse exploitation regimes in tropical forests all over the world, particularly in the region of the Colombian Pacific. In most cases, both extractive and plantation regimes have caused great ecological damage in these fragile ecosystems. Hegemonic discourse has presented these vast territories as uninhabited and inhospitable, wild lands that need to be subdued in order to contribute to the economy and production of the national states containing them. More recently, the abundance and heterogeneity of tropical rainforest species and their bio-chemical, genetic, and molecular structure began to be considered as valuable resources over which different and conflictive use-strategies compete— interests represented by the state, capitalists, and social movements.

Inhabitants of these extremely humid wooded areas—whether tribal natives, forcefully displaced populations, such as labor for extractive com-panies, or peasants from other regions—have, in most cases, developed highly sustainable production forms that have low impact on the ecological system.

Recently, local rainforest populations have invoked the defense of their ancestral territories and the protection of the environment as their most noteworthy form of resistance against capitalist projects of exploitation of natural resources. They have demanded low-scale production systems based on reciprocity and cooperation, with an enormous symbolic load in terms of the relationship between society and nature.

The reason why so much attention is given to the rainforest nowadays is based on what we could call "the irruption of the biological" as a central social fact in twentieth-century global policies. After two hundred years of systematic destruction of life and nature, survival has emerged as an aspect of crucial interest for both capital and science through a dialectical process initiated by capitalism and modernity. Conservation and sustainable development have become pressing issues for capital, forcing it to modify its prevailing logic of destruction.

Events that have taken place during recent years in tropical rainforests suggest that what is at stake transcends policies for the defense of resources and the environment, or even policies concerning representation. One crucial point is defined by the multiplicity of constructions of nature in its most complex dimension: the contrast between the meaning/use practices of the various social groups. The existence of a cultural politics of nature in the social movements of rainforest inhabitants is evident, and it is also clear that its lessons extend beyond the forest itself. One of the most noteworthy aspects of this cultural politics is the resulting organized response in the shape of social movements.

"Cultural politics" is understood as the process that takes place when conflict arises between social actors who are shaped or characterized by different meanings and cultural practices. The notion of cultural politics is based on the assumption that both cultural meanings and practices—in particular those theorized as marginal, oppositional, minority, residual, emergent, alternative, dissident, etc., all with respect to a dominant cultural order—are sources of processes that can be considered political (Álvarez et al., 1988). This cultural politics alters the practices and familiar understandings of nature, at the same time as it attempts to free local ecologies, both mentally and in nature itself, from systems deeply rooted in class, gender, ethnic, and cultural domination.

The concept of biodiversity has transformed the parameters through which nature is valued, and also the disputes over the access to natural resources. The idea of biodiversity emerges from a quantification of the number of species in determined areas. These areas acquire a new visibility that makes them the object of a renewed interest on the part of actors as diverse as environmental movements, scientific and academic establishments, and indigenous organizations. Views of the environment acquire a rationality factor in which both the intervention of expert and technical knowledge and the sophisticated character of capitalist intervention sharply contrast with the control of natural resources on the part of local inhabitants (Instituto Humboldt, 1998: 18–22). The assignment of patents to living organisms or their components, deliberately disregarding the authorship of native peoples, is defined and argued in detail by Shiva (2000: 13–24) as outright biopiracy.

Projects for the "conservation of biodiversity"—almost invariably financed by northern NGOs and the World Bank's Global Environment Facility (GEF)—involve national planners and local communities in the complex policies of technoscience, which consider the genes of certain wild species as the key to the conservation of fragile ecosystems; this occurs in countries as different as Costa Rica, Thailand, Ivory Coast, Colombia, Malaysia, Cameroon, Brazil, and Ecuador. According to the basic argument, the genes of wild species constitute a precious library of genetic information, a source of wonderful medicines, and, perhaps, a stock of foodstuffs that could become very valuable products through biotechnology. Thus, the rainforest would be preserved at the same time that substantial profits were obtained, which would also benefit local inhabitants. The increasing interest in biodiversity is the result of a problematization of the biological, since it places rainforest areas in a crucial bio-political global position.

The key to biodiversity conservation, according to the view of the dominant institutions, resides in finding ways of using tropical forest resources that guarantee their long-term preservation. Such use must be based on a scientific knowledge of biodiversity, appropriate management systems, and adequate mechanisms that establish intellectual property rights protecting discoveries that might have commercial applications. Also known as "gene hunting," the prospecting of biodiversity presents itself as a respectable protocol for saving nature (WRI, 1993), since it is considered that the source of benefit and profit in terms of conservation resides in the genes of those species. Prospecting activities are already taking place in some "hot spots" of the Third World, with prospectors from North American and European botanical gardens, pharmaceutical companies, independent biologists, and Southern NGOs among others.

The apparatus for biodiversity production involves a series of different actors—ranging from northern NGOs, international organizations, botanical gardens, universities, and corporations to recently created Third World institutions for biodiversity, Third World planners and biologists, as well as local activists and communities. All of these have their own interpretive frame concerning biodiversity—what it is, what it should be, or what it could become. This discursive formation can be theorized as a network with a multiplicity of agents and places where knowledge is produced, debated, used, and transformed.

Thus, there are conflicts about how to get to know biodiversity and the ways in which it is known. Both scientific knowledge about the chemical components of species and traditional knowledge of the medical or economic use of those species are avidly pursued by pharmaceutical and biotechnological multinational companies, research centers, and state institutions. The biodiverse dimension of nature generates new fields of attraction for these varied actors and their respective interests. Commercial companies work on one of the most dynamic lines of contemporary capitalist accumulation in pharmacology, biotechnology, and genetics. State agencies manifest contradictory positions, oscillating between opening access to biological resources to national and multinational companies, placing biological resources under state control, or protecting the rights of the native inhabitants of biodiverse areas. In scientific and academic centers, some studies focus on the strictly biological while others conceive of biodiversity as part of a social reality that, in its turn, can be considered either as an unproblematic space or as the arena of conflict over access to and control of natural resources (GRAIN-GAIA, 1998).

A critical perspective on biodiversity from the viewpoint of political ecology includes the following set of propositions:

1) Although biodiversity has concrete biophysical referents, it should be considered as a recent discursive invention. This discourse is articulated through a complex network of actors, from northern international organizations and NGOs to scientists, prospectors, local communities, and social movements.

2) Through the cultural politics they generate, social movements propose a particular vision for the conservation and appropriation of biodiversity. By linking biodiversity to the defense of culture and territory, these movements offer an alternative framework for political ecology.

3) Particular aspects of the debates about biodiversity—namely, territorial control, alternative development, intellectual property rights, local knowledge, and conservation itself—acquire new dimensions; they can no longer be restricted to the technocratic and economistic prescriptions of the dominant positions. Marginal localities such as communities and social movements have begun to be considered as centers for innovation and emergent alternative worlds.

At the risk of oversimplification, it is possible to distinguish four main positions produced thus far by the biodiversity network. Each of these positions is in itself heterogeneous and diverse, and the network as a whole is therefore extremely dynamic and changing (Escobar, 1997a):

1. *Resource management: the "global-centric" perspective.* This is the vision of biodiversity produced by dominant institutions, particularly the World Bank and the major northern environmentalist NGOs backed by the G-8 countries (World Conservation Union, Nature Conservancy, World Resource Institute, and World Wildlife Fund, among others). It offers a set of prescriptions for conservation and the sustainable use of resources at inter-

national, national, and local levels. It also suggests appropriate mechanisms for resource management, including scientific research, *in situ* and *ex situ* conservation, national biodiversity planning, and the establishment of appropriate mechanisms for compensation and the economic use of biodiversity resources, mainly through intellectual property rights. This position originates in dominant views of science, capital, and management (WRI/IUCN/UNEP, 1991; WRI, 1994: 149–151). The Convention on Biological Diversity (CBD) has a preeminent role in disseminating this perspective.

2. Sovereignty: Third World national perspectives. Although the positions of Third World governments vary considerably, the existence of a national Third World perspective can be asserted. Without fundamentally questioning the global-centric discourse, this position seeks to negotiate the terms of the treaties and the strategies concerning biodiversity. Aspects not yet agreed upon—such as *in situ* conservation and access to *ex situ* collections, sovereign access to genetic resources, ecological debt, and the transfer of technological and financial resources to the Third World—are important topics in negotiation agendas.

3. Biodemocracy: the perspective of progressive NGOs. An increasing number of southern NGOs consider the dominant and global-centric perspective to be a form of bio-imperialism. Bio-democracy sympathizers emphasize local control of natural resources, the suspension of development mega-projects and subsidies for capitalist activities that destroy biodiversity, support for practices based on the logic of diversity, a redefinition of productivity and efficiency, and the acknowledgement of the cultural base of biological diversity.

4. Cultural autonomy: the perspective of social movements. The social movements that construct a political strategy for the defense of territory and of culture and identity tied to specific places and territories generate a cultural politics mediated by ecological considerations. Aware of the fact that "biodiversity" is a hegemonic construction, activists nevertheless acknowledge that its discourse opens up a space for the configuration of culturally appropriate developments, which can oppose more ethnocentric and exploitative tendencies. Theirs is the defense of a whole lifestyle project, and not only of "resources" or biodiversity (Escobar, 1997b).

From the four discourses about biodiversity just outlined, a fundamental asymmetry can be inferred between science and modern economy, on the one side, and the practices of nature, on the other.

The current phase of the globalization of capital implies that crucial issues

294 ANOTHER KNOWLEDGE IS POSSIBLE

related to the legal frameworks within which capitalist transactions are carried out (especially those that concern commercial and industrial property rights and trade regulations) are formulated in multilateral international arenas upon which core capitalist countries and multinational companies exert vast influence and power.

Conferences of Parties on the Convention on Biological Diversity (CBD) have been taking place around the world since the establishment of the Convention by more than 150 countries at the 1992 Earth Summit in Rio de Janeiro. In 1994, Colombia ratified CBD through Law 165, known as the Biodiversity Law. In the conferences, it was agreed that information and access to resources would be gradually opened for developed countries and private companies, but there is not yet protection for poorer countries and their local populations. There is strong pressure on the part of multinational pharmaceutical companies and the governments of advanced capitalist countries concerning controversial issues such as intellectual property, biotechnological patenting, and the privatization of biological phenomena, which are yet to be decided upon (Flórez, 2000; Instituto Humboldt, 2000: 56–59).

Nevertheless, CBD agreements, as well as those to be approved in the future, cannot affect previous conventions between countries. For this reason, the few international agreements for the protection of biodiversity, the rights of people bearing traditional knowledge, and long-term inhabitants of highly diverse environments, are subject to the WTO-regulated market dictatorship and regional agreements, with the risk of commercial sanctions. The imposition of purely capitalist criteria which ignore the consultation and debate processes has taken place, for example, in Andean countries that signed the Cartagena Agreement and that had already accepted biological patenting and exclusive commercial property of new plant varieties (see Andean Pact Decision 391 of 1996). In these agreements, the Andean Community declares the state as the sovereign owner of tangible genetic resources, i.e., of organisms in themselves (plants, animals), whereas traditional knowledge associated to indigenous and peasant groups is considered as an intangible component owned by such groups. Thus, it is the state that controls natural biological resources, disregarding the collective intellectual authorship of ancestral inhabitants in the development of species. According to Andean Pact agreements, when issuing licenses or patents to private companies, the state protects tangible patrimony, whereas local populations that own intangible patrimony must establish private agreements with the commercial companies (Instituto Humboldt, 2000: 59–60).

Thus, the future of the rights of ethnic minorities to control their own biological resources as well as their traditional knowledge depends to a great extent on the mobilizing of ethnic organizations and other sectors of civil society such as NGOs at the international and national levels, since within the current institutional framework the positions in favor of the market are predominant and also count on better resources to impose their points of view. Few governments, especially in Latin America, are willing to question the WTO or risk their reputation as sensible commercial partners of advanced capitalist countries. Those governments will not dare to challenge the WTO's free market principles in order to privilege the rights of local communities to control their traditional knowledge and to be recognized as the authors of the genetic realities of the varieties that they have domesticated.

The general position of the governments of core capitalist countries, as well as multinational companies, is cynically advantageous: free access to all natural resources but private property and restricted access to them once they have been appropriated and processed by industrial companies. Millennial knowledge about use, the domestication of species, or diversity conservation in traditional territories is not considered to be the patrimony of ethnic groups for which they should be given recognition and adequate compensation.

Intellectual property rights and patents are fundamental legal artifacts for the capitalist economy. These rights must be registered and enforced by special entities; they not only protect inventiveness and effort on the part of individuals and companies, but they also frequently entail a privatization of social use-values for individual profit. For ethnic groups, the privatization of components or biological properties derived from their knowledge or use also involves intrusion and threats to their territory and their autonomy, even if, as in the Colombian case, the rights to their land and autonomy have already been legally established.

Within a Western framework, profit emerges from innovations, which must be protected by intellectual property rights. However, in many peasant communities, innovation springs from within tradition. When a language of intellectual property rights is imposed on peasant systems, the benefits from community innovations end up increasing external capital (Gudeman and Rivera, 1990; Gudeman, 1996).

REDISCOVERING A REGION:
THE COLOMBIAN PACIFIC REGION

The Colombian Pacific region is a vast tropical rainforest area around 960 km long, its width fluctuating from 80 to 160 km (roughly 700,000 km^2). It extends from Panama to Ecuador, and from the slopes of the western mountain range (*Cordillera Occidental*) to the Pacific ocean. An approximate 60 per cent of the population inhabits a few cities and large towns, while the remaining population dwells in riverbank areas along the more than 240 rivers flowing from the mountains to the ocean. Afro-Colombians, descendants of slaves brought from Africa at the beginning of the seventeenth century for gold-mining activities, form the majority of the population, although the number of indigenous inhabitants amounts to approximately 50,000. The latter belong primarily to the Embera and Wounan ethnic groups and inhabit the northern part of the department of Chocó. Indigenous communities have maintained specific material and cultural practices, such as multiple economic and survival activities (involving agriculture, fishing, hunting, collecting, and small-scale mining), extended families and kinship relations, strong oral traditions and religious practices, particular forms of knowledge, and the use of diverse ecosystems, etc.

The black groups maintain and have developed cultural practices of African as well as of indigenous and Spanish origin: complex systems of rainforest utilization, extended families, special dances, oral and musical traditions, funerary rituals, witchcraft, etc. These activities are increasingly articulated with modern urban forms, due in part to internal and external migrations as well as to the impact of commodities, the mass media, and development programs. Although the region has never been isolated from world markets—gold and platinum bonanza cycles, precious woods, rubber, and timber industries (Whitten, 1986), and, as we soon will see, genetic resources, have linked the ethnic communities to the world economy—it was only during the 1980s that the region began to be taken into consideration and that policies were devised for its development.

What is now taking place in the Pacific region is unprecedented: large-scale development plans, new fronts opening for capital accumulation (such as African palm tree plantations and shrimp nurseries), and numerous indigenous and black mobilizations. Within this emerging imaginary, the Colombian Pacific region occupies an important place as a launching platform for the macroeconomy of the future (Escobar, 1996). The discovery of biodiversity in this region is one of the main components of this new imaginary.

Three main actors—the state, capital, and social movements—struggle to define the future of the region. Behind these actors stand different political and cultural orders whose genealogies and whose connections with socioeconomic and cultural rationales must be clarified. The study of each actor's cultural politics is important because the future of the region will depend, in great measure, on the ways in which it will be defined and represented. The cultural politics concerning nature in this region is based on three fundamental processes, which were simultaneously developed after 1990: 1) radical policies of opening to world markets, favored by the government in recent years, with special emphasis on the integration of Pacific-basin economies into those of the rest of the country; 2) new sustainable development strategies and biodiversity conservation; 3) more numerous and increasingly visible mobilizations among black and indigenous populations.

The present situation in the Colombian Pacific region is very special because the various factors involved in the debates about biodiversity, patents, and intellectual property rights over the use of biological species are deeply interconnected here. This area has been acknowledged as one of the most biodiverse in the world (García Kirkbride, 1986); its rural zones constituted by rainforests are inhabited by ethnic indigenous and Afro-Colombian groups deeply engaged in organizing themselves in defense of their rights. Moreover, the fact that the Colombian Constitution and Colombian laws acknowledge the rights of ethnic groups, and that Colombia officially participates in international fora about biodiversity, make the Colombian Pacific region one of the most crucial arenas for contemporary debates about biodiversity.

Since the late 1980s, the government has been pursuing a wide-ranging policy of integration with other economies of the Pacific basin. The Pacific Ocean—renamed "the sea of the twenty-first century"—is perceived as the socio-economic, and to a lesser extent cultural, space of the future.

ETHNIC MOBILIZATION IN THE PACIFIC REGION

Since the early 1970s, indigenous groups from all over the world, especially Colombia and elsewhere in Latin America, have renewed with particular intensity their struggle for survival. They now demand specific rights based on ethnic difference and no longer solely as agrarian social sectors in search of basic rights. These mobilizations have had an impact on multilateral arenas such as UNESCO, the ILO, and the UN. In particular, ILO agreement #169 involved a detailed acknowledgement of the rights of indigenous peoples of the world, and was sanctioned as law by many of the signatory countries. This was the case in Colombia, with the approval of Law 21 of 1991. However, as Flórez (2000: 5) notes, there is no national legislation or international agreements for the explicit protection of traditional knowledge from undue appropriation by multinationals buttressed by the governments of capitalist metropolises. The regulation of such activities is thus one of the urgent issues that ethnic movements see the need to target.

The irruption of the concept of biodiversity and its varied consequences has taken place in Colombia within a context of three decades of indigenous struggle and one decade of black community struggle for the collective ownership of their territory, respect towards their socio-cultural particula-rities, and autonomy of indigenous authorities. As a result of this collective mobilization of indigenous and black communities, Colombian legislation, by way of different constitutional regulations, laws, and decrees, now acknowledges these rights. But the ability of the Colombian state to enforce its own laws is extremely weak.

Indigenous peoples from the region are the minority group. Numbering around 50,000, they are almost all located in the northern portion of the department of Chocó. A much smaller group is based in the southern departments. In Chocó, black inhabitants have been organized since 1980 through the Embera Wounan Regional Organization (Organización Regional Embera Wounan, or OREWA). OREWA includes 150 local community councils or governments (cabildos). In the southern portion of the Pacific coastal forests there are much smaller regional organizations made up of Embera groups, known in the region as eperara siepidara. There are around 7000 Embera organized under the Antioquia Indigenous Organization (Organización Indígena de Antioquia, or OIA) and in the larger communities of the Chamí area in Risaralda. They inhabit the slopes of the mountainous range adjacent to the northern part of the Pacific coastal plain, in the departments of Antioquia and Risaralda, areas that have been the object of intensive colonization for almost a century. In the space between the mountain range and the Pacific jungle, in the Department of Nariño, around 5000 members of the Awá community are organized around the Union of the Awá People (Unión del Pueblo Awá, or UNIPA).

The organization of rural populations from the Pacific started to develop twenty years ago. At the time, a group of young indigenous high school students, supported by Catholic missionaries and inspired by the emerging organizations of indigenous peoples from the Cauca department in Colombia and other parts of Latin America, created the Embera Wounan Regional Organization of Chocó. This organization engaged in a struggle for the recognition of indigenous territories, respect for their culture, and the organizational linkage of all indigenous communities in the region. Two decades later, OREWA successfully registered property titles in reservations corresponding to the majority of indigenous lands and established local councils (cabildos) in almost all of the indigenous communities in Chocó (Pardo, 1997: 233). Throughout, OREWA has had to confront timber companies, mining businesses, road construction, hydroelectric projects, and, more recently, attempts to develop research on biological and genetic resources without previous consultation. The above-mentioned processes of organization in the areas adjoining the mountain range in the departments of Antioquia, Risaralda, and Nariño, as well as in the lowland coastal forests of Valle, Cauca, and Nariño, are somewhat more recent.

In the early 1980s, black population groups of the Atrato River, organized under the Atrato Integral Peasant Association, or ACIA (Asociación Campesina Integral del Atrato), involved the association, with missionary support, in the defense of their territory and natural resources against large timber companies, which had obtained great concessions from the state. After intense mobilization and tortuous negotiation with the government, ACIA achieved the acknowledgment of the communities' right to access and protection of enormous territorial extensions vital for their survival, and which previously had been considered wastelands. Only in recent years has the banner of cultural difference become the most important element of this black organization, particularly as a result of a new movement in the Pacific region. In this sense, there are two main factors: first, the developmental and capitalist assault on the region, fueled by the process of economic opening and the region's integration into the country; and second, the constitutional reform process that culminated in the election of the National Constituent Assembly and the replacement of the Constitution of 1886.

For the black communities of the Pacific, this was a unique opportunity to construct their identity according to cultural, political, and socioeconomic demands and proposals. Given the fact that blacks did not succeed in securing their own representatives to the 1991 Constituent Assembly, their situation was presented by the indigenous representatives. The cultural and territorial rights of black communities were finally included in Law 70 of 1993, two years after the promulgation of the new Political Constitution.

ACIA's experience in the middle Atrato region and its demands for the recognition of the collective character of the territory and its cultural distinctiveness were crucial in the process that led to the recognition of the rights of black populations in the 1991 Constitution. They were also fundamental for the emergence of a dynamics that led to the organization of the black communities in the whole Pacific area. In Chocó, shortly after ACIA, other organizations began to form along other rivers, such as the Baudó, the upper and lower San Juan, and the lower Atrato. Later on, as a sequel to Constituent Assembly discussions, activist organizations emerged in the greater urban centers with the aim of stimulating the organization of black rural communities within departments.

The new constitution gave unprecedented rights to ethnic and religious minorities and explicitly recognized specific rights for indigenous peoples, granting them unalienable territories in the form of reservations and recognizing their political autonomy. The constitutional change provided a new context for a series of social processes, black and indigenous organizations being the most visible among these. The new constitution ordered the promulgation of a law for the safeguarding of the territories, society, and culture of the black communities in the rainforests of the Pacific and similar areas. As a consequence, the government presented Law 70 of 1993, which was approved. This law established the creation of collective territories for the black communities of the Pacific, their administration by community councils, and other measures for the protection of the culture and society of these social groups.

The actions undertaken by black populations ten years ago with the aims of presenting their case to the Assembly, exerting pressure for the promulgation of Law 70, and participating in their own development, have extended the organizational process to the majority of black populations of the Pacific. These started as nuclei of urban activists, which disseminated information and educated black river-dwellers on the possibility of securing their territories as well as their own cultures. Later, in 1992, in order to promote debate on legislation related to black communities, the government provided resources for organizing workshops in the whole Pacific area. These resources were mainly awarded to incipient organizations in the departments, a fact that allowed them to consolidate their influence.

Mobilization and discussion during the Constituent Assembly (1990–1991) in preparation for the drafting of Law 70 (1992 and 1993) and its later disclosure were financed by the government, with significant leadership on the part of some fluvial basin organizations from Chocó and organizations from the departments of Valle, Cauca, and Nariño. In the latter, between 1993 and 1998, the Process of Black Communities—PCN—a network made up of more than 140 local organizations, played a leading role in the struggle for constitutional rights for black communities and the defense of their territories.

The PCN's most distinctive feature is the articulation of a political proposal whose character and base are mainly ethno-cultural. Their vision is not that of a movement based on a catalogue of "needs" and demands for "development" but that of a struggle presented in terms of defending cultural differences. Therein lies its most radical character. The PCN coordinated departmental organizations known as *palenques* in Valle, Cauca, Nariño, and on the Atlantic coast. With the advancement of the process of registration of collective territories, the influence of the PCN at the national level and that of the *palenques* at the departmental level has diminished as community councils consolidate.

At the third National Assembly of Black Communities (Asamblea Nacional de Comunidades Negras), where the PCN was formally constituted in September of 1993, the participants proposed goals such as the following: 1) reaffirming identity (the right to be black); 2) the right to the land; 3) autonomy, especially in the realm of politics; 4) the right to construct an autonomous perspective of the future based on black culture (Grueso et al., 1998).

Considerations about biodiversity and the rights of local populations over the region's biological and genetic resources occupy a prominent position in the mobilization agendas of both indigenous and black organizations of the

Pacific. Very important among contemporary anti-hegemonic expressions, the ethnic-territorial movements of the Pacific, be they Amerindian or black, have succeeded in removing vast territories from private, individual, and mercantile land property regimes and in placing them under local population control for sustainable use.

The struggle of these groups for controlling their territory and their natural resources has developed on several fronts: against the crudest extraction methods such as strip-mining and forest devastation; against infrastructure work such as roads, ports, and hydroelectric plants threatening community welfare; against capitalist forms of agro-industrial exploitation that endanger ecological viability or access to land (such as shrimp nurseries, palm tree plantations, and palmetto trunk heart exploitation); against attempts to explore genetic resources on the part of multinational companies; or against state regulations (such as in the case of access to mangrove areas and their inclusion in collective territories or the viability of including artisan mining in the mining code).

Thus, these movements have been struggling against different forms of exclusion, domination, and exploitation. Analogous to what Santos and Santos (2000: 18) observe, the movements have achieved creative results regarding the contradictions that emerged in the process of collective action, and have developed emancipatory relationships while confronting established power in different situations.

For activists, the defense of particular cultural practices of riverbank communities is a strategic decision, inasmuch as these practices are seen not only as forms of resistance against capitalism, but also as elements of an alternative ecological rationality. In this way, the movement is constructed on the basis of networks of cultural practices and meanings that are deeply rooted in riverbank communities and are part of their active construction of worlds (Melucci, 1989). Nevertheless, the movement conceives these networks as bases for the political configuration of an identity related to the encounter with modernity—the state, capital, science, biodiversity—rather than to timeless essences.

As prescribed by Law 70 (1993), the registration of Black Collective Territories in the Pacific has been taking place since 1997. The first title was granted to some localities of the Lower Atrato river in March of 1997; in February of 1998, the government gave ACIA the collective ownership of around 650,000 hectares in the Mid Atrato. Since then, smaller collective territories in different parts of the Pacific area have been legalized, in a process that has considerably changed organizational patterns in the three southern departments. The leadership of urban activists from the main towns and cities of the Pacific (Buenaventura, Guapi, and Tumaco) has progressively receded to give way to the community councils created by Law 70 as collegiate administrators of collective territories.

Most of these community councils have formed in sub-regional organizations, which, although they have not explicitly given up departmental organization, have gradually gained independence and autonomy. As collective property is legalized, urban activists lose their influence on rural communities, in spite of the fact that they are still quite visible and maintain communication with governmental institutions. Thus, the organizing pattern that has prevailed in northern Chocó since the mid-1980s, when the movement started—sub-regional associations of adjacent riverbank communities joined in the struggle for collective territory—is gradually consolidating in the southern part of the Pacific region (Pardo, 2000: 339). This is what activists and analysts of the black community movement have labeled "ethnic-territorial organizations."

Indigenous and black movements are thus involved in complex networks of national and international relations that help them deal with the isolation and anomie that the hegemonic system has imposed on them. Not only have they joined networks of anti-hegemonic globalization, but also several alliances and strategic coalitions have been implemented among black and indigenous organizations. Since indigenous communities began organizing seven years before black populations, this previous experience enabled them to support emerging black organizations in 1987, particularly ACIA. Shortly thereafter, in 1989, ACIA and OREWA promoted the creation of the Peasant Association of the San Juan River (ACADESAN), which led to the first meeting between black and indigenous communities. As a result of this meeting, the bold idea of creating an inter-ethnic collective territory was proposed (OBAPO, OREWA, and ACIA, 1990–1991). OREWA and other black organizations continued coordinating mobilizations to the point of jointly supporting the indigenous candidate of the Chocó region to the Constituent Assembly of 1991. The indigenous representative was elected and had a significant role in securing the titling of collective territories for black populations (Wade, 1995). Currently, in the Chocó region, these organizations continue coordinating their positions regarding certain issues, as well as their participation in public entities as mandated by legislation.

In the region to the south of Chocó, the indigenous population is considerably smaller and their organizations more recent. In this area, black organizations have formed in departmental federations (the so-called *palenques*), many of which are coordinated at the national level by the PCN (Process of Black Communities). These organizations' joint actions have recently produced important results regarding demands to include mangrove areas in the collective titles. The Ministry of the Environment argued that mangrove areas were considered public and therefore could not be part of collective titles. However, the organizations stated that the public status of the mangroves was violated when the state itself permitted shrimp companies to construct gigantic pools that seriously altered the mangrove ecology. Finally, in 2000, the government accepted the demand to include the mangroves in the titles, although not as unalienable property. In claiming control over mangrove areas, the movements continue to broaden their conception of nature-territory as a vital space of complex and varied interactions between populations and the environment, therefore fighting against the increasing incursions of capital to commodify nature.

Indigenous organizations form part of the Colombian National Indigenous Organization (ONIC), which maintains active and permanent international contacts with other ethnic, human rights, and environmental organizations that support grassroots movements. Black organizations have also established relations with international entities. International committees, mainly European, have visited the areas struck by war and violence. Both indigenous and black organizations have developed projects funded by international organizations from different countries. European Catholic organizations have been constant sponsors of indigenous organizations and of ACIA. Both black and indigenous leaders regularly participate in international forums and voice their positions. PCN activists, for example, have attended numerous international meetings, as part of both anti-globalization networks as well as black and environmental activist networks (Escobar, 2000). More recently, black and indigenous movements have been forced to appeal to all possible national and international contacts to seek solidarity and support in view of the brutal impact of war on the populations and territories of the region.

THE WAR EXTENDS TO THE PACIFIC

For six years, the struggles of grassroots organizations of the Pacific for the control and humanist use of their territories and natural resources have been dramatically affected by the irruption of the war that has devastated many other Colombian regions. The intensification of military confrontations has revealed that in addition to the economic, geopolitical, and biotechnological dimensions that led to different disputes for the region's control, its military character must also be considered. The region's characteristics make it a privileged space for the circulation of illegal weapons and drugs. The vast wilderness areas are ideal sites for armed groups to operate in. Within the geopolitics of war, military control of this territory has become immensely valuable. Paramilitaries are striving to extend their control towards the northwestern part of Colombia and in this way insure domination over the strategic Panamanian border. All armed groups want to control the passageways to the Pacific as well as the fast-growing coca plantations in areas inhabited by the black communities that are expanding towards the north of Nariño.

Furthermore, activities carried out by social movements regarding territorial control have affected the interests of capitalist investments in the region, which include timber, gold, and palmetto extraction industries, as well as extensive cultures of shrimp and African palm trees. This situation easily results in the emergence of armed groups that seek either to blackmail the companies or to harass social movement activists, which quickly degenerates into open confrontation between paramilitaries and guerrillas, with the occasional presence of the army.

As illustrated in the works of Romero (2000) and Uribe (2000: 25–26), confrontations among armed groups rarely lead to direct combat between their protagonists. The most generalized tactic is to insure territorial control by manipulating the local population through terror. When one of these armed organizations attacks another, it does so by eliminating or expelling the civilian population that had been previously subdued by their adversaries. For years, the northern sector of the Pacific region had been a rearguard for FARC. As part of the paramilitary project to dominate the Colombian northwest, in late 1996, these groups began raiding the populations of the lower Atrato, killing numerous people and leaders as well as forcefully displacing the majority of the population. The surviving leaders of the local black peasant organization, the Peasant Organization of the Lower Atrato (OCABA), which had received the first title for collective territories established by Law 70, were forced to flee and the organization virtually disappeared (interview with OCABA leaders, Quibdó, 1998). Thousands of inhabitants from the Lower Atrato River and the Chocoan Urabá were displaced, resulting in tremendous overcrowding at Quibdó, the capital of the department. Faced with governmental inefficiency, other social organizations expressed their solidarity by stepping in to obtain funding for meeting the basic needs of the affected population. The paramilitaries continued to move southwards, and by early 1999 were already in control of the principal populations.

For years, the Antioquia Indigenous Organization (OIA) proclaimed an "active neutrality" towards the armed conflict. This reluctance to get involved led to retaliation from FARC, which killed various indigenous authorities in Urabá and the western part of the department. This has deeply affected Emberá-Katío communities, whose members constitute the greater part of the organization. Shortly after, paramilitaries were making similar accusations and killing other community leaders.

In March of 2000, FARC tried to recuperate the lost territory by destroying the towns of Vigía del Fuerte and Bellavista in the mid-Atrato region, the heart of ACIA territory. A few months after the death of the Bellavista parish priest and a secular missionary, their boat having been attacked by a paramilitary motorboat, the entire population of the village of Neguá had to flee to Quibdó.

There is a permanent anxiety, and new confrontations are expected to happen at any given moment (Wouters, 1999: 265).

In the Nariño department, the southernmost part of the Pacific region, the war has also arrived with devastating consequences. The trajectory between Pasto and Tumaco, one of the two roads that connect the Andes with the coast in Colombia, has been a war area for approximately five years. In the neighboring area of Barbacoas, there is a strong ELN presence, and in the outskirts of Tumaco there have been threats and selective assassinations of black leaders who have denounced the abusive expansion of palm tree plantations and shrimp nurseries (Agudelo, 2000).

On the other road that leads to the Pacific, from Cali to the Buenaventura international port, the situation is also quite serious. FARC and ELN have been attacking this area for two years, and the paramilitaries have also begun to dispute the region. Similar situations have been occurring in the Pan-American route between Cali and Popayán. As is often the case, local communities have been the victims of killings, the destruction of towns, massacres, displacement, and generalized terror.

Thus, the region's situation is grim; the majority of the territories in which black and indigenous grassroots organizations operate are sites of armed confrontation. Armed groups aim to gain territorial control by inflicting terror on local communities. Faced with this situation, the priorities of the ethnic organizations often tend to center primarily on survival and denunciation, while the projects of territorial and natural resource protection have to be put on hold.

Accordingly, black and indigenous organizations have had to rely on previously constituted networks of national and international groups that support grassroots and human rights organizations. The Chocó organizations, particularly ACIA, have joined a campaign that gathered diverse sectors of the population together with the goal of declaring the region a "Peace Territory." The PCN has proposed the creation of "Protection Territories" for the southern departments, in which attacked or threatened civilian populations can seek shelter and rely on international monitoring systems (Agudelo, 2000). In recent years, displaced black communities have formed organizations that work closely with the ethnic-territorial organizations.

In mid-2000, the situation of indigenous communities in western Antioquia and in other parts of the country was so serious that the United Nations made a special appeal to the Colombian government to protect these communities caught in the middle of war. Nevertheless, towards the end of 2000, a FARC squad killed an OREWA leader, as well as the mayor of Juradó, on the coastal Panamanian border. Practically all major international human rights organizations have asked the Colombian government to act and protect defenseless populations caught in the crossfire.

However, the situation of displacement and aggression towards civilians has reached such dimensions in Colombia that the cases occurring in the Pacific region are just a few of the many in the rest of the country. Indeed, today Colombia is experiencing one of the most serious situations of displaced communities in the world, with more than two million people forcefully expelled from their homes.

ETHNIC MOVEMENTS AND BIODIVERSITY

Will social movements from the tropical forest be able to become important actors within the discourses that are shaping the future of the wilderness? Will they be able to jointly participate in the production of both technoscience and society, of nature and culture, which has been set in motion by the biodiversity network?

The adoption of cultural difference as the articulating concept of political strategy was the result of several historical factors, and was also linked to the wide-ranging debates fostered by constitutional change. In their re-interpretation of regional history, activists from the Pacific not only departed from an integrationist perspective, strongly rejecting the myth of racial democracy, but also highlighted the fact that black and indigenous communities from the Pacific have historically favored their isolation from both the national society and economy. They recognize, however, that such an ethics of isolation and independence is less and less plausible under current integrative tendencies and in view of the unavoidable presence of the mass media, modern commodities, etc. In this sense, the relationship between territory and culture is of the greatest importance. Activists conceive the territory as "a space for the creation of futures, of hope, and continued existence." The loss of territory is equated with "a return to the era of slavery."

It is from this recognition that an interest in diversity both emerges and provides a gateway to the future. It is not by chance then that several black professionals linked to the movement have decided to participate in a national project for biodiversity. Negotiations with the Bio Pacific Project (Proyecto Bio Pacífico, or PBP), a governmental conservation and research project financed by the Global Environment Facility, led black and indigenous organizations to participate in the planning process by disseminating strategies for the awareness and divulgation of biodiversity throughout the region. The activism of social ethnic movements has also succeeded in securing the participation of their representatives in the general assemblies and boards of directors of the regional corporations, which are the environmental authorities at department level. They also participate in the Institute for Environmental Research in the Pacific (Instituto de Investigaciones Ambientales del Pacífico), which inherited from the PBP both the archives and the mission of research and conservation of biodiversity in the Pacific region.

Even though they are aware of the risks that such participation entails, they are convinced that the discourse on biodiversity opens up possibilities that they cannot afford to ignore. Biodiversity can also be an important element in the formulation of alternative strategies for development. As activists themselves point out, they do not want any kind of conventional development, and yet they are less clear about what they do want. They also recognize that experts—ecologists, anthropologists, biologists, planners, etc.—can be important allies, which points to the possibility of a collaboration between experts and activists from social movements.

The notion of "territory" is a new concept in social struggles in tropical forests. Peasants are involved in struggles about land throughout Latin America. The right to a territory—as an ecological, productive, and cultural space—is a new political demand, which is presently promoting an important re-territorialization, i.e., the formation of new territories motivated by new perceptions and political practices. Discourses on biodiversity and capitalist dynamics in its ecological phase open up spaces that activists attempt to use as elements of struggle. This dialectic presents a series of paradoxes for the movement, including contradictory aspects such as defending local nature and culture by means of a language that does not reflect the local experience of nature and culture.

There are theoretical grounds for anticipating alliances between local communities and technoscience. The political advantages of such alliances cannot be discarded beforehand. The case of a certain number of Third World NGOs that have succeeded in articulating opposing views circulating inside the network, mainly due to new practices and new means such as electronic networks and preparatory UN meetings, can be instructive.

The ways in which nature has been understood and related to in the Pacific region are being transformed by the increasing penetration of capital, development, and modernity—including discourses about sustainable development and biodiversity. Present-day landscapes of both nature and culture are characterized by their hybrid character. Hybrid natures supposedly assume special forms in tropical forest areas. There, popular groups and social movements would seek to defend, through new practices, organic nature from attacks on the part of capitalist nature, in a possible alliance with techno-nature. In places such as the Colombian Pacific region, struggles for cultural difference are also struggles for biological diversity. What types of nature will it be possible to design and protect under these circumstances? Is it possible to construct a cultural politics about biodiversity that does not further promote the colonization of natural and cultural landscapes so typical of modernity? (Escobar, 1997b).

The struggles in the tropical forests of the world are positioned precisely at the point of convergence of different historical epistemic regimes, whose hybridization constitutes a unique form of postmodernity. These struggles would have exemplary stories to tell us about what "nature" has been, about what it now is, and about what it will become in the future. If it is true that philosophical practice is the creation of concepts—the construction of possibilities for life through new ways of thinking, imagining, and understanding (Deleuze and Guattari, 1993)—and that nowadays such a task implies renewing resistance against capitalism, activists in the tropical forests might be able to keep the dreams of other lands and peoples alive for the future. Utopian? Perhaps. But let us keep in mind that "utopia designates the conjunction of philosophy with the present. [. . .] Through utopia, philosophy becomes politics, bringing to an extreme the critique of its era" (Deleuze and Guattari, 1993: 101). Some of these utopias of nature and culture can be seen in the dissident practices of indigenous and black activists in the Colombian Pacific region.

DISPUTES OVER BIODIVERSITY IN THE PACIFIC REGION

In the face of national and international pressure related to the natural and genetic resources of this region, organized black and indigenous communities have prepared to wage an unequal and strategic struggle for control over the last territorial space in which they still have significant cultural and social influence. With respect to the possibility of diminishing state and capital predatory activities, discussions on biodiversity are of the greatest importance for indigenous and black movements. They have amply demonstrated the lesser impact of traditional systems on biodiversity, while deconstructing the perception that forests are being destroyed by poor indigenous people and blacks. Future developments related to biodiversity will be conditioned by three factors: the issue of peace and violence in Colombia, the ability to imagine and implement alternative development strategies, and the persistence and strength of the movement.

The construction of notions of territory and region in the Colombian Pacific is very recent. Early response on the part of black communities and organizations to the capitalist assault on the region of the middle Atrato (in timber and mining, especially) from the mid-1980s on was important for the construction of such notions. This assault, following William Villa's (1998) correct analysis, not only promoted the erosion of traditional production practices and the communities' modes of settlement and appropriation of the environment, but also forced these communities to delimit and defend their territory from outside invasion. This appropriation of the territory took a definitive turn when ACIA (Asociación Integral del Atrato) entered the scene; ACIA not only introduced the issue of ethnicity into the discussion but also started questioning the state. These struggles mark "the beginning of a new territorial order for the Pacific and the verification of the efficacy of a political discourse that articulates black cultural identity with a specific form of territorial appropriation" (Villa, 1998: 441).

It can be said that this articulation between cultural identity and territorial appropriation underlies the political ecology of the social movement of black and indigenous communities. The demarcation of collective black territories and indigenous reservations has led activists to develop a conception of territory that emphasizes articulations between settlement patterns, uses of space, and meaning/use practices concerning resources, which are expressed, in the case of indigenous populations, in ancestral cosmologies.

The "traditional production systems" of riverine communities, more oriented towards local consumption than towards the market and accumulation, have operated as forms of resistance. They have been sustainable to the point that they have allowed for the reproduction of cultural and biophysical ecologies and the definition of biodiversity as "territory plus culture." A vision of the Pacific as a "territory-region of ethnic groups" is closely related to this definition: a cultural and ecological whole that constitutes a space laboriously constructed through the daily cultural and economic practices of black and indigenous communities.

The territory-region is a conceptual unity as well as a political project. It is an attempt to explain biological diversity from within the eco-cultural logic of the Pacific. The territory is the space where communities appropriate the ecosystem through complex interactions with it. In contrast, the territory-region articulates the communities' life project with the social movement's political project; in other words, it is a political construction in defense of the territory and its sustainability. The territory-region strategy is essential to the strengthening of specific territories in their diverse ecological, economic, and cultural dimensions.

Could we say that this represents an alternative approach to biodiversity or even a legitimate political ecology? If the territory is an assemblage of projects and representations from which a whole series of behaviors and commitments can pragmatically emerge in aesthetic, social, cultural, and cognitive time and space—i.e., an existential space of self-reference from whence "dissident subjectivities" can emerge (Guattari, 1995a, 1995b)—then it is clear that the movements in the Pacific are promoting such a project. In this sense, what is at stake with respect to indigenous reservations and black collective territories is not "land," or even this or that community's territory. It is the concept of territoriality itself as a central element in the political construction of reality based on the cultural experience of ethnic groups. The struggle for territory is therefore a cultural struggle for autonomy and self-determination.

Territory, political autonomy, natural resources, authorship of developments, and biological uses are therefore all part of the same complex problem. The continued existence of rural ethnic groups is concomitant with access to their traditional territories and control over the natural resources contained in such traditionally managed territories. Therefore, the survival of ethnic groups also depends on the implementation of legislation protecting and guaranteeing cultural specificity and political autonomy. In this context, the struggles of ethnic groups to exert control over the uses of the biodiversity found in their territories, as well as over the applications of traditional knowledge associated with biodiversity, constitute an essential factor for their cultural and political survival.

In order to promote innovation in local emergent communities such as those in the Colombian Pacific region, while considering as well the applications of their knowledge in the global economy, it is necessary to consider the ways in which global knowledge can be linked to local practices in a positive manner. This approach directly opposes dominant proposals based on intellectual property rights and is related with the political ecology that social movements have configured. As Martínez Alier argues (1996), the conflict inherent to the debates on biodiversity, between economic and ecological reasoning, needs to be politically resolved. Otherwise, conservation strategies will result in the commodification of biodiversity. Is it possible to defend a post-economistic ecological production rationale? In practice, it appears that social movements are the strongest champions of "ecological economies." At least they refuse to reduce their territorial and ecological demands to the exclusive terms of the market, and this is a valuable lesson for any strategy aimed at biodiversity conservation (Varese, 1996).

Analogous to what Visvanathan concludes in his research in India, the ethnic movements of the Colombian Pacific face capitalist rationality with the logic of age-old production practices. These practices are in many aspects incompatible with the institutionality and discursivity of development grounded on a particular predatory and instrumental version of science and economy. Visvanathan states that the issue of traditional knowledge should be founded on a corpus of principles that questions Western knowledge; in other words, a worldview grounded on the creative use of nature and the moderate satisfaction of the needs of every society (Visvanathan, 2000: 36–42). Attempts to establish a fragmented vision of life (as genetic or biochemical components) and traditional knowledge (as having only potential capitalist value) in national legislations and international agreements can lead, according to Santos (2000: 22–24), to the rejection of native peoples' rights to be acknowledged as integral societies, carriers of non-fragmented knowledges and non-separable biological, economic, or social practices.

The ethnic groups of the Pacific region and their organizations have taken important measures with respect to biodiversity management and its related knowledge. The indigenous organizations OREWA, of Chocó, and OIA, of Antioquia, have issued bylaws on both the use and dissemination of traditional knowledge, whereby demands for those interested in researching natural resources are established. These organizations declare that traditional knowledge is the collective property of indigenous peoples. They affirm that all research projects must clearly benefit their community and that they must be submitted to previous consultation and analysis within local communities and the organization. Finally, all ulterior uses of research results must be agreed upon with the organization. OREWA has gone even further, indefinitely prohibiting any investigation related to traditional knowledge and genetic resources. Black organizations have also become aware of the importance of controlling the access to and use of traditional knowledge and research in collective territories. Most organizations require a consultation process for research projects.

Indigenous and black leaders have started taking part in international debates about biodiversity. The Conference of the Parties of the CBD, in Buenos Aires in 1996, for example, included indigenous and black delegates from Colombia who together agreed to propose a moratorium for research projects on biodiversity until the collective rights of ethnic groups are guaranteed. Colombian ethnic groups have already been able to see at close hand examples of uncontrolled bio-prospecting, such as an attempt to patent in the US some components of *yagé,* a sacred hallucinogenic, and the non-authorized collecting of blood samples from indigenous groups that were later sent to the US.

Biodiversity is a construction that constitutes a powerful interface between nature and culture, giving rise to a vast network of localities and actors through which concepts, policies, and ultimately cultures and ecologies are debated and negotiated. This construction is increasingly present in the strategies of social movements around the world. The social ethnic movement from the Colombian Pacific region, as we have seen, has generated a cultural politics that has significant ecological concerns, including biodiversity. It progresses through the slow and laborious construction of Afro-Colombian identities and the re-affirmation of indigenous identity, both of which are interconnected with alternative constructions of development, territory, and biodiversity conservation.

Although still incipient and precarious, the articulation of a linkage between culture, nature, and development represents an alternative framework of political ecology for discussions about biodiversity. One thing is clear: the distance that separates dominant discourses on biodiversity conservation and the political ecology of social movements is enormous and perhaps increasing. As we have shown, these movements' struggles have different and complex facets. They challenge the nation-state in order to achieve the right to exist as different societies with their own authorities and norms. They confront numerous economic agents who seek to profit from their territories and ancestral knowledge. They resist the irruption of war agents who do not respect any right. They create and extend local and international circuits of dissident actors that question the hegemonic order. These aspects of their struggles join the efforts of others who are building and connecting anti-hegemonic projects of diverse origins. Thus, these social movements are, to a greater or lesser degree, emancipatory expressions that strive for "the transformation of power into shared authority, the transformation of despotic might into democratic rights, and the transformation of regulatory knowledge into emancipatory knowledge" (Santos and Matias, 2000: 36).

BIBLIOGRAPHY

Agudelo, Carlos Efrén (2000). "El Pacífico Colombiano: de 'Remanso de Paz' a Escenario Estratégico del Conflicto Armado." Paper presented at the symposium "La Société Prise en Otage. Stratégies Individuelles et Collectives Face à la Violence—autour de Case Colombien." Marseille, November.

Álvarez, Sonia, Evelina Dagnino, and Arturo Escobar, eds. (1998). *Cultures of Politics/Politics of Cultures: Re-visioning Latin American Movements.* Boulder, CO: Westview.

Alonso, Margarita Flórez, (2000). "Can We Protect Traditional Knowledges?" Paper presented at the symposium "Reinventing Social Emancipation," U of Coimbra, 23–26 November. [Revised version reprinted in this volume: Chapter 9.]

Deleuze, Gilles, and Félix Guattari (1993). *¿Qué es la Filosofía?* Barcelona: Anagrama.

Escobar, Arturo (1996). "Viejas y Nuevas Formas de Capital y los Dilemas de la Biodiversidad," A. Pedrosa and A. Escobar (eds.), *Pacífico ¿Desarrollo o Diversidad?* Bogotá: Ecofondo—Cerec. 109–131.

——————— (1997a). "Biodiversidad, Naturaleza y Cultura: Localidad y Globalidad en las Estrategias de Conservación." *Colección El Mundo Actual.* México, DF: Unam/Ciich.

——————— (1997b). "Política Cultural y Biodiversidad: Estado, Capital y Movimientos sociales en el Pacífico Colombiano," M. V. Uribe and E. Restrepo (eds.), *Antropología en la Modernidad.* Bogotá: ICAN.

——————— (2000). "Notes on Networks and Anti-Globalization Social Movements." Paper presented at the session "Actors, Networks, Meanings: Environmental Social Movements and the Anthropology of Activism," 99th American Anthropological Association annual meeting. San Francisco.

García Kirkbride, Cristina (1986). *Biological Evaluation of the Chocó Biogeographic Region in Colombia.* Washington, DC: World Wildlife Fund.

GRAIN–GAIA (1998). "TRIPS o CDB: Conflicto entre comercio global y biodiversidad." Discussion document in the Fourth Conference of the Parties, CBD. Bratislava.

Grueso, Libia, Carlos Rosero, and Arturo Escobar (1998). "The Process of Black Community Organizing in the Southern Pacific Coast Region of Colombia," S. Alvarez, E. Dagnino, and A. Escobar (eds.), *Cultures of Politics, Politics of Cultures*. Boulder, CO: Westview. 196–219.

Guattari, Félix (1995a). *Chaosmosis*. Bloomington: Indiana UP.

——————— (1995b). *Chaosophy*. New York: Semiotext(e).

Gudeman, Stephen (1996). "Sketches, Qualms, and Other Thoughts on Intellectual Property Rights," Stephen Brush and Doreen Stabinsky (eds.), *Valuing Local Knowledge*. Washington, DC: Island Press. 102–121.

———————, and Alberto Rivera (1990). *Conversations in Colombia. The Domestic Economy in Life and Text*. Cambridge: Cambridge UP.

Instituto Humboldt (2000). "La Protección del Conocimiento Tradicional. Propuesta de reglamentaciónde la Decisión Andina 391 de 1996." Unpublished document. Bogotá.

——————— (1998). *Colombia, Biodiversidad Siglo XXI*. Bogotá: Instituto Humboldt, Minambiente, DNP, PNUMA, UICN.

Martínez Alier, Joan (1996). "Merchandising Biodiversity," *Capitalism, Nature, Socialism* 7(1): 37–54.

Melucci, Alberto (1989). *Nomads of the Present*. Philadephia: Temple UP.

OBAPO, OREWA, and ACIA (1990–91). "Etnocidio de Indígenas y Negros." *Ecológica* 6: 12, 19.

Pardo, Mauricio (2000). "Escenarios Organizativos e Iniciativas Institucionales en Torno al Movimiento Negro en Colombia," M. Archila and M. Pardo (eds.), *Movimientos Sociales, Estado y Democracia en Colombia*. Bogotá: CES/ Universidad Nacional—ICANH. 321–345.

——————— (1998). "Movimientos sociales y Actores No Gubernamentales," M. V. Uribe and E. Restrepo (eds.), *Antropología en la Modernidad*. Bogotá: ICAN. 207–252.

Restrepo, Eduardo (1996). "Cultura y Biodiversidad," A. Pedrosa and A. Escobar (eds.), *Pacífico ¿Desarrollo o Diversidad?* Bogotá: Ecofondo—Cerec. 220–243.

Romero, Mauricio (2000). "Los Trabajadores Bananeros de Urabá: De Súbditos a Ciudadanos?" Paper presented at the symposium "Reinventing Social Emancipation," U. of Coimbra, 23–26 November. [Revised, translated, and published as "The Banana Workers from Uraba: From 'Subjects to Citizens'?" chapter 9 in volume 1 of this collection, entitled *Reinventing Social Emancipation: Towards New Manifestos*: Boaventura de Sousa Santos, ed. (2006). *Democratizing Democracy: Beyond the Liberal Democratic Canon*. London: Verso.]

Santos, Boaventura de Sousa, and Ana Cristina Santos (2000). "The Homosexual Movement in Portugal: Subjects, Projects and Strategies." Paper presented at the symposium "Reinventing Social Emancipation," U. of Coimbra, 23–26 November.

Santos, Boaventura de Sousa, and Marisa Matias (2000). ' "Don't Treat Us Like Dirt': The Fight Against the Co-Incineration of Dangerous Industrial Waste in the Outskirts of Coimbra." Paper presented at the symposium "Reinventing Social Emancipation," U. of Coimbra, 23–26 November.

Santos, Laymert García dos (2000). "When Technoscientific Knowledge Becomes High-Tech Predation. Genetic Resources and Traditional Knowledge in Brazil." Paper presented at the symposium "Reinventing Social Emancipation," U. of Coimbra, 23–26 November. [Revised version reprinted in this volume: Chapter 6: "High-Tech Plundering, Biodiversity, and Cultural Erosion: The Case of Brazil"].

Shiva, Vandana (2000). "North–South Conflicts in Intellectual Property Rights." Paper presented at the symposium "Reinventing Social Emancipation," U. of Coimbra, 23–26 November. [Revised version reprinted in this volume: Chapter 10: "Biodiversity, Intellectual Property Rights and Globalization"].

Uribe, Maria Teresa (2000). "San José de Apartadó: A Peace Community or a New Foundational Pact." Paper presented at the symposium "Reinventing Social Emancipation," U of Coimbra, 23–26 November. [Revised and published as "Democratic Self-Determination: San José de Apartadó as a Community of Peace," chapter 10 in volume 1 of this collection, entitled Reinventing Social Emancipation: Towards New Manifestos: Boaventura de Sousa Santos, ed. (2006). Democratizing Democracy: Beyond the Liberal Democratic Canon. London: Verso.].

Varese, Stefano (1996). "The New Environmentalist Movement of Latin American Indigenous People," Stephen Brush and Doreen Stabinsky (eds.), Valuing Local Knowledge. Washington, DC: Island Press.

Villa, William (1998). "Movimiento Social de Comunidades Negras en el Pacífico Colombiano. La Construcción de una Noción de Territorio y Región," A. Maya (ed.), Los Afrocolombianos. Geografía Humana de Colombia. Vol. VI. Bogotá: Instituto Colombiano de Cultura Hispánica. 431–448.

Visvanathan, Shiv (2000). "Between Cosmology and System: A Heuristics for Globalization." Paper presented at the symposium "Reinventing Social Emancipation," U. of Coimbra, 23–26 November. [Revised version reprinted in this volume: Chapter 7: "Between Cosmology and System: The Heuristics of a Dissenting Imagination".]

Wade, Peter (1995). "The Cultural Politics of Blackness in Colombia," American Ethnologist 22(2): 341–357.

Whitten, Norman (1986). Black Frontiersmen: Afro-Hispanic Culture of Ecuador and Colombia. Prospect Heights: Waveland.

Wouters, Mieke (2000). "Derechos Étnicos bajo Fuego: El Movimiento Campesino Negro frente a la Presión de Grupos Armados en el Chocó," M. Pardo (ed.), Acción Colectiva, Estado y Etnicidad en el Pacífico Colombiano. Bogotá: ICANH—Colciencias. 259–285.

WRI (World Resources Institute) (1993). Biodiversity Prospecting. Oxford: Oxford UP.

————————, IUCN (World Conservation Union), and UNEP (United Nations Environment Program) (1991). Global Biodiversity Strategy. Washington, DC: WRI/IUCN/UNEP.

Part IV

THE RESISTANCE OF THE SUBALTERN: THE CASE OF MEDICINE

12

Marginalized Medical Practice: The Marginalization and Transformation of Indigenous Medicines in South Africa

Thokozani Xaba

INTRODUCTION

The collision of African political, economic, social, religious, and cultural practices with modern civilization has had an overwhelming and lasting impact on Africans. Within a short period of time, Africans were transformed from being peasants living on the produce of the land and their cattle to being forcibly incorporated into a universalistic, mono-economic, and mono-cultural world economic system. Together with such economic changes, their lives went through political, social, and cultural transformations through which the cultural, social, economic, and political practices and institutions were suppressed and marginalized.

This chapter is about the socio-cultural impact of the marginalization of African medical practices. It argues that modern development, which is intolerant of competing points of view, sought to change or supplant indigenous medical beliefs and practices with modern ones. Consequently, Africans find themselves constantly destabilized while the benefits derived from the holistic approach and the egalitarian nature of indigenous medicines are not being realized. Instead, Africans are subjected to modern practices, among which are the *invasive techniques* of "scientific" medicines.

This chapter also argues that, while some proponents of modern civilization believed in and practiced it like a religion, their dogmatism blinding them to the value of indigenous practices, others were motivated by economic competition, which spurred them to remove any form of competition emanating from indigenous practices. Among the historical bastions of development were political institutions represented by the state, the religious institutions represented by missionaries, and the medical and pharmaceutical institutions representing "scientific" medicine.

The argument in this chapter is divided into five sections. The first section provides the theoretical trajectory of the arguments for and against development. The second section discusses the "ideal typical" African indigenous medical practices that had evolved before the advent of colonialism. The third section shows how African indigenous medical systems were undermined, circumscribed, and prevented. The fourth section addresses the consequences of the disruption of and the restrictions on indigenous medical practices. The last section is the conclusion.

DEVELOPMENT AND ITS MALCONTENTS

This chapter looks at "development" as a descendent of what has been referred to as "modern civilization." "Modern" in "modern civilization" refers to the epistemological foundation of the worldview that is considered "scientific." The concept "development" has been (and continues to be) a bone of contention and has metamorphosed from colonialism/imperialism, modernization or civilization, and development/underdevelopment/dependent development to globalization. However, it remains that development still largely refers to the Westernization of the world. That is, making the rest of the world conform to the economic, socio-cultural, and political norms that have developed in the "West."

The advocates of this view and their followers saw colonialism as a catalyst to bringing the advantages of development to people in other parts of the world (the "South").[1] They identified the economic, political, cultural, religious, and social institutions of the people in the "South" as a stumbling block to the potential progress realized in the "North"[2] (Hoselitz, 1960; McClelland, 1961; Inkeles and Smith, 1974). They prescribed ways and means to manipulate, alter, and destroy those institutions and aspects of the "South" that blocked progress to development (Huntington, 1968; Parsons, 1951). In pursuing such a project, they did not always agree among themselves. However, originating from people who held similar beliefs regarding the appropriateness of propagating the advantages of development, the critiques were meant to strengthen the argument for the proliferation of the practices, values, and institutions of development.

There were various detractors of the promise and the strategy of development. One set of opponents of modern civilization rejected the superiority of "modern" values and institutions implied in the propagation efforts. They renounced the claims of progress and popular welfare implied in neo-classical economics (Hobsbawm, 1963; Scott, 1976) and politics (Myrdal, 1968), as well as the displacement of traditional behavior and practices and their replacement with practices based on "rational" individualism (Hirschman, 1965). Instead, they tried to uncover the rationality of the behavior and institutions of the people in the "South" (Scott, 1976; Popkin, 1979).

The more radical critics identified the state as an arena of conflict that reflects power relations in society and not as a custodian of popular welfare or a representative of democratic sentiments (Baran, 1952; Frank, 1967; Cardoso, 1972). They argued that the causes of such conditions were not unrelated to the relations of the "center" and the "periphery." This group considers alienation, resistance, and protest in the "South" as an expression of the loss of control by ordinary people as opposed to the dominant groups (especially, ordinary people's relation to technology and the organization of work and life). This argument is best represented by the writers of the Frankfurt School (e.g., Marcuse, 1964, and Habermas, 1984).

Writers in the "South" and their supporters highlight the role of culture in development. They argue that the "scientific" proclivity of modern civilization leads to the technocratization of society, which not only does not serve popular interests but is inimical to them (Parekh, 1989; Verhelst, 1987; Nandy, 1987; Marglin, 1990; Nandy and Visvanathan, 1990). Gandhi decries the mechanization that was followed by technological inventions, and which turned humans "into helpless and passive victims of its inexorable momentum" (Parekh, 1989: 23). The social, cultural, and natural environmental deterioration is blamed on the bureaucratization of society that removes decisions from ordinary people and vests them in the bureaucratic institutions of the state. Consequently, Gandhi continues,

> Modern man has become abstract and empty, he is not internally or organically related to others and his relations with them were not grounded in the sentiments of fellow feeling and good will. [. . .] Morality has been distorted, other people matter not because one cares for them but because the laws demand it, rather than a fulfillment of man's nature, morality is seen as a necessary but painful restriction on freedom, morality has been reduced to its barest minimum i.e., the need to prevent people from destroying one another. [. . .] A society of unrelated beings gets dominated by fear, hostility and tension [. . .]. Modern man spends most of his time trying to steady himself in a hostile and unsteady environment. He lives outside himself and exhausts himself physically and spiritually [. . .]. The exploitation of others was built into the foundation of modern civilization [. . .]. That is why modern civilization rests on and is protected by massive violence (against others, animals and the environment) (Parekh, 1989: 23, 24, 25).

While Gandhi throws light on the consequences of the technocratization of society, Banuri (1990) maintains that the development of the "South" has been disadvantageous, not because of bad policy advice or malicious intent of advisers, nor because of the disregard of neo-classical wisdom, but rather because the project has constantly forced indigenous people to divert their energies from the *positive* pursuit of indigenously defined social change, to the *negative* goal of resisting cultural, political, and economic domination by the West. [Emphasis in original]

He goes on to insist that, to improve welfare in the "South," the West should stop imposing measures of "development" (such as "quality of life" indices) because such measures "disenfranchise people," "make it unnecessary for their opinion to be sought," and "make it impossible for them to change their preferences in the face of manifest problems."[3] He insists that the right to define welfare and progress should be "unconditionally restored to indigenous people." Along the same lines, Verhelst (1987) insists that "poor people have a right to be poor" (i.e., to remain outside the "world system" that oppresses them). Banuri is, however, under no illusion that the people in the "South" will necessarily succeed where development professionals have failed, and maintains that, "unlike the latter, they will learn from their mistakes and they will adjust their behavior, instead of continually trying to rationalize their errors, or to justify their actions, their privileges, and their right to intervene."

This chapter is interested in that process of "disenfranchisement" that forced Africans to abandon what was useful in the indigenous cultural and medical systems for the products of "scientific" medicine. It argues that the universalizing process of development in South Africa disembedded Africans from their epistemological foundations. Consequently, the decentered Africans have lost and are losing some of the essential qualities of their cultural practices. One such cultural practice is a holistic view of health and illness and of the causes and cures of illnesses. The "scientific" medicine that has been imposed on them, however, not only ignores the remedies of indigenous medicines and practices but also seeks their suppression. Therefore, some of such remedies have been lost and are increasingly being diminished among the compendium of medicines consulted by Africans when they face "manifest (medical) problems." Consequently, the advantages of a *holistic, non-invasive,* and *egalitarian* medical system are being systematically undermined. Also, as a consequence, the possible benefits of the cooperation between indigenous medical practitioners and the practitioners of "scientific" medicine remain unrealized.

The chapter also maintains that "scientific" medicine has achieved its elevated position not because of its superior powers but because of the power of the state to proscribe and marginalize indigenous medicines and practices and also because of the dominant position of those who espouse modern ideas of health and progress. There is a tendency among the critics of development to always impute ideological interests to its proponents. However, in South Africa, many of the zealous proponents of "scientific" medicine are spurred by the threat to their pecuniary interests. Such interests are presented in the ideology of modern civilization that does not accommodate other points of view.

INDIGENOUS AFRICAN SYSTEMS OF HEALING

Long before the advent of Europeans on the African landscape, Africans had developed "medical systems" that they used in the prevention and cure of diseases and illnesses. Those medical systems were founded on the archeology and epistemology of African religions. In such religions, a person is more than the body that stands in front of you but the personification of past, present, and future relations between the living and the dead. As such, those types of ailments and suffering that seem to have no evident cause and that defy recognized forms of relief are considered to originate from fractures in the relations among the living or between the living and the dead or the spirit world. Accordingly, the solutions for such suffering emerge from the restoration of the *status quo ante*.

The system of medical knowledge that evolved was egalitarian and not all the preserve of specialists. As part of this system, the average person and household were exposed to general medical knowledge that enabled them to remain healthy and to cure minor ailments. Each household had a designated "medicine man" who looked after the health of the family. When the family's "medicine man" was not successful, the patient was referred to the professional medicine man. The practice of having a "medicine man" in each household ensured that medical knowledge and skills were widely available. The ready availability of medicines in plants and animals ensured the egalitarian nature of the system.

When an illness was considered to be more than just a body ailment and seemed to have no understandable material cause, a *sangoma* (diviner) and an *inyanga* (herbalist) were consulted.[4] Steeped in the understandings of African cosmology and cosmogony as well as in the epistemology of African religion, *izangoma*[5] and *izinyanga*[6] practiced a holistic approach to medical treatment. The *sangoma* would identify the origins and causes of the ailments or sickness, would advise the family of the causes of the ailment and the necessary rites that had to be fulfilled, if any, and would then refer the ailing person to a medicine man who would help him or her. In the event that the solution to the ailment or suffering lay in the performance of certain rites, a designated person or the *sangoma* herself or himself could assist the person or the family in the performance of such rites.

In the event that the suffering required the interventions of an *inyanga*, a *sangoma* would refer the person to a qualified *inyanga*, who would provide him or her with the necessary medicines to cure the ailment. As part of their arsenal against ailments, *izinyanga* produced medicines from various types of plants, roots, and animals as well as mixtures of such plants and animal products. *Izinyanga* were assisted by their students in the procurement, preparation, and administration of medicines. Such assistance was part of the students' education, which was understood to take anywhere between ten years and a lifetime (Gumede, 1990: 154)

The causes of suffering for which *izangoma* and *izinyanga* were consulted ranged from *abathakathi* (wizards and witches), *izigigaba* (calamities or catastrophes), *izimila* (swellings and tumors), *imikhuhlane* (colds), *izishayo* (visitations), *imimoya emibi* (wanton spirits), to *abaphansi* (ancestral spirits) (Gumede, 1990: 43–47). There were specialists for the various kinds of ailments from which Africans suffered (Ngubane, 1977: 105–106).

Izinyanga and *izangoma* treated their patients both as in- and outpatients. The inpatient came to live with the indigenous healer at his or her home. Often, a relative accompanied the sick person and stayed with them at the healer's lodge until the sick person got well (Ngubane, 1977: 106). The presence of a relative during treatment provided emotional and psychological support to the sick person.[7] The outpatients traveled between their home and the healer's residence or place of practice.

When *izangoma* were banned through various Anti-Witchcraft Acts (discussed below), the need for divination and healing did not suddenly disappear. Some of the work done by *izangoma* was taken over by *abathandazi* (Christian diviners) who, because they were a new phenomenon and largely unknown, could function under the cover of church garments. *Abathandazi* function in that liminal space between *izangoma* and Christian religious healers or mediums. Their knowledge is informed by (and balances) both African and Christian epistemology and cosmology. Their methods of intervention range from prayer, using the name of *Jesu* (Jesus) or *Mariya* (Mary, Jesus' mother), to the use of blessed water and other objects, as well as the use of indigenous medicines.

Most notable among *abathandazi* are Mr. Isaiah Shembe, the 1911 founder of *Isonto LamaNazaretha* (the Nazareth Church), who became an eminent religious leader, prophet, and a prolific religious songwriter, as well as Mr. Maphithini Thusi (a child of *isangoma* [Gumede, 1990: 192] who in the 1930s founded the *eMakhehleni*[8] Church, which adopted the Zulu code of living and social structure). There were many other *abathandazi* who worked during the times of Prophet Shembe and Prophet Thusi, and there have been many others since then. Those who became successful started their own African Independent Churches, such as the African Faith Mission, the African

Free Bapedi Church, the African Native Ndebele Church, the African St. John Baptising Church, and the New Jerusalem Church, among various other Zionist and Ethiopian churches. Many others did not start any churches but serviced the public from their own houses and even from the backyards of their rented houses.

Unlike "scientific" medicine—which requires a person to hand over the custody of their body to the experts to do with it what they like so that the patient learns nothing from his or her ailments, develops them again, and is treated in the same manner (Parekh, 1989: 27; Jarret-Kerr, 1960: 36–37)— the methods of treatment of indigenous medicines are less invasive and have greater advantages for the patient. Their advantage is that they assist people to "acquire a greater understanding and control of their bodies by explaining to them the causes and etiology of their ailments, how to prevent them and how they [are] integrally related to their way of life" (Parekh, 1989: 26–27). They also activate and energize the body's internal rhythms, resources, and built-in intelligence necessary for self-protection and healing. Scientific medicine, on the other hand does not

> see ailments as a cry by an overworked body for rest and discipline, but as an unacceptable interference with its routine, requiring an immediate and effective response. The body is not allowed to cope with illness at its own pace. The body is turned into a battlefield where armies of ailments fight armies of chemicals in a deadly contest in which the body becomes the casualty (Parekh, 1989: 26–27).

The system of indigenous medicine that had developed prior to the arrival of Europeans on the African landscape had three main characteristics.[9] It had a *holistic* approach to health and illness. Its *egalitarian* nature ensured that the medicines were readily available and that the knowledge was not the preserve of only specialists. Its methods of treatment were *non-invasive* and relied on the participation of patients in the healing process.

That system of healing was affected by the challenges to African culture and beliefs that were systematically introduced through labor, education, conversion, and the administration of African affairs by the state. This is the point to which we now turn.

THE "TROJAN HORSE" STRIKES

The marginalization of African religions, customs, and practices was methodical and was effected by means of the "Trojan Horses" of labor, Christianity, missionary education, and the roles that both the state as well as the medical and pharmaceutical establishments played. In reality, these four processes were not always in harmony with one another. In fact, at times, colonizers and missionaries found themselves on opposite sides of important issues. However, what united them was the zeal to "develop" Africans (i.e., to change not only the manner in which Africans lived and behaved but also the way they looked). These four issues are considered separately here for analytical reasons. Together, they reveal that, in order to disembed Africans from their epistemological anchor and to entrench modern civilization, the integrity of African ideas of civilization, culture, and morality had to be discredited and destroyed.

Labor and the marginalization of African practices

Africans were distanced from their religious and cultural practices through the systematic erosion of those practices. One way in which this happened was by the forcible removal of Africans from their cultural setting and by compelling them to labor in the mines and factories. This section addresses the role played by forced labor and the work environment in distancing Africans from their practices. As Lord Selborne said, "There will be no surer way of teaching them [Africans] to work than by increasing their wants, and especially the wants of the women. These wants can be engendered, and are engendered constantly, by contact with whites; but education wisely directed, may do much to assist the movement."[10] The wants to which Selborne refers are some of what Atkins (1993) refers to as "gates of misery." They were part of a larger strategy to deprive Africans of their means of livelihood so that they would seek employment either on farms or in urban areas. The accompanying strategy was to require that every African man above the age of 18 pay a certain amount in direct taxation to the central government.[11] The requirement was vigorously and implacably applied; the penalty for failure to pay taxes being imprisonment. Jabavu (in Schapera, 1967) discusses the case of men who were arrested while attending services in churches and of funeral processions that were disrupted due to men being arrested for failure to produce evidence of tax payment.

The mines and factories to which Africans were driven in order to fulfill their wants curtailed their freedom and degraded their humanity. The work they did was not only meaningless and unfulfilling but was also dehumanizing. The functions they performed at work were disembedded[12] from the social context that they left behind and only became meaningful in as much as the wage could be used to pay taxes, buy food, and pay rent. Their socialization into the rhythms of industry (such as living in cramped quarters and altering the relations between young and old) represented not only the denigration of their cultural practices but also their subjugation to the repressive "laws of industry."

Not only were Africans expected to work in disembedded conditions, they were also expected to dress differently (i.e., to discard their indigenous clothes and to wear "European" clothes). The command that "All [Africans] should be ordered to go decently clothed" (Magubane, 1979: 61) was made for various reasons. Christians and other Victorian Europeans considered Africans to be unclothed and, having been taught to be ashamed of their bodies, considered it scandalous that Africans should be allowed to walk "naked."

The requirement for Africans to wear European clothes brought the missionary and the clothing manufacturers closer together since the requirement served the economic interests of those who stood to benefit from selling clothing to Africans.[13] The enforcement of a "dress code" was supported by other positive reinforcements that rewarded Africans for "washing their bodies" and covering their "nakedness." Not being arrested was reward enough. The fact that employers increasingly insisted that workers be "decently" clothed made it imperative for those seeking employment and those seeking to keep their employment to discard their African attire, if only for the duration of their employment. The demand for clothing was made even though it was detrimental to the lives of Africans.[14]

Africans were not only expected to change their outward appearance, they were also expected to change the manner in which they perceived themselves. The pass offices, labor bureaux, and other employment offices were disinclined to give work-seekers permits to Africans with African names. In order to get a permit, one had to fill out government forms that required a "Christian name," and this was understood to refer to an English or Afrikaans name. A Christian name, up until the 1990s, was a sign that one was a member of a church. Therefore, Africans were forced to buy church membership at a price, after which they would be given a baptism certificate with a Christian name. In the early days, when many Africans could not read and write, the official bureau took the Christian name from the baptism certificate or simply gave one to the African. While the names may have been forced on people initially and some may have even disliked their English or Afrikaans names,[15] the urban environment made such names more acceptable than African names. Some even developed a dislike for their given African names.

All the foregoing work-related factors conspired to ensure that urbanized Africans tended to move closer to the "modern" culture of the cities and away from their African religion and cultural practices. The recently arrived African who still held on to African religion and practices was increasingly considered a relic of the past (Mayer, 1961). Because he/she did not understand the ways of the city, he/she was considered "stupid" and "backward." The lack of understanding the city was thrown into the same pot with his/her belief in African religion and practices and together produced an attitude that looked down upon African religious and cultural practices. How else could African religion and cultural practices be considered if the people who practiced them were considered "stupid" and "backward"? Claiming belief in African religion became the equivalent of claiming "stupidity" and "backwardness."

While compulsion was used to force Africans to discard their "nakedness," Christianity and education were used to make them sufficiently ashamed of their bodies and embarrassed by their own culture so that they would always be clothed, in the Christian sense. A discussion of this subject follows.

"Missions" and the marginalization of African religion

The stream of missionaries who descended upon Southern Africa were inspired, among other things, by the ideal of bringing light to the "dark continent" (see Gelfand, 1984). They condemned African beliefs as inferior to their own and instilled a spiritual dictatorship that mandated Christianity as the one and only true religion. They systematically worked towards uprooting and destroying all "heathen beliefs," customs, and practices in order to replace them with Christian ideals and Christian ways. In their campaign against heathen practices in South Africa, missionaries found support from the state[16] and almost every European (miners, farmers, diamond diggers, and other fortune seekers) (Eiselen, in Schapera, 1967: 65). They, however, were on their own in spreading the gospel to Africans.

The activities of the missionaries did not go without opposition. Since they attacked the organization, customs, religion, and practices of Africans, their efforts were resisted. They were resisted because they exercised authority over converts in ways that challenged the authority of amakhosi[17] (chiefs) and izinduna[18] (headmen) (Eiselen, in Schapera, 1967: 69–70). They separated converts from their group and harbored them as refugees. In such internal colonies, called "missions," the missionaries had free reign to distance Africans from their institutions, culture, customs, and practices. The "mission" refugees were not sufficient. Missionaries continued to proselytize among those who had not decided to emigrate, mentally and physically. They used all manner of subterfuge to convert Africans. For instance, they used medical missionaries[19] to draw Africans to Christianity (Gelfand, 1984: 20–21). While preaching the brotherhood of man, they instilled religious intolerance towards African religion and assaulted the organization of the African family, the socialization of children, as well as the rites of passage conducted at different stages of the lives of Africans. To lure Africans to the refugee camps of missions, some missionaries even dangled political and social rights (which were, supposedly, enjoyed by "mission" Africans) in front of unconverted Africans (Eiselen, in Schapera, 1967: 80).

The triumph of the missionaries' work among Africans was realized in the proliferation of churches of different denominations among Africans, Christian Societies and Associations, as well as in the numbers of those who proclaimed themselves either "Christian" or "saved." The success of the "scare tactic" of threatening burning in an eternal fire of brimstone can be seen in the numbers of people who were "afraid of dying without being baptized" (Jarret-Kerr, 1960: 22). The many denominations and churches signified the numbers of Africans who had finally been persuaded that their own religion was nothing but obscurantism and superstition. Such people discarded their pagan ways and adopted "civilized" and Christian morals and conduct.

The manner in which better educated and Christian Africans see themselves *vis-à-vis* the poor and "uneducated" African was aptly captured in the comments of one of Mayer's respondents:

> The difference between a Red man and myself is that I wear clothes like White people's, as expensive as I can afford, while he is satisfied with old clothes and lets his wife wear a Red dress. After washing, I smear Vaseline on my face: he uses red ochre to look nice. He is illiterate whereas I can read and write. I want to educate my children, but he just wants to circumcise his boys so that he should have a daughter-in-law. A Red man attends sacrifices but I attend church. I pray for my sins when I am sick. He knows nothing about sins and approaches a diviner for his illnesses. I was baptized, he was sacrificed for. I must not use any words that are obscene, but he uses any type of words, even in the presence of his elders without fear of rebuke (Mayer, 1961: 21).

It is doubtful whether many contemporary African Christians would express the differences between themselves and those who "do not believe" as clearly as Mayer's respondent.

However, the conversion to the new faith was not completely total. For many, the Christian message had to be tempered with the message of African epistemology, cosmology, and cosmogony. Through such a view, African Independent Churches (AICs) were born. The open acknowledgement of the value of African beliefs in AICs allowed the believer to claim both African beliefs and Christianity. As such, the believer who is a member of an AIC may not have a religious reason to deny consulting *izinyanga* or *izangoma*.

For the most part, the African leadership of the other Christian Churches (Methodists, Lutherans, Catholics, etc.) does not openly acknowledge the value of African traditional beliefs. Nonetheless, the behavior of "believers" in these churches suggests a belief system that is much more nuanced than that which is preached by the church leaders. The behavior of African Christians, by and large, reveals that they do not subscribe to the Christian view that sees the world in terms of the polar opposites of "Christian" and "heathen." Such an environment leads to believers saying one thing and doing another. It is most likely that it is believers in such churches who would deny their consultation of *izinyanga* and *izangoma*.[20] The followers of Reverend Livingstone September are among those who have found comfort in a mixture of Christianity and the practice of African cultural healing rituals, and they are not ashamed to show it:

Reverend Livingstone September is a St. Joseph's Apostolic Church spiritual father and faith healer. People bring water, in various containers, to him to bless. Sometimes, owners of the containers of water even attach notes with special wishes that they expect fulfilled. People sprinkle the blessed water on whatever they want blessed or protected from evil, such as their homes, cars, themselves, etc.

> Over and above the blessed water, people can get various medicines; such as ashes of burnt wood to cure sores and cancer, diluted vinegar for drinking and bathing which cures broken bones, help the paralysed walk, and the barren give birth. The reverend also helps people who have marital problems, do not get along with their employers, or cannot find work. A white rope worn around the waist helps in the prevention of worries, a red one across the forehead wards off bewitchment. (*Sunday Life Magazine*, 4 February 1996: 16–19).

From the outside, Reverend September's church looks like any other Christian church. But from close up, it appears quite different. Some of the practices conducted in the church may be considered by some to be even un-Christian.

This section has discussed the work of missionaries in converting Africans to Christianity. While many converted, many more tempered their conversion with African cultural practices, thus subverting the notion that the two forms of beliefs are mutually exclusive and that one is superior to the other.

The education of Africans

The missionaries' initial motivation to "educate" Africans was largely in order that they could learn to read the Bible. As Africans progressed in their education, and as this bore the fruit of more Christianized Africans, missionaries accelerated their advocacy for the education of Africans. As more missionaries were allowed to establish schools and as more and more Africans were persuaded to go to school, increasing numbers of Africans became exposed not only to the new education but also to Christianity.[21]

Therefore, it was not accidental that the extent of one's education was measured in the distance that one had created between oneself and African indigenous religion and cultural practices. And, most importantly, evidence of continued belief in African religion and the performance of cultural practices became the mark of a lack of "education." It is clear how anyone who wants to be considered as educated would respond to the question of whether they are Christian or not.

Also, the association of education with "science" and the products of modern development, such as electricity, running water, and the modern transportation infrastructure impresses upon the educated African the distance that he/she should put between him/herself and the rural areas. Because he or she considers it to be "unscientific," the educated African disregards African epistemology, metaphysics, and axiology and their criticism of "science" and "Christianity." His or her world is the world founded on the epistemology of modern civilization. Is it any wonder, therefore, that teachers, nurses, doctors, and other educated Africans are disinclined to work in rural areas?

The medical establishment and African practices

Medical missionaries were used by the missions to draw Africans to Christianity (Gelfand, 1984: 20–21). They were the first to come across African beliefs and the use of indigenous medicines (Sundkler, 1948). While most of them, like their fellow brethren, condemned such beliefs and practices, some sought to understand the practices, if only to prove their uselessness or harmfulness. A few, however, found value in such beliefs and practices, so much so that Etherington (1987) refers to some such relations as "characterized by [. . .] mutual understanding." Such "mutual understanding," if not tolerance, is evident in Father Apolinaris's admonitions to Dr. Max Kohler:

> The African lives in a world of his own and it will take a long time until the correct relation between a white physician and an African patient is established, which in most cases, I think, is the *sine-qua-non* of successful treatment. Doctor, for the time being you must be satisfied with being the last resort in the health problems of the African. Before they come to you they have been consulting their medical experts, especially the illegal diviner or *isangoma*. (in Schimlek, 1957: 91; emphasis in original)

Missionary doctor and medical superintendent at Charles Johnson Memorial Hospital in KwaZulu (Nquthu), Anthony Barker provides an explanation for the doctor who may need to know the difference between the African world (that about which Father Apolinaris talks) and his world:

> For these men and women our medicine is too small. It is too cold, too materialistic. We should cease from scorning those who pass our hospitals for the care of the traditional medicine men, or seeing this moment as necessarily retrogressive. It is nothing of the kind, but rather a barometer of our failure to satisfy that part of a sick man's consciousness which he reserves for himself (Barker, 1959: 33–34).

The continued consultation of indigenous healers by Africans may be partly an index of the failure to satisfy the sick African's consciousness. It may also be partly due to the lack of confidence in "scientific" medicine, as medical missionary Jarret-Kerr noticed (1960: 30–32), and to the recognition of the power of indigenous medicines (1960: 43–44, 47–48).

In urban areas, the practices of indigenous doctors came in direct conflict with the practices of "scientific" doctors and pharmacists. Indigenous practitioners who wanted to be successful in urban areas modeled their practices after the practices of "scientific" medical practitioners. They set up their practices in towns and referred to themselves as "doctors." Those who produced medicines called themselves "pharmacists." The doctors of "scientific" medicine as well as pharmacists were financially threatened by such practices and demanded that the state proscribe the use of indigenous medicines.[22] As will be mentioned below, the state pursued an ambiguous policy that resulted in the proliferation of indigenous practices in urban areas.

The doctors of "scientific" medicine were not alone in marginalizing indigenous healers. They worked hand in hand with psychologists and psychiatrists who were similarly threatened by *izangoma* and their practices. It is not an overstatement that psychologists and psychiatry have done very little or nothing for the African in South Africa. It is true also to state that, save for those confined in mental institutions, the African has generally not needed the services of psychologists or psychiatrists. In *izangoma*, Africans have psychologists and psychiatrists who not only come from the same cultural environment but who are also steeped in the belief systems of their patients. *Izangoma*'s role in keeping many Africans sane during the darkest periods of apartheid rule has never been acknowledged and most probably never will be. The upheavals of the late 1980s and early 1990s not only destabilized the former state, they also destabilized people's psychological anchors. Here too, *izangoma* have not been recognized as contributors to the psychological stability of many during those turbulent times.

This lack of recognition stems from the marginalization of all indigenous practices. It has deprived the practitioners both of systems of psychological help along with the advantages arising from the cross-pollination of these practices. Here too, the cooperation that one sees between practitioners trained in the "scientific" method and the practitioners of eastern forms of psychiatric treatment, such as yoga, is not replicated in South Africa or anywhere in Africa. The general South African psychiatrist, if he or she has dared to search, has seen nothing valuable in the indigenous systems. Jungian psychotherapist Dr. Verah Buhrman is among the minority who think:

> Ritual and skill of black healers are not the mumbo-jumbo or witchdoctor's magic some whites think but are based on the same sound principles that underlie Western Psychology. Contact between black and white healers should be approached in a spirit of mutual respect [. . .]. There is the use of dreams by the black traditional healer to get contact with the unconscious mind. It is of powerful value in giving another dimension to healing—the aid of the ancestral spirits [. . .] (*Sunday Express*, 13 January 1985).

Unlike Dr. Buhrman, Dr. Barker, and Father Apolinaris, the doctors of "scientific" medicine and psychotherapy were willing to abandon the principles of scientific investigation (i.e., making deductions from observable facts) and propound their uninformed beliefs and superstitions regarding indigenous medicines and practices. The marginalization of indigenous medicines had little to do with their efficacy or their hygiene and more to do with the religious and cultural superstitions of doctors as well as the threat posed by competition from indigenous healers.

The results of the activities and campaigns of missionaries and the medical establishment can be appropriately realized in the legislation that was enacted over time.

The state and African practices

The South African state (in all its former incarnations) played an active and ambiguous role in the marginalization of African practices. On the one hand, the state was influenced by missionaries and the medical establishment to curtail the practices of *izinyanga* and *izangoma*, and became interested in protecting Africans from the "primitive ill" perpetrated by *izangoma* and *izinyanga*. On the other hand, reconciling the state's ideologies of separate development and apartheid meant that some African cultural practices had to be tolerated. In Natal, *izinyanga* were recognized and licensed from as early as the 1890s through the Natal Code (Section 268 of the Natal Code of Native Law, No. 19 of 1891) and the Zululand Proclamation (No. 7 of 1895).

However, those practices that were purely religious and psychological (i.e., practices of *izangoma* and other mediums) were prohibited and criminalized. Thus the practice and trade in "philtres, charms, divining and witchcraft" were prohibited. The Natal Code was, however, a compromise between the demands of missionaries and the imperative to maintain some semblance of African culture as well as a rational response to the shortage of doctors of "scientific" medicine in Natal. The Natal Code, however, restricted African herbalists to treating only Africans and only in African areas.

While the recognition of *izinyanga* did not herald an era of full acceptance and support, it created an environment that fostered the survival of medical practices in urban areas. The Natal Code created conditions for indigenous medical practitioners to apply for annually renewable licenses.[23] A provision was made for practitioners to charge *ugxa* (consultation fees) between two, six, and ten shillings, and to charge for other services as well, if necessary. The exorbitant license fees (initially one pound, but which was later raised to three pounds) discouraged many from applying.[24] The restrictions placed against the practice of indigenous medicines were not sufficient for missionaries. In the early 1910s, the Natal Missionary Conference opposed (and worked for the reversal of) the decision to license indigenous medical practitioners.

Over the years, missionaries, the medical establishment and the pharmaceutical industry found common cause in the prohibition and marginalization of indigenous medical practice. Together, they put pressure on the state to curtail the practice. In 1912, the license fee for indigenous medical practitioners was raised three times and the chiefs (on whose recommendations licenses were renewed) were encouraged not to recommend renewal of licenses (Dauskardt, 1994). To stop *izinyanga* from competing with practitioners of "scientific" medicine and pharmacists, the Black Administration Act (No. 38 of 1927) formally restricted the advertising of indigenous medicines (Nesvag, 1999). The Medical, Dental and Pharmacy Act (No. 13 of 1928) was enacted to restrict the economic functions of herbalists (by recognizing biomedicines only) as well as to stop the activities of the organizations of indigenous medical practitioners, which sought to defend indigenous medical practitioners and to strengthen their position.

Competition between indigenous practitioners and the practitioners of "scientific" medicines and pharmacists had led to indigenous practitioners advertising themselves, through their "mail-order" advertising, as "doctors" and "chemists." Complaints and appeals to the state by modern medical practitioners and pharmacists resulted in Proclamation No. 168 of 1932, which prohibited *izinyanga* from "assuming the European title of 'doctor' or 'chemist'" and restricted the issuing of new licenses to the order of the Minister of Public Health.

The apartheid government, which came to power in 1948, continued with the steps of the previous governments. The Witchcraft Suppression Act (No. 3 of 1957) re-established the government's position of recognizing indigenous medical practice as part of the "cultural heritage" of Africans and the suppression of the practice of divining.[25] The Pharmacy Act (No. 53 of 1974) was passed to protect pharmacists from competition from indigenous pharmacists ("herbalists").[26] The Medical, Dental and Supplementary Services Act (No. 56 of 1974) was introduced to replace the Medical, Dental and Pharmacy Act (No. 13 of 1928). The Homeopaths, Naturopaths, Osteopaths and Herbalists Act (No. 52 of 1974) was passed to regulate the activities of medical practitioners who were not officially considered to be doctors or pharmacists. The Associated Health Services Act (No. 63 of 1982) established the Associated Health Service Professions Board to control homoeopathic activities.

There are three major consequences of the actions of the missionaries, the medical and pharmaceutical industries, as well as of the state. The first was that the prohibition of *izangoma* meant that each *inyanga* had to do his own divining.[27] Also, some *izangoma* applied for licenses as *izinyanga* (Berglund, 1976: 190)[28] and had to prescribe medicines for the ill and injured.[29] Second, the practice of divining was driven underground, and in urban areas—despite gallant resistance from some of the members—even *izinyanga* were eventually marginalized. The marginalization of *izinyanga* and the driving underground of *izangoma* impressed upon African practitioners the need to protect their practices. Therefore, from as early as 1930, indigenous doctors Solomon Mazibuko[30] and Mafavuke Ngcobo established the Natal Native Medical Association (later known as the Natal Inyangas Association), which sought to protect the interests of indigenous practitioners as well as to campaign for the acceptance of indigenous medical practices.

It is in the light of the foregoing discussion that Vachon's (1983) caustic remarks regarding the development mission become understandable:

> our sanctimonious missions of civilization, development, conscientization, modernization, social change, democratization, liberation, social justice and even of co-operation and international solidarity, are often Trojan horses vis-à-vis the traditions of Africa, Asia and the Americas. It is in the sense that, in the name of literacy, the oral traditions of the local people are destroyed; in the name of agricultural reform, of the best distribution of land, wages and full employment, we destroy their original, non-monetary economic culture which is bound in a co-operative partnership with Mother Earth; in the name of our democracies, we destroy their *dharma*-cracies; in the name of the acquisition of national sovereignty and the Nation State, we destroy their anti-state organizations; in the name of a democratic taking of power, we destroy their original consensual political culture of leaders without power;

that finally, in the name of human rights, we destroy their traditional judicial world which sees man not as a subject of rights but primarily as a subject of grace, of gratitude and cosmic responsibility (Verhelst, 1987: 18).

And, in the name of "scientific" medicine, indigenous systems of medicine have been systematically undermined and destroyed, with far-reaching consequences.

SUBVERTING THE "TROJAN HORSE"

The efforts to marginalize African religion, customs, and practices were not completely successful. While the destruction of the old ways of life facilitated labor, education, and Christianization, as well as distanced Africans from their systems of medical practice, resistance to such destruction, albeit disarticulated by disembeddedness, was relatively successful. The success was in large part due to the socioeconomic conditions of Africans. However, in order to respond to the changed conditions of Africans, indigenous medical practice and medicines had to be transformed. This section highlights the socioeconomic conditions of Africans that led to the successful resistance of indigenous medical practice and the conditions that led to the transformation of the practice.

The socioeconomic and socio-political environment from the mid 1980s to the mid 1990s produced high levels of political violence and violent crime (Sitas, 1986; Mare and Hamilton, 1987). The economy was in a recession[31] and consequently many people lost their jobs while many others could not find work.[32] The drought during this period seems to have pushed large numbers of people out of rural areas to seek opportunities in urban areas.[33] The political conflict between the two main political parties in KwaZulu-Natal, coupled with the rising level of property crimes owing to the poor economic conditions, left most people feeling vulnerable (Mare and Hamilton, 1987: 181–216). Consequently, the demand for indigenous medicines to be used as protection against the consequences of the recession, as well as against crime and violence, increased. Such demand resulted in changes in indigenous medicines themselves. Medicines were improved and made to respond to the new socioeconomic and socio-political conditions of Africans at the time.

There were two notable sets of changes that occurred. The first set of changes related to the use of indigenous medicines. The second set of changes related to the practice itself. This discussion is limited to medicines used to procure employment and to protect property and oneself from both physical and metaphysical harm.

New medicines in old bottles

Changes in the use of medicines reflected the manner in which people felt vulnerable and the various needs for protection during a time when there were high rates of violence and crime and the state institutions seemed unwilling or unable to address their concerns.

A job by any means

The first set of changes had to do with people consulting practitioners. The recession saw large numbers of people losing their jobs as well as many being put on reduced-time. The numbers of the jobless swelled as recent graduates failed to find employment. It became harder and harder to find employment, particularly permanent employment. Those who were looking for work could rely on the extra advantage that indigenous medicines gave them to find employment. For instance, there were medicines to make one attractive to employers. Since during this time better-educated Africans could apply for employment—which meant that they could be called for interviews, many used indigenous medicines, such as *isimatisane* (*Odenlandia corymbosa*),[34] not only to make themselves attractive to employers but also to enable them to "sweet-talk" them. *Isimatisane* and love charms were used by those who were lucky enough to be employed and who still wanted to keep their employment.

Also, known forms of medicines were modified to respond to new conditions, and new medicines, which did not exist before, were developed to respond to such conditions. An example of a known medicine that was modified for use in the new environment was medicine used in courting women. Normally, young men would break a small piece off of the medicinal root and keep it under his tongue while talking to a woman. The medicine was supposed to make his voice sound musical to the woman and thus make the woman fall in love with him. During the 1980s and 1990s, the same medicine was prescribed for people going for interviews. At interviews, the medicine was expected to make the voice of the interviewee sound musical to the interviewers and, in this way, make them choose the person for the job.

The following case reveals that people in troubled relations with their employers seek solutions from indigenous medicines, as well as the potential threat to indigenous healers when their medicines fail to produce the desired results.

A Mpumalanga security guard is reported to have gunned down a 78 year-old traditional healer, Mrs. Eldah Mokoena, and critically wounded her supplier, the 70 year-old Mr. Nelson Sibiya, after claiming that Mrs.

Mokoena gave him the wrong "medicine." The man had problems at work that affected his relationship with his employer. He wanted "medicines" to help him improve relations with his employer. Mokoena is supposed to have told the man that, if he washed himself with the "medicine," the relationship with his employer would improve. Police spokeswoman, Sergeant Thabisile Gama, reported that the "medicines" "apparently did not have the desired effect, and in a rage, the man went to Mokoena's home and accused her of witchcraft, [. . .] shot her four times, killing her instantly." He then went to Mr. Sibiya's house, accused him of supplying the wrong "medicine," "fired seven shots hitting Sibiya in the body and jaw." The man later handed himself over to the police and surrendered his 9mm pistol.[35]

What is important in this case is that the man sought relief for his troubles in indigenous medicines. For him to have done so, he must have either witnessed or heard of indigenous medicines producing such relief. While the report does not mention the name of the "medicine" used, various medicines that in the past had been used to make men likeable to women were modified during the 1980s and 1990s to make people get and keep employment.

Property shield in the time of need

The high rates of crime and violence, as well as the seeming reluctance and inability of the police to curb it, led many to seek the powers of indigenous medicines to protect themselves as well as their property. It is during this time that medicines to protect such property as one's house and car, as well as one's family, proliferated. The case of Doom's car provides evidence for what people did when they lost their property and found that the police could not help them. Doom was born in Greytown and grew up in the Durban townships. After working for sometime, he started a taxi business with his co-worker, Zitha, a man from the Midland of KwaZulu-Natal. One day, Doom's taxi was stolen from his yard and he tried to use the help of indigenous healers to find it.

After trying a few "seers," a fellow taxi owner advised him to see a man from an informal settlement outside Umlazi. Doom was not encouraged when he saw the shack in which the man was living. However, since he had traveled a long way, he went in to see the man. The man was something between a *sangoma* and *umthandazi*. He used water divination but did not call the names of *Jesu* and *Mariya*. Instead, he called on Doom's relatives to help reveal where the car was. He gave Doom a calabash full of water and asked him to look for his car in the water. When Doom looked at the water, he saw a "picture" of a white minivan parked under a red plastic port behind a shack. After some discussion and after the man had consulted his own ancestors, the man asked Doom to accompany him to go get the car. Doom was surprised at this since most "seers" only tell you where you can find your property.

They took a taxi to Durban and then to Inanda. After traveling on foot a long distance from where the taxi had dropped them, they came to a ravine across which was the red carport, but the minivan was not under it. They asked a woman who was washing clothes at a tap nearby whether she had seen a white minivan parked under the red carport. She said that the driver of the minivan was her younger brother and that he was a "troublemaker." She even told them that she suspected that her brother and his friends had stolen the minivan. They told the woman that the minivan belonged to Doom. On their way back, Doom reported the matter to the police in Inanda, who told him that there was nothing they could do since he (Doom) did not know where the thief was. When he got to Umlazi, he again reported the matter to the police, who told him that the matter was outside their jurisdiction. After numerous attempts of staking out the red carport, neither Doom nor Zitha managed to get the minivan back. On one of their visits, they discovered that the minivan had been chopped up and sold for parts. The two front doors under the red carport told the story.

During the mid-1980s and the early 1990s, when violent crime engulfed large parts of South Africa, people who lost their property could not rely on the police. Indigenous medical practitioners served both to protect people's property as well as to find it when lost. In the case above, Doom found out what happened to his car although he did not find either his car or the man who stole it. If Doom wanted to punish the person who stole his minivan, he would not have gone to the police. The police had already demonstrated their impotence to him. Like many others, he would have both sought out and punished the person himself, assisted by either relatives or friends, or he would have sought such assistance from the powers of indigenous medicines.

The body of iron

The ubiquitous crime and violence that seemed poised to strike at any person anywhere impressed on many the need for protection should they become victims of crime and violence. One way in which this was done was to use *intelezi* to ensure that bullets would not penetrate a person's body. *Intelezi* was used to strengthen and protect warriors during wars. In the 1980s and 1990s, it was used to protect ordinary people from violence. The case of Madlangala, who needed protection from some people who wanted to take his house, provides evidence for the use of medicine to protect both one's body and house. Madlangala and his wife were asked by an elderly neighbor to look after her because she could not look after herself. To thank them, she bequeathed her only possession, her house, to them. The woman passed away a year and seven months after the date of the will. After the woman passed away, her niece came, claiming to be the woman's daughter, and demanded to get the woman's body so that she could get it buried. After about a week of arguing, Madlangala gave the body to the niece.

A week later, the niece came to claim the house. When Madlangala refused to vacate the house, she went away threatening to return with "people who would force you out." Fearing for his family's well-being, Madlangala and his family consulted an *inyanga* in Stanger, who told them that, if the threat was real, they, together with their house, needed protection. Their bodies were strengthened with the application of medicines into incisions that had been made on all the major joints of their bodies. He then promised them to come to strengthen their house as well as the old woman's house the following weekend. He indeed came on a Saturday evening of that weekend. After dark, he began by sprinkling "fortified medicine" inside and outside of Madlangala's house. He then buried some of the medicines in the four corners of the house. They went to the old woman's house at the corner where he repeated the same process. He then promised them: "no one will touch you now."

The following Thursday the woman arrived at the house with three minibus vans. Six men clad in long overcoats—a mark of armed men during the heyday of armed attacks on people's houses—disembarked from the different cars and approached the old woman's house. By this time, Madlangala had asked his wife and children to go stay with relatives at Umlazi. (His wife refused to leave but sent the children to the relatives.) He had told some of the men from his village that he thought he would be attacked that evening. Four of the men came—armed with guns, one of which was given to Madlangala—to wait for the attack with him. The six men in overcoats came to the house and knocked. Their leader asked for a Mr. Mkhize's house. Madlangala asked them which Mkhize they were referring to since there were quite a few in the area. The leader said that the Mkhize they were looking for was a taxi owner. Madlangala told them that he did not know any Mkhize who owned taxis. The leader mumbled something about "the wrong house" and then they left, got into the minibus van, and took off.

According to Madlangala, the men were lucky because there was a gun pointing at each and every one of them. If they had tried to attack, none of them would have survived. He believes that what made them lose their plan to attack was the fortification of the house on the previous Saturday. He said that the fortification "confused them" and that "they babbled like babies." "We could have killed them all, and they would not have known what happened."

In this case, the fortification of Madlangala's family as well as his houses seems to have worked in protecting them from a planned assault. What appears to have happened to the men who came in the minibus vans is commonly known as *ukudungeka kwengqondo* (befuddlement of the mind),[36] which is understood to be induced by certain types of indigenous medicines. In this case, it was used to protect Madlangala's family's property and lives.

New practices for new problems

Changes to the practice were evident in two areas. The hard economic conditions in rural areas coupled with the drought forced large numbers of women into the informal economy. Some of these women traded in ingredients used in preparing and producing indigenous medicines. On the other hand, the economic conditions in urban areas led many to establish themselves as "indigenous" healers when they had neither the training nor the know-how.

Chopping trees for survival

The second set of changes occurred in the practice of indigenous medicines. Economic conditions were difficult for most Africans in the mid-1980s and early 1990s but were felt even harder in rural areas that relied on remittances from people working in urban areas. Over the years, rural communities could resort to supplementing remittances with food grown in their fields. However, the drought of the early 1990s eliminated that option (Padayachee, 1997). It was during this time that many women, forced by poverty in rural areas, were catapulted into the "informal economy." Most women sold fruit and vegetables. But many started cutting indigenous medical plants for sale in urban areas. The entry of these women into the economy changed the nature of harvesting indigenous plants and the manner in which medicines were sold. Anyone could then buy medicines from the women in the Durban's established Muthi Market[37] and then set themselves up as indigenous healers. The sales of indigenous medicines proved very lucrative for many sellers.[38]

According to *amakhosi* who participated in the 1915 hearings,[39] a healer or diviner traditionally found indigenous medicines through the help of his or her ancestors. Once the medicines had been found, rituals for harvesting— such as prayer and giving thanks to the ancestors—were performed. In most cases, the person would only harvest the part of the tree or plant (such as bark, leaves, roots, etc.) that he or she needed. The rest of the tree would be saved for future use. Medicines were harvested at particular times of the year, mostly during the time when harvesting would do the least damage to the tree or plant. The "just-in-time" nature of such use meant that people harvested only the medicines they needed.

However, the entry of large numbers of women who were only traders and not healers or diviners completely changed such a relationship with the environment. Interested in the money they received for the medicines, praying to the ancestors for the medicines would not be the first thing that came to their minds. To lower their transport costs to urban areas, it became necessary for them to transport the medicines in bulk. Competition with others meant that medicines were harvested throughout the year and that the whole tree or plant would be harvested instead of its primary parts. Such processes resulted in the over-exploitation of indigenous medicines and threatened the survival of some species (Cunningham, 1992).

Charlatans and their magic cures

There were also people who entered the practice as practitioners when, in fact, they had not gone through the training or been called to the practice. The worsening economic conditions led many to set themselves up as indigenous medical practitioners. People who, for one reason or another, did not want to go to hospitals, were susceptible to being taken advantage of by such self-styled "traditional healers." The case of Mrs. Ndlovu shows how charlatans promised false relief to a woman suffering from cervical cancer.

Mr. and Mrs. Ndlovu were married for about twenty-nine years and had four children and five grandchildren. By and large, except for colds and the flu, they had not had any serious illnesses in the family, until Mrs. Ndlovu fell ill early in 1994. Initially she complained about a stomach-ache that kept her awake at night and did not seem to respond to painkillers. A neighbor suggested that she be taken to a hospital for examinations. She would have none of that. She feared that the doctors would say that she had either ulcers or, even worse, cancer, and that they would then operate on her.[40] Mr. Ndlovu also considered an operation as a dicey undertaking.[41] They both agreed, instead, to see an *inyanga*.

After trying a few healers without success, Mr. Ndlovu was prepared to go to a Zanzibari *inyanga* who lived in Phoenix—an Indian township east of Kwamashu. He had been told that this *inyanga* had cured many people's illnesses. On the afternoon of the visit, Mr. Ndlovu came to ask me to accompany them to the *inyanga* in Phoenix. When we got to the *inyanga*'s house in Phoenix, the *inyanga* was away. We had waited for about fifteen minutes when a new white 7-series Mercedes Benz arrived. I did not quite get to see what the *inyanga* looked like, since we were ushered into a waiting area before he got out of his car.

While we waited, I noticed a certificate that declared that the *inyanga* was a member of the United African Herbalists Organization. A card pinned next to the certificate boasted that the *inyanga* cured all sorts of illnesses and diseases, that even he cured AIDS and had medicine for "Lotto Luck" and "Casino Luck." When we went into his consulting room, the *inyanga* asked Mr. Ndlovu whether he wanted *ukubhula* (i.e., divination to find out what the problem was with his wife and family]. Mr. Ndlovu agreed. He was to use *abalozi*[42] to find out what was wrong with Mrs. Ndlovu and with Mr. Ndlovu's family. The *inyanga* then left the room and a boy (about 15) walked in. The young man started spraying and smearing concoctions on the small drums (situated inconspicuously at one corner of the room) through which the *abalozi* were to speak. After the spraying and smearing, the *inyanga* came in and the boy left the room. The *inyanga* then asked the drums to speak. After some time, a voice came through the drums greeting Mrs. Ndlovu. It was a raspy young woman's voice, which spoke slowly and deliberately. It told Mrs. Ndlovu what was wrong with her and that her condition was a result of a jealous neighbor. Mrs. Ndlovu asked how she could get help and the voice told her that the *inyanga* was going to help her.

Before we could leave, Mrs. Ndlovu was "strengthened against evil spirits" and given medicines to use at her house; Mr. Ndlovu had to pay R310.00 (R50.00 for divination and R260.00 for the rest). The *inyanga* guaranteed that Mrs. Ndlovu was going to be well within six days. This astonished me: no *inyanga* ever creates such stringent conditions for his or her medicine to work. Six days later, Mrs. Ndlovu's stomach pains were completely gone and the swelling in her legs was going away. But two days after that, her legs were swollen again. Mr. Ndlovu did not know what else to do. After further visits to numerous other "healers," Mrs. Ndlovu's condition did not improve. She was, eventually, admitted to a hospital in Durban, where radiation therapy was administered to her. However, she passed away not too long after admission to the hospital.

Mrs. Ndlovu's case reveals how some of the self-styled "healers" work. They claim to have solutions to all the problems that people present to them.[43] They invariably claim to have "medicines" that address people's shortage or lack of money, good luck, employment, and good social relations. Further, their charges are exorbitant. Quite a few have "certificates" that claim to be from some "association" or "organization" of "traditional healers." They are notorious for claiming to use human body parts in their medicines. Speculation over the use of body parts cast away in bushes, over which parts were used for what, as well as over the effect of such "medicines" captivated the nation in the early 1990s. The discovery of mutilated bodies (especially the bodies of children) during this time added to the increasing calls for the proscription of all forms of indigenous medical practice.

In sum, the period 1980–94 saw indigenous medical practice play a role in assisting Africans to cope, first, with the repression and, later, with the rise in crime and violence. Changes in the practice of indigenous medicines around this time pertained to the use of medicines to procure and keep employment, the use of medicines to protect oneself as well as one's relatives and property from crime and violence, and to the proliferation of charlatans who preyed on a besieged, unsuspecting population. As this period drew to a close, there were calls for the proscription of the indigenous medical practice.

Calls to proscribe indigenous medical practice

People's increased resort to indigenous medical practice between the mid-1980s and early 1990s, coupled with the distorted coverage by a sensationalist mass media,[44] spurred interest in the practice from various quarters. Such interest led to a call to proscribe indigenous medical practice. The proliferation of charlatans and the seemingly burgeoning specter of "witch killings" and "muti killings" resulted in calls for the proscription of witchcraft, such as that made in the *Ralushai Commission Report* (discussed below).[45] During this period, numerous studies (such as that conducted by the Institute for Multi-Party Democracy) were conducted and conferences (such as the conference on the Witchcraft Suppression Act of 1957, called by the "Gender Commission") as well as hearings were held in order to determine the dangers of indigenous medical practice.

Most notable among the calls for some control over the practices of indigenous healers was the report of the Ralushai Commission. In 1996, after a spate of "witch killings," the Northern Province government instituted a commission of inquiry, chaired by Professor N. V. Ralushai, to investigate the reasons behind and the causes of the widespread "witch killings." The report presented a plethora of macabre practices in human mutilation, which some of the "traditional healers" supposedly practiced. Among the recommendations of the commission were 1) the institution of a code of conduct for traditional healers; 2) the liberation of people through education from belief in witchcraft; 3) the institution of different penalties for witches and those who sniff them out; and 4) the criminalization of the forced collection of money required to pay *izangoma*.

In 1998, the Institute for Multi-Party Democracy (IMPD) initiated a review of the Anti-Witchcraft Act of 1957 by talking to stakeholders in various communities, particularly the affected Northern Provinces. In 1999, the IMPD issued a discussion document entitled *Witchcraft Summit, Towards New Legislation*, in which it recommended and drafted a Witchcraft Control Act meant to replace the Anti-Witchcraft Act. Among the recommendations were the creation of "special witchcraft courts as appendages to the formal court system" to work with the Departments of Health and Justice, as well as the imposition of fines for people "making reckless or self-serving witchcraft accusations and on those found actually practicing witchcraft."

In 1999, the Commission on Gender Equality hosted the Legislative Reform Conference, which sought to make recommendations on the reform of the Witchcraft Suppression Act of 1957. Among the key presentations made at the conference were those from Dr. Esther Njiro, the advocate Seth Nthai, and Professor Ralushai. Dr. Esther Njiro, the director of the Centre for Gender Studies at the University of Venda, presented a paper entitled "Witchcraft as Gender Violence in Africa," in which she argues that the "smelling of witches," who are mainly females, by youth (who are mainly males) is a form of gender violence (Njiro, 1999). Advocate Nthai's paper contrasted the manner in which previous governments had treated "traditional healers" and appealed to the government established in 1994 not to address its relations with "traditional healers" in the same manner (Nthai, 1999). Professor Ralushai briefly discussed the findings of the commission over which he presided in 1996.

The recommendations from the Ralushai commission, the IMPD's Witchcraft Summit, and the Commission on Gender Equality's Legislative Reform Conference were largely for controls to be exercised on the practices of indigenous practitioners, especially those accused of either practicing or "smelling" those who practice witchcraft. The recommendations included the establishment of traditional courts to adjudicate matters related to witchcraft, the establishment of traditional police to investigate witchcraft-related crimes, and the sentencing of people who practice witchcraft or those who "smell out" the witches.

Calls for the normalization of indigenous medical practice

The second response, however, appealed for the "normalization" of indigenous medical practice, pointing to the benefits that would be lost should the practice be banned. There were three aspects to the second response. First, the government instituted its own review of existing legislation that pertained to indigenous medical practice, such as the Anti-Witchcraft Act of 1957. On 4 August 1998, the Select Committee on Social Services tabled its report with recommendations relating to indigenous medical practice. One of the most important recommendations was for the "formation of a statutory national traditional medical council."

The second aspect of the second response was the establishment of "research centers" that sought to identify the biological properties and medicinal advantages of various indigenous medicines. Most notable among these was the establishment of a collaborative Medical Research Council-supported project between the pharmacology departments of the Universities of Cape Town and the Western Cape to test plants supplied to them by indigenous healers for medicinal qualities.[46]

The third aspect on the second response was an attempt by practitioners to institutionalize indigenous medical practice.[47] First was the establishment of indigenous medical hospitals. In Durban, five "Traditional Hospitals" were established between 1994 and 1998. Since the "traditional hospitals" did not get subsidies from the government and relied only on fees paid by patients, they soon found it difficult to continue operating. Owing to lack of funds, all five hospitals had ceased to function by the year 2000. Second was the acceptance of indigenous medical practice by some employers and the agreement to allow indigenous medical practitioners to claim against medical aid funds.[48] Third was the establishment of the KwaZulu-Natal Traditional Healers' Council (KZNTHC). The KZNTHC brought together various Traditional Healer's Associations from KwaZulu-Natal.[49] One of its major functions is to give practical tests to its members before they are issued with the Health Ministry-recognized "certificates of competence" as well as "membership cards."[50]

In sum, the socioeconomic conditions of Africans and the lack of support from state institutions were such that Africans had to rely on the protections of indigenous medical practices. The proliferation of charlatans during this time led to calls for the proscription of witchcraft, which to many meant the proscription of indigenous medical practice. The call for proscription was accompanied by a call for the normalization of indigenous medical practice. The process of normalizing indigenous medical practice was supported by the state, some research institutes, and the practitioners themselves.

CONCLUSION

This chapter has argued that agents of modern development sought to marginalize the medical practices of Africans. Such agents included, but were not limited to, missionaries, the medical and pharmaceutical establishments as well as the state. The marginalization they sought was implemented through the processes of labor, religion, education, and law. While the attempts at marginalization achieved some success, they also faced resistance. For our purposes, resistance took the form of people either refusing to be converted or tampering with the Christian message by inserting African religious and cultural practices. Such practices included the use of indigenous medical services.

What contributed greatly to the successful resistance was both the non-responsiveness of state institutions to the needs of Africans as well as their socioeconomic conditions. However, the practices of the mid-1980s to the mid-1990s were such that calls were made for the proscription of witchcraft. Since no distinction was made between indigenous medical practice and witchcraft, all forms of indigenous medical practice were threatened by such calls for proscription. One response to such calls was a different call, one for the "normalization" of indigenous medical practice.

The "normalization" of indigenous medical practices has thus far meant the normalization of the practices of *izinyanga* and the shunning of the practices of *abathandazi*. The Select Committee recommended the exclusion of *abathandazi* (Christian spiritual healers) "because they are not traditional in nature and their training and accreditation is unclear and ill-defined." The exclusion of *abathandazi* was rooted in the lack of knowledge and understanding of their practices by the Select Committee. Was this not the main reason for the exclusion of *izangoma* by previous legislation? Thus, we have gone full circle from the Natal Code of Native Law (No. 19 of 1891), which legalized the practices of *izinyanga* and banned the practices of *izangoma*. However, today, while the practices of *izangoma* are accepted, the practices of *abathandazi* are banned. This is despite the work done on the value of the practices of *izangoma* and *abathandazi* in diagnosing the causes of illness, in resolving psychiatric disorders, as well as in treating mental illness.[51]

The normalization of indigenous medical practices may produce far-reaching changes in the practice of indigenous healing. However, not only is such "normalization" based on an old understanding of indigenous medical practice, and fails to take account of its transformations and commodification, but it is also predicated on indigenous medical practitioners subjecting themselves and their practices to "scientific" tests. Such a view presupposes the superiority of one form of medical system over another. While there are fields in which "scientific" medicine is far superior to indigenous medicine, there are other fields in which indigenous medicines are unrivalled. Therefore, the medical emancipation of Africans from unnecessary suffering will be realized when indigenous medical practice is recognized and accepted as a form of medical help in its own right and as an occasional alternative to "scientific" medicine. Such recognition should include the establishment and support of necessary institutions and facilities for indigenous medical practice. The social emancipation of Africans will be assured when their cultural practices are allowed to flourish and be useful to them if and when Africans deem so.

The lack of communication between the two systems, which owes its origin to the reluctance of "scientific" medicines to interface with indigenous medicine, is such that people in South Africa suffer and die from illnesses and diseases that might be mediated and cured were the two medical systems to combine their efforts or, at least, to recognize each other. The benefits that Gumede (1990) and others have reaped from their collaboration with indigenous healers remain accessible only to the maverick fringe and assist only those desperate enough to try anything. The program in which indigenous healers and "scientific" doctors cooperate in the healthcare of the residents of the ODI District (run by Associate Professor D. J. Oberholzer of the University of Pretoria's Department of Psychiatry) was certainly groundbreaking (Oberholzer, 1985). As such, despite the successive reports of the World Health Organization (1978 to 1983) on collaboration between the two fields of medicine, the South African public continues to be denied the benefits of such collaboration as well as other related medicines and treatment.

The losers in this are the users of indigenous medicines who, unlike the users of "scientific" medicines, which benefit from state subsidies for research and development, solicit the services of a system that has been suppressed, undermined, never funded, and not properly researched. The effect of marginalization is that some of the accumulated knowledge of cures remains unresearched, poorly developed, and continues to be lost.[52] As a result, some of the users of indigenous medicines continue to die unnecessarily from curable diseases. Their emancipation lies in the establishment and support of institutions for the research, development, and propagation of appropriate indigenous medical practices.

BIBLIOGRAPHY

Atkins, K. E. (1993). *The Moon is Dead! Give Us Our Money!* Portsmouth, NH: Heinemann.

Banuri, T. (1990). "Development and the Politics of Knowledge: A Critical Interpretation of the Social Role of Modernisation," Marglin and Marglin (eds.), *Dominating Knowledge: Development, Culture and Resistance.* Oxford: Clarendon. 73–101.

Baran, P. (1952). "On the Political Economy of Backwardness," *Manchester School* 20: 6–84.

Barker, A. (1959). *Giving and Receiving: An Adventure in African Medical Service.* London: Faith Press.

Berglund, A. (1976). *Zulu Thought-Patterns and Symbolism.* Uppsala: Swedish Institute of Missionary Research.

Bryant, A. T. (1966). *Zulu Medicine and Medicine Men.* Cape Town: C. Struik.

Cardoso, F. H. (1972). "Dependency and Development in Latin America," *New Left Review* 74: 83–95.

Chavunduka, G. L. (1992). "The Development of African Medicine: The Case of Zimbabwe," *African Medicine in the Modern World.* Edinburgh: Centre for African Studies.

Cunningham, A. B. (1992). "Imithi IsiZulu: The Traditional Medicine Trade in Natal/KwaZulu." M.A. thesis. Durban: University of Natal.

Dauskardt, R. P. A. (1994). "The Evolution of Health Systems in a Developing World Metropolis: Urban Herbalism on the Witwatersrand." M.A. thesis. University of the Witwatersrand, Johannesburg.

Etherington, N. (1987). "Missionary Doctors and African Healers in Mid-Victorian South Africa," *South African Historical Journal* 19: 77–91.

Frank, A. G. (1967). *Development and Underdevelopment in Latin America.* New York: Monthly Review Press.

Gelfand, M. (1984). *Christian Doctor and Nurse: The History of Medical Missions in South Africa from 1799–1976.* Durban: Marrianhill Mission.

Gumede, M. V. (1990). *Traditional Healers: A medical practitioner's perspective.* Johannesburg: Skotaville.

Habermas, J. (1984). *The Theory of Communicative Action.* Boston, MO: Beacon.

Hirschman, A. O. (1965). "Obstacles to Development: A Classification and a Quasi-Vanishing Act," *Economic Development and Cultural Change* 17(4): 384–389.

Hobsbawm, E. J. (1963). *Primitive Rebels.* New York: Praeger.

Hoselitz, B. (1960). *Sociological Aspects of Economic Growth.* London: Free Press.

Huntington, S. (1968). *Political Order in Changing Societies.* New Haven, CT: Yale UP.

Hutchings, A., A. H. Scott, G. Lewis, and A. Cunningham (1996). *Zulu Medicinal Plants—an Inventory.* Scottsville: U of Natal P.

Inkeles, A., and David Smith (1974). *Becoming Modern.* Cambridge, MA: Harvard UP.

Jarret-Kerr, M. (1960). *African Pulse.* London: Faith Press.

Kiev, A. (1964). *Magic, Faith and Healing: Studies in Primitive Psychiatry Today.* New York: Free Press.

Maclean, U. (1971). *Magical Medicine: A Nigerian Case Study.* London: Penguin.

Magubane, B. M. (1979). *The Political Economy of Race and Class in South Africa.* New York: Monthly Review Press.

Marcuse, H. (1964). *One Dimensional Man.* Boston: Beacon.

Mare, G., and G. Hamilton (1987). *An Appetite for Power: Buthelezi's Inkatha and the Politics of Loyal Resistance.* Johannesburg: Ravan.

Marglin, F. A. (1990). "Small Pox in Two Systems of Knowledge," Marglin and Marglin (eds.), *Dominating Knowledge: Development, Culture and Resistance.* Oxford: Clarendon. 1–28.

Mayer, P., and I. Mayer (1961). *Townsmen and Tribesmen.* London: Oxford UP.

McClelland, D. (1961). *The Achieving Society.* Princeton, NJ: D. Van Nostrand.

Myrdal, G. (1968). "The Beam in Our Eyes," *Asian Drama: An Inquiry into the Wealth of Nations.* London: Penguin. 5–35.

Nandy, A. (1987). "Towards a Third World Utopia," *Traditions, Tyrannies and Utopias: Essays in the Politics of Awareness.* New Delhi: Oxford UP. 154–184.

———, and V. Shiv (1990). "Modern Medicine and Its Non-Modern Critics: A Study in Discourse," Marglin and Marglin (eds.), *Dominating Knowledge: Development, Culture and Resistance.* Oxford: Clarendon.

Nesvag, S. I. (1999). "D'Urbanised Tradition: The Restructuring and Development of the Muthi Trade in Durban," M.A. thesis. University of Natal-Durban.

Ngubane, H. (1977). *Body and Mind in Zulu Medicine.* London: Academic.

Njiro, E. (1999). "Witchcraft as Gender Violence in Africa," paper presented at the Legislative Reform Conference, Pietersburg, 28–30 November.

Nthai, S. (1999). "Witchcraft Violence: Legislative Framework," paper presented at the Legislative Reform Conference, Pietersburg, 28–30 November.

Oberholzer, D. J. (1985). "Co-operative venture with traditional healers in providing community health in ODI District, Bophuthatswana: A preliminary review," in *Psychotherapy and Psychiatry in Practice* 36: 41.

Padayachee, V. (1997). "The Evolution of South Africa's International Financial Relations and Policy: 1985–95," J. Michie and V. Padayachee (eds.), *The Political Economy of South Africa's Transition.* London: Dryden.

348 ANOTHER KNOWLEDGE IS POSSIBLE

Parekh, B. (1989). *Gandhi's Political Philosophy*. London: Macmillan.
Parsons, T. (1951). *The Social System*. New York: Free Press.
Peek, P. M. (1991). *African Divination Systems: Ways of Knowing*. Bloomington: Indiana UP.
Popkin, S. (1979). *The Rational Peasant*. Berkeley: U of California P.
Preston-Whyte, E., and J. Beall (1985). "How Does the Present Inform the Past? Historical and Anthropological Perspectives on Informal Sector Activity in Early Twentieth Century Natal," conference paper on the history of Natal and Zululand, University of Natal, Durban.
Schapera, I. (1947). *Migrant Labour and Tribal Life*. London: Oxford UP.
————— (1967). *Western Civilisation and the Natives of South Africa*. London: Routledge and Kegan Paul.
Schimlek, F. (1957). *Medicine versus Witchcraft*. Marrianhill: Marrianhil Mission.
Scott, J. (1976). *The Moral Economy of the Peasant: Rebellion and Subsistence in South East Asia*. New Haven, CT: Yale UP.
Sitas, A. (1986). "Inanda, August 1985," *South African Labour Bulletin* 11(4): 85–121.
————— (1995). "Exploiting Phumelele Nene: Post Modernism, Intellectual Work and Ordinary Lives," *Transformation* 27: 74–87.
Sundkler, B. G. M. (1948). *Bantu Prophets in South Africa*. London: Lutteworth.
Verhelst, T. G. (1987). *No Life Without Roots: Culture and Development*. London: Zed Books.
Weber, M. (1930). *The Protestant Ethic and the Spirit of Capitalism*. London: Allen and Unwin.
World Health Report (1983). *Traditional Medicine and Health Care Coverage*. New York: United Nations.

Notes

1 The "South" refers to the group of African, Asian, and Latin American countries considered to be at various stages of the development trajectory followed by the "North."

2 The "North" refers to the countries of Northern Europe and North America that are considered to be far ahead of others in the development trajectory. This group of countries includes Japan, Australia, and New Zealand. These countries are sometimes referred to as the "West."

3 Marglin maintains that "once people are reduced to quantifiable targets, it is difficult to take their freedom seriously" (Marglin and Marglin, 1990: 140).

4 This paper uses examples found among *AmaZulu*. Similar examples are found among other African ethnic groups.

5 Plural for *sangoma*.

6 Plural for *inyanga*.

7 Something that is denied to the patients at "scientific" institutions.

8 *Emakhehleni* literally means "at the place of the grandfathers or ancestors."

9 Indigenous medical practice also had a darker side. *Abathakathi* (who were variously referred to as wizards, witches, witchdoctors, etc. by missionaries) used their knowledge of indigenous medical practice to harm others or to help those who wanted to harm others (Bryant, 1966; Douglas, 1970; Marwick, 1970; Niehaus, 1995; Ashforth, 2000).

10 These are the words of the High Commissioner for South Africa and

Governor of the Transvaal and Orange River Colony from 1905 to 1919, Lord Selborne (in Magubane, 1979: 62). On the new wants of Africans, see also Schapera, 1947: 122.

11 This form of direct taxation—which did not distinguish either by ability to pay or by age—was paid by no other group of people in South Africa (Jabavu, in Schapera, 1967: 286).

12 See Marglin (1990: 217–282) for a discussion of how Judeo-Christian and Greek traditions disembed meaning from work.

13 This does not necessarily mean that the missionary and the industrialist always saw eye to eye. In fact, they sometimes got in each other's way.

14 A report in the newspapers found that clothing was "dangerous to the Native" because it "deprived them of the vitamins from the sun which are lacking in their diet." (*Daily News*, 6 December 1937).

15 One of the slogans of workmen in the streets or on railway lines goes: "*Abelungu o swine. Basibiza ngo Jim.*" Literally, "White people are swine. They call us Jims" (i.e., they give us English names).

16 Without the state weakening and corrupting African institutions of rulership and administration, and without the state forcing Africans through the "gates of misery" (Atkins, 1993), missionaries would have found a much more resilient population supported by strong and vibrant institutions.

17 The singular for *amakhosi* is *inkosi*.

18 The singular for *izinduna* is *induna*.

19 To be sure, medical missionaries provided an invaluable service to Africans when the state did not concern itself with their medical needs.

20 Ari Sitas (1995: 77, 85) tells the story of Phumelele Nene (a Christian) who, when the crop she had planted wilted, sought answers from, among many sources, an *inyanga*. Of relevance here is that someone who was a Christian had consulted an *inyanga*.

21 Schools normally started with prayer (usually "The Lord's Prayer") and ended with prayer. The teaching was infused with Christian beliefs and morality, to which students were expected to adhere or, at least, to behave as though they did.

22 For similar reasons, doctors of western medicine opposed the training of Africans in Western medicine.

23 Natal was the only province that allowed the licensing of *izinyanga*.

24 Among the reasons for licensing was a combination of raising funds for the colonial government, limiting the number of practitioners, and pressure from the white population for curtailment.

25 See also Gumede, 1990: 135.

26 In order to attract more customers, some herbalists had been found to also stock "scientific" medicines.

27 Normally, *izangoma* are restricted to divining and *izinyanga* are restricted to prescribing cures.

28 See also Preston-Whyte and Beall (1985: 31) who provide evidence of a male *inyanga* who petitioned against female *izinyanga* being granted licenses.

29 Combining the two practices proved lucrative during the time when license fees were becoming prohibitive. Because the person would normally be proficient in one or the other practice, increasing fuzziness and slippage

increasingly characterized the practice. The practice of combining the two aspects of treatment has survived to this day and is one of the main reasons for the proliferation of charlatanry.

30 Indigenous doctor Solomon Mazibuko became the life president of the association until his death in 1986, at 116 years of age, when he was buried at his residence in Ndedwe district. He was a veteran of two wars, the South African War and World War I, during which he served in France (Gumede, 1990: 179, 217).

31 *South African Reserve Bank Quarterly Bulletin* (June 1995).

32 *South African Reserve Bank Quarterly Bulletin* (March 1994).

33 The severity of the drought was such that South Africa received an IMF Compensatory and Contingency Financing Facility of $850 million to support "the balance of payments following decline in agricultural exports and the increase in agricultural imports caused by the prolonged drought" (Padayachee, 1997: 31–32).

34 Hutchings (*et al.*) says that the leaves of *isimatisane* are chewed as protective charms when passing the hut of an enemy (1996: 294).

35 *Independent on Line*, 29 March 2000, and *African Eye News Service*.

36 There are numerous other examples of what happens to people who are exposed to this condition. These include attackers who search in vain for houses that have "disappeared" and others who find inanimate objects (such as pools of water or forests) where they expect to find houses. In some cases, the attackers find themselves shot at from the "pool" or "forest." Bryant (1966) mentions *izimpundu* as the medicine that was used to confuse *abathakathi* (19–20).

37 A market for indigenous medicines at *eMatsheni*, which was situated at the Victoria Street beer hall, was closed by the Durban Corporation in 1920 after complaints from doctors, pharmacists, and *amakhosi* (traditional leaders). (See the Chief Native Commissioner's report CNC-193–149/1915). Today's "Muthi Market" on Russel Street over the Warwick Junction was started in 1990 and formalized in 1998.

38 In 1997, the Provincial Minister of Traditional and Environmental Affairs estimated that trade in indigenous medicines in the province was worth R61 million a year (*Daily News*, 14 May 1997).

39 See the Chief Native Commissioner's report (CNC-193–149/1915).

40 The Zulu word for an operation is *ukuhlinza*, a word that is also used to refer to the act of killing and cutting open a cow, goat, or sheep.

41 People in the township normally hear of an operation only when something has gone wrong. There is not much interesting and, therefore, worth talking about in the case of an operation that went without a hitch.

42 Africans believe that the spirits of the dead live among us and that the dead, who know all and see all, can be conjured to speak to the living. The use of *abalozi* (ventriloquists) is one way of conjuring the dead.

43 In fact, by and large, this is a measure of someone who is not very helpful to the people who consult him or her.

44 An article entitled "Human parts that heal," based on hearsay, provides an example of how the alleged practices within a small community can be presented as though they applied to the whole country (*Mail & Guardian*, 9 Dec. 1994). Another article had prices for various body parts (*Mail & Guardian*, 9 October 1998).

45 Since many people could not distinguish between witchcraft and indigenous medical practice, such calls were understood to refer to the proscription of indigenous medical practice as well.

46 The project is popularly known as the 50–50 project because royalties will be shared equally between the universities and people providing the plants (*Mail and Guardian*, 5 March 1998).

47 Such attempts became possible because the Select Committee on Social Services, which reviewed the *Anti-Witchcraft Act* of 1957, recommended the institutionalization of traditional medical practice.

48 In its investigations, the Select Committee found that the electricity-providing para-statal (Eskom) was reported to be recognizing medical certificates from indigenous medical practitioners (*Select Committee on Social Services Report*, 4 August 1998).

49 Although the relationship is not clearly delineated presently, the KZNTHC is likely to be the KwaZulu-Natal organ of the "Statutory National Traditional Healers Council," the formation of which was proposed by the *Select Committee on Social Services* in 1998.

50 Chavunduka (1992: 70) suggests that certification will be a sure way to prevent charlatans from operating.

51 See, for instance, among others, Chavunduka (1992: 70–71), Peek (1991), Kiev (1964) and Maclean (1971).

52 A good example here is the knowledge of traditional birth attendants, which has been usurped by "scientific" medicine.

13

"When there are no problems, we are healthy, no bad luck, nothing": Towards an Emancipatory Understanding of Health and Medicine

Maria Paula G. Meneses

INTRODUCTION

When we speak of rival knowledges today, most analyses begin by presenting modern knowledge systems—such as biomedicine—as globalized forms of knowledge (Chavunduka, 1994; Wynne, 1994; Mappa, 1998). In several studies produced in Africa, the act of situating the "other's" knowledge becomes the key moment in the production of a relationship of inequality; from this standpoint, pre-modern forms of healthcare are characterized, *en bloc*, as traditional therapies, frequently of only local relevance (Ngubane, 1981; Hewson, 1998). The definition of traditional midwifery and of healing and herbal medicine as the main components of "traditional medicine" (WHO, 1996) manifests an extreme simplification of the concept of health, which fails to take note of the historical, social, economic, political, and cultural specificities underlying the development of knowledge about health (Meneses, 2000).

In Mozambique, in most of the work on "traditional medicine," the dominant discourse confers on modern science a hegemonic status, which is defined and protected by the state as "official knowledge."[1] In contrast, local, native forms of knowledge are given a secondary position (Marrato, 1995; Tsenane, 1999; Instituto Nacional de Estatística, 1999). The search for a definition of "traditional medicine" that goes beyond the diversity and heterogeneous character of its therapeutic practices and knowledges is inscribed in the social order resulting from the process of colonization of knowledge itself. What transforms these practices into objects is simply the state's refusal to recognize them (Santos, 1995).

The alternative hypothesis that I would like to discuss in this study is based on the argument that the forms and practices of so-called "traditional" knowledge constitute in fact legitimate knowledge, a status that is conferred on them by the considerable number of patients that seek traditional doctors.

This fact may help explain the enormous vitality and persistence of such practices, both in the colonial period and the present day, notwithstanding the repeated attempts at "epistemicide"[2] to which these forms of knowledge about health have been subjected. Yet many other aspects have to be explored: for example, what is alternative medicine? Alternative in relation to what and whom? What should be considered legitimate knowledge? Legitimate in whose eyes? For knowledge to transform itself into solidarity, which guarantees the liberty and equality of each culture, it is necessary to give that "other" culture the status of subject.[3]

Questioning the dichotomous relationship between local and global forms of knowledge, seen from the perspective of the evolution of "traditional" medicine, is the main analytical focus of the present research. The data and ideas presented here are the product of a research project that I have been carrying out for over eighteen months in the city of Maputo, especially in the neighborhood of Polana Caniço (in the city's suburban area). This is an extraordinarily complex region, of considerable cultural wealth, where there are various health systems that frequently intersect and interpenetrate. To analyze this plurality of medical systems (MacCormack, 1986) is not an easy task, since the interaction of elements of different medicines and the differing perceptions of individuals and social groups about health, well-being, and disease create an immensely complex fabric that manifests itself in forms of "inter-medicine."[4]

In a world of permanent production of cultural differentiation, this process acts as a catalyst of spaces crossed by political and economic relations deeply rooted in inequality. Therefore, in this study, the initial discussion will be focused on the questioning of the reasons that have led to the construction of this difference. Who is the "other," the one that produces and preserves other forms of knowledge?

In order to evaluate existing perceptions about the distinct medical systems in place, several interviews were carried out, both with practitioners of traditional medicine and their patients as well as with participants in the elaboration of health policies in Mozambique (governmental organizations and NGOs). The in-depth interviews involved about thirty people, whose ages varied between 22 and 60 years. Most were interviewed separately. Most of the data presented and discussed comes from interviews with "traditional doctors" from the new board of directors of AMETRAMO,[5] who shared with me, almost on a daily basis, their ideas about their practice and knowledge, their problems and doubts.

To write a text using as a narrative basis "other" perceptions of knowledge was not an easy task.[6] While adapting myself to another, quite complex and dynamic, world, I came to realize that a reflection on how to emancipate this knowledge could only be achieved by producing a *mestizo* text. This explains my decision to write a text that shifts from a situated narrative to a more detailed analysis of the topic, avoiding the elaboration of a stereotyped image of the "other"; this was made possible by presenting the subjects in their own words and perspectives, each with his/her own individual identity. The choice of personal narratives allows me to present the process of construction of the particular "self" of each subject while also evaluating the narrators' biases. In this text, the "I's" became an active component of the discourse, a part of the analysis of the phenomenon, and not the phenomenon itself, raising many questions still to be explored in the future. This has required a detour through the interpretative field of the very concept of health, a reconsideration of the place and role of existing medicines in Mozambique, in which the voices of several of the actors involved in this question are heard.

MEDICINE AND MEDICINES

In the midst of several conversations that I had with a traditional doctor, she would say to me: "there are our diseases, traditional [diseases], but there in the college [Faculty of Medicine] they don't know what these are. But when there are problems we don't understand, we send them to the hospital."[7] These words underline the statement made by several authors about how illnesses or maladies are explained: etiologies are a direct expression of the norms and representations that sustain social structures (transgressions of prohibitions, manifestations of ancestral spirits, aggression by witches, etc. [Dozon, 1987; Hess, 1994]).

In a country like Mozambique, with an extremely complex socio-cultural fabric, there is an unquestionable mixture of medical subcultures, each with its own characteristics and structures, although, through ignorance, biomedicine describes them as a homogeneous entity, resulting in the general reference to a single traditional medicine (Nordstrom, 1991; Jurg, 1992; FRELIMO, 1999). This stereotype, the product of colonial situations, is still very prevalent today.

As I shall discuss in the body of this chapter, it has been possible for some time to detect the development of medical hybridization in Mozambique, a hybridization that accepts the modern model of medicine and even creates space for its practice. Seen from this angle, the vitality of traditional medicines reflects the difficulties of a biomedicine that seems to be unable to achieve its objectives. The hybridization of therapeutic knowledges constitutes a complex diversity of transformed appropriations that are not by any means fixed in space and time, as so often is imputed to "traditional values."[8]

As a starting point, the analysis of this plurality of medical systems is made through the cautious use of the variables official/non-official, traditional/modern. Caution is necessary precisely because of the situation of inter-medicine, of the constant mixing and intersecting of decisions that give rise to a multiplicity of hybrid situations.

The official/non-official dichotomy is defined by the state, which establishes by law—among the wide variety of therapeutic forms—a more or less explicit distinction between what is legal and what is illicit, if not illegal. Everything recognized as official medicine is the object of support by the state. Medicine not recognized as official is tolerated, but most frequently ignored, due to its low permeability to the impositions and control of biomedicine.

The ongoing formalization of traditional medicine is the cause of its own fragility, and this normative process is a reflex of the character of the state in Mozambique. From the perspective of modern medicine, traditional medicine encompasses several knowledges, such as biology and chemistry (i.e., plants and their extracts used as remedies), biomedicine (the treatment and curing of the body), justice (the resolution of problems and conflicts that express themselves in bodily illnesses), and religion (explanations for beliefs described in terms of a magico-religious set of concepts). This reduction of the complexity of knowledge to a list of scientific fields, through the compartmentalization and normalization of knowledge, is the most visible expression of the state's formalization.

Indeed, in the "traditional" sphere, the institutions that take on the healing of illness are simultaneously political, therapeutic, juridical, and religious; they cover an extensive field of competencies and functions that place the efficacy of treatment within a more enveloping efficacy, bringing into play institutions of authority, normative and symbolic structures, and relations of force, knowledge, and power (Fisiy and Geschiere, 1990, 1996; Geschiere, 1995, Fisiy and Goheen, 1998; Comaroff and Comaroff, 1999).

This requires that we make a careful evaluation of the traditional/modern variable when we look at the origin and development of medicines in Mozambique. In the modern, Eurocentric view, the qualifier "traditional" applied to medical practices is used to refer to collective knowledge that has "always" existed, thus reinforcing the object status of those who produce it. In Mozambique, the traditionalization of local knowledges emerges in parallel with and in opposition to the biomedical paradigm that began to be introduced in the late nineteenth century. Depending on the social concerns of each pillar of this dichotomy, the traditional can be seen as an invention of the modern, or the modern a creation of the traditional. As the traditional doctor Carolina Tamele told me, "traditional medicine is ours, we cannot write, it is not like over there at the university. But we study a lot to learn how to heal; we know things they do not teach in school."[9]

Modern medicine appears only as another therapeutic practice in this region, and it does not constitute, even today, a real competitor to other medicines,[10] which have maintained their vitality. The common denominator is to be found, paradoxically, in the fact that these "traditional" medicines have the advantage of not constituting an autonomous domain, enclosed by a body of rules, knowledge, practices, and specialists. In fact, so-called "traditional" medicines are embedded in many other sectors of social life—in this sense, they require that we redefine the concept of "illness," of "malady," which goes beyond the notion of misfortune or unhappiness, and which includes cognitive, symbolic, and institutional aspects of society.

As mentioned above, the fundamental question to be posed is how the dynamics of hybridization of these medicines developed. This universe testifies to the coexistence in the social sphere of the institutions that treat illness and malady in general, at the same time that they treat society itself—whether such treatment is to ensure the reproduction and maintenance of the existing order (norms, representations) or its perturbation (tensions, conflicts, collective misfortunes). In this process lies the heart of the internal resilience of traditional medicines in Mozambique.

THE INVENTION OF TRADITIONAL MEDICINE

Illness, as a sign of maladjustment, of individual and social imbalance, is, like other signs, the object of ambiguous and fluid representations, constructed as practices of knowledge and the exercise of power (Appadurai, 1999; Santos, 1995, 2000). In a world where the hegemonic imposition of scientific knowledge is widely present but in contest with other forms of knowledge, one of the main battles concerns what needs to be known (or ignored), how to represent this knowledge, and for whom.

In Mozambique, the search for a definition of "traditional medicine," beyond the evident diversity and heterogeneity of therapeutic practices, has to be inscribed in the social order resulting from the process of the colonization of knowledge itself—what turns these practices into an object is simply their non-recognition by the state[11] and its institutions.[12] This process implies the creation of the "other" as non-knowledge, included in the natural world and excluded from the civilized world (see, for example, Liengme, 1844–1894; Maugham, 1906; Pina, 1940; Silva Tavares, 1948; Santos Reis, 1952). Therapeutic knowledges and practices are then fragmented according to the classification systems of modern science. This compartmentalization of knowledge allowed the colonial system to appropriate the pharmacological principles of various products used by local therapists, as is shown in various records of Portuguese scientists working in Mozambique: "The remedies employed by indigenous doctors are numerous; they use them in many illnesses and at times with notable success. There is much to study in local plants, some of which may be of use" (Santos Junior and Barros, 1952: 615). At the same time, the process of situating this knowledge, and then restricting it to a symbolic content, invests the communities that possess it with an exotic aura, making them relevant for anthropological study, as well as for ethnic tourism (Meneses, 2000). In identifying local knowledge as "sacred," the focus of action is diverted from its creators, while at the same time the barriers between Self and Other are continuously reinforced, thus sustaining knowledge as colonization. The excerpts presented below constitute examples of the subterranean continuity of a discourse in which the opposition between medicine and magic is reinforced through the division between biomedicine and traditional medicine. Both in the past and in the present, "traditional medicine" is associated with localized, native, or indigenous knowledge (Batalha, 1985; Green, 1996; Hewson, 1998; Green et al., 1999).

> The witchdoctor does not offer anything out of the ordinary. He is a black like the others [. . .], he is only smart enough to win their respect, inducing in them a mystified respect for his clinical procedures, divination abilities, and resources to resolve various difficulties in life. [. . .] But in general he is no more than a swindler (Cruz, 1910: 140).

In this excerpt, it is important to observe the hostility with which medical practices are evaluated, and also how the traditional doctor and the witchdoctor are conflated.

> After the diagnosis, in which the physical symptoms are always downplayed, the sick are advised [by the "black doctors"] according to whether their conditions were caused by spirits of gods, witches, pollution by the dead. [. . .] However, the "black doctor" is not generally a charlatan; he works conscientiously and is confident in his knowledge (Schwalbach and Schwalbach, 1970).

Another characteristic aspect of modern medicine is its low degree of openness towards other possible forms of diagnosis, which, because they are different, are not recognized as equally important as auxiliary means of detecting illnesses.

> There are healers who actually perform cures by using certain medicines obtained from roots, plants, etc., but spiritual healing is, from all viewpoints, negative and obscurantist par excellence [. . .] (Castanheira, 1979: 12).

> [Traditional medicine is] a collection of unorganized empirical knowledge, distorted in its contents by the process of oral transmission, and often surrounded by obscurantist practices, such as rites, etc. [It is the function of the GEMT[13]] to cleanse such existing knowledge of all obscurantist ideas with which it is usually impregnated, and thus promote its value as scientific knowledge to the benefit of the people as a whole (Serviço de Nutrição, 1981: 3–5).

These last two extracts, both produced in Mozambique after independence, illustrate the attempt to impose modern knowledge through the annihilation of practices that did not fit the project of development proposed by the FRELIMO party (in power since independence) and supported by the state.

Finally, the next quotation, while trying to make a clearer differentiation between traditional and modern medicine, reinforces the above proposal of FRELIMO's government (regarding the duality of practices), implicitly supporting the subordination of tradition to modernity:

> In many traditional cultures [of southern Africa], illness is thought to be caused by psychological conflicts or disturbed social relationships that create a disequilibrium expressed in the form of physical or mental problems. In contrast, medical science rests on the axiom of Cartesian dualism, or the separation of mind and body [. . .]; the primary concern is healing the body and eliminating physical suffering. (Hewson, 1998: 1029)

By mediating between the performance of an act and the intention of those who select the content of representations, it is possible to produce phenomena that are a distortion of reality, and which justify the preservation of the binary and geographically specific opposition we/others (Goody, 1979: 35; Barth, 1995; Santos, 2000).

The hegemony of modern science results in the local confinement of knowledge, which can be both the cause of discrimination as well as the basis of resistance to this form of globalization. But how do traditional doctors see themselves? Localism appears as a form of security and affirmation of what is specific to themselves, of a knowledge that belongs to them and that thus enables them to acquire space for maneuvering, spaces of empowerment.

For traditional doctors, their "medicine" is what happens "here, in our space."[14] The patients themselves establish a very clear distinction between the limits and application of biomedicine and those of traditional medicine. The distinction is made according to the context of production/reproduction of knowledge about good and evil.

TRADITIONAL DOCTORS AND TRADITIONAL MEDICINE: THE CONCEPT OF HEALTH[15]

"To have good health is to have a good life . . ."

For the majority of the population of Maputo city, and even the whole of southern Mozambique, the concept of health is very broad, referring implicitly to the existence of a social balance, a concept not unique to Mozambique or Africa, since it is present in various cultures with distinct medical systems.

"To have a good life" are words that best summarize what is meant by being in good health. A good life translates into "having a well-built house, enough food, money for clothing, for soap, for the children to go to school, for the hospital;"[16] "we feel good when there are no problems, when we have food, and when the family is fine."[17] The expression of these feelings suggests that in order to be in good health it is necessary to achieve an internal balance, to be at peace with one's family (including one's ancestors), with neighbors, with one's own body (including hygiene); to be properly fed (which means having employment to ensure income) and protected from ills, whether natural or "visited." When someone produces a lot, has a good harvest, finds a good job or has a good house, a member of the family or a friend may envy such wealth and resort to a traditional therapist to cast a spell against that person. "People today suffer much from bad luck, and even die as a result of jinxes, without deserving such a fate [. . .]."[18]

These conceptions about the role of traditional doctors require a deeper analysis, as well as a re-evaluation of both the ethical and emic principles underlying the emergence of concepts concerning traditional medicine.

Medicine and witchcraft

A discussion of the ethical boundaries of a medical system that extends far beyond the established limits of biomedicine implies broadening the analysis to the field of so-called witchcraft.

As mentioned above, the process of negation of knowledge of traditional medicine involved the identification of the image of the healer with that of the witchdoctor.[19] But these are in fact entirely different, as both patients and practitioners of traditional medicine attest:

> There is a difference between a healer and a witchdoctor. A healer cures, and a witchdoctor kills. A witchdoctor knows potions that kill. But we healers cure, because that is our duty [. . .]; otherwise the spirits may punish us.[20]

To overcome misfortune or bad luck it is necessary to get the help of the traditional healer so as to re-establish individual balance. But a traditional healer can also be used with malicious intent:

> [. . .] spells result from ambition and hatred between people [. . .]. There are poisonous plants and animals that, when used malevolently, can cause evil [. . .]. There are harmful roots [. . .]. There are directors who contact us to help them resolve problems in government, or even when they need to have more power for governing. There are plants that help resolve social problems and complications at work.[21]

The constant demand for traditional medicine is more visible today because there are many more individuals on whom the fortunes of modern or, indeed, traditional society have not shone, and who are searching for success—through promotion, wealth, and business opportunities, for example.

The very classification of illnesses being treated by traditional doctors working in Maputo is very different from that used in biomedicine. Side by side with epilepsy, scabies, tuberculosis, and "eye pain," there are also other pathologies such as "marital problems," "witchcraft," "bad luck," and "evil spirits." In the "traditional" sector of society, if things do not go well, when production fails, when there is "misfortune," the traditional doctor is consulted to find and explain the source of the problem, and also to give medicines either to eliminate it or to restore relations with the ancestors.

The primary available sources for the analysis of witchcraft consist of accusations and rumors,[22] which raise numerous problems in the evaluation of its persistence and efficacy.

> Since crimes of this nature are not resolved by the authorities or the courts because of lack of material evidence, [. . .] people die, fall sick, and remain paralyzed as a result of these Dantesque barbarities perpetrated by witch-doctors who rule and proliferate in our villages and towns. The law ignores them, and sometimes even goes so far as to defend them. What is the difference between an assassination through witchcraft and that through stabbing or shooting? Is it not the same crime? Just because the former is done furtively and through the spirits? Or is there fear on the part of the authorities when they distance themselves from the serious problem of tradition lest they find out that after all witchdoctors operate even within the legal system? (Phaindanne, 2000)

First, we should notice the pertinence of the opposition between scientific knowledge and local representations in the discourse about the "other." Although today this idea is prevalent in many studies, what is important to see is who benefits from these situations and how witchcraft is related to the reproduction or the rupture of the social order. The persistence of the phenomenon of accusations of witchcraft—while implying a marked ambiguity insofar as it is related to some form of power—shows that it is essential to the functioning of society, providing a supplementary force that may even serve constructive ends. Thus, witchcraft should be seen as constituting a possibility for resisting change and continuously emerging inequalities; it may also stimulate attempts to appropriate new resources.

> There are people who become rich at the expense of their family or work colleagues. To become bosses, to succeed better in life, they go to the healer.

The [traditional] doctor throws the bones,[23] invokes the ancestors' help for increasing the power of the ambitious person over his "enemy." No one can then do anything, unless it is to find a more powerful doctor than the one who made the medicine for him to prosper and have more power at work, to be a greater boss [. . .]. I came here just because I want to keep straight with my family, I came to be "vaccinated," if not all will go awry at work, there is so much envy [. . .].[24]

The tenacity with which witchcraft prevails in Mozambican society means that conceptions of power and its exercise have specific implications, since these situations are symmetrical in terms of feelings of power (protection—traditional doctor) and impotence (envy—witchcraft). Traditional medicine offers means to build up power but at the same time reflects feelings of impotence, since it appears to serve to conceal the sources of power. In societies in which the role of family networks is very strong, witchcraft and the appeal to the traditional doctor for social promotion show how closely connected these two phenomena are, a subject analyzed in more detail below.

The discourse on witchcraft is not exclusive to Mozambique (Geschiere, 1995; Englund, 1996; Mappa, 1998; Comaroff and Comaroff, 1999) or even to Africa (Taussing, 1987; Escobar and Pardo, 2000). However, in the region where this study took place, witchcraft operates as a privileged mirror that permits greater manipulation of the "traditional" in the struggle for the construction of "another modernity."

Discourses concerning witchcraft do not express a resistance to modern development; rather, they are reflexes of a constant struggle for a better life. Because traditional medicine is an open system, formally delimited only at the level of the statutes of one association,[25] there are innumerable possibilities for explaining the problems that people experience in life. This enables an anthropophagic interaction of different elements that are part of the project of the creation of "another modernity" (Ong, 1996; Santos and Trindade, 2000). In this sense, witchcraft accusations, far from reinforcing a radically different otherness due to the strange exoticism of witchcraft, constitute a discourse of struggle concerning problems that affect the family, the community, and society.

From the brief collection of opinions presented above, what seems to emerge specifically is the fact that in a context of searching for solutions for misfortune or malady, the concepts of conflict and social imbalance are the central axis around which the whole process of the treatment and cure of the person affected revolves. It is this social space that is occupied by the figure of the traditional doctor.

Who is the traditional doctor?

Although there are various designations for traditional therapists, the most common is "*nyàngà*."[26] The *nyàngà* is a doctor who heals, who knows the power of medicines and how to heal with the help of ancestral spirits. In a text that seeks to give voice to distinct actors, it is necessary to allow traditional doctors to introduce themselves, to define their specificity as well as areas of contact with modern doctors.

An interesting aspect is the fact that all traditional doctors refer to the initial period in "their calling" by their ancestors' spirits to learn to be healers as a very difficult period, one of pain and suffering:

> I was in South Africa working in the mines and I fell very sick, I could not work [. . .]. Then I came to Mozambique, I consulted a doctor who told me that I had spirits that wanted to come out [. . .]. I took the course and I became a traditional doctor. [. . .] I learned a lot, because it is not just spirits, it is knowing how to heal with plants, to help people.[27]
>
> In order to have the spirits that today help me being a healer, first I became very ill, very, very ill . . . I did not do anything for almost three years, I couldn't work in the fields, I could not even eat. They took me to the hospital [. . .]. Then I was told I had the spirits, and [my family] sent me to become a healer.[28]

The selection of the future traditional doctor occurs through a mechanism of painful rupture (simultaneously physical and spiritual)[29] with his/her family and community, a mechanism that seems to be beyond the control of the would-be healer. During the process of perception of his/her new social role, the candidate suffers from innumerable physical and psychological maladies that have no plausible explanation (and which thus cannot be cured within the biomedical paradigm). This unexplained malady works as a password for admission into a different universe of knowledge, which is the basis of the doctor's power of decision in the solving of problems he/she will have to deal with in his/her therapeutic practice.[30] This ritual rupture happens whenever a problem of some gravity occurs, a problem that requires great seriousness and knowledge: "[. . .] afterwards, even when we are working and the spirits come out, it hurts a lot, I lose the power of my arms and legs, I cannot move or do anything at all. It is really painful when they come out in us."[31] As several traditional doctors mentioned, ancestral spirits[32] momentarily occupy the therapist's body in order to help him/her with the diagnosis and detection of the roots of the problem, as well as with the selection of the necessary medication.

The period of apprenticeship of a "*thwasana*"[33] usually lasts from two to five years, and may be even longer. Under the supervision of his/her ancestors (who have chosen this person to perpetuate their knowledge), the candidate has to select the "*b'ava*"[34] with whom he will learn to become a qualified therapist.

> It is hard to be a healer. We have to learn a lot. We have to learn to know the origin of the problem, know the plants that cure, know the different illnesses and how to cure them, with what plants, animals, and many other things. You have to be very careful not to make mistakes. We learn to recognize and distinguish all of this, and afterwards in meetings we talk with our colleagues.[35]

It is not easy to learn to become a traditional doctor, and the ethical principles involving human beings are shown both in the concern about avoiding errors and in the professional secrecy about the patient's ailments, among other aspects.

Illness is something abnormal installed in the body, which, as it comes to be felt as pain or discomfort, alters the person's normal balance.[36] It is therefore necessary to locate and treat the physical or spiritual source of the problem and re-establish normalcy. The ailment may be derived from not fulfilling social rules (such as "*timhamba*"[37]), from the dead not having been properly buried, contagion from impure objects, and the action of malevolent spirits (the "*valòyi*"[38]).

> Often people come here to consult me because of wrongs they did, and because things are going badly, because there is misfortune in their lives. There are also many men with diseases they get from women; this is a great problem here in Maputo, even AIDS [although she refused to say whether she can treat AIDS]. I use the "tinholo." Sometimes the reply comes quickly, at other times not. Each occasion is different. But it is only like this that I manage to find out properly what the person has got. [. . .] In other cases, "kufemba"[39] is necessary, to see what spirits the patient has. They will say what they want. Past problems that they have not solved. During the war, in Gaza, many people died, even our people were killed. Now you may be passing through, and a spirit comes out and stays inside you, needing to resolve its problem. You become really sick, get thinner and thinner, and no one in the hospital can help. Only the traditional doctor can, s/he has to do the treatment to allow these spirits to come out and give them what they need to be happy.[40]

Thus, the cause of the ailment is defined by identifying the alien object that has got into a person's body through different means (touch, sight, or smell). To alleviate the ailment, it is necessary to use medicines—"*mìrhri*"[41]—that allow the patient to recover their full state of health. These medicines are used to heal the body, to cure the pain that assails a particular part of the person, and at the same time to restore self-confidence. The "*nyàngà*" cures the body, heals the wounds, and eliminates the suffering of the organism by using the knowledge he/she has of nature, and simultaneously treats the perturbations of the mind and spirit that are caused by socioeconomic imbalances or by traumas at work.

About illnesses

Traditional doctors seem to know best how to deal with so-called "traditional" illnesses—i.e., illnesses with a heavy emotional component—because they deal with the body and the spirits that "invade" the body and cause diverse problems to patients. Thus, the "*nyàngà*" plays a double role—divinatory and curative—based on a broader conception of illness, understood at two levels: as a social phenomenon, resulting in deep changes in everyday life; and as a physical phenomenon, a manifestation of changes in someone's body. The divinatory function seeks to treat the causes of the illness, prescribing several means to solve it. The curative function seeks to eliminate the physical symptoms. These two functions complement each other, and both help cure the patient. For the traditional doctor, healing means removing all the impurities or imbalances from the patient's life, and thus each treatment normally ends with a purification ceremony that aims to prevent similar situations from happening in the future.

In Mozambican society, as in other societies, witchcraft acts as a regulatory element for dissonant social pressures (Meneses, 2000; Santos and Trindade, 2000). Those who have a lot of money or power do so because they have taken it from someone else with the help of somebody. Those who die, those who suffer "misfortunes," do so because they are "sick," have problems with success, or there is someone who dislikes the fact of their being different; it may also be somebody trying to break away from his/her social group.

For example, infertility is sometimes interpreted as having been caused by someone who does not want a woman to stick with her husband, which in the last instance would imply the annulment of the marriage and the weakening of family and community ties. For the resolution of this problem, all possible means are employed, including "non-traditional" medicines:

> [. . .] when a woman does not conceive, we treat her, and after a month we advise her to go to the hospital to have it checked. Then she returns and we carry out a treatment to "secure" the pregnancy, the baby in the mother's womb. All this is important, the hospital in addition to our medicines. Then there are no problems.[42]

Traditional doctors recognize that they are not able to resolve all cases presented to them, and frequently, after several failed attempts to treat a problem, they suggest that the patient consult practitioners of other medicines, including biomedicine (symbolized by the hospital).

Thus, the plurality of medical systems makes it possible to resort simultaneously to different forms of "treatment" that can identify problems with a physical expression. In parallel, there is also a system that punishes and regulates maladies. They are two sides of the same coin, the physical and the social ills, the individual and community conflicts and tensions, in a system still very much in transition (and quite often at the brink of collapse) to a capitalist society of individual accumulation.

The way in which illnesses are perceived and the attempts to cure or prevent them have to be understood and discussed within the context of each of the existing systems of knowledge—that of biomedicine and that of traditional medicine—since the notions of causality (etiology) do not always coincide. Like their patients, traditional doctors do not necessarily distinguish between healing and treating, between objective and subjective symptoms, between measurable and non-measurable clinical data, which are essential questions to the practice of biomedicine. The traditional doctor is interested in resolving the problem and controlling the symptoms, in restoring the physical functions and social relations that have been affected. As M. F. Zimba puts it, "when the head doesn't work the body suffers," thus summarizing the main premise of his work as a traditional doctor. Although other forms of medicine also advocate the principle that the cause of an illness lies in a person's imbalance or disorder, for biomedicine, when the body is healed, order is re-established. Among the traditional doctors whom I have interviewed, the question that always cropped up was that the harmony, the well-being of an individual, is a reflex of the well-being of the group, of the network of friends and relatives, and that illness alters the relationship of the individual with others. In this sense, while studying a specific case, the "*nyàngà*" promotes the reintegration of the individual into the solidaristic interplay of group interests, seeking to control emerging conflicts so as to ensure the maintenance of the group. As Lewis Carroll (1977) would say, there has to be continuous movement for the group to maintain itself as it is.

Another factor to keep in mind is that of contamination, since frequently an illness—if it results from the contagion of "unsatisfied" spirits, and if it is not effectively treated—can affect other members of the group. If obligations to ancestors are not fulfilled, they can withdraw protection from an individual, a family, or even a community, since their spirits continue to be a part of the family structure. The ailment caused by this absence of protection is seen as a demand made by ancestral guardians that broken ties be re-established, thus calling attention again to the question of witchcraft as a regulatory system of social imbalances.

The considerable dynamics of traditional medical action can be contrasted with the Ministry of Health's[43] project of collaboration with practitioners of traditional medicine, a part of its health policy (Jurg et al., 1991; FRELIMO, 1999). The system of public health developed by the state after independence places special emphasis on prevention. It seeks to reach the majority of the population, rural or peri-urban, through the establishment of a vast network of basic health units and agents capable of offering elementary healthcare, as well as by promoting health through education and the improvement of conditions of hygiene. The effect of such policies depends in the first place on the participation of the targeted populations.[44] For this reason, the WHO (1978) has recommended the inclusion of "practitioners of traditional health" within national health systems. Since this policy considers populations as partners in its implementation and not merely as passive recipients, the rehabilitation of local therapists, who have long been directly involved in such practices within communities, is essential.

The state has been using this justification to legitimize its interest in so-called traditional medicine, although this alone does not explain the underlying ambiguities that affect both the notion of valorizing "traditional medicine" and the practical experiments that are recommended. In promoting a discourse that supports the integration of traditional medicine with modern medicine, the state and WHO itself (Jurg, 1992; Monekoso, 1994; World Bank, 1994; Aregbeyen, 1996; WHO, 1996; Friedman, 1996) aim to remove from traditional therapists the control over the treatment (in its various forms) of the majority of the population. In supporting the formalization of "traditional medicine" according to the tenets of modern medicine, the former is circumscribed into a collection of empirical knowledge (medicinal plants, pharmacopoeia, and practical know-how), physical techniques and epidemiologies (Tomé, 1979; Marrato, 1995; Lambert, 1997). The knowledge of the traditional doctor is only seen to be valid as a complement to biomedicine; further, the traditional doctor is seen as one who needs to be trained, but who does not participate in the training of biomedical doctors (Nordstrom, 1992; Cunningham, 1995). This fact has resulted in a certain condescending resentment among traditional doctors: "We have no bitterness toward them [i.e., practitioners of modern medicine] but we also want recognition; they have to respect us [. . .]; we want to work with them, but also to teach what we know: it is not just plants."[45]

All these aspects suggest that we should make a deeper evaluation of the importance and legitimacy of different bodies of knowledge.

THE IMPORTANCE OF TRADITIONAL MEDICINE

Between legitimation and legitimacy

It is necessary to conduct a brief analysis of the privileged role of the state, the arbiter that attributes to itself the special status of establishing the rules as well as of playing the game. By looking at who is authorized and/or favored by the state, what knowledges are tolerated or suppressed, what practices are recognized or even ignored, it is possible to get a stronger and clearer idea of the logic of the state's action. This implies analyzing the fields of power from the point of view of the social recognition of different categories of health practitioners, in the complex interplay between competition and complementarity (Fassin and Fassin, 1988).

For the state, in the present as in the past, the delimitation of what is knowledge and magic, of the official and the non-official, is done according to normalized practices that the state itself controls. In the perspective of rational legitimation imposed by the colonial system, only those who study in formal institutions of learning are authorized to practice medicine. This must have been one of the main reasons that led many traditional doctors, at the beginning of the 1990s, to establish their own association (AMETRAMO).

People legitimate the health practitioners that they consult, whether those practitioners are trained in biomedicine or in so-called traditional medicine. Usually, traditional legitimacy is spontaneously associated with the "*nyàngà*" and rational legitimacy with the modern doctor (depending on his/her certificates). The acceptance of traditional doctors depends on the loyalty and confidence of those who recognize them as the inheritors of wisdom. Their legitimacy, the recognition of their competence within a field of knowledge, is ensured by those who constantly consult them. Among the traditional doctors themselves, legitimacy is reinforced by belonging to and sharing an ancestral knowledge, which is retrieved during the "visitations" of the spirits. The commitment to curing a patient as well as the ethical behavior of the traditional doctor reflect on his/her professional success: "When you do good work, it becomes known. People know that I can cure illnesses; they come from long distances [. . .]. They have heard of a healer in Maputo who cures this or that illness. That is how people know that I can heal properly, because I've healed many people."[46]

One of the most notorious forms used by biomedicine to disqualify traditional medicine lies in the characterization of the latter as an illegal practice, as well as in demonstrating the absence of "scientific" procedures (such as experimentation) or the lack of an understanding of epidemics or contagion (Polanah, 1967–68; 1987; Junod, [1917] 1996). All these factors confirm the "local" negative characterization of traditional medicine from the modern "scientific" point of view, which in effect omits references to their work procedures so as to bolster the "scientific" status of biomedicine. However, work on and with traditional doctors has shown that there is a continuous process of inquiry and search for new medicines and solutions, as well as the exchange of information among therapists. All of this implies the existence of experimentation, which, furthermore, is not a recent phenomenon:

> My grandfather, who was a well-known doctor in his time, taught me to heal as a child [. . .]. When he died, I devoted myself to the studies he left, doing various experiments, first with dogs, then with cats, and after being convinced of the usefulness of these medicines, I applied them to treat illnesses arising in our family. Thus I came to be known as a doctor many years ago [. . .] and I saved many people from certain death, acquiring more practical experience from my work and, due to my patience and tenacity, I came to enjoy a great reputation (Madão, [1921] 1971: 9).

What stands out in this brief historical analysis is that traditional medicine seems to be able to adjust to new therapeutic systems, seeking to negotiate positions and maintain or gain recognition and status, while biomedicine is still searching for ways and means to demonstrate its competencies.

The vitality of traditional medicine

The various attempts to suppress traditional medicine, or at least to limit its practice to "uncivilized native subjects," led to changes in the traditional doctors' field of action, a process that in fact constitutes evidence of the extraordinary capacity of this medicine to adapt itself and appropriate the mechanisms created by the state for its own benefit (Meneses, 2000). Like any attempt at social imposition, this type of interference has resulted in periodic crises of vulnerability.

With the implantation of the colonial system, the Portuguese state attempted to eliminate traditional therapists, condemning their activities as superstition and magic (di Celerina, 1846; Cunha, 1883; Junod, [1917] 1996; Silva Tavares, 1948). This resulted in the imprisonment and banishment of numerous "healers," particularly during the 1920s and 1930s. However, because of the scarcity of doctors and nurses in the territory, the colonial state rapidly came to accept the presence of healers, since it could not provide for the healthcare needs of the population:

> Indigenous medicine has been and must continue to be tolerated while medical assistance cannot fully reach all the villages of the interior [. . .]. If ancestral medicine has to be tolerated in some areas of the colony, it would

not be logical to use full punitive sanctions in respect of the clinical errors of *nyàngàs* of good faith. Apart from this, in a certain way, they should be considered useful in their social milieu because, with the lack of a better medicine, what they do is not so abominable (Gonçalves Cota, 1946, Art.68).

As a result of the fragility of the Portuguese colonial system, traditional doctors were able to request and obtain formal authorization (by the state) to act as therapists in areas where there were no practitioners of modern medicine, or where confidence in these was not very high.[47]

In the period immediately after independence (late 1970s and 1980s), the first movement of traditional therapists attempted to gain more space for action. Among the proposals made in 1975 by a group of traditional doctors to the Transitional Government Commission for Restructuring Health Services[48] was the creation of a School of Tropical Medicine to train more traditional practitioners. This was refused, in the period after independence, "because traditional medical practices are limited to empirical knowledge mixed with obscurantism. The official recognition of a healers' organization would amount to the institutionalization of obscurantism [. . .]. This implied the practice of private medicine, which was not legal at the time."[49]

Because it was important "to make use of the knowledge, but not the person, for the attitude of the person was obscurantist,"[50] and as a result of pressure exerted by various traditional practitioners on government and FRELIMO party organs, the National Directorate of Preventive Medicine at the Ministry of Health was given the task of creating the necessary means to research and collect plants used by traditional health practitioners (Castanheira, 1979; Tomé, 1979). At a juncture in which the field of action of healers was severely limited, the collection of plants and discussion of their use with the GEMT and INIA[51] was one of the few possibilities for the continuation of their activity, albeit with a semi-legal character.

Although the traditional doctors expected greater openness, since "now the country was finally ours,"[52] both doctors and magistrates of the post-independence period, due to their western education and the political objectives of the time, looked on witchcraft and the practices of healers as a shameful phenomenon. It was necessary to abandon them in order to construct a new knowledge, free of superstition and obscurantism. Once again, in the post-independence period, the state emerged as the unwitting ally of witchcraft by maintaining the prohibition of ordeals and legitimizing their application by traditional authorities and institutions.[53] If in the colonial period some forms of practice by traditional doctors were still permitted, now their prohibition was instituted, with healers being persecuted (even those who could solve cases of witchcraft and cure people). In this hostile environment, "traditional therapists" were now called "obscurants," with old mentalities (Castanheira, 1979; Tomé, 1979; Machel, 1981; Serviços de Nutrição, 1981).[54]

In M. F. Zimba's words, this was a very difficult period, and only the formation of an association of traditional doctors could alter the situation:

> Early on I went to talk with Machel [the first President of Mozambique] to help us get organized. It was necessary to organize ourselves so as to work properly, to avoid prosecution [. . .]. He sent me to talk with Hélder Martins [the then Minister of Health]. He was not helpful [. . .], he threatened us, but I kept insisting [. . .]. Then we managed to set up the Office for Support to Traditional Medicine. I worked a lot with Leonardo Simão [a doctor, and the present Minister of Foreign Affairs] in his office in the Ministry. Afterwards I stopped working there. At present I am working at home.[55]

At the end of the 1980s, with the introduction of neoliberal policies, the opening toward traditional medicine widened, until in 1991 the practice of private medicine was liberalized. As I mentioned, this made possible the formation of AMETRAMO—the Association of Mozambican Traditional Doctors.

The state and AMETRAMO

The evaluation of the traditional should not be seen only from the legal and formalistic position of the state. Several traditional therapists mentioned that it was common to meet with their seniors—the *mab'ava*—in order to analyze problems about which they were uncertain, a practice that is currently being reinforced by AMETRAMO.[56]

Thus, AMETRAMO has not come to fill a totally empty space in the relations between traditional therapists. During the meetings ("*mavandla*"[57]) for the graduation of the "*mathwasana*," the therapists come together to discuss the matters affecting them. AMETRAMO has merely reinforced and amplified these connections. Another important aspect is the constitution of AMETRAMO as a space for claiming social recognition for traditional medicine. In this case, the members of the association show themselves to be not in a position of weakness, but one of strength, due to the social role they represent. The concern of the current leadership of AMETRAMO in acting as the representative for the interests of all Mozambican traditional doctors in the rehabilitation of traditional medicine contributes toward its own legitimation; the power that derives from this representation acts as a confirmation of their concern and as a means of achieving their objective.

The paradox that many insist constitutes an obstacle to development—the persistence of "traditional" values—should not be seen as an antinomy.

Traditionalism is only what it is to the extent that it is distinguished from modernity by difference, but in fact it continuously feeds on modernity. Encounters occur at various levels: the state ignores traditional doctors while its functionaries frequently resort to them; the medical and law faculties do not recognize their knowledge, while many nurses and other medical personnel and lawyers do not hesitate to consult these therapists. This paradox is only an apparent contradiction: the norm established and imposed by the state is based on a legal and rational model of legitimacy. The agents that make up these institutions, on the contrary, dispense with these principles when acting as patients, obeying only practical rules. As one of the patients told me, "anything goes, you never know if they will work, but one certainly will; we just cannot risk not doing so."[58] For the patient, the need for legitimacy diminishes in the face of an ailment, social problems, or misfortune. When they consult a traditional doctor to solve a problem or cure an ailment, the university professor, the minister, or the lawyer are not considering the question of legitimacy, but looking for a practical effect. For this reason, it is impossible to divide society into "traditional" and "modern" in terms of medicine and the search for healing. The "civilized" businessman and the peasant woman with a sick child have similar itineraries, differing only in the financial means involved, and, consequently, in the prestige of the traditional practitioners consulted.

WHERE IS THE ALTERNATIVE?

Returning to the beginning of this text, I pose the same question: is traditional medicine really an alternative to biomedicine? The argument developed to this point leads to the suggestion that the struggle of bio-medicine for a limited incorporation of traditional medicine (only in the restricted sense of medicines and techniques), as well as its resistance to the recognition of the wide spectrum of efficacy of traditional medicine, are really a recognition of the strength of this other medicine, which is called, by opposition, traditional. The major reason for the tremendous vitality of traditional medicine seems to lie in the fact that "traditional medical institutions" treat disease and at the same time resolve society's problems, whether they are related with order (representations, norms) or with conflicts (tensions, collective misfortune). They are figures of modernity, but of another modernity, not imposed but composed of compromises with previous orders. Far from embodying the stasis of tradition, traditional medicine feeds on an eminently problematic modernity, appropriating the gaps and metamorphoses created by the state and giving them new meanings. Traditional medicine acts as a regulatory factor of social rhythms, resolving tensions and ensuring the reproduction of the social fabric.

The main focus of interpretation consists in demonstrating that modernity is not over, that it does not cease to amplify the "noise" of the traditional. If the treatment of illness is necessarily based on the therapeutic efficacy of symbolic and interpretative procedures, other forms of intervention give it a greater scope. Apart from treating different manifestations of misfortune (failure at school, marital difficulties, financial problems), the traditional doctor also operates in the preventive field, guaranteeing his clients means of protection against various sources of harm. In this sense, the traditional doctor ensures development, inserting him/herself into the heart of a modernity that, through individual aspirations and strategies, attempts to break with previous logical orders. It is for this reason that traditional medicine continues to attract not only patients from rural areas, or the economically disadvantaged; rather, patients from the urban areas increasingly come with their problems and expectations, seeking treatment, protection, success, things which all believe are possible and practicable. One can thus legitimately speak of a counter-hegemonic form of knowledge and power, in which this medicine represents the dynamics and the poles of locally used power.

In order to answer the initial question—whether traditional medicine is an alternative to biomedicine—I think it has been made clear that the strength of this field of knowledge lies in its ability to make use of modernity and modify it according to its needs. The alternative lies not in "other knowledges," classified as complementary, but in a complex interaction between different knowledges, all legitimate in the eyes of those who resort to them and sanction them as a form of power. Inter-medicine is thus synonymous with multiple medical knowledges, which are applied in different spheres— the family, the community, the workplace, and the public sphere of citizenship—thus granting it an emancipatory character.

Would not the recognition of AMETRAMO by the state, via its legalization, thus imply the impossible task of imposing a version of modernity that is exogenous to the one present in the social terrain? For the public powers (both at a national and international level), the political bet seems to favor the valorization and pseudo-legitimation of traditional medicine, refusing, however, to acknowledge the social dimension of this medicine by restricting it to the simple application of drugs and plants.[59] The constant attempts by the state to "promote and valorize" traditional medicine—as a complementary alternative to biomedicine—lead to another point of tension and conflict, the result of efforts to control politically the communities where this knowledge is produced. However, the complexity, fluidity, and ambiguity of the meanderings that compose the social field of traditional medicine make this process very difficult, if not impossible. In normalizing traditional therapeutic processes, in reducing this knowledge to written form, which is repetitive and allows for little innovation, are we not putting into question precisely that ambiguity that is so essential to the dynamic of traditional medicine's transformation and creative appropriation of modernity?

The emancipatory character of inter-medicine derives from its being "under construction" at a stage in which traditional medicine is experiencing a turbulent process of transition while trying to produce "another modernity." In this process, it is the echoes and marks of the traditional world that are most noticeable because they are at odds with "classic Western modernity." The constellation of distinct knowledges that is being created among different therapeutic realities leads to the reinforcement of their performance and legitimacy, as well as to a greater reciprocal control. This mosaic of hetero-geneous knowledges thus emerges as a guarantee of a permanent and open dialogue "in progress," as an exercise of democratic power/knowledge, justifying its emancipatory character. Hence, based on the local forms of resistance, one needs to present the different actors and their contexts of struggle, to build connections between these actors, mobilizing them and supporting their campaigns for a more egalitarian inclusion in the struggle for the diversity of knowledges, for achieving a broader space of action, and for enlarging the shared fields of knowledge. This unity based on difference should constitute one of the cornerstones of the elaboration of a new global counter-hegemony.[60] This kind of research necessarily has to be directed towards political intervention and towards the transformation of contemporary societies.

BIBLIOGRAPHY

Alonso, Margarita. Flórez, (2000). "Protección del conocimiento tradicional?" Draft paper for the Coimbra meeting on Reinventing Social Emancipation. Coimbra, 2000 (mimeo). [Revised version reprinted in this volume: Chapter 9: " Can We Protect Indigenous Knowledges?"]

Appadurai, A. (1999). "Globalization and the research imagination," *International Social Science Journal* 160: 229–238.

Aregbeyen, J. B. O. (1996). "Traditional herbal medicine for sustainable Primary Health Care," *Indigenous Knowledge Monitor* 4.

Barth, F. (1995). "Other knowledges and other ways of knowing," *Journal of Anthropological Research* 51: 65–67.

Batalha, M. M. (1985). "Medicina e farmacopeia tradicionais bantu," *Muntu* 3: 69–84.

Borges Coelho, J. P. (2001). "Estado, Comunidades e Calamidades Naturais no Moçambique Rural." Draft paper for the Coimbra meeting on Reinventing Social Emancipation. Coimbra, 2000 (mimeo). [Revised version reprinted in this volume: Chapter 8: "State, Community, and Natural Calamities in Rural Mozambique."]

Carroll, L. (1977). *Alice do outro lado do espelho.* Lisbon: Estampa.

Castanheira, N. (1979). "Curandeiros espiritistas: desmascarar a mentira, educar o homem," *Tempo* 474: 10–12.

Chavunduka, G. L. (1994). *Traditional medicine in modern Zimbabwe.* Harare: U of Zimbabwe P.

Comaroff, J., and John L. Comaroff (1999). "Occult economies and the violence of abstraction: notes from the South African postcolony," *American Ethnologist* 26: 279–303.

Copans, J. (1990). *La longue marche de la modernité africaine: savoirs, intellectuels, démocratie.* Paris: Karthala.

Cruz, D. (1910). *Em terras de Gaza.* Oporto: n.p.

Cruz e Silva, T. (2000). "Evangelicals and politics in Mozambique: the Universal Church of the Kingdom of God, The United Methodist Church and Maputo Zionists, in Southern Mozambique." Draft paper for the African Region Workshop on Evangelical Christianity and Political Democracy. Harare, Zimbabwe, August 2000 (mimeo).

Cunha, A. d. (1883). *Breve memória acerca da medicina entre os cafres da província de Moçambique.* Mozambique: n.p.

Cunningham, A. B. (1995). "People, plants and health care in Mozambique: background and recommendations on linking ethnobotany, plant conservation and health care." Maputo: Ministério da Saúde (mimeo).

di Celerina, J. d. S. (1846). "Esboço das moléstias da costa oriental d'África," *Annais marítimos e coloniais* 2: 43–72.

Dozon, J.-P. (1987). "Ce que valorizer la médicine traditionelle veut dire," *Politique Africaine* 28: 9–20.

Englund, H. (1996). "Witchcraft, modernity and the person: the morality of accumulation in central Malawi," *Critique of Anthropology* 16: 257–279.

Escobar, A., and M. Pardo (2000). "Biodiversidad, Movimientos Sociales en las Comunidades del Pacífico Colombiano." Draft paper for the Coimbra meeting on Reinventing Social Emancipation. Coimbra, 2000 (mimeo). [Revised version reprinted in this volume: Chapter 11: "Social Movements and Biodiversity on the Pacific Coast of Colombia."]

Fassin, E., and Didier Fassin (1988). "De la question de légitimation a la question de la légitimité: les thérapeutiques 'traditionelles' au Sénégal," *Cahiers d'Études africaines* 28: 207–231.

Fisiy, C. F., and P. Geschiere (1990). "Judges and witches, or how is the state to deal with witchcraft?" *Cahiers d'Études africaines* 118: 135–156.

Fisiy, C., and P. Geschiere (1996). "Witchcraft, violence and identity: different trajectories in postcolonial Cameroon," R. Webner and T. Ranger (eds.), *Postcolonial identities in Africa.* London: Zed Books. 193–221.

———, and M. Goheen (1998). "Power and the quest for recognition: neo-traditional titles among the new elite in Nso', Cameroon," *Africa* 68: 383–402.

Folgosa, J. M. (1956). *A arte de curar em Moçambique: povos, curandeiros remédios. História dos hospitais da província.* Lourenço Marques: n.p.

FRELIMO, Comité Central do Partido (1999). *Proposta de programa do Governo 2000–2004.* Maputo: n.p.

Friedman, E. C. (1996). "Community based sales of Jeito using Traditional healers, Traditional birth attendants and APEs." Maputo: Ministério da Saúde (mimeo).

Galvão da Silva, M. (1955). "Diário das viagens feitas pelas terras de Manica em 1790," A. A. Andrade (ed.), *Relações de Moçambique Setecentista*. Lisbon: Agência Geral do Ultramar.

Geschiere, P. (1995). *Sorcellerie et Politique en Afrique: la viande des autres*. Paris: Karthala.

Gentili, A. M. (1999). *O Leão e o caçador: uma história da África sub-saariana*. Maputo: Imprensa Universitária.

Gonçalves Cota, J. (1946). *Projecto definitivo do Código penal dos indígenas da Colónia de Moçambique*. Lourenço Marques: Imprensa Nacional.

Goody, J. (1979). *La raison graphique: la domestication de la pensée sauvage*. Paris: Ed. Minuit.

Green, E. C. (1996). *Indigenous healers and the African State*. New York: Pact Publications.

——————, Kenneth G. Goodman, and Martha Hare (1999). "Ethnobotany, IPR and benefit-sharing: the Forest People's Fund in Suriname," *Indigenous Knowledge and Development Monitor 7*.

Hess, D. J. (1994). *Science and technology in a multicultural world: the cultural politics of facts and artifacts*. New York: Columbia UP.

Hewson, M. G. (1998). "Traditional Healers in Southern Africa," *Annals of Internal Medicine* 15: 1029–1034.

Hobsbawm, E. (1988). "Introduction: Inventing Tradition," E. Hobsbawm and T. Ranger (eds.), *The invention of Tradition*. Cambridge: Cambridge UP. 1–14.

Honwana, Alcinda M. R. M. (1996). *Spiritual agency and self-renewal in southern Mozambique*. PhD dissertation. University of London School of Oriental and African Studies. London: U. of London.

Instituto Nacional de Estatística (1999). *Inquérito Demográfico e de Saúde, 1997*. Maputo: Instituto Nacional de Estatística and Demographic and Health Surveys.

Junod, H. P. (1939). "Os indígenas de Moçambique no séc. XVI e começo do séc. XVII segundo os antigos documentos portugueses da época dos descobrimentos," *Moçambique Documentário Trimestral* 17: 5–34.

—————— (1996 [1917]). *Usos e costumes dos Bantu*. 2 vols. Maputo: Arquivo Histórico de Moçambique.

Jurg, A. (1992). "HIV, STD and traditional medicine. Approaches in Mozambique." *VIII International conference on AIDS—III STD World Congress*. Amsterdam, 1992 (mimeo).

Jurg, I., J. de Jong, T. Tomás, J. Marrato, M. Wilisone, and G. Kirchner (1991). "Fornecedores e utentes de cuidados de saúde, modernos ou tradicionais, em Maputo, Moçambique: opiniões e preferências mútuas." Maputo: GEMT—Ministério da Saúde (mimeo).

Lambert, J., and Gabriel Albano (1997). "Mozambique's medicinal plants: a proposed draft agenda for sustainable utilization." Maputo: GEMT—Ministério da Saúde (mimeo).

Liengme, G. (1844–1894). "Quelques observátions sur les maladies des indigenes des provinces de Lourenço Marques et Gaza," *Bulletin de la Société Newchateloise de Géographie* 8: 180–191.

MacCormack, C. (1986). "The articulation of western and traditional systems of health care," M. Last and G. L. Chavunduka (eds.), *The professionalisation of African medicine*. Manchester: Manchester UP. 151–162.

Machel, S. (1981). "A escola é uma base científica," *Tempo* 549: 37–42.

Madão, Z. T. (1971 [1921]). "A minha medicina," *A Voz de Moçambique* 18/07/1971: 9, 18.

Manjate, E. (2000). "Na Ametramo: curandeiros em luta," *Savana* (1 September 2000): 13.

Mappa, S. (1998). *Pouvoirs traditionnels et pouvoir de l'État en Afrique: l'illusion universaliste.* Paris: Karthala.

Marrato, J. (1995). *Seminário colaborativo modelo entre a medicina moderna e a medicina tradicional na província de Nampula.* Ministério da Saúde: GEMT.

Maugham, R. C. F. (1906). *Portuguese East Africa: The History, scenery and Great Game of Manica and Sofala.* London: John Murray.

Meneses, M. P. (2000). "Medicina Tradicional, biodiversidade e conhecimentos rivais em Moçambique," *Oficina do CES* 150.

Monekoso, G. L. (1994). "WHO deplores Africa's health crises," *WHO Newsletter* 9(2).

Muthemba, A. S. (1970). "Usos e Costumes do Sul de Moçambique," *O Cooperador de Moçambique* 10.

Nathan, T., and Isabelle Strengers, (1995). *Le médecin et le charlatan. Manifeste pour une psychopatologie scientifique.* Paris: Les Empêcheurs de penser en rond.

Ngubane, H. (1981). "Clinical practice and organization of indigenous healers in South Africa," *Social Science and Medicine* 15B: 361–366.

Nordstrom, C. (1991). "Formalizing traditional medicine." Maputo: Ministério da Saúde (mimeo).

O'Laughlin, B. (2000). "Class and the customary: the ambiguous legacy of the *indigenato* in Mozambique," *African Affairs* 99: 5–42.

Ong, A. (1996). "Anthropology, China and modernities: the geopolitics of cultural knowledge," H. L. Moore (ed.), *The Future of Anthropological Knowledge.* New York: Routledge. 60–92.

Phaindanne (2000). "A feitiçaria não é um mito, é uma realidade," *Demos* (5 July 2000): 14. [Maputo].

Pina, L. (1940). "A medicina indígena da Africa Portuguesa." *Memórias e Comunicações ao IX Congresso Colonial do Mundo Português.* Vol. XIV(1). Lisbon: n.p. 177–207.

Polanah, L. D. (1967–68). "Possessão e exorcismo em Moçambique," *Memórias do Instituto de Investigação Científica de Moçambique* 9(C).

Polanah, L. (1987). *O nhamussoro e outras funções mágico-religiosas.* Coimbra: Instituto de Antropologia da Universidade de Coimbra.

Santos, B. d. S. (1987). "Law: a map of misreading. Toward a postmodern conception of law," *Journal of Law and Society* 14: 279 pp.

————— (1995). *Toward a New Common Sense: Law, Science and Politics in the Paradigmatic Transition.* New York: Routledge.

————— (1998a). *La globalización del derecho: los nuevos caminos de la regulación y la emancipación.* Bogota, ILSA: Universidad Nacional de Colombia.

————— (1998b). "Time, baroque codes and canonization," *Cultural Values* 2: 403–420.

————— (2000). *A crítica da razão indolente: contra o desperdício da experiência.* Vol. 1. Porto: Afrontamento.

—————, J. C. Trindade, et al. (2000). "O Estado Heterogéneo e o pluralismo jurídico," B. S. Santos and J. C. Trindade (eds.), *Conflito e transformação social em Moçambique: uma paisagem das justiças em Moçambique*. Vol. I. Maputo: CEA, CES.

Santos Junior, J. R., and F. Barros (1950). "Notas etnográficas de Moçambique." *XIII Congresso Luso-Espanhol para o progresso das Ciências*. Vol. V. Lisbon: n.p. 609–623.

Santos Reis, C. (1952). "A 'arte indígena de curar' em terras de Zavala," *Moçambique Documentário Trimestral* 71: 37–58.

Schoffeleers, M. (1991). "Ritual healing and political acquiescence: the case of the zionist churches in southern Africa," *Africa* 60: 1–25.

Serviço de Nutrição, DNMP (1981). "Alguns resultados preliminares do trabalho do GEMT (Grupo de Estudos de Medicina Tradicional)," *Cadernos de Saúde* 1.

Silva Tavares, J. A. (1948). "A arte indígena de curar," *Moçambique Documentário Trimestral* 53: 111–132.

Simões Alberto, M. (1965). "Elementos para um vocabulário etnográfico de Moçambique," *Memórias do Instituto de Investigação Científica de Moçambqiue* 7: 171–228.

Schwalbach, M. T. F. S., and João F. L. Schwalbach (1970). "Aspectos gerais da medicina negra de Moçambique," *Revista dos Estudantes da Universidade de Lourenço Marques* 14 pp.

Taussing, M. (1987). *Shamanism, Colonialism and the wild man. A study of terror and healing*. Chicago: U of Chicago P.

Temba, J. (1992). "Mirhi (misinya) ya ku lapha Mavabyi (medicamentos tradicionais)." Maputo (mimeo).

Temba, E. (2000). "Curandeiras: rupturas, descontinuidade ou subalternidades?" *Jornadas de Estudos Africanos* Barcelona (mimeo).

Tique, Saúl (2000). "Em Sofala 'há muito feitiço': os estereótipos dos moçambicanos, segundo pesquisa da UEM," *Imparcial* (18 Oct. 2000): 4. [Maputo].

Tomé, B. (1979). "Medicina tradicional: estudar as plantas que curam," *Tempo* 460: 13–23.

Tsenane, X. (1999). "Plantas: beleza e magia," *Tempo* (7 Nov. 1999): 10–13.

Visvanathan, S. (2000). "Between Cosmology and System. A Heuristics for Globalization." Draft paper for the Coimbra meeting on Reinventing Social Emancipation. Coimbra, 2000 (mimeo). [Revised version reprinted in this volume: Chapter 7: "Between Cosmology and System: The Heuristics of a Dissenting Imagination."]

Xaba, T. (1999). "A disenchanted modernity: the accommodation of African medicine in contemporary South Africa," A. Sitas and T. C. Silva (eds.), *Gathering Voices: Perspectives on the Social Sciences in Southern Africa*. Durban: n.p. 155–170.

Xaba, T. (2000). "Development and its discontents—the marginalization of indigenous medicines in South Africa." Draft paper for the Coimbra meeting on Reinventing Social Emancipation. Coimbra, 2000 (mimeo). [Revised version reprinted in this volume: Chapter 12: "Marginalized Medical Practice. The Marginalization and Transformation of Indigenous Medicines in South Africa."]

World Bank (1994). *Better Health in Africa: Experience and lessons learned*. Washington, DC: World Bank.

WHO (1978). *Primary health care*. Geneva: World Health Organization.
———————— (1996). "Traditional medicine," *WHO Fact Sheet* 134: 3 pp.
Wynne, B. (1994). "Scientific knowledge and the global environment," M. R. Redcliff and T. Benton (eds.), *Social theory and the global environment*. London: Routledge. 168–189.

Notes

1 Here I follow Santos's approach (2000), which refers to similar situations as examples of "globalized localism."

2 The death of local knowledge by an alien science (Santos, 1998a: 208).

3 This subject is also discussed by Xaba (2000), who makes a critique of the negative impact of modern scientific medicine on South African indigenous medical knowledges.

4 Here I follow Santos's theoretical proposal on "interlegality" (see Santos, 1987; Santos and Trindade, 2000), broadening it and projecting it beyond the field of justice to that of health.

5 Associação Moçambicana de Médicos Tradicionais (Mozambican Association of Traditional Doctors).

6 See also Borges Coelho's text (2001), which focuses on the question of rival knowledges in the prevention of natural disasters from the national/local perspective.

7 C. Tamele, personal interview, June–July 2000.

8 In Africa, much has been written on the place of the "traditional" in current epistemological discussions (see Hobsbawm, 1988; Copans, 1990; Gentili, 1999; O'Laughlin, 2000; Santos and Trindade, 2000). In other political contexts, the debate between the "modern" and the "traditional" is seen either as a space of conflict from which new realities can emerge (for India, see Visvanathan, 2000), or as the basis for the creation of spaces of difference and contrast (Flórez, 2000; Xaba, 2000).

9 Personal interview, May 2000.

10 It also happens that imported religions (Christianity and Islam) have generated syncretic movements whose specificity lies in the fact that their religious work includes therapeutic functions, which contribute further to the range of therapeutic options available. Between the local medicines and syncretic movements there is no necessary continuity or proximity; rather, they are examples of the enormous diversity of therapeutic resources currently available for responding to problems of crisis and order in existing structures (see Schoffeleers, 1991, Honwana, 1996, Cruz e Silva, 2000).

11 First the colonial, and subsequently the post-colonial, state (i.e., after 1975).

12 Ministries, medical and law faculties, etc.

13 Gabinete de Estudos de Medicina Tradicional (Office for the Study of Traditional Medicine), founded in the Ministry of Health to promote links with traditional medicine (Serviço de Nutrição, 1981). In a conversation with the director of GEMT, A. Agostinho (a biochemist), the continuity of state policy concerning traditional medicine became evident (May 2000).

14 M. F. Zimba, personal interview, August 2000.

15 In the logic of biomedicine, health has to be understood in the wider context of the development of a country, region, or community (WHO, 1996).

16 A. Fabião, personal interview, April 2000.
17 A. Boane, personal interview, March 2000.
18 P. Salomão, personal interview, July 2000.
19 Another form of discredit is based on the use of the term *"curandeiro"* (healer), which for many practitioners of traditional medicine in Maputo city is synonymous with witchdoctor. Thus, in order to claim powers similar to those of the practitioners of biomedicine, such healers demand to be called "traditional doctors."
20 M. Suzana, personal interview, February 2000.
21 Extract of an interview with Amida Safar Gina, traditional doctor (*Domingo*, 13 January 1991).
22 Tique, 2000.
23 I.e., the *"tinholo,"* the divination bones used by traditional doctors as auxiliary means of diagnosis.
24 L. Augusto, personal interview, May 2000.
25 See the case study of AMETRAMO below.
26 In southern Mozambique, the native term used for traditional doctors is *"nyàngà,"* (Galvão da Silva, [1790] 1955; Simões Alberto, 1965, etc.) The *"nyàngàrùme"* is the herbal doctor who uses plants for treatments, without resorting to spiritual forces to help solve problems (Temba, 1992).
27 M. F. Zimba, personal interview, June 2000.
28 H. Macie, personal interview, February 2000.
29 During the training process the individual remains isolated from his/her family, maintaining few or even no contacts at all with them, even when he/she is married and has children.
30 See also Honwana (1996) and Temba (2000). The latter evaluates the question of traditional doctors from a gender perspective.
31 C. Tamele, personal interview, May 2000.
32 As stated in several texts, one of the main characteristics of "traditional knowledge" seems to be its ancestral roots, which are maintained and transmitted from generation to generation with the support of dead kin (Flórez, 2000; Xaba, 2000).
33 A student of traditional medicine.
34 A term of respect applied to a very wise and esteemed person. In the context of this study, it refers to an experienced or senior traditional doctor, male or female, who has students.
35 P. Cossa, personal interview, June 2000.
36 Hence the fact that many illnesses are explained as "the head aches" or "the leg hurts."
37 Prayers to ensure the maintenance of connections with the ancestors.
38 Plural of *"nòyì."* The *nòyì* is a spirit with evil power, who can even provoke trouble from a distance, through the help of somebody whose body he uses. Usually the *valòyì* act at night, through the introduction of alien parts (bones, blood) into somebody's body; as a consequence, the person withers and dies. During the day, the evil spirit can act through elements he has previously contaminated. The *nòyì* can still use a person whose body he "opened" and penetrated, enslaving him/her. These people can be transformed into animals, such as leopards, hyenas, and serpents, or be forced to work in

the fields for this spirit, or to steal goods to feed the spirit (Muthemba, 1970; Polanah, 1987; Honwana, 1996).

39 I.e., to "sniff out" the evil spirits, so as to get hold of them, since they are the origin of the problem. The spirit can only be identified by its odor, and this explains the need to "sniff out" the souls of unsatisfied ancestors or of the valòyi.

40 Interview with C. Tamele, March 2000.

41 Plural of "mùrhi," i.e., "plants." In a broader sense, it also means medication.

42 M. Yussufo, personal interview, December 1999.

43 The state entity that is most directly related with traditional medicine.

44 It should be mentioned that in Maputo, in terms of provision of hospital care in modern medicine, there is a ratio of one doctor to 48–50,000 inhabitants, while the ratio of traditional doctors to patients is one to 1000–1500, a situation that is similar to other countries in the region.

45 M. F. Zimba, C. Tamele, and P. Cossa, collective interview, September 2000.

46 M. F. Zimba, personal interview, April 2000.

47 More censured and persecuted was the practice of "ordeal," i.e., a test of guilt or innocence, which was prohibited according to the precepts of Portuguese justice.

48 I am grateful to L. Meneses for this information.

49 H. Martins (the first Minister of Health in independent Mozambique), personal interview, March 2000.

50 Ibidem.

51 Instituto Nacional de Investigação Agronómica (National Institute for Agronomic Research).

52 M. F. Zimba, personal interview, March 2000.

53 This was equivalent to forbidding the identification and punishment of those individuals considered to hold "evil knowledge," regarded as a source of social instability and therefore harmful to society (see note 51)

54 Several of them were sent to distant forced labor camps, the so-called "re-education camps."

55 M. F. Zimba, personal interview, June 2000.

56 C. Tamele, personal interview, April 2001.

57 Vandla—assembly, gathering, meeting (lit.). Here, the word refers to a group of traditional therapists who had or still have the same b'ava; it also refers to larger gatherings of traditional doctors, called to discuss subjects relating to the "health" of a given community.

58 A. Boane, personal interview, March 2000.

59 In 2004, the Mozambican government recognized traditional medicine as an integral part of the national health system.

60 Research as action, as an exercise in citizenship, is analyzed following Santos's suggestion (2000).

Part V

COMMENTARIES

14

Globalization, Multiculturalism, and Law

Yash Ghai

INTRODUCTION

Racism and multiculturalism are both products of globalization. Racism is generally regarded as the ideological justification and practical effect of imperialism and colonialism. It belongs to the rise of Western, capitalist dominance of the world, which proclaimed the superiority of Western culture and religion, and justified its mission to bring civilization and Christianity to heathen and barbaric peoples. The deliberate denigration of other cultures produced a deep sense of inferiority among those people. This enterprise involved a considerable misrepresentation and stereotyping of cultures, as typified in the concept of "orientalism." Multiculturalism, on the other hand, belongs to the contemporary stage of globalization and is seen as the tool to fight the legacies of racism and ensure a fairer social and political system.

The relationship between globalization and multiculturalism is thus ambiguous. At one level globalization brings different cultures into contact. Through the establishment and organization of states that—both during colonialism as well as in more contemporary migrations—brought diverse peoples together within common borders and a single sovereignty, globalization has led to the development of multicultural states and societies. Even within a state, globalization increases contacts among its different people—as the frontier of the market moves in search of raw materials—and thus many indigenous peoples have been brought into the general sphere of the state. With the current preoccupation with identity, stimulated in considerable part by globalization, it has given recognition and prominence to identities within states that have tended to regard themselves as ethnically and culturally homogeneous, thus giving a new spin to multiculturalism. It changes the context within which multiculturalism operates, bringing it within the confines of a state rather than into a clash/relationship across broad and disparate geographical areas. Some of the most intense and interesting debates about multiculturalism now take place within the borders of a state, relating to the coexistence of its communities.

Today there is greater respect for other cultures. Developments in international law and global economy promote ethnic and cultural consciousness, often as a defense mechanism or response. Dominated cultures are not so vulnerable as previously; they have their own sovereign states, some of them successful economically, so that they are able to challenge the assumptions of the superiority of Western cultures, as in the "Asian values debate" (Ghai, 1994; Langlois, 2001). On the other hand, we must acknowledge the homogenizing influence of global capitalism and markets on cultures. There is ample evidence that market capitalism tends to disrupt and eventually destroy communal or common ownership of land and with it the bonds and cohesion of the community. It introduces new values that displace traditional ways of thinking and behaving. It breaks up the joint or extended family, around which are embedded core values and rituals of culture. It leads to new forms of labor and to new modes of organization. Today, additionally, we have the powerful influence of international media, films, and advertising, supported by trademarks and other forms of intellectual property rights. However, it has indeed been argued that capitalism need not have this kind of impact on a society and its traditional values. It has been suggested that Chinese and other communities in the Far East have developed and nurtured capitalist economies without having to give up Confucian values, and that instead Confucianism itself has been the primary organizing matrix for that capitalism (Redding, 1990). However, it is unlikely that capitalism can develop beyond a rather rudimentary stage in this way, and it is clear that as firms in the Far East achieve a degree of national or global operations they inevitably change their modes of organization, fundraising, and decision-making (Ghai, 1995). The argument that capitalism is consistent with various forms of culture appears untenable. Globalization has fundamentally changed the cultures of many peripheral regions. It has set a new framework within which cultures may coexist, and in which Western ideas of economy, the individual, community, and state dominate. There is resistance to this framework.

The project from which this book results is built around the crucial distinction "between hegemonic globalization, which is dominated by the logic of world neoliberal capitalism, and counter-hegemonic globalization, which includes the local-global initiatives undertaken by subaltern and dominated social groups in an attempt to resist the oppression, de-characterization, and marginalization produced by hegemonic globalization" (Santos, 2000a). Santos asks the question, "Is it possible to unite what has been separated by hegemonic globalization and separate what has been united by it? Is this all that counter-hegemonic globalization entails? Is it possible to contest the forms of dominant social regulation and from there reinvent social emancipation?" (Santos, 2000a). The usefulness of the project lies not just in the intellectual issues it engages with but in its implications for practical struggles as well. Among the issues to be examined in this ambitious project are the roles of constitutions, state structures, and human rights, both as instruments of domination and tools of counter-hegemony. The focus on these topics fits in the general strategy of the project: to examine, from the perspectives of the periphery, local initiatives as they impact on global forces. Constitutions and state structures clearly fall in the local category, although, in the cases studied here, they too reflect international conventions. Human rights occupy a somewhat different position, for they have become central to the rhetoric of international politics and are negotiated internationally with a growing global industry of the production and supervision of human rights, armed with some sanctions and powers of intervention.

Santos recognizes that there are many conflicts, resistances, struggles, and coalitions clustering around cosmopolitanism and the common heritage of humankind, demonstrating "that what we call globalization is in fact a set of arenas of cross-border struggles" (Santos, this volume). Chief among these arenas are emancipatory multiculturalism and alternative forms of justice and citizenship, which oppose in particular unequal identity differentiation, domination, and patriarchy (Santos, 2000a). Essays dealing with multiculturalism explore the revolutionary potential of human rights, including networking on the basis of human rights and local initiatives, the importance of group or collective rights, legal pluralism, and the redesign of state structures to accommodate ethnic, social, and cultural diversities—as well as the forms of struggle that are made possible by these developments. In general, the authors favor special legal regimes for minorities and indigenous people, support constitutional reform and state structures, including regional or cultural autonomy (which accommodate ethnic and cultural diversity), and highlight the benefits of the use of human rights for social movements and networking.

To an extent, as a friendly and sympathetic critic, I take issue with some suppositions that underlie the counter-hegemonic strategies. I do so partly to draw attention to the diversity of situations generated by globalization and to caution against the belief that there can be universal solutions to the challenges it raises. My own conclusions do not always coincide with them, in part because my own experience relates to situations somewhat different from those discussed in these essays. In that regard my approach is similar to the one foreshadowed by Santos, the editor of these studies, when he alerts us to the dangers of generalization or of the prescription of universal remedies. He writes:

It is actually possible that some initiatives that present themselves as alternatives to global capitalism are themselves a form of oppression as well. By the same token, an initiative that, in a given country at a given moment, may be seen as counter-hegemonic, may be seen as hegemonic in another country or another moment. [. . .] Just like science, is not social emancipation multicultural, definable, and valid only in certain contexts, places, and circumstances (since what is social emancipation for one social group or at a particular historical moment may be considered regulation or even social oppression for another social group or at a different moment in time)? Are all struggles against oppression, whatever their means and objectives, struggles for social emancipation? Are there degrees of social emancipation? Is it possible to have social emancipation without individual emancipation? And social emancipation is for whom, for what, against whom, against what?" (Santos, 2000a).

The value of the studies in this book is precisely that they are so carefully located in their specific contexts.

HUMAN RIGHTS

The complexity and contradictions of globalization allow its ideologies, institutions, and processes to be used to facilitate as well as fight globalization. Nowhere is this more obvious than in the case of human rights. Human rights has become a highly contested terrain, assisted by the multiplicity of norms and international and regional conventions, the plurality of enforcement or supervisory mechanisms, differing political and moral justifications for the primacy of rights, and the modes of challenge to the very concept of rights (Ghai, 2002a). The concept of human rights, legally formulated as entitlements, is generally accepted as Western in origin. The dominant tradition of human rights—civil and political rights—derives from western philosophy, and is closely connected to liberalism, individualism, and the market. Rights inhere in the individual and protect against the acts of the state, not private parties or corporations. The ideology and rhetoric of human rights are often regarded as a tool of Western domination, which provide critical support to globalization. The following are some of the ways in which the regime of human rights is seen to assist the assertion of Western hegemony.

—Using the notion of universalism, human rights enable western values to masquerade as universal, thus denigrating other cultures and values, particularly insofar as they retard the market economy;
—the notion of human rights as supreme over other rights, claims, or policies privileges Western values;

—Western personnel and institutions maintain supremacy in the interpretation of rights, through adjudication and educational processes;

—the values promoted through human rights assist in the globalization of economies: property rights (now enormously expanded), equality (discouraging discrimination against non-citizens), bringing corporations within the categories of beneficiaries of rights (but not duties), freedom of contract, independent judiciaries, etc.;

—weakening the state and strengthening civil society/economic corporations, defining a narrow role for the state, thus benefiting the already advantaged (also through questioning the status as rights of economic, social, and cultural rights—the concept of rights is determined in substantial part by intellectuals, and the West has the resources to fund intellectuals and their centers of learning);

—extending the range of interventions in other states through promoting and directing international NGOs and through support to local movements and NGOs, often under the hegemony of Western-based organizations;

—allowing sanctions against or "humanitarian" intervention in other states;

—selectivity or double standards, which allows an opportunistic use of rights, condemning states hostile to the West (such as Iran), but ignoring or glossing over the shameful record of its allies (Suharto's Indonesia), assisted by the Western media;

—possible for a powerful state, partly through its hegemony over international institutions, to get away with violations of rights (as regularly in the US), but not for weak states.

Equally, human rights can be or have been used as counter-hegemony, in the following ways:

—independence movements in the post-war period were based on the language of rights, particularly self-determination;

—challenging the notion of western values as universal and positing other values (the Asian values debate); using cultural relativism arguments to demonstrate the culture specificity of human rights; infusing notions of differential cultures in human rights regimes (compare the interpretations of Article 27 of the International Convention on Civil and Political Rights [see below]);

—gaining more space for derogations of and limitations on rights;

—denigrating the whole idea of rights, for example by reference to the primacy of duties, or the primacy of the community;

—downgrading rights through assertions of state sovereignty;

—seeking more democratic methods for the formulation of rights;

—expanding the notion of rights, e.g., self-determination, indigenous peoples' rights, rights of minorities and migrants, the right to development,

economic, social, and cultural rights, and gender rights; these rights challenge
the hitherto dominant tradition of civil and political rights, some of which
are closely connected to market economies;

—using rights for networking (particularly successful examples of which
include campaigns by women and indigenous peoples);

—developing notions of collective rights (and arguing that the state
personifies the collective);

—exposing Western hypocrisy over rights by demonstrating the uneven
record of Western states (China, for example, has issued two official papers
documenting and criticizing the reality of rights in the US);

—using ideas of universalism and interdependence to locate responsibility in
the richer countries;

—using the concept of economic, social, and cultural rights to resist aid and
other conditionalities, structural adjustment programmers, and the directives
of the WTO, etc.

It would be evident from the above list that not all the "counter-
hegemonic" strategies are directed against globalization. Tensions often arise
among different local groups and forces, or between local actors and national
forces and institutions. In some cases, the state is seen as an ally or surrogate of
"external" forces (see Arenas, this volume). In others, the confrontation of
the local with the national aims at securing gains at the local level, extracting
concessions from the state, and granting or extending rights to local self-
government. Counter-hegemonic strategies are often the product of debates
or conflicts between East–West/North–South, which are neither intellec-
tually sustainable nor capture the complexity of globalization. For example,
the severest critic in Asia of human rights and the strongest proponent of
Asian values is Lee Kwan Yew, who is also an ardent supporter of
globalization. Other states infused with Confucian cultures have chosen
to integrate their economies into the international system. The collusion of
the US (and some other Western states) with "Southern" dictators in the
suppression of rights and in cover-ups has been the most important factor in
the oppression of their people. The blanket denigration of rights or the
exposure of the failure of Western states to honor human rights may do little
for counter-hegemony. To keep emphasizing the superiority of a society
animated by the concept of duty may merely be a device to maintain
patriarchy, male chauvinism, and other forms of social or family oppression
(Ghai, 1998). It is clear, as studies in this book suggest, that many subaltern
groups in the South benefit or can benefit from rights, that rights have played
a valuable role in conscientising and mobilizing the oppressed, that rights
have facilitated the articulation of local protests with international organizations, helping to establish the commonality of interests between the peoples

of the South and the North—for example, in the preservation of the environment or even the culture of faraway communities—and that the violation of rights has been instrumental in forcing international intervention to stop the slaughter of minorities. Counter-hegemonists should therefore beware of being seduced or entrapped by high-moral-sounding persons whose commitment to justice and diversity is questionable. If rights are to play a liberating and counter-hegemonic force, they have to be treated with respect. Equally, the potential of rights has to be carefully reviewed and then strengthened. As Santos rightly points out, the "tenuous line between emancipation and regulation oscillates according to the ambiguity of the "partnerships," which, for tactical reasons, may combine the emancipatory initiatives of the struggle with instruments of social regulation" (Santos, 2000b: 19).

Strengthening the regime of human rights

Human rights provide the most powerful and coherent challenge to the ideology of globalization. Globalization is individual-oriented, glorifying in the greed of and incentives to individuals, at the same time as it treats people as commodities (labor) or consumers, is profit driven, fragments, and destroys communities, and appropriates commons, producing vulnerability and insecurity, without common values. Globalization is based on monopolies and hierarchies. The regime of human rights, on the other hand, emphasizes democracy and participation, solidarity, collective action, and responsibility, aims to ensure basic needs, dignity, social recognition, and security. It offers an alternative vision of globalization in which social justice and solidarity are emphasized. In fact, sometimes, human rights are the only weapons that the weak and the victims of different kinds of oppression and violence can draw upon. In its hegemonic version, however, the regime of human rights is a homogenizing device, and thus it does tend towards the suppression of cultures that are not dominant in the emergence of modern rights theory; but there are possibilities of its extension to other values and thus cultures. The human rights framework also offers options to individualism, which is contrary to community values: a kind of cosmopolitanism, freedom of association for communities to semi-opt out of the dominant culture and pursue their own culture, and some recognition of collective identity and goals.

Counter-hegemonic approaches to human rights often criticize the double standards in the upholding of these rights. But this should not be turned into an attack on human rights. The more productive approach to rights as "counter-hegemonic" is to develop the framework of rights in a balanced way. This can be done by focusing on the problems of the disadvantaged or the oppressed (international conventions on indigenous peoples and migrants, women, and children are examples), by exploring the cultural dimensions of rights, promoting collective or group rights, with the capacity to remedy injustices of the past, taking seriously economic, social, and cultural rights, building on their interdependence (as in the conventions on women and children), mainstreaming rights into development policies and institutions, and emphasizing the obligations of the international community to protect and ensure equal rights to all (especially social and economic rights). This last point is particularly important in the age of globalization, when the ability of states to provide welfare has been eroded under neoliberal doctrines, and with the consequent transfer of decision-making power over key social and economic issues to international financial and trade organizations and transnational corporations (see Ghai, 1999, for the relationship between rights and globalization). We need to move away from the traditional notions that rights are organized within state boundaries and that their protection is the responsibility of state institutions—the concept of global citizenship vests that responsibility in the global community, especially with the transfer of key economic and political power to regional and international institutions. Equally, to the same effect, one can invoke the classical conceptualization of human rights as inherent, universal, and indivisible. Responsibility for the protection of human rights can also be ascribed to corporations, as the logical development of the rise of private economic power. Rights can also provide a better framework for competing forces in globalization if its cultural foundations can be broadened. Santos, in this volume, shows one method for enriching the corpus of human rights by drawing on the virtues and strengths of different cultures, as an aid towards fusion. Another method towards achieving interculturalism has been indicated by Charles Taylor, who, using Rawls's concept of overlapping consensus, aims at the convergence of specific rights by looking at common values and practices in different cultural, rather than their philosophical or religious, bases (Taylor, 1999). Yet a third approach is that of Abdulahi An-Nai'm, who advocates reinterpretations of tenets of religious traditions to fit in, where possible, with internationally accepted norms (An-Nai'm, 1990). Each of these approaches has of course different implications for multi-culturalism, but they all point to the need for an intercultural consensus on rights. Santos's approach is the most imaginative and fruitful of those developing a bridge or synthesis. Whereas Taylor and An-Nai'm aim at finding commonality, Santos looks at differences in order to build a more complete conception of human rights. Restriction of space prevents a full discussion of these strategies for counter-hegemony. I propose to examine developments in international norms only in four related areas: self-determination, cultural rights, indigenous peoples' rights, and the right to development, which show the possibilities and potential of counter-strategies.

Self-determination

The broadest source of autonomy is self-determination, in itself a difficult and controversial concept, but which is increasingly being analyzed in terms of the internal, democratic organization of a state rather than in terms of secession or independence. The marked bias of the international community of states against the use of self-determination, other than for classical colonies, is well known (Franck, 1993). The UN General Assembly resolved many years ago that autonomy is a manifestation of self-determination. The greater involvement of the UN or a consortia of states in the settlement of internal conflicts has also helped to develop the concept of self-determination as implying autonomy in appropriate circumstances, such as in Bosnia, Eastern Europe, and Kosovo (Rosas, 1993; Franck, 1993; Higgins, 1993). However, the birth of new states following the collapse of the communist order in the Soviet Union, Eastern Europe, and the Balkans has removed some taboo against secession, and the international community seems to be inching towards some consensus that the extreme oppression of a group may justify secession. This position has served to strengthen the internal aspect of self-determination, for a state can defeat the claim of separation if it can demonstrate that it respects the political and cultural rights of minorities. A further, and far-reaching, gloss has been placed on this doctrine by the Canadian Supreme Court, which decided in 1999 that Quebec has no right under either the Canadian Constitution or international law to unilateral secession, but that if Quebec were to decide on secession through a referendum, Ottawa and the provinces would have to negotiate with Quebec on future constitutional arrangements (*Reference re Secession of Quebec* [1998] 2 SCR 217). However, these rules or understandings are not accepted everywhere and they are unlikely to persuade leaders in Africa or Asia. As for Latin America, the contributions by Souza Filho, Neves, and Arenas in this volume underline some of the ambiguities of the notion of self-determination as it relates to the rights of indigenous peoples.

Such a view of self-determination has some support in certain national constitutions, indicating no more than a trend at this stage. Often, constitutional provisions for autonomy are adopted during periods of social and political transformation, when an autocratic regime is overthrown (when there is considerable legitimacy for autonomy), when a crisis is reached in minority–majority conflicts, or when there is intense international pressure (in which case legitimacy is granted rather grudgingly). Propelled by these factors, a number of constitutions now recognize some entitlement to self-government, such as the Philippines in relation to two provinces, one for indigenous people and the other for a religious minority; Spain, which guarantees autonomy to the regions; Papua New Guinea, which authorizes provinces to negotiate with the central government for substantial devolution of power; Fiji, which recognizes the right of indigenous people to their own administration at the local level; and, recently, Ethiopia, which gives its "nations, nationalities, and peoples" the right to seek wide-ranging powers as states within a federation and guarantees to them even the right to secession. The Russian Constitution of 1993, in the wake of the breakup of the Soviet Union, provides for extensive autonomy to its constituent parts, whether republics or autonomous areas (Agnew, 1995; Lynn and Novikov, 1997; Smith, 1996). The Chinese Constitution entrenches the rights of ethnic minorities to substantial self-government, although in practice the dominance of the Communist Party negates their autonomy (Ghai, 2000a). In other instances, the constitution authorizes, but does not require, the setting up of autonomous areas, with China again an interesting example (Art. 31) in its providing a constitutional basis for "One Country Two Systems" for the reunification of Hong Kong, Macau, and Taiwan. It should also, on the other hand, be noted that some constitutions prohibit or restrict the scope of autonomy by requiring that the state be unitary or some similar expression; such a provision has retarded the acceptance or the implementation of meaningful devolution in, for example, Sri Lanka, Papua New Guinea, and China.

Indigenous peoples

The Convention on Indigenous Peoples adopted in 1991, representing a reversal of the paternalistic and assimilationist approach followed in the 1959 Convention, recognized the "aspirations of these peoples to exercise control over their own institutions, ways of life, and economic development and to maintain and develop their identities, languages, and religions, within the framework of the States in which they live." Their cultural and religious values, institutions, and forms of traditional social control are to be preserved (Art. 4). The system of land ownership and the rules for the transmission of land rights are to be protected (Arts. 14 and 17). The Draft UN Declaration on the Rights of Indigenous Peoples (submitted by the UN Sub-Commission on Minorities, August 1994) goes even further and proclaims their right to self-determination, under which they may "freely determine their political status and freely pursue their economic, social and cultural development" (Art. 3). The principle of self-determination gives them the "right to autonomy or self-government in matters relating to their internal and local affairs," which include social, cultural, and economic activities, as well as the right to control the entry of non-members (Art. 31). It recognizes their "collective rights" (Art. 7) and the right to maintain and strengthen their distinct political, economic, social, and cultural characteristics (Art. 4). These ideas have already formed the basis of negotiations between indigenous peoples and the states in which they live, giving recognition not only to their land rights (as in Australia and New

Zealand) but also to forms of autonomy (as in Canada), although Asian and African governments deny the existence of indigenous peoples in their states and the instruments have had little impact there (Brölmann and Zieck, 1993; Stavenhagen, 1990; Alfredson, 1998; and Kingsbury, 1999). The proposal for "autonomy" put forward by the indigenous movement of Brazil is a way of overcoming exclusion, which, in the field of inter-ethnic relations, shaped the "exclusive/defensive communities" closed in upon themselves in defense against the domination (social, cultural, environmental, agrarian, political, epistemological, etc.) of the state, as an "exclusive-aggressive community" (Santos, 2000b: 14). This statement is undoubtedly true—even in Hong Kong, autonomy, however flawed, gives a sense of empowerment and a base from which to attack Mainland hegemony—which also explains China's reluctance to give true autonomy to Tibetans and other cultural minorities (Ghai, 2000a). Much of the struggles of cultural communities today takes the form of demand for autonomy. This critical issue needs more attention. Indigenous people, particularly in North America, also base their claims on other legal bases: (a) their "inherent sovereignty," which predates colonization, and (b) treaties with incoming powers (for what has been called "treaty federalism," see Henderson, 1994). In several Latin American countries, the claims of indigenous peoples have given rise to the recognition of their collective identities, linked to specific territories (Souza Filho, Neves, and Arenas, this volume). It would be important to pursue the differences between indigenous people and other groups/minorities (in terms of legal instruments, public sympathy, historical context, their relative isolation from other communities and norms, etc.).

Cultural rights

When the UN began work on an international regime of rights, it emphasized individual rights and carefully avoided giving rights, particularly political rights, to groups. There are trends now, however, towards a greater recognition of the cultural and ethnic bases of autonomy. Article 27 of the International Covenant of Civil and Political Rights, until recently the principal UN provision on minorities, was drafted in narrow terms. It reads:

> In those States in which ethnic, religious or linguistic minorities exist, persons belonging to such minorities shall not be denied the right, in community with the other members of their group, to enjoy their own culture, to profess and practice their own religion, or to use their own language.

There is a grudging acknowledgement that minorities may exist, giving states a way out by denying that minorities exist. The rights belong not to minorities as groups, but to individual members, denying minorities a legal or corporate status. Rights given to members of minorities are negative, prohibiting the state from suppressing their culture or language, but imposing no positive obligations on it to promote minority culture, religions, or languages.

However, in recent years, the UN Human Rights Committee (which supervises the implementation of the Covenant) has interpreted the article in a more positive way, using it to develop the collective rights of minorities, including a measure of autonomy, and some positive obligations on the states (Spiliopoulou Åkermark, 1997). In a series of decisions, the committee has interpreted the article as a basis for collective minority rights,[1] as a basis for the preservation of the culture and way of life of a minority group,[2] and as a basis for protecting and developing the traditional way of life of minorities.[3] The committee summarized its view of the purpose and reach of Article 27 in a General Comment (*Rights of Minorities*, General Comment 23, 1994). The committee distinguished Art. 27 rights from the right to self-determination, the latter being a group right, so that complaints of its violation are not admissible under the Optional Protocol (which allows individuals to lodge complaints with the committee). On a more positive note, the committee accepted that in some situations Art. 27 rights may be associated with a territory, as when cultural rights consist of a way of life that is closely associated with territory and the use of its resources. The committee stated that Art. 27 rights are available to non-citizens resident in the state. Whether a group is a minority depends upon objective criteria and not upon a decision of the state. The committee has given a broad meaning to "culture," noting that "culture manifests itself in many forms, including a particular way of life associated with the use of land resources, specially in the case of indigenous peoples. That right may include such traditional activities as fishing or hunting and the right to live in reserves protected by law." The committee has also interpreted the right to have elements of group rights. "Although the rights protected under Art. 27 are individual rights, they depend in turn on the ability of the minority group to maintain its culture, language or religion. Accordingly positive steps may also be necessary to protect the identity of a minority and the rights of its members to enjoy and develop their culture and language and to practice their religion, in community with the other members of the group" (para. 6.2). The committee regards Art. 27 rights directed at the survival and continued development of the cultural, religious, and social identity of minorities. From this analysis, it draws the conclusion that despite the negative language of the article, it implies a positive obligation on the state to ensure the protection of the rights against their denial or violation by the state through its legislative, judicial, or administrative authorities, or by other persons. From the same analysis, particularly the nexus between culture and territory, the committee also draws the right of minorities to participation, observing that the enjoyment of cultural and other rights implies the "effective participation of members of minority communities in decisions which affect them" (para. 7).

This broader approach is reflected in a UN Declaration on the Rights of Minorities adopted by the General Assembly in 1992. Unlike the ICCPR, it places positive obligations on the state to protect the identity of minorities and to encourage "conditions for the promotion of that identity" (Art. 1). The Declaration places particular emphasis upon the right of minorities to participation. It states that "[p]ersons belonging to minorities have the right to participate effectively in cultural, religious, social, economic and public life" (Art. 2.2). They have the "right to participate effectively in decisions on the national and where appropriate, regional level concerning the minority to which they belong or the regions in which they live, in a manner not incompatible with national legislation" (Art. 2.3); presumably such legislation may not deny them the right to participation (Art. 4.1). Three further specific participation rights are guaranteed: the right to establish and maintain their own associations (Art. 2.4), the right to maintain free and peaceful contacts with members of other minorities, as well as, across frontiers, with citizens of other states to whom they are related by national or ethnic, religious or linguistic ties (Art. 2.5), and the right to participate fully in economic progress and development (Art. 4.5).

Right to development

The promotion of the concept and text of the right to development was one of the most sustained forms of the challenge of the South to Western versions of human rights based primarily on civil and political rights. After considerable efforts and time, a UN Declaration on it was adopted. The declaration states that the "right to development is an inalienable human right by virtue of which every human person and all peoples are entitled to participate in, contribute to, and enjoy economic, social, cultural and political development, in which all human rights and fundamental freedoms can be fully realised" (Art. 1.1). It also states that the human person "is the central subject of development and should be the active participant and beneficiary of the right to development" (Art. 2.1). While all human beings have a responsibility for development, states have the "right and duty to formulate appropriate national development policies that aim at the constant improvement of the well being of the entire population and of all individuals, on the basis of their active, free and meaningful participation in development and in the fair distribution of the benefits resulting therefrom" (Art. 2.3). The Declaration also states clearly the obligation of the international community to assist in development; international cooperation is a central theme of the declaration. This international aspect was emphasized at the Vienna UN

World Conference on Human Rights, which emphasized the obligation of states to "cooperate with each other in ensuring development and eliminating obstacles to development [. . .]. Lasting progress towards the implementation of the right to development requires effective development policies at the national level, as well as equitable economic relations and a favourable economic environment at the international level" (para. 10 of the Vienna Declaration and Programme of Action).

The Right to Development has not been well received by some Western governments, and its endorsement at Vienna was due to horse-trading, whereby Southern states were persuaded to accept the universality and interdependence of rights. However, the document proclaiming the Right to Development is valuable for establishing a broad and humanistic definition of development as "a comprehensive economic, social, cultural, and political process, which aims at constant improvement of the well-being of the entire population and of all individuals" and "in which all human rights and fundamental freedoms can be fully realized." It provides a basis for the integration of various strands of rights, pointing to conditions under which all kinds of rights can be enjoyed. It prescribes the specific obligations of states and the international community that flow from the right, including the obligation to "eradicate all social injustices." The international community is enjoined to take collective steps to "ensure the full exercise and progressive enhancement of the right to development."

It is, however, necessary to temper enthusiasm for this declaration, for it has been promoted by many states whose commitment to human rights is suspect. Its detailed formulations could easily be used to obscure or evade the obligations of states for ensuring human rights, attribute the failure to ensure rights to wrong causes, and close off international scrutiny of the national record of the observance of human rights. By itself the declaration scarcely adds new rights, and its usefulness in providing a means to balance different kinds of rights or as a framework for achieving rights in a globalizing world with new powerful actors is limited. However, with refinement, and consensus, it could provide a useful basis for an integrated approach to human rights, and of course it does have considerable emotional appeal in developing countries.

The pluralism of human rights

The consequence of these developments is that the human rights regime is no longer focused exclusively on the individual—it includes strong norms of social justice, via economic and social rights; it is no longer indifferent to cultural differences; it engages with poverty and alienation; and the concept of equality has been enriched to include affirmative action and other forms of group rights. Some of these developments may exist solely at the level of theory, but that is not a bad starting point. That the framework of human rights can be employed to negotiate inter-ethnic claims and to acknowledge diversities of cultures and values in a way that is broadly defensible and acceptable is evident from the experiences of India (see Randeria, this volume), Canada, South Africa, and Fiji when designing their constitutional orders (Ghai, 2000b). The cases of several Latin American countries are discussed in the contributions to this volume by Souza Filho, Neves, and Arenas. These countries not only represent different cultural and religious traditions but also share the common experience of struggling to manage conflicts arising from their ethnic and religious diversity. They also typify countries with gross disparities of access to resources, wealth, and opportunities, raising acute problems of social justice.

From the perspectives of this project, the most interesting case is Canada. Cairns says of Canadians, "Those issues that have most deeply divided us, and have agitated our passions to the point of frenzy, have revolved around race, ethnicity, religion, and language, all of which have pervasive symbolic overtones" (1992: 59). "Rights" have not traditionally been employed to cope with these issues. When Canada was constituted a state in 1867 through the British North America Act, the principal issue concerned the respective identities and privileges of the English and the French communities. It was resolved through the grant of a significant autonomy (particularly in relation to civil law and education) to the francophone community residing in Quebec by federalization. The solution lasted for a very considerable time, but it came under stress a few decades ago. Several factors seem to have contributed to the stress: an increasing role of the state, which generated controversy on social policies; a rising francophone professional class in Quebec resentful of economic domination by English speakers; the immigration of other national groups, from Europe but more particularly from Asia, which diluted the proportion of francophones and challenged the notion of the two "founding races"; and the politicization of the first nations advancing their economic and cultural claims. Canadians seemed threatened with fragmentation but it was the stridency of francophone claims, backed with the threat of Quebec separatism, that started the search for new constitutional solutions, in which a bill of rights came to play an important role (Cairns, 1992; Russell, 1992).

The Canadian Charter was adopted only in 1982, over a century after Canada was constituted a federal state. The primary aim of the charter does not seem to have been the strengthening of rights, for they were on the whole well protected under the law and traditions of Canadian polity (criminal law has been a federal subject, thus ensuring uniformity and allowing courts to review the criminal process in provinces).

The push for the charter came from the then Prime Minister, Pierre Trudeau, who was worried about a growing feeling of provincialism and wanted to offer Canadians an identity that they could all embrace. That identity was to come from a bill of rights. It was to infuse a new identity for Canada as a bilingual and multicultural state; in other words, it was intended to overcome narrow parochialism. The association of rights with the idea of the nation-state has, of course, an ancient pedigree.

Trudeau's aspirations towards universalism for the charter are reflected in the general rules for the qualifications of rights. Rights may be subject to "only such reasonable limits prescribed by law as can be demonstrably justified in a free and democratic society" (Sec. 1). In so far as culture is relevant, it is "political culture," though of course the initial choice of rights is to some extent determined by "culture." But the context for the charter is also reflected in the rules of interpretation—human-rights guarantees not to be construed to abrogate or derogate from aboriginal treaties or rights or freedoms (Art. 25); the charter to be interpreted in a manner consistent with the preservation and enhancement of the multicultural heritage of Canada (Art. 27, which may become more problematic than envisaged with the increase in Asian and African immigrants—the original understandings of multiculturalism developed in the context of newer European immigrants); and the rights and privileges of "denominational, separate or dissentient schools" are not affected (Art. 29).

In the event, Canada accepted an even more complex regime of rights than perhaps even India (even if by exclusions from the regime—fragmenting rather than uniting). It has a greater orientation to group rights than India. It seeks to accommodate the francophones and the first nations through forms of collective rights. In another respect as well the charter recognizes groups, not just individuals. Article 15 allows derogation from equal rights in respect of "any law, programme or activity that has as its object the amelioration of conditions of disadvantaged individuals or groups including those that are disadvantaged because of race, national or ethnic origin, colour, religion, sex, age or mental or physical disability." Two Canadian scholars have argued that section 15(2) is intended to redress the imbalance against those groups that have been subject to persistent disadvantage, by pointing to the grounds on which discrimination has been based. They also state (like the current Indian Supreme Court position) that the right to equality and the provision for affirmative action should be seen as serving a common purpose rather than as incorporating two inconsistent conceptions of equality (Black and Smith, 1996: 14–22).

The Canadian Supreme Court's view of the charter is of rights as governed by "respect for the inherent dignity of the human person, commitment to social justice and equality, accommodation of a wide variety of beliefs, respect for cultural and group identity, and faith in social and political institutions which enhance the participation of individuals and groups in society" (saying "to mention a few").[4]

All these concessions and compromises have not eased Canada's problems of identity and cultural differences. It was realized early that the repatriation process (and the charter) were not the end of the problem but rather the beginning and, in one sense, even a cause of the difficulties. The political process, long drawn out as it has been, has so far failed to resolve outstanding issues. Issues that were up for negotiations included a clearer recognition of the distinctiveness of the francophones and the greater acknowledgment by the first nations of the imperative of gender equality. The task of reconciliation has been complicated by the multiplicity of claims that have been advanced (themselves promoted by the introduction of the notion of rights as a framework), cutting across class, ethnic, and gender distinctions, pointing to the limits of the flexibility of that framework. The listing of interests, values, and groups that must be taken into account in interpreting the constitution that was contained in the Canada clause of the Charlottetown Accord provides a clear indication of the difficult burden placed on the charter. However, the impasse of that effort means that, at least for the time being, the baton has to some extent been passed to the courts, which have begun to grapple with the challenges of multiculturalism, distinct society, and aboriginal claims.

It is not possible to summarize other case studies, but the general conclusions that emerge from them may be stated. In all these countries, there were serious ethnic conflicts or competing claims. It might have been possible to deal with them through negotiations and compromises. However, at least in South Africa and Fiji, where the conflict was intense and a clear framework for the settlement of competing claims was hard to establish, the process would have been protracted and even then might not have succeeded.

In all cases, the relevance of human rights to the construction of the state was acknowledged. In South Africa and Fiji a prior agreement on this question was a prerequisite to the start of negotiations on other matters. It was in Fiji that there was perhaps the greatest initial resistance (by the indigenous Fijians) to accepting rights as the framework. The use of the framework of rights facilitated the application of norms that enjoyed international and some domestic legitimacy, and which were sufficiently malleable to provide broadly satisfactory outcomes.

The contents and orientation of rights were drawn from external sources: in India's case from foreign national precedents (the Universal Declaration of Human Rights had just been adopted), but in other instances from international instruments. A comparison of precedents used in India (1947) and

Fiji (1995) provides an insight into the periodization of rights that speaks to the concerns of universality. At the time of Indian independence, there was no internationally accepted body of norms or procedures. Nor was there a consensus that constitutions had to include a bill of rights. By the 1990s there was both a substantial body of internationally negotiated norms and a consensus that they had to be implemented in national constitutional systems. Likewise, between the Canadian Bill of Rights (1960) and the Charter (1982), a certain distance had been traveled in the use of international norms. In this way international law and procedures of human rights have the effect of binding states into a common regime and building a presumption of "universality" into the negotiating process.

"Culture" has nowhere been a decisive element determining attitudes to rights, though it has been important in Fiji, Canada, and South Africa. But it has been important in different ways. The francophones do not object to the philosophical basis of rights (indeed they could hardly object to an instrument that draws its inspiration from the French revolution), but see their "universalizing" tendency as a threat to the survival of their culture (closely connected with language). In that sense it can be seen as a defensive reaction. In Fiji, on the other hand, rights were presented as antithetical to the underlying values of indigenous social and political organization. "Culture" itself, as already indicated, was very broadly defined. It was used in an aggressive rather than a defensive way—as justifying claims to Fijian "paramountcy." Paramountcy implied then a wide degree of political and economy supremacy that had little to do with culture as such. Using human rights as a framework helped to pare down but not eliminate "paramountcy." Demands by South African traditional leaders and the Inkatha Party were based on culture, and the ability of the latter to derail the transition to democracy gave an importance to its demands that otherwise seem to have had little support. It was perhaps in the stance of the Canadian aboriginals that "culture" was most crucial. It was central to their demands of autonomy, the settlement of outstanding claims, and the preservation of their internal social organization. It was also the hardest case of the accommodation of cultural claims within the general framework of the charter. The accommodation was secured through wide exclusions from the charter rather than through forms of balancing as in other instances discussed in this text.

With the exception of the Canadian first nations, the proponents of the cultural approach to rights were not necessarily concerned about the general welfare of their community's cultural traditions. They were more concerned about the power they obtained from espousing those traditions. It is widely recognized that Quebec's separatist politics were mobilized by young francophone professionals who found it difficult to compete with the more established English-speaking professionals. The manipulation of "tradition" by the Inkatha Party is well documented. Fijian military and politicians who justified the coup were accused of similar manipulations by a variety of respectable commentators.

Difficult questions arise if the culture of a group can only be maintained at the expense of the rights of another community, or via the agency of the state, as is the consequence of Fijian claims of paramountcy. The cultural relativism argument in a homogenous community (where the issue is purely between local values and international standards) is less problematic than in a multicultural state, where it can be divisive, lead to the subordination of one community by another, etc. Thus the debate about relativism in Tonga or Samoa (both homogeneous Polynesian societies) is of a different dimension than in Fiji. The aboriginal claims in Canada are easier to negotiate because, for the greater part, aboriginal peoples live in reservations where contact with other communities is minimal (and this may explain why the accommodation of Metis people, more spread and less well anchored in one culture, has proved more problematic).

In my view, the more interesting issues arose when the question of the relationship of rights to culture was debated *within* the cultural community itself. In most of the cases women opposed the claims of the "traditionalists," as with the first nations in Canada, the Muslims in India in regard to the application of the *shariah*, and the traditional leaders in South Africa. Hindus in India were divided over reforms of Hindu law, which followed from the mandate to codify and unify personal laws. More generally, significant numbers within the cultural community were anxious to build a more inclusive community instead of isolating their own community from the mainstream of developments. Such divisions provided opportunities for using rights to interrogate culture, and gave interesting insights into the nature of rights.

In no case are rights seen merely as protections against the state. They are instruments for the distribution of resources; a basis for identity; hegemony; and a social vision of society. Rights are not necessarily deeply held values, but a mode of discourse, of advancing and justifying claims, etc. Thus, important sectors of the white community in South Africa opt for group rights when it comes to autonomy, but settle for individual rights when it comes to economic rights.

Groups present their claims in different paradigms of rights: individual versus group; equality versus preference; uniformity versus group identity. This comes out clearly in the contributions by Souza Filho, Neves, Arenas, and Randeria. In Fiji as well, the conflicts between the two communities are played out in the competing currencies of human rights (universal human rights versus indigenous peoples' rights).

These case studies also undermine the myth that those who push for universalism are westerners and those who oppose it are easterners. It was the

British who resisted a bill of rights in India; it was the whites in South Africa who set up one of the most repressive regimes of this century. Both of them believed in the relativism of rights—one for whites and another for coloreds. The most powerful resistance to the charter has come from French Canadians. Indians wanted a universal regime, but had to make concessions to accommodate the claims of the historically disadvantaged minorities. The majority of the blacks in South Africa showed the greatest commitment to a universal regime. In Fiji it was the dominant majority within the Methodist Church that most strenuously resisted the regime of rights.

Constitutional settlements in multi-ethnic societies require the balancing of interests. This balancing is particularly important if there are prior, existing disparities of economic, social, or political resources, and particularly if these disparities are the result of state policies. Achieving this balancing has various implications for the regime of rights.

> (a) It involves the recognition of corporate identities as bearers of rights (an issue, however, that remains deeply controversial, as does the scope of the recognition). It is in that sense that one can talk of collective rights. But we also find individual rights that are connected to being a member of a group. Most rights of affirmative action in India perhaps fall into this category.
>
> (b) There cannot be, in relation to most rights, a notion of the absolutism of rights; there must be an acceptance of qualifications on rights.
>
> (c) This exercise of qualification forces constitution-makers to try to understand and define the core of the rights concerned, in order to establish the qualifications that may be made consistent with maintaining that right.
>
> (d) The appropriate formulation and protection of social, economic, and cultural rights, emphasizing the "positive duties" of the state, is often fundamental to a settlement, both to acknowledge the importance of culture and to redress ethnic inequalities. This is perhaps less so in Canada where the charter is more oriented towards civil and political rights, but there too problems associated with first nations are dealt with through redistributions. Thus, for this (and other reasons of "ethnic" management) there arises the necessity for an activist state.
>
> (e) Since inter-ethnic relations are so crucial to an enduring settlement, and past history may have been marked by discrimination or exploitation, a substantial part of the regime of rights has to be made binding on private parties.

Juridically, there are a few important means for balancing:

> (a) the traditional one of limitation clauses;
> (b) closely associated is the direction as to interpretation;

(c) balancing of one right against another (what Galanter has called "competing equalities" [Galanter, 1991]); the most difficult task in this regard is the balancing of "negative" with "positive" rights (e.g., the protection of property versus affirmative action or other forms of social justice); and

(d) overcoming these dichotomies by a new conceptualization, e.g., "equality" defined in substantive terms as in India and South Africa.

(e) The Indian technique of the juxtaposition of rights with directive principles has not been followed elsewhere, perhaps because of the difficulties that the technique presented there.

A particular consequence of using the framework and language of rights and the juridical techniques mentioned above is the increase in the power and responsibility of the judiciary for the settlement of claims and disputes. It then falls ultimately to the courts to perform the balancing of interests and rights that is an essential part of using the human rights framework. They may represent a different understanding of the permissible limits of the balance, and may come in conflict with determinations by the legislature or the executive. This was the Indian experience with the courts taking a different view from that of the other branches as to the primacy of property rights over social rights. On the other hand, vesting the final authority in courts means that close attention is paid to the framework of rights and that the balance between the core of the right and its modification is done in a reasoned and principle way. Usually, the prestige of the courts helps also to bring the dispute to some resolution, although the Indian experience with the *Shah Bano* case (1985—2 Sup. Ct. Cases 556 [see below]) suggests that judicial decisions can themselves be a source of conflict.

On the more general question of universalism and relativism, it is not easy to generalize. It cannot, for example, be said that bills of rights have a universalizing and homogenizing tendency, for, by recognising languages and religions, and by affirmative policies, they may in fact solidify separate identities. On the other hand, there may be some necessity for a measure of universalism of rights to transcend sectional claims for national cohesion. Simple polarities—universalism vs. particularism, secular vs. religious, tradition vs. modernity—do not easily work; a large measure of ambiguity is necessary for the accommodations that must be made. Consequently, most bills of rights are Janus-faced (looking in the direction of both liberalism and collective identities). What is involved in these arrangements is not an outright rejection of either universalism or relativism but an acknowledgment of the importance of each, as well as a search for a suitable balance, using for the most part the language and parameters of rights (see Santos on rights in this volume).

DESIGN OF STATES

The criticism of the liberal theory of rights from the perspectives of multi-culturalism is also reflected in the criticism of the liberal state. The argument is that the modern state, with its lineage of the market-oriented and homogenizing regime, built on the principle of individualism and equal citizenship, is inherently incapable of dealing with the ethnic and social diversity that characterizes most countries. Constitutionalism associated with the modern state was concerned at first with limits on power and the rule of law, to which were later added democracy and human rights. For the purposes of the present argument, it is argued that constitutionalism is not primarily concerned with the relations of groups to the state, or relations between groups.

Noting different communities or groups that are seeking constitutional recognition of their cultural or social specificity—immigrants, women, indigenous peoples, religious or linguistic minorities—James Tully concludes that what they seek is participation in existing institutions of the dominant society, but in ways that recognize and affirm, rather than exclude, assimilate, and denigrate, their culturally diverse ways of thinking, speaking, and acting. He says that what they share is a longing for self-rule: to rule themselves in accordance with their customs and ways (Tully, 1995: 4). The modern constitution is based on the assumption of a homogeneous culture, but in practice it was designed to exclude or assimilate other cultures and thus deny diversity (Tully, 1995: 58).

He argues that a constitutional order, which should seek to provide a framework for the resolution of issues that touch on the concerns of the state and its various communities, cannot be just if it thwarts diverse cultural aspirations for self-government (Tully, 1995: 6). Symmetries of power, institutions, and laws that define the modern state are inconsistent with the diversity of forms of self-government that Tully considers necessary for a just order in multi-ethnic states. The necessity of a constitution that is based on the mutual recognition of diversity is reinforced by the consideration that there is no escape from multi-ethnic states, as the alternative of over 1,500 "nation-states" is not feasible. Such a constitution should be "a form of accommodation" of cultural diversity, of intercultural dialogue, in which the culturally diverse sovereign citizens of contemporary societies negotiate agreements on their forms of association over time (Tully, 1995: 30).

A similar approach is taken by Bikhu Parekh, who argues that the theory of the modern liberal state presupposes a culturally homogeneous society and becomes a source of disorder, injustice, and violence when applied to culturally heterogeneous societies. He identifies various institutional and structural features of the modern state that impose uniformity and ignore diversity. The organizing principle is state sovereignty, which justifies the centralization of power and displaces local and group sites of power. This sovereignty operates on a territorial basis, with hard boundaries. Rules for the exercise of this sovereignty are biased towards majoritarianism, stifling the voices of minorities. Much of his criticism is encapsulated in his view of sovereignty as "a rationalised *system of authority*, is *unitary* and *impersonal* in nature, is the *source* of all legal authority exercised within the state, is not *legally* bound by the traditions, customs, and principles of morality, and is not subject to a higher internal or external authority" (Parekh, 1997: 183). People relate to the state through the concept of citizenship, based rigidly on equal rights and obligations of all persons, premised on loyalty to the state, and acknowledging no distinctions of culture or tradition. Citizens have rights but these are rights of individuals, based on an abstract and uniform view of the human person. The state operates through the medium of the law, but it is the law created by the state rather than by pre-existing bodies of customs or local law. The state favors the uniformity of structures and seeks to achieve the homogenization of culture and ideology, propagating them as universal values. The domain of the state is the public space, with an ever-shrinking area of private space, which alone allows some expression of cultural diversity.

Despite its claims of universality, both Tully and Parekh demonstrate the specificity of this system by contrasting it with pre-modern polities. Those polities cherished cultural diversity. It was no function of the state to impose moral or religious order, much less to impose conformity. The public sphere was narrow and the private extensive, allowing ample space for diverse cultural and religious traditions. Nor did the center aim towards a tight or detailed regulation of society, but rather was content with a large measure of decentralization, frequently based on cultural communities. It accepted pre-existing bodies of customs and laws. There were multiple layers of authority and borders were porous, adding to the flexibility of the polity. Similar accounts of the diversity and flexibility of pre-modern or pre-colonial polities have been presented by other authors (for example, Kaviraj, 1997; Tambiah, 1992). It is not my purpose to engage directly with this thesis—except to remark that it exaggerates the uniformity in the modern state and the flexibility and diversity in the pre-modern. Pre-modern China's experience, where the centralization of authority and the confucianization of the emperor's subjects were vigorously pursued, seems inconsistent with the picture sketched by Tully and Parekh. Several modern states have different categories of residents, there are differential spatial distributions of power, and religious and cultural affiliations are recognized for many public purposes. Many multi-ethnic states recognize diversity through a variety of devices, including differential citizenship rights, as in Israel (Peled, 1992), Malaysia, and Fiji. Even "modern states" like the US, Canada, Australia, and the Nordic countries had less than a uniform system of laws, citizenship, or institutions when they dealt with indigenous communities; and if Lijphart (1977) is right about the prevalence of consociationalism in several parts of Europe, then also the monopoly of the centralized modern state is questionable. Several recent instruments and recommendations of the Organisation of Security and Cooperation in Europe and the Council of Europe seek to promote linguistic and religious diversity: decentralization, cultural councils, special voting rolls, language rights, and so forth. The general international law has come to recognize various categories of collectivities, such as minorities and indigenous people, with varying group rights. Even the regime of human rights, castigated for its obsession with the individual, has increasingly recognized group entitlements (Ghai, 2000b). There is considerable flexibility in the design of states, such as Bosnia-Herzegovina—perhaps in response to the kinds of criticisms leveled at the modern state by Tully and Parekh. Liberalism's tolerance of difference (admittedly a doctrine developed in the west for—relatively—culturally homogeneous societies) has some potential for being turned to use for the design of multicultural arrangements.

Nor is recognition of diversity always a virtue. The colonial state was *par excellence* a state of diversity and discrimination, deeply acknowledged, indeed entrenched, in constitutional and legal systems. While denigrating local cultures, colonial regimes sponsored numerous anthropological studies of "tribes." Anthropologists became the handmaidens of the colonialists in using indigenous cultures and institutions to establish more effective domination over them, often through indirect rule, often involving the preservation of these cultures and institutions, suitably modified to suit the aims of imperialism, which included the practice of "divide and rule" (Ghai and McAuslan, 1970; Mamdani, 2000). Traditional cultures and institutions were also "preserved" to avoid the uncontrollable social and political consequences of capitalism and to use them to absorb the costs of imperialism and the market economy. The organization of the apartheid regime in South Africa, which "glorified" racial and cultural diversity, used these distinctions to build its edifice of oppression. Jewish control over Israel is maintained through various legal institutions and distinctions that discriminate against Arabs or fragment the political community. More benignly, the essential principle for the organization of the political, social, and economic system of colonial Fiji was race: legislative representation and participation in the executive was allocated racially; indigenous Fijians had their own system of administration and the right to review legislative proposals before they reached the legislature, and there were several institutions to safeguard Fijian customs and laws. The division of labor was also structured along racial lines.

Many features of the colonial system survived into the independence period, not always with positive effects on racial harmony. The separation of the political and economic organization of indigenous peoples in the US, Canada, Australia, and much of Latin America had the effect, as was the intention, of marginalizing them. The preservation of indigenous cultures and the development of pluralistic legal orders in which various regimes of personal and customary laws were recognized produced a spurious kind of multiculturalism.

However, it is not my contention that the political recognition of diversity is always fragmenting or oppressive. Special regimes for communities based on sensitivity to their vulnerabilities, or the recognition of the centrality of cultures to them, or of past injustices, have contributed to justice as well as improvement in inter-ethnic relations. Whether the political recognition of diversity is fair or beneficial depends on the context, the preferences and aspirations of the various communities, and the forms that political recognition takes. Moreover, support for it depends on differing theories of ethnicity.

The principal modifications to the liberal state are in the forms of representation (as in Bosnia-Herzegovina, where ethnic groups are separately represented in the executive and the legislature, using separate electorates), territorial autonomy, and cultural autonomy—of which, for reasons of space, only cultural autonomy is discussed here (for a wider discussion, see Ghai, 2002b). To some extent, globalization has helped in these developments, both by the practical consequences of globalization for economic policies and choices, and by sanctioning, through the authority of international or regional institutions, interventions in "troubled states" not only to bring the fighting to an end but to impose solutions. Globalization makes states less salient in some respects, leads to regional economic integration, which facilitates regional autonomy, and enables small territories to carve out niches in the global economy. A new but uneven element in the spatial organization of government is the emergence of international regional organizations in which national sovereignty has been traded for a share in participation and decision-making in these organizations. Common policies over larger and larger matters are determined by the regional organization, so that a measure of control of the affairs of a national region has been transferred from national to supranational authority. The consequences are that the diminution of the salience of national sovereignty opens up possibilities of new arrangements between the state and its regions, the state feeling less threatened by regions in a multilayered structure of policy-making and administration and the region being more willing to accept the national sovereignty that may be the key to its participation in the wider arrangements. This trend is most developed in the European Union, with its developing concept of the Europe of Regions (Bullain, 1998), which is helping to moderate tensions between states and border regions previously intent on secession, as in Spain and Belgium, and which has facilitated the interesting spatial arrangements for policy, administration, and consultation in the two parts of Ireland, each under separate sovereignty, which underlie the new peace settlement. Attempts to provide for unified Nordic arrangements for the Saami people, including a substantial element of autonomy, regardless of the sovereignty they live under, are another instance of similar kind (Hannum, 1990: 256–62).

Several initiatives have been taken in Europe, through the Organisation of Security and Cooperation in Europe (OSCE) and the Council of Europe and the European Union (EU) to promote the concept of autonomy, although its impact so far is restricted to Europe. This is manifested both in formal declarations and interventions to solve ethnic conflicts in Europe (such as in the Dayton Accord over Bosnia-Herzegovina or the Rambouillet proposals for Kosovo). Article 35 of the Copenhagen Declaration on Human Dimension of the OSCE recognizes "appropriate local or autonomous administrations" "as one of the possible means" for the promotion of the "ethnic, cultural, linguistic, and religious identity of certain minorities." The principal instrument of the Council of Europe is the Framework Convention for the Protection of National Minorities (1994), which protects various rights of minorities, obliges the state to facilitate the enjoyment of these rights, and recognizes many rights of "identity." It obliges state parties to "create the conditions necessary for the effective participation of persons belonging to national minorities in cultural, social and economic life and in public affairs, in particular those affecting them" (Article 15). There is no proclamation of a right to autonomy, but the exercise of some of these rights implies a measure of autonomy. The Copenhagen Declaration and statements of principle by the Council of Europe, although not strictly binding, have been used by the OSCE High Commissioner for Minorities and other mediating bodies as a basis for compromise between contending forces, and have thus influenced practice, in which autonomy has been a key constituent (Bloed, 1995; Packer, 1998; Thornberry, 1998; see also the Lund Recommendations on the Effective Participation of National Minorities in Public Life, 1999, issued by the OSCE High Commissioner).

Globalization threatens or facilitates the reorganization of a state through the activities of the diasporas of the state, which fuel the manifestation of the discontent of particular communities with the state. A common form of assistance is money and the purchase of weapons, which facilitates political violence back home. Many a reorganization of states has taken place after long or short periods of violence or civil strife. But, equally, globalization forces do not favor violence, for that creates disorder, which on the whole is not congenial to trade and the economy.

Cultural autonomy

A major limitation of the territorial devolution of power, its restriction to circumstances where there is a regional concentration of an ethnic group, can be overcome by "corporate or cultural autonomy" whereby an ethnic group, dispersed geographically, is given forms of collective rights. There are different forms and uses of corporate autonomy. Rights or entitlements protected under such autonomy can be personal, cultural, or political. They can be entrenched or subject to the overriding authority of the government. They normally consist of positive and substantive rights and entitlements, but they also can be negative, such as a veto. They form the basis of the communal organization of politics and policies and of the collective protection of their rights. The Cyprus Constitution of 1970 was an example of expansive corporate autonomy, while the current constitution of Bosnia-Herzegovina combines more traditional federalism with corporate shares in power and communal vetoes.

Cultural autonomy was a significant feature of old and modern empires. Modern examples include provisions in the constitutions or laws of Estonia, Hungary, Slovenia, and the Russian Federation, which countries provide for the establishment of councils for national minorities that assume responsibility for the education and cultural affairs of the minorities (Eide, 1998: 256–9). In principle, a council can be set up if a majority of the community desires it, as expressed in votes. Once established, its decisions bind members of the community throughout the state, except that a member can opt in or out of membership—the important principle of self-identification is maintained. Within the areas in relation to which powers are vested in it, the council's regulations prevail over those of the state. The council has the power to levy a tax on its members and also receives subsidies from the state. It has authority over the language, education, and culture of the minority. The principal objective of the system is the maintenance or strengthening of the identity of the minority, based on language and culture. The objective is to take culture out of "politics" and leave other matters to the national political process, in which minorities may or may not have a special status through representation. It is too early to evaluate their experience, as the few councils established so far, often under external pressure, have existed for only a short period. However, it would seem that the distinction between culture and politics may be too simplistic, especially today when the survival of culture is closely connected to the availability of resources and to national policy in several areas.

More central reliance on group autonomy through cultural councils is found in the developing constitutional dispensation of Belgium. In 1970, separate councils were established for Dutch-, French-, and German-language speakers with competence over aspects of cultural and educational matters; their competence was considerably extended in the 1980s (Peeters, 1994; Murphy, 1995). In some new constitutions group autonomy is related to, or is part of a package of, federal or other devices for the protection of ethnic communities, frequently in consociational arrangements, such as in Belgium, Bosnia-Herzegovina, and Fiji.

Cultural autonomy can take the form of the application to the members of a community of its personal or religious laws, covering marriage and family, and occasionally land, particularly for tribal communities (see Ghai, 1988: 52–9; for a historical account of its use in Europe, see Eide, 1998). The application of personal laws, and thus the preservation of customary law or practices, is considered important for maintaining the identity of the community. When India tried, during the drafting of its constitution, to mandate a common civil code for all of the country, some Muslim leaders objected. The supporters of a common code argued that common laws were essential for national unity. The opponents argued that it amounted to the oppression of minorities and the loss of their communal identity. The result was that the constitution merely set a common code as an objective of state policy, and it is now a well-established convention that the *shariah* will continue to apply to Muslims so long as they desire it.

The scope of the application of personal laws, quite extensive during the colonial period in Africa and Asia, is now diminishing under the pressure of modernization, although it is being reinforced in some countries committed to a more fundamentalist view of their religion. However, one place where regimes of personal laws still apply with full vigor is Israel, where each of the major religions has its own laws on personal matters (Edelman, 1994, on which the following account is principally based). Israel has civil courts, military courts, and courts of fourteen recognized religious communities. The principal and exclusive jurisdiction of religious courts is over matters relating to marriage and divorce, there being no civil marriage or divorce in Israel. These courts also resolve other personal- and private-law issues. Since legislative authority over these matters is rarely exercised, courts have a profound effect on shaping the country's political culture, involving the rights of women, contacts between members of different communities, and more generally the lives of Israelis. For the Jews, most matters of personal law fall exclusively within the rabbinical courts, while Muslims are subject to the jurisdiction of *shariah* courts applying the *shariah*. Although linked to and supported by the state, these courts are administered independently of the state. For the Muslims, the presence of *shariah* courts has reinforced their sense of community and the values they want to live by, and has helped in the social reproduction of the community—an important factor for a minority, many of whom live under foreign occupation. These conclusions corroborate an argument for cultural autonomy, namely, that it "supports political stability by providing non-dominant (and unassimilable) groups with mechanisms that enable them to minimize the effects of their inferior position in the larger society" (Jacobsohn, 1993: 30). But the separate regime of Muslim law has isolated Arabs from the mainstream of Israeli politics. For the Jews, the rabbinical courts have been deeply divisive, symbolizing the fundamental schism between orthodox and secular Jews. In both instances the courts give the clergy, committed to the preservation of orthodoxy, a specially privileged position. The law is slow to change in these circumstances and can lag well behind social attitudes and social realities. In contrast to civil courts, which have sought to promote a democratic political culture based upon the rule of law, religious courts and personal regimes of laws have sharpened distinctions among Israel's communities, and retarded both social relations among them and the development of a unifying political culture. Edelman (1994: 119) concludes that religious courts have emphasized group identity and solidarity at the expense of a unifying political culture: "Yet without a shared political culture and the concomitant sense of a shared national identity, the prospects for a sustained, peaceful national existence are not bright." This view is not endorsed by Jacobsohn, who says that studies of Jewish public opinion in Israel reveal that shared ethnicity and a shared set of religious symbols are much more important than a shared set of values in providing unity for Israeli society. "Thus, the subordination of cultural aspects to individual liberties on the basis of the assertion that the latter are 'principles' has less justification in a polity where cultural imperatives may legitimately demand principled consideration" (1993: 37).

One of the major problems with cultural/religious/legal autonomy of this kind is that it puts certain sections of the relevant community at a disadvantage. Edelman (1994) shows how both Jewish and Muslim women come off worse in their respective autonomous courts. In India, Muslim women are unable to benefit from the more liberal legal regime that has applied to other Indian women after the reforms of the 1960s. One aspect of their disadvantage was illustrated in 1985 by the famous *Shah Bano* case (above), where the Supreme Court held that the maintenance that a Muslim divorced woman could claim from her former husband was to be determined under the general national law, which provided a higher amount than she would get under the *shariah*. This decision provoked a violent reaction from a section of the Muslim community, which considered that its identity was thrown in jeopardy. The government gave way to pressure from the Muslim clergy and other sections of the Muslim community and legislatively overruled the decision. The rise of Hindu nationalism is often ascribed to this "capitulation" by the government to Muslim minority demands. In Canada, the application of the customary law of Indian bands has also disadvantaged women; the UN Human Rights Committee has held invalid the law that deprived an Indian woman of her land and other community rights if she married an outsider, men who marry outside the community not incurring a similar liability (*Sandra Lovelace v. Canada*—Report of the Human Rights Committee. GAOR. Thirty-sixth session, Supplement No. 40 [A/36/50], 166–75). In South Africa, demands by traditional leaders for the continuation of customary laws were resisted by African women because of the discriminations against them, such as in relation to custody and inheritance. The South African solution was to provide for the application of customary law but subject to the Bill of Rights.

CONCLUSION

The cases studied here show that no simple judgment on the utility or justice of the political recognition of ethnic diversity is possible. Separate legislative representation has sometimes been worthwhile, as the Indian example shows; but mostly it has been harmful. Asymmetrical federalism has great capacity to respond to the varying circumstances and needs of ethnic groups. But it is hard to negotiate and sometimes hard to operate. Cultural autonomy can give a beleaguered community a sense of identity and moral cohesion, and assist in preserving its traditions. But as with other asymmetrical devices, it can cause injustice to both the members of the autonomous community and those outside it. All three can produce resentment and conflict.

Each of these devices has supporters and opponents. Even if it were agreed that none of them was the preferred approach, it may be hard to generalize about the usefulness of particular modalities. The choice between these options may depend, in many situations, less on their inherent merits than on circumstances and constraints. The objective circumstances as well as the aspirations of minorities vary from place to place and from time to time. For example, the size of the minority is a material factor: a substantial and economically well-off minority might not require special rules for legislative representation, but a small minority might. Moreover, in the former case special rules might be resented or mistrusted by the majority, but not necessarily in the latter case. Several of the studies in this book concern indigenous peoples—which may be regarded as a special case. Indigenous minorities have a strong moral case for special treatment—few groups have suffered as much as they from the oppression of outsiders, to which they are still vulnerable, their cultural traditions and community life is still strong, they have a strong affinity with land and nature, and they have a firm desire to continue with their traditions.

The choice of approach and modalities would depend on the ultimate goals that the state and minorities have set themselves. The problem arises when there is no consensus either between the majority and the minority or within either group. One section of a minority may want to preserve its social structure and culture at all costs; another may wish to escape the constraints or even the oppression of the community and seek its identity in a cosmopolitan culture. The choice would also depend on the balance between individual and communal rights. Nor are particular solutions valid for all times; they may need to be reviewed as the socio-economic and demographic situation changes. It is worthwhile to caution against reifying temporary or fluid identities, which are so much a mark of contemporary times. There is a danger of enforcing spurious claims of primordialism and promoting competition for resources along ethnic lines, thereby aggravating ethnic tensions. Separate representation and institutions tend to lead to ethnic manipulation or extremism. Many proposals for diversity that have been made in recent years are untried; and, even when tried, it is too early to assess their success. Many of them are concerned excessively with management conflict, and perhaps not sufficiently focused on long-term objectives.

Nevertheless, these studies highlight some aspects of the constitutional recognition of diversity that pertain to policy on this matter. Several examples of legal recognition of cultural diversity were imposed rather than sought by minority groups—for example, apartheid structures, or divide-and-rule mechanisms used by colonial authorities. Historically, diversity arrangements have been connected with discrimination and domination. Often, if a culture or religion is constitutionally recognized, it is the culture or religion of the majority, resulting in the domination of the culture of others—as in Sri Lanka and Malaysia. Separate cultural systems are also a way of privileging some members of a community, such as traditional elites—usually male—or the wealthy, over others. For similar reasons, emphasis and efforts that go into developing separate systems for separate cultures mean that urgent social problems, whether of a community or of all the people, may be neglected. One might conclude that while multiculturalism does require the re-consideration of traditional legal and constitutional orders, it is not so clear what in each case the emergent reconfigurations will be.

BIBLIOGRAPHY

Agnew, John (1995). "Postscript: Federalism in the Post-Cold War Era," in Graham Smith (ed.), *Federalism: The Multiethnic Challenge*. London: Longman.

Alfredson, Gudmundur (1998). "Indigenous Peoples and Autonomy," Markku Suksi (ed.), *Autonomy: Applications and Implications*. The Hague: Kluwer.

An-Nai'm, Abdullahi (1990). *Toward an Islamic Reformation*. Syracuse, NY: Syracuse UP.

Black, William, and Lynn Smith (1996). "The Equality Rights," in Gerald Beaudoin and Errol Mendes (eds.), *The Canadian Charter of Rights and Freedoms*. 3rd ed. Scarborough, Ont.: Carswell.

Brölmann, C. M., and M. Y. A. Zieck (1993). "Indigenous Peoples," in C. Brölmann et al. (eds.), *Peoples and Minorities in International Law*. Dordrecht: Martinus Nijhoff.

Bullain, Inigo (1998). "Autonomy and the European Union," in Markku Suksi (ed.), *Autonomy: Applications and Implications*. The Hague: Kluwer.

Eide, Asbjorn (1998). "Cultural Autonomy: Concept, Content, History and Role in the World Order," in Markku Suksi (ed.), *Autonomy: Applications and Implications*. The Hague: Kluwer.

Franck, T. M. (1993). "Comments: Postmodern Tribalism and the Right to Secession," in C. Brölmann et al. (eds.), *Peoples and Minorities in International Law*. Dordrecht: Martinus Nijhoff.

————— (1994). *Human Rights and Governance: The Asia Debate*. Occasional Paper No. 1, San Francisco: Center for Asian Pacific Affairs, Asia Foundation.

————— 1995. "Asian Perspectives on Human Rights," in James T. H. Tang (ed.), *Human Rights and International Relations in the Asia-Pacific Region*. New York: St. Martin's Press. 54–66.

————— (1998). "Rights, Duties and Responsibilities," in J. Cauquelin et al. (eds.), *Asian Values: Encounter with Diversity*. Richmond, Surrey: Curzon.

————— (1999). "Rights, Social Justice and Globalisation in East Africa," in Joanne Bauer and Daniel Bell (eds.), *The East Asian Challenge for Human Rights*. Cambridge: Cambridge UP.

————— (2000a). "Chinese Minorities: Autonomy with Chinese Characteristics," in Yash Ghai (ed.), *Autonomy and Ethnicity: Negotiating Claims in Multi-Ethnic States*. Cambridge: Cambridge UP.

————— (2000b). "Universalism and Relativism: Human Rights as a Framework for Negotiating Interethnic Claims," *Cardozo Law Review* 21(4): 1095–1140.

————— (2002a). *Human Rights and Social Development: Towards Democratization and Social Justice*. Geneva: UNRISD.

————— (2002b). "Constitutional Asymmetries: Communal Representation, Federalism and Cultural Autonomy," in Andrew Reynolds (ed.), *The Architecture of Democracy: Constitutional Design, Conflict Management and Democracy*. Oxford: Oxford UP.

Ghai, Yash, and J. P. W. B. McAuslan (1970). *Public Law and Political Change in Kenya: A Study of the Legal Framework of Government from Colonial Times to the Present*. Nairobi, Kenya: Oxford UP. (Reprinted 2001).

Hannum, Hurst (1990). *Autonomy, Sovereignty, and Self-Determination: The Accommodation of Conflicting Rights*. Philadelphia: U. of Philadelphia P.

Henderson, James (sákéj) Youngblood (1994). "Empowering treaty federalism," *Saskatchewan Law Review* 58: 241–329.

Higgins, R. (1993). "Comments: Postmodern Tribalism and the Right to Secession," in C. Brölmann et al. (eds.), *Peoples and Minorities in International Law*. Dordrecht, Martinus Nijhoff.

Jacobsohn, Gary J. (1993). *Apple of Gold: Constitutionalism in Israel and the United States*. Princeton, NJ: Princeton UP.

Kaviraj, Sudipta (1997). "The Modern State in India," in Martin Doornbos and Sudipta Kaviraj (eds.), *Dynamics of State Formation*. New Delhi: Sage.

Kingsbury, Benedict (1999). "Rights: The Applicability of the International Concept of Indigenous Peoples in Asia," in Joanne Bauer and Daniel Bell (eds.), *The East Asian Challenge for Human Rights*. Cambridge: Cambridge UP.

Langlois, Anthony J. (2001). *The Politics of Justice and Human Rights: Southeast Asia and Universalist Theory*. Cambridge: Cambridge UP.

Lijphart, Arend (1977). *Democracy in Plural Societies*. New Haven, CT: Yale UP.

Lynn, Nicholas, and Alexei Novikov (1997). "Refederalizing Russia: Debates on the Idea of Federalism in Russia," *Publius* 27(2): 187–203.

Mamdani, Mahmood, ed. (2000). *Beyond Rights Talk and Culture Talk: comparative essays on the politics of rights and culture*. New York: St. Martin's Press.

Murphy, Alexander (1995). "Belgium's Regional Divergence. Along the Road to Federation," in G. Smith (ed.), *Federalism: The Multiethnic Challenge*. London: Longman.

Packer, John (1998). "Autonomy within the OCSE: The Case of Crimea," in Markku Suski (ed.), *Autonomy: Applications and Implications*. The Hague: Kluwer.

Parekh, Bhiku (1997). "Cultural Diversity and the Modern State," in Martin Doornbos and Sudipta Kaviraj (eds.), *Dynamics of State Formation*. New Delhi: Sage.

Peled, Yaiv (1992). "Ethnic Democracy and the Legal Construction of Citizenship: Arab Citizens of the Jewish State," *American Political Science Review* 86: 432–43.

Peeters, Patrick (1994). "Federalism: A Comparative Perspective – Belgium Transforms from a Unitary to a Federal State," in Brutus de Villiers (ed.), *Evaluating Federal Systems*. Cape Town: Juta.

Redding, S. Gordon (1990). *The Spirit of Chinese Capitalism*. Berlin: W. de Gruyter.

Rosas, A. (1993). "Internal Self-determination," in Tomascat (ed.), *Modern Law of Self-Determination*. Dordrecht: Martinus Nijhoff.

Russell, Peter (1992). *Constitutional Odyssey: Can Canadians Become a Sovereign Nation*. Toronto: Toronto UP.

Santos, Boaventura de Sousa (2000a). "Reinventing Social Emancipation: An Overview" (typescript). Published as "General Introduction: Reinventing Social Emancipation: Toward New Manifestos," in Santos (ed.) 2006.

————————— (2000b). "Toward A Multicultural Conception of Human Rights." Published in this volume (Chapter 1) with the title "Human Rights as an Emancipatory Script? Cultural and Political Conditions."

————————— (ed.) (2006). *Democratizing Democracy: Beyond the Liberal Democratic Canon*. London: Verso.

Smith, Graham (1995). "Mapping the Federal Condition," G. Smith (ed.), *Federalism: The Multiethnic Challenge*. London: Longman.

Smith, Graham (1996). "Russia, Ethnoregionalism and the Politics of Federation," *Ethnic and Racial Studies* 19(2): 391–410.

Spiliopoulou Åkermark, Athanasia (1997). *Justifications of Minority Protection in International Law*. Uppsala: Iustus Förlag.

Stavenhagen, Rudolfo (1990). *The Ethnic Question*. Tokyo: United Nations Press.

Tambiah, Stanley J. (1992). *Buddhism Betrayed? Religion, Politics, and Violence in Sri Lanka*. Chicago: U. of Chicago P.

Taylor, Charles (1999). "Conditions of an Unenforced Consensus on Human Rights," in Joanne Bauer and Daniel Bell (eds.), *The East Asian Challenge for Human Rights*. Cambridge: Cambridge UP.
Thornberry, Patrick (1998). "Images of Autonomy and Individual and Collective Rights in International Instruments on the Rights of Minorities," in Markku Suski (ed.), *Autonomy: Applications and Implications*. The Hague: Kluwer.
Tully, James (1995). *Strange Multiplicity: Constitutionalism in an Age of Diversity*. Cambridge: Cambridge UP.

Notes

1 *Kitok vs. Sweden* (1988), document CCPR/C/33/D/197/1985. Internet: http://www.unhchr.ch/tbs/doc.nsf/(symbol)/CCPR.C.33.D.197.1985.En?Opendocument.
2 *Bernard Ominayak, Chief of the Lubicon Lake Band vs. Canada*, (1990), document CCPR/C/38/D/167/1984. Internet: <http://www.unhchr.ch/tbs/doc.nsf/(symbol)/CCPR.C.38.D.167.1984.En?Opendocument.
3 *Länsman vs. Finland* (1995), document CCPR/C/58/D/671/1995. Internet: http://www.unhchr.ch/tbs/doc.nsf/(Symbol)/CCPR.C.58.D.671.1995.En?Opendocument.
4 *R. vs. Oakes* [1986] 1 SVCR 103, at p. 136.

15

People-Based Globalization

Tewolde Berhan Gebre Egziabher

INTRODUCTION

Professor Boaventura de Sousa Santos has challenged me with an unusual and most enjoyable project. This consists, first, of reading eight thought-provoking chapters from this volume, which concern what we are doing to biodiversity and the consequent crisis; second, of being inspired by those chapters; and, lastly, of presenting my comments on them. Yet the best aspect of the challenge involves my inspiration to write a chapter that overarches the contents of the eight chapters. I will now briefly relate the contents of these chapters, and follow that with what they have provoked me to write.

A BRIEF REVIEW OF THE CHAPTERS

All of the eight chapters deal largely with biodiversity, how our lives are linked to it, how indigenous and local communities use it in a sustainable manner (as noted by Article 8[j] of the Convention on Biological Diversity [CBD]), and how the modalities of use have been, and are being, changed by the globalization currently occurring under the impetus of corporate privatization enshrined in the agreements of the World Trade Organization (WTO), especially in its Agreement on Trade Related Aspects of Intellectual Property Rights (TRIPs). This globalization is a continuation of the plundering of human life and labor by the colonialism and neocolonialism of the last 500 years and its enslavement, not just of human freedom, but of the natural resources and the fruits of labor of other humans as well.

The eight chapters are case studies from five countries from the South. From these chapters we gather that in Mozambique the attempts of Portuguese colonialism to make basic changes in the use of biodiversity were not very effective. In South Africa, the colonial impact was also minimal. Yet later, during apartheid, the changes were more brutally imposed and were more effective. As in Mozambique, the former colonial power of Brazil is also Portugal. Unlike Mozambique, Brazil has been independent for almost two centuries. Also unlike Mozambique, people of European origin dominate the establishment in Brazil, followed by people of African origin, with the indigenous Americans being a minority. In Colombia, which along with Brazil remained the longest under European rule and in which the most influential and normative portion of the population is now of European origin, more systematic attempts at accommodating indigenous cultures have been consciously attempted than has been the case in Brazil. In India, a country that was under colonial rule for centuries but which now is not dominated by Europeans, there has been the most marked shift on thinking about systems of knowledge and technology. This happened through the spread of the European scientific tradition to a non-European culture. Nevertheless, this new infusion of thought and knowledge has not effectively destroyed the knowledge, technologies, and practices of Indian indigenous and local communities. Due to these observations, I will, following a very brief exposition of all of the chapters, summarize first the chapters about Mozambique, followed by those about South Africa, Brazil, Colombia and India. I will end with Vandana Shiva's treatment of globalization and biodiversity, and finally focus on an overall view of globalization and biodiversity, indigenous and local communities, and, in general, development in the South.

A QUICK GLIMPSE AT THE CHAPTERS

Mozambique is a low-lying country of diverse environmental conditions and ethnic and cultural groups. The heterogeneous environment is prone to flooding, cyclones, and drought. João Paulo Borges Coelho shows us clearly how the diversity of cultures has equipped the inhabitants with equally diverse environment-specific systems of predicting calamities and dealing with them. Paula G. Meneses portrays a similarly effective and culturally diverse system of health care, with traditional doctors not only treating physically sick people but also people dissatisfied psychologically or otherwise, even those complaining of ill luck.

Both authors tell us that during the long colonial period, dislocation and community breakdown as a result of the demands of the colonial governments for labor in commercial agriculture as well as the active assaults on the traditional medical systems as obscurantist, weakened these knowledge systems. Following independence, the Marxist Frelimo government intensified the problems by insisting on collective farms and modern medicine, thus disregarding the community knowledge and technology systems, which fell into disuse. The subsequent ideological liberalization and the consequent reduction in persecution have helped improve conditions for traditional medicine, although it is still seen as inferior, and perhaps undesirable. The intensification of floods, droughts, and cyclones still continues to disrupt settlements, to displace people, and to thus render the traditional systems of coping with calamities ineffective.

Thokozani Xaba describes in a well-written and well-referenced chapter how traditional medicine has been very seriously disrupted and depleted in South Africa. Similar to the situation in Mozambique, the negative impact of the colonial period was serious, but not total. This intensified during the apartheid period, and it has seriously impaired traditional medicine in South Africa.

In both Mozambique and South Africa, the traditional knowledge and technology systems are described as versatile, incorporating new facts and adapting to new conditions as they come. The local communities in both Mozambique and South Africa are portrayed as able to quickly identify emerging opportunities to try to obtain recognition of their right to their knowledge and technologies as well as to their biodiversity. Laymert Garcia dos Santos informs us that the conditions are similar in Brazil. He describes how corporate capitalism disrupts and appropriates community knowledge, technologies, and biodiversity. He describes the attempts that have been and are being made in Brazil to legally recognize the rights of communities to their knowledge, technologies, and biodiversity and to protect them from corporate plunder. The interplay among corporate, community, and national pressures for and against such recognition are described.

The rights of indigenous communities to the ownership and management of their natural resources is recognized in the constitution of Colombia. This has caused the maintenance and control of community knowledge, technologies, biodiversity, and territory by indigenous and local communities, as well as the struggles for the specific legal recognition of those rights and protection from corporate plunder, to develop a distinct dynamic. The chapter by Margarita Flórez Alonso and that by Arturo Escobar and Mauricio Pardo give us complementary information about the nature of the knowledge, technologies, and biodiversity of the indigenous and Afro-American communities of the Pacific coastal lowlands and piedmonts of Colombia and the history of their struggle for recognition. Thanks to the Colombian Constitution, these communities have achieved the recognition that they have fought for. Yet the violence so prevalent in the area, caused by rebel movements, has targeted many of the community leaders.

All these authors implicitly or explicitly show us how the social and knowledge system values of conquering Europe suppressed, and then marginalized, traditional knowledge systems, science, and technology, and how, in the desire to progress towards becoming like Europe, even post-independence national governments continued and still continue this mar-

ginalization, usually more effectively than their predecessor colonial governments had.

Shiv Visvanathan shows that even science is not value-neutral, and that it has
European religious and cultural values ingrained in it. He convincingly points
out that thermodynamics, especially its Second Law, is merely an expression of
European economic values and that, as a consequence, the application of the
concept of entropy favors the individual over the community, the rich over the
poor, the urban over the rural, and the industrial over the subsistence producer.
He also gives the same view as the other authors in their respective countries of
study of an embattled system of knowledge and technology in India. Perhaps
owing to the large size of the Indian scientific community, however, there has
been much more conscious debate on the issue in India than has been the case in
most other countries. Vandana Shiva's chapter focuses on the current scene in
international law and on other norms (most notably, intellectual property
rights) that help to maintain in the present the ravaging that dominated the past,
and which seem set to insure its continuance.

I now take it as my duty to make use of all of these authors' insights and to
add, hopefully, some useful dimension to their excellent analyses. The very
nature of attempting to find commonalities among all the chapters necessarily
brings my focus to the international, in many ways parallel to and overlapping with the ground covered by Vandana Shiva.

INDIGENOUS AND LOCAL COMMUNITIES

Farmers produce most of the food we eat. Some food is merely hunted or
gathered, not raised or cultivated. Hunters and gatherers collect and use it. But,
in absolute terms, farmers probably gather more uncultivated food than those
we formally call gatherers. Even laborers, executives, and intellectuals from
towns gather some uncultivated food, e.g., mushrooms and berries. Conversely, there probably are few, if any at all, hunters or gatherers that never have
access to food produced by farmers. Differences between farmers and non-
farmers are therefore quantitative, not absolute, and their interests overlap.

Some hunters, gatherers, and farmers live in countries controlled by
powerful newcomers with different value systems. Therefore, we collectively
call them indigenous peoples. Many farmers are, thus, also indigenous
peoples. Other hunters, gatherers, and farmers are of the same culture as
those who are in power over them and who oppress them. We collectively
call these hunters, gatherers and farmers local communities (Egziabher,
1996). That is why Article 8(j) of the Convention on Biological Diversity
recognizes indigenous and local communities as the owners of biological
diversity and the knowledge and technologies for its sustainable use.

FEUDALISM: OLD AND NEW

My interest here is in the oppressed indigenous community and in the local community. Therefore, in the following discussion, I will use images from the community world rooted in the past to describe the modern world. I hope that this will help us better understand indigenous and local communities, their service to humanity, and their plight. Since the majority of indigenous and local communities are farming communities, my emphasis in this text will be on agriculture and agricultural biodiversity, knowledge and technologies.

In the past, virtually all farmers were subjected to powerful armed oppressors who extracted a large share of their produce. These oppressors came mostly from among the farmers themselves but often also from foreign conquerors. We call the oppressors aristocrats, and we call the farmers serfs. Now that the aristocrats have been largely eliminated, the serfs have no landlords and we call the farmers peasants. The aristocrats greatly modified the farming community by breaking it up into portions to constitute their respective manor houses and serfs tied to them. Even if restricted to the lands of the manor house, however, these serfs maintained their community values, which they had developed prior to feudalism. The feudal lords extracted produce but interfered little in the production systems.

With industrialization, some of the aristocrats have become, or have been replaced by, farmers who are not oppressed, and who, unlike the freed serfs or peasants, have large landholdings. Most agricultural production in the North and a growing amount in the South is now by this new breed of farmers who have replaced and are replacing peasants. They are important members of the *status quo*. They employ laborers who are often of peasant origin and continue to be as oppressed as peasants. "Modern farmers" and peasants are, therefore, incompatible and not capable of being direct allies despite the fact that both are farmers. However, farm laborers and peasants suffer similar fates and would be natural allies if they could establish a liaison.

But of course modern farmers and peasants have some commonalities too. They both want to produce biomass as food or as raw material. However, the peasants want it primarily for themselves, while the modern farmers want it for the market. To cultivate and produce biomass, the modern farmer and the peasant want seed. The peasant primarily generates and maintains his/her seed through a system of cooperation and exchange with other farmers. The modern farmer primarily buys it. From whom? From seed companies.

With the entrenchment of the industrial culture, seed companies have thus emerged. They supply seed to the modern farmer, and always seek to "modernize" the peasant when they think of his/her role as a biomass producer who could buy their seed. These companies have recently been consolidating into smaller and smaller numbers of larger and larger North-based corporations. But the seed they sell has largely been generated by the serf and peasant,[1] and if he/she were "modernized," in the long run there would remain little variety to use in breeding, and thus also little commercial seed to sell. However, the long run is not always easy to appreciate and, bent on immediate private gain, the seed corporations eliminate farmers' varieties merely to cut off their own noses only to spite their own faces and starve us all in the process.

To get seed that is good, both the modern farmer and the peasant want to generate new varieties, to select the best from the existing, and to combine the best traits from different varieties. We have now come to call this process research.[2] The peasant does his/her own research. The modern farmer has it done for him/her. By whom? By the life-science corporations.

The old feudal system was run by aristocrats who became landlords and exacted produce and obedience from the peasants/serfs. The aristocrats and the peasants/serfs constituted the antithetical but complementary major groups in feudal society. The production system they created required some inputs that the two could not generate on their own: implements from artisans, treatment from those who had medical lore, records from scribes, spiritual reassurance from clerics, etc. The old feudal system, therefore, allowed the existence of these specialized actors in guilds of varying degrees of autonomy.

DEMOCRATIZATION AND CORPORATIONS

It was the ideals of democratization, the desire to be free, that caused the demise of the old feudal order. The pursuit of this ideal liberated the peasants and the aristocrats alike. All of them could become farmers or warriors, smiths or scribes (or authors), or even dream up new professions. Freed from strict regimentation by individual aristocrats, the ingenious and the devious found the opportunity to accumulate money and other resources from the honest and the industrious. Though the state was strengthened to deal with the increasing need for regulation, it did not try to stop the unequal accumulation of wealth. In fact, since the state machinery was usually run by the wealthiest, it protected wealth. In the North now and progressively also in the South, individual property is hallowed. One can insist on human rights, but only as subordinate to private property rights.

With the state protecting personal property and with persons accumulating wealth, a new power base and a new aristocracy was established. Steel armor was replaced by the gold bar; feudalism has re-emerged as corporate capitalism. This corporate capitalism with its global agenda fits the role of the agent of imperialism expounded by Marx in his many writings more than colonialism did at its height. We are now back full spiral one level removed upwards (downwards?) from feudalism: the knight yeoman is replaced by the chief executive officer (CEO) and the manor house is replaced by the corporation.

The old feudal system was simple and the new one is complex. In the old system, peasants constituted the workforce, the serfs, who were organized under a manor house to cultivate food crops. The rest of the aristocratic structure was built hierarchically upwards all the way up to the king or emperor. In the new feudal system, the crafts, which in the old system had been organized in autonomous guilds, have been incorporated into the mainstream and many more types of economic activity have been created. The capitalist system is thus made up of many major groups partially antithetical and partially mutualistic among themselves. Each economic activity has its manor house or corporation commanded by the CEO, a new golden knight. His power is commensurate with his wealth. He does not have to understand the work done by his white-collar and blue-collar serfs (workforce); specialists attracted (press-ganged) by his wealth can do it for him (note that it is usually not for her). The hierarchical arrangement above the company headquarters bears no relationship to geography. It thus creates a reticulate system, one that could be likened to a net with the knots randomly assigned to represent manor (business) houses. Even the once powerful states of the North have now been entangled by this net and left with little room for maneuver. Meanwhile, the self-employed majority, the peasant (subsistence) farmers of the South, have been marginalized by this reticulate global power surreptitiously operated by a relatively few shadowy CEOs.

The old aristocrats, when knights in armor, saved damsels, and, when rogues without official attire, raped them. The new aristocrats have no time for either. Most of us save money for later use, as the squirrel saves nuts in autumn for use in winter. The wealthy are constantly accumulating: they have no leisure and presumably little pleasure. Who is more depraved, the old or the new aristocrats? In the old feudal system, successively higher and thus fewer aristocrats fought for the topmost position, that of the king or emperor. In spite of continually trying, they never established a worldwide emperor. Even the huge British Empire was only a blip in history, and ruled only one-fifth of the earth. The new aristocracy has succeeded where the old failed: it has crowned the World Trade Organization as the supreme ruler; never mind that its CEO is not called an emperor. Nevertheless, the new aristocrats continue to fight more viciously than those of old, the casualties are at least as numerous, and the instabilities are definitely greater and growing.

AND THE PEASANT?

The peasants' new counterparts, the corporation's employees, are now all entangled in the global net. If they wriggle, the golden corporate sword severs them with its sharp blade of unemployment. The modern farmer, when small enough, gets squeezed for money by the seed company owner, who charges the

424 ANOTHER KNOWLEDGE IS POSSIBLE

maximum possible price through royalties and conditionalities (Clunies-Ross, 1996: 20–24). The supermarket owner pays her/him the minimum possible for her/his produce sold and charges her/him the maximum price possible for necessities bought. The seed company and the supermarket become increasingly owned by the same corporation. The breeder gets squeezed by the seed company, which pays the lowest salary possible, and by the supermarkets, which charge the highest price possible for necessities bought. The relic peasant in the North who wants to stay out of the new corporate feudal system is entangled with legislation that makes it impossible for him/her to continue planting seed of his/her choosing (Clunies-Ross, 1996: 32). In the South, the peasant is "helped" through credit systems into desperation and the abandonment of his/her land (Shiva, 1994: 176–183). Can the peasant, especially in the South, slip through the holes in the global corporate net and survive, or is he/she doomed? Will the humans running the North-based corporate minority, who have now effectively marginalized the Southern self-sustaining majority, succeed in the logical next step: the elimination of self-sustenance and the global rule by compulsory dependence?

The Southern peasant would be the first to doom himself/herself if that would change his/her lifestyle. In spite of the myth to the contrary, peasant farmers do not want to remain poor. They want greater comfort and an easier life. They are not impermeable to new knowledge and thinking if it becomes accessible enough to them and in a form that makes it understandable to them—just like everyone else. They are not static but can change values and organization when they see these as useful. Peasant farmers are not conservatives who have opted out for the sake of opting out. They are the global majority who have been marginalized by the aggressive globalizing minority. For this reason peasant farmers want to remain in control of the process that is to lift them out of poverty—just like any of us. Above all, just as with their colonial masters, they have been let down so often by the modern state, which is supposed to be their own, that they are skeptical about offers of improvement in lifestyle—just like any of us would be. They want greater comfort, but they want to know the price they will pay for it and if they will at all be able to afford it—just as any of us would want to.

In short, as also pointed out in the chapters by Coelho and by Meneses for Mozambique and by Alonso and by Escobar and Pardo for Colombia, peasants are not conservative out of obstinacy; they merely want to keep the best of the little they have—just like any of us. And are we, their counterparts of the industrial culture cohabiting their countries, also similarly obstinate? Our morale is down the drain, and we are so suppressed by the aura of the might of the North that we are unable to be obstinate. Most of us have turned into automatons that chime "yes" to whatever is suggested from the North.

AND THE EMPLOYEE?

When the old feudal system was destroyed by people's desire to be free, and when the accumulation of wealth was rather limited, most people could continue the peasant and artisan traditions of being self-employed. With greater accumulation of wealth, the means for their self-employment came to be owned more and more by the wealthiest and they became wage laborers. This process began with the buying up of and eviction from the land, and has now culminated in transnational buy-ups and mergers. With the space for self-employment virtually all bought up by the wealthy, the employee is weak and easy to dismiss. Unemployment is the sharp golden sword that the new corporate golden lord or CEO of the corporate manor uses to keep his modern serfs, the corporation's white- and blue-collar employees, obedient.[3]

How did the worker and the professional, who took over from the peasant, have their prospects for gainful employment so reduced? This is not the main thrust of my quest here and I will only briefly point out three correlated processes:

—The accumulation of knowledge and technologies supported by shifts in value made it possible for the honest and industrious individual to be self-employed.

—The worship of private property and the disregard, beyond mere lip service of social justice[4] made it inevitable that a relatively reduced number of individuals would accumulate a growing proportion of the wealth generated by the population and hence control people's lives.

—The very small cartel of wealthy men found it useful to have a docile workforce and instituted "structural" unemployment, with the consequent feeling of dispensability of the employee.

The process that initially made the self-employed of the North lose his/her livelihood through the accumulation of wealth by others is the same that is now destroying the livelihood of the peasant, the pastoralist, the gatherer, and the hunter of the South. The disadvantaged, both in the North and in the South, suffer the same fate meted out by the same doom.

THE PEASANT'S PRODUCTION SYSTEM
AND ITS PRIVATIZATION

The early farmers chose the plants and animals that gave food and other needed products and helped these chosen plants and animals grow at the expense of other plants and animals. The set of technologies they used in achieving this gave us agriculture. In agriculture, therefore, one plant species (a crop) occupies the specialized environments in which many other species of plants naturally grew. The situation is similar with domestic animals, which have replaced many other species of wild animals in our pastures and rangelands.

By excluding most species, therefore, agriculture harms the local ecosystem,[5] and therefore the natural environment. This weakness of agriculture forced the early cultivators to learn the roles of the excluded species and to find ways of substituting for those roles. They learnt to use seed heterogeneity to maximize variation in a response appropriate for the variation in the environment. They thus gave plasticity to their crops. They rotated different crops to vary demands on nutrients. They fallowed the land to bring it under the influence of the natural or semi-natural large range of plant species. They planted a range of trees in and around fields (now called agroforestry) to benefit from forest conditions where decaying leaves yield nutrients. They manured and composted to maximize nutrient release at the required place and time.

Plasticity has been the most important adaptive trait of crop species ever since agriculture was adopted, replacing much of the role of the many species unwanted in terms of biomass that the crop displaced from agroecosystems. Modern agriculture has got rid of plasticity. How did it do so?

With the demise of the aristocracy of the old feudal order, the deserved liberation of both the aristocrat and the peasant came about. The social fences of exclusion erected around the artisan guilds also broke down. Human choice of lifestyles increased. Freedom is surely good! With increased freedom, the types of crafts increased and, irrespective of class origin, the predisposed became artisans by choice. This expansion in the scope of the making of crafts was mirrored by a corresponding increase in the trade in the tools and goods made by the artisans. Then came industrialization: the means of privatizing the crafts made by artisans and the transformation of the self-employed to wage laborers. Services also grew in kind and magnitude. Finally, one of the oldest of services, trade, led the way to the accumulation of sufficient wealth to buy up factories, and to further privatize from the industrialists the already privatized crafts of the wage laborers. This is the basis of the present industrial culture of the North. Of course, I would never quarrel with industrialization, only with the privatization that has attended it in the North.

Parallel developments occurred in agriculture. Among the easiest to privatize from the peasant and from which to create new professions was the making of farm implements, the epitome of which is now the tractor. Then followed other farm inputs. The role of agriculture has always been seen as so obviously overriding that privatization was not the stated motive in the developments that occurred. With regard to seed, Clunies-Ross (1996) has traced the development of seed privatization in the United Kingdom, the birthplace of industrialization. A genuine desire to protect the farmer from being swindled by merchants who sold bad seed led to the development of seed standards and tests. This gave rise to both seed sellers and regulators of what used to be produced and exchanged by farmers themselves. Then developed the express desire to help the farmer choose the best seed, which led to a massive exclusion of seed heterogeneity and hence also to a loss of plasticity. It also led to plant breeders as professionals distinct from farmers. Finally, in the name of encouraging the research to keep improving seed, the farmers were made to pay royalties and to obey conditionalities of use of seed, management of crop in the field, and the use and marketing of the harvest. This was enforced by law, and farmers can now plant only "authorized" seed bought from seed corporations if they want to sell their produce to anyone.

This privatization of seed was made possible by creating a myth of creativity of the plant breeder different from that of the peasant farmer (see note 2). The elimination of plasticity from seed was paraded as creative and as one of the measures of the plant breeder's achievements is "uniformity." The requirement for uniformity does not explicitly oppose plasticity, but it limits its extent so much that now, for a breeder's variety to be grown extensively, massive efforts are needed to make the environment correspondingly homogeneous. This is done through the provision of irrigation water and chemicals. The logic is simple: since the seed has been made homogeneous, the environment must also be made homogeneous so that it becomes suitable for the crop's growth.

The other two measures of the plant breeder's presumed creativity are the distinctness and the stability of the variety. Distinctness has no value other than enabling the breeder to identify the variety as his/her own. In the context of producing food, it is trivial. Its existence is a reflection of the homogeneity, and hence the limited plasticity and adaptability, of the breeder's variety. Stability is equally an outcome of homogeneity: no matter what selection pressure changes in environment apply, a stable (homogeneous) seed either succeeds in the narrowly defined suitable environment, or fails everywhere else. It cannot adapt and change with changes in the environment. Is stability really needed to ensure food production? Like distinctness, it is merely a consequence of genetic poverty, a desire to cut up genetic diversity into portions amenable to privatization.

Which, then, is more creative? Which is more useful? Which is more environmentally friendly? The breeder's or the farmer's variety? The answer would be clear if we did not live in a topsy-turvy world where privatization reigns supreme and communal cooperation is tantamount to sedition. In my view, therefore, the values of the status quo are obviously flawed. The steps needed to counter these values are not obvious, but they must be found if we are to continue feeding ourselves. It should be remembered, however, that, as clearly explained in Shiva's chapter, a patent originally was (and it is now

clear that it still is) a written permission given by the powerful to plunder at
will. The excuse of "creativity" is thus a historical afterthought to cater to
postcolonial sensitivities without changing the fact. Will we, then, be able to
continue feeding ourselves? I wonder.

WHAT IS AT STAKE?

We have a world minority status quo in which efforts at freeing the
individual from the oppressive old feudal order has culminated in some
individuals (even if merely based on the inheritance of wealth their pro-
genitors unfairly privatized) determining all international values and relationships. As aptly and clearly explained in Visvanathan's chapter, even scientific
laws are not free from private commercial values. He shows this clearly in
thermodynamics, which considers the energy that brings us rainfall as
degenerate, and the energy that can fire a bullet as of high quality. He
points out that this view makes sense only in the commercialization of
energy, not in its inherent nature. I am grateful to Visvanathan because he has
helped me restore my confidence in myself. In college, I did very well in
physics and mathematics, but entropy always eluded me. Now I know that it
exists only in the commercial mind! In the context of biodiversity and the
knowledge and technologies based on it, the global imposition of such values
and norms has resulted in the following injustices.

INTELLECTUAL PROPERTY RIGHTS PROTECTION (IPRS)

Northern corporations take biodiversity and technologies from the South
and own them. Their ownership is sealed with breeder's rights and patents.
These IPR systems are forced on the whole world through TRIPs (Trade
Related Aspects of Intellectual Property Rights). Ancient farmers eliminated
most species and created a poorer environment in order to produce more
food for humans. That was bad for nature, but it looked good for humans.
Soon the ancient farmers realized that what was bad for nature was also bad
for humans and corrected this defect in agriculture. Yet modern breeders are
eliminating most genetic variation in order to enable them to stake claims on
seed. This destroys the ancient correction of the defects in agriculture, and it
is thus bad both for nature and for humans, especially for those in Southern
countries, most of whom are peasants. But it is obviously good for the bosses
of breeders, the now fewer and fewer life-science corporations. It enables
them to have breeders combine and recombine the farmers' varieties from
the South in order to choose uniform, distinct, and stable breeder's varieties,
to patent these (Egziabher, 2001: 28), to charge royalties on them, to impose
conditionalities on their use, to destroy the rest in the name of conserving

them in gene banks (Fowler and Mooney, 1990: 161–172)—the diversity they do not as yet want to claim, the very foundation of their breeding—and, eventually perhaps, to destroy most of us.

Southern peasants are seen by these transnational corporations as an unexplored market for their degenerate seed. In the name of free trade they globally push the degenerate seed. The "free market" rules of the World Trade Organization make this possible for them. I cannot see what is "free" in a market where countries and peoples are forced to import things that they would rather not. In the name of development, but for ensuring dependency, these transnational corporations force the acceptance of this "free market" through loan and aid conditionalities enforced by Northern governments directly and/or through the World Bank and the IMF.[6]

As shown in Shiva's chapter, the grotesque instrumentality of robbery through these IPRs is shown by the fact that the farmers' varieties, whose integrity as seeds has been safeguarded by peasants the world over, are considered not worthy of a comparable protection because they are not degraded into being uniform, distinct, and stable. At the same time, even less uniform, distinct, and stable categories of seed are now being patented by these same transnational corporations merely for having one trait (e.g., resistance to the herbicide glyphosate) genetically engineered into them. A patented transgene from a transgenic variety unintentionally but certainly does get into other cultivars through pollination, and all the cultivars are sunk into the patented variety.[7] What a world of inconsistency! That is why, as vividly described for Brazil in the chapter by Santos, national debates in the South on the issue are tortuous and apparently interminable. Even the more specific case of traditional medicine embroils society in debate, as well documented by Xaba for South Africa and Meneses for Mozambique.

The breeder will always need the peasant's heterogeneous seed. Otherwise corporate breeding would stop. The new corporate feudal system should, therefore, learn from the old and allow peasant communities to survive even if only as guilds. It should thus forgo its intellectual property rights system at least with regard to indigenous and local communities. Or else, as suggested by Shiva in her chapter, it should allow a counterbalancing Community Rights (Farmers' Rights) system that protects the indigenous and local community's biodiversity, knowledge, and technologies. Otherwise, the new corporate lord will be like the old feudal lord without his smiths and knights, and thus without sword and armor. Intellectual property rights protection could then become the way to the destruction of the supposedly protected corporate lord and his retinue, the stakeholders.

And what of the peasants, pastoralists, and gatherers who have generated and maintained the biodiversity, knowledge, and technologies? The Northern status quo considers them invalid owners because they are organized into cooperating communities and it is appropriate that only individuals should own anything. They claim that, therefore, something owned by communities is there for the taking by any individual. Some of them at least maintain that communal ownership should not be allowed since, as can be noted from the now defunct Soviet Union, it is non-viable (Clunies-Ross, 1996: 36–37). Of course this is rubbish. Communities have existed for millennia. It is only the emergence of the new feudal system, corporate capitalism, which is based solely on individually amassed wealth, that is destroying communal ownership. Even thus, as clearly described by Meneses and by Coelho for Mozambique, by Xaba for South Africa, by Escobar and Pardo and by Alonso for Colombia, communal ownership is viable. It is the individually based new corporate feudal system itself whose viability has not yet been fully tested.

Privatization through IPRs is working by default: communities now know what is hitting them, while their governments, if they know, do not want to help because the government officials themselves are in positions that maximize their opportunity to join the privatization foray. The intellectual property protection game has all its fickle rules set by the other (Northern and corporate) side, and the rules change as we learn the game—e.g., a variety has to be homogeneous in order to be given a Breeders' Right protection; yet all the different varieties into which a patented gene has entered through pollination enjoy the same patent protection (see note 7). What should we do? We should make our own rules, first for the rural communities of the South. Then perhaps the actually and potentially unemployed and unemployable of the North, trying to rediscover self-employment, may join us. The Organization of African Unity has tried to respond to this challenge. In 1998 its Summit in Ouagadougou endorsed an African Model Law on the Rights of Local Communities, Farmers, and Breeders and on the Regulation of Access to Biological Resources (Ekpere, 2001: 78). African countries are domesticating this model law by passing national laws. Article 9 of the model law stipulates that the rights to be protected are those recognized by the community itself as its customary rights and that such rights are not to be determined *de nova* by the state.

The International Treaty on Plant Genetic Resources for Food and Agriculture, adopted in Rome in November 2001, is the first international law to recognize the rights of countries to provide community rights to farmers through national law (Farmers' Rights).

MISGUIDED RESEARCH STRATEGY

As explained well in the chapters by Shiva and Santos, all plant breeding now aims at homogeneity by producing uniformity, distinctness, and stability. Within this constraint, it tries to maximize plasticity or adaptability to a wide range of environments. If it had not bowed to the dictates of privatization and abandoned the age-old strategy of using heterogeneity to maximize plasticity, it would have had more impact.[8] Considering that most agricultural research is now in the hands of corporations, a reversal of this research paradigm is unlikely in the short run.

Nevertheless, agricultural research should focus on maximizing the use of biodiversity and on enhancing the natural ecological processes to maximize soil fertility. When inputs are needed for this enhancement, they will almost always be locally available in the ecosystem. How a system to achieve this can be created should be debated nationally, involving multidisciplinary professionals, the public, and, especially, indigenous and/or local communities. Agricultural research possibly could then have the competence to support subsistence (peasant) agriculture. Currently, there is a national policy and concerted political effort to make this happen in Ethiopia. Since Ethiopian agriculture has been in serious crisis, this experiment is needed, and will be ecologically instructive towards sustainable agriculture.

QUICK FIXES

The logic of the quick fix that is used to try to solve specific manifestations of the problem caused by the privatization of the seed goes as follows: if corporations need to make seed homogeneous in order to exclude peasant communities as well as other corporations, it must be done. But the seed corporations must also make the heterogeneous environment homogeneous by adding water and chemicals. Otherwise their homogeneous seed will not suit the environment. Besides, the situation creates new business opportunities for the corporation. Unfortunately, the environment is changing quickly because of this onslaught of homogenization, and even the chosen homogeneous seed is regularly failing (Fowler and Mooney, 1990; Pretty, 1995: 7). It is time that the corporations went back to heterogeneous seed in order to suit the reality of the heterogeneous environment. The appeal of genetic engineering may well thus lie in enabling the corporations to restore heterogeneity by introducing through pollination one transgene into a whole crop genome and yet still be able to claim the complete control that patenting a transgene gives.

Agrochemicals and seed are now mostly controlled by the same seed-controlling corporations. Chemicals should be used in agriculture when indispensable, but only so long as they can help natural processes and not oppose them and undermine the prospects for the continuation of life. But a reduction in the use of chemicals would proportionately reduce the power of control and the income of the seed/chemical corporations. Therefore, genetically engineering the need for chemicals into the seed, e.g., herbicide tolerance, will continue to intensify in the future.

GENETIC ENGINEERING AS THE NEXT QUICK FIX

Genetic engineering is thus with good reason now being seen as the quick fix to overcome the failure of the discredited chemical quick fix of the Green Revolution. Genetic engineering should be used if proven useful, but not to hastily cover up failures. Suppose it also fails? And in this respect I think it will fail. The problem with the present use of agrochemicals is that the environment becomes poisoned. In a poisoned environment, all life deteriorates. Even what we get through genetic engineering is life. Thus even transgenics would do better in a good environment. In a ravaged environment, it is possible that temporarily we may be better off with genetic engineering than without. But I have no doubt that we would be better off still in an environment whose integrity we have safeguarded. And, as pointed out by all the authors that have contributed chapters to this book, indigenous and local communities safeguard environmental integrity even when their governments implementing the globalization agenda make it difficult for them. In any case, genetic engineering is only just over a decade old. We do not as yet know how well it works. We do not know its long-term impacts. Should we plunge into the unknown in the dark? I would have thought that it would be safer to retrace our steps into ecological agriculture and wait for daylight!

BIOSAFETY

In the meantime, we should make sure that the unseen does not get out of control and cut off our route for going back into ecological agriculture. That is why we have the Cartagena Protocol on Biosafety. That is why, in spite of the pressure from the United States of America to accept their doctrine of the substantial equivalence of genetically engineered organisms with non-engineered counterparts, we should subject genetic engineering to the precautionary principle as stipulated in articles 10.6 and 11.8 of the Cartagena Protocol on Biosafety.

There should also be national biosafety legislation in each country to safeguard human health and the natural biota. Peasants would then have their newest fear about their own health and biodiversity reduced. Realizing this, and spurred by the fact that genetically engineered organisms, like all other organisms, recognize no national borders, the Organization of African Unity has developed a Model Law on Safety in Biotechnology (Organization of African Unity, 2002: 42) to help its member states develop national biosafety laws of a regionally compatible rigor. This is a good example that I think all regions should emulate.

WHAT SHOULD BE DONE:
HOMEMADE RULES FOR FAMILY GAMES AND
INTERNATIONAL LAW AND ACTION FOR LOCAL LEEWAY

The Northern status quo that so dominates us is made up of individuals with standard human sensibilities and sensitivities. I am sure that, in the absence of a slaughterhouse, most of them would have a lunch of bread and cabbage rather than butcher the ox earmarked for their steak. I am convinced that the "international" norms that they impose upon us arise as much by default as by design, because we offer none of our making. These norms continue from the past of Northern institutions, from their slavery and colonial periods. I, therefore, believe that Southern countries should legislate at home what they want internationally. At least at home the family will then play the game by rules of its own making, and some of those home rules may find their way into the international arena. As shown by Shiva in her chapter in this book with regard to the fight against the *neem* patents, it is persistent efforts from the South that are needed. Of course, corporate interests will oppose these home rules by stating that WTO agreements override national law. Of course, some individuals from the North will also personally oppose us. These individuals should be treated as enemies worse than their colonizing ancestors. Some will support us. We should cultivate our alliances with them. Most will be so preoccupied with the routine of living that they will not be bothered. These are potential allies who will see our need also to live, just as they live. We should work hard to inform them, and to stimulate them to react. What does this mean in the context of biodiversity and indigenous and local communities?

Africa has started a strategy, which looks appropriate to me, to achieve this. Nationally, African countries have started to pass laws that recognize community rights and farmers' rights. They are also making their breeders' rights laws subordinate to community and farmers' rights. Thanks to persistence, their position is now being strengthened by the International Treaty on Plant Genetic Resources for Food and Agriculture. Article 9 of this treaty empowers countries to recognize farmers' rights under national law. Such national legislation will give indigenous and local communities leeway to keep generating and managing their community knowledge, technologies, and biodiversity. The African members of the WTO have also now, followed by the least developed country members of the WTO, which are mostly African, tabled at the TRIPs Council their objection to patenting as it is now provided for in TRIPs, and asked that Article 27.3(b) of TRIPs be revised to forbid the patenting of plants or animals as well as to forbid the patenting of life processes. Their position has a strong scientific basis, since it is only what is invented and not what is discovered that is patentable, and since the cells, organelles, chromosomes, genes, and nucleic acid molecules used to claim patents are all natural, and since there has not been one life form that has been constructed out of the non-living (Egziabher, 2001).

This fight to free biodiversity from corporate control should not stop at attacking patenting. In addition to patents, very restrictive contracts are now a norm between seed corporations and farmers in North America. It is likely that seed corporations will try to use the protection to undisclosed information given by TRIPs in order to bypass patenting and yet control farmers through contracts that ensure their obedience to arbitrary orders and the protection of information. Of course the grain will be there for anyone to access and test to determine its identity. But if information is kept confidential, testing will be difficult, especially in a transgenic variety. In any case, I think that anyone can analyze and find out what Coca-Cola is constituted of; however, since its composition is legally a secret, reconstituting it would break the laws governing confidential information. It is for this reason that the composition of one of the commonest substance on earth, Coca-Cola, "remains a secret." Therefore, I feel certain that seed corporations will keep finding newer and newer methods of biodiversity control, and thus finding equally newer and newer ways of combating their control will be needed. And, as shown by Santos for Brazil, their ways are not restricted to the norms they create; they also destabilize national debate in southern countries.

Perhaps the most critical strategy in this struggle will be information exchange. Corporate globalization itself has made this information exchange possible. Opposition to corporate biodiversity control exists not only in the South. Opposition to it is growing among the northern public, especially among researchers who are now finding it more and more cumbersome to negotiate the use of patented varieties, constructs, and genes. It is said that the now well-known Golden Rice of Professor Potrykus and his team now carries over fifty patents. Even though awareness is as yet low, what this means is that developing genetic engineering, or even continuing with traditional breeding, will become virtually impossible in the South. Activists in the South should, therefore, try to raise awareness on these issues in the South, and liaise with those in the North who oppose biodiversity control by corporations. This can all be done through the internet, and it may take no more than enthusiasm and a few websites.

BIBLIOGRAPHY

Alexander, Titus (1996). *Unravelling Global Apartheid*. Cambridge: Polity.
Clements, Frederic E. (1905). *Research Methods in Ecology*. Lincoln, NE: University Publishing.
Clunies-Ross, Tracey (1996). *Farmers, Plant Breeders and Seed Regulations*. Sturminster Newtown, UK: Ecologist.
Duvick, Donald N. (1995). "Plant breeding and biotechnology for meeting future food needs," in *Population and Food in the Early Twenty-First Century:*

Meeting Future Food Demand of an Increasing Population, in N. Islam (ed.). Washington, DC: International Food Policy Research Institute.

Egziabher, Tewolde Berhan Gebre (1996). "The Convention on Biological Diversity, Intellectual Property Rights and the Interests of the South," in *The Movement for Collective Intellectual Rights*, Solomon Tilahyn and Sue Edwards (eds.). Institute for Sustainable Development: Addis Ababa and London: Gaia Foundation, 15–42.

———————— (2001). *The Inappropriateness of the Patent System for Life Forms and Process*. Penang, Malaysia: Third World Network.

Ekpere, Johnson A. (2001). *The African Model Law for the Protection of the Rights of Local Communities, Farmers, Breeders and for the Regulation of Access to Biological Resources*. Addis Ababa: Organization of African Unity.

Fowler, Cary, and P. Mooney (1990). *Shattering*. Tucson, AZ: U. of Arizona P.

Goldsmith, James (1994). *The Trap*. London: Macmillan.

Hancock, Graham (1989). *Lords of Poverty*. London: Mandarin.

Korten, David C. (1995). *When Corporations Rule the World*. London: Earthscan.

Linthurst, R. A, P. Bourdeau, and R. G. Tardiff (eds.) (1995). *Methods to Assess the Effects of Chemicals on Ecosystems*. Baffins Lane, Chichester, UK: John Wiley & Sons.

McIntosh, R. P. (1976). "Ecology since 1900," in *Issues and Ideas in America*, B. J. Taylor and T. J. White (eds.). Norman, OK: U. of Oklahoma P.

Organization of African Unity (2002). *African Model Law on Safety in Biotechnology*. Addis Ababa: Organization of African Unity.

Pretty, Jules (1995). *Regenerating Agriculture*. London: Earthscan.

Shiva, Vandana (1994). *The Violence of the Green Revolution*. Penang, Malaysia: Third World Network.

UNDP (2001). *Human Development Report 2001*. New York: Oxford UP.

Notes

1 Fowler and Mooney, in their book entitled *Shattering*, have given details of the diversity in farmers' varieties and shown that all the crops grown by modern farmers and peasants now depend on this diversity.

2 The specially trained plant breeders who produce the homogeneous varieties for industrial agriculture have been denying the fact that farming communities are breeders, maintaining that farming communities merely select what nature provides. This is indeed true, not only of farming communities, but also of plant scientists. That is why, to conjure up a distinction, the industrial agriculture breeders call the varieties produced by farming communities "land races," connoting that it is the land and not the farming community that produces the variety. Albeit grudgingly, even industrial agriculture plant breeders are now recognizing farming communities as breeders. For example, Duvick (1995: 221–222) recognizes both as breeders and distinguishes their contributions as "professional plant breeding" and as "plant breeding by farmers".

3 Goldsmith (1994: 15–46) gives the magnitude of unemployment in industrialized Europe at the time. I have no recent statistics, but I have the impression that unemployment has increased.

4 The squeeze by seed companies on the potato growers of Scotland, which has been described by Clunies-Ross (1996: 20–28), and the refusal of the British Government to do something about it, can be cited as an example.

5 Any introductory textbook on ecology will give sufficient information to understand an ecosystem. A brief but sufficient analytic description is found in the proceedings of a workshop (Linthurst, Bourdeau and Tardiff [1995: 13–34]). Though views on the degree to which an ecosystem can be seen as a loose assemblage of organisms with complementary requirements (e.g., McIntosh, 1976: 353–372), or as a superorganism with the component species as its clearly determinable parts (e.g., Clements, 1905), the ecosystem as a unit maintained at more or less the same condition, even if changing over the long term, through homeostasis maintained by the interactions among all the components, is accepted as ecological fact.

6 It is understandable that official Northern publications, even those of the UN, IMF, and World Bank, which should know this best, do not contain much information about conditionalities imposed on the South except in broad terms, for instance, on the debt of developing countries (e.g., UNDP, 2001: 191–194). Many individuals have, however, written on these issues. An easily readable account on how developed countries, especially through international lending institutions, exact conditionalities, including structural adjustments, has been written by Hancock (1989: 37–75). The private sector also exacts obedience to its conditionalities, including those within its own home base, and pressures governments effectively to do what it wants. This has been described by many authors, e.g., Korten (1995). Another author, Alexander (1996: 54–84), describes how industrialized countries usually force developing countries through economic means to do what they are asked. On pp. 120–145, he describes the role of the IMF and the World Bank in this. In particular, on pp. 126–128, he describes how "structural adjustment" is used to open up a developing country's markets. In this way, it is only developed countries that use the right to keep out goods that is granted them by the Multilateral Agreement on Trade in Goods of the WTO. Structural adjustment denies developing countries this right, which international law entitles them to have. Obviously, economic might is the ultimate right. Many other authors have also written in a similar vein on the issue.

7 Percy Schmeiser (2001), personal communications. Schmeiser maintains that he planted non-genetically modified rape (canola). Pollination from other fields introduced Monsanto's Roundup-Ready Canola genes into his rape. Monsanto took him to court for infringement. In return, he sued Monsanto for contaminating his field. The judge found Schmeiser guilty, saying that however the genetically engineered gene got into his crop, the fact that it is there is sufficient guilt on his part! Mad, but that is what comes out of a combination of patenting a gene or species, and adhering to Article 34 or TRIPs, which assumes that the accused is an infringer unless he can prove otherwise. How can anybody prove or disprove that a bee or a butterfly flew from Monsanto's field to Schmeiser's? Would it not make sense to accept what happens in nature as true rather then what TRIPs says? Which is more likely to be wrong: the law of nature, or the law of industrial man?

8 Dr. Tesfaye Tessema and his colleagues, in an unpublished report, have shown that, at the Debre Zeit Agricultural Research Centre, they combined selected farmers' varieties of durum wheat and obtained yields without chemical inputs comparable to those obtained from homogeneous "improved" varieties grown with chemical inputs.

Contributors List

Luis Carlos Arenas, Wisconsin Coordinating Council on Nicaragua (USA)
João Arriscado Nunes, University of Coimbra (Portugal)
Tewolde Berhan Gebre Egziabher, Environmental Protection Authority of Ethiopia (Ethiopia)
João Paulo Borges Coelho, University Eduardo Mondlane (Mozambique)
Arturo Escobar, University of North Carolina (USA)
Margarita Flórez Alonso, Latin American Institute for Alternative Legal Services (Colombia)
Yash Ghai, University of Hong Kong (China)
Carlos Frederico Marés de Souza Filho, Pontific Catholic University of Paraná (Brazil)
Maria Paula Meneses, Centre for Social Studies, Coimbra (Portugal)
Lino João de Oliveira Neves, University of Amazonas (Brasil)
Mauricio Pardo, Colombian Institute of Antrophology (Colombia)
Shalini Randeria, University of Zurich (Switzerland)
Laymert Garcia dos Santos, State University of Campinas (Brasil)
Vandana Shiva, Research Foundation for Science, Technology and Ecology (India)
Boaventura de Sousa Santos, University of Coimbra (Portugal)
Shiv Visvanathan, Centre for the Study of Developing Societies (India)
Thokozani Xaba, University of Natal (South Africa)

Index